Springer Studies in Alternative Economics

This book series offers an outlet for cutting-edge research in alternative, heterodox and pluralist economics. It features scholarly studies on various schools of thought beyond the neo-classical orthodoxy, including Austrian, Post Keynesian, Sraffian, Marxian, Georgist, Institutional-evolutionary, as well as feminist, radical, social, green, and ecological economics. It aims to promote pluralism of economic ideas, methodological approaches, and topics.

The series also welcomes works that seek to develop alternative visions of the economy, economic structures and new approaches that aim to serve society, for example by embedding the economy within the ecosystem, or to enrich economic thought by advancing diversity, gender, race, and social equality. All titles in this series are peer-reviewed.

Ali Ari
Editor

Capitalism at a Crossroads

A New Reset?

Springer

Editor
Ali Ari
Department of Political Science and Public Administration
Marmara University
Istanbul, Turkey

ISSN 2731-5908 ISSN 2731-5916 (electronic)
Springer Studies in Alternative Economics
ISBN 978-3-031-23256-5 ISBN 978-3-031-23257-2 (eBook)
https://doi.org/10.1007/978-3-031-23257-2

This Springer imprint is published by the registered company Springer Nature Switzerland AG
The registered company address is: Gewerbestrasse 11, 6330 Cham, Switzerland

Contents

Part II Quest for Rebuilding the Capitalism

Contributors

Elife Akiş Department of Economics, Istanbul University, Istanbul, Turkey

Emre Akusta Department of Economics, Kirklareli University, Kirklareli, Turkey

Ali Ari Department of Political Science and Public Administration, Marmara University, Istanbul, Turkey

Laurent Baechler Centre, Nice, France

Ünal Çaglar Department of Economics, Kirklareli University, Kirklareli, Turkey

Serhat Çakmak Department of Economics, Manisa Celal Bayar University, Manisa, Turkey

Elif Selin Calik London Institute of Directors, London, UK

Raif Cergibozan Department of Economics, Kirklareli University, Kirklareli, Turkey

Murat Çetin Department of Economics, Istanbul University, Istanbul, Turkey

Caner Demir Department of Economics, Manisa Celal Bayar University, Manisa, Turkey

Charalampos Efstathopoulos Department of International Politics, Aberystwyth University, Aberystwyth, UK

Olivier Gajac Centre Émile Durkheim de Bordeaux, Pessac, France

Saim Karabulut Ostim Technical University, Ankara, Turkey

Ali Osman Karci Ostim Technical University, Ankara, Turkey

Hakan Mehmetcik Department of International Relations, Marmara University, Istanbul, Turkey
University of Notre Dame, Kellogg Institute for International Studies, Notre Dame, IN, USA

Betül Mutlugün Department of Economics, Istanbul University, Istanbul, Turkey

Süleyman Emre Özcan Department of Economics, Manisa Celal Bayar University, Manisa, Turkey

Ata Ozkaya Department of Economics, Galatasaray University, Istanbul, Turkey

Murat Öztürk Department of Economics, Kirklareli University, Kirklareli, Turkey

Abdüsselam Sagin Department of Economics, Kirklareli University, Kirklareli, Turkey

Semanur Soyyigit Department of Public Finance, Kirklareli University, Kirklareli, Turkey

Dogukan Taskiran Department of International Relations, Marmara University, Istanbul, Turkey

Mehmet Hanefi Topal Department of Public Finance, Kirklareli University, Kirklareli, Turkey

Jean-Claude Vérez University of Artois and International Centre for European Training, Arras, France

Murat Yülek Ostim Technical University, Ankara, Turkey

List of Figures

Chapter 4

Chapter 5

Chapter 6

List of Tables

Chapter 14

Introduction

Ali Ari

Abstract Over the last three decades, the world economy has faced several complex and interrelated problems such as global climate change, food and energy scarcity, rising inequality, poverty, and more frequent and severe financial and economic crises. However, the capitalist system has been struggling to bring responses to those increasing problems and uncertainty. This has generated lively debates on the sustainability of the liberal capitalist economic system. Therefore, this book aims first to assess current problems of the world economy from a theoretical and empirical perspective, then to propose plausible answers from different points of view to restore the capitalist economic system.

Keywords Capitalism · Sustainability · Growth · Climate change · Global warming · Agriculture · Energy · Inequality · Debt · Financial crises · Financialization · Poverty · Trade wars · COVID-19 · Political crises · Economic security · Artificial intelligence · Technological change · Great reset · Degrowth · Green deals · Solidarity economy · Balance of power · Smart cities

The capitalist world economy has faced several complex and interrelated problems over the last three decades. These problems have generated lively debates on the sustainability of the liberal capitalist economic system. Some even have predicted the end of capitalism (i.e., Boldizzoni, 2016; Streeck, 2016). However, this is not the first time the economists had predicted the end of capitalism. Marx, for instance, indicated that disequilibrium between demand and supply (overproduction or underconsumption)—due to high competition among capitalists leading firms to replace labor by machines to increase efficiency—results in falling rate of profit. There appears an economic crisis, exacerbating the inequality between rich and poor. Excessive wealth for the few along with widespread poverty for the many will lead to a revolutionary crisis—as the state controlled by the wealthy cannot reform the

A. Ari (✉)
Department of Political Science and Public Administration, Marmara University, Istanbul, Turkey
e-mail: ali.ari@marmara.edu.tr

A. Ari (ed.), *Capitalism at a Crossroads*, Springer Studies in Alternative Economics,
https://doi.org/10.1007/978-3-031-23257-2_1

political economic system (Elwell, 2013). Mill thought that capitalism would gradually settle into a "stationary state" when the capitalist economies reach the limit of demographic and environmental sustainability (Boldizzoni, 2016). This is actually a chance for the society, get rid of the tyranny of need, to pursue social justice and continuous progress toward higher human and social achievements. Keynes, nearly a century later, predicted the end of capitalism when people would reach saturation of their needs or in other words loose passion for capital accumulation.[1]

However, contrary to predictions of different economists, the capitalist system survived despite serious crises in the nineteenth (1857, 1866, 1873, 1882, and 1890–93) and twentieth centuries (1929 and 1973),[2] through adapting itself to changing economic and political environments and reinventing a new growth model. For instance, following the 1929 Great Depression, capitalism transformed itself by proposing an original mode of production—Fordism—based on mass production, real wage increases, productivity gains, and growth. After leading to exceptional prosperity between 1945 and 1973, the Fordist system entered, in turn, into crisis. The stagflation of the 1970s brought the advent of a new form of capitalism—financial or neoliberal capitalism—based on deregulation. At first, financial expansion positively affected economic growth, but then it has become a source of imbalances and crises. The global financial crisis of 2007–08 is the perfect example, feeding discussions on the reform of the global economic and financial architecture.

Now we stand at a crossroads! Nearly four decades of economic liberalization and privatization have generated more negative consequences for the world economy. Higher return on capital for shareholders along with stagnating real wages has led to increasing inequality within most advanced countries, which would cause underconsumption. To avoid it, governments chose enhanced borrowing hence a debt-driven growth strategy with the effects that we know!

Moreover, liberalization policies implemented to increase the competition among financial and nonfinancial companies resulted in a higher degree of concentration in several sectors. This produces systemic risk; hence, public authorities are de facto forced to bail out these "too big to fail companies" in case of difficulties as we clearly observed following the global crisis of 2007–08. This leads to moral hazard issues as those actors take excessive risks, since their losses are socialized.

Furthermore, privatization of state-owned enterprises (SOEs) and of public services such as education and health, coupled with increasing inequality, has jeopardized social mobility and social cohesion, increased health problems, and reduced

[1] There are also other mechanisms put forward for the end of capitalism. Polanyi underlined the rising resistance to further commodification of life and society; Kondratieff emphasized technological stagnation; Hilferding insisted on the suspension of liberal markets by monopolistic firms; Schumpeter and Hayek highlighted bureaucratic suppression of entrepreneurialism. See Hartwell and Engerman (2003) and Streeck (2016) for an extensive review of previous predictions on the end of capitalism.

[2] See Gilles (2004) for an extensive review on crises occurred in capitalist economies in the nineteenth and twentieth centuries.

life expectancy for low-income households. At the end, all these issues have lowered productivity and growth rates. The COVID-19 pandemic—started in China in late 2019 and spread to the whole world in early 2020—put evidence on the incapacity of health services in most advanced countries and inflamed debates on the "return of state" in economic sphere.

On the other hand, constantly increasing world population (from 2.5 billion in 1950 to nearly 8 billion in 2022 and projected to reach 9.8 billion in 2050) and their rising energy and food demand have led CO_2 emissions to reach record levels. Hence, climate change and global warming have started to affect our daily lives. Non-implementation of necessary policy actions at international level would lead to irreversible consequences for the earth such as melting of glaciers and loss of biodiversity that threaten the human life. However, those problems are likely to affect much more underdeveloped parts of the world. This will cause more immigration to developed countries which have been already struggling with increased political tensions.

In short, we are heading to a collision and need radical changes to prevent a catastrophe. Therefore, this book aims first to assess current problems of the world economy from a theoretical and empirical perspective, then to bring plausible answers from different points of view to restore the capitalist economic system.

The first problem of the capitalism, that we treat in the book, is slowing growth rates in advanced economies (from 4.5% on average in the 1960s and 1970s to 2.9% in 1980s). In "golden" 1990s, high-income countries recorded a growth rate of 2.7% and this rate was even lower in the 2000s (1.8%). We observe the same trend in the world growth rates (from 4.5% in the 1960s and 1970s to 2.9% in 2000s).[3] This generates debates on the end of the endless growth regime. M. H. Topal, in Chapter "End of Endless Growth Regime: Accumulation and Technology", deeply analyzes the two opposing theoretical views on whether endless growth is possible. He shows that the proponents of endless growth underline capital accumulation, technological progress, and efficiency as key drivers for continuous growth. On the other hand, opponents consider the limits of economic growth, particularly in the context of its impact on environment, social inequalities, and human well-being. Topal claims that there are two aspects on which the two opposing approaches have reached some consensus: the reduction of the carbon footprint and the indispensability of technology. But he indicates that continuous technological development, alone, cannot resolve environmental crisis and increasing inequalities. For that we also need a social and political transformation.

R. Cergibozan and E. Akusta analyze, in Chapter "Energy, Economic Growth, and Ecological Collapse", the impact of economic growth on energy demand, hence carbon emissions, climate change, and biodiversity. In other words, they assess environmental limits of economic growth. They show that from the Industrial Revolution onwards along with increased population, the need and demand for energy continuously increased. As the biggest part of the energy is produced from

[3]The data are gathered from World Bank–World Development Indicators.

non-renewable sources such as oil, natural gas, and coal, increased growth harms the environment. The global warming leading to the loss of biodiversity threatens the sustainability of the ecosystem and the humanity. Therefore, to be successful in the fight against climate change, we must increase the use of renewable energy sources in electricity production and in other areas such as transportation, heating, and cooling activities. They conclude that it would be appropriate to switch to environmental-friendly growth instead of growth at all costs.

M. Çetin and M. Öztürk, in Chapter "Agriculture and Food Problems and Solutions: Challenges and Capacity of the Capitalist System in the 21st Century", analyze another problem of the capitalist system: deficiencies of capitalist agro-food system such as difficulty in access to food, price fluctuations, unsustainability of production, decline in biodiversity, and climate change. The authors indicate that current failures, increasing pressures—rapid economic development in some developing countries (i.e., China and India) and continuous increase in world population—and supply shocks such as the COVID-19 pandemic and Russia–Ukraine war are likely to exacerbate food issues. They claim that these deficiencies are related to the structure of contemporary agro-food system based on corporate concentration in the global input and distribution markets. The authors also claim that the globalization of food industry reduces the resilience of the agro-food system as seen during the food crises of 2008 and 2011 that led to huge increases in prices and commodity speculation. Because of those uncertainties and instabilities, some poor people and countries could not access to enough food, putting in danger food security of the import-dependent countries, in particular. They suggest that proposed solutions by international organizations such as the UN-FAO, IMF, and World Bank through the perspective of food security and sustainability cannot mitigate the food problem. Thus, what is required is the reset of the agro-food system on a global scale. However, as this radical change is difficult, an important step would be to accept the rights to nature and to food as basic human rights and to gain institutional and legal guarantees for this.

Financialization and finance-driven capitalism constitute a major threat for the future of capitalism. As analytically discussed in Chapter "Financialization and Finance-Driven Capitalism" by B. Mutlugün, the role of finance has changed beyond its traditional function of providing capital for the productive investments. The new order of the financial sector with its sophisticated financial instruments (i.e., derivatives), new digital technologies, and high-frequency trading has removed the accumulation of capital from the sphere of production and has created a rent-seeking society. This "transformation" has on the one hand limited growth leading to higher unemployment rates, and on the other hand, it reinforced the instability of capitalism as illustrated by the increasing number, frequency, and cost of financial crises occurred in both developing and advanced countries with devastating social and economic consequences such as increasing income inequality.

Income inequality is not solely caused by the increasing number of financial crises. As extensively discussed in Chapter "Income Inequality, Household Debt, and Financial Crises" by A. Ari and R. Cergibozan, income inequality has significantly increased within most developed countries over the past four decades due to globalization, technological development, and reduced bargaining power of labor as a result of free-market policies. The authors theoretically and empirically show that increasing inequality led to excessive borrowing—facilitated by growing financial development, expansionist monetary policies, and low inflationist framework, particularly over the last two decades—thus higher household debt stock. Higher debt-to-income ratios of low- and middle-income households, in particular, fed spending booms and asset bubbles in the US and other advanced countries. These imbalances played then a crucial role in the outbreak of the global financial crisis of 2007–08, which in turn exacerbated the inequality in income distribution. The authors suggest that income inequality emerges as a structural problem of the neoliberal capitalist system. Thus, temporary solutions (i.e., low interest rates and excessive borrowing) aggravate structural problems of the economy by leading to boom-bust cycles, creating supply-side distortions, reducing productivity, slowing growth, and preparing the ground for next financial crises.

Beside income inequality, an important part of the world population, particularly in Africa and South Asia, suffers from poverty (about 750 million people living on $1.90 a day), aggravated by the recent COVID-19 pandemic (more 250 million people fell into poverty). J. C. Vérez examines this issue in Chapter "Health Crisis, Income Poverty and Public Policies in the World". He shows that the COVID-19 pandemic has impacted all countries in the world—by leading to the most synchronized recession since the Great Depression of 1929—but to varying degrees. The less-developed countries were severely affected by increasing poverty, food insecurity, rising food prices, and geopolitical tensions that dampened demand and slowed down growth. These countries with no public health protection systems along with increasing debt problems could only have reached to very low vaccination rates—exposing them to new waves of the pandemic. Because unlike advanced countries, governments in less-developed ones did not have sufficient policy space to sustain economic activity and mitigate social shocks. Therefore, the author underlines that public policies should be redesigned in several fields such as education, health, transport, and communication, to increase growth prospects and the resilience of their economies. As their budget constraints do not allow these countries to deploy extensive infrastructure investments, public–private partnerships could be an option.

Chapter "Trade Wars and the Changing Balance of Power", prepared by C. Efstathopoulos, enquires the ways in which the current US–China trade wars affect the world economy and the balance of power in the capitalist system. Trade wars are caused by core economic interests, such as market and technology access, but are also linked to strategic and geopolitical criteria. The potential intensification of the US–China trade war in the next decade cannot only cause loss of GDP for the USA and China (estimated at -1.35% and -1.41%, respectively), but also affects global GDP that can decrease by -$450 billion when global value chains are accounted for. On the other hand, trade wars can mark a shift to a new phase of international economic relations in the capitalist system such as economic revisionism and neo-mercantilism in both the USA and China. Moreover, trade wars redefine not only relations between major powers, but also affect the economies of middle powers that may benefit from trade diversion and higher revenues but also experience adverse effects in terms of GDP and inequality. Therefore, different middle powers endeavor to maintain security alliances while maximizing economic opportunities in the capitalist system. This has shaped the policymaking options of middle powers, not only in economic but also in foreign policy, as they are constrained by an increasingly polarized global economy.

M. Yülek, S. Karabulut and A. O. Karci, in Chapter "On Economic Security and the Political Economy of Neocolonialist Capitalism: The Case of France and Niger's Uranium Resources", analyze the impact of another "political" issue—neo-colonialism—on the sustainability of the capitalist economic system. The authors suggest that neo-colonialism is an evolved version of colonialism and neo-colonial practices of powerful nations ensure the transfer of economic wealth and welfare from economically less-developed nations although they are *de jure* independent. This issue is considered a threat to the economic security of weaker nations that make them a victim of unfair international trade, as the more powerful side of the exchange has the power to set terms. The authors show through a value chain analysis on Niger's raw uranium transactions with France that Niger has received only 3.2% of the ultimate value-added electricity that the French energy firms have generated in 2020 using Niger's raw uranium. Therefore, the authors suggest that unfair resource and welfare transfer in favor of economically and technologically more powerful nations make the capitalist system vulnerable and possibly unsustainable over the long term.

H. Mehmetcik and D. Taskiran, in Chapter "Political Crises of Capitalism", analyze how economic issues such as income inequality, poverty, inflation, and unemployment lead to new types of political crises in both developing and advanced countries. The authors show that globalization and financialization of the world economy since the late 1970s have increased financial and economic instability and generated higher inequalities. Economic and financial downturns in 2008 and 2020 have exacerbated those problems as many lost their jobs, saw the decline of their living standards but had to pay for the bailout of failing financial and nonfinancial institutions. Now they are forced to bear most of the consequences of environmental problems mainly caused by the production process. Therefore, the modern economy's failures rise discontent in several societies and deteriorate political legitimacy. Those who feel left behind in increased economic insecurity and social hardship have fostered a broad hostility toward the state and traditional political parties. Therefore, we have been observing the rise of populism and retreat of democracy, the rise of neo-mercantilism and state capitalism, and the legitimacy crisis in global governance over the last two decades, particularly. Brexit, Trump's election, and the rise of the extreme right in European democracies as well as xenophobic rhetoric and anti-migration sentiments are all visible indications of a long-run crisis.

What could be the solutions to these complex and interrelated problems of the capitalist system? Is it possible to restore the capitalist structure by some "radical" changes and/or reforms that would build equitable and sustainable economies? Or are those efforts doomed to failure? How will the global economic order evolve: into more globalization, deglobalization, or more interventionist (state capitalism)? These are the questions that we aim to answer in the following chapters.

As the technological progress is considered the main driver of economic growth, hence welfare, in modern macroeconomics, it would be better to start the analysis of the probable solutions to restore the capitalist system with the fourth industrial revolution. Industry 4.0 has many dimensions such as the Internet of things, cyber-physical systems, smart factories, big data, cloud technology, 3D printing, artificial intelligence (AI), and augmented reality, and these components operate in an interactive and integrated way with each other. As the AI is considered the most important component of the industry 4.0, the fair question here is whether the AI is an opportunity to pull out the capitalism from its structural problems. That is the question that C. Demir and S. Çakmak try to answer to in Chapter "Artificial Intelligence, Technological Change, and the Future of Capitalism". The authors first analyze the capitalist growth process through technological developments from a historical perspective, then examine the probable impacts of the AI on the future of capitalism. They indicate that unlike other technological systems, the ability to think and act makes AI different. The AI, by substituting labor, may cause a decrease in labor demand. Decreased demand for labor will reduce wages, hence lower private consumption. Moreover, as technological progress produces proportionately more high-skill, better-paid jobs, benefiting those with the required skills, it may exacerbate the already-high-income inequality. Furthermore, AI brings fundamental changes in the financial markets. AI-based decision-making systems would increase efficiency in financial markets. However, considering that the biggest shareholder in these markets is the capital owner class, there is a potential to cause more income inequality. At this point, governments have an important regulatory role to play. The universal basic income may be a remarkable alternative for income distribution. On the other hand, lower wages may lead to the emergence of new jobs as observed during the previous industrial revolutions. Moreover, the increase in productivity brought by AI may boost the profit appetite of the capitalist class and encourage new investments. Therefore, this process should be managed carefully in cooperation with private sector to maximize the opportunities brought by the industry 4.0.

A. Ozkaya, in Chapter "Endless Growth Regime: The Role of Elasticity of Substitution and Extraordinary Economy Policies", revises the neoclassical growth model introduced by Solow (1956) to assess whether the capitalist economies can have endless growth. The author focuses on the effect of elasticity of substitution on output per capita, growth rate of capital–labor ratio, and the growth rate of output per capita, respectively. Contrary to early findings, he mathematically proves that output per capita and growth rate of capital-labor ratio are decreasing functions of elasticity of substitution. In other words, increasing the minimum marginal product of labor and an increase in the ratio of minimum marginal product of labor to minimum marginal product of capital enhance the growth rate of per capita income. These policies, which can be set either independently or jointly, may be an appropriate tool to ensure endless growth rate of output in capitalist economies. On the other hand, the author proposes a model of economic disequilibrium under extreme events causing demand and supply shocks such as the COVID-19 pandemic. To do this, the author exemplifies both fiscal policy of US government and monetary policy of Federal Reserve amid COVID-19 pandemic. The model results suggest that the US fiscal policy and monetary policy do not optimally match and hence the fiscal policy should be calibrated. To be more precise, instead of increasing minimum marginal product of labor (i.e., increasing minimum wages as done by the US government in February 2022) which leads to an increase in minimum marginal price of labor, increasing maximum marginal product of capital would be a better policy choice in terms of fiscal approach. Monetary policy, on the other hand, aiming to increase the sensitivity of demand to price level is efficient to establish price stability.

S. Soyyigit and E. Akis, in Chapter "Covid-19: An Assessment in the Context of its Economic Impacts and Market-State Relationship", discuss different points of view about the future of capitalism following the COVID-19 pandemic. They first show how the pandemic has exacerbated the ongoing problems of the capitalist system such as underemployment, income inequality, and poverty, then, how vulnerable and unable is the neoliberal approach—based on profit maximization—in providing necessary products for the well-being of the people. As we clearly saw during the pandemic, the free-market mechanism could not satisfy the need for medical products and vaccines, healthcare services remained insufficient to respond to the increasing number of cases, and all these happened in advanced countries. As during the global financial crisis, governments largely intervened in economy to bailout companies but, this time, also to help households through social insurance measures (i.e., sick leave, health insurance provision, expanded pension schemes), social assistance scheme (i.e., cash assistance, food and other in-kind assistance, childcare assistance), and labor market measures (i.e., wage subsidy, labor intermediation and training, emergency employment programs). This shows the need for a "bigger" state in the economic system. Therefore, the authors suggest that there will a rising tendency toward state capitalism, deglobalization, and increasing populism and nationalism in the future.

One of the "popular" ideas to remedy the capitalist system is the "great reset" proposed by Klaus Schwab of World Economic Forum (WEF) following the COVID-19 pandemic. Schwab, the founder and director of the WEF, indicates that the pandemic made the weaknesses of the current global economic system more evident, and the fourth industrial revolution that will impact growth, unemployment, market structure, and political system in the near future will force the world economic order toward a great reset. Through the great reset, we could create a new social and economic order more resilient and sustainable. For that we need a transition from shareholder capitalism to stakeholder capitalism: this will be the end of neoliberalism with more interventionist governments. A. Sagin and Ü. Çaglar, in Chapter "Great Reset", discuss whether the great reset proposal can be a remedy for the crises of capitalism. The authors first show how the pandemic has affected the world economy in terms of growth, unemployment, income inequality, and how the fourth industrial revolution will change it. Then, they indicate that the great reset idea proposed by the WEF is a must, but as such, it is far from bringing the necessary changes to the world economy. The authors suggest that the great reset should be participatory and inclusive in the sense that it must be planned through international cooperation rather than by an elite. However, the authors are somehow pessimistic about a "successful" great reset since the world's great powers are not willing to give up their privileges. Therefore, they opt for power shifts or great reset by war rather than cooperation and collaboration.

Another approach to eliminate the negativities arising from capitalist system is degrowth. S. E. Özcan and C. Demir discuss, in Chapter "Degrowth Strategy to Sustain the Capitalist System", whether the degrowth movement can ensure the sustainability of capitalism. They first analyze from a theoretical perspective how economic growth may be assured and then show the externalities of growth-addicted approach of the neoliberal system such as income inequality and environmental issues. They indicate that degrowth has emerged as a response to the triple crisis: environmental, social, and economic. Hence, the degrowth movement seeks to deliberately downsize economies to create a life of greater social welfare by addressing climate change and working less or increasing leisure time. Degrowth is not synonymous of negative growth or stagnation. Although GDP decreases with degrowth, there will be positive qualitative, social, and environmental changes that we cannot use in the measurement of GDP. However, it will be not that easy for households and companies to settle for less consumption and less profit rates, respectively. Thus, to establish a "new capitalism" based on the degrowth concept, microeconomic agents, national institutions, and international organizations should league together in a common acceptance.

L. Baechler, in Chapter "Can Green Deals Save Capitalism from Ecological Collapse?", discusses whether green deals implemented by many countries can save the capitalist system from an ecological collapse. The author first underlines the dramatic increase in ecological pressures of all kinds within a few decades in the post-World War II period, then examines green deals implemented by the USA and the EU from the perspective of financial capacity, institutional reforms, and international cooperation. The author underlines that the first green deals were put into action mostly with the prospect of exiting developed countries from the 2007–08 global financial crisis. The second wave of green deals which have been implemented following the COVID-19 crisis are far more ambitious, both ecologically and economically because they set major objectives with numerous targets (i.e., reducing net greenhouse gas emissions by 55% by 2030, reaching the share of renewable energy sources by 40% in the EU's overall energy mix by 2030, etc.) and they mobilize greater economic resources to achieve these targets. However, achieving these targets in a relatively short run is a huge challenge that involves a radical transformation of energy production and consumption systems, along with the preservation of biodiversity. The ecological transition cannot be based exclusively on a plan devised by governments, but also markets should fully contribute to this fundamental reorientation of individual and collective behaviors. Besides, there should be an international cooperation to equally share the burden of transforming the global economic system. The failure of this process would certainly be a catastrophe for the sustainability of modern economic systems.

E. S. Calik analyzes, in Chapter "Green Technology and Smart Solutions for Capitalist Cities in the 21st Century", how smart cities can save the capitalist system from an ecological disaster, since the urbanization represents one of the most pressing environmental challenges we face today. As the author underlined, the number of people living in cities has reached around 59% of the total population worldwide and it is estimated that this figure will reach 70% by 2050. The increased urbanization along with the explosion of the world population has led to an increase in energy consumption and carbon emissions. With a growing number of vehicles on the road and increasing traffic congestion, many cities have become increasingly polluted environments. In this context, sustainable development has emerged as a new paradigm for urban planning and design. A sustainable or smart city is one that can meet the needs of its population in terms of social equity, economic prosperity, and environmental conservation. However, most smart city initiatives still lack clear strategies and are often limited to isolated projects with little impact on the overall development of their regions. Therefore, green technology should be considered as the future of smart cities, since it will help us to improve our cities and make them cleaner and better places to live. In other words, green technology will make smart cities more efficient, productive, and better places to live, hence ensure sustainable development.

O. Gajac, in Chapter "Solidarity Economy", examines whether solidarity economy can be an alternative to the dominant market economy. The author first considers terminological and linguistic aspects associated with the solidarity economy in the different parts of the world, from a historical perspective, from its associationist roots to the present day, to highlight the forces and characteristics that would bring it closer to and/or distinguish it from the social economy, the non-profit sector, and the popular economy. The author then highlights the solidarity economy to compensate the shortcomings of the neoliberal order and its externalities. He shows that since the 1990s, the solidarity economy has invested in many sectors such as proximity services, management of urban services by inhabitants, knowledge exchange networks, self-production, sustainable agriculture, organic shops, collective kitchens, solidarity tourism, solidarity finance, fair trade, creation of activities by unemployed people and other forms of collective entrepreneurship. And today, it contributes to the emergence of innovative solutions in new sectors such as renewable energy, short circuits, circular economy, new forms of employment, housing, shared mobility, and digital. Although the solidarity economy is marked by a great diversity of initiatives, due to geographical areas and political contexts, whose scale of intervention can vary from local to international, the solidarity initiatives are driven by the idea of changing the neoliberal world into a more humane, caring, compassionate, and cohesive world. This more democratic and egalitarian model of social protection tends to reduce the power of individuals to self-organize in a non-lucrative way and to democratically lead to a social change reconciling politics and economy and providing individuals to better social conditions of existence and the consideration of nature. However, the central and/or local public authorities have difficulty in recognizing their utility and legal statutes and tend to limit their field of actions by laws and other administrative obstacles.

So, there are solutions and recommendations to rebuild a more humane, egalitarian, democratic, sustainable, socially cohesive, environmental-friendly capitalist system. What it lacks, however, is the political will, social transformation, and international cooperation to equally share the burden of transforming the global economic system. Otherwise, we are heading at full speed to a collision with the future.

References

Boldizzoni, F. (2016). *Foretelling the end of capitalism*. Harvard University Press.

Elwell, F. W. (2013). *Socio-cultural Systems*. Athabasca University Press.

Gilles, P. (2004). *Histoire des Crises et des Cycles Economiques*. Armand Colin.

Hartwell, R. M., & Engerman, S. L. (2003). Capitalism. In J. Mokyr (Ed.), *The Oxford encyclopedia of economic history* (Oxford University Press) (Vol. 1, pp. 319–325). New York.

Streeck, W. (2016). *How will capitalism end?* Essays on a Failing System.

Solow, R. M. (1956). A contribution to the theory of economic growth. *The Quarterly Journal of Economics, 70*(1), 65–94.

Part I
Current Problems of the World Economy

End of Endless Growth Regime: Accumulation and Technology

Mehmet Hanefi Topal

Abstract One of the most important moral questions of our time is how to ensure the endless growth despite some of its limits. The question of whether endless growth is possible is not only on the agenda of advanced capitalist economies. It is also a fundamental problem for less developed economies and capitalist industrial civilizations as a whole. In the economic literature, there are two opposing views on whether endless growth is possible. According to proponents of capitalism and endless growth, it is possible through the creation of accumulation based on technological progress and efficiency. On the other hand, opponents consider the limits of economic growth, especially in the context of green thinking and human well-being. This study attempts to answer the question of whether we have reached the end of the ideology of endless growth and capitalism by presenting the arguments of the two opposing views.

Keywords Endless growth · Capitalism · Accumulation of capital · Technological progress

1 Introduction

One of the most important moral issues of our time is whether endless growth is possible despite some of its limitations. The question of whether endless growth is possible is not just an agenda of advanced capitalist economies, but also a fundamental problem of less developed economies and the capitalism as a whole. The ideology that societies need endless growth in order to increase their welfare is a fairly recent one. However, this ideology dates back to the 1950s. Prior to that, neither the political arena nor the academic discussions focused on the idea of endless growth (Pansera & Fressoli, 2021).

M. H. Topal (✉)
Department of Public Finance, Kirklareli University, Kırklareli, Turkey
e-mail: mtopal@klu.edu.tr

A. Ari (ed.), *Capitalism at a Crossroads*, Springer Studies in Alternative Economics,
https://doi.org/10.1007/978-3-031-23257-2_2

The necessity of endless growth first came to the fore in the political scene in the USA with the new political climate as a result of the Cold War. Then, there were academic discussions about it. The promotion of economic growth was seen as a solution to several issues such as unemployment and welfare. Thus, it became a policy that guaranteed the political legitimacy of capitalist regimes. In the early years of the idea of endless growth, technological development and capital accumulation were emphasized the most. In a very short time, the paradigm of growth was embraced by all parts of the political spectrum and Western world. The main expectation from growth was that it would improve welfare and decrease poverty and social inequalities. Some even expected that class conflicts would cease with growth over time (Higgs, 2017; Barry, 2020). Today, many segments such as international economic organizations, media, universities, thinktanks, and political parties strongly embrace the idea of endless growth and reproduce it. Advanced countries, emerging economies, and even planned economies like China adopt the ideology of endless growth as the inevitable way of creating wealth for everyone.

Criticisms of economic growth are as recent as the idea of economic growth. More recently, however, criticisms have focused on the ideology of endless growth. The endless growth regime is criticized by different segments for its negative effects on environmental pollution, global climate change, global poverty, inequality (Meadows & Randers, 2012; Piketty, 2014; Hickel, 2017), and its natural (Georgescu-Roegen, 1971; Daly, 1974) and social (Hirsch, 1977; Kallis et al., 2018) limitations. Indeed, global inequalities, poverty, social instabilities, and conflicts have increased continuously since the second half of the twentieth century, when the growth ideology began to settle and capitalist expansion rose (Milanovic, 2012; Piketty, 2014; Cairo-i-Cespedes & Castells-Quintana, 2016). In addition, environmental pollution continues to increase due to the excessive use of non-renewable natural resources, and in parallel, natural resources are constantly depleted. Disruption of biogeochemical cycles, global warming, biodiversity, and dramatic losses in ecosystem are growing threats to humanity (Rockström et al., 2009; Steffen et al., 2015).

On the other hand, some authors even proclaim that endless growth and capitalism have expired or will soon end. There are multiple reasons for this expiration put forward by scholars. These are, namely, capital accumulation based on diminishing marginal returns (Bonaiuti, 2014), depletion of technological innovations (Gordon, 2012), and inability to create effective demand for capital and new investments (Harvey, 2010). In addition, Mason (2015) thinks that technological transformations jeopardize capital accumulation while Cairo-i-Cespedes and Castells-Quintana (2016) hold that there is a multidimensional systemic crisis stemming from the dynamics of capital accumulation. However, mainstream economics continues to strongly defend the ideology of endless growth based on capital accumulation and technical progress. Although there are obviously serious criticisms, the ideology of endless growth and capitalism still maintain their place as dominant ideologies.

Discussions on the endless growth regime have divided the economics literature into two camps. According to the defenders of the first (orthodox or mainstream) view, endless growth is possible with capitalism. As in the early years of the idea of endless growth, advocates of this view frequently emphasize two elements, which are technological development and accumulation of capital. The opponent (critical and ecologist) view, on the other hand, oppose the idea of endless growth by considering the limitation of growth especially in the context of green thinking and human well-being. Critical economists object to the techno-optimistic stance of the mainstream and characterize capital accumulation as the harm of crises.

The purpose of this study is to present the arguments of two opposing views related to capital accumulation and technological development, the traditional drivers of endless economic growth, and to discuss whether we have reached the end of the growth paradigm and capitalist industrial civilization.

The study is organized as follows. Section 2 presents the background of growth in the political economy based on the historical framework. Section 3 explains how the new growth models justify the endless growth ideology. Section 4 presents the critical arguments of the opponents of the ideology of endless growth. Section 5 presents the defense of mainstream economics against the criticisms. Section 6 provides a general assessment of whether we have reached the end of the growth paradigm and capitalism.

2 The Origins of Endless Growth: Accumulation, Technical Change, and Capitalism

Capitalism is an economic and social system based on private ownership of the means of production. The capitalist system differs from feudalism or socialism with its unique features such as the ownership of the means of production by a minority, commodification of labor, production of goods and services for the market, monetary exchange and market coordination, and production which is motivated by profit (Andreucci & McDonough, 2014). Unlike other systems, continuous growth is considered a necessity, the only way, to meet the growing needs in the capitalist system (Gordon & Rosenthal, 2003; Jackson, 2009).

The most important difference between the industrial capitalism that emerged after the Industrial Revolution and the preceding commercial capitalism is that industrial capitalism redirects the surplus to investment and creates an ongoing accumulation process, which is indispensable for industrial capitalism (Higgs, 2017). As early political economists, although Smith and Marx have different economic views, they agree on the importance of capital accumulation in the process of economic growth. Both agree that for wealth to be transformed into further accumulation, there must be an initial accumulation. In addition, according to Marx, the crises or the end of capitalism is due to the accumulation process. Smith, on the other hand, lays the foundations of the paradigm of growth by arguing that economic growth sustained by capital accumulation is the source of all wealth. On the other hand, he mentions a phenomenon called steady state and emphasizes that there is a saturation point of economic growth and wealth.

In fact, many classical political economists such as Ricardo, Malthus, and Mill, as well as Smith, share the idea that economic development has an endpoint defined as a steady state, and that endless growth is impossible. According to classical political economists, economic growth slows down as the marginal returns of natural resources and profitable investment opportunities decrease. Growth reaches its inevitable limit when profit rates reach their minimum, wages stabilize, and capital accumulation ceases. When this limit is reached, welfare improves no more and the population remains stable (Rose, 2020).

While the idea that there is a limit to growth is a perspective shared by political economists, classical political economists have different views on when this limit will be reached, whether it is possible to delay reaching the limit, or whether it is good or bad for the economy to be at a point of steady state. Among these economists, Malthus is the most pessimistic in terms of the future of development, societies, and technological progress. Malthus radically argues that there was a limit to growth in the late eighteenth century, even before great industrial expansion took place. Malthus argues that population growth would inevitably outpace the growth in food production and that sustainable improvement in living standards would not be possible. He even goes further with this concern to the point that egalitarian social arrangements would only accelerate the growth of the poor population and exceed the food supply, thus harming the rich population. For Malthus, the steady state is clearly an undesirable disaster. In his theory of population, however, Malthus makes no criticism of industrial growth, resource depletion, or environmental degradation (Higgs, 2014). On the other hand, although his ideas had shortcomings and the policies he proposed were not adopted, he became the most inspirational economist in the studies on the limits of growth in the following years.

Ricardo believes that England is a prosperous and progressive society, far from the steady-state point, and is not very interested in the idea of the end of growth. Mill, like other political economists, sees the endless growth as possible, but contrary to other political economists, he claims that the end of growth is not actually a bad condition. According to him, the end of economic growth will present the opportunity for continuous progress toward higher human and social achievements than ever before, and a steady-state society is the most ideal one. While this ideal society does not increase production, consumption, and wealth anymore, it spends its energy on aiming and achieving progress in more civilized areas (Rose, 2020).

In fact, the concern that pushed classical political economists to distance themselves from the endless growth approach was the limited availability of fertile agricultural lands, which was a fundamental factor in production at that time (Bonaiuti, 2014). However, before the end of the century, mainstream economics disproves the steady-state argument. According to mainstream economics, supply and demand is balanced by market relations. The relationship between the limitations of land and growth is undermined as the structure of the economy is transformed from agriculture to industry, along with practices such as rapid industrialization, excessive use of natural resources, and exploitation of colonies (Hiroi, 2019). In addition, the experience of tremendous technological progress has a serious impact on the economists' conception of steady state. As a factor of production, land is not important as labor and capital. After these developments, the classical political economists' concern about the limits of growth is replaced by the understanding of endless growth. The steady state is also turned into an analytical concept rather than a reality (Kerschner, 2010).

As a political economist outside of this tradition, Marx focuses his research on how a real equilibrium might be possible beyond capitalism. Marx mainly focuses on how the end of economic development will come rather than its limit. He characterizes the capitalist mode of production by a continuous technological change that revolutionizes the productive forces in pursuit of profit, and this process has a constant tendency to expand. Marx's system analysis not only explains the dynamics of capital accumulation, but also emphasizes the role of capital accumulation process and technical progress on economic growth and the crisis of the system. To analyze the inner nature of capitalism, Marx deals with aspects of growth such as income distribution, reserve army of labor, mechanization (technical progress), and labor productivity (Nikolaos & Tsaliki, 2021). However, Marx is never able to reject the material progress ideology of industrial capitalism and does not foresee serious limits to economic growth (Higgs, 2014).

Marx predicts that the end of capitalism would come because of its own contradictions, including growing inequality and impoverishment of labor. Particularly at this point, he puts a special emphasis on capital accumulation and technological change that lead to greater economic productivity. Marx argues that technological change will bring with it decreases in wages and profits and ultimately the end of the process of capital accumulation. Investing in new technologies will reduce the need for labor and, accordingly, lower wages. Due to poverty and unemployment, the demand for the goods will decrease, diminishing then profits. Decreasing profits, on the other hand, are the harbingers of the end of endless growth and the system.

Nonetheless, the capitalist system continued to expand until the Great Depression of 1929; thus, Marx's prophecy did not come true. But the depression revealed a reality that is hardly discernible. This reality was that for mass production to be profitable and constant, it must either meet demand (Say's law) or be in demand (Higgs, 2017). Keynes was the first economist who observed this situation best. He convincingly explains that the production bottlenecks and widespread unemployment that emerged in economies are due to insufficient spending. Keynes also argues that government interventions are important to increase spending. However, he pays little attention to the role of investments in expanding the economy's productive capacity (Victor, 2014). He only states that the increase in the consumption tendency will lead to an increase in investment demand. Later, economists such as Harrod (1939) and Domar (1946) discuss how the changes in consumption and aggregate demand affect investment demand, capital accumulation, and long-term economic growth. Harrod and Domar's growth model, which argues that the capital-output ratio and growth are related to the level of savings and investment, starts to popularize capital accumulation at the end of the 1940s (Escobar, 2014).

Around the same period, Schumpeter (1942) challenges the assumption of mainstream economic thought that economic growth is based on capital accumulation. According to him, the source of the cycles faced by capitalism is the crisis of capital accumulation. Technological change is the real instrument of growth, capitalist expansion, and overcoming crises of capital accumulation. Technological developments that bring dynamism and stability to the free market economy also create permanent revolutions (creative destruction) in the way goods and services are produced and presented. The main representatives of these processes are visionary entrepreneurs seeking competitive advantages. Seeing the rising wave of technological development after World War II, Schumpeter changes his mind and brings that the R&D departments of large companies become the core of industrial innovations (Pansera & Fressoli, 2021).

With Schumpeter's work, concerns about capital accumulation decrease. The importance of investments, capital accumulation, and technological change in the growth process by increasing labor productivity is again discussed in the early 1960s and is re-expressed by (especially mainstream neoclassical) mathematical growth models. During these years, development economics emerges as a new academic field and human welfare is defined by economic growth and the use of resources. In these early years of the Cold War, development economists especially regarded technology and capital accumulation as the main elements of human progress and indispensable for capitalism (Higgs, 2014). As one of the development economists of the period, Lewis (1954) draws attention to the fact that progress depends on capital accumulation and that people who save should be protected during the creation of the first accumulation. In addition, Rostow (1960) writes about what stages a self-sustaining growth process would go through and how to formulate development as capitalism.

3 Modern Growth Theories and Endless Growth

After Schumpeter's work, mainstream economics realizes that the view that growth is based solely on capital accumulation is incomplete. In this new era, modern growth theories start to put innovations and technological progress at the center of their analysis. Capital accumulation is also considered important in new growth models, but it is not overemphasized as in the views of classical political economists. Instead, the self-regulatory characteristics of the market are highlighted. These modern growth theories have long regarded technological development as the most important determinant of economic growth. In addition, these new theories are divided into two groups as neoclassical and endogenous growth theories. These theories differ in terms of their assumptions about the role of technology, factors of production, and human capital in economic growth.

Neoclassical growth theory predicts that the long-term growth of living standards depends on the economy's own dynamics, such as the rate of population growth, the rate of savings, the rate of technical progress, and the capital-to-depreciation ratio. On the other hand, endogenous growth theories explain technological change with endogenous factors. In addition, the endogenous growth models try to go beyond neoclassical explanations, which do not adequately capture the endless growth regime. The endogenous models consider human capital and innovations to explain economic growth.

The work of Solow (1956) and Swan (1956) on growth is the beginning of neoclassical and modern growth models. This neoclassical model, also called as the Solow-Swan growth model, assumes that only two factors of production (labor and capital) are used in production with decreasing returns. They also assume that initial saving rates, technological development, and population growth rate are exogenous and constant, and the capital is depreciated at a constant rate. The most important inference of the model is that endless growth is only possible with external technological changes. On the other hand, it does not neglect the function of capital accumulation in the growth process, which is the only internal factor since the growth in output is related to the accumulation of capital. In the short run, both technological progress and capital accumulation can make a positive contribution to the growth rate. However, capital accumulation is associated with savings. Due to diminishing returns in the long run, capital accumulation is passive at best and only functions as a growth promoter. Therefore, the growth rate in the long run is determined only by technology. Capital accumulation, on the other hand, affects only the level of output, not the growth rate. In short, productivity-enhancing technological progress is an inevitable necessity for the continuity of growth (Howitt & Aghion, 1998).

Structural economic policy recommendations of the model are to reduce the population growth rate, increase savings, encourage technological development, and reduce the depreciation rate of capital. According to one of the well-known implications of the model, the long-run growth rate of output, capital, and consumption per capita will be equal to zero under a given level of technology, saving rate, population growth rate, and depreciation rate. Since it is assumed in the model that every economy has roughly the same basic characteristics, economies will surely encounter this steady-state growth (absolute convergence) in the long run. Another well-known implication of the model is conditional convergence. Conditional convergence suggests that countries with lower per capita output grow faster than developed countries and that differences in terms of development levels between countries will disappear over time when other conditions are similar.

The neoclassical growth model mainly emphasizes technological progress for endless growth but does not adequately explain how this can be achieved. The model assumes that firms have perfect and complete knowledge of the best available technology at any given time and considers technology as an exogenous and constant parameter. This insufficient explanation is one of the weakest aspects of the model. On the other hand, the model implicitly predicts that the population growth rate should remain constant or decrease so that growth is continuous. Because, when productivity decreases, despite technological progress, per capita output, consumption, and capital stock can only increase if the population growth rate is constant or decreases. Decreased returns constitute another weak point of the model. In addition, the model assumes that the rise of per capita consumption and even of the capital stock are not subject to any limits. On the other hand, the parameters that determine the return on investment and how realistic the inferences of the model will be in cases of low savings and high depreciation rates are other issues that remain unclear (Strauss, 2010).

The AK model provides the first explanation about how to overcome the problem of diminishing returns in production, which is an important obstacle to endless growth. This model is the forerunner of later endogenous growth theories. The model asserts that as long as the saving rate is greater than the population growth rate and the depreciation rate, a positive growth in capital per capita and hence output is possible. This model regards investments as the most important factor in the growth process. An increase in investment (growth in capital accumulation) is associated with a permanently higher growth rate. Thus, the model explains how economic growth is possible in the long run even at an external and stable technology level (Barro & Sala-i-Martin, 2005; Bond et al., 2010; Yildiz, 2018).

Dissatisfaction with the explanations of the neoclassical growth model motivated the construction of new growth theories in the mid-1980s. These new theories claim that key determinants of growth are intrinsic. As prominent figures of these theories, Romer (1986) and Lucas (1988) claim that long-term growth is determined by internal factors, rather than external factors. The focus is on explaining how long-term and endless growth is produced internally by suggesting new channels such as human capital, innovation, and knowledge and how the problem of diminishing returns can be overcome.

There are two types of endogenous growth approaches: capital accumulation-based (AK type) and innovation-based (R&D, innovation). AK-type endogenous growth theories focus on the endogenous accumulation of physical and human capital and emphasize the importance of investments in both types of capital (e.g., Romer, 1986; Lucas, 1988; Rebelo, 1991; Mankiw et al., 1992). Following Uzawa (1965), these theorists claim that the growth rate of countries will slow down or increase, especially depending on whether human capital is scarce or abundant. In addition, endogenous growth theorists such as Aschauer (1989), Pecorino (1993) and Zeng (2003) draw attention to the important functions of the public sector in this accumulation process.

Innovation-based endogenous growth theories, on the other hand, focus on innovation and spillover effects based on Nelson and Phelps' (1966) technological spillover theory (e.g., Romer, 1990; Grossman & Helpman, 1993; Aghion & Howitt, 1992; Benhabib & Spiegel, 1994). In this approach, innovations come to the fore as the source of growth. According to these models, R&D investments of companies create innovations which spread then to the economy over time. Ultimately, technological changes caused by increases in the stock of knowledge rescale the production function by increasing the productivity of labor and capital.

In endogenous growth models, the main economic agents are producers, inventors, and consumers. Inventors are the drivers of economic growth. These agents invest resources in continuous research to improve quality. When the time comes, producers and consumers, on the other hand, face creative and disruptive change because of technological progress and replacement of old goods by new ones (Aghion & Howitt, 1992). Although there are differences between endogenous growth models in terms of factors such as patent periods and innovation costs, there is a consensus that increases in human capital and innovation will drive the growth rate away from zero. The most important way out of zero growth is to reduce innovation costs (Romer, 1990; Grossman & Helpman, 1993). Especially R&D investments are of critical importance in reducing innovation costs. In addition, endogenous growth models explain why conditional convergence is not possible with technological changes. Differences in technological change are explained by human capital, knowledge externalities, and spillover effects.

More recently, endogenous growth models such as Aghion and Howitt (1998, 2017), van Marrewijk (1999), and Zeng (2003) bring together capital accumulation and innovation, suggesting that both are important in growth dynamics. More capital accumulation is needed for R&D investments, and technological progress is needed for more capital accumulation. For-profit firms, entrepreneurs, and investors allocate resources to technology and innovation to reduce factor costs, meet or steer changing consumer preferences, maintain or expand market share, and survive in the market. Increasing the assortment of goods increases the productivity of capital goods, which in turn leads to capital accumulation. Capital accumulation in turn increases the productivity and profitability of the development process of new products. Increases in productivity and profitability lead to inventions, which in turn increases capital accumulation.

Some other modern growth theories focus on how to reduce the differences in growth rates between countries and how convergence is possible (i.e., Nelson & Phelps, 1966; Krugman, 1979; Aghion et al., 2001; Acemoglu et al., 2010). These new models are also optimistic about endless growth. They explain how growth is possible in the long run using assumptions such as clusters, intellectual property rights, communication, integration of supply chains, fertility preferences, government intervention, and labor preference for work and leisure (Strauss, 2010).

Growth accounting research (e.g., Crafts, 2010) also significantly confirms modern growth theories. According to the results of the studies, technical change is the main driver of growth and dominates other sources of growth, especially physical and human capital accumulation. But technical change is not the only factor that increases output, since output also increases due to increased capital accumulation that is depending on increases in output (Smulders et al., 2014).

4 The Limits of Endless Growth

The ideology of endless growth is very popular and continues to dominate strongly. However, there is also a rich literature claiming that endless growth is impossible and that growth is subject to natural and social limits. While the growth ideology is mostly criticized by social opponents in the early period, the harshest criticism in recent years comes mostly from environmental economists. Relatively few studies explain why endless growth is not possible through the methodological flaws of growth theories (e.g., Ponzi et al., 2003; Gomes, 2006; Strauss, 2010). Some opponents criticize capitalist endless growth, arguing that growth does not necessarily or automatically lead to more prosperous societies (e.g., D'Alisa et al., 2014; Kallis, 2014; Piketty, 2014; Kallis et al., 2018).

The strongest argument for limits to growth comes from the ecological approach, which claims that the planet we live on has a limited capacity. Environmental economists such as Boulding, 2015[1966], Georgescu-Roegen (1971), Daly (1974, 1991), Meadows et al. (1972) and Ayres (1998) question the foundations of mainstream economic principles and propose a serious deconstruction which reveals that the idea of endless growth is wrong. Environmental economists point out that economic activities have a limited planetary capacity, which is called natural capital. Their common concern is that a system that requires endless economic growth (capitalism) is unsustainable on a planet with limited resources. On the other hand, although environmental economists have a common concern (environmental collapse) and similar criticisms, they also significantly diverge at certain points. Although it is not easy to make a classification, the most basic environmentalist criticisms toward endless growth are about Georgescu-Roegen's (1971) bio-economics, Daly's (1974) steady-state economics, and the discussions of the Club of Rome.

Georgescu-Roegen's (1971) theory of bio-economics is a basic starting point. In this approach, the limits of economic growth are related to the entropic nature of economic processes. According to the law of entropy, every productive activity involves the irreversible decay of increasing amounts of energy. Since economic processes take place in the natural environment and require use of non-renewable resources (energy and material), it leads to two consequences (Bonaiuti, 2014); (1) The fact that the endless growth of production and consumption contradicts the laws of thermodynamics, and (2) the unrealistic expectation that there will be an infinite cycle where demand creates production and production creates new demand through income.

The law of entropy also applies to all natural resources to some extent. Based on this idea, Georgescu-Roegen proposes a new law, which is called the fourth (or economics) law of thermodynamics. According to him, while all natural resources are subject to entropic depletion, economic production occurs as a physical process that inevitably accelerates dispersion (Foley, 2012). Economic production leads to the consumption of material resources and energy and creates a large amount of waste. Although some materials are potentially recyclable unlike energy, this recycling is never fully realized (Kerschner, 2010). This also means that even if the self-renewal process of the universe is supported by human beings, complete recycling is out of question as long as economic production continues.

Georgescu-Roegen's student Daly (1974) draws attention to the physical limitations of growth, saying that infinite growth requires an ever-growing ecosystem. Like his teacher, he builds his steady-state approach in thermodynamics. Daly (1974) first states that the physical world we live on is indispensable for economic activities. However, production requires resource inputs and sinks in the physical world where waste can be absorbed. An economy that produces large quantities of material artifacts requires large resources and large sinks. If these sinks are insufficient, exhaustion and pollution become inevitable. The scale of economic enterprise must therefore be proportional to the scale of the natural world. Daly argues that standard economic models do not contain variables to represent resources or waste and are therefore incapable of reflecting thermodynamic limits (Higgs, 2017).

Daly proposes steady-state economics as a solution to the scaling problem. Steady-state economics requires the following five principles to be met: (1) the depletion of resource stocks should be prevented (there should be regeneration), (2) waste emissions should not exceed the waste absorption capacity, (3) the basic needs of the population should be met without non-renewable resources by current technologies, (4) resource extraction and waste emissions should not threaten the ecosystem, and (5) population stability should be ensured. Thus, achieving a steady-state economy can only happen in two ways. First, there should be low but stable resource stocks and subsistence consumption considering large human populations. Second, there should be rich resource stocks and high per capita consumption considering a small population. The model obviously suggests that the growth rate should stop at the point where the marginal costs of production equal the marginal returns (Farley, 2014). This means that growth in both population and material production is zero (Higgs, 2014).

Another environmental critique of the endless growth regime is "The Limits to Growth Report," which is based on systems theory and an estimate of the biophysical limits of the universe. The report is written by a team of scientists at the Massachusetts Institute of Technology. The main concern is that economies would continue to grow exponentially on a finite planet. Researchers identify five key areas of potential crisis: rapid industrialization, rapid population growth, widespread malnutrition, depletion of non-renewable resources, and a deteriorating environment. The main conclusion of the report is that endless growth is almost impossible. The report also includes models of computer simulations (World3) which reveal that if no action is taken, we will encounter a global stagnant situation in about a century (by 2070) (Meadows & Randers, 2012; Higgs, 2014).

However, this warning of the Club of Rome and other environmentalist in the 1970s is not taken seriously in the following years. Since the 1980s, the development of technology and innovation-based information and communication technologies, the development of financial markets and globalization, and the trend of neoliberalism undermine the fact that there are environmental costs of growth. In addition, increases in industrialization and economic expansion in the developing world in the second half of the twentieth century suppressed objections to endless growth. It is only at the beginning of the new century that the debate regained vitality.

One of the key promises of the endless growth ideology is a better standard of living for all. A more prosperous life for all means a world without inequalities, poverty, and exclusion. However, critics of growth and capitalism point out that inequalities increase in every period of capitalism (Bourguignon & Morrisson, 2002). In fact, even after 1980s when capitalism expanded with continuous growth, there was no decrease in inequalities (Milanovic, 2012). Rodgers (2011) defines inequality as the most important problem of our time and states that it is the primary threat to humanity. According to critics, with economic growth and production relations, capitalism produces its own contradictions as it expands. In addition to the unsustainability arising from the society–nature relationship, these contradictions manifest as poverty or inequality arising from the labor-capital relationship. On the other hand, inequalities become a transmission channel of human development that reinforces environmental and socio-political crises that drag capitalism into crisis (Cairo-i-Cespedes & Castells-Quintana, 2016).

In fact, mainstream economic theory accepts that inequality is inevitable to some extent in growing economies. This theory considers inequality as a development problem and argues that inequalities will decrease with economic development. The claim is that in the long run there is a positive relationship between a decrease in income inequality and increases in capital accumulation and growth. As physical capital accumulation is the main source of growth in the early stages of development, inequality accelerates the growth rate and development process due to the transfer of resources to capital owners with a higher propensity to save. However, as the return on human capital increases at advanced development levels, human capital and a more egalitarian distribution become incentives for growth (Galor & Weil, 1999). In addition, equity may be a necessary condition for growth in advanced stages of development due to skill- or talent-based technological change caused by human capital accumulation. Because the effect of inequality on growth depends on the relative returns of human and physical capital. In the long run, equality may be an incentive for sustainable growth, depending on the propensity to save, constraints on credits, and whether the relationship between human capital and physical capital is complementary (Galor & Moav, 2004). However, empirical research is far from providing strong evidence for the implications of mainstream theory on the relationship between inequality and growth (Alesina & Rodrik, 1994; Persson & Tabellini, 1994; Banerjee & Duflo, 2003).

On the other hand, mainstream theory also neglects the effects of income inequalities on aggregate demand and income. Decline in living standards also causes a decrease in consumption, aggregate demand, capital accumulation, and profits by narrowing the demand for goods and services. Therefore, this regression will cause a decrease in growth rates. In addition, greater inequality threatens growth by becoming a cause of social conflict, social instability, decreases in well-being (Bonaiuti, 2014) and environmental losses (Cairo-i-Cespedes & Castells-Quintana, 2016). On the other hand, Piketty (2014) suggests that inequalities are not the result of growth but the result of the falling growth rate after the 1970s. In this period, the growth rates decreased at a lower level than the rate of return on capital, and this led to an increase in the capital-income ratio. Piketty points out that reduced labor returns for households will result in worse inequality and stagnant or decreased wages.

Certain indicators show that income inequalities are constantly increasing on a global scale, and the Gini coefficient is rising. Inequalities seem to have become the cause of higher unemployment rates and lower growth. While growth has increased the size of the middle class in the developing world, there is no strong evidence that it has lifted millions out of poverty. Half of the world's population still lacks material security for living, and the wealth that is created is concentrated more in a privileged minority (Hickel, 2017). In short, poverty continues to rise in the world despite growth. Billions of people still do not have access to basic human needs such as drinking water, hygiene, food, health, shelter, and education. The decline in quality of life as a whole continues. In addition, the created wealth is concentrated in the hands of a minority, including developed economies. The disproportionate concentration of income and wealth in a few hands leads to the accumulation of power and resistance to policy change (Kallis, 2014).

5 Mainstream Stance against Critical Challenges

Mainstream economics does not remain indifferent to environmentalist arguments in its early years. Early neoclassical growth models assume that technological progress increases inexhaustible resources and that there is a perfect substitution between resources. These models assert that capital accumulation has no limits and continues to legitimize the regime of endless growth. Solow and the mainstream economists who followed him deny the physical limits to endless growth by drawing particular attention to the role of technical progress. Early neoclassical growth models (e.g., Dasgupta & Heal, 1974; Solow, 1974; Stiglitz, 1974) rescale the production function by adding natural capital consisting of non-renewable resources. The main purpose of the proposed models is to identify the principles which would ensure that at least per capita consumption does not decrease and the ways to make the best use of natural resources. Considering that the substitution between resources is flexible, these economists argue that economies can grow if there are technical changes, despite production bottlenecks that may result from shortages of raw materials. In short, the main implication of these models is that sustainable growth is possible even in conditions of exhaustible, limited, and necessary resources, and positive population growth.

Solow (1974) argues that advanced economies can eliminate all harmful waste and that economic growth will certainly provide the necessary technology. According to him, industrial production does not necessarily produce waste and it cannot be subject to thermodynamic limits. Pollution is not a condition related to production. Pollution is caused by flaws in the price system. In fact, Solow believes that pollution could be easily corrected through waste management and public intervention (Higgs, 2014). In response to the argument of thermodynamic limits to growth in later years, some mainstream economists (e.g., Smulders, 1999) try to overcome physical limits by suggesting many channels such as expanded technical progress through innovation, renewable natural capital, productivity improvement, as well as the optimism of flexibility of substitution (Strauss, 2010).

Endogenous growth models also try to explain how endless growth is possible by adopting assumptions such as the limited natural capital, the decreasing returns as a result of thermodynamic laws, the unlimited technological progress, and the perfect substitution between natural capital and physical capital. According to these models, endless growth will result in decreasing environmental quality as an alternative cost (e.g., Stokey, 1998). However, most models suggest that an ecologically sustainable growth is possible (e.g., Smulders, 1999). In addition, endogenous growth models allow the transition from goods to services by incorporating knowledge and human capital into capital accumulation, which enables endless growth. Thus, the models try to explain how sustainable growth is possible even in the presence of non-renewable resources (Grimaud & Rouge, 2008). Mainstream economics regards the environmental pessimism of critical economics to be excessive. Because waste problems will be solved by the development of cleaner or more efficient technologies (Bovenberg & Smulders, 1995; Aghion & Howitt, 1998; Kornafel & Telega, 2020) or a structural shift from manufacturing to services (Rodrigues et al., 2005).

Technological progress always has a key role in the mainstream economics, both for increasing energy efficiency (or for reducing pollution) and for other resources. The source of technological progress is improvements and innovations. Technological advances can help us to overcome the physical limits of energy resources and delay depletion times. Technological progress and innovations can increase efficiency by leading to lower energy use intensity (de-materialization) in the long run. However, increasing efficiency still depends on regulatory interventions and adequate price incentives. Human capital is at the core of these processes. Investments in improvements and innovations result in reductions in unit costs of factors and energy, and yield productivity gains. However, since the information is not homogeneous for all sectors in the economy, the emergence of new technologies excludes certain sectors. In addition, achievements and accumulation in knowledge will occur in the economy over time. These will cumulatively increase the efficiency of capital types and energy, ensuring the continuity of positive growth (Saunders, 2016).

Although there are different perspectives, opinions on innovations are shaped around two presuppositions; innovation (1) induces growth and thus prosperity for all, and (2) expands the limits of growth imposed by scarcity of resources. In addition, the claims about innovation include technological innovations and changes bring more social benefits than risks and harms; innovation creates more and better jobs; the efficient use of technical systems ensures less use of natural resources and environmental sustainability (Strand et al., 2018). These assumptions lead to two basic beliefs. The first is technological determinism: technological advances are inevitable. Second, productivity innovations lead to economic growth, increased welfare, and job creation, and in itself is a good thing (Pansera & Fressoli, 2021).

Mainstream economics does not deny the importance of clean energy from renewable energy sources such as solar or wind to prevent environmental degradation but considers that it is not the only solution. Alternative and clean energy from renewable energy sources is relatively more expensive in terms of production costs. It also has costs such as interruptions and storage problems (Smulders et al., 2014). There are also a number of barriers to relying on renewable energy. First, renewable energy offers a lower return on energy investment under current technology compared to fossil fuels. Second, even for the transition to renewable energy, a large amount of conventional energy expenditure is required. Third, renewable energy is more suitable for small economies (Kallis et al., 2018).

Mainstream economics directly challenges critical economics' objection to inequality by presenting itself as a recipe for endless growth. According to mainstream thought, if growth is sustained and wealth is distributed fairly, slow but endless growth can make everyone better off forever (Rose, 2020). Because only with sustained growth, wealth increases and people have more opportunities to achieve their goals and satisfy their basic needs (Baumol et al., 2007).

It is assumed that the growth process yields more returns in favor of capital and wages stagnate or begin to decline. Saunders (2016) states that increases in labor mobilization and technology-induced productivity gains in developed economies erode the power of labor. However, he also claims that this process lowers the real prices of goods and services. This process increases the purchasing power of all segments of the society. Inequalities experienced in developing economies are seen as a development problem arising from the inadequacy of capital accumulation. As a manifestation of the inequalities in these countries, poverty and exclusion are claimed to be related to their delayed involvement in growth and development processes that are seen as progressive and universal. It is believed that rising income and prosperity with growth will also prevent poverty and exclusion by expanding freedoms, opportunities, individual abilities, and capacities (Nussbaum, 2011; Tomasi, 2012). It is claimed that inequality will decrease, wages will converge, and the problem of poverty will be overcome in developing countries with industrialization and capital mobility (Saunders, 2016).

According to mainstream economics, the pursuit of endless growth also encourages innovation and technological developments that increase people's opportunities and protect societies against future risks. Mainstream economics argues that increasing innovations and technological advances with economic growth will offer opportunities for people to develop their talents and shape their lives in more enjoyable and meaningful ways. In addition, advances in technology protect societies against risks that have devastating effects on a large scale (such as natural disasters, epidemics, global warming, and climate change). On the other hand, according to mainstream economics, endless growth is a moral imperative. Endless growth also has moral benefits such as attitudes of openness, tolerance, and generosity that is necessary for the functioning and continuity of a liberal democratic society (Baumol et al., 2007).

Nevertheless, critical economists regard endless growth as a moral problem and strongly argue against the growth fetishism of mainstream economics and its justifications. According to critical economics, growth needs to be evaluated differently. However, although they have similar arguments about how this evaluation should be, they do not have a common consensus (for the contrary claim, see Kerschner, 2010). The critical approaches are zero-growth, which follows Daly's steady-state economics (e.g., Jackson, 2009; Blewitt & Cunningham, 2014; Farley, 2014) and degrowth, which adopts Georgescu-Roegen's view of entropy (e.g., Latouche, 2009; D'Alisa et al., 2014; Bonaiuti, 2014; Kallis et al., 2018).

However, both approaches have the notion that endless growth is neither desirable nor actually feasible. They argue that greening is not possible with the market-based solutions of capitalism and growth. They strongly criticize the proposed technical improvements for ecological modernization. Contrary to what is claimed, they argue that energy efficiency based on technical advances will not reduce the use of energy and materials but will increase energy and material consumption as resources become cheaper (Andreucci & McDonough, 2014; Kallis, 2014; Farley, 2014). According to them, increasing energy efficiency can lead to an increase in both output and energy use, as it reduces the cost of output, as predicted by the Jevons paradox. Therefore, technical progress is not the magic formula for humanity to get completely rid of its dependence on energy (Brannlund et al., 2007).

The value of technical progress and innovation is not denied by critical economists. However, they oppose the idea that the only way to generate new ideas and technologies is endless growth. They also state that although technical progress and innovations offer new opportunities, this may not be beneficial and may create greater risks for societies, such as nuclear energy, instead of protecting society against risks (Rose, 2020). They think that economic growth supported by innovations in an endless growth regime actually increases inequality. They are skeptical of the argument that innovations create more and better jobs. They argue that even if innovations increase labor productivity, they are not sufficient to provide prosperity or to remove poverty.

Critical economists challenge mainstream economics' view that bases the expansion of the capitalist system and the destiny of humanity on endless accumulation. They also think that sustained growth is often sustained by the higher sacrifices of the worse off. Most environmental (and critical) economists recommend moving to a carefully planned steady-state economy through a more socially equitable and democratic, but also environmentally sustainable degrowth. The main policy recommendations for this are to stabilize the population and consumption. In addition, environmental economists who defend the degrowth suggest that reducing consumption alone is not sufficient. Consumption should also be redistributed equally, and production should be collectivized.

6 Conclusion: The End of the Growth Paradigm and Capitalism?

In the century we live, the devastating effects of capitalism on the well-being of humanity and the future of our planet have become much more evident. Social inequalities have increased, as have environmental disasters. Anti-capitalism has become synonymous with anti-growth. Many approaches (e.g., degrowth, steady-state economics, bio-economics) have been developed that attempt to explain what the alternative to growth ideology and capitalist industrial civilization might look like. The main message of these anti-growth approaches is that endless growth is impossible on a finite planet and that if growth is indispensable, humanity faces a major collapse. Their main proposals are to push economic production to its natural and social limits and to reformulate economic prosperity and human development. On the other hand, proponents of growth and the capitalist system continue to reproduce the growth by proposing various frameworks (e.g., green growth, Green

New Deal, and circular economy) that they deem appropriate for the conditions of the time.

Although they make opposing claims about growth, there are two aspects on which the two ideologies have reached some consensus: the reduction of carbon footprint and the indispensability of technology. Both parties agree that the second aspect is important to achieve the first. However, there are different claims about the function of technological development. Capitalist liberal thought sees the progress of civilization and prosperity in a gradual and progressive context. It argues that technological innovations can continue to produce useful things in the future, as they have in the past. According to mainstream thinking, technological progress is the primary driver of growth and prosperity and promotes economic growth by creating new resources. Resource efficiency can be accelerated through technological innovation, and the ecological and material impacts of consumption and production can be mitigated without sacrificing growth. Simply put, technological progress and wealth creation are the inevitable path to overcoming all problems. Even the opponents of growth are aware that degrowth will not be possible without technological innovation, even in the most optimistic downsizing scenarios. However, they do not sufficiently consider that the new relations of production created by technological innovation also require a transformation of social systems. However, ending economic growth without social transformation increases instability even more.

The emphasis on technology in the two opposing views is, of course, important. However, the way they position technological progress is problematic in terms of the processes they offer. First, as far as we know, no technology has yet been discovered that is decoupled from carbon emissions and enables sustainable growth based on resource efficiency. No appropriate technological solutions have yet been found to overcome at least one of the negative aspects such as global warming, climate change, plastic and toxic pollution, or extinction of species. Even countries that are making efforts to decarbonize continue to emit emissions into the atmosphere. Even a green growth strategy alone is not enough to reduce emissions. Even new investments and renewable energy technologies can only partially reduce emissions. If growth continues, emissions will inevitably increase worldwide. On the other hand, technological innovations in the capitalist system cannot be seen as the savior for eliminating inequalities. Not all masses have access to new technologies, and only a limited segment of society will continue to benefit from the technological blessings of the new growth strategies.

Technological progress is necessary for the abandonment of growth and planned degrowth, but that alone is not enough. First, opponents have not explained how the necessary resources for new technologies can be created without growth. Moreover, as far as we know, there is no strong evidence that degrowth, supported by technological change, will be a solution to the environmental crisis. On the other hand, it is likely that the redistribution of resources in anti-growth, green economies will also raise issues of social and environmental justice (e.g., ownership and conflict). As in mainstream thinking, anti-growth approaches cannot provide clear solutions for reducing social inequalities.

Two opposing ideologies are content to offer us their predictions about where capitalist industrial civilization and our growth framework should go. They cannot, however, provide accurate information about whether we have reached an inevitable end to growth and whether human history is changing. Proponents of growth believe that environmental and humanitarian crises can be overcome with growth. Opponents of growth, on the other hand, fear that a major collapse is in store for humanity if the current style of growth continues as it is and suggest that a way out of the collapse is only possible by turning away from endless growth and capitalism. It must be admitted that the views of the proponents of growth and capitalism still dominate, despite all the challenges of the latter, and it seems that they will maintain this position in the years to come. One can even argue that this liberal thinking is moving toward new neoliberalism.

In the history of mankind, many civilizations have developed and then collapsed. The collapse of civilizations occurred when they reached their limits and a combination of complex social factors. When the production and organizational systems of civilizations lost the ability to produce solutions to their problems, their collapse was inevitable. The process of civilization has been characterized by the successful development of technological transformations. Now, can we speak of an end reached for the present capitalist industrial civilization? It is very difficult to answer this question. We do not know with certainty whether we have already reached an end. But we do know that there is no complete global political and social consensus that capitalism has reached its natural and social limits.

Capitalist industrial civilization continues to reach its limits as it grows. The visions of organizations such as the United Nations (e.g., United Nations Framework Convention on Climate Change; 2030 Agenda for Sustainable Development; and Sustainable Development Goals) and the European Union (e.g., EU Climate Law and European Green Deal) that seek green and sustainable growth are based on the belief that it is possible to delay reaching this limit. In the process of delay, the creation of accumulation and technological development are seriously accepted as the main driving forces. Moreover, the search for new technologies ranges from speculative and marginal solutions such as nuclear fusion to deep geothermal technologies to space technologies based on the search for water and life. The zero-growth or degrowing economies envisioned by opponents of growth are subject to strict social and institutional constraints. These practices, which require holistic changes in production and organizational systems, involve serious difficulties and high capitalist opportunity costs. These alternative proposals are far from being a political and social choice. To summarize, capitalist industrial civilization will continue to reach its limits by following the indispensable path of growth. While it is clear that growth will continue and that, like previous civilizations, we are headed for collapse, it is uncertain when we will experience that collapse.

References

Acemoglu, D., Griffith, R., Aghion, P., & Zilibotti, F. (2010). Vertical integration and technology: Theory and evidence. *Journal of the European Economic Association, 8*(5), 989–1033.

Aghion, P., & Howitt, P. (1992). A model of growth through creative destruction. *Econometrica, 60*(2), 323.

Aghion, P., & Howitt, P. (1998). *Endogenous growth theory*. MIT Press.

Aghion, P., & Howitt, P. (2017). Some thoughts on capital accumulation, innovation, and growth. *Annals of Economics and Statistics, 125/126*, 57–78.

Aghion, P., Harris, C., Howitt, P., & Vickers, J. (2001). Competition, imitation and growth with step-by-step innovation. *The Review of Economic Studies, 68*(3), 467–492.

Alesina, A., & Rodrik, D. (1994). Distributive politics and economic growth. *The Quarterly Journal of Economics, 109*(2), 465–490.

Andreucci, D., & McDonough, T. (2014). Capitalism. In G. D'Alisa, F. Demaria, & G. Kallis (Eds.), *Degrowth* (pp. 87–90). Routledge.

Aschauer, D. A. (1989). Is public expenditure productive? *Journal of Monetary Economics, 23*(2), 177–200.

Ayres, R. U. (1998). Eco-thermodynamics: Economics and the second law. *Ecological Economics, 26*(2), 189–209.

Banerjee, A. V., & Duflo, E. (2003). Inequality and growth: What can the data say? *Journal of Economic Growth, 8*(3), 267–299.

Barro, R., & Sala-i-Martin, X. (2005). *Growth theory*. MIT Press.

Barry, J. (2020). A genealogy of economic growth as ideology and cold war core state imperative. *New Political Economy, 25*(1), 18–29.

Baumol, W. J., Litan, R. E., & Schramm, C. J. (2007). *Good capitalism, bad capitalism, and the economics of growth and prosperity*. Yale University Press.

Benhabib, J., & Spiegel, M. M. (1994). The role of human capital in economic development evidence from aggregate cross-country data. *Journal of Monetary Economics, 34*(2), 143–173.

Blewitt, J., & Cunningham, R. (2014). *The post-growth project: How the end of economic growth could bring a fairer and happier society*. Green House.

Bonaiuti, M. (2014). *The great transition*. Routledge.

Bond, S., Leblebicioğlu, A., & Schiantarelli, F. (2010). Capital accumulation and growth: A new look at the empirical evidence. *Journal of Applied Econometrics, 25*(7), 1073–1099.

Boulding, K. E. (2015). The economics of the coming spaceship earth. In V. Lippit (Ed.), *Radical political economy: Explorations in alternative economic analysis* (pp. 357–367). Routledge.

Bourguignon, F., & Morrisson, C. (2002). Inequality among world citizens: 1820-1992. *American Economic Review, 92*(4), 727–744.

Bovenberg, A. L., & Smulders, S. (1995). Environmental quality and pollution-augmenting technological change in a two-sector endogenous growth model. *Journal of Public Economics, 57*(3), 369–391.

Brannlund, R., Ghalwash, T., & Nordström, J. (2007). Increased energy efficiency and the rebound effect: Effects on consumption and emissions. *Energy Economics, 29*(1), 1–17.

Cairo-i-Cespedes, G., & Castells-Quintana, D. (2016). Dimensions of the current systemic crisis: Capitalism in short circuit? *Progress in Development Studies, 16*(1), 1–23.

Crafts, N. (2010). The contribution of new technology to economic growth: Lessons from economic history. *Revista de Historia Económica, 28*(3), 409–440.

Daly, H. E. (1974). The economics of the steady state. *American Economic Review, 64*(2), 15–21.

Daly, H. E. (1991). *Steady state economics: The economics of biophysical equilibrium and moral growth* (2nd ed.). W. H. Freeman.

Dasgupta, P., & Heal, G. (1974). The optimal depletion of exhaustible resources. *Review of Economic Studies, 41*(5), 3–28.

Domar, E. D. (1946). Capital expansion, rate of growth, and employment. Econometrica. *Journal of the Econometric Society, 14*, 137–147.

D'Alisa, G., Demaria, F., & Kallis, G. (2014). *Degrowth*. Routledge.
Escobar, A. (2014). Development: Critiques of. In G. D'Alisa, F. Demaria, & G. Kallis (Eds.), *Degrowth* (pp. 72–76). Routledge.
Farley, J. (2014). Steady state economics. In G. D'Alisa, F. Demaria, & G. Kallis (Eds.), *Degrowth* (pp. 100–104). Routledge.
Foley, D. K. (2012). Dilemmas of economic growth. *Eastern Economic Journal, 38*(3), 283–295.
Galor, O., & Weil, D. N. (1999). From Malthusian stagnation to modern growth. *American Economic Review, 89*(2), 150–154.
Galor, O., & Moav, O. (2004). From physical to human capital accumulation: Inequality and the process of development. *The Review of Economic Studies, 71*(4), 1001–1026.
Georgescu-Roegen, N. (1971). *The entropy law and the economic process*. Harvard University Press.
Gomes, O. (2006). Routes to chaos in macroeconomic theory. *Journal of Economic Studies, 33*(6), 437–468.
Gordon, R. J. (2012). *Is US economic growth over? Faltering innovation confronts the six headwinds*, NBER Working Paper, No. 18315.
Gordon, M. J., & Rosenthal, J. S. (2003). Capitalism's growth imperative. *Cambridge Journal of Economics, 27*(1), 25–48.
Grimaud, A., & Rouge, L. (2008). Environment, directed technical change and economic policy. *Environmental and Resource Economics, 41*(4), 439–463.
Grossman, G. M., & Helpman, E. (1993). *Innovation and growth in the global economy*. MIT Press.
Harrod, R. F. (1939). An essay in dynamic theory. *The Economic Journal, 49*(193), 14–33.
Harvey, D. (2010). *The enigma of capital and the crises of capitalism*. Oxford University Press.
Hickel, J. (2017). *The divide: A brief guide to global inequality and its solutions*. William Hienemann.
Higgs, K. (2014). *Collision course: Endless growth on a finite planet*. MIT Press.
Higgs, K. (2017). Limits to growth: Human economy and planetary boundaries. *The Journal of Population and Sustainability, 2*(1), 15–36.
Hiroi, Y. (2019). Science as care: Science and innovation in post-growth society. In S. Lechevalier (Ed.), *Innovation beyond technology* (pp. 301–324). Springer.
Hirsch, F. (1977). *Social limits to growth*. Routledge.
Howitt, P., & Aghion, P. (1998). Capital accumulation and innovation as complementary factors in long-run growth. *Journal of Economic Growth, 3*(2), 111–130.
Jackson, T. (2009). *Prosperity without growth: Economics for a finite planet*. Routledge.
Kallis, G. (2014). Social limits of growth. In G. D'Alisa, F. Demaria, & G. Kallis (Eds.), *Degrowth* (pp. 217–221). Routledge.
Kallis, G., Kostakis, V., Lange, S., Muraca, B., Paulson, S., & Schmelzer, M. (2018). Research on degrowth. *Annual Review of Environment and Resources, 43*, 291–316.
Kerschner, C. (2010). Economic de-growth vs. steady-state economy. *Journal of Cleaner Production, 18*(6), 544–551.
Kornafel, M., & Telega, I. (2020). Dynamics of natural capital in neoclassical growth model. *International Journal of Sustainable Economy, 12*(1), 1–24.
Krugman, P. R. (1979). Increasing returns, monopolistic competition, and international trade. *Journal of International Economics, 9*(4), 469–479.
Latouche, S. (2009). *Farewell to growth*. Polity Press.
Lewis, W. A. (1954). Economic development with unlimited supply of labour. *The Manchester School, 22*(2), 139–199.
Lucas, R. E. (1988). On the mechanics of economic development. *Journal of Monetary Economics, 22*(1), 3–42.
Mankiw, N. G., Romer, D., & Weil, D. N. (1992). A contribution to the empirics of economic growth. *Quarterly Journal of Economics, 107*(2), 407–437.
Mason. (2015, July). The end of capitalism has begun. *The Guardian*, Accessed Sep 02, 2021, from http://www.theguardian.com/books/2015/jul/17/postcapitalism-end-of-capitalism-begun

Meadows, D. H., Meadows, D. L., Randers, J., & Behrens, W. W. (1972). *The limits to growth: A report for the Club of Rome's project on the predicament of mankind*. Universe Books.

Meadows, D., & Randers, J. (2012). *The limits to growth: The 30-year update*. Routledge.

Milanovic, B. (2012). *Global income inequality by the numbers: In history and now- an overview*. World Bank Policy Research Working Paper, No. 6259.

Nelson, R. R., & Phelps, E. S. (1966). Investment in humans, technological diffusion, and economic growth. *American Economic Review, 56*(1/2), 69–75.

Nikolaos, C., & Tsaliki, P. (2021). The dynamics of capital accumulation in Marx and Solow. *Structural Change and Economic Dynamics, 57*, 148–158.

Nussbaum, M. C. (2011). *Creating capabilities: The human development approach*. Harvard University Press.

Pansera, M., & Fressoli, M. (2021). Innovation without growth: Frameworks for understanding technological change in a post-growth era. *Organization, 28*(3), 380–404.

Pecorino, P. (1993). Tax structure and growth in a model with human capital. *Journal of Public Economics, 52*(2), 251–271.

Persson, T., & Tabellini, G. (1994). Representative democracy and capital taxation. *Journal of Public Economics, 55*(1), 53–70.

Piketty, T. (2014). *Capital in the twenty-first century*. Harvard University Press.

Ponzi, A., Yasutomi, A., & Kaneko, K. (2003). A non-linear model of economic production processes. *Physica A: Statistical Mechanics and its Applications, 324*(1–2), 372–379.

Rebelo, S. (1991). Long-run policy analysis and long-run growth. *Journal of Political Economy, 99*(3), 500–521.

Rockström, J., Steffen, W., Noone, K., Persson, Å., Chapin, F. S., Lambin, E. F., et al. (2009). A safe operating space for humanity. *Nature, 461*(7263), 472–475.

Rodgers, D. (2011). Introduction: The politics of poverty and inequality. *European Journal of Development Research, 23*(4), 511–512.

Rodrigues, J., Domingos, T., Conceição, P., & Belbute, J. (2005). Constraints on dematerialisation and allocation of natural capital along a sustainable growth path. *Ecological Economics, 54*(4), 382–396.

Romer, P. M. (1986). Increasing returns and long-run growth. *Journal of Political Economy, 94*(5), 1002–1037.

Romer, P. M. (1990). Endogenous technological change. *Journal of Political Economy, 98*(5), 71–102.

Rose, J. L. (2020). On the value of economic growth. *Politics, Philosophy & Economics, 19*(2), 128–153.

Rostow, W. (1960). *The stages of economic growth: A non-communist manifesto*. Cambridge University Press.

Saunders, H. (2016, June). Does capitalism require endless growth? Marx and Malthus reconsider. *The Breakthrough Institute*. Accessed Sep 02, 2022, from https://thebreakthrough.org/journal/issue-6/does-capitalism-require-endless-growth

Schumpeter, J. (1942). *Capitalism, socialism, and democracy*. Harper & Row.

Smulders, J. A. (1999). Economic growth and environmental quality. In H. Folmer & H. L. Gabel (Eds.), *Principles of environmental and resource economics* (pp. 602–664). Edward Elgar Publishing.

Smulders, S., Toman, M., & Withagen, C. (2014). Growth theory and 'green growth'. *Oxford Review of Economic Policy, 30*(3), 423–446.

Solow, R. M. (1956). A contribution to the theory of economic growth. *Quarterly Journal of Economics, 70*(1), 65–94.

Solow, R. M. (1974). The economics of resources or the resources of economics. *American Economic Review, 64*(2), 1–14.

Steffen, W., Richardson, K., Rockström, J., Cornell, S. E., Fetzer, I., Bennett, E. M., et al. (2015). Planetary boundaries: Guiding human development on a changing planet. *Science, 347*(6223), 1259855.

Stiglitz, J. E. (1974). Growth with exhaustible natural resources: The competitive economy. *Review of Economic Studies, 41*, 139–152.
Stokey, N. L. (1998). Are there limits to growth? *International Economic Review, 39*(1), 1–31.
Strauss, W. (2010). *The myth of endless growth: Exposing capitalism's unsustainability*. Lulu Press.
Strand, R., Saltelli, A., Giampietro, M., Rommetveit, K., & Funtowicz, S. (2018). New narratives for innovation. *Journal of Cleaner Production, 197*, 1849–1853.
Swan, T. W. (1956). Economic growth and capital accumulation. *Economic Record, 32*(2), 334–361.
Tomasi, J. (2012). *Free market fairness*. Princeton University Press.
Uzawa, H. (1965). Optimum technical change in an aggregative model of economic growth. *International Economic Review, 6*(1), 18–31.
van Marrewijk, C. (1999). Capital accumulation, learning, and endogenous growth. *Oxford Economic Papers, 51*(3), 453–475.
Victor, P. A. (2014). Growth. In G. D'Alisa, F. Demaria, & G. Kallis (Eds.), *Degrowth* (pp. 180–184). Routledge.
Yildiz, F. (2018). Theoretical approach to economic growth. In A. Gulmez & F. Besel (Eds.), *Economic growth: Theory and practice* (pp. 3–27). Cambridge Scholars.
Zeng, J. (2003). Reexamining the interaction between innovation and capital accumulation. *Journal of Macroeconomics, 25*(4), 541–560.

Energy, Economic Growth, and Ecological Collapse

Raif Cergibozan and Emre Akusta

Abstract Economic growth is at the core of all countries' economic policies. In order to ensure the continuity of the targeted economic growth, the use of energy needs to be increased day by day. Large part of the energy use is obtained from non-renewable sources like fossil fuels. The increase in the use of fossil fuels carries carbon emissions to serious levels, leading to changes in global climate patterns. Biodiversity is one of the most basic elements that show the sustainability of an ecosystem. With the effect of increasing global temperature, we observe that biodiversity is exposed to more threats today than in the past. The loss of biodiversity can cause an irreversible ecological collapse for the humanity. In this chapter, we analyze the relationship between economic growth, energy use, and environment by using available data. Thus, we assess the environmental limits of economic growth.

Keywords Energy use · Ecological economics · Climate change · Economic growth · Biodiversity loss

1 Introduction

Energy is one of the indispensable elements for meeting humans' basic needs and raising their standard of living. Therefore, energy is a typical global issue and has always managed to find an important place for itself throughout history. As seen in Fig. 1 that presents the evolution of industrial civilization, societies usually employed the power generated from human and animal bodies until the Industrial Revolution. Following the Industrial Revolution, mechanical power gained importance with the invention of machines. The rapid mechanization process brought an increase in energy demand and significantly changed the components of energy. In order to meet the increasing energy demand, fossil sources such as coal and oil

R. Cergibozan (✉) · E. Akusta
Department of Economics, Kirklareli University, Kirklareli, Turkey
e-mail: raif.cergibozan@klu.edu.tr; emre.akusta@klu.edu.tr

A. Ari (ed.), *Capitalism at a Crossroads*, Springer Studies in Alternative Economics,
https://doi.org/10.1007/978-3-031-23257-2_3

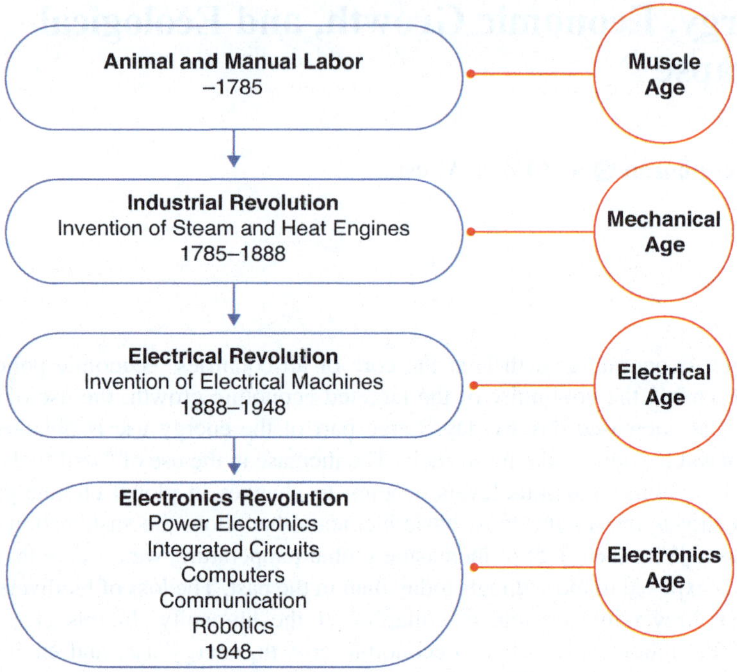

Fig. 1 Evolution of Industrial Civilization. Source: Authors' calculations based on Bose (2010, p. 2)

gained importance and their use became widespread. On the other hand, electricity gained great importance with the electric revolution and the invention of electric machines. In this period, fossil energy sources are not only used directly in machines, but they are also converted into electricity. Electricity has become more important with the electronics revolution from 1948 onwards.

In today's modern and industrialized societies, technological development, economic indicators, and defense determine the development level of countries. One of the most important resources for the sustainable development is energy because energy is an important input for production, which is a driving force for development and an element to increase welfare. As the economic growth provides a significant improvement in living standards (Jackson, 2016), economic growth has become the most important policy goal for all countries. Hence, governments design their policies to promote economic growth.

More growth leads to more energy use. Empirical studies confirm this relationship between these two variables. For instance, Kadoshin et al. (2000) find that a significant increase in energy consumption in the last half-century is related to increasing population and economic growth in both developed and developing countries. Other studies show that the most important factor causing an increase in energy consumption is economic growth (i.e., Ozturk et al., 2010; Eggoh et al., 2011; Al-Mulali & Sab, 2012; Gozgor et al., 2018; Thomas & Rosenow, 2020).

However, because of the enthusiasm for higher economic welfare, growth policies implemented with higher use of energy produced from fossil sources have caused environmental problems and climate change. Therefore, when choosing energy sources, the greater attention is paid not only to the amount of energy output, but also to their impact on the environment and their sustainability.

Environmental problems concern the whole world as a global problem, so do the solutions. In order to prevent environmental problems and climate change, the Kyoto Protocol and Paris Agreement ask countries to reduce their greenhouse gas emissions. For this reason, countries started to focus on renewable energy sources by limiting traditional energy sources that cause environmental pollution, greenhouse gas emissions, and global warming.

On the other hand, the environmental effects of energy consumption and the exploitation of resources have led to the emergence of economic growth debates. At this point, the environmental limits of economic growth are the focus of the discussion. From that perspective, is continuous growth possible or will it become impossible for countries to grow after a certain point? In order to respond to this question, this study analyzes the relationship between energy use, economic growth, and environment in the light of both theoretical and empirical studies in the literature.

The study is organized as follows. Section 2 discusses energy sources and consumption in the world and examines the relationship between energy and sustainable development, along with the issues of energy consumption during COVID-19. Section 3 analyzes the relationship between energy and economic growth with an emphasis on the findings of empirical studies. Section 4 presents the environmental limits of economic growth through a theoretical and historical discussion. Section 5 concludes with some policy implications.

2 Energy

In order to examine the relationship between energy, economic growth, and environment more clearly, it would be appropriate to first present the level of energy use in the world and the sources of energy. This will enable us to observe the trends of energy use in the historical process. We observe that throughout history the improvement in technology and welfare caused a rise in energy use with an expanding rate. The type and amount of energy resources vary according to the economic, technical, natural, political, and environmental conditions of the period.

In the following sub-section, we investigate energy perspectives and discuss the relationship between energy and sustainable development. We also show the impact of COVID-19 on energy consumption.

2.1 Energy Perspectives

Although fossil fuels are exhaustible, they are the world's most used energy sources. The damage of fossil fuels to the environment eased the use of alternative energy sources. In Fig. 2, worldwide energy consumption is shown by energy sources.

Figure 2 shows that fossil sources such as oil, natural gas, and coal form the first three sources for the world energy consumption. When we look at the historical process of energy consumption, we see that 64.72 exajoules of energy consumption were obtained from petroleum in 1965. This figure increased to 167.12 exajoules in 2009, to 191.89 exajoules in 2019, and decreased to 174.20 exajoules in 2020. Between 1965 and 2019, petroleum-based energy consumption increased by 196%, while in the 2019–2020 period it decreased by 9.5%.

In 1965, 22.69 exajoules of energy consumption were produced from natural gas. This figure increased to 105.91 exajoules in 2009, to 140.54 exajoules in 2019, and decreased to 137.62 exajoules in 2020. In other words, we observe that natural gas-based energy consumption increased by 519% while in the 2019–2020 period, it decreased by 2.3%.

In 1965, 58.10 exajoules of energy consumption were stemmed from coal. This figure increased to 144.57 exajoules in 2009, to 157.64 exajoules in 2019, and decreased to 151.42 exajoules in 2020. Considering the change between 1965 and 2019, coal-based energy consumption increased by 171% while in the 2019–2020 period it decreased by 4.2%.

In 1965, 9.23 exajoules of energy consumption were produced from hydroelectricity. This figure increased to 30.72 exajoules in 2009, to 37.69 exajoules in 2019, and to 38.16 exajoules in 2020. This means that hydroelectric energy consumption increased by 308% from 1965 to 2019 and by 1% between 2019 and 2020.

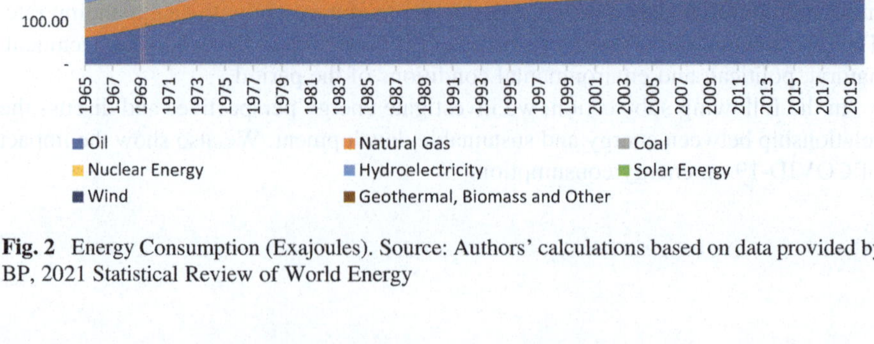

Fig. 2 Energy Consumption (Exajoules). Source: Authors' calculations based on data provided by BP, 2021 Statistical Review of World Energy

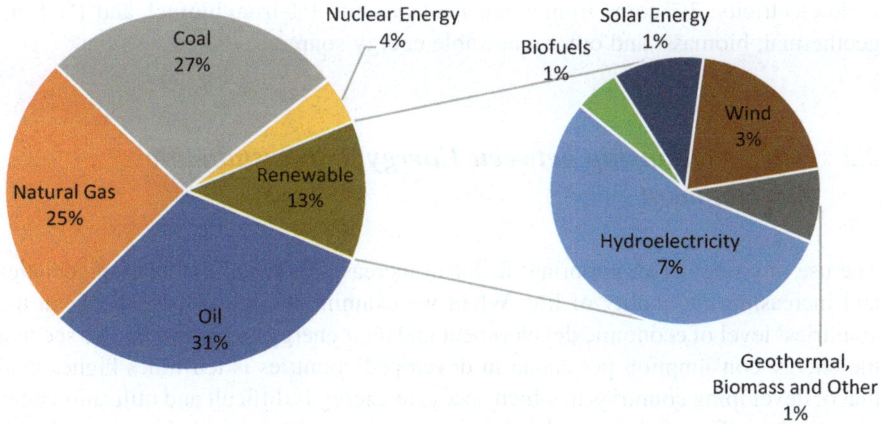

Fig. 3 Energy Consumption by Source (2020). Source: Authors' calculations based on data provided by BP, 2021 Statistical Review of World Energy

In 1991, 0.01 exajoule of energy consumption was obtained from the sun. This figure increased to 0.20 exajoule in 2009, to 6.31 exajoule in 2019, and to 7.60 exajoule in 2020. This shows that solar energy consumption increased by 630-fold from 1991 to 2019 and by 20% between 2019 and 2020.

In 1989, 0.03 exajoule of energy consumption was provided by wind. This figure increased to 2.61 exajoules in 2009, to 12.63 exajoules in 2019, and to 14.13 exajoules in 2020. This shows that wind-based energy consumption increased by 420-fold during the 1989–2019 period and by 14% from 2019 to 2020.

In 1965, 0.18 exajoules of energy consumption came from geothermal, biomass, and other renewable sources. This figure increased to 3.20 exajoules in 2009, to 5.91 exajoules in 2019, and to 6.22 exajoules in 2020. This shows that energy consumption from geothermal, biomass, and other renewable resources increased by 31.8-fold between 1965 and 2019 and by 5% from 2019 to 2020.

The main reason behind the decrease in total energy consumption in 2020 is the COVID-19 pandemic. The unprecedented cessation of economic activities due to the COVID-19 has had a great impact on global energy use and CO_2 emissions.

Obtaining energy from fossil sources dates back to ancient times. Today, most of the produced energy come from fossil sources. However, environmental problems and climate change have led to the necessity of taking precautions for fossil resources and the tendency to renewable resources has risen. In line with the explanations above, the amount of energy produced from renewable sources remains low compared to fossil sources, but its growth rate is considerably high.

Figure 3 presents world energy use figures by source for 2020. We see that 31% of the energy consumed in the world come from oil, 25% from natural gas, 27% from coal, 4% from nuclear, and 13% from renewable sources. If renewable energy sources are examined in detail in 2020, 7% of the energy consumption is met by hydroelectricity, 3% come from wind, 1% from sun, 1% from biofuel, and 1% from geothermal, biomass, and other renewable energy sources.

2.2 The Relationship between Energy and Sustainable Development

The use of energy is an important factor in increasing the welfare level of societies and increasing the quality of life. When we examine the relationship between the countries' level of economic development and their energy consumption, we see that the energy consumption per capita in developed countries is ten times higher than that of developing countries in which access to energy is difficult and utilization rates are very low. Therefore, more labor-intensive production is carried out in underdeveloped and developing countries. This shows that the amount of energy consumption and the level of development are directly proportional. In such a case, energy consumption has a direct impact on the welfare, and vice versa. However, beside raising the welfare level and increasing the quality of life, energy should be produced at low cost and in a way that causes the least damage to the environment. Governments should try to provide the energy to society uninterruptedly, safely, at low cost, and with the minimum damage to the environment (Mahmutoglu, 2013, p. 10). The main reason for energy-related environmental problems is the continuous increase in energy demand. The deep and complex relationships between energy, environment, and development have been explained by the International Energy Agency as follows (IEA, 2004): "The economic, social and environmental aspects of energy and human development are interlinked. Energy is an important input for both human development and economic activities. However, increasing energy demand leads to an increase in greenhouse gas emissions and climate change on a global scale."

Global scale issues require solutions on a global scale. The relationship between energy use and human development is very complex. There is no doubt that the complementary relationship between energy use and economic growth is clear; however, wrong investments or inefficient use of energy hinder economic growth and increase environmental problems. In many poor countries, inefficient public investment, ineffective management, and unsuccessful private investment cause energy shortages and reduce economic growth and development. The main components of sustainable development are given in Fig. 4.

Sustainable development has three main elements: economic, social, and environmental sustainability. There is a close relationship between global climate change and these three elements of sustainable development. Through economic sustainability, we aim to increase the welfare of the society through increases in the production of goods and services, while through environmental and social sustainability we try to preserve the integrity of the ecological system and improve human relations in the society, respectively. From this point of view, energy emerges as one

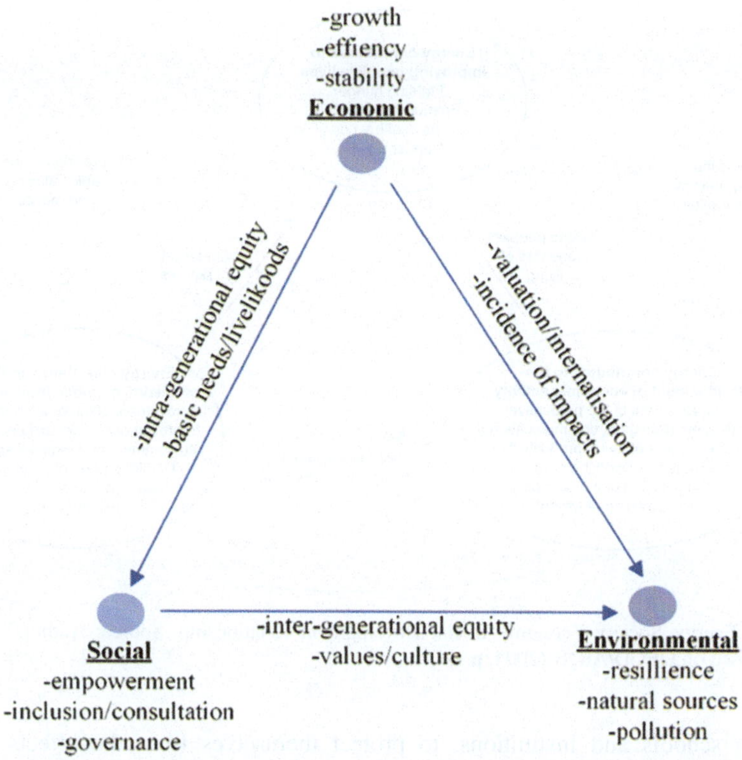

Fig. 4 Elements of Sustainable Development. Source: Authors' calculations based on Munasinghe (2002, p. 127)

of the important sources that affect the economic, social, and environmental dimensions of sustainable development. Therefore, this requires a significant analysis of the relationship between energy, economic growth, and environment.

The relationship of energy with society, economics, and social development is summarized in Fig. 5. Energy contributes to the important cycle of human, economic, and social developments necessary for sustainable development. Adequate supply of clean energy is the basis for raising living standards, increasing the quantity and quality of human capital, improving the business and natural environment, and increasing the effectiveness of government policies (OECD, 2007, p. 17).

2.3 Impacts of COVID-19 on Energy Consumption

The COVID-19 appeared in China spread rapidly in a short period of time, causing then a global crisis. All countries suffered great harm from health, social, and economic perspectives. Countries took gradual and/or radical measures, such as

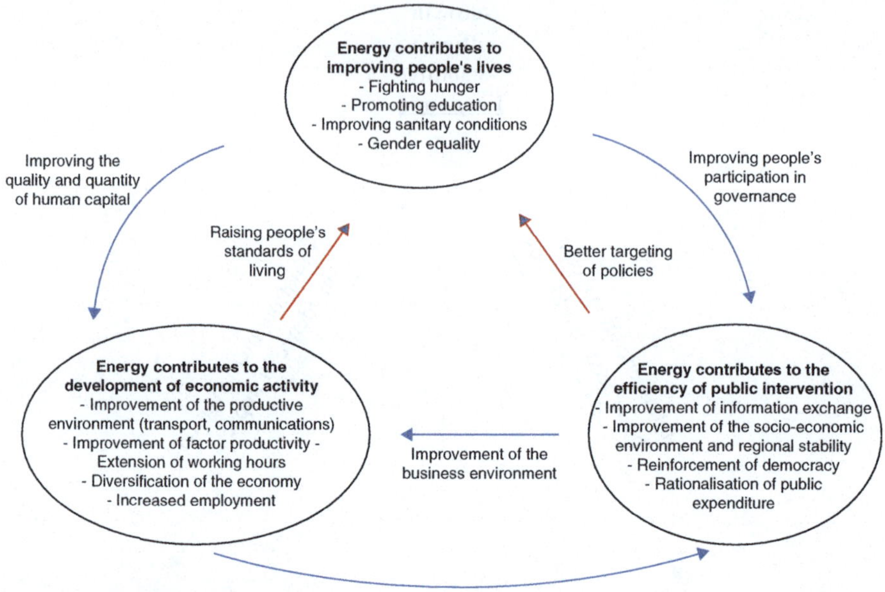

Fig. 5 Energy–Society–Economy–Social Development Relationship. Source: Authors' calculations based on OECD/AfDB (2004, p. 44)

closing schools and institutions, to protect themselves from the effects of the COVID-19 pandemic (BBC, 2020). Then, many countries stopped domestic and international flights and closed borders. In many countries, cities were quarantined, curfews were imposed, national and international land and air traffic were stopped. The first signs of the pandemic showed itself in the field of economy. The decline in economic activities and the contraction in trade volume reached serious levels (Kabir et al., 2020; Li et al., 2020, UNCTAD, 2020). Thus, governments put into action emergency in the economic field.

Figure 6 shows the relationship between world energy consumption and world GDP during the pandemic period. The primary axis of the graph is carbon dioxide in million tons, while the secondary axis includes world GDP in billions of US dollars. With the onset of the pandemic, the measures taken by the countries directly affected the production and caused disruptions in the supply chain. The decrease in production led to a decrease in energy consumption, which in turn caused a decrease in global CO_2 emissions.

As a matter of fact, the studies conducted during this period concluded that the COVID-19 lockdowns significantly reduced carbon emissions in countries. Wu et al. (2021) show that there was a sharp decrease in CO_2 emissions in the short term in Xi'an, China, and emissions began to return to normal levels after the quarantine measures were lifted. Saadat et al. (2020) claim that the COVID-19 pandemic quarantine resulted in improved air quality in most of the world and reduced water pollution in some regions. Wang and Su (2020) state that the COVID-19 outbreak

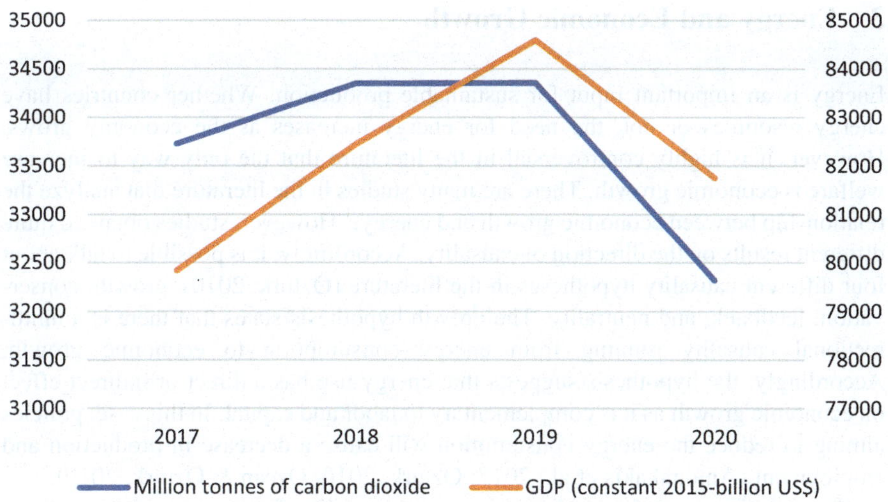

Fig. 6 Impact of the Pandemic on Energy Consumption and CO_2 Emissions. Source: Authors' calculations based on data provided by BP, 2021 Statistical Review of World Energy

improved China's air quality and played an important role in reducing global carbon emissions. This effect manifests itself especially with the reduction in energy consumption and NO2 emissions based on the decrease in economic activities.

Han et al. (2021) find a reduction of 257.7 Mt. CO_2 (11.0%) compared to the first quarter of 2019. They also conclude that the secondary industry contributed 186.8 Mt. CO_2 (72.5%) to the overall reduction, largely due to low coal consumption and cement production. Andreoni (2021) analyzes 23 European countries and 10 economic sectors. Findings from the study show that 195,600 thousand tons of CO_2 were avoided in the first 6 months of 2020, which represents a − 12.1% change in emissions. The study conclude that the largest decreases occurred in the Manufacturing, Wholesale, Retail Trade, Transportation, Hospitality and Food Service sectors, accounting for more than 93.7% of the total CO_2 change. Ray et al. (2022) indicate that the total carbon emissions of 184 countries were reduced by 438 Mt. in 2020 compared to 2019. Sarfraz et al. (2021) suggest that curfew contributes to the reduction of toxic emissions in the short term, but is not a permanent solution for environmental sustainability. Anser et al. (2020) highlight that COVID-19 measures significantly reduced carbon emissions due to the worldwide industry lockdown. Most of the studies agree that the effect of the COVID-19 quarantine measures in reducing emissions is short term that carbon emissions will return to their previous levels after the loosening of the measures. They reach a conclusion that a lasting emission reduction is only possible if the authorities design long-term viable strategies for transport, climate, and environmental policies globally (Ray et al., 2022; Sarfraz et al., 2021).

3 Energy and Economic Growth

Energy is an important input for sustainable production. Whether countries have energy resources or not, the need for energy increases as the economy grows. However, it is highly controversial in the literature that the only way to increase welfare is economic growth. There are many studies in the literature that analyze the relationship between economic growth and energy.[1] However, studies obtained quite different results on the direction of causality. Accordingly, it is possible to talk about four different causality hypotheses in the literature (Ozturk, 2010): growth, conservation, feedback, and neutrality. The growth hypothesis states that there is a unidirectional causality running from energy consumption to economic growth. Accordingly, the hypothesis suggests that energy use has a direct or indirect effect on economic growth as it is complementary to labor and capital. In this case, policies aiming to reduce the energy consumption will cause a decrease in production and employment (Antonakakis et al., 2017; Ozturk, 2010; Ozcan & Ozturk, 2019).

Conservation hypothesis claims one-way causality from economic growth to energy use. If this hypothesis is valid in the economy, energy conservation policies can be applied to reduce CO_2 emissions without adversely affecting economic growth (Antonakakis et al., 2017; Ozturk, 2010). The feedback hypothesis states that there is a bidirectional causality between energy consumption and economic growth. To be more precise, there is a relationship of complementarity and interdependence between energy use and economic performance. In such an economy, it would be appropriate to plan the policies to be implemented in a way that covers the two-way effect (Antonakakis et al., 2017; Ozturk, 2010; Ozcan & Ozturk, 2019). The neutrality hypothesis indicates no significant relationship between energy use and economic growth. In this case, it is expected that the energy policies to be implemented will not affect the economic growth (Ozturk, 2010).

Some of the studies that analyze the severity, level, and direction of this inevitable relationship between economic growth and energy consumption are given below. For instance, Mehrara (2007) shows a unidirectional relationship from economic growth to energy use for both in the short and long run in emerging countries. Chontanawat et al. (2008) find a causality from energy consumption per capita to real GDP per capita in 21 OECD and 36 non-OECD member countries. Azam (2020) shows that in 10 Asian economies energy leads to economic growth. As shown above, there is no consensus on the direction of the causality between energy use and economic growth.

However, as the total output of the economy increases, the need for energy also increases accordingly. Because energy is an important input especially for the industrial sector, the growth in the level of development of the economy increases energy consumption in every sector. Economic growth increases energy consumption, and energy consumption affects economic growth (Aydin, 2010).

---

[1] For a detailed review, see Tiba and Omri (2017).

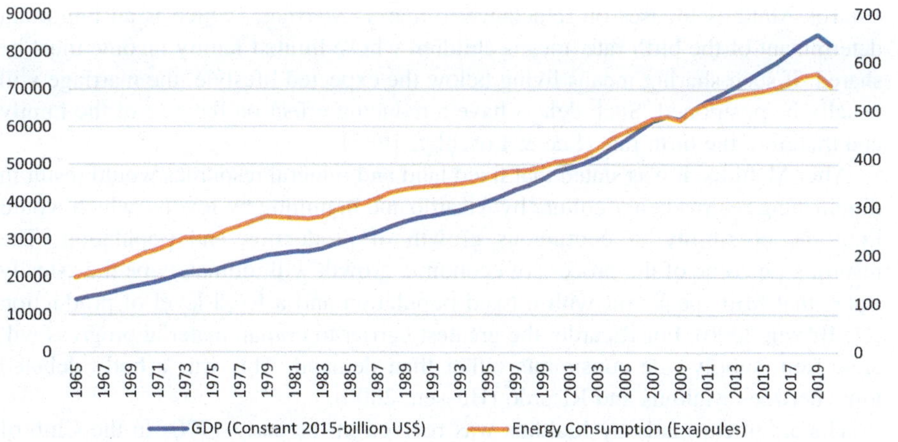

Fig. 7 World Energy Consumption and Economic Growth. Source: Authors' calculations based on data provided by BP, 2021 Statistical Review of World Energy

Figure 7 shows the relationship between world energy consumption and economic growth. As can be seen in Figure, there is a parallelism between energy consumption and GDP. In 2009, energy consumption and GDP started to rise again after some decline. In 2020, a decrease is observed in both energy consumption and GDP with the effect of the COVID-19.

4 Environmental Limits to Economic Growth

The history of discussions on the relationship between economic growth and environment is quite old. It is possible to trace the beginning of these discussions back to Malthus' work "An Essay on the Principle of Population" written in 1798. Malthus states in his book that if the population is not controlled, it will increase geometrically. As food products only increase arithmetically, it does not seem possible for food growth to catch up with population growth. He also claimed that in case of imbalance between population and food products, two types of control can occur: positive and preventive controls (Malthus, 1798). Here, positive controls mean wars, pandemics, natural disasters. If these do not succeed in bringing the population to the same level with food products, eventually famine will arise and equality will be achieved. Malthus also suggested preventive controls such as birth control, late marriage, and "moral restraint." Positive controls increase the mortality rate, while preventive controls decrease fertility. According to Malthus, the population can be prevented from exceeding its food supply, if late marriage, birth control, or moral restraint are applied; but without these less painful checks, the population would grow rapidly to the point where so-called Malthusian forces would be mobilized by famine, disease, and war (Avery, 2005). In discussing preventive control, Malthus focuses on reluctance to marry. Marriage, which is an important determinant of the birth rate, means children whose limited family income must be shared. If such sharing means living below the expected lifestyle, the marriage will usually be postponed. Such delays have a reducing effect on the size of the family and therefore the birth rate (Lee & Loschky, 1987).

After Malthus, it was stated that fixed land and mineral resources would result in diminishing returns in agriculture by Ricardo and in mining by Jevons, which would limit the possibility of continuous growth of production and population. The resulting outcome of the process of economic growth will ultimately be the "steady state" that Mill speaks of, with a fixed population and a fixed level of production (De Bruyn, 2000). For Ricardo, the greatest barrier to human material progress will arise from supply-side constraints rather than demand. This was a hotly debated topic between Malthus and Ricardo (Hussen, 2000).

The argument made by Malthus was revived in the early 1970s in the Club of Rome's report "The Limits to Growth" (Saunders, 2016). This report significantly re-popularized the Malthusian view in the academic world. At this stage, it would be appropriate to briefly touch upon the process of the report's emergence.

In 1968, a group of 30 scientists, business people, and government officials from 10 countries met in Rome to discuss the main problems threatening humanity. At this meeting, the Club of Rome, which was not an official organization, emerged. The Club of Rome decided to initiate an important project in various meetings it held. The Club named this project "The Project on the Predicament of Mankind." This project took its final form at the meetings held in Bern and Cambridge in 1970. At the Cambridge meeting, Professor Jay Forrester of MIT proposed a world model based on system dynamics that allows for the clear identification of the main problems threatening the world. Afterward, the system dynamics model was reported by the MIT team led by Professor Meadows in a way that anyone interested in world problems can understand. In 1972, this report was published as "The Limits to Growth." In this report, population, agricultural production, natural resources, industrial production, and environmental pollution issues that limit economic growth are analyzed. The report also aimed to create a system that reveals the interdependence and interaction between these five critical factors. In the study, it is emphasized that population, food production, industrialization, environmental pollution, and the use of non-renewable natural resources, even all activities of people, increase exponentially. If the current growth trend continues, the growth limit will be reached in the next century. However, it is emphasized that if this growth trend is changed, it will be possible to establish an ecological and economic balance in the future. The report proposes a non-growth state for human society. Here, the situation in which population and capital are fixed is defined as equilibrium. Meadows et al. (1972) define the equilibrium state as:

> ... the most basic definition of the state of global equilibrium is that population and capital are essentially stable, with the forces tending to increase or decrease them in a carefully controlled balance.

In addition, the minimum conditions for ensuring world balance are specified in the report (Meadows et al., 1972);

- Capital and population are constant in size.
- All input and output rates, births, deaths, investments, and depreciation are kept at their lowest levels,
- The arrangements of capital and population and their ratio to each other are stated in accordance with the values of the society.

It is possible to say that the results of the report indicate that after more than 100 years, humanity is facing the problems expressed by Mill's theory (Hiroi, 2019). In addition, although the results of the report were mostly considered as a doomsday scenario, the message the Club of Rome wanted to convey was actually more optimistic. The main emphasis of the report was to warn that if the current economic growth trend continues, the limits of the planet will be reached by about 2070, hence humanity must take action as soon as possible to prevent negative effects (Higgs, 2014). Similarly, in his book "The Population Bomb" Paul R. Ehrlich (1968) stated that hundreds of millions of people would starve to death in the 1970s and 1980s. Hence, many lives could be saved by increasing food production and ensuring a fairer distribution of available food. In addition, taking decisive steps toward population control is of critical importance in ensuring success.

After the environmental discourses that emerged in the 1960s, a new approach began to take shape. This approach took its final form with the establishment of The International Society for Ecological Economics in 1988. This new approach is called ecological economics (Røpke, 2010). Ecological economics combines elements of economics, ecology, thermodynamics, ethics, and a range of other natural and social sciences to provide a biophysical perspective on the interaction of the environment and economy (van den Bergh, 2001). It would be appropriate to assess some important work in the field for a clearer understanding of the economics and environment relationship approach of ecological economics.

Kenneth E. Boulding examines the relationship between economics and environment in his 1966 book "The Economics of the Coming Spaceship Earth." In this study, Boulding states that primitive people believed that the world they lived in was unlimited. The view claims that there are always new places for people to go in case of deterioration of the natural environment or in similar cases. Boulding refers to the open world of the past as the "cowboy economy." In the study, the closed world of the future is called the spaceman economy, in which the world becomes a single spaceship. The cowboy economy means a world where human behavior is reckless and exploitative, where resources are unlimited and environmental pollution problems are ignored. The spaceman economy, conversely, describes a world with limited resources, unlike the cowboy economy. According to Boulding, the closed world of the future will be quite different from the open world of the past. In the cowboy economy, production and consumption are always seen as a good thing. In this system, the success of the economy is measured by the amount of output obtained from the factors of production. In space economy, on the other hand, production and consumption are factors that should be minimized, not maximized (Boulding, 1966).

Nicholas Georgescu-Roegen analyzed the relationship between economic growth and environment by using the laws of thermodynamics in his book "The Entropy Law and the Economic Process" published in 1971. The first law of thermodynamics states that we cannot create or destroy energy and matter, we can only transform them. For example, coal consumption in any given year should equal the amount of waste gases and solids produced by coal combustion. Some of these substances will appear as slag, carbon dioxide, etc. But we can take some of this waste and recycle it. As a matter of fact, used bottle collection boxes are everywhere to recycle them. However, most of these wastes cannot be recycled. The second law of thermodynamics shows us the answer to why not all wastes can be recycled. Materials used in economics tend to be used entropically. There is also a category of non-recyclable resources, which are energy resources. Therefore, entropy presents a physical barrier to redesigning the economy as a closed and sustainable system (Čiegis & Čiegis, 2008).

Georgescu-Roegen refers to the entropy law expressed by the second law of thermodynamics as the most economic of all physical laws. Economic production transforms low entropy of goods and services into high entropy of final goods and services. It is a very convincing explanation of the fact that low entropy is responsible for the utility of a particular good. Therefore, only thermodynamics can explain why goods have economic value. Low entropy resources, which are constantly decreasing in the human environment, are the main cause of scarcity of goods. Production processes are characterized by reducing resources with low entropy, so the main feature of economic phenomena is that they are irreversible. This leads one to the conclusion that economic flows do not create a circular income stream—contrary to what traditional economics advocates—but it is rather unidirectional. High entropy can be released into the environment both by natural physical processes and economic processes (Jakimowicz, 2020).

However, it is important to note that both Georgescu-Roegen and Boulding are not opposed to the idea technological progress. There are two concerns in this regard. First, it must be recognized that there is a limit to technological progress. Second, technology can be abused or misused. On the other hand, technology can be beneficial when used judiciously. For example, a technological advance that reduces the need for production while maintaining the standard of living at a desirable level is really important. If technological progress is geared toward producing more goods and services with no apparent limit, such a strategy can be quite dangerous for long-term sustainability. Therefore, the prudent use of technology requires recognition of natural limits imposed by nature (Hussen, 2000).

Daly (1993) defines the ecosystem as a finite, non-growing closed system. A closed system is a system in which matter and energy enter and exit, and the economy is a subsystem of the world ecosystem. Here, the economy makes a living by taking useful raw materials and energy with low entropy, and by giving waste, that is, high entropy materials and energy back to the environment. What remains of the economic subsystem in the world's ecosystem absorbs the emitted waste and

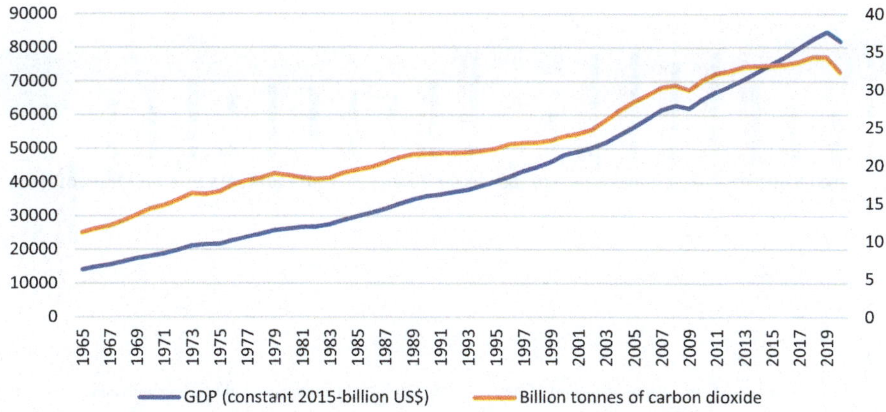

Fig. 8 World GDP and CO_2 Emissions. Source: Authors' calculations based on data provided by BP, 2021 Statistical Review of World Energy

converts most of the waste into reusable raw materials through biogeochemical cycles powered by the sun. As the economic subsystem expands, more total living space becomes economic space. Accordingly, as the economy grows, less living space remains. Daly suggests that the world adapts itself to the uneconomic growth model. Here, uneconomic growth means qualitative growth without quantitative growth. This structure proposed by Daly is called the steady-state economy.

After mentioning the thoughts of some important academics of ecological economics above, it would be appropriate to analyze the current state of the environment with some data. Population growth causes an increase in energy demand. The increase in energy demand causes an increase in resource use. Thus, a chain cycle occurs with the use of more fossil fuels. This cycle causes an increase in CO_2 emissions and other greenhouse gases that cause climate change and global warming.

Global warming is a concept that refers specifically to the impact of human activities on the climate, such as the burning of fossil fuels and large-scale deforestation. Such gases prevent the Earth from reflecting back the sun rays and keep it warmer than usual. Changes in climate can be seen as more frequent heat waves, increases in precipitation, and an increase in the frequency and intensity of many extreme climate events (Houghton, 2005). This global climate change problem affects almost all countries, regardless of the level of development.

Figure 8 shows the relationship between world GDP and CO_2 emissions. As shown in Figs. 3, 83% of the energy consumed in the world is obtained from fossil sources. Therefore, the increase in production causes an increase in CO_2 emissions. During periods of increased production, we observe an increase in world CO_2 emission rates. On the contrary, during periods of global crisis and epidemics, production decreases throughout the world, and accordingly, CO_2 emissions decrease. This is more clearly seen in Fig. 9.

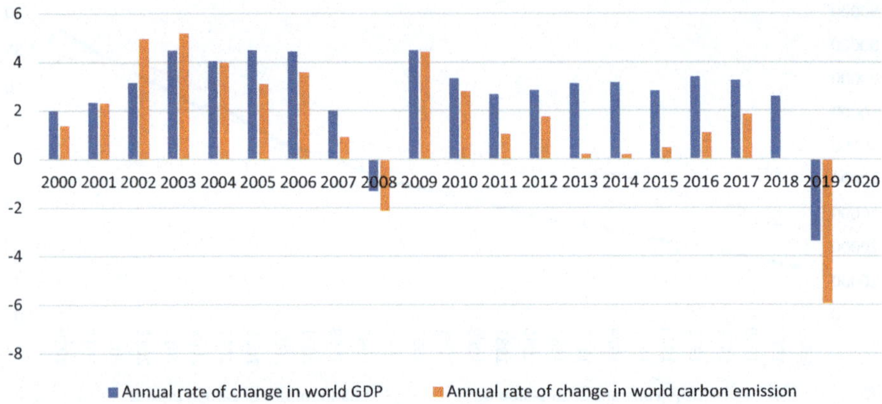

Fig. 9 Annual Rate of Change in World Carbon Emissions and GDP. Source: Authors' calculations based on data provided by BP, 2021 Statistical Review of World Energy

Figure 9 shows the annual rate of change in world GDP and CO_2 emissions. The 2007–08 economic crisis, which initially appeared as a financial crisis, caused a recession in most countries, stagflation in some countries, and depression in others. With the shrinkage of production worldwide, a decrease in world GDP was observed, followed by a decrease in world CO_2 emissions. In 2020, the COVID-19 pandemic also caused a global crisis. In this period, there was a decrease in world GDP with the shrinkage of production around the world, followed by a decrease in world CO_2 emission rates.

There are various opinions on the speed and magnitude of the change in climate. According to the Intergovernmental Panel on Climate Change (IPCC) report, it is accepted that there was a 0.74 ± 0.18 °C change between 1906 and 2005 (Güner & Turan, 2017). Studies indicate that climate change will directly or indirectly affect human health, agricultural lands and products, the quantity and quality of water resources, coastal areas, and natural habitats (Davis et al., 2007). Raftery et al. (2017) conclude in their climate change scenario analysis that the global temperature increase will vary between 2.0–4.9 °C until 2100, and the median temperature will be 3.2 °C. Liu and Raftery (2021) estimate the median temperature for 2100 to be 2.8 °C. The temperature estimates vary between 2.1–3.9 °C. The IPCC report (Begum et al., 2022) states that for the very high greenhouse gas emission scenario for 2081–2100, there will be an increase in temperature between 3.3–5.7 °C, and in the scenarios for the intermediate and high greenhouse gas emissions, there will be a temperature increase between 2.1–3.5 °C and 2.8–4.6 °C, respectively. According to the Paris Agreement signed in 2015, it is aimed to absolutely keep the temperature increase below 2 °C or 1.5 °C preferably (UNFCCC, 2015). As seen in the scenario analyses above, temperature forecasts are made above the target. At this point, one can conclude that the significant impact of global temperature increases on biodiversity will rise in the future. Nunez et al. (2019) argue that even a moderate temperature increase of 1–2 °C causes significant reductions in biodiversity.

Hence, it is recommended to keep the global temperature increase below 1.5 °C in order to protect biodiversity. Habibullah et al. (2022) reach the conclusion that temperature, precipitation, and the number of natural disaster variables, which they used as climate change variables in their analysis for 115 countries, reduce biodiversity. The IPCC estimates that 20–30% of species will be at an increasingly high risk of extinction if global temperature rise exceeds pre-industrial levels by 2–3 °C (Warren et al., 2013). The decrease in biodiversity, on the other hand, affects humanity through different channels, leaving it with the danger of extinction. Biodiversity supports food security and sustainability of nutritional health. It also provides important resources for medical research. It has an important role in the control of diseases. It has social, cultural, and spiritual importance for societies. It is very important for adaptation to climate change. A healthy ecosystem can reduce disaster risks (COHAB, 2010). Accordingly, it will be difficult to talk about the existence of humans in a world where there is no biological diversity. For this reason, it is of great importance for the future of humanity to design existing policies in a way that minimizes the damage to the environment.

5 Conclusion

In this study, we analyzed the relationship between energy use, economic growth, and environment. When we observe the data on energy use, we see that energy use has significantly increased especially after the Industrial Revolution. The biggest part of the energy source comes from the fossil fuels such as oil, natural gas, and coal. The energy obtained from fossil fuels harms the environment. Because of increase in the use of fossil fuels, carbon dioxide emissions reach serious levels and make the problem of global warming increasingly important. This increase in energy use and its problems pushed researchers to find the factors that increase energy demand. In many empirical studies, economic growth is found to be the most important factor causing the increase in energy use (i.e., Ozturk et al., 2010; Eggoh et al., 2011; Al-Mulali & Sab, 2012; Gozgor et al., 2018; Thomas & Rosenow, 2020). The strong belief that economic growth will improve the standard of living led all countries to determine the main target of their economic policies as economic growth. Unquestionably, the intended economic growth effects were first seen on the excessive use of energy. Afterward, the most important negative effect of energy, which is mostly provided from non-renewable sources, was seen on the environment with increasing carbon emissions. Extreme increases in carbon emissions have caused global warming, after which the increasing temperature has become a significant threat to biodiversity. If this process eventually causes the collapse of the ecological system, it may lead to the end of humanity.

For a clearer understanding of the debate on whether there are environmental limits to economic growth, it would be appropriate to look at the thoughts of the two schools of economics. These schools are Ecological Economics and Environmental Economics. Ecological Economists are more pessimistic than environmental economists about the effects of economic growth on the environment. Population growth, which is increasing at an unsustainable level, is one of the issues that ecological economists approach with skepticism. Increases in population exceed the carrying capacity of the world. Second, there is the issue of increasing inequality both within and between countries. Another issue that ecological economists care about is the use of highly entropy-enhancing technologies that poison the air, water, and soil. Finally, it is land conversions that destroy habitat and diversity of species, and increase soil erosion (Costanza et al., 2015). Environmental economists, on the other hand, argue that finding substitutes to prevent scarcity of natural resources, discovering new resources and the emergence of new technologies that increase productivity will be sufficient to prevent scarcity. Unlike Malthusians, they believe that economic growth through increases in per capita income and advances in technology will offer solutions to environmental and population problems. Neoclassical economists believe that the signals of emerging resource scarcity will be provided in a timely manner by the efficiency of the market system (Hussen, 2000). When the current situation and future scenario analyses are examined, we see that both sides have right and wrong views. The current situation is neither as bad as the Malthusians claim, nor as smooth as environmental economists think. In the current situation scenario, it is stated that the global temperature will increase between 2–5.7 °C in 2100 (Raftery et al., 2017; Liu & Raftery, 2021; Begum et al., 2022). These temperature increases will thus greatly reduce biodiversity. But biodiversity is the key element to provide the healthy functioning of the ecosystem. For this reason, instead of targeting economic growth without questioning, determining alternative policies compatible with the environment will play an important role in ensuring the future of the ecosystem. Looking at the literature, some alternatives to economic growth are presented. We can list these alternatives as the steady-state economy, degrowth, and green growth. By utilizing renewable energy sources, it is possible to reduce CO_2 emissions arising from global energy use. Doubling the share of renewable energy by 2030 could reduce about half of CO_2 emissions. Combined with this effect and energy efficiency, the average rise in global temperature can be kept below 2 °C and climate change can be prevented from becoming a global catastrophe (Masson-Delmotte et al., 2018). In order to be successful in the fight against climate change, renewable energy sources should continue to increase in electricity production, while their use in transportation, heating, and cooling activities should be increased. In addition, the policies to be implemented in every field should be designed in such a way that the damage to the environment is kept minimal and thus the future of humanity should be guaranteed. As a result, we think that it would be appropriate to switch to environmental-friendly growth instead of growth at all costs.

References

Al-Mulali, U., & Sab, C. N. B. C. (2012). The impact of energy consumption and CO_2 emission on the economic and financial development in 19 selected countries. *Renewable and Sustainable Energy Reviews, 16*(7), 4365–4369.

Andreoni, V. (2021). Estimating the European CO_2 emissions change due to COVID-19 restrictions. *Science of the Total Environment, 769*, 145115.

Anser, M. K., Yousaf, Z., Khan, M. A., Voo, X. H., Nassani, A. A., Alotaibi, S. M., et al. (2020). The impacts of COVID-19 measures on global environment and fertility rate: Double coincidence. *Air Quality, Atmosphere & Health, 13*(9), 1083–1092.

Antonakakis, N., Chatziantoniou, I., & Filis, G. (2017). Energy consumption, CO_2 emissions, and economic growth: An ethical dilemma. *Renewable and Sustainable Energy Reviews, 68*, 808–824.

Avery, J. (2005). *Malthus essay on the principle of population*. Accessed Jan 1, 2022, from http://learndev.org/dl/MalthusEssay-Avery.pdf

Aydin, F. (2010). Enerji tüketimi ve ekonomik büyüme. *Erciyes Üniversitesi İktisadi ve İdari Bilimler Fakültesi Dergisi, 35*, 317–340.

Azam, M. (2020). Energy and economic growth in developing Asian economies. *Journal of the Asia Pacific Economy, 25*(3), 447–471.

BBC. (2020). *Koronavirüs (Covid-19): Salgına karşı hangi ülke, ne tür önlemler aldı?* Retrieved from https://www.bbc.com/turkce/haberler-dunya-51864424

Begum, R., Lempert, R., Ali, E., Benjaminsen, T. A., Bernauer, T., Cramer, W., Cui, X., Mach, K., Nagy, G., Stenseth, N. C., Sukumar, R., & Wester, P. (2022). Point of departure and key concepts. In H. O. Pörtner, D. C. Roberts, M. Tignor, E. S. Poloczanska, K. Mintenbeck, A. Alegría, M. Craig, S. Langsdorf, S. Löschke, V. Möller, A. Okem, & B. Rama (Eds.), *Climate change 2022: Impacts, adaptation and vulnerability. Contribution of Working Group II to the Sixth Assessment Report of the Intergovernmental Panel on Climate Change*. Cambridge University Press.

Bose, B. K. (2010). Global warming: Energy, environmental pollution, and the impact of power electronics. *IEEE Industrial Electronics Magazine, 4*(1), 6–17.

Boulding, K. E. (1966). The economics of the coming spaceship earth. In H. Jarrett (Ed.), *Environmental quality in a growing economy* (pp. 3–14). Resources for the Future/Johns Hopkins University Press.

BP. (2021). *Statistical review of world energy*. https://www.bp.com/content/dam/bp/business-sites/en/global/corporate/xlsx/energy-economics/statistical-review/bp-stats-review-2021-all-data.xlsx

Chontanawat, J., Hunt, L. C., & Pierse, R. (2008). Does energy consumption cause economic growth?: Evidence from a systematic study of over 100 countries. *Journal of Policy Modeling, 30*(2), 209–220.

Čiegis, R., & Čiegis, R. (2008). Laws of thermodynamics and sustainability of the economy. *Engineering Economics, 57*(2), 15–22.

COHAB. (2010). *The importance of biodiversity to human health*. The COHAB Initiative (Co-operation on Health and Biodiversity. Policy brief. Retrieved from https://www.cbd.int/doc/health/cohab-policy-brief1-en.pdf

Costanza, R., Cumberland, J. H., Daly, H., Goodland, R., Norgaard, R. B., Kubiszewski, I., & Franco, C. (2015). *An introduction to ecological economics*. Cambridge University Press.

Daly, H. E. (1993). Steady-state economics: A new paradigm. *New Literary History, 24*(4), 811–816.

Davis, C. P., A. D. Joroff & C. F. Jenks, (2007, January 4) Climate change strategies for the financial services industry, goodwin procter.

De Bruyn, S. M. (2000). *Economic growth and the environment: An empirical analysis*. Springer Science & Business Media.

Eggoh, J. C., Bangaké, C., & Rault, C. (2011). Energy consumption and economic growth revisited in African countries. *Energy Policy, 39*(11), 7408–7421.
Ehrlich, P. R. (1968). *The population bomb*. Ballantine Books.
Georgescu-Roegen, N. (1971). *The entropy law and the economic process*. Harvard University Press.
Gozgor, G., Lau, C. K. M., & Lu, Z. (2018). Energy consumption and economic growth: New evidence from the OECD countries. *Energy, 153*, 27–34.
Güner, E. D., & Turan, E. S. (2017). Yenilenebilir enerji kaynaklarının küresel iklim değişikliği üzerine etkisi. *Doğal Afetler ve Çevre Dergisi, 3*(1), 48–55.
Habibullah, M. S., Din, B. H., Tan, S. H., & Zahid, H. (2022). Impact of climate change on biodiversity loss: Global evidence. *Environmental Science and Pollution Research, 29*(1), 1073–1086.
Han, P., Cai, Q., Oda, T., Zeng, N., Shan, Y., Lin, X., & Liu, D. (2021). Assessing the recent impact of COVID-19 on carbon emissions from China using domestic economic data. *Science of the Total Environment, 750*, 141688.
Higgs, K. (2014). *Collision course: Endless growth on a finite planet*. MIT Press.
Hiroi, Y. (2019). Science as care: Science and innovation in post-growth society. In S. Lechevalier (Ed.), *Innovation beyond technology* (pp. 301–324). Springer.
Houghton, J. (2005). Global warming. *Reports on Progress in Physics, 68*(6), 1343.
Hussen, A. (2000). *Principles of environmental economics*. Routledge.
IEA. (2004). *World energy outlook 2004*. Chapter 10. http://large.stanford.edu/courses/2018/ph241/lin1/docs/WEO2004.pdf
Jackson, T. (2016). *Prosperity without growth: Foundations for the economy of tomorrow*. Routledge.
Jakimowicz, A. (2020). The role of entropy in the development of economics. *Entropy, 22*(4), 452.
Kabir, M., Afzal, M. S., Khan, A., & Ahmed, H. (2020). COVID-19 pandemic and economic cost; impact on forcibly displaced people. *Travel Medicine and Infectious Disease, 35*, 101661.
Kadoshin, S., Nishiyama, T., & Ito, T. (2000). The trend in current and near future energy consumption from a statistical perspective. *Applied Energy, 67*(4), 407–417.
Lee, M. L., & Loschky, D. (1987). Malthusian population oscillations. *The Economic Journal, 97*(387), 727–739.
Li, K., Qin, Y., Wu, J., & Yan, J. (2020). Containing the virus or reviving the economy? Evidence from individual expectations during the COVID-19 epidemic. In S. Agarwal, Z. He, & B. Yeung (Eds.), *Impact of COVID-19 on Asian economies and policy responses*. World Scientific.
Liu, P. R., & Raftery, A. E. (2021). Country-based rate of emissions reductions should increase by 80% beyond nationally determined contributions to meet the 2°C target. *Communications Earth & Environment, 2*(1), 1–10.
Mahmutoglu, M. (2013). Türkiye'nin Enerjide Dışa Bağımlılığı ve Buna İlişkin Çözüm Önerileri. *Türkiye Kalkınma Bankası Yayını, 67*, 1–60.
Malthus, T. (1798). An essay on the principle of population. St. Paul's church-yard.
Masson-Delmotte, V., Zhai, P., Pörtner, H. O., Roberts, D., Skea, J., Shukla, P. R., et al. (2018). *An IPCC special report on the impacts of global warming of 1.5 C*. UNCC.
Meadows, D. H., Meadows, D. L., Randers, J., & Behrens, W. W. (1972). *The limits to growth*. Universe Books.
Mehrara, M. (2007). Energy consumption and economic growth: The case of oil exporting countries. *Energy Policy, 35*(5), 2939–2945.
Munasinghe, M. (2002). The sustainomics trans-disciplinary meta-framework for making development more sustainable: Applications to energy issues. *International Journal of Sustainable Development, 5*(1–2), 125–182.
Nunez, S., Arets, E., Alkemade, R., Verwer, C., & Leemans, R. (2019). Assessing the impacts of climate change on biodiversity: Is below 2°C enough? *Climatic Change, 154*(3), 351–365.
OECD. (2007). *Energy for sustainable development*. OECD Contribution to the United Nations Commission on Sustainable Development 15.

OECD/AfDB. (2004). *African economic outlook 2004*. OECD Publishing. https://doi.org/10.1787/aeo-2004-en

Ozcan, B., & Ozturk, I. (2019). Renewable energy consumption-economic growth nexus in emerging countries: A bootstrap panel causality test. *Renewable and Sustainable Energy Reviews, 104*, 30–37.

Ozturk, I. (2010). A literature survey on energy–growth nexus. *Energy Policy, 38*(1), 340–349.

Ozturk, I., Aslan, A., & Kalyoncu, H. (2010). Energy consumption and economic growth relationship: Evidence from panel data for low and middle income countries. *Energy Policy, 38*(8), 4422–4428.

Raftery, A. E., Zimmer, A., Frierson, D. M., Startz, R., & Liu, P. (2017). Less than 2°C warming by 2100 unlikely. *Nature Climate Change, 7*(9), 637–641.

Ray, R. L., Singh, V. P., Singh, S. K., Acharya, B. S., & He, Y. (2022). What is the impact of COVID-19 pandemic on global carbon emissions? *Science of the Total Environment, 816*, 151503.

Røpke, I. (2010). Society's nature: Ecological economics and the combined challenge of environment and distribution. *Journal für Entwicklungspolitik, 26*(4), 14–35.

Saadat, S., Rawtani, D., & Hussain, C. M. (2020). Environmental perspective of COVID-19. *Science of the Total Environment, 728*, 138870.

Sarfraz, M., Mohsin, M., Naseem, S., & Kumar, A. (2021). Modeling the relationship between carbon emissions and environmental sustainability during COVID-19: A new evidence from asymmetric ARDL cointegration approach. *Environment, Development and Sustainability, 23*(11), 16208–16226.

Saunders, H. (2016). *Does capitalism require endless growth? Marx and Malthus reconsidered*. The Breakthrough Institute, Summer 2016. Accessed Jan 1, 2022, from https://thebreakthrough.org/journal/issue-6/does-capitalism-require-endless-growth

Thomas, S., & Rosenow, J. (2020). Drivers of increasing energy consumption in Europe and policy implications. *Energy Policy, 137*, 111108.

Tiba, S., & Omri, A. (2017). Literature survey on the relationships between energy, environment and economic growth. *Renewable and Sustainable Energy Reviews, 69*, 1129–1146.

UNCTAD. (2020). *Investment policy responses to the COVID-19 pandemic*. Retrieved from https://unctad.org/en/PublicationsLibrary/diaepcbinf2020d3_en.pdf

UNFCCC. (2015). *The Paris agreement*. Bonn United Nations framework convention on climate change. Accessed Aug 27, 2022, from https://unfccc.int/process-and-meetings/the-paris-agreement/the-paris-agreement

Van den Bergh, J. C. (2001). Ecological economics: Themes, approaches, and differences with environmental economics. *Regional Environmental Change, 2*(1), 13–23.

Wang, Q., & Su, M. (2020). A preliminary assessment of the impact of COVID-19 on environment–a case study of China. *Science of the Total Environment, 728*, 138915.

Warren, R., VanDerWal, J., Price, J., Welbergen, J. A., Atkinson, I., Ramirez-Villegas, J., et al. (2013). Quantifying the benefit of early climate change mitigation in avoiding biodiversity loss. *Nature Climate Change, 3*(7), 678–682.

Wu, S., Zhou, W., Xiong, X., Burr, G. S., Cheng, P., Wang, P., et al. (2021). The impact of COVID-19 lockdown on atmospheric CO_2 in Xi'an, China. *Environmental Research, 197*, 111208.

OECD/NEA/IEA. (2020). *Nuclear energy outlook 2020*. OECD Publishing. https://doi.org/10.1787/[illegible]
Ozcan, B., & Ozturk, I. (2019). Renewable energy consumption-economic growth nexus in emerging countries: A bootstrap panel causality test. *Renewable and Sustainable Energy Reviews*, [illegible].
[illegible]
Öztürk, [illegible], A., Kılınç, [illegible], H., [illegible]. Energy consumption [illegible] ecological footprint nexus [illegible] and middle income countries. *Energy Policy*, [illegible].
Raupach, M. R., [illegible], D. M., [illegible]. The dangers of meeting [illegible] CO₂ emission targets. *Nature Climate Change*, [illegible].
Rao, R. L., Singh, A., [illegible], H., & [illegible]. Decline in the impact of COVID-19 pandemic on global carbon dioxide emissions. *Science of the Total Environment*, [illegible].
Rees, W. E. (2010). Ecological footprints and appropriated carrying capacity: What urban economics leaves out. *Environment and Urbanization*, 4(2), 121–130.
Saadat, S., Rawtani, D., & Hussain, C. M. (2020). Environmental perspective of COVID-19. *Science of the Total Environment*, 728, 138870.
Saidi, K., [illegible], M., [illegible], [illegible]. [illegible] relationship between carbon emissions, [illegible] consumption and economic growth: A [illegible] ARDL [illegible] approach. *Environmental Science and Pollution Research*, [illegible].
Saunders, H. (2014). *Toward a neoclassical theory of sustainable consumption*. In [illegible] (Ed.), The [illegible]. Retrieved from https://thebreakthrough.org/[illegible]
[illegible], S., & [illegible]. (2012). [illegible] energy consumption and economic growth [illegible] policy implications. *Energy Policy*, [illegible].
[illegible]. (2017). [illegible] relationship between energy, environment and economic growth. *Renewable and Sustainable Energy Reviews*, 69, 1129–1146.
UNCTAD. (2020). *Impacts of the coronavirus (COVID-19) pandemic*. Retrieved from https://unctad.org/[illegible]
UNFCCC. (2015). *The Paris Agreement*. United Nations Framework Convention on Climate Change. Accessed [illegible] 2022, from https://unfccc.int/process-and-meetings/the-paris-agreement/the-paris-agreement
Van den Bergh, J. C. (2011). Environment versus growth—A criticism of "degrowth" and a plea for "a-growth". *Ecological Economics*, 70(5), 881–890.
Wang, Q., & Su, M. (2020). A preliminary assessment of the impact of COVID-19 on environment—A case study of China. *Science of the Total Environment*, 728, 138915.
Wiedmann, T., Lenzen, M., Keyßer, L. T., & Steinberger, J. K. (2020). Scientists' warning on affluence. *Nature Communications*, 11(1), 1–10.
Yu, S., [illegible], Y., Chen, Y., [illegible], Cheng, F., Wang, P., et al. (2021). The impact of COVID-19 lockdown on [illegible]. *Environmental Research*, [illegible].

Agriculture and Food Problems and Solutions: Challenges and Capacity of the Capitalist System in the Twenty-First Century

Murat Çetin and Murat Öztürk

Abstract The many problems of and linked to the hegemonic capitalist agro-food system—such as world hunger, price fluctuations, unsustainability of production, decline in biodiversity, and climate change—have become more pressing in recent years. The system cannot offer satisfactory solutions to these problems, but alternative approaches are not yet sufficiently strong to replace it. Thus, there is a multiplicity of agro-food problems and an ongoing search for solutions within the present system that brings different approaches to the agenda. This study first presents some special characteristics of the current agro-food system and its problems. Then, it reviews the history of policies introduced within the framework of the hegemonic system by its actors to mitigate the food problem through the perspective of food security and sustainability. Finally, it concludes that a solution to the food problem and related issues demands a radical choice between either profitability and national policies or a global approach to food and nature rights. What is required is a thoroughgoing reset of the agro-food system.

Keywords Food security · Global food crises · Commons · Agro-food system reset

1 Introduction

Agro-food systems have specific characteristics that make them different from other economic and political phenomena, even within the framework of the capitalist economic system. First, they use natural sources converted into food, foodstuffs, and other products. Thus, agro-food economies have established a reciprocal bond with nature and society. Then, the main actors of the system—farmers, food

M. Çetin (✉)
Department of Economics, Istanbul University, Istanbul, Turkey
e-mail: mcetin@istanbul.edu.tr

M. Öztürk
Department of Economics, Kirklareli University, Kirklareli, Turkey
e-mail: mozturk@klu.edu.tr

A. Ari (ed.), *Capitalism at a Crossroads*, Springer Studies in Alternative Economics,
https://doi.org/10.1007/978-3-031-23257-2_4

manufacturers, transporters, and other intermediaries—aim to secure a livelihood by producing food items within the framework of the natural resources. These activities must be carried out by considering the laws of nature and society, on the one hand, while, on the other hand, they themselves have a strong impact upon nature and society. Finally, agro-food systems must reproduce natural resources, labor force and the material, and cultural patterns that govern the consumption of food and the production of knowledge about the food system (van der Ploeg, 2016, p. 1).

As a result of all these factors, food systems need to reproduce the natural resources and ecosystems that are employed in order to maintain ecological balances—or to secure sustainability. The specific needs in this respect vary according to the ecosystems and the technological repertoire. Also, the necessity of agro-food systems to enable to secure livelihoods for their actors is not an optional objective, and this, too, needs to be sustained or reproduced. Typically, it involves a variety of skills and decentralized loci of control. In summary, agro-food systems are based on living nature and produce food—they involve the conversion of one into the other. Thus, farming implies a double exchange, an ecological exchange and an economic one, and these two need to be balanced carefully.

This double exchange means that farming cannot be seen as a "simple extension of the general economy" (van der Ploeg, 2016, p. 2). However, today's primary agro-food system has become controlled by exchangeable elements in the global process of capital accumulation under complex forms of corporate control, while the sciences conventionally conceptualize agro-food economies as basically governed by markets and technology. Inevitably, this system is not effective, as is evident from the litany of negative impacts and poor results.

The current agro-food system is manifestly ineffective. Moreover, the various environmental and food-provisioning crises appeared in the present system are manifesting not only a crisis of the model but also a huge philosophical and ethical challenge. For example, the iniquitous distribution of wealth increasingly reconfigures the world in the service of short-run profit, which constitutes a crisis in the institutions of governance (McMichael, 2000, p. 31). At both global and national level, societies currently face a major problem with food supply (production and distribution) and the sustainability of natural resources. When we look at to the history of attempts to deal with these problems, we cannot say that solutions have been found and that the problems will end; on the contrary, we can say the opposite. But there are some solutions in the human knowledge and experiences. Before discussing alternative solutions in the following sections, we first review, in Sect. 2, the current system based on the three main features of agro-food systems (natural resources, food production, and the relationship between the two, i.e., conversion of resources to food) and review, in Sect. 3, current issues of the capitalist agro-food system. Then, we consider, in Sect. 4, mitigation strategies, while in Sections 5 and 6 we present reform strategies directed at the current problems in the agro-food system. Section 7 discusses those contesting approaches and Sect. 8 concludes with some policy recommendations.

2 Features of Agro-Food Systems

2.1 *Natural Resources*

As D'Odorico et al. (2018, p. 457) note, "Anthropogenic pressure on the Earth system has reached a point where abrupt environmental change is feared with global sustainability becoming a mere utopia." Food production brings environmental costs involving land conversion and deforestation, topsoil and biodiversity loss, aquatic and terrestrial ecosystem pollution, water resource degradation, and the production of greenhouse gases (GHGs). Here, a brief note highlighting just the last two of this list may suffice for further detail.

Despite limited replenishable water sources, countries continue to increase dam construction, which has many kinds of environmental and social consequences on this vital resource for agriculture—which itself places pressure on water sources through, for example, animal production methods, bio-fuel production, and food waste. Meanwhile, agro-food system activities taken as a whole—agricultural production, transport, storage, processing, packaging, and retail along with food loss and waste have a huge impact on man's contribution to atmospheric GHGs. The Intergovernmental Panel on Climate Change (IPCC, 2019, p. 13) "Report on Climate Change and Land" states with "medium confidence" that the "estimated share of food systems in global anthropogenic [GHG] emissions is between 21 and 37%."

2.2 *Food Production*

In recent years, supply- and demand-based problems manifesting as issues with food production, distribution, and food access have become a growing concern. As a result of rapid economic development, such as in China and India, immense pressure has developed on the demand side with the increased consumption of all foods in excess of the continuing population increase worldwide. Although economic theories generally accept food demand as relatively inelastic, the rise in population and disposable income and changes in the composition of food consumption (notably, demand for meat) have significantly raised food demand. As a result, huge and increasing inputs are devoted to agriculture (see Fig. 1).

The increased demand in combination with supply issues has caused continuous changes since the 1970s resulting in food price volatility (see Fig. 2). The main reasons for the fluctuation of food prices on the supply side are natural disasters and climate change, increases in energy and input costs, and bio-fuel production, along with war and internal conflicts. The increase in food prices and the fragilities within the context of the capitalist food system have provided profit opportunities leading to an increase in investments; speculative behavior on food products in financial markets has also caused food prices to rise and fluctuate artificially. These negative developments contribute to increases in the welfare gap between the richer and

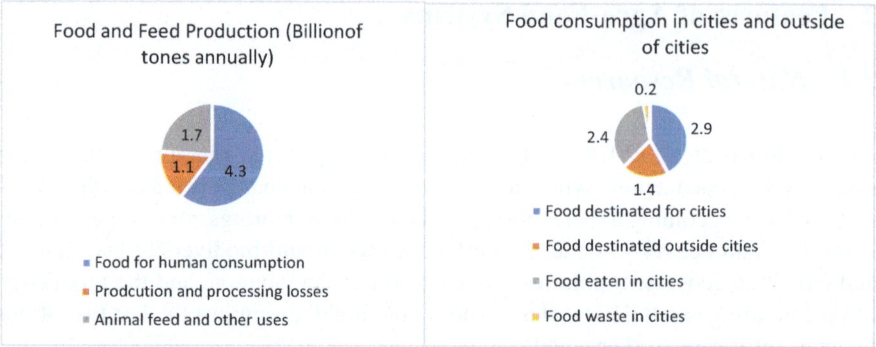

Fig. 1 Food, feed production materials, and consumption (billions of tons per annum). Source: Authors' calculations based on Weforum, https://www.weforum.org/agenda/2019/01/how-to-build-a-circular-economy-for-food

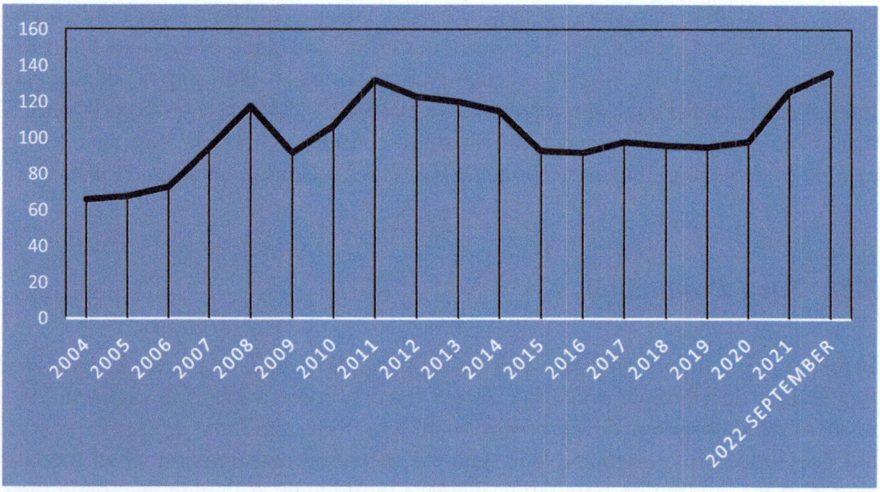

Fig. 2 FAO food price index, 2004–2022. Source: Authors' calculations based on FAO data, https://www.fao.org/worldfoodsituation/foodpricesindex/en/

poorer parts of the world, which, in turn, have devastating consequences on small and medium-sized agricultural enterprises in developing and underdeveloped countries.

Some 10% of the world population currently lives in conditions of hunger. Basic needs are not met on a massive scale even though world food production and crop supply have more than tripled, and animal production has increased 2.5-fold in the recent past. Even though dairy and meat production are expected to increase by 65% and 76%, respectively, by 2050 (D'Odorico et al., 2018, p. 460), in addition to the increasing wealth-based demand, UN world population projections estimate a continued rise to some 10 billion people by 2050 (UN, 2019). These numbers only

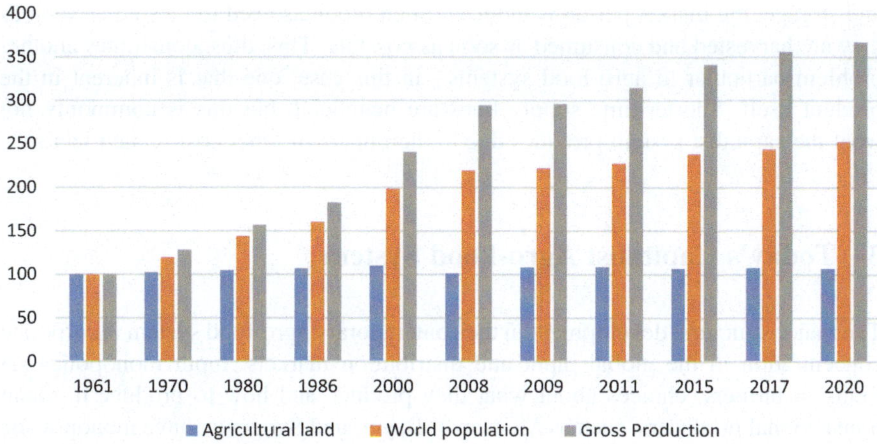

Fig. 3 Changes in food production, population, and agriculture land 1961–2020, (1961 = 100). Source: Authors' calculations based on FAOSTAT data

continue the recent historical trends in which per capita food production has risen faster than population (Fig. 3). Overall, the current failures and increasing pressures alone are enough to show that the global agro-food system as a whole will face immense difficulties in the near future.

2.3 *Conversion of Natural Resources into Food Requirements*

The problems of the current agro-food system are not only rooted in the human-nature relationship. Rather, this system works in the context of policies related to, in addition to agriculture, those concerned with finance, trade, and other institutional arrangements that involve the cultural, educational, and economic dimensions of food consumers (D'Odorico et al., 2018, p. 458). Crucially, however, these largely neglect to take properly into account considerations of natural and social justice, while the socio-economic structure of the system is also the root of many problems. These problems do not only subsist in the social and ecological contradictions of capitalism but are also represented through price and credit relations leading to "accumulation through dispossession" (McMichael, 2005, p. 269), which is a kind of primitive capital accumulation.

Additionally, many foods are consumed in their natural state—that is, as fresh produce. This brings specific issues with perishability, supply and demand uncertainty, and GHG emissions produced throughout the supply chain due to the cooling, transportation to producer and retail markets, and disposal of fresh produce. Perishable-foods markets operate under time limits determined by the life of the products. Because of the short product life, storage costs, and costs of transportation and storage, the market period is reduced. Such products need to be sold as soon as they are harvested and consumed as soon as possible. This, thus, constitutes another problem particular to agro-food systems—in this case, one that is inherent in the product itself. Shorter-time supply lines are beneficial, but this is commonly not what the capitalist system provides due to the impact of other cost-related factors.

3 Today's Capitalist Agro-Food System

The major structural development in the contemporary agro-food system is corporate concentration in the global input and distribution markets. Input monopolies set limits to farmers' choices about what they produce and how to produce it. Giant transnational producers, such as Monsanto, Bayer, and Syngenta, have monopolistic power in the input markets. These companies aim further to gain control over the genetic material of seeds and use this monopoly power to limit other producer activities and product choices. On the other side, the concentration of the retail markets determines which foods are available, accessible, convenient, and desirable for consumers. Giant supermarkets also have the power to control food supply chains and directly affect production by developing own brands as well as by managing food safety and quality standards (Dörr, 2018, p. 200). In this economic environment, farmers and suppliers are subject to the double price squeeze of both input and retail markets (ibid, p. 205).

The structure of the world food and beverage industry is fragmented. Companies in the EU, the US, New Zealand, China, Brazil, and Australia have market dominance. Along with the US, France and the Netherlands are the home countries of 45 of the top 100 large food and beverage companies and realize 57% of the total food and beverage sales (TÜSİAD, 2007, p. 44). According to food regime scholars, corporate concentration and private standards-setting are directly linked with a global governance deficit.

The neoliberal approach of the Washington Consensus is to advocate freedom of trade and enterprise for market efficiencies. Experiences in the recent past, however, have refuted this strategy. When global food crises emerged in 2008 and 2011, crop prices and commodity speculation rose. Some poor people and countries could not access to enough food, and some exporting countries imposed measures like export bans, which led the import-dependent countries into a state of food insecurity.

As can be seen in this example, the globalization of food trade and the intensification of trade dependency can reduce the resilience of the agro-food system because markets sporadically fail for a variety of economic and political reasons (D'Odorico et al., 2018, p. 498). Thus, there are deeper structural roots linked to the globalized agro-food system with its scaling of food trade, trade channels between countries and topological properties of the trade network, and its financialization and facilitation of capital transfers linked directly and indirectly to agriculture (food production, distribution, and markets). Indeed, according to the UN Food and

Agriculture Organization (FAO), the system itself has become increasingly vulnerable (FAO, 2013).

Another important tendency in today's agro-food system is that of globalization. Some 23% of food is currently traded internationally, and about 85% of countries rely on food imports to meet domestic demand (D'Odorico et al., 2018, p. 460). The globalization of food is not limited to trade since it also extends to investments and acquisition of agricultural lands (ibid, p. 494). Global arable land acquisitions since 2008 are estimated to have exceeded 40 million hectares (Anseeuw et al., 2012; Nolte et al., 2016). Foreign agribusiness companies, national corporations, mixed ventures, and foreign governments, as well as retirement funds, are all involved in such land-acquiring investments (Cotula, 2013a, 2013b; Kugelman & Levenstein, 2013; Robertson & Pinstrup-Andersen, 2010). Land acquisition investments lead to many problems, in developing countries particularly. Corporations may turn farmers into employees and increase their vulnerability to food price volatility (e.g., De Schutter, 2011), or they may force the dispossession of traditional users and populations and with various violations of human rights and negative impacts on women and rural livelihoods generally (D'Odorico et al., 2018, p. 496).

Globalization enables dominance and the hegemony of a single agro-food system. Intimately linked to worldwide trade and transnational corporations in this regard is the capitalist imperative of scale. Extensive as well as intensive large-scale farming is rising and causing severe problems in agro-food production. The default to scaling-up gains driven by capitalism, however, ignores the claims of smallholder and medium-size (traditional, family) farms, which are—actually, still—responsible for most of the global calorie and nutrient production (Herrero et al., 2017; Samberg et al., 2016). In fact, smaller farming units can be very productive (D'Odorico et al., 2018, p. 503). There is presently additional competition for land between food and fuel crops (Borras Jr. et al., 2011), and accelerated land grabbing (White et al., 2013)—but also a growing awareness of ecosystem degradation resulting from large-scale farming practices (monocropping, chemical input usage, etc.) (Millennium Ecosystem Assessment, 2005). In other words, we are at a juncture at which the capitalist agro-food hegemony is under pressure for its failures and the future in doubt.

4 Mitigation: UN-FAO Approaches to Food Systems

The biggest representative of the international community for food issues, the UN-FAO organized a summit, United Nations Food Systems Summit (UNFSS), convened by the UN Secretary-General in late 2021. This, however, was much criticized: Although few people will dispute that global food systems need transformation, it has become clear that the Summit is instead an effort by a powerful alliance of multinational corporations, philanthropies, and export-oriented countries to subvert multilateral institutions of food governance and capture the global narrative of food systems transformation. (Canfield et al., 2021, p. 1).

The determination of a system in need of transformation and the opinions expressed at the end of the summit also provide a good indication of the UN-FAO's approach to world food problems—as supported by other international agencies, both in the UN and the World Health Organization (WHO), and managing trade and supplying capital, like the World Trade Organization (WTO), International Monetary Fund (IMF), and World Bank (WB), and overseeing the system as a whole, such as the World Economic Forum (WEF)—and how this reflects the current trends of the capitalist economic system on food issues at the global level. The approach proposed in 2021 can be more clearly understood when considered in the context of the events and policies followed since the establishment of the FAO after World War II (Table 1).

The number of food-insecure people have risen since 2014. According to the FAO, 746 million people were suffering from severe food insecurity in 2019, and an additional 1.25 billion people experienced moderate food insecurity (FAO et al., 2020), These two figures combined reach to a quarter of the world's population. Meanwhile, the Covid-19 pandemic is anticipated to add between 83 and 132 million more people into food insecurity (FAO et al., 2020).

Change to a country's food security status varies according to different insecurity measurements involving not only national food supply and demand and human health, but also agricultural land supply and off-farm income urbanization, economic growth, and capital resources (including social capital), and literacy and access to information (internet connectivity).[1] If a country has low-income levels, and agricultural production is the major source of GDP, for example, economic growth and higher literacy increase food availability. According to the FAO's resilience index measurement and analysis (RIMA), access to sanitation and safe drinking water and schools, hospitals, and agricultural markets provide important support enabling household resilience, particularly in very arid zones and in pastoralist households.

Contrary to the neoliberal promotion of free trade, market openness has not had a meaningful effect on food security (Dikshit & Gopinath, 2021). According to the advocates of free trade in agriculture and food, the efforts to protect small, local producers are barriers to trade that need to be eliminated. Therefore, the agreements made, and measures taken to curtail such supports benefit the multinational corporations that already dominate the world production and exchange of goods. Food system crises are a part of and generally a result of the current crisis of the world political economy that began with the dismantling of the Bretton Woods system established to regulate the world economy, including trade. In the absence of rules governing international trade, Northern countries raised agricultural protections, and

[1]The main measures of food security used by the FAO are (1) the traditional measure, which considers food supply and consumption needs of a country's population—first, production, stock changes, and net imports of food (including food aid) are calculated, then, domestic product and estimated demand or calories per person are assessed, referred to as the minimum dietary energy requirement (MDER)—and (2) the alternative method, which uses anthropometrics, such as body mass index (BMI) and stunting or wasting, especially among children (Dikshit & Gopinath, 2021, p. 1).

Table 1 Post-WWII developments in the world food system and its governance

Date	Developments	Actors	Aims	Actions/policies
Mid 1940s	Food shortages	FAO-UN	To stabilize and manage food security on a world scale	Food, an essential of life rather than primarily merchandize Food, a human right in UN declaration, 1948
1963	End of shortages Food surplus of the US and the EEC (later EU)	FAO world food congress	Worldwide hunger campaign	Food, a development issue Bilateral aid programs Extension of green revolution techniques
1974	Big rise in grain and oilseed prices Famine in India, Bangladesh, Ethiopia, the Sahel Global food crisis.	FAO, UN conference on trade and development (UNCTAD): UN world food conference	To mitigate rises in food prices and famine To reduce hunger	Universal declaration on the eradication of hunger and malnutrition FAO's public vision of food security Food production and distribution linked to explicit humanitarian food aid via grants Adopted green revolution program
1986	Uruguay round started	World Bank US secretary of agriculture US Department of Agriculture (USDA)	To introduce neoliberal policy changes and comparative advantages	Ability to purchase food Food security seen as best provided through a smooth-functioning world market
1995	Uruguay round ended	WTO, 123 states	Free trade regime	Removal/reduction of custom barriers on food trade
1996	UN-FAO world food summit	FAO, 185 states	To reduce world hunger by half by 2015	Food security conceptualized but no plan implemented Global south farmers lost price supports Large-scale grain farmers in the west retained huge subsidies Food dumping in southern markets Second half of the 1990s: Up to 30 million peasants dispossessed in the south

(continued)

Table 1 (continued)

Date	Developments	Actors	Aims	Actions/policies
1996	Opposition to UN-FAO world food summit	International NGOs and La via Campesina (LVC)	Food sovereignty	A vision of democratic, territorially controlled food systems not subject to the market-control of the global north and its transnational food corporations
2000	Hunger and negative impacts on southern agriculture from Uruguay round	International planning Committee for Food Sovereignty (IPC)	To encourage FAO to convene a multilateral forum to address issues of food security	This vision came to pass following "food crisis" of 2007–08
2008	Food crises, Serious legitimacy crisis for the UN	UN-FAO-UN industrial development organization (UNIDO), UN agencies, funds and programs, international financial institutions, and other international organizations WTO, WB	To establish a high-level task force (HLTF) on global food and nutrition security	Reflected the coalescing of a market-based vision of food governance Held the line against the food sovereignty movement
2009	Food crises, rising world hunger, and unacceptable poverty	Committee on world food Security (CFS)	To reform CFS to enhance its capacity to govern global food security To create greater inclusivity and evidence-based decision-making	Stated four pillars of food security (availability, access, utilization, and stability) Established civil society and indigenous peoples' mechanism (CSM) and a private sector mechanism (PSM), both self-organized. Established a high-level panel of experts as a science-policy interface to provide scientific evidence on issues affecting food security and nutrition
2021	Food crises, rising food prices, world hunger, and poverty Covid-19 Green consensus	FAO	To reformulate agro-food system governance	Five aims: (1) to ensure access to safe/nutritious food (2) to shift to sustainable consumption patterns

(continued)

Table 1 (continued)

Date	Developments	Actors	Aims	Actions/policies
				(3) to boost nature-positive production (4) to advance equitable livelihoods (5) to build resilience to vulnerabilities, shocks, and stress

Source: Authors' calculations based on Canfield et al. (2021)

chaotic competition built in agricultural commodity markets. Thus, there was a reconstruction of North-South relations that resulted in the hegemony of the Northern agro-food companies and Southern countries' rising food dependency.

Centralization, the monopolization process of Northern agro-food companies, and the governance of the agro-food system under the auspices of the IMF and the General Agreement on Tariffs and Trade (GATT), become the two main pillars of the world agro-food system. In this system, the primary strategy for food security was to increase food production for greater food availability. Fertilizer, pesticide, and water usages were raised to boost production, but this approach also saw food security reduced for billions of people (de Raymond et al., 2021, p. 5). The system produced much more of some products but at the same time led to many fluctuations and shocks that affected both consumers and producers. The most affected groups from these shocks and fluctuations are small-scale farmers, fishers, pastoralists, landless rural workers, urban poor's, women, and indigenous people. The food security of these households is the main indicator[2] of the agro-food system resilience and efficiency (FAO, 2021, p. 61).

Another aspect of the hegemonic agro-food system is regional specialization in certain products and animal husbandry. Specialization in industrial agro-food production (monoculture herbs and single-animal production) provides an ideal space for the spread of parasites, diseases, and pests. As can be seen from recent viral spreads, zoonosis is a rising and major global risk (de Raymond et al., 2021, p. 4).

Food shortages and rising food prices have brought in their wake rising popular revolts in many countries of the Southern hemisphere and politicized food movements worldwide, including in the US. While a sixth of the world's population is now hungry, the same proportion in the US is deemed "food insecure". The dimensions of the hunger and insecurity show that the root causes are in the political economy of the global, corporate food regime (Holt-Giménez & Wang, 2011). When we look at the root of the problem, the contradictions of agricultural capital accumulation and the WTO agricultural policies targeting subsistence agriculture become clear, and the increasing influence of transnational corporations and their various lobbying mechanisms become a cause for deep concern. In this context, it should be

[2]For a detailed discussion on food securiy indicators, see Poudel and Gopinath (2021).

noted that the funds that are a part of the world's economy-political structure, circulating between countries to earn income from interest rate differences, speculating on energy, minerals, and food products as well as securities are a major cause of the fluctuations in the market prices of agricultural products. These realities indicate that food security is not just a food problem but, on the contrary, is intimately tied to all economic, cultural, and international relations and institutions.

5 Approaches to Reform of the Agro-Food System

Proposals to reform the agro-food system can be grouped into two. In the first approach, linked to food security, the agro-food system is handled only as an economic sector that produces food, while in the second, linked to food sovereignty, it is handled in the context of the integrity of the human-nature and human-human relationships. Although these two perspectives may be similar to each other insofar as they seek solutions not only to food but also to related climate and ecological problems connected to agriculture and share many suggestions for ways to go about this, the fundamental distinction remains important.

The differences between the proposed policies of approaches to the bundle of food and environmental issues reveal the difference between whether they support a radical change to the system, as well as the ideological and political positioning of defending or criticizing the capitalist system in general. In other words, the political perspectives expressed as differences between reformist efforts for food security and radical efforts for food sovereignty characterize the direction demanded of food-systems change. Different approaches to the food justice concept, definitions, and practices either express structural changes to resource redistribution or blur its political meaning by focusing on food accessibility (Holt-Giménez & Wang, 2011).

More concretely, reform and solution proposals in the agro-food system manifest themselves as giving priority to the laws of nature, profitability, and industrial agriculture or to traditional small production and agroecological agriculture methods. In this context, we can see the differences and intersections between two approaches more clearly by looking briefly at the policy recommendations and justifications.

5.1 Food Security

The fundamental injunction of the food security perspective can be expressed as the following: to increase domestic production and improve food supply chains and physical access to food through transport networks and thus the livelihoods of agro-food systems' actors. It supports enhancing human rights, including the right to food and inclusiveness in systems, and asserts that agro-food systems need to adopt agroecological farming and other resource-conservation practices. Sustainable subsidies, the involvement of government institutions, investments in public goods that reduce risks, such as in irrigation and drainage systems, and high-yielding, high-resistance crop varieties are promoted.

The food security approach advocates development of the nonfarm economy for household resilience and improvements to risk management and resilience capacities, including interventions directed at food supply chains, governance, and institutions, as well as the infrastructure necessary to support them. It encourages diversity, connectivity, and flexibility; promotes dialogue, transparency, and collective learning in food supply chains and networks; and seeks to ensure that vulnerable households have access to healthy diets, even when incomes are affected by a shock. Public policies should focus on helping small-scale producers, small and medium enterprises, and vulnerable households to gain access to the business tools they need to enhance their resilience (FAO, 2021, p. 94).

What the food security approach does not involve is a rejection of the hegemonic agro-food system. This is capitalist, global, monopolistic, and increasingly controls the production, processing, distribution, and consumption of food. Now, agro-food corporations aim to gain control of genetic material, too. The corporate regime of the monopolistic agro-food system has five basic food-security-oriented claims in this respect: biotechnology's potential for feeding an increasingly hungry or food-deficient world population, sustainable agriculture, efficient agriculture, moving government out of business, and leveling the playing field (although the latter is quite belied by the lopsided relations between North and South (McMichael, 2000).

Overall, the assumption is that the current track of biotechnology is toward greater food security—yet, aiming for complete dominance, the primary drivers of the hegemonic system, the transnationals, seek to monopolize even the capacity to do agriculture (through genetic modification and associated proprietary rights). Given their primary and bottom-line motivation of monetary profit and the record of food insecurity to date; however, it is apparent that we certainly cannot expect the benefits of biogenetics developments to be well shared, let alone fairly. In other words, we should not place much faith in the emerging future of the current system to deliver food security for all, with biotechnology offered as a promissory note, a Green Revolution-type silver bullet, which is already badly tarnished.

In the face of the mounting pressures on food-provisioning linked to population growth and increased consumption coupled with climate change with its somewhat unpredictable trajectories and unexpected shocks, the agro-food system needs to be particularly resilient. The promise of resilience may be regarded as another key feature of the development of biotechnology for food security. However, resilience also involves the economic and political dimensions of agricultural trading, price dynamics, and only finally, the availability, accessibility, and adequacy of food. Thus, a more radical analysis is implied.

5.2 *Food Sovereignty*

In the recent past, individuals, states, and social movements have tried to introduce public regulatory institutions with the capacity to promote food security and the human right to food. However, public global food governance has been sabotaged by powerful actors. These actors have forced and enforced the introduction and maintenance of industrial agriculture, productivism, and trade liberalization. The cost of this effort has been a weakening of food self-sufficiency and the impoverished livelihoods of small-scale farmers and agricultural workers. Indeed, industrialized agricultural methods using synthetic inputs and proprietary technologies bear a major responsibility for the crisis that is now unfolding and threatens ever-greater food insecurity.

The very structure of the hegemonic agro-food system causes the over-use, misuse, and abandonment of natural resources. Against this, the food sovereignty approach focuses on socio-ecological crisis and aims at a "re-specialization" of social and economic relations (McMichael, 2005, p. 298). The main initiator of the food sovereignty approach, La Via Campesina (LCL), upholds the "independence and food sovereignty of all of the world's peoples" and "advocates that food to be produced through diversified, farmer-based production systems":

"Food sovereignty is the right of peoples to define their own agriculture and food policies, to protect and regulate domestic agricultural production and trade in order to achieve sustainable development objectives, to determine the extent to which they want to be self-reliant, and to restrict the dumping of products in their markets. Food sovereignty does not negate trade, but rather, it promotes the formulation of trade policies and practices that serve the rights of peoples to safe, healthy, and ecologically sustainable production" (Via Campesina, 2001).

Food sovereignty is not the antithesis of food security but rather represents an alternative principle to food security as currently defined by the corporate food regime. Food sovereignty is a premise for genuine food security since "food is first and foremost a source of nutrition and only secondarily an item of trade" (Via Campesina, 2001). The six pillars of food sovereignty listed by the European Coordination Via Campesina (2002) state that it

- Focuses on food for people.
- Values food providers.
- Localizes food systems.
- Puts control locally.
- Builds knowledge and skills.
- Works with nature.

As an alternative to the corporate food regime, the main views expressed from the perspective of food sovereignty build on the global peasant and human rights movement spearheaded by the LVC. The LVC is a broad-based social conglomerate made up of activist peasants, farmers, fisher peoples, farmworkers, women, environmentalists, and indigenous peoples committed to social justice and human rights. It directly challenges the globalization project and protests at the WTO and other international forums. It rejects the WTO food security approach based on free trade and corporate rights and instead seeks to develop coalitions for improving agro-food self-sufficiency using the traditional, grounded, and responsive capacities of indigenous knowledge and initiatives—or indigenous food-ways.

The food sovereignty movement or perspective proposes to remedy the global metabolic rift through a repossession and regionalization of the agro-food system. The food supply problem, it argues, can be solved through ecological modernization and sustainable intensification. Its land sovereignty ontology views land through an ecological, cultural, and multifunctional lens rather than the commodity lens. It recognizes small-to-medium-scale agroecological farming as more resilient to climate shocks than conventional agriculture and domestic-based production as the better path to food security than global commodity chains. It internalizes the environmental costs of farming and advocates for a rights-based rather than market-centered framework, where rights are defined as collective rather than individual (Constance et al., 2014).

While food monopolies control markets, peasant and smallholder movements look to create new local markets based on the principles of food sovereignty and defending the democratic access to living nature. Thus, the food sovereignty movement presages an ontological alternative to neoliberal capitalism. It stands for how the world and its inhabitants might be organized according to ecological principles emphasizing equitable human relations and sustainability instead of the economic principles of commodification, efficiency, and private interest (McMichael, 2016). Essentially, the argument from food sovereignty against food security as an agro-food system philosophy is that the former naturally incorporates the latter; sovereignty is a basic principle while security is just an outcome and thus easily compromised (as currently witnessed). With the Covid-19 exacerbating food insecurity and malnutrition, global social movements demanding public global food governance see an opportunity to further their cause.

6 Postcapitalist Futures: Agroecology

There is not yet an answer to the question of how to sustainably meet the food, energy, and water needs of the rising demand, but the answers must include technology, water, energy, and cultural and institutional dimensions. One approach that incorporates all these is that of agroecology. Agroecology is effectively an efficiency in production, but for peoples' movements and civil society organizations that are struggling for food sovereignty, its meaning is more inclusive.

One focus of agroecology is on the soil. While more than 90% of our food production depends on the soil, soil is itself coming under increasing pressure, and fertile land is becoming scarce. Therefore, healthy soil is very important for food sovereignty. A transformation of the global food system is also related to climate impacts, to which agroecology presents solutions, and agroecology also has a potential trade-off by building resilience through diversification.

Second, advocates of small-scale agriculture argue that it has many advantages. Small-scale farmers can be competitive and resilient, employ sustainable production practices, and have capacities to adopt and adapt to resource-conserving practices—in short, tend to practice agroecology. There are many research results that do not justify the conventional assumption that small-scale agriculture is less productive than large-scale agriculture. If the small-scale farmer is supported, that support yields improved food production, technology transfers, secures poverty alleviation, and enhanced food system resilience. The FAO (2021: pp. xiv-xv) remarks that household supports in areas such as health services, education, and training can strengthen livelihoods and incomes, with positive impacts on agro-food systems, too.

Since smallholders are the primary food producers globally, for an end to hunger and malnutrition and to increase food production, it is necessary to support them and enhance their role in national food provisioning under the liberal trade regime; however, they have generally lost price supports and food subsidies, which have disproportionately harmed the global South. In the same period, large-scale farmers in the US and Europe have retained huge subsidies, leading to cheap food dumping in Southern markets. Currently, therefore, we observe the incongruence wherein cheap food relations result in dispossession and displaced small-scale farmers even as it is this group that is still feeding the majority of the world's population and cultivating the larger part of its land.

7 Discussion: Contesting Approaches

It is possible to reach some clear conclusions by discussing the approaches to the agro-food system in the context of the pro-capitalist corporate food regime represented by the major international organizations and the food sovereignty movement represented by LVC. The WEF is trying to seek to redesign multilateral global governance as part of the "Great Reset." However, the multistakeholder approach undermines the responsibilities of governments and does not have sufficient political participation or clear rules of participation, and it (further) subverts traditional means of political representation and erases mechanisms of accountability.

The partnerships of the WEF does not only allow corporations to set the agenda but also serves as a "path to value" for corporations that sense they are losing their public legitimacy (Canfield et al., 2021). Meanwhile, the UN's Millennium Goals (MGs), now expanded and refitted as the Sustainable Development Goals (SDGs), are a gift for agro-business because the economic rewards for delivering them are probably worth at least $12 trillion and can generate up to 380 million new jobs each year up to 2030 (ibid.). It seems that, via the Great Reset approach, the WEF aims to promote the interests of the world's largest corporations and allay the growing opposition to neoliberal globalization, including opposition to the hegemony of capitalism as the world's agro-food system.

In the food security perspective, there is a consensus that transforming the agro-food system to achieve efficiency, resilience, inclusiveness, and sustainability is necessary for realizing the 2030 Agenda for Sustainable Development. For example, the UNFSS call to action in September 2021 aimed at building resilience to vulnerabilities, shocks, and stresses to ensure the continued functioning of healthy, sustainable agro-food systems. Peoples and movements struggling for food sovereignty, however, wonder whether the outcomes of the UNFSS are baked into its structure and actions to date. They wonder about the policies of the FAO and WEF that focus on handling food system transformation as a technological change, diminishing the role of international intuitions, blurring democratic participation and inclusivity, excluding the voices of producers and workers, undermining accountability for violations of human rights and eco-health degradation, and supporting the illusion that a single global food system based on trade and the "economic integration" of smallholders into global markets will ensure sustainable food security. They defend the need to strengthen the vision of public global food governance to end hunger.

Presently, there is an ongoing reduction of governmental support for agriculture that supports unsustainable patterns of production and consumption, along with GHG emissions, and is economically inefficient. Policy conditionality that ties support to the adoption of environmental-friendly but lower-yielding farm practices could potentially reduce emissions. However, national policies should not focus solely on the impacts of reforms on GHG emissions; international coordination is vital for achieving reductions in global emissions from agriculture. Meanwhile, definitions of sustainability and inefficiency need to be closely interrogated.

The promotion of food sovereignty and indigenous food-ways, identifying pathways to facilitate agroecology and regenerative approaches, and accepting food as a public good hold the promise of a future postcapitalist approach to agro-food systems. Relatedly, five priorities for a transformative research and action agenda involve philanthropy, multilateral donors, researchers, and policymakers playing a uniquely impactful role when working in partnership with farmers' and indigenous peoples' organizations, civil society, the private sector, and others. The transformation envisaged needs to create a future of food that is sustainable, inclusive, equitable, and resilient.

Other recommendations of the food sovereignty approach, agroecology, regenerative approaches, and indigenous foodways, represent a continuous source of knowledge that can inform a repaired relationship between people and nature to accelerate systemic transformation and build equitable, sustainable food systems, decolonize, and democratize knowledge systems for education, research, and innovation. Participatory, transdisciplinary research, and action agendas that bring together farmers, researchers, policymakers, donors, consumers, and other actors across food systems are key to leveraging food systems transformation (GAFF, 2021).

In general, it is accepted there is a huge potential for agroecology, regenerative approaches, and indigenous food-ways to contribute to transformative change. On the other hand, although the weaknesses and failures of the corporate food system have been exposed, the future remains highly contested. Efficiency comes first among the criticisms of ecological farming methods. It is argued that the ever-increasing world population will make them insufficient to meet consumption.

However, there are many studies that show the advantage of the regenerative, agroecological farming (McMichael, 2013).

Although agroecological approaches to agriculture and food security offer similar solutions on many issues, the food system issue is basically political. The interests of capital groups and transnational companies, the main actors of the current system, do not match the interests of poor farmers and people, the requirements of capital accumulation, sustainability, and the measures needing to be taken against climate change. Undoubtedly, there are different groups, interests, and policy proposals on both sides, but still one can talk about the interests of capital, on the one hand, and nature, poor farmers, and people, on the other. In the current situation, it would be naive to expect institutions such as the FAO and WEF to put forward an approach that contradicts the requirements of capital accumulation. The great reset discourse is currently ideological.

Therefore, if the food-system changes, it will come from powerful and sustained social pressure that forces reformists to roll back neoliberalism in the agro-food system. Much of this pressure could come from the food movements. These are not a single bloc, of course. While some may adopt more radical attitudes, others are more reformists. Yet, this may be a strength since their strategic alliance may go a long way toward overcoming the hurdles necessary to shift away from the hegemonic twentieth-century model toward a multiplicity of postcapitalist agro-food systems for the still-new millennium.

8 Conclusion

It is clear that the problems of hunger, environmental degradation, global warming, sustainability of production, and food security urgently require solutions. Unforeseen developments, such as the current Russia-Ukraine war, only magnify and worsen the situation. The hegemonic agro-food system and its representative institutions acknowledge the problems but are unable to find deep and permanent solutions. Such solutions necessarily involve setting priorities and making fundamental policy choices regarding the allocation of resources in a context where motivating interests differ among different segments of society and countries. The dilemmas faced require principled, policy-level choices in determining attitudes toward the use of food and natural resources. Will nature and food be used and (re)produced in line with the needs of humanity (the commons), or will it be (re)-produced according to the profitability principles of the current system?

In this context, one observes that issues related to nature, the climate, and the environment, as well as food sovereignty, poverty, and the situation of agricultural villagers cannot be addressed and resolved on a national scale. The world is a single system, as has recently been graphically revealed by the Covid-19 pandemic. We are increasingly interdependent, including in respect of food products. Poverty and hunger in one part of the world can spread across the world with migrations and wars. Thus, there is a need to choose between national and international approaches to agro-food and related issues. Nature and food must be treated as a global concern, not a national one.

Within the framework of this basic choice, the ideal for all humanity to live in a sustainable world without hunger is waiting to be adopted and defended as a primary and basic universal goal. The dazzling measures of the current food emperors, the "midcourse guidance" attitudes of international institutions, are insincere approaches that avoid permanent, radical solutions, even though they express ideas that sound good at first. In fact, there is an abundance of tools and a wealth of experience for the realization of agroecological approaches that promise alternative solutions. The problem is actually one of fundamental principles and political choices. Thus, what is required is a thoroughgoing reset of the agro-food system.

Under the present capitalist system, one cannot imagine that the necessary solutions will be adopted. Rather, the fundamental transformation needed by humanity will have to be developed through the struggle of all the peoples of the world, farmers, the poor, and activists for and supporters of a just and healthy future. Without waiting for a total economic and social system change, an important step will be to accept the rights to nature and to food as basic human rights and to gain institutional and legal guarantees for this.

References

Anseeuw, W., Wily, L. A., Cotula, L., & Taylor, M. (2012). *Land rights and the rush for land: Findings of the global commercial*. ILC.

Borras, S. M., Jr., McMichael, P., & Scoones, I. (Eds.). (2011). *The politics of biofuels, land and agrarian change*. Routledge.

Canfield, M. D., Andersson, M., & McMichael, P. (2021). UN food systems summit 2021: Dismantling democracy and resetting corporate control of food systems. *Frontiers in Sustainable Food Systems, 5*, 661552. https://doi.org/10.3389/fsufs.2021.66155

Constance, D. H., Friedland, W. H., Renard, M.-C., & Rivera-Ferr, M. G. (2014). Alternative agrifood movements: Patterns of convergence and divergence. *Research in Rural Sociology and Development, 21*, 346.

Cotula, L. (2013a). *The great African land grab? Agricultural investments and the global food system (248 pp.)*. Zed Books Ltd..

Cotula, L. (2013b). The new enclosures? Polanyi, international investment law and the global land rush. *Third World Quarterly, 34*(9), 1605–1629. https://doi.org/10.1080/01436597.2013.843847

de Raymond, A. B., Alpha, A., Ben-Ari, T., Daviron, B., Nesme, T., & T'etart, G. (2021). Systemic risk and food security. Emerging trends and future avenues for research. *Global Food Security, 29*, 100547.

De Schutter, O. (2011). The green rush: The global race for farmland and the rights of land users. *Harvard International LJ, 52*, 503.

Dikshit, P., & Gopinath, M. (2021). Exploring the disparity in global food security indicators. *Global Food Security, 29*, 100549. https://doi.org/10.1016/j.gfs.2021.100549

D'Odorico, P., Davis, K. F., Rosa, L., Carr, J. A., Chiarelli, D., Dell'Angelo, J., et al. (2018). The global food-energy-water nexus. *Reviews of Geophysics, 56*, 456–531. https://doi.org/10.1029/2017RG000591

Dörr, F. (2018). Food regimes, corporate concentration and its implications for decent work. In C. Scherrer & S. Verma (Eds.), *Decent work deficits in southern agriculture: Measurements, drivers and strategies. Labor and globalization (Vol. 11)* (pp. 178–208). Rainer Hampp Verlag.

European Coordination Via Campesina. (2002). *Sovereignty now. A guide to food sovereignty.* viacampesina.org/en/wp-content/uploads/sites/2/2018/02/Food-Sovereignty-A-guide-Low-Res-Vresion.pdf

FAO. (2013). *The state of food insecurity in the world 2013. The multiple dimensions of food security.* FAO.

FAO. (2021). In FAO (Ed.), *The state of food and agriculture 2021. Making agrifood systems more resilient to shocks and stresses.* https://doi.org/10.4060/cb4476en

FAO, IFAD, UNICEF, WFP, and WHO. (2020). The state of food security and nutrition in the world 2020. Transforming food Systems for Affordable Healthy Diets. www.fao.org/3/cb4474en/cb4474en.pdf.

GAFF. (2021). *The politics of knowledge: Understanding the evidence for agroecology, regenerative approaches, and indigenous foodways.* Global alliance for the future of food. www.futureoffood.org

Herrero, M., Thornton, P., Power, B., Bogard, J., Remans, R., Fritz, S., et al. (2017). Farming and the geography of nutrient production for human use: A transdisciplinary analysis. *The Lancet Planetary Health, 1*(1), e33–e42. https://doi.org/10.1016/S2542-5196(17)30007-4

Holt-Giménez, E., & Wang, Y. (2011). Reform or transformation? The pivotal role of food justice in the US food movement. *Race/Ethnicity: Multidisciplinary Global Contexts, 5*(1), 83–102. Food Justice.

IPCC. (2019). *Climate change and land. summary for policymakers.* Intergovernmental panel on climate change. ipcc.ch/site/assets/uploads/sites/4/2020/02/SPM_Updated-Jan20.pdf

Kugelman, M., & Levenstein, S. (2013). *The global farms race: Land grabs, agricultural investment, and the scramble for food security.* Island Press.

McMichael, P. (2000). The power of food. *Agriculture and Human Values, 17*, 21–33.

McMichael, P. (2005). Global development and the corporate food regime. *New Directions in the Sociology of Global Development Research in Rural Sociology and Development, 11*, 269–303.

McMichael, P. (2013). *Food regimes and agrarian questions.* Fernwood Publishing.

McMichael, P. (2016). Food regime for thought, *An international colloquium 4-5 February 2016 Colloquium Paper No. 56*, at International Institute of Social Studies (ISS) Kortenaerkade 12, 2518AX The Hague.

Millennium Ecosystem Assessment. (2005). *Ecosystems and human Well-being: Synthesis.* Island Press, World Resources Institute.

Nolte, K, Chamberlain, W., & Giger, M. (2016). *International land deals for agriculture. Fresh insights from the Land Matrix: Analytical report II.* Centre for Development and Environment; Centre de coopération internationale en recherche agronomique pour le développement; German Institute of Global and Area Studies; University of Pretoria; Bern Open Publishing.

Poudel, D., & Gopinath, M. (2021). Exploring the disparity in global food security indicators. *Global Food Security, 29*, 10054.

Robertson, B., & Pinstrup-Andersen, P. (2010). Global land acquisition: Neo-colonialism or development opportunity? *Food Security, 2*(3), 271–283. https://doi.org/10.1007/s12571-010-0068-1

Samberg, L. H., Gerber, J. S., Ramankutty, N., Herrero, M., & West, P. C. (2016). Subnational distribution of average farm size and smallholder contributions to global food production. *Environmental Research Letters, 11*(12), 124010. https://doi.org/10.1088/1748-9326/11/12/124010

TÜSİAD. (2007). Uluslararası Rekabet Stratejileri: Türkiye Gıda Sanayi, Yayın no:TÜSİAD/T-2007-09-442.

UN. (2019). World: Total population, *World population prospects* (UN Department of Economic and Social Affairs, Population Dynamics). population.un.org/wpp/Graphs/Probabilistic/POP/TOT/900

Van der Ploeg, J. D. (2016). Theorizing Agri-food economies. *Agriculture, 6*(30). https://doi.org/10.3390/agriculture6030030

Via Campesina. (2001, November 1). Our world is not for sale WTO: shrink or sink. *Statement network: "Our world is not for sale" (OWISNS),* Bulletin. viacampesina.org/en/statement-network-qour-world-is-not-for-saleq-owinfs/.

White, P. J., George, T. S., Dupuy, L. X., Karley, A. J., Valentine, T. A., Wiesel, L., & Wishart, J. (2013). Root traits for infertile soils. *Frontiers in Plant Science, 4*, 1–7. https://doi.org/10.3389/fpls.2013.00193

Financialization and Finance-Driven Capitalism

Betül Mutlugün

Abstract This chapter discusses the discourses and consequences of finance-driven capitalism from a political economy approach by employing an analytical eclecticism. For this aim, we bring together diverse approaches to frame the understanding of financialization and how it influences the behavior of different actors. First, we critically assess the financialization theories from various historical perspectives. Then, we examine periodization issues of financialization by looking at historical patterns to uncover how different trajectories of the role of finance can offer insights in answering whether financialization constitutes a shift toward a new paradigm in capitalist accumulation, or a tenacious regularity of economic bubbling up. We claim that despite institutional and formal differences, financialization has been unfolding in the centuries-long history of finance. Its pace can be moderated or accelerated by particular policies, institutional changes, and the state of the economy, similar to those implemented during the Golden Age of capitalism or repeal of the Glass-Steagal act. Financialization is a global phenomenon and situated within unproductive activities by creating a rent-seeking society and reflects actual workings of modern capitalism rather than constituting a new epoch in capitalism.

Keywords Finance-driven capitalism · Financialization · Contemporary capitalism · Financial crises · Capitalist accumulation

1 Introduction

The phenomenon of financialization received wider scientific and public attention after the 2007–08 financial crisis. The contemporary research on financialization has entered a new phase as the tentacles of finance reach into the lives of billions of ordinary people, while financial markets are shrouded in mystery arising from extremely complex financial instruments and unbridled intensification of speculative

---

B. Mutlugün (✉)
Department of Economics, Istanbul University, Istanbul, Turkey
e-mail: betul.mutlugun@istanbul.edu.tr

A. Ari (ed.), *Capitalism at a Crossroads*, Springer Studies in Alternative Economics,
https://doi.org/10.1007/978-3-031-23257-2_5

economic activities. According to the most recent data from the (2022a), for the first half of 2021, the total notional amount outstanding for contracts in the global over-the-counter (OTC) derivatives market was an estimated $610 trillion. However, the gross market value of all contracts is stood only at approximately $12.6 trillion. Considering that global GDP was amounted to about $84.5 trillion in 2020, the global derivatives markets are not only large in absolute terms but also when compared with the size of the global economy and global financial markets.

The financialization discussion emphasizes on how the role of finance changed beyond its traditional function of providing capital for the productive investments, its altered linkages to the real economy, and its transformative power on the behavior of various social actors and workings of the society (Lapavitsas, 2013; Orhangazi, 2008; Epstein, 2005; Onaran et al., 2011; Hein, 2013; Tori & Onaran, 2018). For some scholars, the crisis suddenly made it clear that capitalism has changed in recent decades, and financialization is the most significant determinant of this transformation (Krippner, 2005; Van Treeck, 2009; Lapavitsas, 2012). The new order of the financial sector with its range of sophisticated and increasingly abstruse financial instruments, new digital technologies, and high-frequency trading combined with the rentier behavior had further removed the accumulation of capital from the sphere of production. But when did financialization start?

To be sure, the Great Financial Crisis was not a one-off event. It has a long past that goes back to the Tulipmania in 1637, the South Sea Bubble in 1720, followed by many other historical bubbles. The recent financial crisis may remind the instability inherent to capitalism and the current economic system, but the global financial market muddles on. Moreover, the crises will likely have a long future, coming in various frequencies with different severities. So here we are. Marx (1894) could hardly have imagined the extent to which financial capital has gained purchase over everyday life in the twenty-first century. The financial system has indeed been transformed in the context of contemporary capitalism. This is evident from the root of the recent financial crisis that hits the real economy eventually on a global scale: the financialization of worker's income and mortgage lending in the US, in particular.

Nevertheless, the tendency to frame financialization as a radical departure from a nonfinancialized norm and characterizing financialization as a shift toward a new paradigm by accompanying it with financial globalization can be misleading (Christophers & Fine, 2020). Financial speculation in today's digitized economy is such that one can trade hundreds of securities while casually sipping a coffee. However, efforts of generating income through unproductive activities without undertaking a risk in the production circuit existed throughout history using money. Financialization is a more sophisticated practice of creating financial products by securitizing loans and tangible assets, pooling various types of loans together, and selling them as a bond to "mitigate risks" where algorithmic agents carry out the transactions. It carries the activities of fractional reserve banking one step further. In contemporary capitalism, these financial innovations are of extreme complexity, and financial logic penetrates every aspect of economic activity. If the financier Mr. Merdle in Dickens's Little Dorrit is a personification of Marx's nineteenth-century capitalism, depicting the pitfalls of finance capital with the mindless pursuit of money, imprisoning effects of debt, and financial insolvency, Patrick Bateman in American Psycho can account for the contemporary iteration of financialization portraying the workings of fictitious capital in today's digitized economy.

Our study views the phenomenon of financialization from a political economy approach, highlighting that finance plays an integral but contradictory role in continuing accumulation as discussed by Marx and Keynes. We base this argument on the distinction between productive versus unproductive activities, where financialization is situated within unproductive activities and creates a rent-seeking society. The financial sector strengthens the position of the rentier class to the detriment of the productive sectors of the economy. However, introducing rentiers as a class construct and distinguishing it from producers does not necessarily imply that financialization is the consequence of nonfinancial capitalists escaping low profits in the sphere of production. On the contrary, the higher rent opportunities led up to the rapid growth of circulation compared to production, which in turn reinforced the instability of capitalism.

From the above vantage point, this chapter provides an overview of studies on the history, origins, drivers, and implications of the financialization of the economy. In the following, we examine some major trends related to the finance sector's recent growth compared to the real sector. Then, we explore two approaches that underpin different types of contributions by scholars to the financialization debate: studies investigating the changing role of finance in capitalist accumulation from a historical perspective and studies focusing on the periodization of the trajectory of financialization to find the common patterns in financialization. In doing so, we provide a critical perspective on the competing ideas of conceptual issues in financialization. We also touch upon the consequences of finance-driven capitalism in the context of the recent crises and sustainability of the current system.

2 The Near Exponential Growth of Finance

How big is the global market for financial assets? The past 50 years have witnessed profound changes in the financial sector regarding its volume, impact, and role in real economic activities. The financial deregulation that began in the core capitalist economies in the late 1970s and in developing economies afterward led to the proliferation of new and complex financial products and a simultaneous surge in pervasive indebtedness. Eventually, the financial industry has grown at an unprecedented rate. Today, the size of finance in GDP is at an all-time high in many developed and emerging economies.

According to Palma (2009), between 1980 and 2007, the stock of global financial assets, including equity, private and public debt securities, and deposits, increased from $26.6 to $241 trillion in real terms. This growth is more evident when measuring the financial sector by its share of GDP. The ratio of the stock of financial assets to world output between 1980 and 2007 jumped from 1.2 to 4.4. Using nonconsolidated data for financial assets, McKinsey Global Institute (2021) estimated that between 1970 and 2020, liabilities and their corresponding financial assets had risen relative to GDP from 2.3 to 5.9. From 2000 to 2020, financial assets within the financial sector grew from 4.4 to 6.0 times GDP, while outside of the financial sector, they rose from 4.2 to 6.0 times GDP for the same period. In short, the value of global financial assets outweighs global GDP today, grew by a staggering 10.9% compared with the previous year. It amounted to $468.7 trillion in 2020, representing six times of world GDP (Financial Stability Board, 2021).

The relative size of the total financial assets to GDP is now the highest among many rich countries. For example, Crotty (2008) estimated that the US's financial assets to GDP ratio reached around 950% in the early 2000s from around 400 to 500% from the 1950s until the financial deregulation in the early 1980s. For the UK, this ratio soared even more dramatically, rising from around 700% in the late 1980s to around 1200% by the end of 2009, according to Lapavitsas' (2013) calculations. Figure 1 indicates the notable upsurge in the size of the financial assets held by the financial sector and outside the financial sector before the financial crisis in 2008 and ongoing financial deepening to date. This ratio is huge in European countries, while it remains lower in Mexico as an emerging economy.

Until the 1990s, securitized debt products were not a large part of US and European capital markets. In contrast, such products have a long history in the US. Traditionally, financial intermediaries retained the loans they originated on their balance sheets until maturity to ensure the loan quality. However, starting around the 1990s, this "originate-to-hold" model gradually turned into an "originate-to-distribute" model where banks sold the securitization pools in capital markets known as asset-backed securities (ABS). In addition to subprime securitizations in the US ABS market in the early 1990s, collateralized debt obligations (CDOs) and credit default swaps (CDSs) commenced in the late 1990s. This market remains unregulated and has fundamentally transformed the functioning of capital markets and financial intermediation.

Gorton and Metrick (2013) indicated that the amounts of private securitization and corporate bonds issued in the US reached over $1.7 trillion and $1,1 trillion in 2007, respectively, from around $100 billion in 1990. The total securitization issuance for Europe is estimated to have grown to around $302 million in 1992 and peaked at $1,1 trillion in 2008 before plummeting to $512 million after the crisis. The market for those products in 2010 in Europe is predicted to be around $2.7 trillion (Blommestein et al., 2011). According to BIS calculations, total debt securities outstanding at end-June 2021 for the US were calculated as $47.8 trillion as against $624 billion in 1970, while in the UK, it was $7.2 trillion as against $425 billion in 1987. At the end-June of 2021, the global debt securities market, including domestic and international debt securities, was estimated to exceed $141 trillion (BIS, 2022b). Derivative markets are growing even faster. The notional value of outstanding derivatives rose to $610 trillion for the same period. The gross market value of OTC derivatives which provides information about the potential market

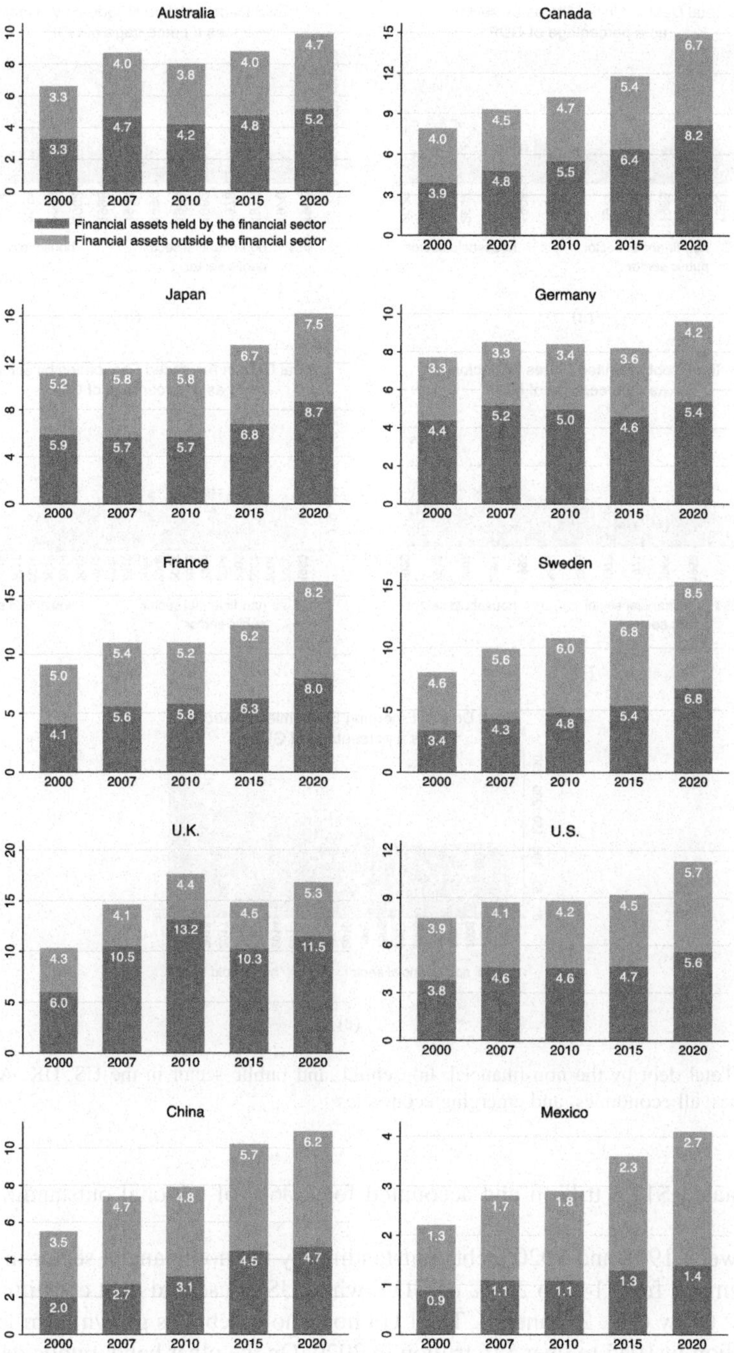

Fig. 1 Financial deepening between 2000 and 2020 in selected countries: the ratio of financial assets held by the financial sector and outside the financial sector (GDP multiple)

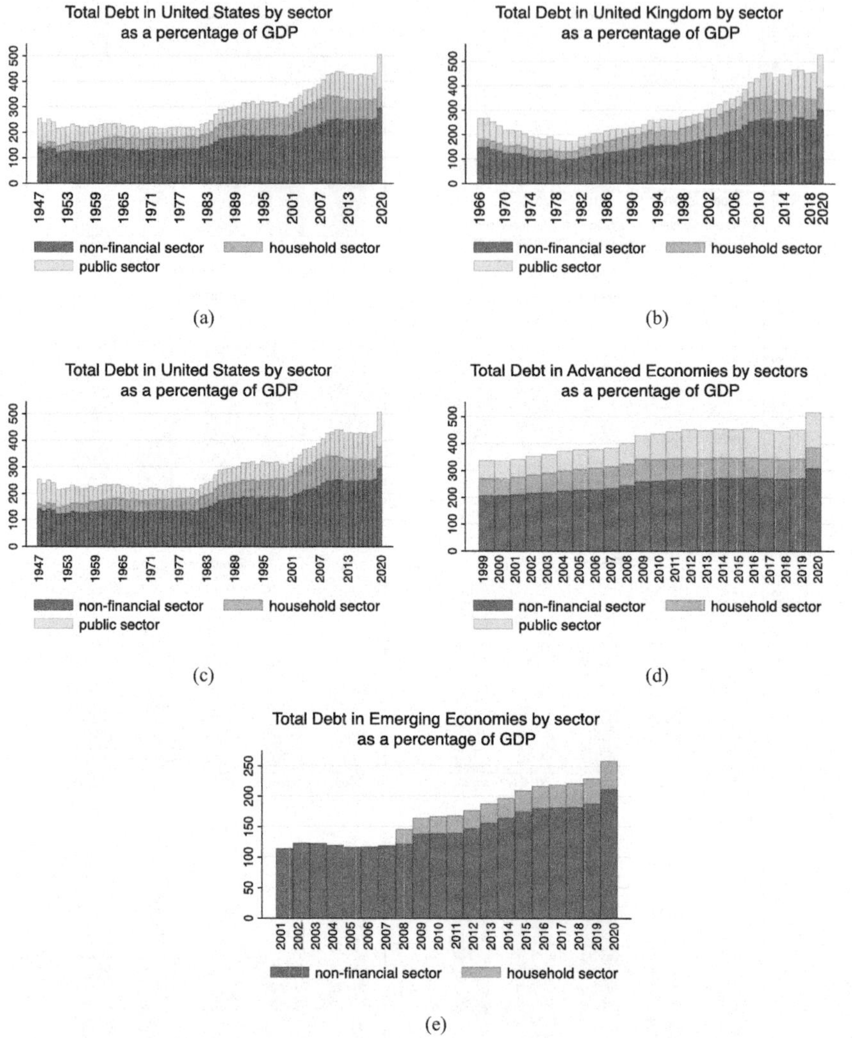

Fig. 2 Total debt by the non-financial, household, and public sector in the US, UK, Advanced economies, all economies, and emerging economies

risk, totaled $12.6 trillion and accounted for 2.06% of notional outstanding (BIS, 2022a).

Between 1947 and 2020, debts outstanding by the nonfinancial sector in the US have jumped from 141 to 296% of GDP, while US household debt constitutes 80% of GDP today (Fig. 2, panel a). Total US household debt has grown from less than $30 billion in 1945 to over $16 trillion in 2020. On the other hand, public debt is up from 94.6% in 1946 to 131% of GDP. The scenario is different in the UK. Total

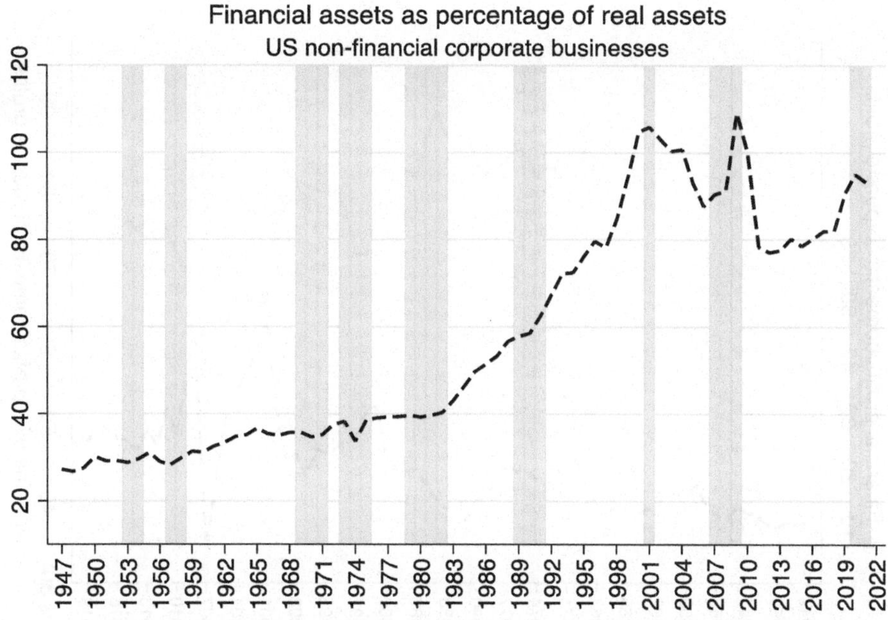

Fig. 3 Financial assets as a percentage of tangible assets for US nonfarm nonfinancial corporate businesses (1947–2021). Source: Board of Governors of the Federal Reserve System (2021), Federal Reserve Statistical Release, Z1 flow of funds accounts of the United States, Table B. 102 (Balance sheet of nonfarm nonfinancial corporate business). Author's calculations

nonfinancial sector debt has accelerated since the late 1970s, climbing from $164 billion to $8.9 trillion in 2020. At the same time, household debt almost tripled, from 32.9% of GDP in 1966 to 88.5% today (Fig. 2, panel b). Comprising 206% of GDP in 1999 and 260% in 2010, nonfinancial sector debt in advanced economies soared from 206% to over 300% of GDP today (Fig. 2, panel c). As a result, total debt for the public sector in advanced economies and total household debt in emerging economies have almost doubled, while nonfinancial sector debt is now over 250% of GDP worldwide (Fig. 2, panels d and e).

The remarkable rise in financial investments of nonfinancial corporations (NFCs) and the transformation of the nonfinancial sector has become a distinguishing feature of financialization since the late 1970s (Stockhammer, 2004; Krippner, 2005; Orhangazi, 2008; Palley, 2013; Lapavitsas, 2013). One key stylized fact reflecting this transformation in the balance sheet of NFCs is an ever-increasing financial asset holding relative to fixed capital in their portfolios. Figure 3 shows the dramatic rise in the ratio of financial assets to tangible assets in total assets of NFCs in the US from 1947 to 2021. The graph indicates that this ratio is rising slightly between 1950 and 1970, but sharply escalates beginning in the 1980s, and peaks at 109.05, surmounting the level of nonfarm NFCs tangible assets in 2009. Today, financial assets as a percentage of tangible assets are more than tripled compared to the postwar decade. The historical rise in the share of financial profits within domestic

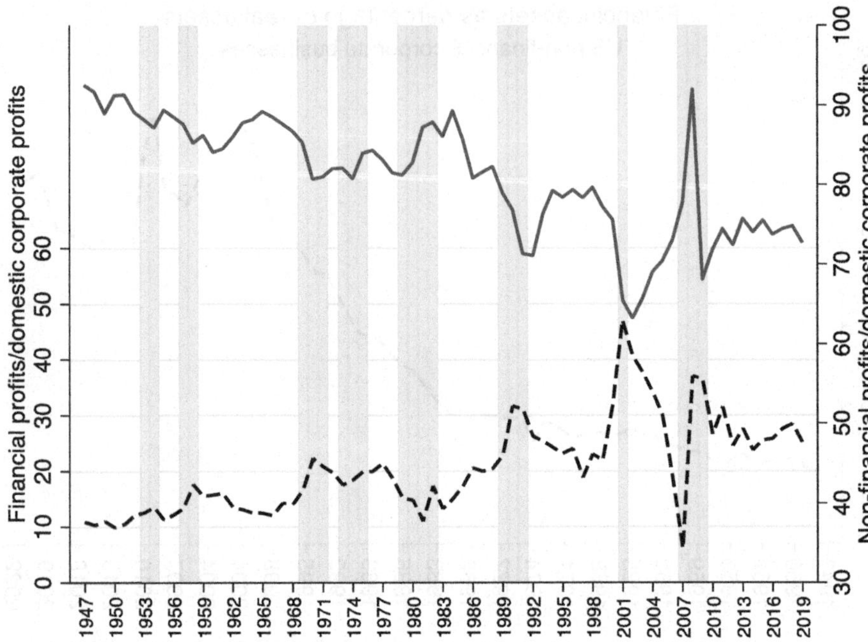

Fig. 4 Financial profits (dashed line) and nonfinancial profits (solid line) as a percentage of domestic corporate profits for US domestic corporations (1947–2019). Source: US Bureau of Economic Analysis (BEA) (2021), National Income and Product Accounts (NIPA), Table 6.16A. Corporate Profits by Industry. https://apps.bea.gov/iTable/iTable.cfm?reqid=19&step=2#reqid=19&step=2&isuri=1&1921=survey

corporate profits throughout the postwar decades is also striking. The share of financial profits in domestic corporate profits peaked at close to 50% in the wake of the collapse of the dot-com bubble (Fig. 4). Conversely, the share of nonfinancial profits within domestic corporate profits declined considerably, dropping from 92% in 1947 to 72% in 2019.

Accumulation scholars who focus on the financialization of modern corporations draw attention to a surge in stock buybacks by NFCs (Lazonick, 2009; Lazonick & O'Sullivan, 2000; Stout, 2012). Using firm-level data, Davis (2016) highlighted the episodic increase in equity repurchases by large NFCs where periods of growth in repurchases correspond to the business cycle. For Davis, this trend had been encouraged by (i) changes to the tax code and (ii) regulatory changes that occurred in 1983, 1991, and 2003 in which Securities and Exchange Commission (SEC) adopted the rules 10b-18, intending to provide a safe harbor for an issuer to reduce liability when they buy back shares of the company's common stock. The sharp fall in the rate of net issues during these periods is most evident from Fig. 5. The issuance of new corporate bonds was negative for most of the 1980s. On average, the rate of net issues of equities for nonfinancial was about 0.007 from 1947 to 1980 but turned to negative and receded to around −0.013 between 1981 and 2020. Recent empirical

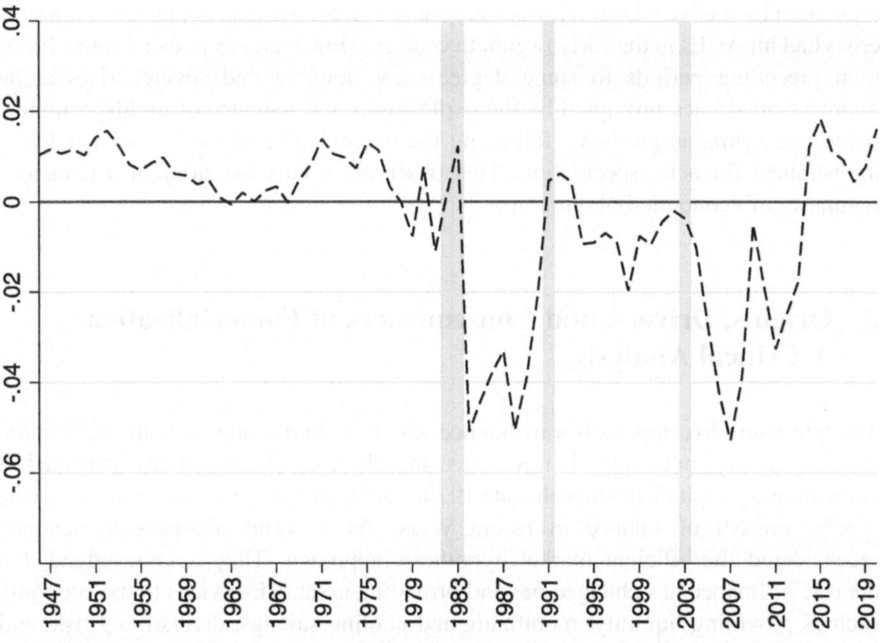

Fig. 5 The rate of net issues of corporate equities for US nonfinancial corporate businesses (1947–2019). Source: Board of Governors of the Federal Reserve System (2021), Federal Reserve Statistical Release, Z1 flow of funds accounts of the United States, Table L. 213 corporate equities (1) and Table F.213 corporate equities (1). Author's calculations

evidence by Mason (2015) suggests that NFCs gradually borrow to finance stock buybacks instead of real investment to maximize shareholder value. Skott and Ryo (2008) calculated that NFCs had spent only about 5% of their gross investment to finance new issues in the 1950s–1970s, but this amount increased to 12% between 1980 and 2005.

The stylized facts of changes in financial variables presented above support the crowding-out thesis advanced by the financialization literature (Orhangazi, 2008; Stockhammer, 2004; Duménil & Lévy, 2005; Akkemik & Özen, 2014). For some scholars, all this meant that a new financial system has emerged in the last four decades (Krippner, 2005; Van Treeck, 2009; Lapavitsas, 2013). The detailed financial data that are available back to the 1940s for the US and other advanced capitalist economies (ACEs) detect the increasing dominance of finance after the 1970s. The lack of reliable historical financial data obstructs the attempt to investigate whether financialization is a new phenomenon or periodic intensifications in the evolutionary process of financialization before the twentieth century which resembles that of contemporary financialization.

Nevertheless, a simple observation offers us an important clue: financial markets expanded benignly, and financial crises were nonexistent in Western economies during the Golden Age era. The stability was achieved with strong financial regulation by the New Deal reforms (such as the Glass-Steagall act in 1933) after the crisis had hit ACEs in the early twentieth century. However, the years after the 1980s (and preceding periods to some degree) saw frequent and severe crises at an unprecedented pace prompted by the explosion in the issuance of highly complex, risky, and synthetic products, following the deregulation of the financial industry unrestrained financial speculation. This observation tells the story of a tenacious regularity of economic bubbling up.

3 Origins, Drivers, and Consequences of Financialization: A Critical Analysis

Though heterodox approaches to finance stand in sharp contrast with mainstream financial theory, both schools now agree that the role of finance has increased in contemporary capitalism since the late 1970s, and the recent crisis is connected to the secular growth of finance in recent years. As a result, mainstream scholars reconsidered the efficient market hypothesis approach. They acknowledged that the role of finance has changed beyond providing essential services to the economy such as providing liquidity, mobilizing and pooling savings, diversifying risk, and acting as a mediator in allocating funds to investment (see Blinder et al., 2012; and Shin, 2010). On the other side, heterodox studies championed the concept of financialization to highlight how finance, intrinsic in capitalist relations, can extend to social, cultural, and economic life and increasingly influences and dominates them, which can sometimes be detrimental on a destructive scale.

The discussion in framing financialization often gravitated around two interrelated broad themes. First, scholars either strived to identify common patterns of financial development and its changing role in capitalist accumulation from a historical perspective or deal with the periodization of the trajectory of financialization. In terms of the former approach, Van der Zwan (2014) has summarized three primary schools in recent financialization debates: financialization as a structural shift in patterns of capitalist accumulation (see Krippner, 2005, 2012; Van Treeck, 2009; Duménil & Lévy, 2005; Stockhammer, 2012; Lapavitsas, 2013); change in corporate governance and objectives of top management toward short-termism in firm decision-making and shareholder value maximization (see Froud et al., 2000; Lazonick and O'Sullivan, 2000; Aglietta & Breton, 2001; Dallery, 2009); and financialization of everyday life (see Martin, 2002; Dixon, 2008; Langley, 2009; Montgomerie, 2006). For the latter, financialization can be periodized in three different ways, following Beck and Knafo (2020) and Vercelli (2014): financialization as a unique historical episode, as a recurrent pattern of development in history, and as a collection of historical financial developments where each has distinctive features of financialization and has different regimes of accumulation.

As these perspectives are interrelated and complementary, we exploit previous contributions to the financialization process in an exclusive and unifying way in the following sections. We emphasize on the consequences of finance-driven capitalism and highlight how financialization influences the behavior of different actors such as nonfinancial corporations (NFCs), households, and states.

3.1 Perspectives on Financialization from a Historical Context

3.1.1 Financialization as a Capitalist Regime of Accumulation

The prevalent thesis in recent decades is that financialization reflects a radical transformation of capitalist accumulation toward a new finance-driven economy, and contemporary capitalism is a unique historical period (Duménil & Lévy, 2004, 2005; Krippner, 2005; Stockhammer, 2007). Many connected the exponential growth of financial markets with the stagnation of industrial production during the economic crisis of the 1970s.

One popular explanation for this assertion belongs to the Monthly Review School. Magdoff and Sweezy (1987) pointed out that the abundance of production that monopoly capitalism cannot absorb implies a systemic tendency toward stagnation. Failure in the exhaustion of surplus and the stagnation of the productive sectors of capitalist economies prompted a shift in the center of gravity of the capitalist economy from the sphere of production to circulation. This instigated investors to have stronger financial and speculative motives after the economic crisis of 1970s.

Brenner (2009), Harman (2010), and Callinicos (2010) gave reference to the overaccumulation theory of Marx in explaining the recent financial crisis. Given the structural inequality in the distribution of income, the consumption and investment markets that saturated with an abundance of production urged businesses to search for new markets and customers, aiming to expand the production and expropriate surplus. The financial sector provides an alternative for the owners of capital to compensate for fewer profitable opportunities in the productive sphere. However, it is unclear how the poor masses representing the majority of the households can afford to invest in stocks and financial derivatives, given the ever-widening inequality of income distribution and weak demand. Lapavitsas (2011) argues that linking stagnation in the sphere of production to financialization and the nature of the recent crisis contradicts the investment banking practices of mortgage lending to the poorest sections of the US working class.

French regulationists traditionally linked the social norms to a regime of accumulation that shaped a country's institutional framework and attempted to explain how this framework helps stabilize the inherently contradictory capitalist economy. By providing a finance-led growth model, Boyer (2000) claimed that ACEs moved from a "Fordist" regime of accumulation based on mass production, consumption, and collective bargaining to a "finance-led" accumulation pattern dominated by the smaller batch production with flexible specialization instead. Here, financialization is considered a process of development in the governance of social and economic reproduction.

The above approaches offer sound arguments about the detachment of finance from the fundamentals of the real economy, which had been an amply emphasized nature of contemporary capitalism. However, defining financialization as a response to stagnation in the real sector neglects the role of government policies. Reverse causality might be at play: financial deregulation is essentially effective in enabling enormous profits in the financial sector in the most direct way, without undergoing a production given its risky nature. Thus, the higher profit opportunities in the financial sector relative to real sector made possible by financial deregulation can pave the way for financialization.

Drawing on the work of Marxist sociologist Arrighi (1994), Krippner (2005) identifies new patterns in the sources of capital accumulation on a macro scale by providing evidence-based historical data for financialized firm behavior and accumulation of profit in the US. The systematic empirical approach she employed triggered a debate over how financialization is fundamentally about a shift in the capitalist regime of accumulation. Empirical studies that examine the weight of the financial industry in ACEs conducted by Marxist and post-Keynesian scholars corroborate Krippner's (2005, p. 202) assertion that "Nonfinancial corporations are beginning to resemble financial corporations – in some cases, closely".

Not only do US NFCs earn an increasing portion of their profits from financial transactions, but they also mobilize a significant portion of their activities to the financial sector through interest and dividends payments and stock repurchases (Crotty, 2005; Krippner, 2005; Lin & Tomaskovic-Devey, 2013). The empirical studies testing crowding-out effect from a microperspective using data at the firm level (Orhangazi, 2008; Tori & Onaran, 2018; Demir (2009); Akkemik & Özen, 2014) or macroeconomic data (Stockhammer, 2004; van Treeck, 2009) highlighted the contradictory relationship between real capital accumulation and the financial sector. While the expansion of the financial sector and the large climb in asset prices crowds out physical investment, it creates a bubble. This artificial boom in financial sector, unbacked by real economic developments, is followed by a spectacular crash. The response of central banks to the burst of the financial bubble with money printing to help the stock prices to rebound increases the risk of the collapse of the entire international payments system.

Many ACEs, in particular the US, can delay the inevitable financial crisis since they can issue debt denominated in their currency. However, given emerging economies' position in the international monetary hierarchy, this unstable system collapses the financialized economy sooner. One of the specific features of financialization in emerging economies is that it generates more local impacts in terms of its consequences, and ACEs can intervene to limit the spread of financial distress. However, this difference is dwindling due to the increasing weight of emerging economies, particularly China, in global and world politics. The integration of global markets gradually eliminates the ability to control the extent of financial sector challenges as regions can generate global-scale impacts.

Substantial increase in finance sector rents not only decreases the share of wages but also returns on capital in the production sector. Financial instruments are, thus, used as particular forms of creating rent. In the nation-state system, the government plays a more prominent role in creating and controlling the rent distribution mechanism, while in many developed economies, the power between the political and business elite is more balanced and maintains on a reciprocal basis. Ashman et al. (2011, p. 189) stated that for developing economies, "there is the added twist of both creating financial elites and strengthening their roles". Engaging in rent-seeking activities eventually became the norm of economic behavior in many developing economies and diverted limited resources away from capital investment to wasteful activities. The fragile economies of developing countries suffering from chronically large budget and trade deficits inevitably exposed to international pressures and indoctrination, including financial globalization.

The recent analyses mentioned above theoretically rely on Keynesian and Marxist assumptions, which delineate the role of finance in capital accumulation as central, immanent, and active (e.g., Crotty, 1990; Palley, 2013; Pollin, 2007). The core argument of these studies is mainly based on the distinction between productive versus unproductive activities. Keynes stresses on the concept of "rentier" capitalism and a "functionless investor" who earns "parasitic" type of income (Keynes, 1936, p. 376). On the other hand, Marxist tradition is more inclined to separate productive labor, which creates value and a source of wealth, from unproductive labor, which does not. Based on this dualistic vision of labor, the financial sector and the labor entangled with this sector are categorically unproductive. This assumption resulted in different and sometimes incoherent perspectives on the nature of financialization. Some scholars pointed out that the expansion in financial profits leads to an inexorable tendency toward economic stagnation as the gains in the financial sector are immaterial, fictitious, and constitute a parasitic entity over the value created by productive labor (Chesnais, 2016; Plihon, 2005). In contrast, for Braga et al. (2017, p. 840), financialization is "a logical and a historical result of a system driven by the incessant search for new ways to accumulate wealth…". Financialization is a structural aspect of a system that reinforces the instability of capitalism.

The understanding of financialization as a new regime of accumulation that transformed capitalism into a "financialized capitalism" is a compelling one. But it faces criticisms. Christophers and Fine (2020) claim that capitalism in recent decades is financialized as the finance sector makes profit by extracting value produced elsewhere in the economy by productive labor while holding on to the understanding of "unchanged" capitalist value "paradoxical." They emphasize that tracing out how different elements of finance such as mortgage lending and currency dealing relate to the production, distribution, and circulation of surplus value which may take increasingly complex forms.

Fine defines financialization as the increasing expansion and dominance of interest-bearing capital, which appropriates surplus at the expense of other forms of capital in the accumulation process (2013, p. 55). In this sense, interest-bearing capital is a "capital in exchange that expands the production and circulation of surplus value, while not producing surplus value, it at most facilitates accumulation (although susceptible to financial crises)…" (Christophers & Fine, 2020, p. 20). Thus, it stands apart from other forms of capital that constitute merely loanable (money) capital and facilitates the circulation of value. From the above specific perspective, financialization has already been identified by Marx. What Fine considers as "new" during the financialization process in contemporary capitalism is both the intensive and extensive penetration of finance into the multiple domains of economic and social reproduction.

It is easy to recognize the workings of contemporary capitalism in a real-world context. As Blackburn (2006, p. 44) found, many NFCs such as General Electric (GE), General Motors (GM), and Ford created financial subsidiaries. They derived much of their profit from financial activities rather than industrial activities (while GM made 80% of its revenues from General Motors Acceptance Corporation in 2005, GE Capital contributed 52% of profits). However, financialization does not imply the "separation" of financial profits from real material production, considering the valorization of capital is based on the value created in the production (Pollin, 1996). The rapid expansion of real accumulation with the growth of global value chains (GVCs) illustrates this point. The value created within developing countries is continued to be extracted in the form of capitalist rents by the ACEs. According to Bhattacharya and Seda-Irizzary (2014), much of the production in developing countries happens within noncapitalist class structures since they operate at the lowest levels of GVCs, and a significant share of resulting noncapitalist surplus-value is retained by mercantile capitalist firms, in Marxian terms. Second, capitalists have not utterly switched their activities toward financial transactions and fictitious capital. Although there have long been companies and various financial institutions that operate exclusively in the financial sector and solely profiting from financial transactions and exploiting NFCs via lending, financial and NFCs are not sharply separated from each other regarding their sphere of activity.

3.1.2 Financialization of the Corporations and Households

In the mainstream discourse, the concerns on the financial system may only arise from the misalignment of interests between firms' managers and shareholders. This view provides a legitimate ground for maximizing shareholder value and short-termism strategies in investment decisions. However, within mainstream literature, financialization is rarely, if ever, mentioned.

Per the mainstream agency theories that provided a theoretical basis for a transformation of corporations, corporate governance mechanisms and practices had undergone a revolutionary change starting from the 1980s. These changes include the hostile takeover movement, which creates a market for corporate control, and shareholder value maximization objectives that prioritize the financial interests of the shareholders. Various aspects of this corporate transformation resulted in a rise in financial investments and incomes of the NFCs, and an ever-growing transfer of resources from NFCs to financial markets in the forms of interest and dividend payments, and stock repurchases. This structural change has attracted the attention of scholars from different disciplines. Later, they formed a coherent body of academic work by locating the origin of financialization within these transformations that accelerated from the beginning of the 2000s.

NFCs' orientation to finance rather than production has been reinforced as the CEO bonuses are often tied to short-term outcomes such as short-term profitability and the corporation's stock market gains (Tomaskovic-Devey et al., 2015). To satisfy the company's investors and raise the corporation's net worth, managers focused on current profitability and adopted short-termism in firm decisions. Engaging in mergers and acquisitions, hostile takeovers, leveraged buyouts, and outsourcing of productive activities have assisted in ensuring this goal significantly since the early 1980s (Davis et al., 1994). In addition, new norms in corporate governance favoring the shareholder value orientation created intense pressures on NFCs to increase dividend payments and share buybacks, reducing retained profits. Eventually, a traditional managerial orientation based on retaining profits and reinvesting has been replaced by downsizing the labor force and distributing profits to shareholders (Lazonick & O'Sullivan, 2000). As an overall outcome, contraction in firms' available funds for long-term investment projects due to lower retention ratios and higher interest payments feeds back on investment (Aglietta & Breton, 2001; Duménil & Lévy, 2004). This corporate strategy implied the "crowding-out" of real investment as NFCs diverted internal funds from real investment to invest in financial assets and proved futile after the collapse of the stock market in 2008.

Financialization has been attributed to the expanding gap between the rates of return on manufacturing versus financial asset investment by some scholars (Duménil & Lévy, 2004; Crotty, 2005). Concerning the rates of return on the financial investments, the deregulation of financial markets and a boost in interest rates due to inflationary conditions in the late 1970s resulted in "disintermediation". In this case, deposited funds at regulated financial intermediaries such as commercial banks, savings and loan associations, and mutual savings banks faced an outflow, and this encouraged banks and money market funds to invest in assets yielding a higher return, such as "junk bonds" (Lazonick & O'Sullivan, 2000, p. 17). For the rates of return on manufacturing investments, the rise of new international competition beginning with Japan and then East Asia squeezed the manufacturing profits and lowered the rate of return on the manufacturing and services sector. These developments from both sides of the finance industry harmed the "retain and reinvest" principle.

The financialization of NFCs from the global aspect engages another vantage point for understanding the consequences of finance-driven capitalism. Technological advances in various fields of production, transportation, and communications allowed domestic firms to expand their operations beyond national borders in response to lower factor costs abroad. This prompted the growing fragmentation of production within GVCs coordinated by multinational companies (MNCs). The internationalization of production fed the transnational corporate profit-seeking activities and intensified the expropriation of the surplus by MNCs. Depending on their powerful positions in the global network, ACEs, especially US firms enjoyed high profits in the early 2000s. However, NFCs in ACEs were reluctant to reinvest in productive activities, since they were able to avoid costly domestic investments in plant and equipment, and inventory costs by transferring these activities to their suppliers in emerging economies. Instead, NFCs in ACEs preferred financial investments and accumulate financial assets through mergers and acquisitions, stock buybacks, and higher dividend payouts. Internationalization of production inevitably deepened the concentration of wealth and other financial instruments in ever fewer hands and strengthened the position of capitalists and rentiers at the expense of the working class. This brought about the problem of the shortfall in aggregate demand due to a falling share of wages and capital in the form of money that cannot be used for productive investments.

As large corporations become increasingly leveraged and rely less on bank loans to acquire financial capital, banks shifted their activities from funding firms' investments and intermediation among various parties toward reaping profit from open financial markets, earning fees and commissions, and lending to households, especially in mortgages. The turn of banks' activities toward households and individuals called some scholars' attention to the phenomenon of financialization of workers' income through mortgage lending, consumption, and pensions (Gabor, 2010; Karacimen, 2016). In addition, the entry of foreign banks into developing economies, especially after the 1990s, exacerbated the process of directing sources from firm investments to individual lending activities and increasing the indebtedness of households (Ashman et al., 2011; Lapavitsas, 2009; Santos, 2013).

3.2 *Periodizing Financialization: A Shift toward a New Era or a Tenacious Regularity?*

Is financialization a recent phenomenon, characterizing a new stage in capitalism, or was it taking place much earlier, with startling parallels to contemporary capitalism? Sawyer (2014) stated that financialization largely varies in form and intensity across time and space. Diverse characteristics of financialization across different episodes require specifying the temporal scope and historical sequence of financialization and articulating whether these episodes have matching parallels (Vercelli, 2014).

Among different ways of periodizing financialization in the literature, one can emphasize three themes that focus on the potentially dysfunctional role of finance within a capitalist society, following Vercelli (2014) and Beck and Knafo (2020). First, one popular theme widely employed by a broad literature labels financialization as a *unique* historical episode. Second, some scholars conceived financialization as a *recurrent* pattern of development in history that occurs in cycles. Third, some followed a strategy of periodizing the *historical financial developments* to reveal the distinctive features of financialization and demarcate it from previous regimes of accumulation, where the work by the Regulationist School is of particular importance.

The first and most adopted approach sees financialization as an epochal departure of the economy from a nonfinancialized form to a financialized one, or a shift in the balance between the realms of production and circulation, on the latter's side in Marxian terms. This way of treatment to financialization portrays an anomaly or a deviation from a normal state of capitalism. It could be rooted in a simple but often neglected observation: ACEs did not hit by any financial and banking crises in the postwar era until the 1970s. This process had been facilitated by heavy regulations on the financial system in recognition of the potential dangers of unfettered financial markets which brought about positive outcomes for growth rates. Provision of loans with longer maturities and lower interest rates in a safe financial environment ensured aggressive productive investments by private- and public-sector firms and delivered a sterling economic performance. For a considerably long time, this might be portraying what a genuine capitalist system looks like. When financial deregulation during what may be called the "interregnum" period laid the foundation for the financial system that we have today, momentous changes in the financial system as described above have been explicated as a radical shift in contemporary capitalism, i.e., financialized capitalism.

What history teaches us is that Western economies had already been hit by many financial crises before with some regularity, and the 2008 financial crash can be placed alongside several similar crises. Understanding this regularity requires investigating the role of money and finance in shaping the relations of exchange, circulation, distribution, and accumulation during different stages of history. The growing influence of money and continuous financial innovations portray the systemic pattern of the capitalist system induced by the constant search of capital for new ways to accumulate wealth, exacerbating the inherent instability of capitalism and eventually contributing to the repeated occurrence of financial crises.

Hyman Minsky's work is one of the most influential sources of financialization in terms of the second approach, which builds upon Keynes' insights to show the recurrence of financial crises by his cyclical analysis of the economy where credit and finance play a crucial role. Minsky's financial instability hypothesis (1986) posits that in a mature stage of the evolution of capitalism, or in his terms, money manager capitalism, the economic system is characterized by highly leveraged financial institutions through money manager's speculative gambles seeking maximum returns in an environment that systematically underestimates risk (Wray, 2009). Moreover, lax supervision of financial institutions and progressive deregulation, such as the one we had since the 1970s until today, feed incentives for excessive risk, fuel optimistic expectations, and spread financial innovations around the world, which generate booms by driving up the prices for the underlying assets. This extreme confidence and foresight eventually unravel the financial instability of the system while asset values decline and collapse the system as a natural outcome of the process.

Minsky's framework of money management capitalism has been applied to the recent global financial crisis by Wray (2009, p. 55), who links "...the crisis to the long-term transformation of the economy from a robust financial structure in the 1950s to the fragile one that existed at the beginning of this crisis in 2007". However, this approach shows financial crises as repeating instances of a familiar pattern generating similar outcomes and fails to elicit what is distinctive about different episodes of financialization that might have specific characteristics. The work of Arrighi (1994) and Perez (2002) stands out because these episodes that occur in different historical periods have novelties and their specific causes and implications need to be uncovered, although some critical parallels may be found. Broadly associated with Marxist theory and inspired by the work of Braudel (1982), Arrighi (1994) frames financialization in terms of a long-wave approach and places it within a cyclical theory of the world system. Financialization represents the autumn of the hegemon as the existing "systemic cycle of accumulation," and productive power declines, and dominant economic centers turn to finance rather than production to extract wealth from others. Arrighi sees the expansion of financial capital as a mean to overcome difficulties in the material economy of hegemonic powers: Genoa, the Netherlands, the UK, and the US all resort to financial activities and enter the last phase of the cycle, i.e., financialization, when they lost their dominant position in production and trade.

Global economic imbalances securing the hegemony of the US to sustain the stock market and housing bubbles have invited financialization scholars to extend the inquiry into the internationalization of capital. Specifically, Arrighi (2003) inspired many scholars within the tradition by highlighting the global power of the US through the functioning of the role of the dollar as quasi-world money in establishing power. From this standpoint, financialization is a phenomenon that sustains the hegemony of the US in the mid-1970s, replacing the Bretton Woods system with the US dollar as the reserve currency petrodollar system. In this sense, Arrighi (2003) and Brenner (2003) link economic restructuring with neoliberalism and the emergence of finance-led capitalism. The use of US dollar-denominated financial innovations, notably derivatives, helps maintain the demand for the US dollar, finances the massive US current account deficits, and provides a global market for fictitious capital. Trade imbalances arising from the national and international supply and demand patterns, international productive chain, and a high volume of trade and US dollar-denominated debt in the face of large current account deficit leave developing economies vulnerable to a reversal of the foreign capital given their dependence on the advanced economies. Today, this has led to boom-bust cycles and exchange rate volatility in developing economies (Epstein, 2005; Kaltenbrunner, 2010).

The final approach periodizes financial developments to uncover different eras of financialization which have different intensities and forms. When mapping out different eras of capitalist development for different regimes of accumulation, they usually rely on the history of Western capitalism, which had been characterized by periods of liberalism in the nineteenth century, Fordism in the post-World War II era, and neoliberalism of the 1980s (Beck & Knafo, 2020). The Regulation theory and specifically the theorization of a finance-led growth regime by Boyer (2000) are notable from this perspective. Linking the social norms to a regime of accumulation that shapes the institutional framework of a country and attempting to explain how this framework helps stabilize the inherently contradictory capitalist economy are the key features of regulationist theory. They conceptualize capitalism in terms of a mode of production and regulation. In contrast, the mode of regulation "acts to guarantee that the dominant mode of production is reproducible in the medium term, through the accommodation, mediation and normalization of crisis tendencies" (Peck & Tickell, 1992, p. 349). Boyer (2000, p. 112) postulates that "a financialized growth regime as the latest candidate for replacing Fordism," in which "the hierarchy among institutional forms is drastically shifted: the financial regime plays the central role that used to be attributed to the wage-labor nexus under Fordism."

Regulationists claimed that while ACEs such as the US and UK moved from a "Fordist" to a "finance-led" accumulation pattern (Boyer, 2000), financialization in emerging economies takes locally specific forms by switching from peripheral Fordism (Becker et al., 2010). Becker et al. (2010) distinguish between financialization based on "fictitious capital" in Anglo-American countries and "interest-bearing capital" in the periphery. While the former depends on the inflation of financial asset prices, the latter rests on the banks and very high spreads between active and passive interest rates. Financialization through interest-bearing capital is particularly relevant for emerging economies due to their dependency on capital inflows. That, in turn, necessitated to offer high-interest payments, overvalued domestic currency, and impose an inflation-targeting regime. Moreover, the neutral domestic currency of many emerging economies in the hierarchic international financial market may lead to dollarization or euroization and strengthen their dependency on capital flows (Becker, 2007). As securitization of public debt, privatization of public institutions and pension system, and focus on rising stock prices had been encouraged, social norms had also been transformed in emerging economies (Coriat, 2006).

Imperative high-interest rates with inflation-targeting regimes disrupt productive investments, deteriorate current account, soar external and public debt, and soon culminate in increasing instability and especially foreign exchange crisis. The debt incurred in the dominant currency to finance consumer durables and real estate may increase the vulnerability of workers, especially middle strata, to the financial crisis (Becker, 2007; Becker et al., 2010). These events in aggregate force emerging economies to follow the advice of international organizations such as the World Bank and IMF and their market-oriented policies.

Aglietta and Berrebi (2007) and Brender and Pisani (2009) mentioned that many peripheral countries adopted reserve accumulation policies as a tool to prevent sudden capital outflows in response to the financial crises that they experienced during the 1990s (Becker et al., 2010, p. 230). These foreign exchange reserves flowed out of emerging economies' central banks to the US financial markets, causing the financial bubble. Forcing the rest of the countries to buildup dollar reserves and leaving emerging economies to bear the burden of this uneven international monetary system were not sustainable and sooner hit the ACEs during the recent crisis.

4 Conclusion

In size terms, it is widely acknowledged that the financial sector has grown too big in most countries. There is now much literature on the increasing dominance of finance in core capitalist economies after the 1970s, a tendency urged by the exponential growth of financial activities and neoliberalization. They discussed how it permeates and shapes the economic and social discourse today in a myriad of ways. While this might serve as a good starting point, a further discussion needs to answer how financialization occurs and what are the appropriate forms and functions of finance within the economy.

Rather than attempting to give a definitive answer to the question of what financialization is and where its origins are located, this chapter has reflected on the two broad and related themes prevalent in analyses of financialization to suggest new perspectives when answering that question. The position taken in this chapter is that (i) to represent the financialization as a different stage and a new accumulation regime in capitalism, the question of what distinctive changes have taken place in the production, distribution, and circulation of surplus value, and the logic of accumulation immanent in capitalism must be addressed, (ii) the process of financialization can be better understood regarding economic history and taking a long-run perspective.

Conceptually, the activity of lending at interest without participating in the production and taking risks and the expropriation of surplus generated through productive activities in the real sector by the individuals or institutions who engage in financial transactions and lending underlies the financialization phenomenon. In this regard, financialization is a global phenomenon. It is simply defined as the increasing transfer of earnings from the real sector to the financial sector, as the real sector progressively falls under financial institutions' control, and the financial sector's growing weight in the economy against the real sector. From this standpoint, financialization is not a phenomenon that belongs to a specific period, but its scope tends to differentiate through different periods of capitalism and may exhibit historical specificities under competitive capitalism, monopoly-finance, financial globalization, and neoliberalism. Sawyer (2014) stated that instead of characterizing financialization as a phenomenon that emerged around the 1980s, it should be seen as a continuation and acceleration of some aspects of previous processes and insertion of some new aspects to these previous processes. The history of money and the role of finance in the accumulation of capital are, on its terms, perfectly accurate. The persistent regularity of economic bubbling comes in waves, linked with different endogenous processes driven by technology, internationalization of production, trade, finance, and capital, or relatively more autonomous developments such as state policies, regulations, political processes, and domestic financial conditions.

References

Aglietta, M., & Breton, R. (2001). Financial systems, corporate control and capital accumulation. *Economy and Society, 30*(4), 433–466.

Aglietta, M., & Berrebi, L. (2007). *Désordres dans le capitalisme mondial*. Odile Jacob.

Akkemik, K. A., & Özen, Ş. (2014). Macroeconomic and institutional determinants of Financialisation of non-financial firms: Case study of Turkey. *Socio-Economic Review, 12*(1), 71–98.

Arrighi, G. (1994). *The long twentieth century: Money, power, and the origins of our times*. Verso.

Arrighi, G. (2003). The social and political economy of global turbulence. *New Left Review*, 20. https://newleftreview.org/issues/II20/articles/giovanni-arrighi-the-social-and-political-economy-of-global-turbulence

Ashman, S., Fine, B., & Newman, S. (2011). The crisis in South Africa: Neoliberalism, Financialization and uneven and combined development. *Socialist Register*, 47. https://socialistregister.com/index.php/srv/article/view/14326

Bank for International Settlements. (2022a). *OTC derivatives outstanding* (Updated 28 February 2022). [Data file]. Retrieved from https://www.bis.org/statistics/derstats.htm?m=6_32_71

Bank for International Settlements. (2022b). *Debt securities statistics* (Updated 28 February 2022). [Data file]. Retrieved from https://www.bis.org/statistics/secstats.htm

Beck, M., & Knafo, S. (2020). Financialization and the uses of history. In P. Mader, D. Mertens, & N. Van der Zwan (Eds.), *The Routledge international handbook of Financialization* (pp. 136–146). Routledge.

Becker, J. (2007). Dollarisation in Latin America and Euroisation in Eastern Europe: Parallels and differences. In J. Becker & R. Weissenbacher (Eds.), *Dollarization, Euroization and financial instability* (pp. 223–278). Metropolis. https://www.metropolis-verlag.de/Dollarisation-in-Latin-America-and-Euroisation-in-Eastern-Europe%3A-Parallels-and-Differences/11262/book.do

Becker, J., Jäger, J., Leubolt, B., & Weissenbacher, R. (2010). Peripheral financialization and vulnerability to Crisis: A regulationist perspective. *Competition & Change*. https://doi.org/10.1179/102452910X12837703615337

Bhattacharya, R., & Seda-Irizzary, I. (2014). *Financialization: A critique of the "Autonomization of capital" thesis* (p. 1). John Jay College of Criminal Justice Department of Economics Working Paper. https://www.academia.edu/6728346/Financialization_A_Critique_of_the_Autonomization_of_Capital_Thesis

Blackburn, R. (2006). Finance and the fourth dimension. *New Left Review, 39*. https://newleftreview.org/issues/II39/articles/robin-blackburn-finance-and-the-fourth-dimension

Blinder, A. S., Lo, A. W., & Solow, R. M. (2012). *Rethinking the financial crisis*. Russell Sage Foundation.

Blommestein, H. J., Keskinler, A., & Lucas, C. (2011). Outlook for the securitization market. *OECD Journal: Financial Market Trends, 2011*(1), 1–15.

Board of Governors of the Federal Reserve System. (2021). *Financial Accounts of the United States–Z.1*. [Data file]. Retrieved from https://www.federalreserve.gov/releases/z1/release-dates.htm

Boyer, R. (2000). Is a finance-led growth regime a viable alternative to Fordism? A preliminary analysis. *Economy and Society, 29*(1), 111–145. https://doi.org/10.1080/030851400360587

Braga, J. C., de Oliveira, G. C., Wolf, P. J. W., Palludeto, A. W. A., & de Deos, S. S. (2017). For a political economy of financialization: Theory and evidence. *Economia e Sociedade, 26*(spe), 829–856. https://doi.org/10.1590/1982-3533.2017v26n4art1

Braudel, F. (1982). *The wheels of commerce, civilization and capitalism 15th–18th century*. University of California Press.

Brender, A., & Pisani, F. (2009). *La crise de la finance globalisée*. La Découverte.

Brenner, R. (2003). The boom and the bubble: The US in the world economy. *Verso*. https://www.amazon.com/Boom-Bubble-US-World-Economy/dp/1859844839

Brenner, R. (2009). *What is good for Goldman Sachs is good for America the origins of the present crisis*. https://escholarship.org/uc/item/0sg0782h

Bureau of Economic Analysis (BEA). (2021). *National Income and Product Accounts (NIPA), Table 6.16A*. Corporate Profits by Industry. [Data file]. Retrieved from https://apps.bea.gov/iTable/iTable.cfm?reqid=19&step=2#reqid=19&step=2&isuri=1&1921=survey

Callinicos, A. (2010). Bonfire of illusions: The twin crises of the Liberal world. *Wiley*. https://www.goodreads.com/book/show/8258835-bonfire-of-illusions

Chesnais, F. (2016). *Finance capital today: Corporations and banks in the lasting global slump*. (Lam edition). Brill Academic Pub.

Christophers, B., & Fine, B. (2020). The value of Financialization and the Financialization of value. In P. Mader, D. Mertens, & N. Van der Zwan (Eds.), *The Routledge international handbook of Financialization* (1st ed., pp. 19–30). Routledge.

Coriat, B. (2006). Moves towards finance-led capitalism: The French case. In P. Petit & G. Schmeder (Eds.), *The hardship of nations: Exploring the paths of modern capitalism* (pp. 69–96). Edward Elgar.

Crotty, J. (1990). Owner–manager conflict and financial theories of investment instability: A critical assessment of Keynes, Tobin and Minsky. *Journal of Post Keynesian Economics, 12*(4), 519–542.

Crotty, J. (2005). The neoliberal paradox: The impact of destructive market competition and modern financial markets on nonfinancial corporation performance in the neoliberal era. In G. A. Epstein (Ed.), *Financialization and the world economy*. Edward Elgar.

Crotty, J. (2008). If financial market competition is intense, why are financial firm profits so high? Reflections on the current 'Golden age' of finance. *Competition & Change, 12*(2), 167–183.

Dallery, T. (2009). Post-Keynesian theories of the firm under Financialization. *Review of Radical Political Economics, 41*(4), 492–515. https://doi.org/10.1177/0486613409341371

Davis, G. F., Diekmann, K. A., & Tinsley, C. H. (1994). The decline and fall of the conglomerate firm in the 1980s: The deinstitutionalization of an organizational form. *American Sociological Review, 59*(4), 547–570. https://doi.org/10.2307/2095931

Davis, L. E. (2016). Identifying the "financialization" of the non-financial corporation in the U.S. economy: A decomposition of firm-level balance sheets. *Journal of Post Keynesian Economics, 39*(1), 115–141. https://doi.org/10.1080/01603477.2015.1116370

Demir, F. (2009). Financial liberalization, private investment and portfolio choice: Financialization of real sectors in emerging markets. *Journal of Development Economics, 88*(2), 314–324.

Dixon, A. D. (2008). *The rise of pension fund capitalism in Europe: An unseen revolution?* (SSRN scholarly paper ID 1090860). Social Science Research Network. https://papers.ssrn.com/abstract=1090860

Duménil, G., & Lévy, D. (2004). Capital resurgent roots of the neoliberal revolution. *Harvard University Press*. https://www.hup.harvard.edu/catalog.php?isbn=9780674011588

Duménil, G., & Lévy, D. (2005). Costs and benefits of neoliberalism: A class analysis. In G. A. Epstein (Ed.), *Financialization and the world economy* (pp. 17–45). Edward Elgar.

Epstein, G. A. (2005). Financialization and the world economy. *Edward Elgar Publishing*. https://econpapers.repec.org/bookchap/elgeebook/3455.htm

Financial Stability Board. (2021). *Global monitoring report on non-bank financial intermediation.* Retrieved from https://www.fsb.org/2021/12/global-monitoring-report-on-non-bank-financial-intermediation-2021/

Fine, B. (2013). Financialization from a Marxist perspective. *International Journal of Political Economy, 42*(4), 47–66. https://doi.org/10.2753/IJP0891-1916420403

Froud, J., Haslam, C., Johal, S., & Williams, K. (2000). Shareholder value and Financialization: Consultancy promises, management moves. *Economy and Society, 29*(1), 80–110. https://doi.org/10.1080/030851400360578

Gabor, D. (2010). (De)Financialization and crisis in Eastern Europe. *Competition & Change, 14*(3–4), 248–270. https://doi.org/10.1179/102452910X12837703615373

Gorton, G., & Metrick, A. (2013). Chapter 1–Securitization. In G. M. Constantinides, M. Harris, & R. M. Stulz (Eds.), *Handbook of the economics of finance* (Vol. 2, pp. 1–70). Elsevier. https://doi.org/10.1016/B978-0-44-453594-8.00001-X

Harman, C. (2010). *Zombie capitalism: Global crisis and the relevance of Marx*. Haymarket Books.

Hein, E. (2013). *The macroeconomics of finance-dominated capitalism–And its crisis*. Edward Elgar Publishing.

Kaltenbrunner, A. (2010). International Financialization and depreciation: The Brazilian real in the international financial crisis. *Competition & Change, 14*(3–4), 296–323. https://doi.org/10.1179/102452910X12837703615454

Karacimen, E. (2016). Consumer credit as an aspect of everyday life of Workers in Developing Countries: Evidence from Turkey. *Review of Radical Political Economics, 48*(2), 252–268. https://doi.org/10.1177/0486613415591806

Keynes, J. M. (1936). *General theory of employment*. Atlantic Publishers & Dist.

Krippner, G. R. (2005). The financialization of the American economy. *Socio-Economic Review, 3*(2), 173–208. https://doi.org/10.1093/SER/mwi008

Krippner, G. R. (2012). *Capitalizing on crisis: The political origins of the rise of finance*. (Gld edition). Harvard University Press.

Langley, P. (2009). *The everyday life of global finance: Saving and borrowing in Anglo-America*. Oxford University Press.

Lapavitsas, C. (2009). Financialisation embroils developing countries. In *Discussion papers* (no. 14; discussion papers). Research on money and finance. https://ideas.repec.org/p/rmf/dpaper/14.html

Lapavitsas, C. (2011). Theorizing financialization. *Work, Employment & Society, 25*(4), 611–626.

Lapavitsas, C. (2012). *Financialisation in crisis*. BRILL.

Lapavitsas, C. (2013). The financialization of capitalism: "Profiting without producing.". *City, 17*(6), 792–805.

Lazonick, W. (2009). *Sustainable prosperity in the new economy?: Business organization and high-tech employment in the United States*. W.E. Upjohn Institute.

Lazonick, W., & O'Sullivan, M. (2000). Maximizing shareholder value: A new ideology for corporate governance. *Economy and Society, 29*(1), 13–35. https://doi.org/10.1080/030851400360541

Lin, K. H., & Tomaskovic-Devey, D. (2013). Financialization and US income inequality, 1970–2008. *American Journal of Sociology, 118*(5), 1284–1329.

Magdoff, H., & Sweezy, P. M. (1987). Stagnation and the financial explosion (economic history as it happened, Vol. IV). *Monthly Review Press*. https://monthlyreview.org/product/stagnation_and_the_financial_explosion__economic_history_as_it_happened_vol_iv/

Martin, R. (2002). Financialization of daily life. *Temple University Press.*. https://tupress.temple.edu/book/3182

Marx, K. (1894). *Capital* (Vol. 3). Penguin Books.

Mason, J. W. (2015). Disgorge the cash: The disconnect between corporate borrowing and investment. *Roosevelt Institute*. https://rooseveltinstitute.org/publications/disgorge-the-cash/

Minsky, H. P. (1986). *Stabilizing an unstable economy*. Yale University Press.

Montgomerie, J. (2006). The Financialization of the American credit card industry. *Competition & Change, 10*(3), 301–319. https://doi.org/10.1179/102452906X114393

Onaran, O., Stockhammer, E., & Grafl, L. (2011). Financialisation, income distribution and aggregate demand in the USA. *Cambridge Journal of Economics, 35*(4), 637–661.

Orhangazi, Ö. (2008). Financialisation and capital accumulation in the non-financial corporate sector: A theoretical and empirical investigation on the US economy: 1973–2003. *Cambridge Journal of Economics, 32*(6), 863–886. https://doi.org/10.1093/cje/ben009

Palley, T. (2013). *Financialization: The economics of finance capital domination (2013th edition)*. Palgrave Macmillan.

Palma, G. (2009). The revenge of the market on the rentiers. Why neo-liberal reports of the end of history turned out to be premature. *Cambridge Journal of Economics, 33*(4), 829–869.

Peck, J. A., & Tickell, A. (1992). Local modes of social regulation? Regulation theory, thatcherism and uneven development. *Geoforum, 23*(3), 347–363. https://doi.org/10.1016/0016-7185(92)90047-8

Perez, C. (2002). *Technological revolutions and financial capital: The dynamics of bubbles and golden ages*. Edward Elgar Publishing.

Plihon, D. (2005). As grandes empresas fragilizadas pela finança. In F. Chesnais, R. Marques, & P. Nakatsni (Eds.), *A finança mundializada: Raízes sociais e políticas, configuração, consequências*. Boitempo.

Pollin, R. (1996). Contemporary economic stagnation in world historical perspective. *New Left Review, 219*. https://newleftreview.org/issues/I219/articles/robert-pollin-contemporary-economic-stagnation-in-world-historical-perspective

Pollin, R. (2007). Resurrection of the rentier. *New Left Review, 46*, 140–153.

Santos, P. L.. dos. (2013). A cause for policy concern: The expansion of household credit in middle-income economies. *International Review of Applied Economics, 27*(3), 316–338. https://doi.org/10.1080/02692171.2012.721755

Sawyer, M. (2014). What is Financialization? *International Journal of Political Economy, 42*(4), 5–18.

Shin, H. S. (2010). *Risk and Liquidity*. Oxford University Press.

Skott, P., & Ryo, S. (2008). Macroeconomic implications of financialisation. *Cambridge Journal of Economics, 32*(6), 827–862.

Stockhammer, E. (2004). Financialisation and the slowdown of accumulation. *Cambridge Journal of Economics, 28*(5), 719–741. https://doi.org/10.1093/cje/beh032

Stockhammer, E. (2007). Some stylized facts on the finance-dominated accumulation regime. In *Working papers (No. wp142; Working Papers)*. Political Economy Research Institute, University of Massachusetts at Amherst. https://ideas.repec.org/p/uma/periwp/wp142.html

Stockhammer, E. (2012). Financialization, income distribution and the crisis. *Investigación Económica, 71*(279), 39–70.

Stout, L. (2012). *The shareholder value myth: How putting shareholders first harms investors, corporations, and the public*. Berrett-Koehler Publishers.

Tomaskovic-Devey, D., Lin, K.-H., & Meyers, N. (2015). *Did Financialization reduce economic growth?* (SSRN scholarly paper ID 2571897). Social Science Research Network. https://doi.org/10.2139/ssrn.2571897.

Tori, D., & Onaran, Ö. (2018). The effects of financialization on investment: Evidence from firm-level data for the UK. *Cambridge Journal of Economics, 42*(5), 1393–1416. https://doi.org/10.1093/cje/bex085

Van der Zwan, N. (2014). Making sense of Financialization. *Socio-Economic Review, 12*(1), 99–129.

Van Treeck, T. (2009). The political economy debate on 'Financialization'–A macroeconomic perspective. *Review of International Political Economy, 16*(5), 907–944.

Vercelli, A. (2014). Financialization in a long-run perspective: An evolutionary approach. *International Journal of Political Economy, 42*(4), 19–46.

Woetzel, J., Mischke, J., Madgavkar, A., Windhagen, E., Smit, S., Birshan, M., et al. (2021). *The rise and rise of the global balance sheet: How productively are we using our wealth?* Retrieved from. https://www.mckinsey.com/industries/financial-services/our-insights/the-rise-and-rise-of-the-global-balance-sheet-how-productively-are-we-using-our-wealth

Wray, L. R. (2009). Money manager capitalism and the global financial crisis. *Real-World Economics Review, 51*, 55–69.

Income Inequality, Household Debt, and Financial Crises

Ali Ari and **Raif Cergibozan**

Abstract This chapter aims to examine why and how rising income inequality in developed countries over the last four decades has led to higher household debt stock which in turn may increase the likelihood of financial crises. To do that, we run simple regressions over a sample of 31 OECD and/or EU member countries over the period of 1980–2020. We find that income inequality leads to higher household debt stock, but mainly in developed countries where the financial sector is more developed and interest rates are lower. These results, in line with the early literature, indicate that governments should implement appropriate tax and benefit policies to decrease income inequality, instead of using monetary policy as a temporary tool to alleviate the consequences of income inequality for low- and middle-income parts of the population.

Keywords Inequality · Leverage · Bank credit · Financial crises

1 Introduction

Over the past four decades, income inequality has significantly augmented within most developed countries (Piketty, 2014; Morelli et al., 2015; OECD, 2015), contrary to the predictions of the Kuznets hypothesis. This rise in inequality has been mainly associated with increasing globalization of trade and capital movements. The relationship between inequality and trade openness is partly explained by the Stolper-Samuelson theorem based on the Heckscher-Ohlin model. When a country endowed with skilled-workers opens to trade, it produces more skill-intensive goods for export, resulting in higher wages for the skilled at the

A. Ari (✉)
Department of Political Science and Public Administration, Marmara University, Istanbul, Turkey
e-mail: ali.ari@marmara.edu.tr

R. Cergibozan
Department of Economics, Kirklareli University, Kirklareli, Turkey
e-mail: raif.cergibozan@klu.edu.tr

A. Ari (ed.), *Capitalism at a Crossroads*, Springer Studies in Alternative Economics,
https://doi.org/10.1007/978-3-031-23257-2_6

expense of the unskilled. Moreover, increased trade with developing countries may lead to deindustrialization in developed countries, resulting in a decline in manufacturing, thus, higher unemployment among the less-skilled (Feenstra & Hanson, 1996).

Financial openness generally brings improvements in the quality and type of financial services, but this mainly benefits high-income individuals and well-established firms (Greenwood & Jovanovic, 1990). Because financial imperfections, such as asymmetric information and transactions costs in financial markets, mostly penalize the poor who lack collaterals, credit records, and networks. Furthermore, the rising delocalization of domestic firms to developing countries—outward foreign direct investment (FDI)—causes job losses, lower wages, and less job security for unskilled workers (Jaumotte et al., 2013).

Technological progress is another factor in explaining the increase in income inequality, since it produces proportionately more high-skill, better-paid jobs, benefiting those with the required skills (Aghion et al., 1999). On the other hand, regulatory reforms in labor markets (i.e., declining union coverage) and a decrease in marginal tax rates for high earners are also crucial to understand the long-term rise in income inequality in advanced countries (OECD, 2015).

Note also that both the global financial crisis of 2007–08 and the recent Covid-19 pandemic exacerbated the inequality of income distribution in both developing and advanced countries. With lower growth and higher unemployment, both crises not only reduced incomes from work and capital but also made their distribution more unequal. Furthermore, higher inflation rates over the last two years—leading to a fall of incomes in real terms—are another important factor in aggravating income inequality.

As underlined by Stiglitz (2012), income inequality results in higher crime and health problems, lower educational achievements, social cohesion, and life expectancy. The social unrest can weaken the social structure and trust in institutions, driving then populist and protectionist feelings, and leading to political instability (OECD, 2015).

Beyond its considerable impact on social cohesion, higher inequality also produces a negative impact on economic growth and its sustainability. Berg and Ostry (2011) indicate that social unrest and political instability may discourage investment which leads in turn to lower growth rates. Moreover, rising inequality may reduce economic opportunity that may limit the growth potential of economies (OECD, 2015). This is mainly materialized through lowering investment opportunities in education of the poorer parts of the population if they cannot afford the fees. This may diminish the accumulation of human capital—which is considered a key factor of economic growth in modern growth theories (i.e., Romer, 1994). This "underinvestment" by the poor or structural demand gap causes lower aggregate output (Akyüz, 2017), on the one hand, and jeopardizes social mobility, on the other.

However, contrary to expected negative outcomes of rising inequality on demand, investment, and growth, many advanced economies, particularly the US, performed well in terms of consumption and economic growth over the last three decades. Cynamon and Fazzari (2016) show that in the decades prior to the global financial crisis unemployment fell, consumption increased, macroeconomic volatility declined, and recessions were modest. This fact actually presents a paradox from the theoretical point of view as discussed above. So, how did consumption and growth increase despite increasing income inequality in the US or other developed countries?

The answer to this question is borrowing by the low- and middle-income households facilitated by easy credit conditions in financial markets due to growing financial development and low inflation rates. This process is also encouraged by financial regulators and policymakers. Because it is an easier way to support growth compared to bringing structural solutions to rising inequalities through reforming tax and benefit policies as well as promoting and increasing access to quality public services. Thus, low- and middle-income individuals incited by low interest rates borrow beyond their means to maintain their consumption. This "overborrowing syndrome" leads in turn to overindebtedness of households in most advanced countries. These overborrowing and overindebtedness, coupled with financial liberalization and deregulation of financial markets, generate then speculative bubbles in stock and real estate markets. When those bubbles burst, countries face a severe economic and financial crisis. Recessions and higher unemployment as a common consequence of crises then exacerbate the unequal distribution of income.

Therefore, this paper aims to empirically investigate the relationship between inequality and household debt, which could be a structural cause of financial crises. To do that, we first clarify how and why inequality leads to higher household debt and financial bubbles which in turn generate a financial crisis by reviewing early literature. Then, we run a regression analysis to assess the role of different macroeconomic factors on household debt accumulation. Our analysis consists of 31 OECD and/or European Union (EU) member countries over a sample period of 1980–2020. Our empirical results show that income inequality leads to higher household debt stock, but mostly in developed countries where the financial sector is more developed and interest rates are lower.

These results are in line with the early literature (i.e., Rajan, 2010; Kumhof et al., 2015). Theoretical work mainly shows that with rising inequalities easy credit conditions helped low- and middle-income households to keep up with the higher consumption levels of top earners (Bazillier & Hericourt, 2017). Van Treeck (2014) proposes two arguments for this macroeconomic trend. First, supply-side argument puts emphasis on the role of government in supporting credit to those households with decreasing relative incomes. Second, demand-side argument points out the active behavior of low- and middle-income households to sustain their consumption level. Empirical studies generally indicate that rising income inequality leads to higher demand for credit (i.e., Malinen, 2016) and higher income-to-debt ratios (i.e., Gu et al., 2019), on the one hand, and engenders financial or banking crises (i.e., Kirschenmann et al., 2016; Bellettini et al., 2019; Gu et al., 2019), on the other hand.

This chapter is organized as follows. Section 2 assesses the causality between inequality, household debt, and crises. Section 3 presents model and discusses estimation results. Section 4 concludes with some policy implications.

2 Inequality and Financial Crises

Nearly all countries faced one or more financial crises during the last three decades with severe negative economic consequences. The increase in frequency and cost of financial crises seem to be related to deregulation of domestic financial markets and liberalization of capital movements.[1] The occurrence of those crises is theoretically and empirically linked to some macroeconomic (i.e., budget and current deficits) and microeconomic factors (i.e., low profitability, asset quality, liquidity, and reserves of financial and nonfinancial institutions) as well as to the structure of financial markets (i.e., asymmetric information leading to adverse selection and moral hazard, integration of financial markets leading to contagion, and quality of regulatory institutions), and psychological factors (i.e., limited rationality leading to myopia, euphoria, and overconfidence).

The same approach is adopted by the large body of literature that analyzes the global financial crisis which started in the US banking system in late 2007. For instance, Acharya et al. (2009) underlined the role of a credit boom and a housing bubble, mainly associated with the FED's loose monetary policy, on the occurrence of the banking crisis in the US. Low interest rates encouraged investors to search for higher yield that further worsened the asset quality, particularly in a lax regulatory framework due to deregulation of the financial system and development of new but complex financial instruments such as securitized assets and derivatives.

Moreover, high growth and low volatility in the world economy led investors to misprice the credit risk and/or take excessive risks. The mispricing could be explained to some extent by the global imbalances: saving surpluses in China and oil-exporting Middle Eastern countries flowed into the US and European assets, leading to excess liquidity, low volatility, and spreads (Ari, 2014). The rise in equity prices increased then the level of perceived wealth, thus reducing domestic savings and increasing current deficits, particularly in the US.

Obstfeld et al. (2009) were one of the first to empirically examine whether the cross-country incidence of the 2007–08 global crisis is related to macroeconomic and financial factors. They found that the excess of reserves over M2 was a statistically significant determinant of currency depreciation during the 2007–09 period. In addition to reserves, real currency appreciation (Frankel & Saravelos, 2012), weak current account positions, high direct financial exposure vis-à-vis the US (Fratzscher, 2009), and bank credit growth (Claessens et al., 2010) were found to be linked to the crisis incidence.

Lane and Milesi-Ferretti (2011) and Berkmen et al. (2012) examined the cross-country severity of the 2007–08 global crisis, and they found that strong credit growth and trade openness affected the crisis severity. Berkmen et al. (2012) also showed that countries with more leveraged financial systems and weak fiscal positions experienced worse crises, while Lane and Milesi-Ferretti (2011) indicated that high current deficits and large precrisis net capital inflows are relevant for understanding crisis intensity. Rose and Spiegel (2011) and Feldkircher (2014) confirmed the findings above: countries with higher current deficits and stronger growth in bank credit suffered worse crises. Giannone et al. (2011) and Rose and Spiegel (2011) found empirical support to the importance of loose banking

[1] See Ari (2010) for a detailed analysis on financial crises.

regulation and high financial leverage in affecting the response of the real economy to the global crisis.

Above explanations on the occurrence and the severity of the global financial crisis seem to focus on "visible" factors such as FED's loose monetary policy, stronger credit growth, high leverage of financial institutions, misprice of credit risk, etc. But the "real" question here is why the FED kept interest rates quite low. One may argue that fears of recession following the dot-com crisis in 2000 and 9/11 terrorist attacks on World Trade Center pushed the FED to lower interest rates. Or others may underline the impact of capital inflows to advanced countries, in particular the US, that increased money supply. However, we argue that FED's loose monetary policy was a response to increasing income inequality in order to allow low- and middle-income groups to maintain their consumption. In other words, it was a medium to support the living standards of those who suffer from stagnating real incomes. However, this policy aiming to temporarily alleviate the consequences of inequality through access to cheap borrowing led to a debt-driven consumption and growth, paving the way for the emergence of the global financial crisis.

There is a growing body of literature focusing on the probable relationship between inequality, leverage, and financial crises. Rajan (2010) argues that increasing inequality, due to technological development and institutional factors in labor market, creates pressures on the political system. To appease this tension, government provides cheap credit to the bottom of the income distribution through government-sponsored enterprises, like Fannie Mae and Freddie Mac, to buy houses. This sowed the seeds of the global financial crisis of 2007–08 through a housing boom as many who bought houses did not have the purchasing power. When the FED started to increase interest rates in late 2005 to contract housing demand, many sub-prime people could not pay back their credits. This is how the banking crisis started in the US in late 2007.

Beside housing boom, Fitoussi and Saraceno (2010a) and Goda et al. (2017) demonstrate the impact of another bubble in asset prices in the outbreak of the global financial crisis. This bubble is mainly linked to the search for higher yield by top earners who benefited from the increase in inequality. Stiglitz (2012) also claims that increasing political influence of the rich and the financial industry contributed to the financial excesses. Hence, net wealth became overvalued, and high asset prices sustained high levels of debt. But when the bubble burst, net wealth radically reduced to unsustainable levels, generating the crisis in the US.

Ahlquist and Ansell (2017) pay attention to countries' institutional and policy context that may impact on demand for credit. They show that higher levels of borrowing are closely related to increasing income inequality, but only in countries where right-wing governments are more frequent. Because in countries with historically more left-wing governments, there exists substantial redistribution to the bottom part of the society. Fiscal redistribution can moderate the effect of inequality on credit demand by reducing the gap in disposable incomes between the rich and poor.

Kumhof et al. (2015) provide a theoretical framework on the mechanisms that link income distribution, leverage, and financial crises. Their model is based on two groups of households: top earners that constitute 5% of the population whose income share has increased over decades and bottom earners who represent 95% of the population with lowering or stagnating incomes. The first group utilizes a large share of the increased income to accumulate financial wealth in the form of loans to bottom earners, rather than using it for higher consumption. This allows bottom earners to sustain their consumption, but their debt-to-income ratio reaches to higher levels, generating financial fragility that eventually makes a financial crisis more likely. The crisis occurs when economic and/or financial conditions change, i.e., an increase in interest rates rising debt burden leads bottom earners to default on their debt. Iacoviello (2008), with a quantitative dynamic model, provides convincing evidence that income inequality was the primary driver of the increase in household debt in the US during the 1980s and 1990s. Cardaci (2018) develops an agent-based model to examine the impact of growing inequality on home equity borrowing. He shows that the resulting debt-financed consumption increases the financial fragility. Rising nonperforming loans deteriorating the banks' balance sheets paves the way for a financial crisis. Note that in those models, the role of government in easing credit conditions is ignored.

On the other hand, we see an increasing number of empirical studies to test the conclusions of theoretical models. First group of studies examine whether income equality leads to higher demand for credit, hence, to higher household debt. Bordo and Meissner (2012) estimate the effect of change in income inequality on the growth of bank credit in 14 advanced countries over the period between 1880 and 2008. They find little evidence relating credit booms to rising inequality. On the other hand, Chang et al. (2020) find different results using same 14 developed countries over the period of 1920–2008, but by employing different estimation techniques and by dividing the sample period into two. Their results indicate a positive relationship between income inequality and credit growth. Using data for the period of 1959–2008 for developed countries, Malinen (2016) also shows that there is a positive long-run steady relationship between income inequality and bank credit. In other words, income inequality contributes to the increase of leverage in accordance with the theories by Rajan (2010) and Kumhof et al. (2015). Perugini et al. (2016) is another study that indicates a robust correlation between private sector credit/indebtedness and inequality. The econometric analysis is performed on a panel of 18 OECD countries for the period of 1970–2007.

The second group of empirical studies indicate that rising income inequality leads to higher income-to-debt ratios, hence, rises the crisis risk. Kirschenmann et al. (2016) assess whether income inequality is a direct driver of financial crises or it indirectly engenders a crisis through credit booms. Their empirical evidence, based on a dataset of 14 developed countries over the 1870–2008 period, presents a high predictive power of inequality on financial crises, but the impact of bank loans is relatively small. Using same 14 developed countries over the 1870–2013 period, Paul (2022) also finds that income inequality is a robust predictor of financial crises. Bellettini et al. (2019) perform an empirical analysis on a panel of 33 advanced countries in the period of 1970–2011. They find a statistically significant and positive relationship between income inequality and the probability of banking crises. Gu et al. (2019) use a relatively short sample period covering the years 1995 and 2007 for OECD countries. Their empirical results show that rising inequality has a significantly positive impact on credit growth and banking crises.

3 Model and Estimation Results

In the study, we aim to empirically demonstrate how income inequality leads to a substantial increase in household debt stock which is considered a structural cause of financial crises in theoretical models and a good predictor of crises in empirical studies. To do that, we use simple regressions on a dataset of 31 OECD and/or EU member countries over the period of 1980–2020.

To measure the indebtedness of households, we use the ratio of household debt over GDP. The data for this indicator are taken from the Bank for International Settlements (BIS) statistics. We use two measures of income inequality: inequality in market income and inequality in disposable income. Inequality in market income is measured by the Gini coefficient and represents the pretax and pretransfer inequality in income. Inequality in disposable income is also measured by the Gini coefficient, but it takes into account taxes and transfers from the government. The Gini coefficient is based on the comparison of cumulative proportions of the population versus cumulative proportions of income they get, and it takes a value between 0 indicating perfect equality and 1 representing perfect inequality The data for Gini coefficients are gathered from the Standardized World Income Inequality Database (SWIID).

As the income inequality is not the only determinant of household debt stock, we use some control variables such as financial development, inflation rates, and interest rates. We utilize two different interest rates, and the data for both are gathered from the Organization for Economic Co-operation and Development (OECD) database. Short-term interest rates are the rates at which short-term borrowings are made between financial institutions or the rate at which short-term government paper is issued or traded in the market. Short-term interest rates are based on three-month money market rates and/or treasury bill rates. Long-term interest rates refer to government bonds maturing in ten years. Rates are mainly determined by the price charged by the lender, the risk from the borrower, and the fall in the capital value. These interest rates are implied by the prices at which the government bonds are traded on financial markets, not the interest rates at which the loans were issued.

Inflation rate measures change in general level of prices. The data for inflation rates are taken from the World Bank–WDI and are based on annual changes of consumer price index (CPI). Financial development may be defined as the improvements in the size, efficiency of, and access to the financial system. A well-developed financial system spurs economic growth because it channels and mobilizes savings into profitable large-scale investments; it reduces the costs of acquiring and evaluating information on prospective projects; and it helps to monitor investments to reduce the risk of resource mismanagement (Levine, 2005; Ari, 2018). However, there is no consensus on how to measure financial development as it is a vast concept and has several dimensions. For instance, total market capitalization and market trading volume are used to measure the sophistication of the stock and bond markets, or ratio of total deposits to GDP and ratio of bank credit to private sector over GDP are utilized for the level of development of the banking system. But all these measures are rough estimation and do not capture all aspects of financial

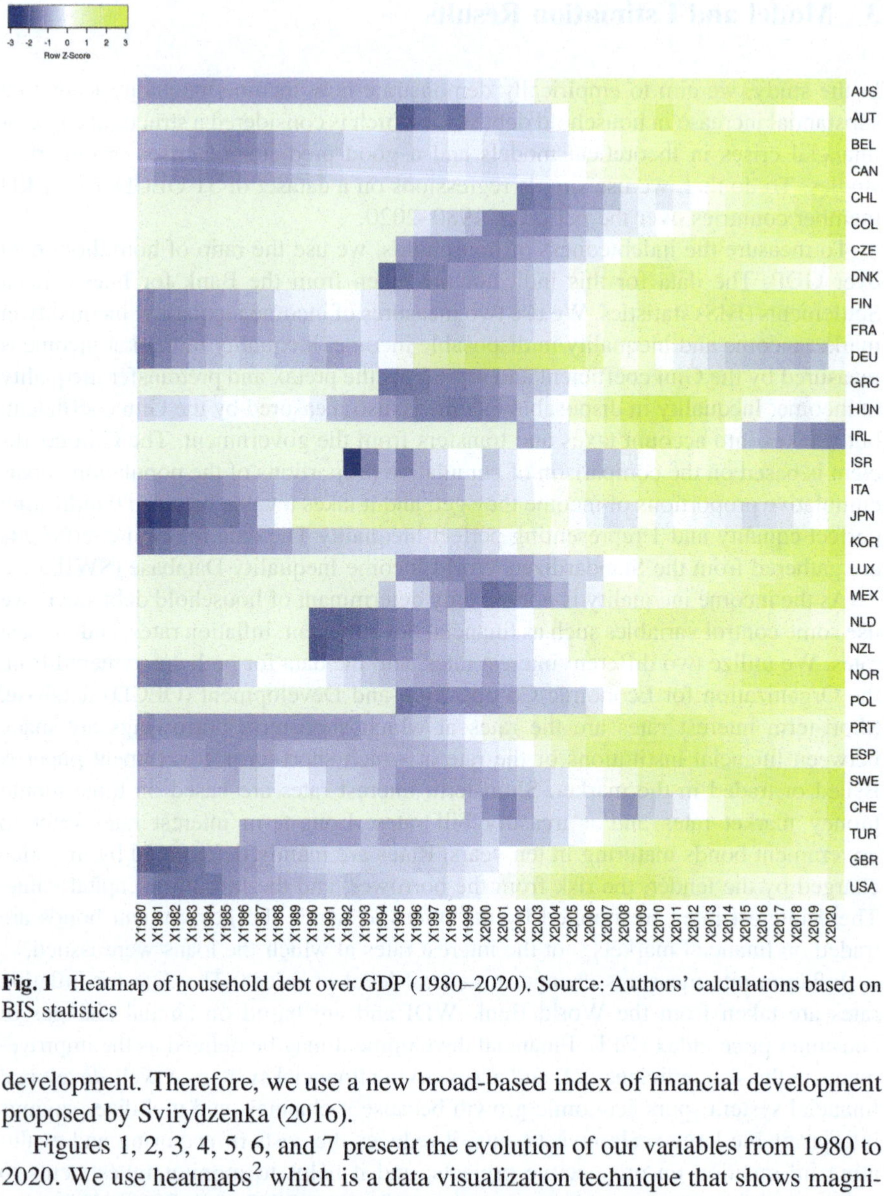

Fig. 1 Heatmap of household debt over GDP (1980–2020). Source: Authors' calculations based on BIS statistics

development. Therefore, we use a new broad-based index of financial development proposed by Svirydzenka (2016).

Figures 1, 2, 3, 4, 5, 6, and 7 present the evolution of our variables from 1980 to 2020. We use heatmaps[2] which is a data visualization technique that shows magnitude of a phenomenon as color in two dimensions. Here blue/yellow colors indicate low/high values that the variables have.

Figure 1 shows the heatmap of the household debt-to-GDP ratio for 31 selected countries. We see that, except for Ireland (over the last 5 years), Germany, Hungary,

[2]For detailed information on heatmaps, see Babicki et al. (2016).

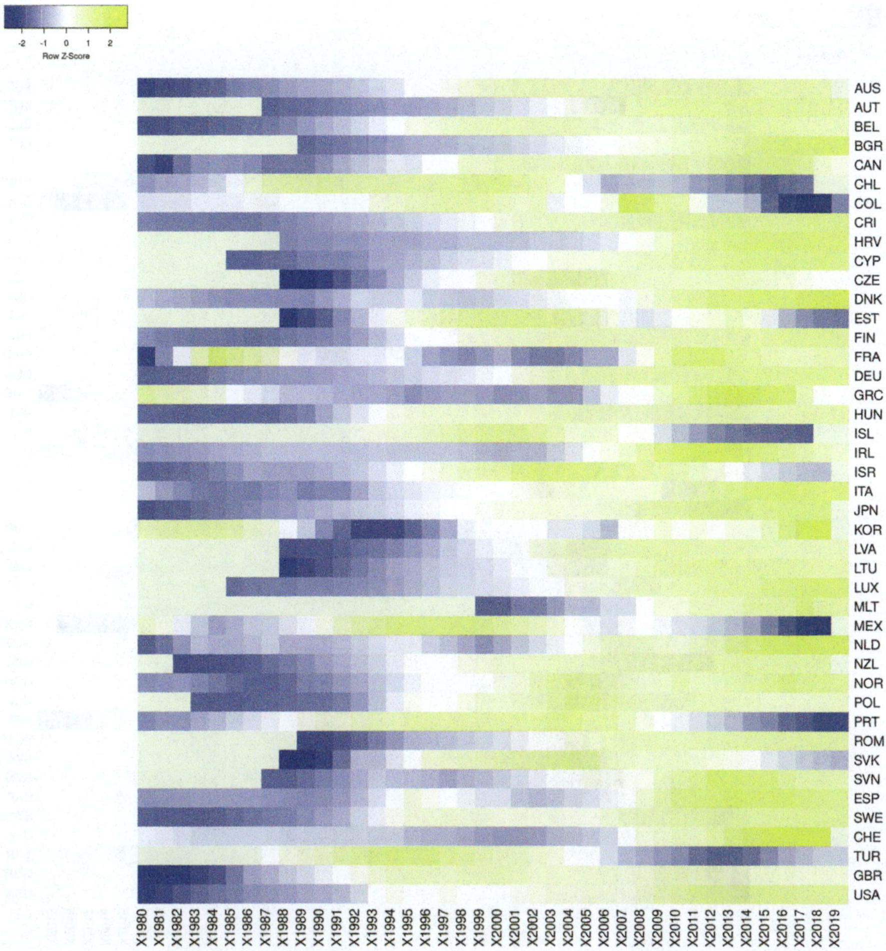

Fig. 2 Heatmap of Gini market (1980–2019). Source: Authors' calculations based on SWIID

and Japan to lower extent, household debt recorded a strong growth, particularly from the beginning of 2000s. It is quite interesting to see that yellow color becomes darker in 2020 reflecting the impact of the Covid-19 pandemic on household debt stock.

Figures 2 and 3 show heatmaps of inequality in market income and inequality in disposable income, respectively for 31 countries over the period of 1980–2019. We observe in Fig. 2 that, except for Iceland and Portugal, income inequality has highly increased in advanced countries, particularly from 1990s. Note that income inequality was higher for both countries before and during the global financial crisis. However, in some emerging countries such as Chile, Czechia, Colombia, Mexico, and Turkey, income inequality has remained constant or declined in 2000s. One may see in Fig. 3 that disposable income inequality considering redistribution policy of

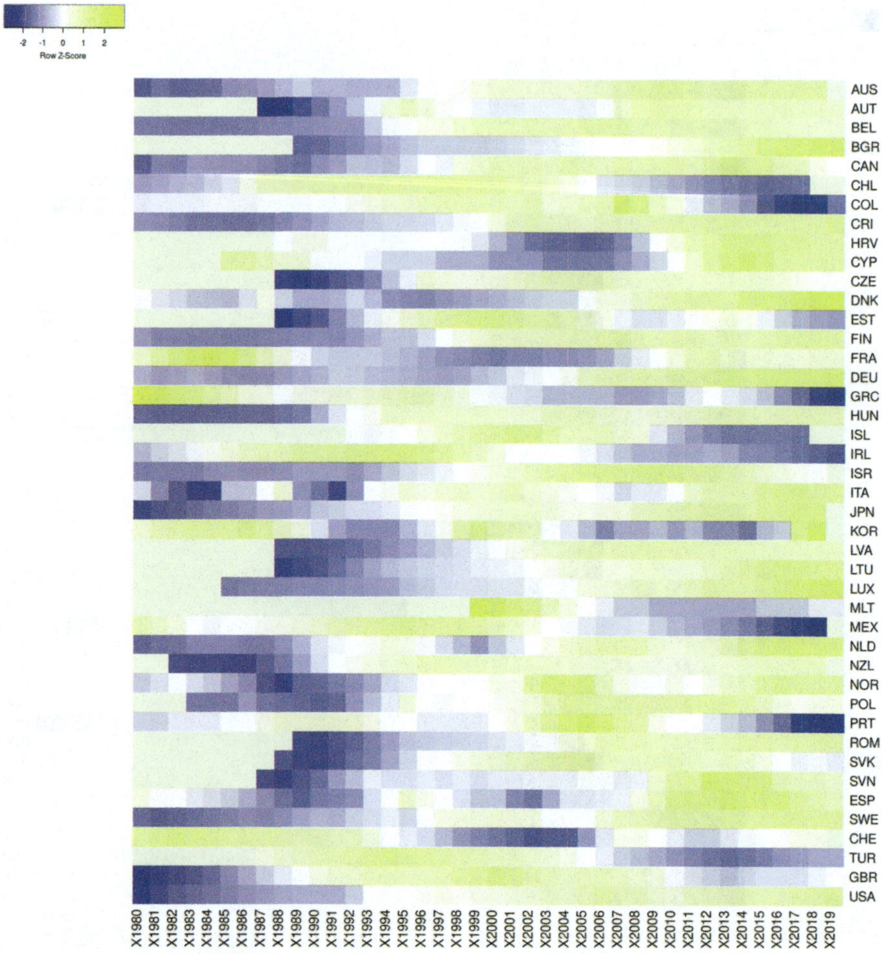

Fig. 3 Heatmap of Gini disposable (1980–2019). Source: Authors' calculations based on SWIID

the governments has only fallen in Estonia, Greece, and Ireland, and remained stagnant in France.

Figure 4 shows heatmap of inflation rates over the period from 1980 to 2020. As seen in Fig. 4, monetary authorities in both developing and advanced countries seem to have resolved the inflation issue in 1990s. We do not ignore growing inflationist pressures in the last two years due to the breakdown of supply chains and excessive money supply following the Covid-19 pandemic. But our data does not cover these last two years.

As seen in Figs. 5 and 6, both short- and long-term interest rates have drastically decreased in all 31 countries included in our sample. This is mainly related to

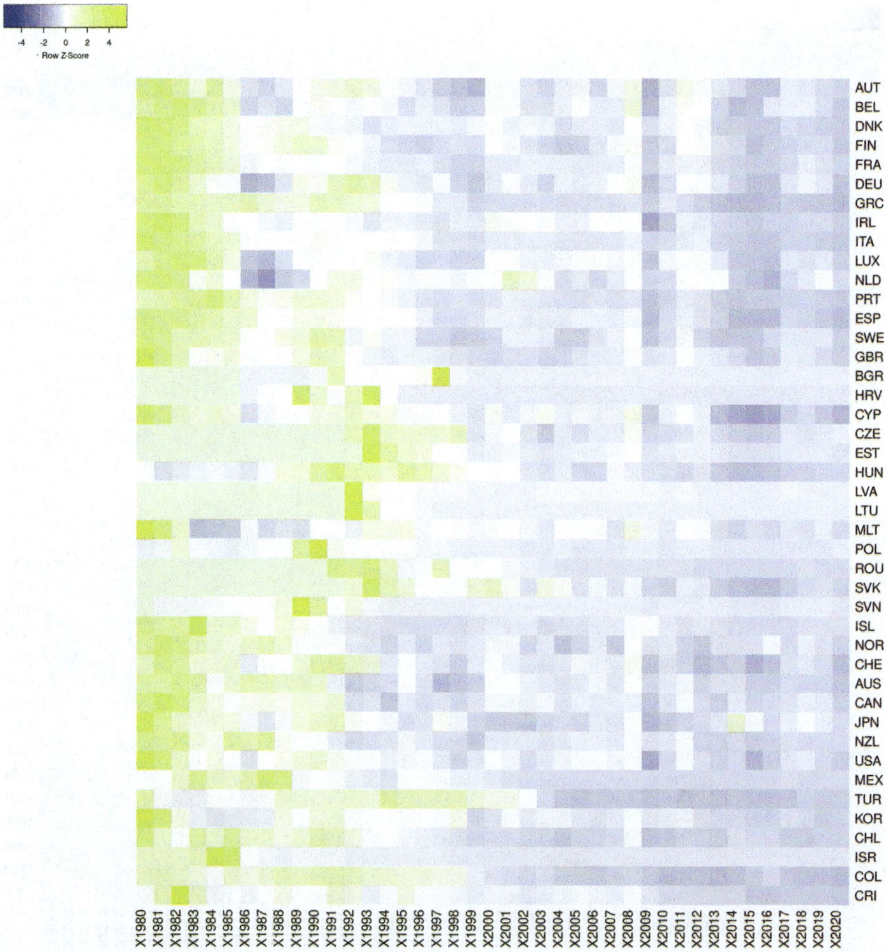

Fig. 4 Heatmap of inflation rates (1980–2020). Source: Authors' calculations based on World Bank–WDI

lowering inflation rates as mentioned above, but also to increasing financial development (see Fig. 7), particularly from the second half of the 1990s.

Figure 8 presents estimation results of our regression analysis on the relationship between household debt and income inequality. As seen in different graphs, there is a statistically significant relationship between household debt and income inequality in 24 countries out of 31. The exceptions are Czechia, Germany, France, Hungary, Ireland, New Zealand, and Portugal. This result is consistent with what we see in Figs. 1, 2, and 3. In Germany, Hungary, and Ireland to some extent household debt stock did not record increases while income inequality remained constant (France) or decreased (Czechia and Portugal).

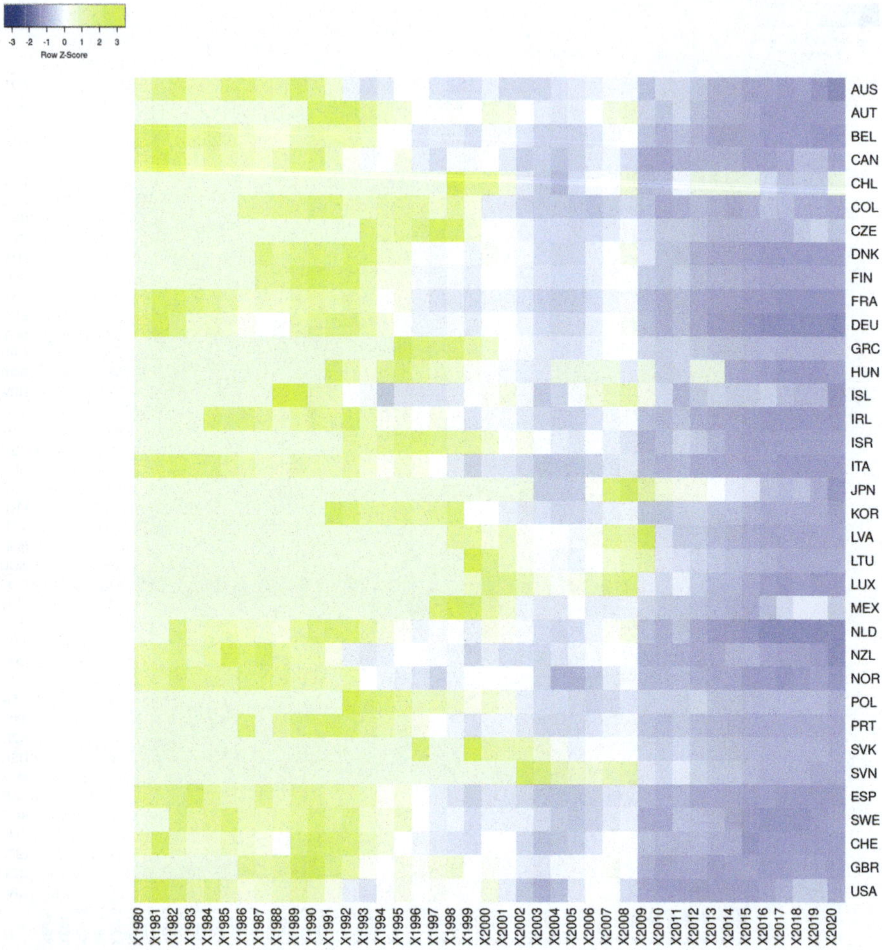

Fig. 5 Heatmap of short-term interest rates (1980–2020). Source: Authors' calculations based on OECD database

An interesting point to underline is the curve is downward/upward sloping for emerging/advanced countries. This means that income inequality leads to higher household debt stock in most developed countries, but it generates lower debt in developing countries. This result would indicate the important role of financial development in easing credit conditions, hence the increasing probability of borrowing for households. Our empirical results confirm this claim as we find a statistically significant relationship between household debt over GDP and financial development. As seen in Fig. 9, except for Czechia, Luxembourg, and Japan, an increase in financial development index leads to a higher household debt-to-GDP ratio in both developing and advanced countries.

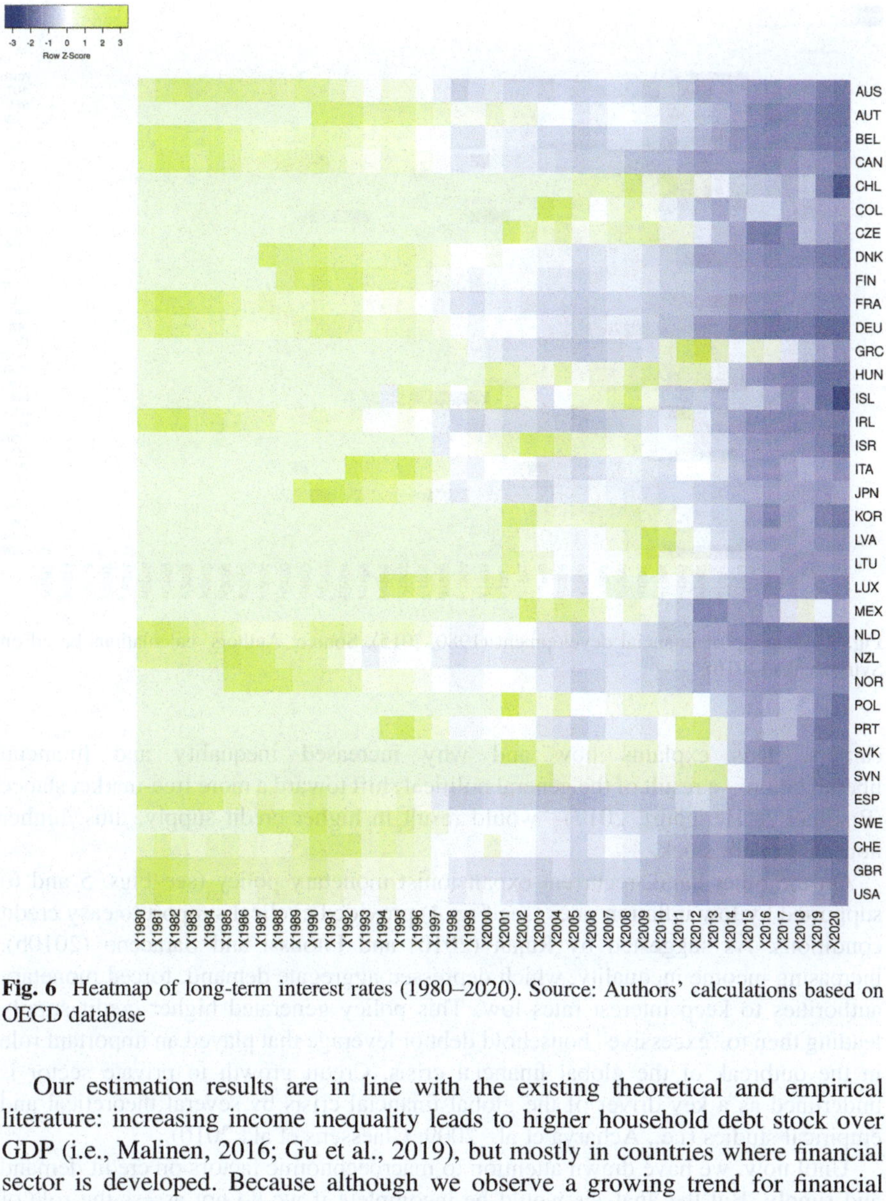

Fig. 6 Heatmap of long-term interest rates (1980–2020). Source: Authors' calculations based on OECD database

Our estimation results are in line with the existing theoretical and empirical literature: increasing income inequality leads to higher household debt stock over GDP (i.e., Malinen, 2016; Gu et al., 2019), but mostly in countries where financial sector is developed. Because although we observe a growing trend for financial development index in all countries of the sample from the 1990s, its level is still quite different between developing and developed countries. Therefore, income inequality increases household debt only in developed countries where borrowing opportunity is higher.

Borrowing opportunity has increased with financial openness, implemented in 1980s. This, by giving banks the possibility to securitize and trade loans (Shleifer & Vishny, 2010) structurally prompted credit supply to low- and middle-income

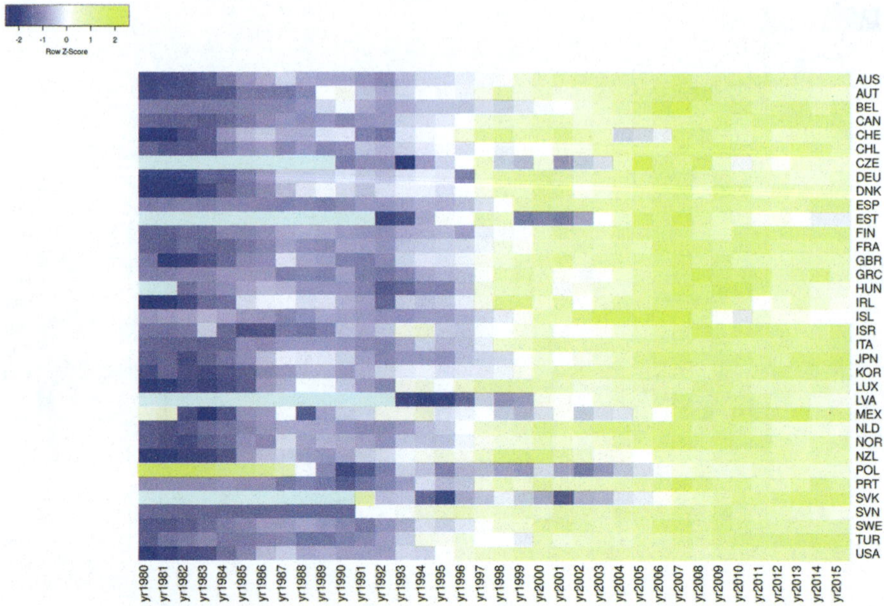

Fig. 7 Heatmap of financial development (1980–2015). Source: Authors' calculations based on Svirydzenka (2016)

earners. This explains how and why increased inequality and financial liberalization—a result of the general political shift toward a more free-market stance (Bazillier & Hericourt, 2017)—would result in higher credit supply, thus, higher household debt stock.

On the other hand, recurrent expansionist monetary policy (see Figs. 5 and 6) supported by low inflation rates (see Fig. 4) provided cyclical support to easy credit conditions. As suggested by Rajan (2010) and Fitoussi and Saraceno (2010b), increasing income inequality, which depressed aggregate demand, forced monetary authorities to keep interest rates low. This policy generated higher credit supply leading then to "excessive" household debt or leverage that played an important role in the outbreak of the global financial crisis. Credit growth to private sector is underlined as a key driver of the global financial crisis by several theoretical and empirical studies (i.e., Acharya et al., 2009; Claessens et al., 2010).

Until now, we have drawn attention to macroeconomic factors on credit demand and supply. But the analysis would be incomplete if we do not assess the role of microeconomic factors (i.e., consumer behavior) on credit demand. There are two approaches that explain why and how credit demand by low- and middle-income households increased prior to the global financial crisis of 2007–08. The first one is often referred to as "keeping up with the Joneses", where the economic agent, described as "outward-looking", pays attention to the average consumption of the overall economy. The second is the relative income hypothesis, introduced by

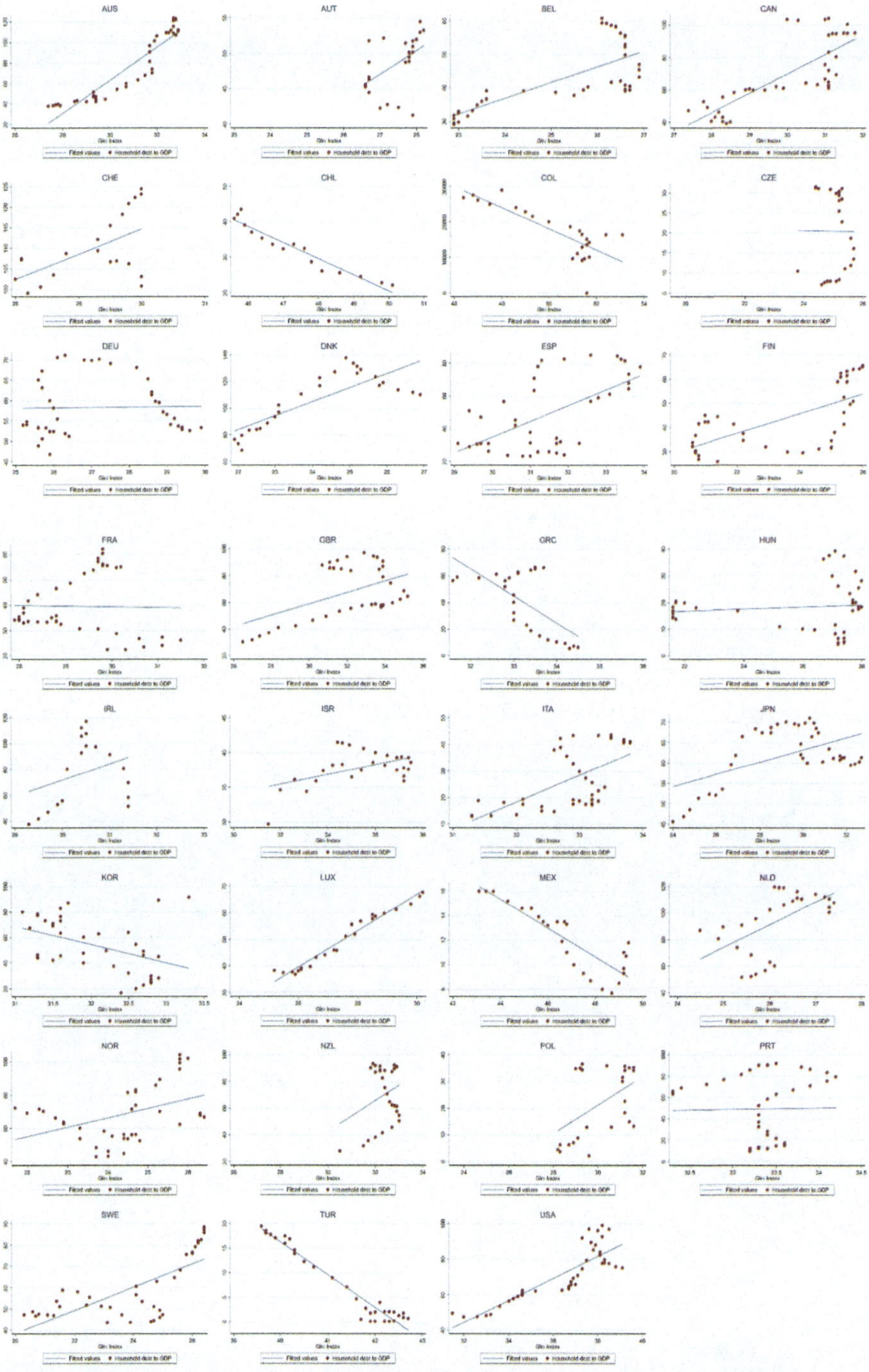

Fig. 8 Scatter plots with trend lines of correlations between household debt and Gini index

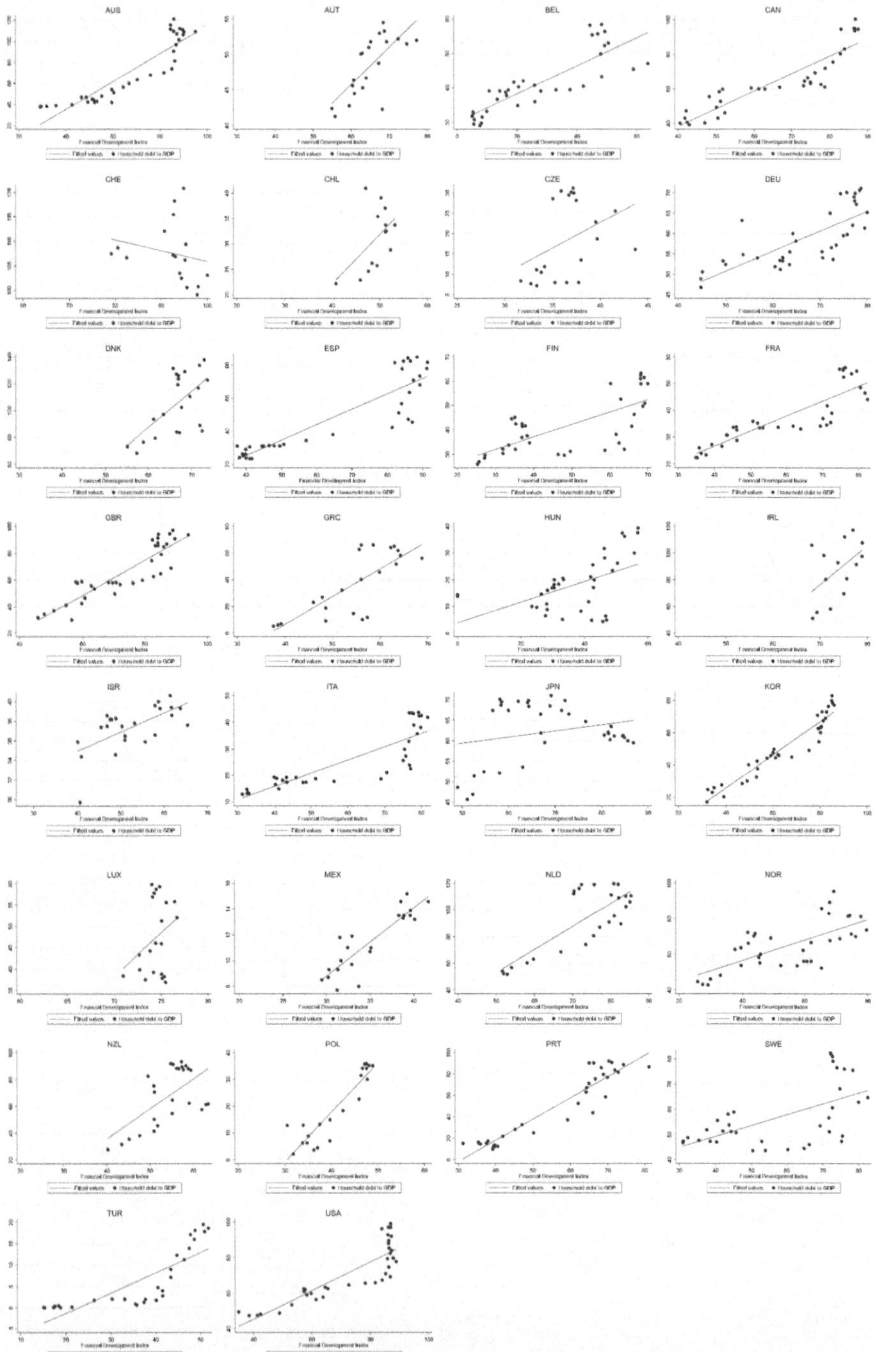

Fig. 9 Scatter plots with trend lines of correlations between household debt and financial development

Duesenberry (1949), in which the demand function of the agent, described as "inward-looking" is based on past income and consumption level. These two arguments show that how increasing inequality between the poor and the rich pushes the poor to borrow in order to maintain the living standards.

4 Conclusion

In this chapter, we examined the inequality-leverage-financial crisis nexus in the light of the global financial crisis of 2007–08. We first explained why the inequality of income distribution has increased over the last four decades in developed countries, putting emphasis on globalization, financialization, and reduced bargaining power of labor due to free-market policies. We then underlined the fact that advanced economies performed well in terms of consumption, investment, and growth despite growing inequality which is expected to lead to negative economic outcomes such as underconsumption. We showed that increasing borrowing, related to financial development and openness, expansionist monetary policies, low inflationist framework, and changing consumer behavior for credit demand, compensated possible negative outcomes of the income inequality. However, we next showed how this excessive borrowing, particularly by low- and middle-income households led to overindebtedness and spending booms, as in the US prior to the crisis. These credit and asset bubbles engendered the global financial crisis, as suggested by the early literature.

In order to test our hypothesis, we ran a regression analysis on a sample of 31 OECD and/or EU member countries over the period of 1980–2020. Our empirical results indicate that income inequality leads to higher household debt stock, but mainly in developed countries where the financial sector is more developed and interest rates are lower. Our results are in line with the theoretical (i.e., Kumhof et al., 2015) and empirical literature (i.e., Malinen, 2016).

Based on literature review and our estimation results, we can affirm that excessive borrowing—encouraged by loose monetary policy and increased financial development—to respond to growing income inequality may only provide partial and temporary solutions to underconsumption, but it may even aggravate the structural problems of the economy. As underlined by Akyüz (2017), excessive borrowing leading to boom-bust cycles creates supply-side distortions, hindering productivity, slowing economic growth, and preparing the ground for financial crises. When the crisis occurs, inequality is exacerbated, and the economy would need bigger bubbles to recover and grow.

Therefore, as Akyüz (2017, p. 51) suggests "the solution is to be found not in monetary policy and negative interest rates but in reversing the secular decline in wages and concentration of wealth, restraining financialization, and assigning a greater role to the public sector in stabilizing aggregate demand." Doing this requires significant increases in wages in real terms, but also a more substantial fiscal policy with additional public spending and a reform on tax policy. As high-income groups will be more taxed, higher levels of public spending would not cause an increase in public debt stocks. However, doing this is not so simple, because it requires not only a structural reform in economic sphere but also a structural change in political area.

References

Acharya, V. V., Philippon, A., Richardson, M., & Roubini, N. (2009). Prologue: A bird's-eye view: The financial crisis of 2007–2009: Causes and remedies. In V. V. Acharya & M. Richardson (Eds.), *Restoring financial stability: How to repair a failed system* (pp. 1–56). John Wiley & Sons.

Ahlquist, J. S., & Ansell, B. W. (2017). Taking credit. Redistribution and borrowing in an age of economic polarization. *World Politics, 69*(4), 640–675. https://doi.org/10.1017/S0043887117000089

Aghion, P., Caroli, E., & Garcia-Penalosa, C. (1999). Inequality and economic growth: The perspective of the new growth theories. *Journal of Economic Literature, 37*(4), 1615–1660. https://doi.org/10.1257/jel.37.4.1615

Akyüz, Y. (2017). *Playing with fire*. Oxford University Press.

Ari, A. (2010). *Crises Financières Turques dans un Monde Globalisé: Développement d'un Système d'Indicateurs d'Alerte*. Editions Universitaires Européennes.

Ari, A. (Ed.). (2014). *The European debt crisis. causes, consequences, measures and Remedies*. Cambridge Scholars Publishing.

Ari, A. (2018). Financial openness, financial stability, and macroeconomic performance in Turkey: A comparative perspective. In A. F. Aysan, M. Babacan, N. Gür, & H. Karahan (Eds.), *Turkish economy between middle income trap and high income status* (pp. 151–169). Palgrave Macmillan.

Babicki, S., Arndt, D., Marcu, A., Liang, Y., Grant, J. R., Maciejewski, A., & Wishart, D. S. (2016). Heatmapper: Web-enabled heat mapping for all. *Nucleic Acids Research, 44*, 147–153.

Bazillier, R., & Hericourt, J. (2017). The circular relationship between inequality, leverage, and financial crises. *Journal of Economic Surveys, 31*(2), 463–496. https://doi.org/10.1111/joes.12150

Bellettini, B., Delbono, F., Karlström, P., & Pastorello, S. (2019). Income inequality and banking crises: Testing the level hypothesis directly. *Journal of Macroeconomics, 62*(C), 103054. https://doi.org/10.1016/j.jmacro.2018.08.007

Berg, A. G., & Ostry, J. D. (2011). Inequality and unsustainable growth: Two sides of the same coin? *IMF staff discussion note*, SDN/11/08.

Berkmen, S. P., Gaston Gelos, G., Rennhack, R., & Walsh, J. P. (2012). The global financial crisis: Explaining cross-country differences in the output impact. *Journal of International Money and Finance, 31*(1), 42–59. https://doi.org/10.1016/j.jimonfin.2011.11.002

Bordo, M., & Meissner, C. (2012). Does inequality lead to a financial crisis? *Journal of International Money and Finance, 31*(8), 2147–2161. https://doi.org/10.1016/j.jimonfin.2012.05.006

Cardaci, A. (2018). Inequality, household debt and financial instability: An agent-based perspective. *Journal of Economic Behavior & Organization, 149*, 434–458. https://doi.org/10.1016/j.jebo.2018.01.010

Chang, X., Li, G., Gu, X., & Lei, C. (2020). Does the inequality-credit-crisis nexus exist? An empirical re-examination. *Applied Economics, 52*(37), 4044–4057. https://doi.org/10.1080/00036846.2020.1730757

Claessens, S., Kose, M. A., & Terrones, M. E. (2010). The global financial crisis: How similar? How different? How costly? *Journal of Asian Economics, 21*(3), 247–264. https://doi.org/10.1016/j.asieco.2010.02.002

Cynamon, B. Z., & Fazzari, S. M. (2016). Inequality, the great recession and slow recovery. *Cambridge Journal of Economics, 40*(2), 373–399. https://doi.org/10.1093/cje/bev016

Duesenberry, J. S. (1949). *Income, saving, and the theory of consumer behavior*. Harvard University Press.

Feenstra, R. C., & Hanson, G. H. (1996). Globalization, outsourcing and wage inequality. *American Economic Review, 86*(2), 240–245.

Feldkircher, M. (2014). The determinants of vulnerability to the global financial crisis 2008 to 2009: Credit growth and other sources of risk. *Journal of International Money and Finance, 43*, 19–49. https://doi.org/10.1016/j.jimonfin.2013.12.003

Frankel, J. A., & Saravelos, G. (2012). Can leading indicators assess country vulnerability? Evidence from the 2008–09 global financial crisis. *Journal of International Economics, 87*(2), 216–231. https://doi.org/10.1016/j.jinteco.2011.12.009

Fratzscher, M. (2009). What explains global exchange rate movements during the financial crisis? *Journal of International Money and Finance, 28*(8), 1390–1407. https://doi.org/10.1016/j.jimonfin.2009.08.008

Giannone, D., Lenza, M., & Reichlin, L. (2011). Market freedom and the global recession. *IMF Economic Review, 59*, 111–135. https://doi.org/10.1057/imfer.2010.14

Fitoussi, J. P., & Saraceno, F. (2010a). Inequality and macroeconomic performance. *OFCE working paper*, 2010-13.

Fitoussi, J. P., & Saraceno, F. (2010b). How deep is a crisis? Policy responses and structural factors behind diverging performances. *Journal of Globalization and Development, 1*(1), 1–19.

Goda, T., Onaran, O., & Stockhammer, E. (2017). Income inequality and wealth concentration in the recent crisis. *Development and Change, 48*(1), 3–27. https://doi.org/10.1111/dech.12280

Greenwood, J., & Jovanovic, B. (1990). Financial development, growth and the distribution of income. *Journal of Political Economy, 98*(5), 1076–1107.

Gu, X. P., Tam, P. S., Zhang, Y., & Lei, C. K. (2019). Inequality, leverage and crises: Theory and evidence revisited. *The World Economy, 42*(8), 2280–2299. https://doi.org/10.1111/twec.12806

Iacoviello, M. (2008). Household debt and income inequality, 1963–2003. *Journal of Money Credit and Banking, 40*(5), 929–965. https://doi.org/10.1111/j.1538-4616.2008.00142.x

Jaumotte, F., Lall, S., & Papageorgiou, C. (2013). Rising income inequality: Technology, or trade and financial globalization? *IMF Economic Review, 61*(2), 271–309.

Kirschenmann, K., Malinen, T., & Nyberg, H. (2016). The risk of financial crises: Is there a role for income inequality? *Journal of International Money and Finance, 68*, 161–180. https://doi.org/10.1016/j.jimonfin.2016.07.010

Kumhof, M., Ranciere, R., & Winant, P. (2015). Inequality, leverage, and crises. *American Economic Review, 105*(3), 1217–1245. https://doi.org/10.1257/aer.20110683

Lane, P. R., & Milesi-Ferretti, G. M. (2011). The cross-country incidence of the global crisis. *IMF Economic Review, 59*, 77–110. https://doi.org/10.1057/imfer.2010.12

Levine, R. (2005). Finance and growth: Theory and evidence. In P. Aghion & S. N. Durlauf (Eds.), *Handbook of economic growth Volume 1A* (pp. 865–934). Elsevier.

Malinen, T. (2016). Does income inequality contribute to credit cycles? *Journal of Economic Inequality, 14*, 309–325. https://doi.org/10.1007/s10888-016-9334-6

Morelli, S., Smeeding, T., & Thompson, J. (2015). Post-1970 trends in within-country inequality and poverty: Rich and middle-income countries. In A. Atkinson & F. Bourguignon (Eds.), *Handbook of income distribution* (Vol. 2, pp. 593–696). Elsevier-North Holland.

Obstfeld, O., Shambaugh, J. C., & Taylor, A. M. (2009). Financial instability, reserves, and central bank swap lines in the panic of 2008. *American Economic Review, 99*(2), 480–486. https://doi.org/10.1257/aer.99.2.480

OECD. (2015). Growth and income inequality: Trends and policy implications. *OECD economics department policy notes*, no. 26.

Paul, P. (2022). Historical patterns of inequality and productivity around financial crises. *Federal Reserve Bank of san Francisco Working Paper*, 2017-23. https://doi.org/10.24148/wp2017-23

Perugini, C., Hölscher, J., & Collie, S. (2016). Inequality, credit, and financial crises. *Cambridge Journal of Economics, 40*(1), 227–257. https://doi.org/10.1093/cje/beu075

Piketty, T. (2014). *Capital in the Twenty-First Century*. Harvard University Press.

Rajan, R. (2010). *Fault Lines*. Princeton University Press.

Romer, P. M. (1994). The origins of endogenous growth. *Journal of Economic Perspectives, 8*(1), 3–22.

Rose, A. K., & Spiegel, M. M. (2011). Cross-country causes and consequences of the 2008 crisis: An update. *European Economic Review, 55*(3), 309–324. https://doi.org/10.1016/j.euroecorev.2010.12.006

Shleifer, A., & Vishny, R. W. (2010). Unstable banking. *Journal of Financial Economics, 97*(3), 306–318.

Stiglitz, J. (2012). *The Price of inequality. How Today's Divided Society Endangers Our Future*. W.W. Norton.

Svirydzenka, K. (2016). *Introducing a new broad-based index of financial development. IMF Working Paper*, 16/5, (Vol. 16, p. 1).

Van Treeck, T. (2014). Did inequality cause the U.S. financial crisis? *Journal of Economic Surveys, 28*(3), 421–448. https://doi.org/10.1111/joes.12028

Health Crisis, Income Poverty and Public Policies in the World

Jean-Claude Vérez

Abstract The pandemic has impacted the world's population to varying degrees. The poorest and most vulnerable populations are particularly affected. Developing countries, especially the least developed countries, the majority of which are located in Africa, are unable to combat income poverty for the first time in 20 years. The challenge for the governments of these countries to overcome the economic and social consequences of the pandemic is enormous and requires a change in public policies, more preventive and better targeted, especially for the poorest.

Keywords Pandemic · Income poverty · Developing countries · Public policy

1 Introduction

In 2020, Covid-19 and its various variants struck countries on all five continents. Faced with this global scourge, the world is trying to contain negative externalities of the pandemic as much as possible, and the governments of the major powers as well as those of emerging and developing countries are seeking to find solutions according to the means at their disposal—vaccination campaigns and access to care for the most affected. At the same time, they are deploying economic support policies for the greatest number of people, even if it means allowing debt levels to rise. The "fashion" is no longer the "Washington Consensus" where many experts praised the merits of laissez-faire while advocating minimalist public intervention.

Of course, the pandemic is more difficult economically and socially for poor people, particularly in developing countries where there are few or no social protection systems. And if they do exist, there is no guarantee that those most at risk will be able to access public and social services. But, conversely, some of those considered poor are less poor than thought because of their informal activities, while households considered non-poor, such as C-level civil servants, are actually poorer than those the recognized as poor. It is therefore particularly difficult to measure the

J.-C. Vérez (✉)
University of Artois and International Centre for European Training, Arras, France

A. Ari (ed.), *Capitalism at a Crossroads*, Springer Studies in Alternative Economics,
https://doi.org/10.1007/978-3-031-23257-2_7

real impact of the pandemic on populations at risk, especially if one wants to conduct a study on the scale of all countries in the world.

This difficulty is all the greater because in developing countries, ethnic, community, or simply village solidarity may come to the aid of the most disadvantaged, whereas in advanced economies, solitude or isolation may prevail. In emerging countries, the two situations may coexist between the more developed urban areas (except for slums) and the rural areas where the popular social categories are more exposed to various shortages.

Finally, when dealing with income poverty, it is always difficult to identify all the causes, as they are numerous, intertwined, and interdependent. For example, in Somalia, people affected by the Covid-19 were also victims of reduced harvests due to recurrent droughts or floods or locust invasions. It is therefore difficult to measure the precise impact of the health crisis on the poorest populations in the same way that it is difficult to measure its effects on income poverty. Despite all these limitations, we first analyze the externalities of the health crisis on income poverty in the world (Sect. 2), before separating the impacts by region or country (Sect. 3). We then examine the short- and medium-term prospects in the world economy in Sect. 4. We discuss the need to redeploy public policies in developing countries in Sect. 5. Section 6 concludes.

2 The Global Increase in Poverty on a Monetary Level

Whatever the methodological problems of measuring income poverty, international institutions including the World Bank identify several criteria for classifying people as extremely poor, poor, or vulnerable. The World Bank estimated in January 2021 that the pandemic had increased the number of poor people in the world to around 120 million in 2020 and between 140 and 160 million in 2021. This includes people living on $1.90 a day. In October 2021, the World Bank also considered that for the first time in over 20 years, the fight against poverty had regressed. With a percentage that remains equal to 10% of the world's population between 2015 and 2020, the number of poor people living on less than $1.90 a day would be around 750 million people (Grown and Sanchez-Paramo, 2021) (Fig. 1).

At the $3.20 a day threshold, according to World Bank estimates in January 2021, the number of poor people would have increased by 228 million for the year 2020, and at the $5.50 threshold, by 177 million. The long-term effects are frightening, as the World Bank estimates that the children of the 120 million people who fell into extreme poverty in 2020 could lose up to $10 trillion of their lifetime earnings (World Bank, 2021, p. 58).

It is also assumed that extreme income poverty has many implications for the satisfaction of people's basic needs. This is particularly the case in the area of food. In 2020, about 720 to 811 million people faced famine according to the World Bank and more than 2 billion people lacked access to sufficient, safe, and nutritious food (ibid, p. 61). This is also the case for education. "Before the pandemic, nearly

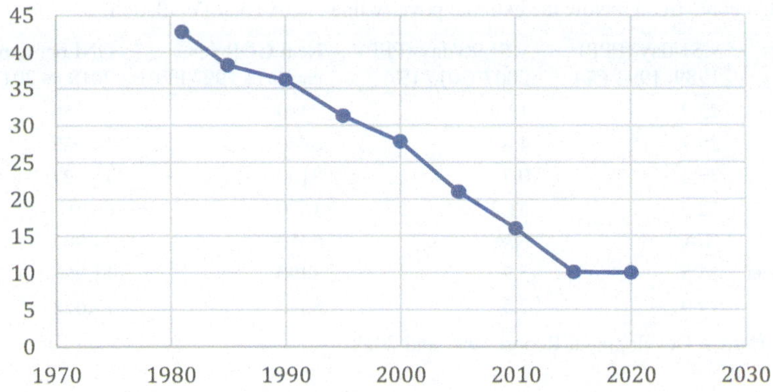

Fig. 1 Population <$1.90 a day (2011 PPP as % of World Population). Source: World Bank (2021)

260 million children and young people were not in school, and in developing countries 53% of 10-year-olds could not write and understand simple text" (ibid, p. 62). The pandemic has forced schools to close: the World Bank estimates that the learning poverty rate in low- and middle-income countries could be as high as 63% and that children suffering from these learning losses could have to forgo a lifetime of income worth $16 trillion, or 10% of global GDP (ibid, p. 62).

The pandemic therefore creates income poverty, deprivation and accentuates pre-existing inequalities. Long before the pandemic, it was known that poverty does not randomly affect people and social categories. "In 2018, four out of five people below the international poverty line lived in rural areas. Half of the poor are children. Women make up the majority of the poor in most parts of the world and in some age groups. About 70% of the poor aged 15 and over have never attended school or have only received a basic education. More than 40% of the world's poor live in countries experiencing fragility, conflict or violence, and this figure could rise to 67% in the next ten years, even though these countries are home to just 10% of the world's population. Some 132 million poor people live in areas at risk of severe flooding" (Grown and Sanchez-Paramo, 2021).

While the pandemic has accelerated deprivation, it has simultaneously delayed the goal of reducing the global extreme poverty rate to below 3% by 2030. If it "was already in jeopardy before the health crisis, it will now be unattainable without swift, meaningful and robust action" (Grown and Sanchez-Paramo, 2021). This negative externality of the pandemic raises questions for economists and policymakers about the mechanisms (existing and/or to be created) to protect against poverty. While we could be pleased with globalization and the emergence of several countries that have opted for a market economy, which has allowed a decline in monetary poverty, we are discovering that Covid-19 has very quickly attenuated this progress. Long before the pandemic, the issue of poverty and extreme poverty was of concern not only to

Table 1 People living below the extreme poverty line (% of Total Population)

Country	<$1/day (PPP) 1989–1994 (%)	<$1.90/day (PPP) 2007–2017 (%)	Real GDP per capita ($ 1997 PPP)	GNI per capita 2018 ($ 2011 PPP)
S. Africa	23.7	18.9	7380	11,756
Brazil	28.7	4.8	6480	14,068
China	29.4	0.7	3130	16,127
India	52.5	21.2	1670	6829
Turkey	N/A	N/A	6350	24,905
Indonesia	14.5	5.7	3490	11,256
Mexico	14.9	2.5	8370	17,628

Source: Human Development Report 1999 and 2019

the people concerned, but also to policymakers and/or international institutions. Table 1 shows the percentage of people living below the poverty line in purchasing power parity (PPP) and the level of wealth created per capita for some emerging countries.

Calculation methods have changed over time including the extreme poverty line which has risen from $1 to $1.90. Comparisons must therefore be made with caution, but some trends can be seen. The percentage of people below the extreme poverty line was on a downward trend while GDP (and then Gross National Income, GNI) per capita increased significantly, particularly in China. As a result of the pandemic and periods of containment, since the spring of 2020, large parts of the world have turned inward, millions of families have been isolated, some people have lost their lives, others their incomes, others their jobs or their occupations in the informal sector. According to the ILO (in Damon, 2021), by May 2020, 1.6 billion workers in the informal economy had been impacted by the pandemic with an estimated two-thirds of their income lost within weeks.

Beyond these general trends, and although the world is complex and plural, it may be useful to identify the factors that influence people's experiences of the Covid-19 crisis: location, social category, health, nutrition, age, education, disability, conflict, and gender.

3 Differentiated Impacts According to Continents, Countries, and Populations

In 2022, it appears that more men have lost their lives while women have suffered from more severe consequences on employment, income, and security. One should remember that from a methodological point of view, it is always difficult to separate the factors that explain such developments. It is known, for example, that men's life expectancy is lower than women's, so measuring the real impact of Covid-19 on men's mortality is risky because of the multiplication of factors that cause death. However, it appears that in South Asia, Latin America and the Caribbean, the Middle

Table 2 Eastern and Southern Africa

Indicators	2000	2010	2015–2020[a]
Total population (millions)	398	518	677
GNI per capita (current $)	628	1376	1365
Population < $1.90 per day (millions)	232	247	281
Pop < $1.90 / Pop. Total (%)	58.2	47.7	43.7

Source: World Bank (2021)
[a]Most recent data between 2015 and 2020

East and North Africa, 60–75% of deaths were among men, but in other countries (Armenia, Pakistan, and Senegal) Covid-19 caused more anxiety among women (Grown and Sanchez-Paramo, 2021).

According to the same study, regions and countries have also been impacted to different degrees by school dropouts, which vary by school level. "According to UNESCO projections from July 2020, boys are more likely than girls not to return to university, primary and secondary school, while the reverse is true in pre-primary and secondary education (Grown and Sanchez-Paramo, 2021).

In another area, employment, women are more likely to lose their jobs in the first months of the crisis, as shown in a recent study by Kugler et al. (2021) based on harmonized data from high-frequency telephone surveys in 40 developing countries. Another study (Cucagna and Romero, 2021) on Latin America indicates that women were 44% more likely to lose their jobs at the beginning of the crisis than men.

In vulnerable countries, especially those affected by conflicts of various kinds (war, coup d'état, ethnic conflict, civil war, terrorism), the pandemic has disrupted health systems, and if social protection systems exist, they are overwhelmed by the considerable needs of the population. "With the help of the International Development Association (IDA), more than 45 countries in sub-Saharan Africa have now set up social safety nets. In Pakistan, the government is turning this crisis into an opportunity: the IDA-funded Pandemic Control Project has launched TeleSchool, a television channel with educational content for primary- and secondary-school students. In countries like Pakistan, where nearly one in three girls has never been to school, distance learning programs offer opportunities to overcome challenges and access educational resources on a continuous basis."

According to IDA (World Bank, 2021), by the end of 2020, "233 million people in IDA countries were food insecure and this number is expected to increase further in 2021 and 2022." The report cites as the main reasons for this are the decline in income due to the pandemic, reduced remittances from abroad due to periods of containment, higher food prices and, in some cases, the depreciation of national currencies. If we combine these causes with the disruptions linked to climate change (water shortages, higher temperatures, lower yields), in certain regions of the world such as the Sahel (Burkina Faso, Chad, Mali, Mauritania, Niger, and Senegal) the human and economic toll of Covid-19 is even greater.

Table 2, divided into major regions, shows the evolution of four economic and monetary indicators. Table 2 presents the data on Eastern and Southern Africa. The

Table 3 West and Central Africa

Indicators	2000	2010	2015–2020
Total population (millions)	267	351	459
GNI per capita (current $)	453	1564	1646
Population < $1.90 per day (millions)	156	165	154
Pop < $1.90 / Pop. Total (%)	56.9	47.1	34.5

Source: World Bank (2021)

Table 4 East Asia and the Pacific

Indicators	2000	2010	2015–2020
Total population (millions)	1816	1966	2105
GNI per capita (current $)	910	3760	8362
Population < $1.90 per day (millions)	632	212	20
Pop < $1.90 / Pop. Total (%)	34.8	10.8	1.0

Source: World Bank (2021)

GNI between 2015 and 2020 is at the same level as in 2010, whereas it had more than doubled between 2000 and 2010. While the percentage of the population affected by extreme poverty has decreased to about 44%, the number of people in millions has increased by 34 million. At the same time, the population has grown by over 150 million since 2010. Hopefully, East Africa, which is seeking to improve the business climate, stimulate investment, and invest in education and skills development, will be able to achieve a sustainable reduction in income poverty, as will Southern Africa, which is seeking to implement an industrialization strategy. Nothing is guaranteed, but diversifying the economies of these two regions can only help to create more economic growth, which in turn can help to fight poverty if and only if the distribution of growth benefits the poorest first.

In West and Central Africa (Table 3), the number of people in extreme income poverty has stabilized and the percentage of people in extreme income poverty has declined, despite an increase in the total population to over 100 million since 2010. However, more than a third of this population remains in extreme poverty. West Africa aims to strengthen rural–urban linkages and develop the private sector, while Central Africa wants to encourage local processing of raw materials and develop its infrastructure. These objectives are essential because one of the obstacles to sustainable growth in Africa, in general, is the low level of processing of exported products while imported products are much more processed, and any processed goods or products contain more added value than the natural resources or raw materials.

China's growth explains much of the fall in extreme poverty, with GNI per capita increasing almost ten-fold in 15–20 years in East Asia and the Pacific (Table 4). The adoption of the market economy by the Chinese authorities explains this success and the growing integration of China in the world trade shows the interest of participating in free trade rather than favoring protectionism. This does not mean that everything is perfect, but no one can dispute that the average Chinese person lives better monetarily than he did at the time of the Great Leap Forward.

Table 5 South Asia

Indicators	2000	2010	2015–2020
Total population (millions)	1391	1639	1857
GNI per capita (current $)	445	1147	1821
Population < $1.90 per day (millions)	577	425	262
Pop < $1.90 / Pop. Total (%)	40	26	15.2

Source: World Bank (2021)

Table 6 Latin America and the Caribbean

Indicators	2000	2010	2015–2020
Total population (millions)	472	535	595
GNI per capita (current $)	4017	7628	7181
Population < $1.90 per day (millions)	66	35	24
Pop < $1.90 / Pop. Total (%)	12.7	6.0	3.7

Source: World Bank (2021)

Table 7 Middle East and North Africa

Indicators	2000	2010	2015–2020
Total population (millions)	279	333	396
GNI per capita (current $)	1596	3996	3163
Population < $1.90 per day (millions)	10	7	27
Pop < $1.90 / Pop. Total (%)	3.5	2	7

Source: World Bank (2021)

The progress made in South Asia (Table 5) is less spectacular than in East Asia, but it is real nonetheless. The growth of the Indian economy should not obscure the persistence of strong inequalities, much more than in China. UNDP (in Jaffrelot and Thakker, 2021) estimates that 260 million Indians will have fallen back into poverty by 2020, almost as many as the 271 million who got out of poverty between 2006 and 2016. This tremendous setback poses significant challenges for the country, particularly in terms of malnutrition.

In Latin America and the Caribbean (Table 6), despite a decline in GNI per capita between the last two periods, the number of extreme poor has fallen in millions and as a percentage of the total population. However, the growth models of the various countries are a source of concern, such as the Brazilian agri-food model because of the environmental problems caused by its intensive agriculture, or the Venezuelan model, which depends on fossil fuels.

In Middle East and North Africa (MENA) (Table 7), GNI per capita fell and the number of poor people living on less than $1.90 a day has increased by 20 million. It correponds to 7% of the total population, twice as much as in 2000. Several countries are in great difficulty, such as Tunisia, whose economy is in a state of collapse for various reasons linked to exogenous shocks (impact of terrorism and the pandemic on tourism) and endogenous shocks (political instability, uncertainty on the evolution of the political regime), and Libya, whose economy is insufficiently divided.

One can observe in tables that it is in Africa and South Asia that the extremely poor populations are concentrated; in relation to the total population, it is in Africa that the challenge is major and one should remember that the population of the continent will double by 2050 before doubling again (or almost) between 2050 and 2100.

4 The Short-Term Economic Outlook

According to the World Bank, global growth could be around 4% in 2022. This outlook seems optimistic because of the persistence of the pandemic here and there, the possibility of a new variant, the reduction of economic support measures, problems linked to the disorganization of transport and supply difficulties, not to mention inflationary pressures that are impacting purchasing power, particularly of the poorest. Another question is the consequences of the Russian invasion of Ukraine: how long will it last and what will be its lasting impact on the sources of supply of many raw materials? We have seen that one month after the outbreak of the war, many countries were suffering from not being able to import what they needed, with the result that prices are rising, causing concern for the poorest, the vulnerable, people with stagnant incomes, households on fixed incomes, etc.

Asia is expected to have the highest growth rate in 2022 and 2023. The trends differ from country to country: impact of border closures and travel restrictions on tourism (Cambodia, Malaysia, Philippines, Thailand), natural disasters (Philippines, South Pacific Islands), continued remittances (Fiji, Solomon Islands, Tonga, Philippines). "Among small Pacific Island countries, per capita incomes are expected to decline, and in many other countries in the region, per capita income growth is expected to lag behind economic growth... Downside risks to the regional outlook prevail." (World Bank, 2021) (Table 8).

Table 8 World Economic Outlook

	2019	2020	2021	2022	2023
World	2.6	−3.4	5.5	4.1	3.2
Advanced economies	1.7	−4.6	5.0	3.8	2.3
Emerging markets and DCs	3.8	−1.7	6.3	4.6	4.4
East Asia and Pacific	5.8	1.2	7.1	5.1	5.2
Latin America and the Caribbean	0.8	−6.4	6.7	2.6	2.7
Middle East and North Africa	0.9	−4.0	3.1	4.4	3.4
South Asia	4.4	−5.2	7.0	7.6	6.0
Sub-Saharan Africa	2.5	−2.2	3.5	3.6	3.8

Source: World Bank (2021)

In the Latin America and Caribbean region, growth is estimated to reach 2.6% in 2022 and 2.7% in 2023, well below the 2021 level. Budgetary and monetary constraints, inflation (especially for food and energy), currency depreciation in some countries, and drought in others (Brazil, Chile) are explanatory factors. "The return of GDP to pre-pandemic levels will be uneven across the region and may be delayed in some countries. According to forecasts to the end of 2023, the region will see its per capita income decline relative not only to advanced countries, but also to countries in the East Asia and Pacific region and the Europe and Central Asia region [...] Supply chain bottlenecks are expected to persist in the first half of 2022." (World Bank, 2021).

The MENA region is expected to experience higher growth across countries and for different reasons: higher oil production in Saudi Arabia and the Islamic Republic of Iran, strong consumer demand in Egypt coupled with rising remittances. Higher oil and gas prices and increased production should benefit energy exporters (Saudi Arabia, Iraq, Islamic Republic of Iran). On the other hand, in Tunisia, the situation is worrying due to the increase in the number of cases of Covid in 2021, confinements and firewalls, and the fact that travel restrictions have severely limited tourism, not to mention the political uncertainties. In Morocco, economic growth is estimated at 3.2% in 2022 and is affected by the slowdown in agricultural production. In short, the MENA region is threatened according to the World Bank by possible new outbreaks of the Covid-19, a risk of social unrest, the high-debt burden, not to mention potential conflicts (as in Libya and Iraq).

In South Asia, growth prospects are good. The economic damage caused by the second wave in India has already been reversed, with output effectively returning to pre-pandemic levels. Growth in Pakistan has surprised on the upside, supported by improved domestic demand and record remittances. Improved domestic demand and a recovery in exports contributed to strong growth in Bangladesh. Risks to the outlook include financing conditions, inflation, the emergence of the Omicron variant and, above all, increasing climate risks (cyclones, floods, droughts). "The region is one of the most vulnerable to climate-related increases in poverty, disease, child mortality, and food prices" (World Bank, 2021).

In sub-Saharan Africa, the recovery in 2021 was not enough to stem the increase in poverty due to the pandemic, while new waves of Covid-19 pose a persistent threat. "The Omicron variant is now fueling the increase in cases across the region. More than 70% of sub-Saharan African countries have reported at least a 50% increase in cases in the last two weeks of 2021. Services, tourism, and manufacturing have been particularly hard hit by the pandemic, with prolonged income and job losses, while inflation has hampered the recovery in consumer spending" (World Bank, 2021). This rises social unrest, insecurity, and internal conflicts, particularly in the Sahel region (Burkina Faso, North-eastern Nigeria, Niger, Mali, Mauritania, and Chad).

Sub-Saharan Africa is undoubtedly the region of the world where the economic outlook is most uncertain due to the multiple above-mentioned uncertainties and the recurrent instabilities. This is not new. The pandemic has only accentuated them, and Africans are used to be confronted with many challenges, which may explain a higher level of resilience than elsewhere. However, it is also true that the challenges that had to be addressed before the health crisis will require additional resources. It is possible that some price developments will be positive, such as commodity prices, oil and other raw materials, and foodstuffs like coffee and cocoa. These high prices will benefit exporting countries. But these desired trends cannot obscure the fact that "the pandemic has undermined progress in poverty reduction and the achievement of key development goals across the region, erasing more than a decade of gains in per capita income for some countries. In more than one-third of the countries in the region, including South Africa, Angola, and Nigeria, per capita income in 2022 will remain below the level of a decade ago. Poverty, food insecurity, rising food prices, and geopolitical tensions could dampen consumer demand and slow growth. Countries facing debt-overhang problems may find it more difficult to access external finance, requiring a sharp fiscal adjustment. Low-vaccination rates against Covid-19 expose countries in the region to a resurgence and worsening of epidemic waves, which could again undermine economic activity. The prolongation of the pandemic risks exacerbating existing development and health problems, undermining structural and fiscal reforms, and leading to sustained losses of human capital." (World Bank, 2021).

Ultimately, the uncertainties linked to the propagation of Covid-19 variants do not allow us to envisage a return to normal in the short term. Depending on the region of the world and the level of development, economic recovery is uncertain in a context marked by tensions on supply, inflation, worrying levels of debt, and an acceleration of inequalities, particularly for the poorest. Unlike industrialized countries, governments in many developing countries do not have sufficient policy space to sustain economic activity and mitigate social shocks.

The latest World Economic Outlook published by by the IMF (2021) identifies three obstacles to a sustainable recovery in developing economies. The first concerns debt: "as Covid-19 has pushed total global debt to its highest level in 50 years, against a backdrop of increasing complexity in the composition of creditors, the report warns that future debt relief efforts will face greater difficulties." The second looks at the implications of sharp fluctuations in commodity prices for emerging and developing economies, most of which rely heavily on commodity exports. Finally, the third examines the impact of Covid-19 on global inequality. It shows how the pandemic has increased income inequality, reversing some of the progress made over the past two decades. Ayhan Kose, Chief Economist and Director of the Prospects Group at the World Bank, says: "Emerging and developing economies will need to carefully adjust their fiscal and monetary policies. They also need to undertake reforms to address the legacy of the pandemic. These reforms should focus on improving investment and human capital, addressing income and gender inequality, and tackling the challenges of climate change."

5 Rethinking Public Policies

The fight against income poverty by governments, international institutions, civil society organizations, and other actors must certainly be rethought. Protective mechanisms to achieve this are no longer sufficient, including in industrialized countries, which are less affected than developing or emerging countries, but they are not spared. The market economy, which can create a great deal of wealth, is undoubtedly at a turning point in its mode of regulation: it will have to anticipate exogenous shocks to a greater extent and, even more so, find ways of allowing the greatest number of people to be included. This is true for all countries, especially emerging and developing ones, which could carry out reforms to reduce their vulnerability to commodity price shocks, reduce inequalities, and improve crisis preparedness.

These constraints can be considered by sector of activity with the support of international institutions, among others. An example is the IDA, which invests in programs to scale up support for restoring degraded land, increasing agricultural productivity and enhancing water security to build climate-resilient food systems and sustainable landscapes. This type of action can be found in Guatemala to improve post-harvest and storage practices to reduce food losses. The work of Sawadogo and Maisonnave (2021) shows that it is possible to assess the impact of a fertilizer subsidy policy on agricultural productivity and poverty in Burkina Faso by studying three different sources of financing (a decrease in public expenditure, an increase in direct business taxes, and indirect taxes), in a context of constrained fiscal space. Their Computable General Equilibrium Model (CGE) takes into account the cross-sectoral effects of this subsidy policy and allows for the evaluation of the implementation of the policy with different financing modes. A micro-simulation model then aims to determine the poverty impacts of each of the financing mechanisms. The financing of the subsidy policy through corporate income tax appears superior in terms of productivity and poverty reduction.

In the field of nutrition, Bérenger and Vérez (2021) analyze the individual and contextual determinants of undernutrition in children under 5 in Senegal. Based on data from the 2005 and 2015 Demographic and Health Surveys, they use multilevel logistic regression models and show that at the national level, nearly 1 child in 5 is stunted, while at the regional level, there are strong disparities. Their analysis shows that beyond individual factors, it is necessary to consider the influence of contextual factors. Although factors such as the age of children may justify actions targeted at children, it appears that other factors, notably the mother's education and household poverty, require specific actions. Furthermore, while the presence of basic services reduces the risk of child undernutrition, it nevertheless contributes to increased disparities in child nutrition between educated and uneducated mothers. This suggests that investments made in some districts contribute to reinforcing inequalities. The results provide useful information for targeting public policies to combat undernutrition.

In the education sector, N'Da Koffi et al. (2021) ask who benefits from education spending in Ivory Coast. Using the Benefit-Incidence method on the basis of the 2015 household survey data and national education statistics, they show that, except for the primary education level, it is the wealthier classes of the population that benefit from the largest share of public spending on education at the secondary, technical secondary and higher education levels. In fact, public spending on education is unequally distributed between different social classes, which creates an asymmetry in favor of the wealthiest social classes in Ivory Coast.

It is possible to cite other examples of the limits of public policies, without minimizing them, and in view of the pandemic and its negative effects on the poor and vulnerable, there is an urgent need to reorient them. But the task is difficult because they are often perceived in the collective imagination as solutions that are quickly available and capable of solving people's daily problems. They are still perceived as a way to reduce worries, inequalities, and uncertainties, so that expectations are such that they are unlikely to satisfy the various households and actors. If, in addition, states are fragile and associated with rentier behavior whose power is tainted by illegitimacy, everything is in place for public policies to be a source of discouragement or even disillusionment without limit (Bourgain and Vérez, 2021).

The contradiction lies in the fact that the poor in less advanced and developing countries need a state to protect them, but they distrust it and cannot control it. Most of these states remain subject to clans, ethnic groups, and clienteles, and are predatory, relying on some of their corrupt officials. Covid-19 did not invent these practices, but it reinforced their devastating effects. "Public policies are no less necessary. Once we accept that the market cannot satisfy all needs, nor provide a solution to all imbalances; once we accept that the sum of individual behaviors does not de facto allow us to reach an overall balance, public policies have their place in the city. However, on the part of politicians, civil servants (or the interest groups which they are linked to which) and users alike, public policies hardly provide a collective solution commensurate with the implemented investments" (Bourgain and Vérez, 2021). It is therefore necessary to try to ensure that poor and very poor people really feel the benefits of public policy, and if this is not the case, if public policy does not improve the daily life of the targeted population, it is necessarily a failure.

Sectors such as education and health provide a good understanding of the issues. It is not enough for pupils to go to school, even regularly throughout the year, for them to become literate. Access to a health clinic in a rural area, designed to receive expectant mothers, does not, in fact, reduce maternal mortality. There are many concrete examples, taken from everyday realities. Furthermore, it should be remembered that all public expenditure needs to be financed and, given the weight of the informal economy and/or corruption, mobilizing revenue is in itself a major challenge. The indicator of fiscal resources in relation to GDP is around 15% in sub-Saharan Africa compared to a world average of 27 and 40% for OECD countries (Bourgain and Vérez, 2021). According to Courade (2021), South Africa is the only country in Africa to have a social security system financed by taxes and contributions. Once tax resources are acquired, their transparent and efficient use is another challenge, which also has implications for resource mobilization.

For the World Bank (2021), several avenues must be explored to improve the lot of the most disadvantaged; some of these are mentioned below by means of a categorical classification and concrete examples.

- Bringing producers closer to consumers. In the agricultural sector, farmers should at least be brought closer to the market by strengthening supply chains, which would avoid imbalances between supply and demand and thus losses of activity and income.
- Developing energy, transport, and telecommunication networks. In Madagascar, the rehabilitation of roads has enabled farmers who were displaced by the pandemic to return to labor-intensive activities or jobs. In India and Kenya, digital platforms are made available to farmers so that they can obtain market information before accessing it, thereby reducing waste.
- Encouraging the development of human capital through distance education as in India: the idea is to reduce dropouts and delays. In rich countries, there would be a tendency to complain about distance learning, preferring face-to-face learning. Here, for very poor, poor, and vulnerable people, the challenge is not to lose touch with the initial learning that is so essential for a better life.
- In terms of social protection, before the pandemic 45% of the world's population had some form of social protection, but in the poorest countries one in five people had access to it (World Bank, 2021). The pandemic has only accentuated these disparities, particularly for those in the informal sector who have great difficulty in obtaining social protection, which the World Bank estimates to be in the billions. To finance real social protection, it would be appropriate to resort to financing based on a general tax rather than a contributory system in which the majority of informal-sector workers cannot participate. Social protection in health should monitor diseases and pandemics by improving access to care, improving family planning, reducing teenage pregnancies, screening for serious diseases such as cervical cancer. The provision of remote counselling services can be very useful for health workers. Finally, the treatment of many non-communicable diseases that have been "neglected" as a result of the surge in demand for intensive care and the shortage of hospital beds should not be overlooked.

The global health context has reminded us of the need to rely on public authorities when they have the means or can obtain them to counteract the negative effects of an exogenous shock. At the same time, it revealed how vulnerable the market economy is to an exogenous shock such as a pandemic. In a short period of time, "the machine has gone haywire" and no one has a quick and effective solution. Neither economics nor other disciplines have the capacity to claim competence on the coronavirus. Medical specialists are still groping, although there have been substantial advances in vaccination and the pandemic is still running in 2022. They are in a situation of uncertainty and these uncertainties can only complicate the task and the decisions to be taken by the public authorities. In fact, some users will continue to complain because they will find that decision makers do not provide a satisfactory response to their concerns and/or problems and/or constraints. This is particularly the case in high-income countries. In developing countries, depending on the political context, people no longer expect much from their leaders, but at the same time, revolts may arise when distress is at its peak and living conditions are close to survival.

If we "let it happen," the contamination would have no limit. And although there are many uncertainties about the parameters of the epidemic, we must continue to make choices while taking them into account. These choices are as much sanitary as economic or political. They also affect many aspects of daily life. Without doubt, one of the most unforeseen choices concerns the imposed and unpopular but widely accepted and understood periods of confinement, with numerous impacts. "For an isolated individual ("Robinson Crusoe"), not working means not producing, not consuming. What is true at the individual level is also true at the collective level. We cannot distribute wealth that we have not produced. Confinement leads to a degraded version of work, and often to a complete stop of production. Fortunately, for many people, telework allows them to maintain a value-creating activity, but it is still very difficult to measure its impact on activity" (Gollier and Straub, 2021). It is the rich countries that have tended to have periods of containment, due to the extent of the pandemic but also due to the degree of potential and then actual intervention by the public authorities.

Wherever possible, public intervention limits the negative effects of containment, but despite this, the most precarious households, casual workers, undeclared actors, isolated people in rural areas or at high altitudes, etc., are more penalized. Similarly, some sectors of economic activity (e.g., tourism) are more directly impacted than others so that "the containment strategy is a collective sacrifice necessary for the common good. This effort must be equitably shared from an economic and financial point of view. It is as much a moral imperative as an economic one" (Gollier and Straub, 2021). For this to happen, the market economy has no other means than to resort to the state, which is the only one capable of establishing an insurance mechanism, and we join the authors who call for "systematic socialization of economic and financial losses due to containment." But we know that this analysis of the facts is only valid for high-income countries; it cannot be deployed in developing countries and even less in less-developed countries because of budgetary constraints. It is therefore appropriate to ask whether it is possible to ensure the common good mentioned above. The challenge of ensuring the common good for all requires upstream thinking and acting in common, which is obviously not the case.

6 Conclusion

The consequences of the pandemic are numerous, affecting all countries but to varying degrees, and reinforcing inequalities to the detriment of the poor and the extreme poor. While high-income countries have the opportunity to mobilize substantial budgetary resources, and to intensify their research, particularly in the area of vaccination, the situation is different for developing countries, including the least developed ones, and in part for emerging countries, where poverty and extreme poverty persist. The challenges for these countries were numerous before the pandemic and are even more so afterwards. In countries with low-savings rates, poorly developed financial markets and high levels of debt, the issue of financing infrastructure of all kinds is crucial. When combined with demographic dynamics, it is difficult to achieve sustainable economic growth that leads to progress in human development, reduces inequality, and anticipates violent shocks such as a pandemic.

However, the pandemic has also revealed capacities for resilience. There is reason for hope, provided that young people, who are very numerous in developing countries, have access to basic goods and services in a sustainable manner. That access to primary schooling becomes more widespread through the use of new technologies, that community health clinics multiply, that international aid for immunization develops, that the most remote villages, where the poorest people are often to be found, are opened up, and that transport and telecommunications infrastructures continue to develop. Public–private partnerships have the merit of being more respectful of good governance and the funds made available allow for more ambitious financing. The development of digital technology is also an opportunity; in any remote village, the poor population has access to a mobile phone and therefore to information, knowledge, advice, and prevention.

The pandemic has forced people to step back and separate the essential from the superfluous. It has shown that while much progress has been made against extreme poverty, nothing is definitive and far too many people have moved very quickly from poverty to extreme poverty. Others, vulnerable, became poor and so on. Covid-19 requires authorities to anticipate future shocks in order to protect the weakest and most fragile populations. The urgency is to end the pandemic if we are to have any hope of halting the rise in poverty. The coronavirus epidemic and its economic consequences have called into question the optimism of the last decades. The situation and the prospects remind us of the importance of public policies, including official development assistance for the least developed countries.

References

Bérenger, V., & Vérez, J.-C. (2021). Can public policies fight against child undernutrition? Application in Senegal. *Developing Worlds, 195*, 29–52.

Bourgain, A., & Vérez, J.-C. (2021). Public policies in sub-Saharan Africa. *Developing Worlds, 195*, 7–10.

Courade, G. (2021). The Africa of poverty during Covid-19. *Politique Etrangère, 186*, 39–52.

Cucagna, E., & Romero, J. (2021). *The gendered impacts of COVID-19 on labor Markets in Latin America and the Caribbean*. World Bank.

Damon, J. (2021). Global poverty: The shock of COVID-19. *Foreign Policy, 86*, 11–22.

Gollier C., & Straub S. (2021, March 21). *The economics of the coronavirus: Some insights*, Toulouse School of Economics, www.tse-fr.eu

Grown C., & Sanchez-Paramo C. (2021). *Covid-19 does not affect men's and women's lives in the same way*. Accessed Jan 15, 2022, from blogs.worldbank.org

IMF. (2021, October). *World economic outlook.*

Jaffrelot C., & Thakker H. (2021). *India: Covid causes a new wave of poverty*. Alternatives Economiques. Hors-série, 50-51. hal-03090139.

Kugler M. D., Viollaz M., Vasconcellos Archer Duque D., Gaddis I., Newhouse D. L., Palacios-Lopez A., & Weber M. (2021). *How did the COVID-19 crisis affect different types of workers in the developing world. World Bank* Policy Research Paper, no. 9703.

N'Da Koffi, C., Kouadio, A., & Aka, F. (2021). Who benefits from education spending in Ivory Coast. *Developing Worlds, 195*, 95–108.

Sawadogo, B., & Maisonnave, H. (2021). Fertilizer subsidy policies in Burkina Faso: A comparison of impacts by financing mode using a computable general equilibrium model. *Developing Worlds, 195*, 11–28.

World Bank. (2021), *Annual report 2021*.

Trade Wars and the Changing Balance of Power

Charalampos Efstathopoulos

Abstract This chapter enquires the ways in which the current US–China trade wars are affecting the balance of power in the capitalist system. The discussion analyzes the emergence of US–China trade wars and shows how protectionist trade policies are increasingly deployed by the two leading economies of the globe to exercise greater political pressure against one another. Such trade wars are understood as targeted mechanisms that increasingly comprise a key diplomatic tool in US–China economic relations, and which are also used to promote diplomatic and security objectives in the capitalist system. The chapter also focuses on how middle powers reassess their options when encountering US–China economic frictions. It is argued that middle powers seek to retain access to both US- and China-led economic agreements, but polarization and geopolitical imperatives are increasingly propelling middle powers to provide their own leadership in the negotiation of new trade agreements in the capitalist system.

Keywords Trade wars · US · China · Middle powers · Trade agreements

1 Introduction

The process of power transition that has unfolded since the end of the Cold War in the capitalist system has now culminated with the emergence of economic wars between the two leading economies of the globe, the US and China. Nevertheless, this latest phase of trade wars is not permanent or definitive, and scholars debate on how the processes of cooperation and competition in the global economy are being reconfigured by such current tensions (Yeung & Quek, 2022). The phenomenon is not new, as previous historical periods have also witnessed diplomatic tensions in the capitalist system that are triggered by changes in the distribution of power in the global economy. In the second half of the twentieth century, the post-war system of

C. Efstathopoulos (✉)
Department of International Politics, Aberystwyth University, Aberystwyth, UK
e-mail: che15@aber.ac.uk

A. Ari (ed.), *Capitalism at a Crossroads*, Springer Studies in Alternative Economics,
https://doi.org/10.1007/978-3-031-23257-2_8

embedded liberalism, which entailed a substantial degree of flexibility and consensus-building in terms of international commitments (Ruggie, 1982), allowed states in the Western Europe and South-East Asia to initially reconstruct and then attain technological and economic supremacy that remained unchallenged until recently. It was only with the emergence of the BRICS and other emerging economies like Indonesia, Mexico, and Turkey that the Western monopoly over the governance of the capitalist system came under challenge. The global financial crisis of 2007–2009 was understood to further accelerate this process of power transition as the Western economies encountered problems like debt, inequality, and unemployment that were mostly endemic in the non-Western world in the previous decades (Helleiner, 2010).

It would, however, be a simplification to argue that current tensions in the capitalist system are mostly emerging along a North–South divide. Current trade wars are centered on the US and China, and other established and emerging economies seem to have different options vis-à-vis the two leading economies that do not necessarily fall under North and South lines. Complicating the options of such middle powers are not only economic interests, but also security imperatives that may override economic considerations but also follow an economic rationale. The very nature of US–China economic competition is also unpredictable. The trade wars of the past mostly remained confined to the economic, technological, and bargaining realms. In the 1980s and the 1990s, the US registered disagreements with what were then deemed as free-riding practices by Japan and the European Community (EC), and such disagreements affected the global trading system. Relations between these economies, however, did not collapse mainly because all parties comprised like-minded states that disagreed over the distribution of responsibilities and burden-sharing, but not about the fundamental organizing principles of the capitalist system itself, such as privatization, liberalization, and deregulation, even though the same countries often strategically opted out from some of these principles in certain sensitive sectors.

The US–China conflict is qualitatively different and bears ideational and security dimensions that distinguish it from the trade wars of the past. First, China's economic rise in itself is generating uncertainty. One the one hand, economic rise is presented by China's leadership as an endeavor towards peaceful development, but the US and many Western states are concerned that a revisionist China will seek to re-write the rules that underpin the capitalist system, while at the same time making the Western economies more dependent upon China's trade, investment, and financial structures (Johnston, 2019). Second, the US shift towards a more assertive and aggressive trade policy towards China has been perceived as partly justified across the West but has also raised concerns that the US is shifting towards unilateralism and even revisionism, and does not prioritize institutional commitments as those of the World Trade Organization (WTO) (Chan, 2021). Third, US–China relations are not divorced from security imperatives but are very much fueled by those, and in this respect, key strategic initiatives such as the US pivot to the Indo-Pacific and China's One Belt–One Road, are also affecting trade relations (Scobell, 2021). Finally, both the Western and Southern middle powers are increasingly affected by US–China trade wars and strive to balance between security and economic objectives as they seek to manage the pressures and the opportunities generated by trade wars in order to improve their position in the capitalist system (Jeong & Lee, 2021).

Based on these initial observations, this chapter addresses the research question: how is the US–China trade war affecting the balance of power in the capitalist system? To address this question, the discussion proceeds as follows. First, it seeks to enquire the current state of US–China trade wars, placing particular attention at recent developments especially during the Biden administration (Sect. 2). Second, it aims to account for the positions of middle powers in a capitalist system characterized by trade wars, enquiring the degree to which middle powers can retain their autonomy when trade wars intensify (Sect. 3). The discussion shows that trade wars play a catalyst role in affecting the balance of power in the capitalist system as the US and China increasingly deploy novel and aggressive trade policies to defend their economic primacy in the capitalist system. In response, different middle powers strive to secure themselves against such tensions and some states, such as certain Asian middle powers, achieve some level of autonomy through new trade agreements, while maintaining a commitment to supporting key institutions of the capitalist system. Finally, Sect. 4 concludes.

2 The Emergence of US–China Trade Wars

The recent outbreak of US–China trade wars has not only affected the bilateral relationship between the world's two leading economies, but also the stability of the capitalist system and its key regimes, such as the global trading system. The main body for managing global trade, the WTO, is now facing an extensive deadlock because of the US–China trade war. Deadlocks in WTO negotiations are not a new phenomenon. Since the 1970s, the emergence of new trading powers, first within the Western world and then with the cases of emerging economies such as the BRICS, has complicated the multilateral negotiating process. In the 1970s and the 1980s, the re-launch of the European Economic Community (EEC) as one trading bloc and the rise of Japan and the newly industrialized countries (NICs), as well as the middle power leadership of exporters such as Australia and Canada, all led to a more multilateral process of decision-making as the US could no longer dominate multilateral negotiations. However, all such economies acted as Western like-minded states favoring open markets, and at critical junctures demonstrated the resolve to advance the capitalist system through new economic agreements and new rounds of global trade negotiations (Bailin, 2005). The completion of major negotiating rounds such as the Tokyo Round (1973–79) and the Uruguay Round (1986–94) demonstrated the increasing complexity of global trade negotiations, but also the capacity of the Western world to find new patterns of cooperation that allowed for the continuous liberalization of global trade. The flexible and ad hoc decision-making structure of the General Agreement on Tariffs and Trade (GATT) allowed for changes in the balance of power in the global economy to rapidly translate into new configurations of power in the GATT system through the so-called "Green Room" diplomacy. The role of the Quad (US, EEC, Japan, and Canada) in the Uruguay Round negotiations (1986–94) is reflective of this process. At the same time, the gap between the capacities of developed and developing economies remained a key aspect of the capitalist system.

The rise of the Southern economies in the post-Cold War era complicated the governance of global trade in new ways. The launch of the Doha Development Agenda (DDA) in 2001 was a result of both the collective resistance of developing countries to Western agendas and the ability of leading economies such as the US and the EU to devise new negotiating platforms. The new round promised to deliver development across the global South, but it soon became apparent that emerging economies did not necessarily share the same challenges as other less-developed countries (LDCs). The BRICS economic phenomenon emerged around 2003 and posed as a new bloc that had the economic capacity and bargaining influence to counter-balance the traditional G7 economies (Schott, 2009). States such as the BRICS were emerging from the margins of the capitalist system and now possessed the bargaining capacity to engage US hegemony, exercise leadership within their respective regions while demanding for greater reform of the Bretton Woods institutional architecture (Hurrell, 2006). The results of such emergence became rapidly evident in WTO negotiations. While new schemes emerged to accommodate emerging economies, such as the G4 in 2005 and the G7 in 2008, all these processes ended up in deadlock. The July 2008 collapse in Geneva is an illustrative case (Blustein, 2008). Repeated deadlocks eventually meant that the DDA negotiations were scaled down to specific packages for LDCs, with the major established and emerging economies seeking new ways to revitalize negotiations. The rise of regional trade agreements and the increasing complexity of the negotiating agenda itself also contributed to the weakening of trade multilateralism (Jones, 2010).

It is in this context that the rise of China in the global trade regime of the capitalist system can be understood. For many years, China's rise was "hidden" within the collective stance of the BRICS where some states, such as Brazil and India were often more vocal than China in their criticisms against Western economic practices (Hopewell, 2015). For the first decade of the DDA negotiations, it was mostly Brazil and India that exerted leadership of the global South and assumed the role of representing the interests of developing countries (Efstathopoulos, 2012; Hurrell & Narlikar, 2006). China joined the WTO in 2001 and for the first decade of its WTO membership it mostly focused on re-adjusting its international trade policy within the legal system of the WTO, while pooling resources with other more experienced states such as Brazil and India, which were original GATT members since 1947. Coalition building often served as the primary platform for such forms of collaborations, with notable examples including the G20 coalition of developing country agricultural exporters and the G33 of developing country food importers (Narlikar & Tussie, 2004), with China being a leading member of both groups. Therefore, China's negotiating stance during the first decade of its WTO membership was mostly seen as an integral part of the collective stance of emerging economies.

China's own narrative of peaceful rise and then peaceful development also contributed to such perceptions (Qingguo, 2005).

Such developments also contributed to shaping how China's role in the developing world could be understood. In the earlier years of the DDA, the common interests amongst different emerging economies were understood as mostly developmental and trade related. The politicization of trade negotiations was essentially a product of historical grievances regarding North–South negotiations and chronic problems like unequal access to markets, the lack of inclusion of developmental issues into the WTO agenda, and the problematic implementation of existing agreements in ways that did not benefit all developing countries (Drahos, 2003). In this respect, China was seen as having common challenges with major developing countries like Brazil, India, Indonesia, and Turkey in terms of importing and exporting policies, while it was also acknowledged that such emerging economies were using veto diplomacy and coalitions of developing countries (such as the G20 and the G33) as platforms for projecting their authority at the multilateral level (Heldt, 2017). Emerging economies sought to re-balance decision-making processes in international institutions, and such prospect of reform was integral to most emerging economies' trade diplomacy, including China. States such as the BRICS were often perceived as "difficult," "irrational," and "irresponsible stakeholders" (Patrick, 2010). However, there was still belief, especially amongst liberals, that in the long run emerging economies would eventually integrate to the capitalist system because of their open-market policies and because the capitalist system was facilitating their economic rise and accommodating their demands (Ikenberry, 2009, 2010). In such systemic context, China's rise was to be understood as an integral part of the "rise of the rest" rather than as a revisionist force in its own right (see for example Zakaria, 2008).

Such perceptions gradually changed under the two Obama administrations, and especially the second one (2012–2016), and, even more rapidly, under the Trump administration (2016–2020). China's greater assertiveness during the 2008–2009 global financial crisis and the belief that China's rise was facilitated by the economic problems (like debt) affecting the Western economies, triggered a re-adjustment of US trade policy (Zhao, 2012). The policy of the second Obama administration, understood as a "Pivot to Asia", entailed establishing plurilateral trade agreements with US allies, such as the Trans-Pacific Partnership (TPP), in order to contain China's economic impact across the Indo-Pacific and create a new set of advanced trade rules that China would be forced to accept at the WTO level (Allee & Lugg, 2016). China promoted its own projects of institution building, with major initiatives such as the One Belt–One Road (OBOR) and the Asian Investment Infrastructure Bank (AIIB) aiming to expand China's circle of economic partners in Asia while containing US presence in the region (Cai, 2018). Since US and Chinese approaches to economic multilateralism allowed for broader participation, it could be argued that despite increased competition and mutual mistrust, the policies of re-balancing allowed for the maintenance of a cooperative relationship (Zhao, 2012).

The Trump administration accelerated economic competition between the US and China and marginalized the option of cooperation with China. The trade wars launched under President Trump have largely redefined bilateral relations between the two leading economies and have affected the stability of the capitalist system. The trade war started in 2018 when the Trump administration initiated an additional tariff of 25% on many goods imported from China and led to further rounds of tariff additions. China retaliated to US tariffs in a proportional way. The Phase One Agreement, signed in 2020, offered a way towards settlement but was quickly disrupted by new tensions, especially because of the outbreak of Covid-19 that further added to US–China frictions. Overall, US tariffs and Chinese counter-tariffs have affected half of US–China bilateral trade, and the Phase One agreement signed in January 2020 has not changed this trend given the wide tariff mechanisms that are now operationalized by both parties (Bown, 2021). Most importantly, the trade wars reflect a deeper, underlying process of undermining the ideational foundations of the capitalist system and key regimes like the WTO system, where a shift to economic revisionism and neo-mercantilism can be identified in both the US and China (Drezner, 2019).

The launch of trade wars reflects the now established perception in the US that China is a threat. Rather than viewing China as a member of developing country coalitions that share the same worldviews and interests, US trade policymakers now understand that China is a major threat to the capitalist system, and in this respect, a major obstacle to progress in WTO negotiations. The case of agricultural subsidies demonstrates this change. The issue was initially framed as a North–South negotiation that was politicized due to notions of justice and fairness but has been re-framed in recent years as an US–China conflict, where China has emerged as the world's largest subsidizer and the US seeks to tackle China's unfair agricultural policies (Hopewell, 2019). The same pattern emerges in other areas of trade like manufacturers. The sources of the conflict derive from trade flows but are also aggravated by the process of power transition that is now seen as imminent in the US and where China is understood to be manipulating trade to accelerate such transition.

The reasons for the outbreak of US–China trade wars are therefore multiple. It has been noted that the trade imbalance between the US and China, domestic political factors in the US (such as the midterm elections), and the rivalry over global economic governance are all key factors (Chong & Li, 2019). Additional reasons include US attempts to target China's industrial policy, and especially its subsidy, technology transfer, and intellectual property policies, which China promotes through projects such as Made in China 2025, and US efforts to alleviate the perceived negative effects on US economy in terms of employment and welfare (Qiu et al., 2019). Political considerations of national security strongly affect the US stance, and major policy areas such as the exchange rate imbalance and bilateral investment flows are perceived as a zero-sum game where retaliation rather than settlement is the best approach (Liu & Woo, 2018). The official rhetoric of US governments towards China has also shaped domestic US perceptions that now view the use of trade wars as an acceptable measure even if simultaneously there is continuous belief that US–China trade can be mutually beneficial (Jin et al., 2022). Overall, US perceptions about China's unfair economic practices combined with considerations of power projection appear to have decisively shifted opinion in the US foreign policy establishment towards a confrontational strategy that can be more effective in shielding US primacy in the capitalist system.

The effects of the trade wars have also been the focus of numerous analyses. Analyses vary on whether it is the US or China that suffers the greater costs, but they agree on the fundamental point that in purely economic terms both parties suffer losses, and reciprocal trade liberalization continues to entail greater benefits than trade retaliation (see for example Archana, 2020; Li et al., 2018). While US imports from China have been diverted to other markets (Germany, Japan, Mexico) and China's imports from the US have also been diverted to other economies (such as Argentina, Brazil, Canada, Germany, Japan, the UK), trade diversion has not been sufficient to cover for revenue losses in the sectors of machinery and electrical products (for the US), and soybeans and automobiles (for China) (Tu et al., 2020). The potential intensification of the US–China trade war in the next decade can not only cause loss of GDP for the US and China (estimated at −1.35 and − 1.41%, respectively), but also affect global GDP that can decrease by −$450 billion when global value chains are accounted for (Itakura, 2020). China has been forced to re-evaluate its domestic economic policies to consider how institutional reforms and high-quality economic growth can be maintained in the face of continuous external pressure by the US (Liu, 2020). Chinese firms have also had to re-adjust their trade policy in the face of increased uncertainty because of higher tariffs (Benguria et al., 2022).

The trade wars are inextricably linked to the need to maintain US technological leadership in the capitalist system. While US national security strategies were marked by a considerable delay in countering China's technological challenge (compared to the urgency of countering the Soviet Union and Japan in the second half of the twentieth century), economic statecraft is now re-emerging as a principal tool of great power rivalry and aims to retain US primacy in critical sectors, such as semiconductors, and generate numerous projects that enjoy bipartisan support and aim to reverse the offshoring of US industrial capacity (Weiss, 2021). The Trump administration's aggressive stance has exposed China's weaknesses in the development of critical technology (such as semiconductor manufacturers), has exerted greater pressure on China's economy and has redefined the US–China relationship as an inherently competitive one (Yang, 2021). However, the shift to competition is not merely a result of Trumpism but reflects rising concerns across the US foreign policy establishment about China's capacity to access the economic benefits of the capitalist system, like trade, investment, and technology, while rejecting the democratic norms that many capitalist states uphold (Lukin, 2019). The intensity and determination of US retaliation has surprised China's leadership that maintained that the US would always favor restraint and interdependence. China has therefore underestimated US willingness to use protectionist measures to halt China's rise at a current historical juncture where the US is still in the leading position in the capitalist system (ibid).

The new Biden administration now faces the task of managing this reality. After assuming office in January 2021, the Biden administration showed no urgency in dismantling existing tariffs that remained in place and maintained that China would have to buy an additional $200 billion of US products (Hsu, 2021). The Biden administration also announced it would review in detail trade and investment policies towards China, although the trade war was soon affected by the outbreak of the Covid-19 pandemic. By September 2021, the Biden administration had not formulated yet a comprehensive trade policy towards China as the issue was under review, and the timeline of the policy is not yet to be finalized or published, according to current USTR Katherine Tai (Kaplan & Rappeport, 2021). Recalibrating US trade policy is a balancing act as the Biden administration seeks, on the one hand, to maintain pressure on China in order to bring it at the negotiating table and enforce the deals struck under Trump (such as the Phase One deal), while, on the other hand, exempting US companies from duties and other economic costs (Leonard, 2021). Such recalibration, however, also entails a broader reassessment of the political and economic objectives of the US in the capitalist system. As with the previous two administrations, the Biden administration continues to view trade with China through the lenses of great power transition and competition (a view also shared by both the Democratic and Republican parties), and this continues to make issues such as the trade deficit, bilateral investment, and intellectual property being interpreted as economic problems caused by China's malpractices (Huang, 2021).

The emergence of trade wars does not necessarily signify the breakdown of the global trading system, but it can mark a shift to a new phase of international economic relations in the capitalist system. It has been argued that a system of "competitive coexistence" and "managed great-power competition" now comprises the most realistic bilateral relationship as the US and China formally list issues of disagreement and gradually provide minor adjustments and incremental benefits to each other (Yang, 2021). Nevertheless, the shift to an increasingly competitive relationship, which has been accelerated due to the turmoil triggered by the Covid-19 (Wang & Sun, 2021), demands a new type of international politics for global trade negotiations. This is especially the case as trade wars redefine not only relations between major powers, but also affect the economies of middle powers that may benefit from trade diversion and higher revenues but also experience adverse effects like income inequality (Nugroho et al., 2021). The next section focuses on this dimension to examine how different middle powers, and in particular in Asia, re-adjust their economic diplomacies in order to respond to the threats and challenges generated by US–China economic competition. Such re-adjustment is deemed imperative if middle powers are to enhance their policy-making autonomy in the capitalist system.

3 The Challenges for Middle Powers

The gradual emergence of US–China trade wars raises important dilemmas for both the Western and Southern middle powers. Middle powers have historically acted as conservative agents, seeking to benefit from stability and predictability in the capitalist system while occasionally assuming diplomatic initiatives to restore these conditions when there is a possibility or threat of systemic destabilization. Liberal Western economies like Australia and Canada historically maintained the overriding goal of maintaining the stability of the capitalist system, and through such stability promote their own roles as committed multilateralists and international bridge-builders in key areas like agricultural trade negotiations (Cooper, 1997). The Nordic middle powers also sought to project their humane internationalism and act as bridge-builders in the North–South development dialogue of the 1970s and 1980s in a way that helped open channels of deliberation and negotiation between opposing regional blocs, while diffusing greater polarization that threatened to destabilize the capitalist system (Pratt, 1990). Such cases show that middle power activism on humanitarian grounds raises expectations that it is possible for the international community to engage in consensus-building and dialogue in order to negotiate solutions to global problems. Such a process leads the dissatisfied and deprived members of the capitalist system, such as less-developed countries, to be persuaded that the international community is governed by ethical obligations that allow for gaining valuable concessions (Lovbraek, 1990, pp. 43, 47–48). The key point here is that middle powers may be aligned to major economies like the US but may also provide co-leadership when necessary to support the existing capitalist system. As Cox noted with regards to the case of Japan at the end of the 1980s, middle powers have historically "attached primacy to institutionalizing regularity and predictability, within which their own interests and those of their populations could be pursued in a semblance of order and tranquility" (Cox, 1989, p. 243). This is a role where crisis-management is essential for neutralizing conditions that threatened system stability and where projecting altruism shows that cosmopolitan norms and values, rather than the narrow interests of the hegemon and its allies, govern the capitalist system (Neufeld, 1995).

In the post-Cold War period, the intermediate category of middle powers expanded to include Southern powers, such as Brazil, India, and South Africa. The Southern powers that adopted middle power internationalism could be understood as essentially abolishing transformative agency to become stabilizers and legitimizers of neoliberalism and the socio-economic forces of globalization (Jordaan, 2003). Middle power internationalism was in itself the product of the shift for these states from Third World radicalism (as reflected in previous initiatives such as the Non-Aligned Movement and the New International Economic Order) to a more reformist approach that sought to promote change from within, but not challenge the core norms of the capitalist system (Alden & Vieira, 2005). Middle power internationalism comprised a loose and flexible foreign policy discourse that allowed for addressing different audiences domestically and internationally and allowed for managing the contradictions between seeking a developmental policy space while adhering to neoliberal norms (Van Der Westhuizen, 1998). Adopting middlepowermanship could be the result of political choices as key governments in the global South (like the African National Congress in South Africa after 1994) accepted the inevitability of globalization and sought to take advantage of existing opportunities in order to attain a higher international status, and ideally be accepted as equal partners by the West. Middlepowermanship could equally be linked to the fragile process of economic development that realistically meant that certain Southern powers could mostly advance their interests through participation in existing neoliberal organizations like the WTO and the World Bank. Compared to traditional Western middle powers, the Southern states had a greater legitimizing potential. As developing countries and representatives of regions of the global South, as well as pivotal actors in regimes like trade, the Southern middle powers were ideally suited to diffuse liberalism in their regions and act as liberal models for other developing states. Such view of the Southern middle powers seemed perfectly in tune with the euphoria of the immediate post-Cold War period about the spreading of liberal values beyond the West. The resurgence of US hegemony post-1991 allowed for assigning follower status to pivotal states in the developing world that would contribute to the stability and economic development of their regions (Chase et al., 1996).

While the Southern powers that assumed middle power internationalism were initially expected to act as key partners for the US and the capitalist system, it gradually became apparent that certain states, such as the BRICS, sought a more independent approach as they enhanced their economic growth and capacity. States like Brazil and India emerged as vocal critics of the Western economies and took a combative stance to re-negotiating key agreements such as the Doha Development Agenda (Hurrell & Narlikar, 2006). Such actions appeared to vindicate those sceptics who saw these states as failing to demonstrate the degree of international responsibility needed for joining the capitalist system (Patrick, 2010). Even though such assertiveness did not amount to outright revisionism or counter-hegemony, it was sufficient in some cases to disrupt the functioning of neoliberal institutions like the WTO (Hopewell, 2016). This meant that the moderate approach of a middle power and the increasing assertiveness of an emerging power were effectively seen (and practiced) as incompatible objectives. Such collapse of expectations is of course not simply evident in the case of middle powers but is part of a broader burst of the "hype" surrounding the "rise of the rest," at least in the eyes of the West. It now becomes apparent that it was rather optimistic to expect development and democratization to advance rapidly across the non-Western world and "produce" key partners for the US and the West (Zarakol, 2019).

Today, both the Western and Southern middle powers are in a position of uncertainty, striving to secure their position in the capitalist system in the face of US–China trade wars. Such uncertainty reflects a degree of disorder in foreign policy as middle powers lack a strategic plan and vision to navigate the US–China trade wars and are therefore exposed to economic pressures and costs that derive from US–China competition. However, the argument presented here is that despite economic pressures and degrees of dependency, middle powers can (depending on the case) carve and maintain a meaningful degree of autonomy that secures their economic interests and even influences the choices of the US and China. Middle powers are re-evaluating their options vis-à-vis the US and China to either collaborate more closely with one of these two economic powers or to gain greater space for strategic autonomy where they reduce their dependence on either the US or

China. It would therefore be a simplification to argue that middle powers' roles are reduced to merely reacting to US–China competition, lacking any real agency in the capitalist system.

In this respect, the first key point that can be observed in the academic literature is that middle powers, both Western and Southern, have a potential to support and revitalize key regimes of the capitalist system such as the multilateral trading system. It has been noted that the current crisis of the capitalist system and its liberal institutions is caused by its expansion to include a greater number of states with diverse interests, views, and preferences, therefore causing the loss of the cohesion and identity of the Western community (Ikenberry, 2018). However, the system can potentially be revitalized by a broader coalition engulfing both the developed Western and the developing non-Western middle powers, and reallocating rights and responsibility to grant the Southern states greater authority (ibid). The renewal of the capitalist system and its major liberal institutions requires pragmatism and compromise, and middle powers need to actively participate in sustaining a rules-based order that does not depend on major power leadership (Andersen, 2019). For such concerts to emerge, leadership from the Western middle powers is often seen as the catalyst, in contrast to the more uncertain contribution of the Southern middle powers. Leadership can be provided by informal alliances of developed democracies (such as Japan, Germany, the UK, France, Canada, and Australia), which can potentially expand to include non-Western members like South Africa, South Korea, and Brazil (Rachman, 2018). Such alliances could counter the aggressive unilateralism of the US, China, and Russia, defend a rules-based capitalist system, and even create new institutional arrangements that uphold capitalist values (ibid). Informal alliances of like-minded democracies could vary depending on the issue (i.e., WTO reform), but overall, a coordinated campaign of plurilateralism could allow middle powers to protect the capitalist world economy, provided that its members commit to this objective and provide leadership in specific issue-based coalitions (Paris, 2019).

Critics nevertheless point out that the actual diplomatic practices of middle powers, and especially of the Southern middle powers, do not reveal a strong potential towards international economic leadership in the capitalist system. It has been argued in recent years that "hawkish middle powers" such as Brazil are opting for securing their own economic interests through bilateral agreements with major powers like the US, therefore preferring a nationalist rather than internationalist approach (Gowan, 2018). The participation of Southern middle powers in major regimes, such as global trade, is a dilemma. It could dilute the like-mindedness of a diplomatic campaign for multilateralism and reproduce divisions, but also enhance the representativeness and legitimacy of coalitions led by middle power economies (Paris, 2019). Sceptics note that the Southern middle powers that were admitted to multilateral fora such as the G20 and acted as engines of regional economic growth and institution building, now show signs of slow economic reform and reluctance to contribute definitively to the norms and institutions of the capitalist system (Aydin, 2021). Certain Southern middle powers respond to external factors, such as the changing distribution of power and the relative decline of US hegemony, in order to pursue more revisionist than conformist forms of internationalism (Sucu et al., 2021). Middle powers also deal with their domestic processes of change as democratic backsliding may drive certain middle powers, and especially those with conflict-driven political processes (for example Brazil), to change their foreign policy and abandon previous forms of internationalism (Grzywacz & Gawrycki, 2021). Like-minded middle powers also face collective challenges as they are often confined to ad hoc and issue-based diplomacy that has a limited horizon and lacks the level of coordination and institution-building required to modernize the multilateral economic system (Brattberg, 2021). Therefore, the capacity of different middle powers to contribute meaningfully to the revitalization of capitalist system remains unknown and uncertain, and varies considerably from case to case.

Despite the accounts above highlighting the uncertainly of middle powers, there is evidence of middle power leadership across key regimes of the capitalist system like global trade. It can be argued that middle power commitment to economic multilateralism is stronger compared to other areas of multilateralism as access to trade and investment flows is critical, even for Southern middle powers, such as Brazil, that seek to withdraw from certain international commitments (Efstathopoulos, 2021). For Western middle powers like Australia and Canada, foreign policy can be framed in ways that prioritize trade access rather than humanitarian norms, and which consequently frame engagement with major economies like the US and China (Gravelle, 2022). Economic pragmatism therefore comprises a defining aspect of middle power internationalism in the capitalist system. In recent years, Asian middle powers like Japan, Australia, India, South Korea, and Indonesia cooperate to counter China's hegemony and preserve the capitalist system through the negotiation of new initiatives such as the Comprehensive and Progressive Agreement for Trans-Pacific Partnership (CPTPP) and the Regional Comprehensive Economic Partnership (RCEP) (Heydarian, 2018). Large-scale free trade agreements (FTAs) such as the RCEP allow Asian middle powers to manage the upheaval emanating from US–China economic tensions, and create trade fora that contribute to a rules-based trade system and allow for some form of regulation and communication in economic transactions with the major economies (Kimura, 2021).

Such imperatives generate cooperation dynamics not only within groups of Western or Southern middle powers, which was evident in the previous decades, but also between Western and Southern middle powers that converge in their efforts at shaping new forms of regionalism (such as the Quad in the Indo-Pacific) and placing middle power diplomacy at the center of new regional communities (Das, 2021). States such as India and South Korea have increasing economic links with the US and China and experience the pressure of these major economies, but nevertheless maintain a degree of autonomy in their foreign policy choices and deploy hedging strategies to resist being forced to cooperate under US or Chinese terms (Hwang & Ryou-Ellison, 2021). Such states face the prospect of higher economic costs generated by a generalized trade war but can opt for mediating between the US and China and promoting multilateral and regional rules-based solutions, based on dispute-resolution processes and the norms of established regimes like agricultural trade (Jeong & Lee, 2021). To respond to the challenges of US–China heightened tensions, middle powers such as South Korea face the imperative to "bolster" their diplomacy to enhance multilateralism in the Indo-Pacific community through bridge-building initiatives, while promoting partnerships with like-minded states and with fora like ASEAN (Huynh, 2021). In all such initiatives, the responses of Asian middle powers to the US–China rivalry should not be understood as one-dimensional. For example, Australia and Japan have forged a strategic partnership that allows for maintaining alliance with the US while accommodating trade opportunities with China, but also resisting China's economic presence across the Indo-Pacific (Wilkins, 2021).

While there is evidence of convergence in the diplomatic practices of middle powers as such states share the objective of maintaining their autonomy, middle powers may nevertheless opt for different strategies, and variations are evident between different middle powers. The Quad group in the Indo-Pacific has provided Asian middle powers with the institutional means to counter China's rise, but other middle powers like South Korea and Indonesia opt to develop their own distinct policy options for engaging with the liberal institutions of the capitalist system (Jung et al., 2012). Lee (2021, p. 29) has accordingly noted that there are "temperature differences" between middle powers that are like-minded but not necessarily "like-situated." Australia and South Korea, for example, have both faced trade retaliation from China and are both striving to improve and not simply preserve the multilateral trading system, but Australia aligns more clearly with the US and the EU compared to South Korea's preference for equidistance (ibid).

Variations in middle power agency can be a problem in terms of effective coalition building but may also open new paths to co-leadership as different middle powers prioritize activism in different areas. It can be argued that there is now a renewed possibility for new forms of collaboration between the Biden administration in the US and like-minded middle powers, which would not be limited to middle power followership under US leadership but would entail co-leadership where middle powers maintain greater independence and take the lead in specific issues (Brattberg, 2021). Japan's trade diplomacy in the negotiation and conclusion of mega-FTAs (including the CPTPP, RCEP and the EU-Japan Economic Partnership Agreement) shows that middle power leadership is feasible when a middle power state, as in the case of Japan, can chart a third way between the US-favored style of trade liberalization and the Chinese-favored approach of mercantilism, while carrying out domestic reforms that allow for sustainable economic development (Katada, 2021). However, defensive trade strategies are also required. Australia, for example, has been targeted by Chinese trade sanctions when it requested for an independent enquiry on the outbreak of the Covid-19, but such sanctions have enhanced confidence in Australia's trade policy which has maintained export income levels, achieved greater diversification of exports, and received greater political support through the alliance with the US (Xue, 2021). Overall, the path to securing greater autonomy for middle powers in the capitalist system remains an on-going challenge that demands new forms of middle power leadership and the development of new trade strategies that enhance the ability of middle powers to resist the coercive practices of major economies.

4 Conclusion

The emergence of trade wars in recent years has played a catalyst role in re-defining international economic relations in the capitalist system. The increasing competition between the US and China is driven to a considerable extent by new and more aggressive practices in international trade policy, which comprise a key policy tool for different US administrations and which are also proportionately deployed by China. Trade wars are caused by core economic interests, such as market and technology access, but are also linked to strategic and geopolitical criteria that further contribute to trade conflicts. These new conditions in the global trading system also affect different middle powers that strive to maintain security alliances while maximizing economic opportunities in the capitalist system. The pressures exerted by US–China wars have clearly shaped the policy-making options of middle powers, not only in economic but also in foreign policy terms more broadly, as such states are constrained by an increasingly polarized global economy. Nevertheless, there is evidence that some states, such as certain Asian middle powers, retain a degree of autonomy that allows them to promote new forms of trade agreements, such as the CPTPP and the RCEP, while maintaining a commitment to supporting key regional and international institutions of the capitalist system.

References

Alden, C., & Vieira, M. A. (2005). The new diplomacy of the South: South Africa, Brazil, India and Trilateralism. *Third World Quarterly, 26*(7), 1077–1095.

Allee, T., & Lugg, A. (2016). Who wrote the rules for the Trans-Pacific Partnership? *Research & Politics, 3*(3), 205316801665891.

Andersen, L. R. (2019). Curb your enthusiasm: Middle-power liberal internationalism and the future of the United Nations. *International Journal, 74*(1), 47–64.

Archana, V. (2020). Who will win from the trade war? Analysis of the US–China trade war from a micro perspective. *China Economic Journal, 13*(3), 376–393.

Aydin, U. (2021). Emerging middle powers and the liberal international order. *International Affairs, 97*(5), 1377–1394.

Bailin, A. (2005). *From traditional to group hegemony: The G7, the liberal economic order and the core-periphery gap*. Ashgate.

Benguria, F., et al. (2022). Anxiety or pain? The impact of tariffs and uncertainty on Chinese firms in the trade war. *Journal of International Economics, 137*, 103608.

Blustein, P. (2008). The nine-day misadventure of the most favoured nations: How the WTO's Doha Round negotiations went awry in July 2008, *Brookings Institute*. Accessed May 25, 2022, from https://www.brookings.edu/wp-content/uploads/2016/06/1205_trade_blustein.pdf

Bown, C. P. (2021). The US–China trade war and phase one agreement. *Journal of Policy Modelling, 43*(4), 805–843.

Brattberg, E. (2021). Middle power diplomacy in an age of US–China tensions. *The Washington Quarterly, 44*(1), 219–238.

Cai, K. G. (2018). The One Belt One Road and the Asian Infrastructure Investment Bank: Beijing's new strategy of geoeconomics and geopolitics. *Journal of Contemporary China, 27*(114), 831–847.

Chan, S. (2021). Challenging the liberal order: The US hegemon as a revisionist power. *International Affairs, 97*(5), 1335–1352.

Chase, R., Hill, E., & Kennedy, P. (1996). Pivotal states and US strategy. *Foreign Affairs, 75*(1), 33–51.

Chong, T. T. L., & Li, X. (2019). Understanding the China–US trade war: Causes, economic impact, and the worst-case scenario. *Economic and Political Studies, 7*(2), 185–202.

Cooper, A. F. (1997). *In between countries: Australia, Canada, and the search for order in agricultural trade*. McGill-Queen's University Press.

Cox, R. W. (1989). Middlepowermanship, Japan, and future world order. In R. W. Cox & T. J. Sinclair (Eds.), *Approaches to world order* (pp. 241–275). Cambridge University Press.

Das, S. (2021). Middle power cooperation in the Indo-Pacific: India and Australia at the forefront. *International Studies, 58*(4), 513–529.

Drahos, P. (2003). When the weak bargain with the strong: Negotiations in the World Trade Organization. *International Negotiation, 8*(1), 79–109.

Drezner, D. W. (2019). Counter-hegemonic strategies in the global economy. *Security Studies, 28*(3), 505–531.

Efstathopoulos, C. (2012). Leadership in the WTO: Brazil, India and the Doha development agenda. *Cambridge Review of International Affairs, 25*(2), 269–293.

Efstathopoulos, C. (2021). Southern middle powers and the liberal international order: The options for Brazil and South Africa. *International Journal, 76*(3), 384–403.

Gravelle, T. B. (2022). Framing middle power foreign policy: Trade, security, and human rights frames in Canadian and Australian foreign policy attitudes. *International Relations of the Asia-Pacific, 22*(1), 101–130.

Grzywacz, A., & Gawrycki, M. F. (2021). The authoritarian turn of middle powers: Changes in narratives and engagement. *Third World Quarterly, 42*(11), 2629–2650.

Gowan, R. (2018, 5 November). Rather than saviors, are middle powers like Brazil a threat to multilateralism? *World Politics Review*. Accessed July 19, 2019, from https://www.worldpoliticsreview.com/articles/26677/rather-than-saviors-are-middlepowers-like-brazil-a-threat-to-multilateralism

Heldt, E. (2017). Shaping global trade governance rules: New powers, hard and soft strategies of influences at the WTO. *European Foreign Affairs Review, 22*, 19–36.

Helleiner, E. (2010). A Bretton Woods moment? The 2007–2008 crisis and the future of global finance. *International Affairs, 86*(3), 619–636.

Heydarian, R. J. (2018, 24 October). Middle powers step up in Asia, *China-US Focus*, Accessed July 19, 2019, from https://www.chinausfocus.com/foreign-policy/middle-powers-step-up-in-asia

Hopewell, K. (2015). Different paths to power: The rise of Brazil, India and China at the World Trade Organization. *Review of International Political Economy, 22*(2), 311–338.

Hopewell, K. (2016). *Breaking the WTO: How emerging powers disrupted the neoliberal project*. Stanford University Press.

Hopewell, K. (2019). US–China conflict in global trade governance: The new politics of agricultural subsidies at the WTO. *Review of International Political Economy, 26*(2), 207–231.

Hsu, S. (2021, 3 March). The US–China trade war is still happening, *The Diplomat*. Accessed Sep 15, 2021, from https://thediplomat.com/2021/03/the-us-china-trade-war-is-still-happening/

Huang, Y. (2021, 16 September). *The U.S.–China trade war has become a cold* war, *Carnegie endowment for international peace*. Accessed Mar 23, 2019, from https://carnegieendowment.org/2021/09/16/u.s.-china-trade-war-has-become-cold-war-pub-85352

Hurrell, A. (2006). Hegemony, liberalism and global order: What space for would-be great powers? *International Affairs, 82*(1), 1–19.

Hurrell, A., & Narlikar, A. (2006). A new politics of confrontation? Brazil and India in multilateral trade negotiations. *Global Society, 20*(4), 415–433.

Huynh, T. S. (2021). Bolstering middle power standing: South Korea's response to U.S. Indo-Pacific strategy from trump to Biden. *The Pacific Review*, advance online publication, 1.

Hwang, W., & Ryou-Ellison, H. J. (2021). Taking a side between the United States and the People's Republic of China: Strategic hedging of South Korea and India. *International Area Studies Review, 24*(2), 60–78.

Ikenberry, G. J. (2009). Liberal internationalism 3.0: America and the dilemmas of liberal world order. *Perspectives on Politics, 7*(1), 71–87.

Ikenberry, G. J. (2010). The liberal international order and its discontents. *Millennium, 38*(3), 509–521.

Ikenberry, G. J. (2018). The end of the liberal international order? *International Affairs, 94*(1), 7–23.

Itakura, K. (2020). Evaluating the impact of the US–China trade war. *Asian Economic Policy Review, 15*, 77–93.

Jeong, B., & Lee, H. L. (2021). US–China commercial rivalry, great war and middle powers. *International Area Studies Review, 24*(2), 135–148.

Jin, Y., Dorius, S., & Xie, Y. (2022). Americans' attitudes toward the US–China trade war. *Journal of Contemporary China, 31*(133), 17–37.

Johnston, A. I. (2019). China in a world of orders: Rethinking compliance and challenge in Beijing's international relations. *International Security, 44*(2), 9–60.

Jones, K. (2010). *The Doha blues: Institutional crisis and reform in the WTO*. Oxford University Press.

Jordaan, E. (2003). The concept of a middle power in international relations: Distinguishing between emerging and traditional middle powers. *Politikon, 30*(2), 165–181.

Jung, S. C., Lee, J., & Lee, J. Y. (2012). The Indo-Pacific strategy and US alliance network expandability: Asian middle powers' positions on Sino-US geostrategic competition in Indo-Pacific region. *Journal of Contemporary China, 30*(127), 53–68.

Kaplan, T., & Rappeport, A. (2021, September 1). Businesses push Biden to develop China trade policy, *The New York Times*.

Katada, S. N. (2021, 18 February). *RCEP is concluded and the middle powers carry the torch, Australian institute of international affairs*. Accessed Jan 20, 2022, from https://www.internationalaffairs.org.au/australianoutlook/rcep-is-concluded-and-the-middle-powers-carry-the-torch/

Kimura, F. (2021). RCEP from the middle powers' perspective. *China Economic Journal, 14*(2), 162–170.

Lee, S. W. (2021, October–December, 28-30). Middle power conundrum amid US–China rivalry, *East Asia Forum Quarterly*.

Leonard, J. (2021, 10 September). Biden team weighs China trade probe in bid to press Beijing', *Bloomberg*. Accessed Sep 15, from https://www.bloomberg.com/news/articles/2021-09-10/biden-team-weighs-china-trade-probe-in-bid-to-pressure-beijing

Li, C., He, C., & Lin, C. (2018). Economic impacts of the possible China–US trade war. *Emerging Markets Finance and Trade, 54*(7), 1557–1577.

Liu, K. (2020). China's policy response to the China US trade war: An initial assessment. *The Chinese Economy, 53*(2), 158–176.

Liu, T., & Woo, W. T. (2018). Understanding the U.S.–China trade war. *China Economic Journal, 11*(3), 319–340.

Lovbraek, A. (1990). International reform and the like-minded countries in the North–South dialogue 1975–1985. In C. Pratt (Ed.), *Middle power internationalism: The North-South dimension* (pp. 25–68). McGill-Queen's University Press.

Lukin, A. (2019). The US–China trade war and China's strategic future. *Survival, 61*(1), 23–50.

Narlikar, A., & Tussie, D. (2004). The G20 at the Cancun ministerial: Developing countries and their evolving coalitions in the WTO. *The World Economy, 27*, 947–966.

Neufeld, M. (1995). Hegemony and foreign policy analysis: The case of Canada as middle power. *Studies in Political Economy, 48*, 7–29.

Nugroho, A., Widyastutik, I. T., & Amaliah, S. (2021). Does the US–China trade war increase poverty in a developing country? A dynamic general equilibrium analysis for Indonesia. *Economic Analysis and Policy, 71*, 279–290.

Paris, R. (2019, 18 June). *Can middle powers save the liberal world order?* Chatham House Briefing. Accessed July 29, 2019, from https://www.chathamhouse.org/publication/can-middle-powers-save-liberal-world-order

Patrick, S. (2010). Irresponsible stakeholders? The difficulty of integrating rising powers. *Foreign Affairs, 89*(6), 44–53.

Pratt, C. (1990). Middle power internationalism and global poverty. In C. Pratt (Ed.), *Middle power internationalism: The North–South dimension* (pp. 3–24). McGill-Queen's University Press.

Qingguo, J. (2005). Peaceful development: China's policy of reassurance. *Australian Journal of International Affairs, 59*(4), 493–507.

Qiu, L. D., Zhan, C., & Wei, X. (2019). An analysis of the China–US trade war through the lens of the trade literature. *Economic and Political Studies, 7*(2), 148–168.

Rachman, G. (2018, 28 May). *Mid-sized powers must united to preserve the world order, Financial Times.*

Ruggie, J. G. (1982). International regimes, transactions, and change: Embedded liberalism in the postwar economic order. *International Organization, 36*(2), 379–415.

Schott, J. J. (2009). America, Europe, and the new trade order. *Business and Politics, 11*(3), 1.

Scobell, A. (2021). Constructing a U.S.–China rivalry in the Indo-Pacific and beyond. *Journal of Contemporary China, 30*(127), 69–84.

Sucu, A. E., Safranchuk, I., Nesmashnyi, A., & Iskandarov, Q. (2021). Transformation of middle powers with the decline of world hegemony: The case of Turkey. *Strategic Analysis, 45*(4), 307–320.

Tu, X., Du, Y., Lu, Y., et al. (2020). US–China trade war: Is winter coming for global trade? *Journal of Chinese Political Science, 25*, 199–240.

Van Der Westhuizen, J. (1998). South Africa's emergence as a middle power. *Third World Quarterly, 19*(3), 435–455.

Wang, Z., & Sun, Z. (2021). From globalization to regionalization: The United States, China, and the post-Covid-19 world economic order. *Journal of Chinese Political Science, 26*, 69–87.

Weiss, L. (2021). Re-emergence of great power conflict and US economic statecraft. *World Trade Review, 20*(2), 152–168.

Wilkins, T. (2021). Middle power hedging in the era of security/economic disconnect: Australia, Japan, and the special strategic partnership. *International Relations of the Asia-Pacific, 2021*, lcab023.

Xue, Y. (2021). *China's economic sanctions made Australia more confident,* 22 October, *The Lowy Institute*. Accessed Feb 8, 2022, from https://www.lowyinstitute.org/the-interpreter/china-s-economic-sanctions-made-australia-more-confident

Yang, X. (2021). US–China crossroads ahead: Perils and opportunities for Biden. *The Washington Quarterly, 44*(1), 129–153.

Yeung, E. S. F., & Quek, K. (2022). Relative gains in the shadow of a trade war. *International Organization, 1–25*, online first.

Zakaria, F. (2008). The future of American power: How America can survive the rise of the rest. *Foreign Affairs, 87*(3), 18–43.

Zarakol, A. (2019). 'Rise of the rest': As hype and reality. *International Relations, 33*(2), 213–228.

Zhao, S. (2012). Shaping the regional context of China's rise: How the Obama administration brought back hedge in its engagement with China. *Journal of Contemporary China, 21*(75), 369–389.

On Economic Security and the Political Economy of Neocolonialist Capitalism: The Case of France and Niger's Uranium Resources

Murat Yülek, Saim Karabulut, and Ali Osman Karcı

Abstract In the standard depiction of the capitalist economic system, international and domestic trade and production are supposed to be undertaken by small private agents that do not have the power to set prices. In this "idealistic" version of the capitalist system, trade among nations is made competitively, enhancing all sides' welfare. Implied in this, both sides of the exchange feel "economically secure," thus, the trade is "fair." However, in reality, this may not be the case for different reasons, including neocolonialist practices of economically and technologically powerful nations. Neocolonialism leads to economic security issues for weaker nations, that make them a victim of unfair international trade, as the more powerful side of the exchange has the power to set terms. On the other hand, unfair international trade makes the capitalist system vulnerable and possibly unsustainable over the long term. Therefore, this chapter primarily discusses the relationship between economic security and neocolonialism through a case study. Further, it attempts to link these two issues to the sustainability of the capitalist system. To do these, it examines the neocolonialist threat to national security in Niger, a *de jure* independent country, which has been facing inequitable resource outflows to France for decades. Our value chain analysis demonstrates the unfair resource transfer and indicates that Niger receives only 3.2% of the ultimate value-added of the electricity that the French energy firms generate using Niger's raw uranium. This shows that neo-colonial practices lead to critical economic security issues and have an important bearing on the future of the global capitalist economy.

Keywords Economic security · Neocolonialism · Future of capitalism · Nuclear energy · Uranium

M. Yülek (✉) · S. Karabulut · A. O. Karcı
Ostim Technical University, Ankara, Turkey
e-mail: murat.yulek@ostimteknik.edu.tr; saim.karabulut@ostimteknik.edu.tr; aliosman.karci@ostimteknik.edu.tr

A. Ari (ed.), *Capitalism at a Crossroads*, Springer Studies in Alternative Economics,
https://doi.org/10.1007/978-3-031-23257-2_9

1 Introduction

In the classical theory of the capitalist economic system, international and domestic trade and production are supposed to be exercised by competing and small, non-price setting private agents. In this "idealistic" version of the capitalist system, trade among nations is contemplated to be undertaken competitively, earning zero economic profits, and enhancing all sides' welfare. Implied in this, both sides of the exchange feel "economically secure," thus, the trade is "fair." In other words, both sides are assumed to be both politically and economically independent nations.

However, as the uneven distribution of military power jeopardizes the political security of nations, that of economic power jeopardizes their economic security. When they need to extract economic or political gains, economically more powerful nations have even threatened less powerful ones. In the notorious history of classical colonialism that peaked in the nineteenth century, powerful nations exploited the resources of less powerful nations and transferred economic wealth and resources to their mainland through war or gunboat diplomacy. As the colonized countries gained their *de jure* political independence in the twentieth century, this inequitable transfer of economic resources is supposed to have ended. However, neocolonial practices of more powerful nations ensure that the transfer of economic wealth and welfare from economically less-developed nations towards the more powerful ones remains a fact.

In this study, we contemplate this issue as a threat to the economic security of nations. We argue that neocolonialism is an evolved version of colonialism and is closely related to the capitalist economic system. All nations face economic security threats (as they are under broader national security threats). Neocolonialism, in particular, is a major threat to economic security of nations that have not achieved a level of economic development which can help them protect their economic resources taken away from them.

Globalization is a new phase in the evolution of capitalism. It accentuated both threats and opportunities to nations. However, for developing countries, threats are much more significant than opportunities. In other words, the existence of powerful neocolonialist countries threatens the economic security of poorer countries and leads to a transfer of wealth out of the latter. At the above is the nation (or, micro) level. At the international (macro) level, the economic security issues driven by neocolonialism are an important factor in the future course of the capitalist system. The imposition of economic power on weaker nations will lead to uneven unsustainable economic outcomes at the global level.

This chapter discusses these topics around a case study of Niger, a *de jure* independent country, which has been facing inequitable resource outflows to France for decades. France benefits from its economic and technological power to acquire uranium at unfair prices and convert this critical resource into a precious commodity: electricity. In the process, Niger gets a very little share of the overall economic value created from the output, although it provides the most critical production input, the uranium.

In the organization of the chapter, in Sect. 2, we first discuss the concept of economic security in relation to the concept of national security. We then discuss the relationship between colonialism, neocolonialism, and capitalism. We also set the relationship between neocolonialism and economic security under the globalization phase of the evolution of the capitalist system. In Sect. 3, we discuss neocolonialism as a threat to economic security with the experience of Niger's raw uranium exports to France. In Sect. 4, we report our value chain analysis to calculate the share of Niger in the total value received by French firms from the raw uranium acquired from Niger. Section 5 concludes the chapter and provides a discussion on the impact of neocolonialism on the course of capitalism.

2 Capitalism, Colonialism, and Economic Security

In the standard literature, national security policy has been conceptualized as the set of necessary decisions and actions to protect domestic core values (Bock & Berkowitz, 1966; Leffler, 1990). At the outset, national security is mainly limited to military issues; a nation would have to protect itself from foreign invasion.

We start our discussion briefly by reviewing the concept of national security which has been discussed heavily in academic and political circles since the end of World War II. The concept of national security has remained ambiguous. Baldwin (1997, p. 26) argues that this ambiguity was even abused; "No social science concept has been more abused and misused than national security. . . . Careless use and abuse of the concept may have already rendered it useless for everyone but the politicians." According to Buzan (2007), this was on purpose in order to maximize the power of the "military and political elite."

But we need a working definition of national security to further our discussion on economic security. According to a basic classical definition, national security is "the ability of a nation to protect its internal values from external threats" (Sills, 1968; Romm, 1993). Lippmann (1943) argues that "a nation has security when it does not have to sacrifice its legitimate interests to avoid war and is able if challenged to maintain them by war." In parallel, it is the set of necessary decisions and actions to protect domestic core values (Bock & Berkowitz, 1966; Leffler, 1990). At the outset, national security was considered to have largely been limited to military issues; a nation would have to protect itself from foreign invasion.

A related concept discussed in the literature was "national power." The literature has various angles in discussing this matter. An economist, Hirschman (1945), states that mercantilism was a policy aiming to increase national economic power through the accumulation of wealth (primarily gold). Further, "national power at the expense of rival states, on the one hand, and increased wealth, on the other hand, were brought into complete harmony by the doctrine of the balance of payments which led the mercantilists to assume that in its economic relations a nation can increase its wealth only by reducing that of the other nations" (Hirschman, 1945, p. 4). Balance of payment surplus would mean increased inflow and accumulation of species which was seen to be "the" source of national power (see, for example, Thomas Mun's (1989) seventeenth Century Treatise).

More recently, the SARS-CoV-2 pandemic reminded us that biological risks might pose significant security risks whether the source is natural or artificial (adversarial nation developing biological agents). There has been discussion on whether the Covid-19 was originally developed as a bioweapon (Molano, 2020; Kortepeter, 2020). Over time, domestic security was integrated more strongly into the debate. In the US, domestic security was more and more seen as part of national security, especially after the 2001 terrorist attacks on the World Trade Center in New York (Newmann, 2002).

More importantly, new threats were perceived to challenge the broader concept of national security, such as drug trafficking, climate change, and growing dependence on imported oil (Romm, 1993). Romm claims that the US's declining economic competitiveness was a national security issue. Thus, along with Hirschman, Romm's conceptualization of national security contains economic security issues.

3 Discussion on the Concept of Economic Security

More recently, discussions of economics and national security have further converged: military vs. economic war. For example, on October 15, 2019, then US President Donald Trump threatened to destroy the Turkish economy (Burns, 2019) as diplomatic relations between the two countries soured. In Turkey, Trump's statement was recognized as a threat of launching an economic war if Turkey does not comply with the US's demands. Thus, it was an issue of "economic security." Further, in response to the Russo-Ukrainian military conflict, European countries and the US were defined in an economic war (see for example, Varadarajan, 2022).

The foregoing discussion leads one to define national security policy to cover a wide range of threats, including military threats (conventional, chemical, and nuclear), terrorism, artificial or natural biological threats, climate issues, social issues (e.g., drugs), and economic threats. The last one, economic security, appears as a critical part of the overall national security concept. However, economic threats and economic security have not so far received a significant attention (Baldwin & Kapstein, 2020; Illarionov, 1999). Losman (2001), for instance, argues that economic considerations should not be part of resource allocation for national security considerations.

As for national security, economic security is a slippery concept (Cable, 1995, p. 307). Economic security in the traditional view was defined as security from manipulation by other governments that wielded these instruments; insecurity was thus vulnerability to other states (Kahler, 2004, p. 486). On the other hand, globalization, which led to intensified movements of capital, labor and technology, and ideas, has made economic security even more important. This is because, as globalization proceeds, countries become more and more prone to external economic shocks. As Kahler (2004, p. 485) suggests "globalization has produced a redefinition of economic security in light of the risks posed by cross-border networks of non-state actors and by the economic volatility of the new global environment." Further, Kahler (2004) limits new definitions of economic security to a narrowband; first "economic (largely financial) shocks that can undermine economic growth, increase inequality and threaten political stability" and second illicit financial flows emanating from terrorism, crime, or pollution.

Based on the foregoing discussion, for our purposes, a good working definition of economic security at the national level would refer to the nation's ability to independently make its resource allocation decisions at market prices, which would cover the ability to export domestic resources at market prices. Relatedly, Investopedia (2022) argues that "economic security refers to a country's ability to pursue its own developmental goals, and it is often explicitly linked to national security. This encompasses broad concerns about the balance of trade, impacts of foreign investments on national markets, and private-public partnerships." According to Horrigan et al. (2008), "one general definition of economic security might be the ability of a nation-state to obtain through production or fair trade those goods and services it needs in order to preserve its national security." Studies of economic security policy would focus, therefore, on how a state uses economic mechanisms to maintain territorial integrity, meet citizen demands for goods and services, preserve political and cultural independence, and achieve freedom from the threat of foreign military assault.

4 Political Independence and Colonialism

This takes us to the concept of political independence, which is closely linked to national security and territorial integrity. The notion of political independence covers the non-material elements of state sovereignty and power, namely the freedom of political decision-making and the direction of state organs in respect of the internal and international affairs of a state (Rozakis, 1987). The United Nations Charter, Art. 2(4) reads "Members shall refrain in their international relations from the threat or use of force against the territorial integrity or political independence of any state, or any other manner inconsistent with the Purposes of the United Nations."

In this sense, colonialism has, historically, been a classical breach of independence of colonized nations' political security, but it had economic reasons as its raison d'être. The colonizing nation had the objective of extracting the colonized nation's economic resources and transferring them to its mainland. Colonization was mostly a military phenomenon; the colonizer threatened the colonized nation by military power to overtake the latter's political and economic authorities.

Thus, colonialism led to the *de jure* loss of political independence together with the impoverishment of the colonized peoples as the colonizers attempted to change the economic and social order to one that generated profits for the mainland. Formerly self-sufficient and thriving agricultural regions witnessed famines, and economic collapse as these territories became plantations of cash crops and products under colonizers' commercial strategies who repatriated all the proceeds while relegating indigenous people to slave-workers (see Rodney, 2018; Saravanan, 2008; Gueye, 2018; Bell, 2021; Nally, 2008 among others).

In the twentieth century, all colonized nations gained their *de jure* independence from colonizers. But does this mean that the colonial economic exploitation era is now over? For thinkers such as Sartre, colonization is a continuum over time.[1] In other words, he does not distinguish between "old" colonialism and the "new" (neo) colonialism. However, the two have a major difference; neocolonialism is practiced in politically independent countries, while the "old" colonialism was mostly practiced in countries that lost their political independence.

4.1 The Advent of the Capitalist Economy

How are colonialism and capitalism related? Let us first briefly look at the advent of the capitalist economy. In the Islamic world, merchant capitalism emerged as early in the seventh century (Heck, 2008). Muslim merchants developed the tools of incorporation, which allowed pooling of capital and risks. These forms were subsequently transmitted to Europe (Udovitch, 2011). In Europe, the emergence of merchant capitalism can most reasonably be attributed to around the eleventh century; circa a century after the start of the European Commercial Revolution, which Lopez (1976) places somewhere between the tenth and fourteenth centuries. European merchant capitalism gave way to industrial capitalism after the industrial revolution in the second half of the eighteenth century.

On the other hand, it can be argued that European financial capitalism gained impetus after (i) the invention of the joint-stock company in England and the United Provinces (Netherlands) at the beginning of the seventeenth century, and (ii) the development of Dutch and English capital markets in the seventeenth century (Neal, 1991). So rather than in the traditional Marxist framework, it can be argued that financial capitalism is not a phase that industrial capitalism gave way to. In fact, as Veblen (1904) states, the two are quite different; in industrial capitalism, accumulation is made on manufacturing activity while in financial capitalism it is made on the fruits of the existing financial capital. Braudel (1984) claims that financial capitalism had emerged in Genoa in the sixteenth century and the United Provinces in the seventeenth and eighteenth centuries both from commercial capitalism that it developed.

During the nineteenth century, thus, financial and industrial capitalism developed together though industrial capitalism were much more dominant. No doubt, the

[1] Sartre (1964) criticized French attack and massacres in Algeria, defining it as colonialism attempt without distinguishing it as neocolonialism. For Sartre, colonialism is a time-proof continuum. He argued for France to disengage from its colonial ambitions which was formed by Louis XIV.

twentieth century witnessed a dramatic rise and prevalence of financial capitalism over industrial and merchant capitalism forms.

4.2 Neocolonialism, Capitalism, and Economic Security

A useful definition of neocolonialism is "the current attempts (actual or alleged) of the developed countries to dominate and control the 'emerging' states (as well as all other economically underdeveloped countries), chiefly through economic rather than military or purely political means" (Fatouros, 1965, pp. 714–715). For Sartre, the (neo-) colonialism is a form of capitalist exploitation. This is also the view of Marxist literature (Brewer, 2002). Marx underlined that the rise of the industrial capitalism was enabled by "primitive accumulation" [grabbing lands, natural resources (gold, silver, agricultural produce) and property of the colonized nation by the powerful capitalist nation] and was closely associated with colonization (McIntyre, 2011) and imperialism. Likewise, for Lenin (1917), imperialism is the "Highest Stage of Capitalism."

In the nineteenth century, Marx identified colonial conquest as a capitalist strategy (Naved, 2008, p. 33): "the discovery of gold and silver in America, the extirpation, enslavement, and entombment in mines of an indigenous population of that continent, the beginnings of the conquest and plunder of India, and the conversion of Africa into a preserve of the commercial hunting of black skins, are all things which characterize the dawn of the era of capitalist production. These idyllic proceedings are the chief moments of primitive accumulation" (Marx, 2019, Chap. 31).

Clearly, there is a close association between capitalism and (neo) colonialism. In terms of causality, it is reasonable to agree with McIntyre (2011) who argues that European colonization has preceded capitalism by centuries and thus, capitalism cannot have caused imperialism. According to Nkrumah (1965), "the essence of neocolonialism is that the State which is subject to it is, in theory, independent and has all the outward trappings of international sovereignty. In reality, its economic system and thus its political policy is directed from outside." For him, "neocolonialism of today represents imperialism in its final and perhaps its most dangerous stage."

The above discussion suggests that neocolonialism is an evolved version of colonialism and is closely related to the capitalist economic system. In the case of colonialism, the colonialists breached the political and economic independence of the militarily weaker nation. In the case of neocolonialism, on the other hand, while the *de jure* political independence of the weaker nation is preserved, its economic independence is breached. In other words, neocolonialism is a threat to economic security of economically less-developed nations. Colonialism was more primitive and explicit; neocolonialism is more refined and implicit. In the former, the powerful colonialist takes over the political administration of the weaker nation and subsequently extracts its wealth to the motherland. In the latter, the colonized nation which is *de jure* politically independent loses its resources to the colonizer at submarket prices. Thus, neocolonialism leads to wealth and welfare transfer from less-developed countries to developed countries.

All nations face economic security threats (as they are under broader national security threats). Neocolonialism, in particular, is a major threat to economic security of nations that have not achieved a level of economic development which can help them protect their economic resources taken away from them.

Globalization is a new phase in the evolution of capitalism. It accentuated both the threats and opportunities to nations. For developing countries, the threats are much more significant than opportunities. For example, in a globalized world, the natural resources of the developing countries are easily accessed by the more powerful nations. The latter needs to import natural resources from the developing countries. If fair trade were assured, globalization's offerings would thus be quite beneficial to developing countries. But their underdeveloped state denies them the opportunity to receive full economic compensation.

In other words, the existence of powerful neocolonialist countries threatens the economic security of poorer countries and leads to a transfer of wealth out of the latter. However, economic security (as in the case of national security) and neocolonialism are vaguely defined. A better understanding of the concept and its consequences can, thus, be achieved by using case studies.

4.3 The Neocolonialism and the Future of Capitalism

In the nineteenth century, Marx (2019) underlined the dynamic impact of class struggle in shaping the future of the industrializing European societies. His approach was deterministic in that he believed that the then existing class struggle would lead to the socialist revolution and toppling of capitalism. Note that, we used the verb "believe" to emphasize that Marx did not have a scientific approach as suggested by Popper (2020).

In a globalized capitalist economy, it may be argued that a similar "class" struggle exists between poorer countries and the richer ones that take advantage of their economic power. This could prove a significant dynamic in shaping the future of the world economy and society in the coming decades. The poorer nations will not be able to be patient in losing their resources at prices significantly below opportunity costs.

Thus, there is a close association between the future of neocolonialism and that of capitalism. Unlike in Marxism, it is not reasonable and scientifically acceptable to be deterministic on the neocolonialist trigger of the collapse of the capitalist economic system. However, it is reasonable to expect that the continuation of uneven economic resource transfers will prove to be a major risk to the stability of the capitalist economies.

5 Neocolonialism as a Threat to Economic Security and a Tool of Wealth Transfer: The Case of Niger and France

This section examines the French exploitation of uranium reserves in Niger in the post-colonial era. It is a case study of the neocolonialist threat to Niger's economic security. Colonization is a historical example of a security breach of militarily weaker nations. British and French Empires, among others, colonized a wide range of countries on almost every continent (Harshe, 1980; Laycock, 2012). As a result of the international evolution of capitalism, such colonialist forces created a system of resource exploitation and wealth transfer from colonized nations to their motherland. This led to a systematic impoverishment of those nations as well as enormous amounts of human loss.

In the contemporary world, many of the colonized nations in Africa, Latin America, and Asia have nominally gained their political independence. However, a newer version of politico-economic dominance ensures continued wealth transfer from weaker nations to the stronger Western economies. A good example is Niger, a West African country. Niger's vast uranium resources have been embezzled by a state-owned French company, posing a significant economic security issue. Niger is a low-income country with per capita GDP $550 in 2020. Its economy is primarily rural and agriculture based. Niger also has several minerals and fuels, including uranium, in which Niger has one of the world's largest reserves.

5.1 Background: Niger's History and Economy

5.1.1 The Historical Context

Niger, dubbed as "the frying pan of the world," gained its independence from France in 1960. The Niger River is the origin of the country's name. Niger is the largest country in West Africa and borders seven countries, including Libya, Chad, Nigeria, Benin, Senegal, Mali, and Algeria.

The economy of this Sub-Saharan country is based on subsistence agriculture, livestock, and one of the world's most extensive uranium resources. Niger is one of the poorest countries in the world, despite having a wealth of valuable natural resources.

Present-day Niger originated from the nomadic peoples of the Northern Sub-Saharan region and the settled farmers of the South. When European colonizers arrived in the nineteenth century, the region assembled disparate local kingdoms. The first European explorers, particularly the British and Germans, explored the area in the nineteenth century, looking for the mouth of the Niger River. After agreeing to share the Niger River with the British, France became dominant and created a colonial administration in 1922. Then, in 1960, the country obtained its independence from France, and it was ruled by the military until the beginning of the 1990s (Central Intelligence Agency, 2021).

In the 1990s, Niger faced a painful conflict with the nomadic Tuareg in the north. Several Tuareg insurgent groups emerged, demanding greater autonomy for their territory, and supporting the old but endangered Tuareg culture. In 1995, the government reached a deal with one of the Tuareg tribes on a peace treaty and amnesty. In 1997, the last of them agreed to the conditions of the agreement.

According to the reports, more than 60 thousand Malian migrants fled to Niger after the terrorist attacks. In addition, the UNHCR reported 241 thousand refugees and 300 thousand displaced people (World Bank, 2021). Niger has been troubled by ecological disasters, economic crises, and political instability since its independence in 1960. More recently, a health challenge due to the Covid-19 pandemic deepens country's weaknesses.

The official language is French, and there are eight other languages recognized as national languages (Index Mundi, 2021). The ethnic composition is made up of Hausa 53.1%, Zarma/Songhai 21.2%, Tuareg 11%, Fulani (Peuhl) 6.5%, Kanuri 5.9%, Gurma 0.8%, Arab 0.4%, Tubu 0.4%, other/unavailable 0.9% (Central Intelligence Agency, 2021).

With a 3.8% growth rate in 2021, the country's current population is 26 million. Following South Sudan and Burundi, Niger has the third fastest-growing population. Since the independence of Niger, the country has had three military regimes, seven republics, and two Tuareg rebellions in this composite structure.

The country has one of Western Africa's lowest adult literacy rates. Approximately 70% of the population in Niger is under the age of 25. Only 16.8% of the population lives in urban areas. The infant mortality rate was ranked fourth in the world. Other key issues confronting the nation include inequity in educational chances for women, early marriage, and childbirth. In addition, both the health and welfare of the people are at an all-time low level.

5.1.2 Niger's Economy

The country is the second least developed country globally, and in terms of income classification, it is in the low-income economy category. The country is ranked last in the world on Human Development Index (African Development Bank, 2021). In 2019, Niger was ranked as the 132nd economy in the world in terms of GDP (current USD), 160th in total exports, 167th in total imports, 179th in terms of GDP per capita (current USD). According to the World Bank's "Doing Business" report, Niger ranks 176th among 189 countries globally (OECD, 2019a).

In 2020, the economy grew by 3.6% (13.68 billion USD), accounting for 0.01% of the global GDP. Annual GDP growth in 2021 was 5.5% (approximately 15.6 billion USD), and it is expected to reach 6.2% in 2022.

In 2020, approximately more than ten million people (42.9% of the total population) lived in extreme poverty. Recent gains in combatting poverty are in danger following a 0.2% reduction in per capita income in 2020. On the other hand, the positive economic outlook is predicted to help reduce poverty from 41.2% in 2020 to 37% in 2023. Agricultural products represent 40% of the GDP, which is the

Table 1 Uranium resources by country (2019)

Country	tU	% of world
Australia	1,692,700	%27.5
Kazakhstan	906,800	%14.9
Canada	564,900	%9.2
Russia	486,000	%7.9
Namibia	448,300	%7.3
South Africa	320,900	%5.2
Brazil	276,800	%4.5
Niger	276,400	%4.5
China	248,900	%4.0
Mongolia	143,500	%2.3
Uzbekistan	132,300	%2.2
Ukraine	108,700	%1.8
Botswana	87,200	%1.4
Tanzania	58,200	%0.9
Jordan	52,500	%0.8
US	47,900	%0.8
Other	295,800	%4.8
World Total	**6,147,800**	**%100**

Source: World Nuclear Association (2021)

livelihood of more than 80% of the population. The GDP per capita declined from $563 (2019) to $550 in 2020 (World Bank, 2021).

5.1.2.1 Niger's Uranium Reserves

The world uranium map shows that Australia still dominates the world's uranium resources, accounting for 27.5%. According to the data in 2019, the total world uranium resources are 6,147,800 tU. In this view, Niger ranked eighth with 276,400 tU, which equals 4.5% (see Table 1). As cumulative uranium production, Niger produced 152,352 tU between 1945 and 2020. Global uranium mine production decreased by approximately 11% in 2017 and 2018, while it increased by 1% in 2019. Due to the increasingly stagnant uranium market, major producing countries like Canada and Kazakhstan have reduced their total output. In addition, global pandemic in the early 2020s significantly exacerbated these limits (Nuclear Energy Agency, 2020). Kazakhstan, Canada, and Australia account for more than half of the world's uranium resources. The total amount of the mined uranium resources in the world to date is 3,012,483 tU (seen Table 2).

The global total uranium production in 2020 was 47,731 tU, corresponding to 74% of the world's demand. Kazakhstan produced the largest amount of uranium (40.8% of the global supply). Niger's production peaked at 4116 tU in 2015, then continuously dropped. It produced 2991 tU (6.3%) in 2020, ranking sixth place globally (Table 3) (Nuclear Energy Agency, 2020).

Table 2 Cumulative production on tU (1945–2020)

Country	tU
Kazakhstan/Uzbekistan	542,949
Canada	542,431
USA	374,864
Australia	232,492
Germany	217,161
Russia	176,626
South Africa	165,293
Niger	152,352
Namibia	146,461
Czech Republic	111,214
France	77,015
Ukraine	69,676
China	55,914
Others	148,035
Total	**3,012,483**

Source: World Nuclear Association(2021)

Table 3 Annual Uranium Production (2020)

Country	tU	% of the world
Kazakhstan	19,477	40.8
Australia	6203	13.0
Namibia	5413	11.3
Canada	3885	8.1
Uzbekistan	3500	7.3
Niger	2991	6.3
Russia	2846	5.9
China	1885	3.9
Ukraine	744	1.5
India	400	0.8
South Africa	250	0.5
Iran	71	0.2
Pakistan	45	0.1
Brazil	15	0.03
USA	6	0.01
World Total	**47,731 tU**	**%100**

Source: Nuclear Energy Agency (2020)

5.1.2.2 Niger's International Trade

Niger had a total export of $1.24 billion and total imports of $3.02 billion, leading to a negative trade balance of $1.78 billion in 2020. In 2020, Niger's total uranium exports to the world were worth $285 million (4315 tU). In this context, France is Niger's largest export and import market. Niger's total exports to France were valued at $212 million with 34% of this amount from uranium. In comparison,

Niger's imports from France were valued at $675 million, 22% of its total imports (as seen in Table 4).

As mentioned above, France holds most of the total exported uranium by Niger in 2020. Uranium ores and concentrates, vehicles other than railway-tramway, mineral fuels, oils, distillation products, machinery, nuclear reactors, boilers, pearls, precious stones, metals, and coins are among Niger's top five exported commodities to France (see Table 5).

Niger's total exports of uranium to France amounted to $1.15 billion. However, Niger's uranium exports have been on a declining trend as seen in Fig. 1. The reason for this is that France is diversifying its uranium sources away from Niger. Currently, the other suppliers for France are Australia, Canada, and Kazakhstan. Four countries represent 80–90% of the uranium used in France (Tertrais, 2014). Note also that all uranium extraction in Niger is made by French firms.

6 French Nuclear Energy Policy

Shaped in the 1970s, the French energy policy is based on two pillars (Breteau, 2022). First is the keen interest in achieving energy security. To achieve this, French authorities accord utmost importance to nuclear energy. Having achieved this goal,

Table 4 Niger's exports and imports (2020)

Total uranium exported in 2020				Total share of France in exports		Total share of France in imports	
Country	Value in %	Value in million $	tU	Value in million $	Value in %	Value in million $	Value in %
France	73.5	208.1	3.173	212.4	%34	675,32 Million	%22
Canada	21.3	54.7	921	...	...	...	...
Spain	2.6	11.7	113	...	...	...	...
Japan	2.0	8.9	86	...	...	...	...
Benin	0.5	1.549	22	...	...	...	...
Total	**%100**	**285.1**	**4.315**	...	...	...	...

Source: Trading Economics (2022), International Trade Centre (2022), Republic of Turkey Ministry of Trade (2022) and Nuclear Energy Agency (2020)

Table 5 Niger's Top 5 commodities exported to France (2020)

Commodity	Value in million $
Uranium ores and concentrates	208.1
Vehicles other than railways, tramways	1.71
Mineral fuels, oils, distillation products	1.28
Machinery, nuclear reactors, boilers	0.95
Pearls, precious stones, metals, coins	0.35

Source: United Nations Comtrade Database (2022) and OECD (2019b)

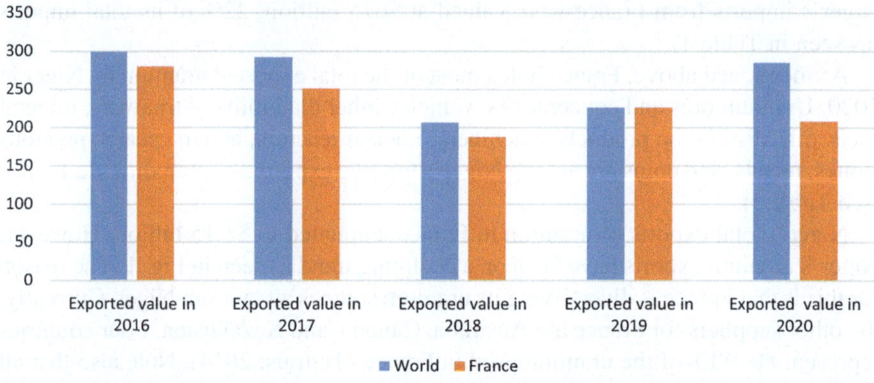

Fig. 1 Niger's uranium exports to France and the World (2016–2020). Source: Trade Map (2022) and UN Comtrade Database (2022)

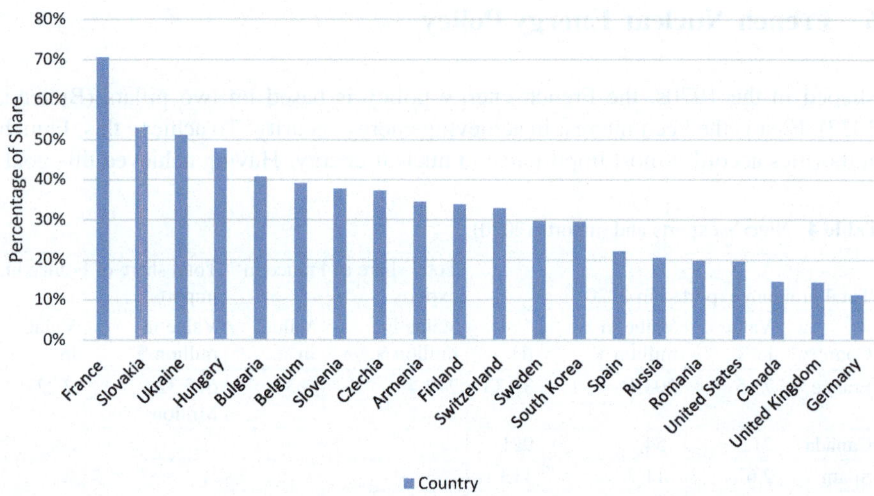

Fig. 2 Share of nuclear power in total energy production (2020). Source: IAEA PRIS Database (2022)

France is the highest in the world, with over 70% in terms of the share of nuclear power in total energy production (see Fig. 2) (World Nuclear Association, 2022). France's second important energy policy is to become an energy exporter, while it was a net importer in the 1970s. Uranium and nuclear energy is the most crucial factor behind this transformation and economic gain. France has now become the world's largest net electricity exporter, and electricity is its fourth-largest export item. Italy and the UK are amongst France's top electricity export markets (World Nuclear Association, 2022). Over the last decade, France has exported up to 70 TWh net each year.

Table 6 Areva and EDF in French Nuclear Energy Production (2012)

	Unit	2012
EDF Sales	Billion Euros	72.7
EDF EBITDA	Billion Euros	16.1
EDF Net Income	Billion Euros	4.2
Share of Areva in EDF electricity sold	%	40–50%
Share of Niger as uranium supplier to Areva	%	40–50%

Source: Authors' calculations based on the data obtained from EDF (2013) and Tertrais (2014)

By 2012, uranium delivered by Areva represented at least 60% of the total needs of EDF. However, with the shift from the EURODIF enriching plant to the new George Besse II enrichment facility, Areva started to supply only around 40% of EDF's uranium acquisitions. Out of the total, 40–50% of Areva's uranium came from Niger by 2012 as seen in Table 6. Thus, in 2012, Nigerien uranium was the source of 20% of EDF's electricity production, according to Tertrais (2014).

Furthermore, Tertrais (2014) argued that "It is true that the total quantity of natural uranium imported by France comes first mostly from Niger (more than 5 tons in 2012) followed by Kazakhstan, Australia, Uzbekistan, and Namibia. But that is because Niger remains an important part of Areva's business as a global company today. Because France also exports uranium (raw and processed), it often imports much more than just the 8 tons a year that are needed for EDF power plants. Thus, from 2006 to 2012, total French imports have ranged from 8 to 14 tons a year."

6.1 French Energy Giant Areva and Its Neocolonialist Operations in Niger

Areva is a multinational corporation based in France and involved in all aspects of the uranium fuel cycle, specializing in nuclear power and renewable energy. The main activities of Areva are uranium mining, enrichment, conversion, fuel recycling, dismantling and engineering, and waste management. It is in the top three companies in terms of mining globally (World Nuclear Association, 2022).

Areva is also involved in military technologies, such as designing the nuclear reactor for the French Barracuda submarine class. The company has a presence in over 30 countries through its subsidiaries and employs more than 19,000 people worldwide (Orano, 2021). Before its corporate restructuring in 2016, Areva was majority-owned by the French state. The structure stands with the French Commission for Alternative Energies and Atomic Energy at 54.4%, Banque Publique d'Investissement at 3.3%, and Agence des Participations de l'Etat at 28.8%. Électricité de France (EDF), where the French state owns a majority stake. The second-largest shareholder after the French state, Kuwait Investment Authority holds 4.8% (European Commission, 2018).

The 2008 financial crisis, the 2011 Fukushima accident, delays in the Olkiluoto-3 nuclear project in Finland, risky acquisitions, corruption, and competition with French energy provider EDF contributed to Areva's rebranding. In 2018, when Areva was renamed Orano, the critics increased due to the company's past scandals. For example, Ali Idrissa, ROTAB Coordinator, stated that "Altering the name should not clear the company and its accomplices from past scandals. The people responsible for the embezzlement must be brought to account and, if necessary, brought to justice" (Tournons La Page, 2020).

Areva's (Now Orano) uranium reserves exist in Niger, Canada, Australia, and Kazakhstan. The company's activities in Niger contain three concessions near Arlit that are run as joint ventures with the Nigerien government's minor partnership and smaller foreign investors. Areva and its subcontractors developed Arlit in the middle of the Sahara Desert to facilitate these operations, and it has a considerable expatriate population. These ventures are SOMAIR and COMINAK.

In addition, Areva had previously obtained a concession in nearby IMOURAREN to augment their production in Niger. However, this project is not activated due to the low-uranium prices. Areva is also under pressure from opening over 100 uranium mining concessions in Niger, primarily to Canadian and Chinese companies. It is also exposed to intense criticism in countries where it operates, especially in Niger. This increasing tension is because of acting as a neocolonialist country and cartel of uranium mines.

Areva remarks that they attach great importance to the environment while carrying out these activities. Moreover, the company claims that its existence significantly contributes to Niger's development. To support this, it is stated that the local people are directly employed in the mines, so the income received is the most significant foreign exchange source for Niger (Orano, 2021). Additionally, it is noted that Areva made a large amount of aid due to the famine in Niger in 2005. However, this aid constituted only 0.05% of Areva's annual profit at that time (Oxfam International, 2014).

In 2008, The Public Eye reported that Areva's work in Niger took place under horrendous conditions and caused radioactive pollution, resulting in the death of many employees. In this vein, the human rights activist group declared Areva as the worst company globally.

EDF, a company that operates as French nuclear power reactors, has made agreements to procure natural uranium from Australia, Canada, Niger, and Kazakhstan: these agreements satisfy about 90% of the demand for 58 French power plants (Tertrais, 2014). In recent years, Areva has provided about 60% of EDF's uranium demand, and 50% of Areva's Uranium is sourced from its mines in Niger.

Recently, Areva's closed mines in the Central African Republic (2012) and one of its mines in Niger (2021) can perhaps be taken as evidence of France's declining influence and control in Africa. However, France's AREVA remains a giant company in the uranium industry. Further, Areva has Africa's largest and the world's second-largest uranium deposit project, "Imouraren" in Niger. Hence, these rumors can also be considered as a communication tool by Areva to negotiate better terms with the government of Niger. Due to the low-market uranium prices and the

Table 7 Orano (2021)

Main activity	Contributing revenue	Employees	Mining sites	Uranium production (2020)
Mining	€1.079 billion	3445	Four mining sites in three countries. (Niger, Canada, Kazakhstan)	6529 tU (the top three of the global market)

Source: Orano (2021)

complex international political conditions, it can be assumed that Areva, in other words, France, may be reanalyzing its overall strategy in Africa.

With 6529 tU produced globally, Areva, known as Orano, is one of the world's biggest uranium producers. In 2020, SOMAIR produced 1879 tU COMINAK produced 1112 tU Cigar Lake produced 3878 tU, and KATCO produced 2833 tU. The company's uranium production locations are in Canada, Niger, and Kazakhstan (see Table 7).

Orano, with its subsidiaries SOMAIR and COMINAK, has extracted 140,000 tU in Niger since its mining activities began. Orano produces enough uranium each year to meet the demands of a country like Spain in terms of power. From the beginning of March 2020, many uranium producers were obliged to reduce, or even interrupt, the activity of their mines due to the Covid-19 pandemic. This drop in uranium supply affected the uranium spot price, which significantly reached $34/lb. at the end of May. During the summer, the improved health situation and the introduction of protective measures by producers allowed the gradual return to regular activity in the fall. The uranium spot price has stabilized around $30/lb. at the end of 2020. The long-term indicator changed slightly during the Covid-19 pandemic to stabilize at $33 at the end of 2020 (compared to $32/lb. at the end of 2019). According to the World Nuclear Association (2022), future projects illustrate that the uranium market is expected to grow, with demand in 2025 predicted to be 17% higher than in 2015.

6.2 The Value of Areva and Niger's Uranium to France

France produces 80% of its electricity consumption from nuclear power plants. However, its local resources are not available to meet the current uranium demand, and it is very costly to extract the extant uranium. In this context, France's need for uranium has made neocolonialism a necessity. Therefore, Paris (especially in the period after the World War II) turned the import of uranium from the French colonies into a suitable form. Furthermore, the oil crisis in 1973 led to power plant projects and thus increased demand for uranium.

In 1976, the French government formed the General Company for Nuclear Materials (COGEMA) in the Atomic Energy Commission's (CEA) production department. Since the cost of domestic production was higher than foreign

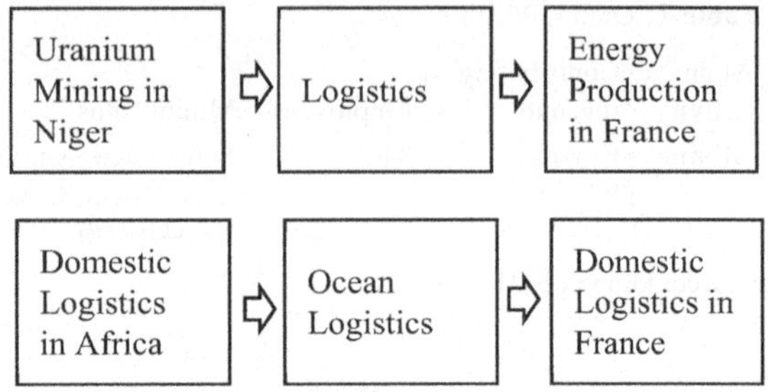

Fig. 3 French nuclear energy value chain and logistics value chain

Table 8 Value of Niger's uranium exports

	2021	1945–2021
Niger's natural uranium exports to		
France (tU) 1/	3173	
The world (tU) 2/		152,352
Electricity produced by Niger's uranium exports to (million kWh) 3/		
France (million kWh)	50,439	
The world (million kWh)		2,421,812
Value of electricity produced by Niger's uranium (until 2020) 4/		
in France (billion $)	8.9	319
in the world (billion $)		434
Niger's export value of raw uranium (million $) 5/	285.1	
Share Niger received from the total value created in France by Niger's raw uranium	3.2%	...

production at that time, COGEMA established Areva in 1983 and 2001 in a two-stage process and incorporated it with other public institutions.

87% of the uranium mined in the Arlit region of the capital Niamey belongs to the French nuclear energy company Areva, which has held the operating rights of uranium in Niger for almost 47 years. The uranium mined here provides nearly a third of France's electrical needs. Therefore, the French government is almost entirely reliant on Niger for the uranium that runs its massive nuclear power system.

Based on the value chain depicted below in Fig. 3, we made a simple analysis of the value generated by France (through the electricity produced by Areva/EDF) and the value received by Niger through exports of raw uranium. In our analysis (as seen in Table 2), Niger exported 152,352 tU of raw uranium globally from 1945 to 2020. Most of these exports were made to France, particularly in earlier years. In 2020, Niger's exports to France amounted to 3173 tU (as seen in Table 4); this represented 73.5% of Niger's total exports of 4315 tU.

As 2021 figures were not available, we inferred they remained the same in 2021. We calculated the electricity equivalent of Niger's raw uranium exports when converted to first U235 isotope and then to electrical energy using theoretical conversion figures. In particular, nuclear fission of 1 kg of U235 yields ca. 19 billion kcal (equivalent to 2700 tU of coal) and a conversion rate of 0.001162 kWh per kcal. For calculating the value of energy produced by Niger's raw uranium, we used mid-2021 market prices per kWh of electricity in France. We assumed half of the energy produced is sold to households and the rest to businesses.

The results of the exercise presented in Table 8 are as follows. At end-user prices (market prices in France), the value of electricity produced by Niger's raw uranium exports to France is calculated as $8.9 billion in France in 2020 (and assumable in 2021), while the country's raw uranium exports (to France) were only $208.1 million in the same year. Between 1945 and 2021, we calculated the value of electricity produced by Niger's raw uranium exports to France as a massive $319 billion and $431 billion to the world. These calculations show that the share received by Niger from the total value creation is only 3.2%. This share does not differ much from other years. So, it can be safely assumed that this is also the share in the cumulative value chain since 1945.

7 Conclusion

Colonialism, along with imperialism, has been an outright breach of the political independence of militarily weaker countries. The colonizers annexed those weaker countries into their colonial empires. A major outcome of the process was a significant wealth transfer from poorer nations to the mainland of the colonial empires.

At the end of the nineteenth century and the beginning of the twentieth century, the colonized nations gained their *de jure* political independence. However, they have not been able to gain economic independence. In the current stage of the evolution of the global capitalist system, neocolonialism is a reality that threatens economically less powerful nations, as demonstrated by Niger's raw uranium transactions with France. Our value chain analysis results indicate that Niger has received only 3.2% of the ultimate value-added electricity that the French energy firms have generated in 2020 using Niger's raw uranium.

France has been able to impose this neocolonialist form of resource transfer in Niger through its economic and technological power rather than its military force. Nevertheless, France has also made military interventions in various African countries when it has considered necessary. All this pose a critical economic security issue for Niger and some other African countries.

Neocolonialist policies pose a significant threat to the economic security of less powerful nations and will continue to have an important bearing on the evolution of capitalism. It leads to unfair resource and welfare transfers in favor of economically and technologically more powerful nations. The uneven and unfair resource allocation will no doubt lead to more questioning of the sustainability of capitalism.

For the least, under the current capitalist world economic order the poorer nations, especially those in Sub-Saharan Africa remain providers of cheap raw materials to the powerful developed countries. This is akin to the Marxist diagnosis of the dynamic impact of class struggle in the industrializing European societies of nineteenth century. Unlike in Marxism, it is not reasonable and scientifically acceptable to be deterministic on the neocolonialist trigger of the collapse of the capitalist economic system. However, it is reasonable to expect that the continuation of uneven economic resource transfers will prove to be a major risk to the stability of the capitalist economic system.

References

African Development Bank. (2021). *Niger economic outlook. African development bank–building today, a better Africa tomorrow*. Retrieved February 3, 2022, from https://www.afdb.org/en/countries-west-africa-niger/niger-economic-outlook

Baldwin, D. A. (1997). The Concept of Security. *Review of International Studies, 23*(1), 5–26. http://www.jstor.org/stable/20097464

Baldwin, D. A., & Kapstein, E. (2020). *Economic Statecraft*. New Edition. Princeton University Press.

Bell, K. (2021). Genocide or disaster: An investigation into the British Empire's role within the great bengal famine of 1770. *Vulcan Historical Review, 25*, 74–81.

Bock, P., & Berkowitz, M. (1966). The Emerging Field of National Security. *World Politics, 19*(1), 122–136. https://doi.org/10.2307/2009846

Braudel, F. (1984). *Civilization and capitalism, 15th–18th century, vol. III: The perspective of the world*. Collins.

Breteau, P. (2022). *L'indépendance énergétique de La France grâce au nucléaire: Un tour de passe-passe statistique*. Le Monde.fr. Retrieved January 27, 2022, from https://bit.ly/3MlVvvt

Brewer, A. (2002). *Marxist theories of imperialism: A critical survey* (2nd ed.). Routledge.

Burns, R. (2019). Trump threatens to 'Destroy' Turkey's economy with sanctions. *AP NEWS*. Retrieved January, 2022, from https://bit.ly/3KKeu23

Buzan. (2007). *People, states & fear: An agenda for international security studies in the post-cold war era* (2nd ed.). ECPR Press.

Cable, V. (1995). What is International Economic Security? *International Affairs, 71*(2), 305–324. https://doi.org/10.2307/2623436

Central Intelligence Agency. (2021). *The world factbook*. Retrieved February 20, 2022, from https://www.cia.gov/the-world-factbook/

EDF. (2013). *2012 full year results: Strong results and commitments delivered*. Globe Newswire News Room. Retrieved February 04, 2022, from https://bit.ly/3rrfPmO

European Commission. (2018). *National accounts treatment of the capital injections into Areva*. In Eurostat (Ares (2018)1221554-05/03/2018). Retrieved February 10, 2022, from https://l24.im/fBznY

Fatouros, A. (1965). Sartre on Colonialism. *World Politics, 17*(4), 703–719. https://doi.org/10.2307/2009329

Gueye, M. (2018). Colonialism in Africa: A revisionist perspective. Africology: The Journal of Pan. *African Studies, 12*(1), 111–122.

Harshe, R. (1980). French Neo-Colonialism in Sub-Saharan Africa. *India Quarterly, 36*(2), 159–178. https://doi.org/10.1177/097492848003600202

Heck, G. (2008). *Charlemagne, Muhammad, and the Arab Roots of Capitalism*. De Gruyter. https://doi.org/10.1515/9783110202830

Hirschman, A. O. (1945). *National Power and the Structure of Foreign Trade*. NBER and University of California Press.

Horrigan, B. L., Karasik, T., & Lalgee, R. (2008). *Security studies. In the encyclopedia of violence, peace, & conflict* (Second Edition).
IAEA. (2022). *PRIS–miscellaneous reports–nuclear share*. The Power Reactor Information System. Retrieved January 10, 2022, from https://pris.iaea.org/pris/worldstatistics/nuclearshareofelectricitygeneration.aspx
Illarionov, A. (1999). The Criteria of Economic Security. *Problems of Economic Transition, 41*(12), 63–92.
Index Mundi. (2021). *Niger demographics profile*. Retrieved February 15, 2022, from https://www.indexmundi.com/niger/demographics_profile.html
International Trade Centre. (2022). ITC. *Trade map*. Retrieved January 25, 2022, from https://www.intracen.org/
Kahler, M. (2004). Economic security in an Era of globalisation: Definition and provision. *The Pacific Review, 17*(4), 485–502.
Kortepeter, M. (2020). *A defense expert explores whether the covid-19 coronavirus makes a good bioweapon. Forbes*. Retrieved January 15, 2022, from https://bit.ly/37jrVHZ
Laycock, S. (2012). All the countries we've ever invaded. *The history press*. Retrieved from https://www.perlego.com/book/1588277/all-the-countries-weve-ever-invaded-pdf
Leffler, M. P. (1990). National security. *Journal of American History, 77*(1), 143–152. https://doi.org/10.2307/2078646
Lenin, V. I. (1917). *Imperialism: The highest stage of capitalism: A popular outline*. Petrograd.
Lippmann, W. (1943). *U.S. Foreign policy: Shield of the Republic*. Little, Brown and.
Lopez, R. S. (1976). *The commercial revolution of the middle ages, 950–1350*. Cambridge University Press.
Losman, D. (2001). *Economic security a national security folly? Policy analysis, 409*. Retrieved February 10, 2022, https://www.cato.org/policy-analysis/economic-security-national-security-folly
Marx, K. (2019). *Das Kapital (Capital): A critique of political economy*. Benediction Classics.
McIntyre, M. (2011). Race, Surplus Population and the Marxist Theory of Imperialism. *Antipode, 43*(5), 1489–1515.
Molano, D. (2020, October 23). *Li-Meng yan: "Coronavirus is a biological weapon."* Retrieved January 18, 2022, from https://en.as.com/en/2020/10/23/latest_news/1603452972_180848.html
Mun, T. (1989). England's treasure by foreign trade, or, the ballance of our foreign trade is the rule of our treasure.
Nally, D. (2008). That Coming Storm: The Irish Poor law, Colonial Biopolitics, and the Great Famine. *Annals of the Association of American Geographers, 98*(3), 714–741.
Naved, S. (2008). The colonial encounter in marxist terms. *Social Scientist*, 33–46.
Neal, L. (1991). *The rise of financial capitalism: international capital markets in the age of reason*. Cambridge University Press.
Newmann, W. W. (2002). Reorganising for national security and homeland security. *Public Administration Review, 62*, 126–137.
Nkrumah, K. (1965). *Neo-colonialism, the last stage of imperialism by Kwame Nkrumah*. Marxists Internet Archive. Retrieved February 10, 2022, from https://www.marxists.org/subject/africa/nkrumah/neocolonialism/introduction.htm
Nuclear Energy Agency and the International Atomic Energy Agency. (2020). *Uranium 2020: Resources, production and demand*.
OECD. (2019a). *The observatory of economic complexity*. Retrieved February 10, 2022, from https://oec.world/en/profile/country/ner
OECD. (2019b). *Balanced international merchandise trade statistics*. Retrieved February 13, 2022, from https://stats.oecd.org//Index.aspx? DataSetCode=BIMTS_HS2017#
Orano. (2021). *Annual activity report 2020*. Retrieved February 10, 2022, from https://www.orano.group/en/finance/publications-and-regulated-information-credit-update-orano

Oxfam International. (2014). *Areva in Niger: Who is benefiting from the Uranium?* Retrieved February 10, 2022, from https://www.oxfam.org/en/press-releases/areva-niger-who-benefiting-uranium

Popper, K. R. (2020). *The Open Society and Its Enemies*. Princeton University Press.

Republic of Turkey Ministry of Trade. (2022). *Kolay İhracat Platformu*. Retrieved February 13, 2022, from https://www.kolayihracat.gov.tr/

Rodney, W. (2018). *How Europe Underdeveloped Africa*. Verso Books.

Romm, J. J. (1993). *Defining National Security: The Nonmilitary Aspects*. Council on Foreign Relations.

Rozakis, C. L. (1987). Territorial integrity and political independence. In *Encyclopedia of disputes installment 10* (pp. 481–487). Elsevier.

Saravanan, V. (2008). Economic exploitation of forest resources in South India during the pre-forest act colonial era, 1793-1882. *International Forestry Review, 10*(1), 65–73.

Sills, D. L. (1968). *International encyclopedia of the social sciences* (17th ed.). Retrieved March 25, 2022, from https://onlinelibrary.wiley.com/doi/abs/10.1002/ncr.4100570915

Tertrais, B. (2014). *Uranium from Niger: A key resource of diminishing importance for France*. Danish Institute for International Studies.

Tournons la Page. (2020). *AREVA and the return of the uranium gate scandal in Niger: Nigerien civil society mobilises in front of the French Justice system*. Retrieved January 10, 2022, from https://tournonslapage.org/en/actualites/areva

Trading Economics. (2022). *Niger exports*. Retrieved January 28, 2022, from https://tradingeconomics.com/niger/exports

Udovitch, A. L. (2011). Partnership and profit in Medieval Islam. In *Partnership and profit in Medieval Islam*. Princeton University Press.

UN Comtrade Database. (2022). *International trade statistics database*. Retrieved January 17, 2022, from https://comtrade.un.org/

Varadarajan, T. (2022). *The West's economic war plan against Russia*. WSJ. Retrieved March 11, 2022, from https://www.wsj.com/articles/the-west-economic-war-plan-against-putin-sanction-ukraine-russia-banks-oil-gas-ruble-central-11647032502

Veblen, T. (1904). *The Theory of business enterprise*. C. Scribner's Sons.

World Bank. (2021). *Country Overview*. Retrieved February 1, 2022, from https://www.worldbank.org/en/country/niger/overview#1

World Nuclear Association. (2022). *Nuclear power in France*. Retrieved February 10, 2022, from https://www.worldnuclear.org/information-library/country-profiles/countries-a-f/france.aspx

Political Crises of Capitalism

Hakan Mehmetcik and Dogukan Taskiran

Abstract This chapter examines the modern political crises of capitalism. Financial imbalances, growing public and private debt, rising inflation, soaring inequalities between nations and within societies, low growth rates, insufficient welfare benefits, and environmental concerns are only a few of capitalism's systemic and converging problems. Over the years, these enduring problems have generated new forms of political crises. Especially, global capitalism has been in a serious structural crisis since 2008, but the current COVID-19 outbreak has aggravated the issues, making it more difficult to build equitable and sustainable economies. The chapter addresses several issues that show how the capitalist world economy produces new types of political crises by examining three interconnected political crises: the rise of populism and the retreat of democracy, the rise of neomercantilism and state capitalism, and the legitimacy crisis in global governance.

Keywords Capitalism · Crises of capitalism · Political crises · Crises of legitimacy

1 Introduction

Today's capitalism is in turmoil, with the processes of financialization and globalization often the obvious targets in attributing blame. Financial services are critical to the global economy today, yet financialization and the spread of financial crises have exacerbated the effect of shocks throughout the global system, resulting in increasing instability. There is rising discontent with the outcomes of successive waves of globalization and technical achievements, which endanger national jobs and living standards. Both globalization and financial capital along with their wider

H. Mehmetcik (✉)
Department of International Relations, Marmara University, Istanbul, Turkey

University of Notre Dame, Kellogg Institute for International Studies, Notre Dame, IN, USA
e-mail: hakan.mehmetcik@marmara.edu.tr

D. Taskiran
Department of International Relations, Marmara University, Istanbul, Turkey

A. Ari (ed.), *Capitalism at a Crossroads*, Springer Studies in Alternative Economics,
https://doi.org/10.1007/978-3-031-23257-2_10

ramifications have already spawned a large body of literature, and it is impossible to provide even a concise summary here. The most significant flaw in the global capitalist system is, however, that it does not appear capable of generating broadly shared prosperity for the majority of people. The social safety nets created in the 1970s are no longer fully functional or adequate. For many years, the link between political legitimacy and political compromise has been weakening, causing the capitalist system to enter an entrenched political crisis mode. Brexit, Donald Trump's election, and the rise of the extreme right in European democracies as well as xenophobic rhetoric and anti-migration sentiments are all visible indications of a long-running crisis.

There are more issues to add to the debate, one of which is inequality, undoubtedly one of the most pressing issues we face today. The uneven development in the world economy of the previous two centuries has resulted in increased inequality in income distribution across nations (Martins, 2011). Inequality within societies is also the most persistent and challenging issue for the economic system, yet even as this inequality is referred to as "the defining problem of our time'" no policy changes have resulted (Krugman, 2013). On the contrary, governments poured money into bailing out the sectors and corporations that precipitated the 2008 crisis, and the biggest chunk of global capital flows was reinvested in banking, insurance, and real estate rather than being spent on creating more equal economies. The financial sector has been draining income from economies, and brains from societies, as corporations reward shareholders through stock-buyback schemes rather than investing to boost long-term growth, and the young and the brightest end up working in the financial sector instead of public services. Furthermore, tax revenues are diminished as a casualty of the intense financialization of capital and multinational firms' routine tax avoidance practices, adding to the structural constraints on welfare state finance.

While the COVID-19 crisis could have provided an opportunity to correct imbalances (Garicano, 2021; Mazzucato, 2020a, 2020b; Murshed, 2020), not only did that chance go to waste, but imbalances in fact grew throughout the pandemic. Overall, inequality, insecurity, a lack of opportunity for those who have been left behind, financial imbalances, expanding public and private debt, rising inflation, and environmental problems are all manifestations of the modern economy's failures. However, the combination of these escalating problems has resulted in a series of full-scale crises in politics and political structures across nations. Traditionally, mutual concessions between ruled and rulers have been used to acquire political legitimacy, which in turn is linked to people's economic prosperity and social well-being. Economic deterioration is always a major factor in the emergence of political discontent and the degradation of political legitimacy in any society. As a result, the gradual increase in contemporary economic failures acts as a harbinger of populism, mercantilism, and state capitalism.

The purpose of this chapter is to analyze and synthesize some of these political crises and the way in which the Covid pandemic has intensified the severity of the crisis mode. We broadly identified three correlated political crises area: rise of populism and retreat of democracy, rise of neomercantilism and state capitalism, and legitimacy crisis in global governance. That is, we undertake a comparative analysis of political crises in the form of populism and democracy, mercantilism and state capitalism, and the legitimacy crisis in global governance. The chapter, however, begins with a very brief overview of the changes in the capitalist system as background reading (Sect. 2). We then address what we describe as the political crises in Sect. 3. In Sect. 4, we discuss the COVID-19 pandemic and how an extraordinary health crisis has rendered these crises more apparent and urgent. Section 5 concludes.

2 The Evolving Capitalist System

The capitalist transition from the 1970s to the present has a distinct character as compared to the post-World War II period when the system was embodied in a Keynesian economic approach focused on full employment and welfare state programs. However, when Keynesian approaches were confronted with the serious challenge of global economic slowdowns that, in practice, were persistent, additional structural changes emerged. Rising inflation, exchange-rate volatility, and rising wages were to blame for the economic slowdowns of the 1970s (Solimano, 2020, p. 94). Slowing growth due to low profitability not only contributed to the 1970s and early 1980s recession but also caused a fundamental transformation of the economic system in the coming years. Traditional pro-labor policies were abandoned, and from the 1970s onwards, a new and profound neoliberal transition began (McNally, 2009). Even though this growing tendency was severely threatened by a series of financial crises in the 1990s and early 2000s, and subsequently by the 2007–08 crisis, capitalism was able to continue on its path of neoliberal policies, all the while generating massive global imbalances.

Various important and systemically relevant characteristics of capitalism have arisen during the last three to four decades. The first is that financial capital, in the form of speculative activities, has become the most important component of economic activity, leading not only to instability but also to income and wealth inequalities (Fine, 2013). These types of speculative activities also produce an exploitative and crisis-driven economic system. The 2007–2008 crisis, in particular, demonstrated that the system was also incapable of generating enough stability to maintain consent and legitimacy between states and their peoples. When a global health crisis becomes a full-blown economic crisis, rising inflation can even lead to a protracted period of increasing prices and economic misery (The Economist, 2021), as happened in the 1970s. However, the political ramifications of such in today's societies are considerably more extensive and long-lasting. The COVID-19 pandemic has starkly revealed that the old capitalist paradigm must be modified for the betterment of the majority through taking into account a wide range of factors, including those that overall have had a beneficial influence on society, such as the technological improvements that are transforming work and social life (Shafik, 2021). Otherwise, the current situation may easily evolve into a series of full-fledged political crises.

3 The Political Crises

In his book "The Globalization Paradox", Harvard Professor Dani Rodrik established his famous trilemma, arguing that it is impossible to attain economic hyper-globalization, national sovereignty, and democracy simultaneously since only two of these are simultaneously attainable (Rodrik, 2012). Indeed, when we look at the broader picture, we see that there is a causal link between what happens at the global level in terms of trade and finance (globalization), and what happens at the domestic level in terms of politics (democratization and sovereignty). The forces of economics and politics stand in opposition to each other at these two levels since the requirements for globalization, national sovereignty, and democracy conflict. Market liberalism encourages increasing openness, free trade, and deregulation to sustain global prosperity and expansion, while in much of the world, ordinary politics calls for increased national protectionism to safeguard individuals against market forces.

Rodrik also underlines that neoliberal market forces lead to patterns of "creative destruction", while technological advancements in domestic markets result in rapid shifts in employment, as well as widening wage and living-standard inequalities. Multinational companies have been taking advantage of Chinese factories' efficiency and low costs to outsource much of their manufacturing to China and other Asian economies. Yet, these practices resulted in extremely complex production chains along with more de-industrialization, as well as the loss of national manufacturing capacity and jobs in Western economies. Another important pattern that has resulted in loss of national manufacturing capacity and jobs is digitalization and automation in work. This is likely a much more significant factor in creating systemic and vast unemployment than anything else. Furthermore, slowing growth in Western economies has exacerbated inequality and increased unemployment, which has fueled anger toward their central and moderate parties and policies (Frieden, 2020). Overall, these circumstances have created a mass of discontented and alienated citizens ready for exploitation by populist political parties. Globalization cannot be realized or managed in the absence of a social safety net to shield individuals from the uncertainties of the global economy. Because governments have not done enough to guarantee that the advantages of globalization are dispersed more equally, these populist groups have thrived (Frieden, 2007). Emerging neo-mercantilist/protectionist policies, as well as state capitalism and global governance legitimacy issues, are all major elements driving global-level reactions to economic and political shifts.

3.1 *Rise of Populism and Weakening Democracy*

It appears that we are living in a populist era. The rise of populist parties has thrown many societies, including industrialized economies and long-established democracies into disarray. According to Global Populism statistics, populism has risen in

Western Europe and North America to almost the same degree as in Central Europe and Latin America (Hawkins et al., 2019). According to the Populism in Power database, there are approximately five times as many populist leaders and parties in power today than there were at the end of the Cold War and three times more since the turn of the century (Kyle & Meyer, 2020). These figures would be enough to sound alarm bells for populism in general.

Even while populism has been driven by a variety of factors, and substantial disparities exist across nations, everyone agrees that significant changes in the economy, in general, have contributed to its emergence (Inglehart & Norris, 2016). As the post-2008 depression in capitalism deepens and the slowdown of economic growth based on profitability declines, subordinated classes become more and more radicalized in their political choices. Anti-system parties capitalizing on popular discontent with global capitalism promote economic nationalism, anti-immigrant, and anti-globalization discourse and policies, and as the world crisis deepens, populists take advantage of nationalist sentiment to consolidate their base. It might also be claimed that in some situations, populist voices develop inside mainstream center-right and center-left parties, which have suddenly shifted their positions on matters such as globalization, migration, and so on.

However, populism is not a new phenomenon in global politics, and the majority of European populist parties have a long history. However, as a result of the 2007–2008 financial crisis, they have gained significant ground in their political landscape. Furthermore, populism has increased even in the most secure countries, such as the UK and the USA, where it has been prominent in the last years and has been firmly linked to economic issues. As a result, we may infer that the economic downturn has played a major role in the formation of democratic discontent and the deterioration of political legitimacy. Those who feel left behind in increased economic insecurity and social hardship have fostered a broad hostility toward the state and traditional political parties.

It is worth considering a few practical examples. For example, the Greek debt crisis of 2010 was probably one instance that is intimately linked to the structural crisis and the subsequent rise of populism. Greece is not alone in this regard. Italy, Spain, and some other Eastern European countries are vulnerable to fiscal and sovereign debt crises not because their governments are frugal (Pérez, 2019), but rather because their economies are unable to compete successfully with imports from the core rich European countries, particularly from Germany (Schmidt, 2011). It is worth noting that, according to some observers, the lack of liberalization rendered these countries vulnerable to the crisis. From the standpoint of certain EU core economies (such as Germany), the crisis impacted the Southern EU nations because these countries were slow to implement neoliberal reforms. However, decades of privatization, outsourcing, and budget cuts in the name of "efficiency" have imperiled governments in these countries in producing responses to the COVID-19 pandemic. Not surprisingly, antagonism to the normative and economic authority of the EU in these countries has been increasing over the years. Opposition to the EU, its restrictive monetary policy, large-scale privatization, EU-led globalization, deregulation, and so on are precisely what lies behind the bolstering of populist factions in these countries (Toplišek, 2020).

Is this a phenomenon that exists only in Europe? Clearly not. A similar, if not identical, trend can be seen over the Atlantic in the USA with President Donald Trump in a fit of similar rage at normative and economic authority (Cox, 2018). Populist leaders have also been on the rise in a number of Latin American, African, and Asian countries over the last decade, and their rise too is related to and boosted by capitalism's modern crises. That is, populism is one of the symptoms of the crisis in the capitalist market economy.

Populism and authoritarianism as mutually reinforcing factors. The data show us that populist governments have amplified corruption, weakened individual liberties, and wrought havoc on democratic institutions (Kyle, 2018). When populists seize control, they have the potential to do long-term economic and political damage. On average, populist-ruled countries see a significant drop in real GDP per capita (Funke et al., 2020). Populists in power everywhere are united by protectionist trade policies, unsustainable debt dynamics, and the erosion of democratic institutions (Funke et al., 2021). It may be claimed that this is also due to the difficulty of implementing populist policy proposals. Populist parties propose bold remedies as opposition parties, but while in government, many of these proposals look naive and impossible to implement. For example, Donald Trump's threat to withdraw from NAFTA and the WTO, the expectation that Brexit would result in a speedy settlement of a trade deal with the EU, and the desire of certain Southern EU members to renegotiate eurozone conditions were all more difficult than anticipated.

While the repercussions of the economic crisis and growing inequities between nations and within communities persist, we are also seeing a weakening of democracy in many countries, a problem that manifests itself in two ways. On the one hand, as voters become increasingly disillusioned with mainstream politics, political party membership and voter turnout are all plummeting (Moffitt, 2020, p. 2). On the other hand, we are witnessing a significant drop in the overall quality and number of democracies. According to the most recent Economist Democracy Index, democratic weakening continued in 2021 (The Economist, 2022). The current pandemic has also emerged as the world's most serious threat to democratic liberty. Citizens have faced emergency restrictions and increased state authority in order to protect themselves against infection, and thus, the pandemic has made the deterioration of democracy much more conceivable and evident.

3.2 *Rise of Neomercantilism and State Capitalism*

In trade, liberalization rather than protectionism has been the prevailing trend during the last fifty years. However, since mid-2018, this pattern began to reverse, and as the COVID-19 pandemic emerged, it became clear that it was about to send the global economy into its worst recession since World War II. As the pandemic disturbed regular economic activity and living throughout the world, global trade dropped by 13% to 32% in 2020. While there was a good recovery in 2021, the global economy is now beginning a sharp downturn, with new risks from COVID-19 variations, as well as increases in inflation, debt, and income inequality, all of which might jeopardize the recovery (World Bank, 2022). The bad news is that, in the short run, governments around the world will become more protectionist to alleviate the economic damage caused by the pandemic than they would have normally governed. However, we must go beyond protectionism to grasp the broader trends and how they connect to capitalism. In this respect, we prefer the term neomercantilism over protectionism because we believe it better describes the overall tendencies. Mercantilism was historically related to nation-states, and neomercantilism is closely associated with the emergence of state capitalism.

We may even distinguish between autarkist and neo-mercantilist trade policies. While the former advocate economic isolationism, the latter advocate strategic protectionism through selective trade restrictions and subsidies as well as other types of government interventions. In today's world, neo-mercantilist economic nationalism is far more prevalent than autarchic economic nationalism (Helleiner, 2019), and indeed, the former may be the case in most countries for a while. This is an essential distinction because neo-mercantilist activities were visible in numerous ways in earlier decades. Since the global depression of 2008, neo-mercantilist tendencies have been gaining ground across the board. As Frieden rightfully pointed out, even for the USA, a country for free trade, the 2016 presidential election marked a turning point. For the first time in 75 years, both parties' presidential candidates were openly hostile to foreign trade, banking, and investment." (Frieden, 2020).

The Economist (2020a) declares that "the big state is back in business" and that the state's economic footprint will continue to grow in the next decade (The Economist, 2020b). State-owned enterprises and sovereign wealth funds are altering international politics and the global economy by shifting greater amounts of economic power and influence on the state's central authority (Bremmer, 2009). Furthermore, the pandemic has enlarged governments' footholds in practically every economy, making a large state the norm rather than the exception. Big states, meanwhile, have embraced neo-mercantilist economic nationalism and promoted state capitalism. In retrospect, the rising pattern of Asian countries, particularly China, has led to a dramatic change in the organization of production. This has accelerated globalization while also making Asian countries and their state capitalism model more alluring (Wade, 2004; White & Wade, 1988; Nölke, 2014).

The increase of state capitalism and the strengthening of neomercantilism is not just a non-European phenomenon. In fact, the strong trading positions of Germany, the Netherlands, Belgium, Austria, and Scandinavia ensure the reproduction of neomercantilism due to persistent trade surplus policies in Europe and beyond (Bellofiore et al., 2011). We may also describe the EU and other several regional organizations as neo-mercantilist initiatives since they provide open trading inside the region while closing the territory off to outside trade flows via rules, regulations, standards, and common tariffs (Hettne, 1993; Mehmetcik, 2019). Both China's state-led developmental economic model and populist conservatism in the USA are neo-mercantilist forms of economic nationalism (Helleiner, 2021). In short, neomercantilism is alive and well in different forms and with different drivers all over the world.

The rise of vaccine nationalism during the COVID-19 pandemic is only one example of how far this trend might go. Some of the world's poorest and most vulnerable individuals are suffering as a result of the worldwide inability to share vaccinations equally. According to the UNDP, WHO, and Oxford University's Global Dashboard for Vaccine Equity, as of September 15, just 3.07% of the world's population in low-income countries has received at least one dose of vaccine, compared to 60.18% in high-income nations (United Nations, 2021). As the Omicron variants verify that infection risks have grown in all nations and "no-one is safe until everyone is safe" (UNHCR, 2021). Pharmaceutical corporations and states are clearly failing to meet their responsibilities and commitments to guarantee that everyone has access to COVID-19 vaccinations. The key factor in the appearance of novel variants and the extension of pandemics is vaccine stockpiling by wealthier nations. The 2007–2008 global financial crisis, along with the COVID-19 pandemic and geopolitical tensions between the USA and China, as well as Russia and the West, created a fertile ground for neomercantilism and protectionism.

3.3 The Legitimacy Crises in Global Governance

Since the global financial crisis of 2007–2008, the US's hegemonic influence has fast waned, while rising powers have ascended to prominence, ushering in a new era in international affairs. Yet, even as the previous order disintegrates, the future seems ever more uncertain. The "post-Western" world order (Stuenkel, 2017), the "rise of the rest" (Zakaria, 2011), an "interdependent hegemonic world" (Xing, 2016), a "decentralized globalism" (Buzan, 2011), "pax-Mosaica" (Narlikar & Kumar, 2012), a "multiplex world" (Acharya, 2017), and the "age of anxiety" (Öniş, 2017) have all been used to explain these tectonic shifts and possible courses happening at international level (Gök & Mehmetcik, 2021a).

The globe is, indeed, witnessing massive and unrelenting transformations in a variety of areas and contexts, including technological, economic, cultural, and institutional. However, the regional and global institutions tasked with managing these transitions are fundamentally ill-equipped and face massive legitimacy crises (Castells, 2005). From the UN to the many and varied regional organizations, we are witnessing vast challenges and legitimacy crises in the global governance (Gök & Mehmetcik, 2021b).

Legitimacy crises in global governance have significant ramifications. One recent example may be seen in the World Health Organization (WHO) during the Covid pandemic (Yang, 2021). The WHO was responsible for planning the global response to pandemics, even though the organization was totally ill-equipped to do so, and already in a deep crisis of legitimacy and functionality. Despite being the most generally recognized worldwide authority and the primary coordinator of international efforts to limit pandemics, the WHO could not respond to this unprecedented crisis in an effective manner. Its handling of the global outbreak of such magnitude has eroded both its political and technical legitimacy, bringing its worldwide public authority into doubt (Yunpeng, 2020). The ineffectiveness of WHO and its legitimacy crises casts itself as vaccine nationalism, protectionism in international affairs.

Similarly, the IMF, World Bank, and WTO, as well as the UN and the EU, and their roles in global governance, are constantly called into question (Chorev & Babb, 2009). Emerging neo-mercantilist/protectionist policies are also damaging global governance credibility, prompting worldwide protests against these institutions. These institutions are the building blocks of the post-World War II international system, yet the current capitalist crisis casts doubt on their viability. This widespread crisis of political legitimacy threatens to destabilize the democratic system, and with it, the ability to deal with the challenges and difficulties of a chaotic world. In the absence of a functional global governance forum, globalization cannot be realized or maintained.

4 Covid-19 and Political Crisis

None would appear to be immune to the Covid-19 virus or the economic consequences of the lockdown measures put in place to stop its spread; rich and poor, powerful and powerless, young and old. As a result, the initial assumption about the pandemic was that it was "the great equalizer" (Owoseje, 2020), devoid of any notions of class, wealth, etc. However, as time goes by, we see that COVID-19 is a class-based, race-based, and gender-based health outbreak, or at the very least makes social divisions distinctly more pronounced and obvious. While a small minority of populations, as in the wealthy and powerful, together with some portion of professional upper-middle classes have fared much better than at any time in their life, the majority of populations, as in poor, non-white, and non-skilled workers have borne the financial, social, and humanitarian costs of the pandemic. Most individuals who do not have college degrees were unable to work from home and thus ran the risk of first-hand exposure to the virus. Women in the service industry, particularly mothers, were more likely to lose their jobs as a result of the pandemic lockdowns. Adults of color were more likely than whites to contract and die from the virus. All these people have also faced disproportionate financial difficulties during the pandemic (Peyser, 2020).

Years of neoliberal austerity policies have shattered public infrastructures, especially in health sectors, that were critical during the pandemic. Furthermore, prior to the COVID-19 catastrophe, Western economies were already in a deflationary trap, in which interest rates were held at historically low levels because central banks were forced to print money through quantitative easing (QE) to inject liquidity into economies. The problem for policymakers was that QE measures and bank bailouts aimed at supporting aggregate demand were benefiting existing asset owners at the expense of wage earners, and this dynamic was only accelerated with the COVID-19 crisis. Now, however, inflation, another—and possibly the most dangerous—enemy of wage earners, has entered the equation, causing even more negative outcomes for the majority of populations. We see a pattern of private companies using public resources and turning these into big gains while giving back little or nothing to the public sphere. For far too long, governments have socialized risks while privatizing gains, and publics have paid the price for cleaning up mistakes, while companies and their investors have reaped the benefits (Mazzucato, 2020a). Initial research and development funds for pharmaceuticals are provided by governments, as was the case with the Covid vaccines, meaning ultimately that public money is diverted into huge profits for large private pharmaceutical corporations (Mazzucato, 2018). The COVID-19 pandemic has also provided fertile ground for neomercantilism and protectionism, which has taken the form of vaccine nationalism.

Covid-19 also contributed to a worsening of already-existing disparities in the international system on four key issues, as indicated by McNamara and Newman (2020); inequality within and across societies, new forms of economic statecraft, existential ecological threats, and the trajectory of the digital revolution. While the COVID-19 crisis may have provided an opportunity to address imbalances, that opportunity was not only overlooked, but imbalances actually expanded during the pandemic. By the end of 2021, wealth concentration in the top 5% had reached its highest level in the post-World War II era, and the rate of wealth concentration accelerated significantly during the pandemic (Coy, 2022). According to statistics, the poorest half of the world's population owns just 2% of total net worth, while the richest half owns 98% of all wealth on the planet. There is even more inequality: the lowest 50% of the global population owns less than 1% of total wealth, while the richest 10% hold roughly 80%. While billionaire wealth in the USA has been gradually growing since 1990, a full one-third of their wealth increase happened during the pandemic (World Inequality Report, 2022). This is happening at a time when, in the battle against Covid-19, governments everywhere have become more indebted than at any time in recent history, debts that surpass even World War II with a figure reaching $19.5 trillion (McCormick et al., 2021). Inflation is at a multi-decade high almost everywhere on earth, and in some countries, it is substantially worse than it has ever been (Greenwood & Hanke, 2021). Yet, all these severe macroeconomic imbalances pale into insignificance when compared to the destruction that comes with climate change, which is only now being seen as urgent. The present pandemic has also had detrimental effects on democratic societies by enforcing emergency limitations and increasing governmental control, making the degradation of democracy much more feasible and visible.

5 Conclusion

This chapter discussed the current political problems of capitalism, offering a summary of the wider debate on the causes and effects of the crisis in political terms. We began by describing the major changes/occurrences that weaken the political compromise in capitalist economies in the first place and connecting them to a series of political crises.

People, particularly in advanced economies, are growing dissatisfied with the results of new waves of globalization and technological breakthroughs that threaten their jobs and living standards. There is a growing sense that democratic support for global governance, free trade, and liberalization is eroding. Domestically, the major structural ramifications of this have been the growth of populism and the erosion of democratic institutions, as insurgent authoritarian populist parties seek to capitalize on dissatisfaction with globalization. Emerging neo-mercantilist/protectionist policies, as well as questions surrounding state capitalism and global governance legitimacy, are all important drivers of global-level reactions to economic and political upheavals. The current economic difficulties pose a number of serious questions about the competency and legitimacy of the international institutions that today manage the global economy.

The broader issues (novel policy frameworks, hurdles, and debt) still hang over the international economy and lie at the root of the erosion of legitimacy and trust those considered responsible for good governance. Finally, it is clear that the COVID-19 pandemic revealed with great clarity that our capitalist economic system in its current form is not simply in crisis, but is, in fact, inherently broken (Mazzucato, 2020a). The COVID-19 pandemic has eloquently demonstrated that the old economic paradigm must be altered for the benefit of the majority. Otherwise, the present situation might quickly deteriorate into a succession of full-fledged political crises. Current political crises are fundamentally different from earlier crises in that they are not merely incidental or easily dismissed. Crises are geographically central and destructive in scale. In this regard, present political crises reflect a rupture or a disintegration of the political organization of the capitalist system (both locally and globally).

References

Acharya, A. (2017). After liberal hegemony: The advent of a multiplex world order. *Ethics & International Affairs, 31*(3), 271–285.

Bellofiore, R., Garibaldo, F., & Halevi, J. (2011). The global crisis and the crisis of European neomercantilism. *Socialist Register, 47*.

Bremmer, I. (2009). State capitalism comes of age - the end of the free market essay. *Foreign Affairs, 88*(3), 40–55.

Buzan, B. (2011). The inaugural Kenneth N. Waltz annual lecture a world order without superpowers: Decentred globalism. *International Relations, 25*(1), 3–25.

Castells, M. (2005). Global governance and global politics. *PS: Political Science & Politics, 38*(1), 9–16. https://doi.org/10.1017/S1049096505055678

Chorev, N., & Babb, S. (2009). The crisis of neoliberalism and the future of international institutions: A comparison of the IMF and the WTO. *Theory and Society, 38*(5), 459–484. https://doi.org/10.1007/s11186-009-9093-5

Cox, M. (2018). *Understanding the global rise of populism. Strategic update. LSE IDeas*. LSE.

Coy, P. (2022, February 2). Wealth inequality is the highest since World War II. *The New York Times*, sec. Opinion. https://www.nytimes.com/2022/02/02/opinion/inequality-wealth-pandemic.html
Fine, B. (2013). Financialization from a Marxist perspective. *International Journal of Political Economy, 42*(4), 47–66. https://doi.org/10.2753/IJP0891-1916420403
Frieden, J. A. (2007). *Global capitalism: Its fall and rise in the twentieth century*. W. W. Norton & Company.
Frieden, J. A. (2020). *Jeffry Frieden on globalization, the rise of populism, and the future of democracy*. Mossavar-Rahmani Center for Business & Government, Harvard Kennedy School. https://www.hks.harvard.edu/centers/mrcbg/programs/growthpolicy/jeffry-frieden-globalization-rise-populism-and-future-democracy
Funke, M., Schularick, M., & Trebesch, C. (2020, October 23). *Populist leaders and the economy*. KIEL Working Paper. https://www.ifw-kiel.de/fileadmin/Dateiverwaltung/IfW-Publications/Manuel_Funke/KWP_2169.pdf
Funke, M., Schularick, M., & Trebesch, C. (2021). The cost of populism: Evidence from history. *VoxEU.Org* (blog). https://voxeu.org/article/cost-populism-evidence-history
Garicano, L. (2021). Capitalism after Covid. Conversations With 21.
Greenwood, J., & Hanke, S. (2021, July 20). Too much money portends high inflation. *Wall Street Journal*, 2021, sec. Opinion. https://www.wsj.com/articles/money-supply-inflation-friedman-biden-federal-reserve-11626816746.
Gök, G., & Mehmetcik, H. (2021a). Global governance and crises of legitimacy: An introduction. In G. Gök & H. Mehmetcik (Eds.), *The crises of legitimacy in global governance*. Routledge.
Gök, G., & Mehmetcik, H. (2021b). *The crises of legitimacy in global governance*. Routledge. https://doi.org/10.4324/9781003128595
Hawkins, K. A., Aguilar, R., Castanho Silva, B., Jenne, E. K., Kocijan, B., & Rovira Kaltwasser, C. (2019). Global Populism Database, V1. *Harvard Dataverse*. https://doi.org/10.7910/DVN/LFTQEZ
Helleiner, E. (2019). Varieties of American neomercantilism: From the first years of the Republic to Trumpian economic nationalism. *European Review of International Studies, 6*(3), 7–29. https://doi.org/10.3224/eris.v6i3.02
Helleiner, E. (2021). The diversity of economic nationalism. *New Political Economy, 26*(2), 229–238. https://doi.org/10.1080/13563467.2020.1841137
Hettne, B. (1993). Neomercantilism: The pursuit of regionness. *Cooperation and Conflict, 28*(3), 211–232. https://doi.org/10.1177/0010836793028003001
Inglehart, R., & Norris, P. (2016). Trump, Brexit, and the rise of populism: Economic have-nots and cultural backlash. *SSRN Electronic Journal*. https://doi.org/10.2139/ssrn.2818659
Krugman, P. (2013). Why inequality matters. *New York Times, 15*.
Kyle, J. (2018, December 26). What populists do to democracies. *The Atlantic*. https://www.theatlantic.com/ideas/archive/2018/12/hard-data-populism-bolsonaro-trump/578878/
Kyle, J., & Meyer, B. (2020). High tide? Populism in power, 1990-2020. *Tony Blair Institute for Global Change*, 2020–2002.
Martins, N. (2011). Globalisation, inequality and the economic crisis. *New Political Economy, 16*(1), 1–18.
Mazzucato, M. (2018, December 3). Putting the public back in public health. *Project Syndicate*. https://www.project-syndicate.org/commentary/big-pharma-health-care-costs-by-mariana-mazzucato-2018-12
Mazzucato, M. (2020a). Capitalism after the pandemic: Getting the recovery right essays. *Foreign Affairs, 99*(6), 50–61.
Mazzucato, M. (2020b, December 28). Covid exposes capitalism's flaws. *Financial Times*. https://www.ft.com/content/9e7b2630-2f67-4923-aa76-0f240a80a9b3
McCormick, L. C., Torres, C., Benhamou, M., & Pogkas, D. (2021, January 27). Global debt grew by $19.5 trillion during the pandemic. *Bloomberg.com*. https://www.bloomberg.com/graphics/2021-coronavirus-global-debt/

McNally, D. (2009). From financial crisis to world-slump: Accumulation, financialisation, and the global slowdown. *Historical Materialism, 17*(2), 35–83. https://doi.org/10.1163/156920609X436117

McNamara, K. R., & Newman, A. L. (2020). The big reveal: COVID-19 and globalization's great transformations. *International Organization, 74*(S1), E59–E77.

Mehmetcik, H. (2019). Bölgeselcilik Çalışmalarında Bölgeler Üstü ve Bölgeler Arası İlişkiler: Avrupa Birliği ve Afrika Birliği İlişkileri Örneği. *International Journal of Political Science and Urban Studies, 7*, 72–84.

Moffitt, B. (2020). *The global rise of populism*. Stanford University Press.

Murshed, S. M. (2020). Capitalism and COVID-19: Crisis at the crossroads. *Peace Economics, Peace Science and Public Policy, 26*(3).

Narlikar, A., & Kumar, R. (2012). From Pax Americana to Pax Mosaica? Bargaining over a new economic order. *The Political Quarterly, 83*(2), 384–394.

Nölke, A. (2014). Introduction: Toward state capitalism 3.0. In *Multinational corporations from emerging markets*, 1–12. Springer.

Öniş, Z. (2017). The age of anxiety: The crisis of liberal democracy in a post-hegemonic global order. *The International Spectator, 52*(3), 18–35.

Owoseje, T. (2020, March 23). Coronavirus is 'the Great Equalizer,' Madonna tells fans from her Bathtub. *CNN News*. https://www.cnn.com/2020/03/23/entertainment/madonna-coronavirus-video-intl-scli/index.html

Pérez, S. A. (2019). A Europe of creditor and debtor states: Explaining the north/south divide in the Eurozone. *West European Politics, 42*(5), 989–1014. https://doi.org/10.1080/01402382.2019.1573403

Peyser, E. (2020). The people who actually had a pretty great year. *The New York Times*, December 14, 2020, sec. Opinion. https://www.nytimes.com/2020/12/14/opinion/sunday/the-people-who-actually-had-a-pretty-great-year.html

Rodrik, D. (2012). *The globalization paradox: Democracy and the future of the world economy*. W. W. Norton & Company.

Schmidt, I. (2011). European capitalism: Varieties of crisis. *Alternate Routes: Journal of Critical Social Research, 22*. http://www.alternateroutes.ca/index.php/ar/article/view/14418

Shafik, M. (2021). Capitalism needs a new social contract. *Oxford Review of Economic Policy, 37*(4), 758–772. https://doi.org/10.1093/oxrep/grab032

Solimano, A. (2020). *A history of big recessions in the long twentieth century*. Cambridge University Press. https://doi.org/10.1017/9781108755276

Stuenkel, O. (2017). *Post-Western world: How emerging powers are remaking global order*. Wiley.

The Economist. (2020a). The new age of interventionism—The big state is back in business. n.d. *Money Talks*. Accessed February 8, 2022. https://www.economist.com/podcasts/2022/01/12/the-new-age-of-interventionism-the-big-state-is-back-in-business

The Economist. (2020b). *The virus means the big state is back*, March 21, 2020. https://www.economist.com/britain/2020/03/21/the-virus-means-the-big-state-is-back

The Economist. (2021). *Is the world economy going back to the 1970s?* October 7, 2021. https://www.economist.com/finance-and-economics/is-the-world-economy-going-back-to-the-1970s/21805260

The Economist. (2022). *A new low for global democracy*. February 9, 2022. https://www.economist.com/graphic-detail/2022/02/09/a-new-low-for-global-democracy?utm_content=article-link-1&etear=nl_today_1&utm_campaign=r.the-economist-today&utm_medium=email.internal-newsletter.np&utm_source=salesforce-marketing-cloud&utm_term=2/9/2022&utm_id=1045717

Toplišek, A. (2020). The political economy of populist rule in post-crisis Europe: Hungary and Poland. *New Political Economy, 25*(3), 388–403.

UNHCR. (2021). *Statement: No-one is safe until everyone is safe – Why we need a global response to COVID-19*, May 24, 2021. https://www.unhcr.org/news/press/2021/5/60a7fc9b4/statement-no-one-safe-safe-need-global-response-covid-19.html

United Nations. (2021, September 19). COVID vaccines: Widening inequality and millions vulnerable. *UN News*. https://news.un.org/en/story/2021/09/1100192

Wade, R. (2004). *Governing the market: Economic theory and the role of government in East Asian industrialization*. Princeton University Press.

White, G., & Wade, R. (1988). Developmental states and markets in East Asia: An introduction. In *Developmental states in East Asia* (pp. 1–29). Springer.

World Bank. (2022). *Global growth to slow through 2023, adding to risk of 'hard landing' in developing economies*. World Bank. January 11, 2022. https://www.worldbank.org/en/news/press-release/2022/01/11/global-recovery-economics-debt-commodity-inequality

World Inequality Report. (2022). //wir2022.wid.world/.

Xing, L. (2016). The nexus between the emerging powers and the existing world order: Interdependent hegemony. Op-Ed. *Rising Powers in Global Governance*.

Yang, H. (2021). Contesting legitimacy of global governance institutions: The case of the World Health Organization during the coronavirus pandemic. *International Studies Review, 23*(4), 1813–1834. https://doi.org/10.1093/isr/viab047

Yunpeng, P. X. (2020, October 1). The COVID-19 pandemic witnessed the weakened authority of the WHO. *California Law Review*. https://www.californialawreview.org/weakened-authority-who/

Zakaria, F. (2011). *The post-American world: Release 2.0*.

Part II
Quest for Rebuilding the Capitalism

Artificial Intelligence, Technological Change, and the Future of Capitalism

Caner Demir and **Serhat Çakmak**

Abstract In this study, the potential effects of artificial intelligence on the future of capitalism are discussed. Artificial intelligence, which has an important place in the transformation process brought by Industry 4.0, has put technological progress discussions on a quite different path. Unlike other technological systems, the ability to think and act makes artificial intelligence different. This situation raises important questions for the future of production and distribution processes. As a result, the demand for labor may decrease, leading to lower household income. Declining household income, on the other hand, could lower consumption which will put capitalism in big trouble. In order to answer these and some other related questions, we discuss the possible effects of artificial intelligence on labor markets and capital accumulation processes and examine the actions that governments can take in this process.

Keywords Artificial intelligence · Capitalism · Technological progress

1 Introduction

We, as humankind, are in a great transformation process called Industry 4.0 in the manufacturing and service sectors, financial and labor markets, and even in the public policies. Artificial intelligence (AI), which is a remarkable component of Industry 4.0, is increasing its impact on the economy day by day. Although the effects of this transformation seem positive at first glance, it is not clear what the long-term effects will be.

Following the Industrial Revolution, which emerged in the early eighteenth century, commercial capitalism was replaced by industrial capitalism. Since then, although many economic issues arose, the capitalist system continued to spread and increase its power. Technological improvements, on the other hand, have always

C. Demir (✉) · S. Çakmak
Department of Economics, Salihli FEAS, Manisa Celal Bayar University, Manisa, Turkey
e-mail: caner.demir@cbu.edu.tr; serhat.cakmak@cbu.edu.tr

A. Ari (ed.), *Capitalism at a Crossroads*, Springer Studies in Alternative Economics,
https://doi.org/10.1007/978-3-031-23257-2_11

been one of the main factors that come to rescue the system in difficult times. In today's terms, the invention of the steam engine is regarded as the first industrial revolution. Then, in the late nineteenth century and the early twentieth century, with increasing energy resources and transition to mass production, the second industrial revolution occurred. Finally, in the second half of the twentieth century, improvements in electronics, industrial automation systems, and information and communication systems led to a new transformation which is now called the third industrial revolution. And as a more recent one, the fourth industrial revolution (also known as Industry 4.0) is the transformation still ongoing in the twenty-first century.

Industry 4.0 process includes many dimensions such as the internet of things (IoT), cyber-physical systems, smart factories, big data, cloud technology, 3D printing, artificial intelligence, and augmented reality. An important point here is that each of these dimensions and components operates in an interactive and integrated way with each other (Saturno et al., 2017).

Among all the industry 4.0 components, AI occupies a privileged position as it has the potential to substitute the human mind. In simple terms, AI refers to the intelligent behaviors of objects made by humans. Thinking rationally like human beings and then acting rationally is the foundation of the AI concept. With the combination of AI and other industry 4.0 components, one may suggest that many production processes will have labor-saving technological improvements. Although this situation is likely to happen, on the contrary, it is also possible that the demand for labor will increase. These differences of opinion will be discussed in more detail in the following sections. This point is directly related to the cost structure of the firms as well as the economic situation of the households. Will the increase in labor savings further increase or decrease the income inequality created by capitalism? In addition, there are possible effects of AI on financial markets and public finance. Will AI be able to play a market expander role in these markets where decision processes are very sensitive and faster than the limits of the human mind? Will the effects of AI on markets, economic agents, and income distribution require some regulations in public finance?

From this perspective, this chapter will discuss the potential impacts of AI on the household's welfare, the accumulation process of the capital owners, financial markets, and the actions of the governments. By making a comparative analysis between different ideas, we will question whether the possible outcomes will be a healer for the future of capitalism. The remainder of the chapter is organized as follows. Section 2 discusses technological progress and transformation of capitalism from a historical perspective. Section 3 discusses the probable impact of AI on different markets and economic actors. Section 4 concludes.

2 Technological Progress and the Transformation of Capitalism

2.1 Technological Development Phenomenon in Economic History

There has always been technological development in human history. The effort to produce new simple inventions even in primitive societies shows the curiosity about technological development and the comfort obtained due to it (Boserup, 1976). Societies have always sought ways to make their lives more comfortable and more productive by pursuing new ideas.

On the other hand, there is a social resistance to technological development. Mokyr (1992) emphasized that technological progress is highly dependent on the social environment. He stated that there had been resistance to innovation in technological development processes throughout history. He stated that this resistance could be observed when an examination was made for the British and French economies during the industrial revolution process. Similarly, Basualdo et al. (2021) also stated that there has always been opposition to technological development breakthroughs in the historical process. In fact, these protests took place in the form of strikes and social revolts. Thus, looking at the historical process, it is possible to suggest that humanity is eager for innovations that make life more comfortable and simpler. However, at the same time, it shows resistance to breaking away from its current habits.

Although technological development is a process of tens of thousands of years, the industrial revolution corresponds to a completely different place terminologically than other technological leaps because it is the beginning of a much more intense and integrated transformation. There are different opinions about when the first Industrial Revolution started. Even so, the widely accepted date range corresponds to the eighteenth century. Great Britain stands out as for the starting place. Great Britain's use of steam power and steam engine played a major role in having such a priority in the industrial revolution. Although the idea of using steam power historically dates back to Egypt in the first century and France in the seventeenth century, machine designs that can be used on an industrial scale emerged in Great Britain (Kitsikopoulos, 2013). Of course, it was no coincidence that this leap came industrially in Great Britain. Mercantilist policies that had prevailed in Europe for nearly three centuries had yielded much more successful results in Great Britain, unlike many other countries such as Germany, France, and Spain. Therefore, it should be no surprise that a country that emerged as much more economically successful than other countries in the period covering the three centuries just before the industrial revolution also pioneered the industrial revolution. In addition, it should be noted that the mercantilist period in Great Britain did not pass as a purely trade-oriented period aiming to have a current account surplus and witnessed significant expansions in the industrial dimension. Briefly, in Great Britain, there was a favorable environment in many aspects for the emergence of the industrial revolution; and this environment paved the way for the transition from commercial capitalism to industrial capitalism.

Today, the industrial revolution is not defined as a one-time event. From the end of the nineteenth century to the beginning of the twentieth century, oil and electric energy began to be used, the use of steel became widespread, transportation and communication networks were developed, and the mass production system was adopted (Boom, 2005; Liffen, 2013). All these developments brought along significant productivity increases. This new transformation period is now referred to as the second industrial revolution.

Following this second industrial revolution, the world wars in the first half of the twentieth century brought along a series of technological developments that were later reflected in the general society. Many developments in electronics, computers, and medicine emerged in this period. In the second half of the twentieth century, advances in engineering and automation systems came together with developments in the chemical industry. Thus, the third industrial revolution emerged. As a result of all these gains, many innovations occurred in the industry, agriculture, health, and services sectors that we benefit from as humanity today (Rifkin, 2011).

When we look at our much more recent history, we see that we are in a new transformation process. For many, this process deserves to be called a new industrial revolution, as it marks much more than conventional technological advances (Kagermann et al., 2011; Drath & Horch, 2014; Hermann et al., 2016). Again, technology is making progress by making a remarkable leap that significantly affects the relations of production, consumption, and distribution. To better understand this new transformation, let us discuss it along with its components in more detail.

2.2 A New Transformation: Industry 4.0

The industry 4.0 process, unlike the previous three industrial revolutions, is not a completed process but a transformation that is still ongoing in our age. Due to the three previous industrial revolutions, production processes had become faster and more complex than ever before. With the inclusion of developments in communication in this advanced structure, the industry 4.0 process has emerged. Kagermann et al. (2013) state that the industry 4.0 process is based on a three-pronged structure in the form of the IoT, cyber-physical systems, and smart factories. These three fundamental components are also related to some other components such as artificial intelligence, big data, cloud technology, blockchain, augmented reality, and three-dimensional (3D) printing that enable the industry 4.0 process to be experienced. In other words, industry 4.0 consists of an interactive operation of all these systems.

Although the concept of the IoT is based on the concept of the industrial internet, which was initially introduced by the General Electric company, it has a much broader scope (Gilchrist, 2016; Hermann et al., 2016). The IoT enables the communication between machines based on very complex calculations by working in coordination with cloud technology and big data, which are other components of

Industry 4.0. In this context, it can be said that it is a component that carries the whole system. Another fundamental component that works in coordination with the IoT is cyber-physical systems. With these systems, machines and other objects in the production process can communicate with each other through related networks. Establishing communication in this way can provide very useful outputs. For example, machines can analyze themselves, make decisions, and transmit them to other machines and objects (Monostori et al., 2016).

With the coexistence of the IoT and cyber-physical systems in the production process, intense communication can occur between the physical capital elements involved in the production, as never before. This new transformation in the production process is called smart factories (Stock & Seliger, 2016). The fact that factories become smart also enable production processes in which the workforce is not involved at all. This transformation is quite possible in a factory where there are only machines and other objects, detection processes are carried out through sensors, and there is absolute communication between units. Although reducing or even zeroing the need for labor may seem like a significant cost advantage at first glance, when the economy as a whole is taken into account, significant problems will likely arise on the consumption side. These effects will be discussed in the following sections.

One of the other essential components of Industry 4.0 is AI. According to Russell and Norvig (2016), there are four different approaches to artificial intelligence; AI is a concept that can think like a human, think rationally, act like a human, and act rationally. The emphasis on "like a human" here undoubtedly indicates that artificial intelligence is a "non-human" entity. These thinking and acting processes are performed by objects (i.e., machines) previously made by humans. Vast amounts of data can be collected through cyber-physical systems and the IoT in the production process. These data are processed by the objects in question, allowing these objects to increase their knowledge. In other words, we are faced with a piece of knowledge and thinking ability that can increase through experiences. This situation points to an "intelligence" even though it was created by artificial means. As stated in the previous paragraph, AI also stands out as a technology that will reduce the need for a workforce. However, since the most prominent point in artificial intelligence is the ability to think, a substitution mechanism will likely emerge for works that are carried out mainly depending on the mind and decision-making processes.

The primary purpose of this chapter is not to cover all the components of industry 4.0 in detail. However, to put it briefly, data with higher dimensions and content than ever before, obtained from the components of industry 4.0, can be obtained and processed with big data. With cloud technology, users can receive various services such as storage, access, and usage remotely without physically owning the necessary hardware and software. Therefore, it has widespread usage area for production as well as consumers. Data obtained through cyber-physical systems can be stored in the cloud system instead of old-style storage at the place of production. In this way, all other units can access this data much more effectively and quickly. With blockchain technology, the tracking of transactions related to tangible or intangible assets has become faster and more systematic than ever before. In the future, this system will be able to spread to every stage of production and minimize the margin of error in many processes. According to Esmaeilian et al. (2020), the bullwhip effect, that is, the inefficiencies and costs that may occur in the supply chain, is reduced with blockchain; hence, it is possible to reduce the increasing responsibilities of the manufacturers and to realize the transportation and shipment times more effectively. In fact, this last benefit becomes even more critical when food safety is taken into account. In addition to these, virtual designs can be combined with the physical environment by using augmented reality and 3D printing technologies. With the developments in augmented reality technology, it can be perceived as if there are designs, drawings, environments that do not physically exist in that place at that time through the necessary equipment. 3D printing technology is another revolutionary invention. With this technology, which enables the production of three-dimensional objects on the printer by spraying the necessary raw material, the design and production of the parts and equipment needed in production will become very effective and fast.

Industry 4.0 and its components are still in an intense development and transformation process. The effects may also lead to a much more complex and powerful transformation in the upcoming years. After presenting some basic information about Industry 4.0, AI, and other components, let us now discuss the effects of technological development on capitalism.

2.3 *Is Technological Progress a Recovery Strategy for Capitalism?*

The current capitalist system is mainly based on the industrial revolution and is called industrial capitalism. In addition, the system in question is currently in a transformation, as stated in the previous section. In fact, since the industrial revolution, it is possible to say that technological development and the effort to produce new technologies have progressed at an increasing rate. In other words, there is a continuous process of technological progress within the capitalist system.

Hugill (2003) emphasized that technology is a fundamental source of capitalism. In his study, which compiles the views of many economic schools on technological development and the continuation of the capitalist system, Hugill touched upon Marx's law of the tendency of the rate of profit to fall and Schumpeter's concept of creative destruction and also discussed the relationship between Kondratiev and hegemonic fluctuations and technological development. He emphasized that with the spread of innovation, the Hegemonic or World leadership cycles system is quite likely to be replaced by another system. Similarly, Smith (2010) discussed the effects of technological development on capitalism by considering some Marxist arguments. According to Smith, technological development will lead to over-accumulation of capital and financial crises. In addition, many adverse effects are likely to be observed in income inequality and environmental dimensions.

De Rivera (2020), on the other hand, emphasized that the current capitalist system can no longer be considered separately from the elements of digital capitalism and that the processes of competition and diffusion in the digital space must be considered in the analyses dealing with capitalism. From this point of view, developments in industry 4.0 and AI, and their effects on the continuation of capitalism gain more importance. The effects of AI on capitalist socialization are also discussed within the framework of Marxist economics and philosophy. According to Engster and Moore (2020), the transformation that AI will create on the means of production will bring both capital and labor to some new forms. At the end of this transformation process, both income distribution and the continuation of the system itself will take different forms. As another possibility, at the end of all these transformation processes, AI can be endogenized within the existing system and may contribute to the increase in the share of capital and the decrease in the share of labor at an increasing rate. From a different perspective, Savul (2020) states that the adverse effects of industry 4.0 on the workforce will be more severe than previously thought. He emphasizes that Industry 4.0 applications should be considered as a new and common strategy of capitalists. According to Savul, the logic of technological progress within the scope of capitalism is to make the value of capital permanent through increasing technological investments.

Lastly, it would be appropriate to mention the intellectual property rights and patent system, which are at the center of today's technological development process. Moser (2013) states that most of the innovation take place outside the patent system in countries where historical evidence has patent laws. She also argues that, in general, the patent system gives a right to the first generation of creative ideas but deters potential later ideas. Considering such alternative approaches and criticisms as well as the mainstream ideology regarding intellectual property rights is important for designing and predicting the future of technological development.

3 Debates on Artificial Intelligence and Capitalism Interaction

Artificial intelligence, with its past experiences and future uncertainties, is still a hot topic for many disciplines. The desired answers to the AI-related questions are whether it will be a repetition of the past or a different matter this time. Of course, if we look at the past, we can see an optimistic result, but it is necessary to discuss the optimistic and pessimistic scenarios when we look at the future.

3.1 AI, Labor Market, and Household Income

The main question in literature is whether machines replace human jobs. One optimistic argument is that technological advancements have not caused mass unemployment yet. Moreover, they brought productivity growth. This productivity growth took place new job opportunities for human labor. In the words of Joseph Schumpeter, technological progress provides creative destruction (Frank et al., 2019). On the one hand, it eliminates some of the existing jobs and tasks, and on the other hand, it generates new jobs and tasks in the economy. However, a distinction emerges between short and long run in the history of technological innovations. Although automation is labor-saving in the short run, it could cause the creation of new jobs and tasks in the long run (Furman, 2019; Furman & Seamans, 2019; Goolsbee, 2019; Stevenson, 2019).

There are also opinions in the literature that automation is not labor-saving. The underlying reason for this view is that automation creates a cost-reducing effect for specific tasks, which lowers the price of all goods and services. Hence, people become relatively more prosperous, and consumption and subsequently demand for labor increase. This is called as productivity effect. Another argument that automation is not labor-saving is the deepening of automation by re-influencing previously affected jobs. This situation also has an increasing effect on the demand for labor due to the increase in productivity (Acemoglu & Restrepo, 2019).

Authors who are pessimistic about automation foresee that a rapid automation process will cause mass unemployment. In the past, economists such as Keynes and Leontief had emphasized that technological developments can lead to unemployment (Furman & Seamans, 2019). Others think that AI negatively affects specific jobs but not whole labor market jobs (Frank et al., 2019). It is thought that machines will replace human labor in low-skill jobs but will not cause unemployment in high-skill jobs (Furman, 2019; Goolsbee, 2019). It is predicted that the number of jobs and wages will increase, especially in information technology-oriented sectors. Another concern about automation is that it will lead to inequality. Compensation for the losers of AI may have difficulty to keep up with the gains of the capitalists. It can take time to create new jobs and tasks. Meanwhile, the countervailing forces of AI may not compensate unemployed workers (Stevenson, 2019).

Another matter is about the speed of automation. If automation replaces too quickly, it may lead to mass unemployment coming to the fore. Moreover, if automation happens faster than expected, it will be challenging to increase productivity and demand to create new jobs and tasks (Korinek & Stiglitz, 2019). In addition to that, a mismatch problem arises in the labor market (Acemoglu & Restrepo, 2019). Structural unemployment tends to people looking for new jobs in other workplace environments. These people are not qualified workers for these jobs, and there will be a retraining process. Thus, the adaptation of workers to new business climates is harder than it looks. This adjustment period will be even more difficult, especially if the education system is not organized to train human capital in areas that will be seen as future professions through AI. Furthermore, it is mentioned that in a rapid automation environment, it will be more challenging to come up with new ideas, and more research resources will be needed (Furman & Seamans, 2019).

Acemoglu and Restrepo (2019) especially emphasize two concepts while mentioning the effects of the automation process on the labor market. The first is the displacement effect. This effect is directly related to the labor-saving feature of automation. The productivity-enhancing technological developments will distort the labor market. The other concept is the reinstatement effect. According to this, automation increases the demand for labor, contrary to the displacement effect. Rapid automation may reduce the share of labor in production and lower wages. In this way, it increases the labor demand appetite of the firms. In addition, AI applications can directly create new jobs and tasks in some sectors such as education and health care. Thus, the reinstatement effect plays a countervailing role even if there is a displacement effect.

Despite all these discussions, it does not seem possible for AI to replace human labor completely. This idea is based on human-specific features (such as empathy, communication skills) and approaches to problems (such as complex reasoning, judgment, abstract problem-solving) that only humans have and are not thought to be possessed by robots (Acemoglu & Restrepo, 2019). Thus, the privilege of being human erodes the idea that AI will cause mass unemployment in the labor market.

Universal Basic Income (UBI) is at the forefront of the solution methods that have emerged in eliminating the fears that arise with AI. UBI is a cash transfer to households to compensate for the loss caused by the displacement effect created by AI, without any additional conditions, based only on criteria such as citizenship and age. In this way, it is aimed that household incomes do not remain below the poverty line in the capitalist new world order. Despite all this focus on income redistribution, UBI is not a program with only pros as it is thought. Whether UBI will be more effective than currently used social security or health programs is still debated. This replacement may adversely affect the incomes of disadvantaged people. Direct cash transfers can also cause using the money in ineffective ways (such as gambling, drugs) compared to an in-kind safety net. In addition, UBI requires a large amount of additional financing. Milton Friedman referred to this additional financing as negative income tax (Goolsbee, 2019). UBI may also cause a decrease in the labor force participation rate of low-wage workers as it will provide people with a stable income. However, there are two alternative solution methods besides UBI. These are wage subsidies and government-guaranteed employment (Furman & Seamans, 2019).

3.2 *AI, Capital Accumulation, and Capital-Owning Class*

Improvements in information technologies such as AI will increase the demand for capital as experienced in the past. This increase in demand will increase capital accumulation. The increased capital accumulation will finally increase human labor, which is seen as a complement to capital up to a certain threshold (Acemoglu &

Restrepo, 2019). Discussions in the literature also begin at this point. Capital accumulation is seen as a countervailing force against the displacement effect. To what extent will wage and employment increases triggered by capital accumulation offset the displacement effect?

The increase in capital accumulation with AI empowers the capital-owning class to make new ideas and inventions. Thanks to this power, new jobs and tasks will be created in the economy, even if jobs have disappeared due to creative destruction. The demand for capital in new jobs and tasks will also increase the capital, and indirectly the demand for labor will increase again, along with the increase in wages.

Some authors say that this process works in reverse and leads to income inequality. Underlying this view is that automation increases the income gap between the rich and the poor. As a result of technological change, the substitution of capital for labor changes in favor of capital, especially in labor-intensive jobs and tasks. This situation reduces both the demand for labor and wages. This increase in demand for capital in jobs and tasks increases the share of the capitalists in production while decreasing the share of workers. It has been observed that the percentage of the richest 1% of the income in developed countries such as the US has increased gradually with technological development (Deskoska & Vlčková, 2018). To eliminate the increasing inequality, Korinek and Stiglitz (2019) argued that taxation of capital would be an additional burden on capital, capitalists would tend to capital augmenting technological innovations rather than labor-saving technological innovations.

3.3 AI and Financial Markets

AI applications affect the financial markets as well as the entire economy. AI leads to an increase in efficiency in financial markets and provides a cost-reducing effect. Thanks to AI applications, this increase in efficiency is achieved by financial institutions' ability to analyze data more quickly and reliably. In addition, financial institutions can provide a more personalized service to their customers by analyzing their customer data, chatbots/virtual assistants, and regulatory compliance, preventing money laundering and fraud, and assessing credit scoring (Fernández, 2019; Mhlanga, 2020).

With the increasing use of AI-based technologies in financial markets in recent years, portfolio management processes have started to be taken more accurately for investors. One of the AI-related technologies emerging in portfolio management is robo-advisor. Robo-advisory is an online automated investment platform that uses quantitative algorithms to manage investors' portfolios. Robo-advisors are designed to manage portfolios made by investment/wealth managers based on customer preferences more impeccable through AI-based algorithms. This automation makes the behavioral investment decision-making process more efficient and less emotional and cognitive bias. Robo-advisors act entirely in the best interests of their clients. Robo-advisors not only help to solve the problems faced by the customer by using algorithms, but also provide architectural choices and online interfaces for them to solve the problems themselves. It is foreseen that robo-advisors will be more involved in the financial markets of the future, as they provide cheaper and more effective service to customers in order to make better investment decisions (Shanmuganathan, 2020; Milana & Ashta, 2021).

3.4 Government Regulations Against Potential Market Imbalances

The automation process brings some potential hazards to the national economy; thus, governments should be ready to regulate these hazards in the next future. We mentioned before that automation might affect the entire labor market or specific jobs and tasks. How should governments struggle with labor-saving technological advances and support countervailing forces against the displacement effect? AI debates continue globally, but which country will be more affected by automation (Frank et al., 2019)? To what extent will the impact of automation on labor markets in developing and developed countries differ? These are still open questions, but some suggestions exist in the related literature.

Public policies should be designed in a way that prevents mass unemployment, does not reduce wages, aggregate demand, and labor force participation rates, and provides income redistribution through negative income tax. Besides, the education policy needs to be reorganized for this transition to avoid mismatch problems due to new jobs and tasks created by AI. Considering the UBI, it should not have an additional cost to governments. Therefore, governments will not support the program very much with extra budget costs. However, if the cost of the program is negligible, it can be considered a policy to be used to compensate for the damage caused by automation (Korinek & Stiglitz, 2019). In addition, the other alternatives (government-guaranteed jobs and wage subsidies) must also be conducted by governments. Thus, governments will play a vital role in this transition.

The private sector is the leading actor in the economy to make innovations, but governments take action against negative consequences of innovation on privacy, cybersecurity, and competition (Furman, 2019). All these market imbalances arise from the customer data held by the companies. With the shift of shopping to online platforms, it has become easy for companies to store customer data thanks to AI-related technologies. Thus, the dominance of market power has passed to firms. Along with this market power, companies try to seize consumer surplus by making price discrimination and apply individualized marketing methods by using customer information without the knowledge of the customers (Goolsbee, 2019). There are some other market imbalances such as information problems, price and wage rigidities, monopolies, insufficient aggregate demand and so forth (Korinek & Stiglitz, 2019). Therefore, antitrust policies are crucial in eliminating market imbalances.

AI needs to be regulated by governments. However, it is still a mystery who and how will make this regulation. For example, governments may be expected to establish a commission or create an economic actor for this purpose. Another question is whether the commission or economic actor will be an enforcement authority or an advisory function (Furman & Seamans, 2019). However, the expectations of governments from technological progress in economic terms are to create productivity gains. In this context, AI or AI-related technologies should be supported, and their use should be encouraged despite all automation discussions. Some governments, such as China, France, and the USA, directly design their development policies based on AI technologies (Agrawal et al., 2019; Frank et al., 2019).

4 Conclusion

In this chapter, we tried to discuss the possible effects of artificial intelligence, an important component of the industry 4.0 process, on the future of capitalism. AI is still evolving and becoming more complex, making all these predictions somewhat hypothetical. However, raising and discussing as many potential impacts as possible is vital for building a future with AI.

When we look at the possible effects of artificial intelligence, we see that the prominent debates are clustered around the most pessimistic and most optimistic ideas. One of the discussion points is on the labor market. The displacement effect which occurs when AI substitutes labor may cause to a decrease in the demand for labor in the future. On the other hand, decreased demand for labor may reduce wages, leading to the emergence of new jobs and models. This situation expressed as the reinstatement effect would mean for capitalism to be reborn from its ashes if it happens.

The productivity increase brought by AI will increase the profit appetite of the capitalist class and will encourage new investments. Although this situation seems optimistic in terms of economic growth, there are different opinions. If the production is done with less labor force, the demand for labor may decrease and there may be a reduction in real wages. This situation will widen the income inequality between the rich and the poor. In the post-Industry 4.0 period, income inequality will create a very different outlook from the income inequality discussed in previous decades. Decreased demand for labor may cause a decline in household income, which in turn may reduce aggregate demand. In this case, there will not be sufficient demand for the goods and services produced by the firms with increasing efficiency. At this point, governments may also have an important regulatory role. The universal basic income idea which has been frequently mentioned recently seems to be a remarkable alternative for the distribution of income. Although the UBI option offered as a solution to this situation has the potential to work, some supportive and counterarguments are put forward in this regard. Possible capital transformations are not limited to physical capital investments. Fundamental changes are also taking place in the financial markets, depending on AI. Making decisions in financial markets, which are getting more and more complex, exceeds the limits of the human mind. At this point, AI-based decision-making systems will be able to ensure that the decisions of those operating in financial markets are much more effective and closer to optimal. However, considering that the biggest shareholder in these markets is the capital owner class, it is possible to state that there is a potential to cause social income inequality.

References

Acemoglu, D., & Restrepo, P. (2019). Artificial intelligence, automation, and work. In A. Agrawal, J. Gans, & A. Goldfarb (Eds.), *The economics of artificial intelligence: An agenda* (pp. 197–236). University of Chicago Press.

Agrawal, A., Gans, J. S., & Goldfarb, A. (2019). Exploring the impact of artificial intelligence: Prediction versus judgment. *Information Economics and Policy, 47*, 1–6.

Basualdo, V., Dias, H., Herberg, M., Schmalz, S., Serrano, M., & Vandaele, K. (2021). Building workers' power in digital capitalism. Trade unions in transformation 4.0. Friedrich-Ebert-Stiftung. http://library.fes.de/pdf-files/iez/18325.pdf

Boom, R. (2005). Iron, the hidden element: The role of iron and steel in the twentieth century. In *The Hatfield Memorial Lectures* (pp. 227–245). Woodhead Publishing.

Boserup, E. (1976). Environment, population, and technology in primitive societies. *Population and Development Review, 2*(1), 21–36.

De Rivera, J. (2020). A guide to understanding and combatting digital capitalism. tripleC: Communication, capitalism & critique. *Open Access Journal for a Global Sustainable Information Society, 18*(2), 725–743.

Deskoska, E., & Vlčková, J. (2018). The role of technological change in income inequality in the United States. *Acta Oeconomica Pragensia, 1*, 47–66.

Drath, R., & Horch, A. (2014). Industrie 4.0: Hit or hype? [industry forum]. *IEEE Industrial Electronics Magazine, 8*(2), 56–58.

Engster, F., & Moore, P. V. (2020). The search for (artificial) intelligence, in capitalism. *Capital & Class, 44*(2), 201–218.

Esmaeilian, B., Sarkis, J., Lewis, K., & Behdad, S. (2020). Blockchain for the future of sustainable supply chain management in industry 4.0. *Resources, Conservation and Recycling, 163*, 105064, 1–15.

Fernández, A. (2019). Artificial intelligence in financial services. *Banco de Espana Article, 03*(19), 1–7.

Frank, M. R., Autor, D., Bessen, J. E., Brynjolfsson, E., Cebrian, M., Deming, D. J., & Rahwan, I. (2019). Toward understanding the impact of artificial intelligence on labor. *Proceedings of the National Academy of Sciences, 116*(14), 6531–6539.

Furman, J. (2019). Should we be reassured if automation in the future looks like automation in the past? In A. Agrawal, J. Gans, & A. Goldfarb (Eds.), *The economics of artificial intelligence: An agenda* (pp. 317–328). University of Chicago Press.

Furman, J., & Seamans, R. (2019). AI and the economy. *Innovation Policy and the Economy, 19*(1), 161–191.

Gilchrist, A. (2016). *Industry 4.0: The industrial internet of things*. Apress.

Goolsbee, A. (2019). Public policy in an AI economy. In A. Agrawal, J. Gans, & A. Goldfarb (Eds.), *The economics of artificial intelligence: An agenda* (pp. 309–316). University of Chicago Press.

Hermann, M., Pentek, T., & Otto, B. (2016). Design principles for industrie 4.0 scenarios. In *2016 49th Hawaii international conference on system sciences (HICSS)* (pp. 3928–3937).

Hugill, P. J. (2003). Technology, its innovation and diffusion as the motor of capitalism. *Comparative Technology Transfer and Society, 1*(1), 89–113.

Kagermann, H., Helbig, J., Hellinger, A., & Wahlster, W. (2013). Recommendations for implementing the strategic initiative INDUSTRIE 4.0: Securing the future of German manufacturing industry; final report of the Industrie 4.0 working group. Forschungsunion.

Kagermann, H., Lukas, W. D., & Wahlster, W. (2011). Industrie 4.0: Mit dem Internet der Dinge auf dem Weg zur 4. industriellen Revolution. *VDI Nachrichten, 13*(1), 2–3.

Kitsikopoulos, H. (2013). From hero to Newcomen: The critical scientific and technological developments that led to the invention of the steam engine. *Proceedings of the American Philosophical Society*, 304–344.

Korinek, A., & Stiglitz, J. E. (2019). Artificial intelligence and its implications for income distribution and unemployment. In A. Agrawal, J. Gans, & A. Goldfarb (Eds.), *The economics of artificial intelligence: An agenda* (pp. 349–390). University of Chicago Press.

Liffen, J. (2013). Telegraphy and telephones. *Industrial Archaeology Review, 35*(1), 22–39.

Mhlanga, D. (2020). Industry 4.0 in finance: The impact of artificial intelligence (ai) on digital financial inclusion. *International Journal of Financial Studies, 8*(3), 45, 1–14.

Milana, C., & Ashta, A. (2021). Artificial intelligence techniques in finance and financial markets: A survey of the literature. *Strategic Change, 30*(3), 189–209.

Mokyr, J. (1992). Technological inertia in economic history. *The Journal of Economic History, 52*(2), 325–338.

Monostori, L., Kádár, B., Bauernhansl, T., Kondoh, S., Kumara, S., Reinhart, G., & Ueda, K. (2016). Cyber-physical systems in manufacturing. *CIRP Annals, 65*(2), 621–641.

Moser, P. (2013). Patents and innovation: Evidence from economic history. *Journal of Economic Perspectives, 27*(1), 23–44.

Rifkin, J. (2011). *The third industrial revolution: How lateral power is transforming energy, the economy, and the world*. Macmillan.

Russell, S. J., & Norvig, P. (2016). *Artificial intelligence: a modern approach*. Pearson Education Limited.

Saturno, M., Pertel, V. M., Deschamps, F., & Loures, E. D. F. R. (2017, March). Proposal of an automation solutions architecture for industry 4.0. In *24th international conference on production research*, Poznan.

Savul, G. (2020). The logic of technological progress under capitalism in the context of industry 4.0. *Journal of Labor and Society, 23*(4), 433–460.

Shanmuganathan, M. (2020). Behavioural finance in an era of artificial intelligence: Longitudinal case study of robo-advisors in investment decisions. *Journal of Behavioral and Experimental Finance, 27*(100297), 1–9.

Smith, T. (2010). Technological change in capitalism: Some Marxian themes. *Cambridge Journal of Economics, 34*(1), 203–212.

Stevenson, B. (2019). 7. Artificial intelligence, income, employment, and meaning. In A. Agrawal, J. Gans, & A. Goldfarb (Eds.), *The economics of artificial intelligence: An agenda* (pp. 189–196). University of Chicago Press.

Stock, T., & Seliger, G. (2016). Opportunities of sustainable manufacturing in industry 4.0. *Procedia CIRP, 40*, 536–541.

Endless Growth Regime: The Role of Elasticity of Substitution and Extraordinary Economy Policies

Ata Ozkaya

Abstract The aim of this study is to analyze the effect of elasticity of substitution on output per-capita, growth rate of capital–labor ratio, growth rate of income per capita, the steady-state capital–labor ratio and the steady-state output per capita, respectively. In addition, we extend our analytical results to make further contribution to the literature. We suggest that the marginal product of input factors can be used as a policy instrument to promote the growth rate of output per capita. Moreover, in case of competitive factor markets, the efficiency of this policy instrument can be measured by the marginal prices for input factors (As an example: under competitive markets minimum wage rate corresponds to minimum marginal product of labor. In February 2022, the US government increased the minimum federal wage rate by %50, signaling the increase in marginal product of labor and expectations on increase in growth rate). Second, we focus on the "magic tool" and one of the crucial results of the modern growth theory that there is a threshold of elasticity of substitution for which there is no steady-state equilibrium and for which perpetual growth is entailed. Finally, we query the future path of the modern growth theory, its inconsistencies, and possible remedies under rare circumstances where the COVID-19 pandemic deteriorated the global supply chains and total demand in the economy.

Keywords Elasticity of substitution · CES production functions · Growth rate · Economic growth · COVID-19

1 Introduction

Solow's famous example on the CES production function (Solow, 1956) demonstrates the condition under which perpetual growth would be possible. This finding leads to an extensive analysis on the relationship between the elasticity of

A. Ozkaya (✉)
Department of Economics, Galatasaray University, İstanbul, Turkey
e-mail: aozkaya@gsu.edu.tr

A. Ari (ed.), *Capitalism at a Crossroads*, Springer Studies in Alternative Economics,
https://doi.org/10.1007/978-3-031-23257-2_12

substitution and the growth rate of output per capita. Based on the empirical findings that the value added per unit of labor used within a given industry varies across countries with the wage rate, Arrow-Chenery-Minhas-Solow (ACMS) (Arrow et al., 1961) derive a unique mathematical function having the properties of (1) homogeneity, (2) constant elasticity of substitution between capital and labor, and (3) the possibility of different elasticities for different industries.

This function is known as CES production function which is based on three parameters identified as the substitution parameter, the distribution parameter, and the efficiency parameter. Arrow et al. (1961) indicate that apart from the efficiency parameter, the CES production function is a class of function known in the mathematical literature as a "mean value of order -ρ", ρ being "substitution between input factors". Second, Arrow et al. (1961) demonstrate that the limiting values of the substitution parameter, ρ, lead to special type production functions: 1) "The case $\rho = 0$ yields an elasticity of substitution of unity and should, therefore, lead back to the Cobb-Douglas function." 2) "…And as $\rho \to \infty$, the elasticity of substitution tends to zero and we approach the case of fixed proportions." The proof of the authors is based on the Weighted Means, theorems of which are proposed by Hardy et al. (1934).

In comparison with Cobb–Douglas-type functions, the application of production functions with elasticity of substitution other than one was hampered by mathematical and theoretical uncertainties on the implications of the structural parameters and on their empirical interpretations.

Recently, there are some attempts to deal with this gap: specifically, the "normalization" of the CES production function is reported to overcome many of those uncertainties (Klump & de La Grandville, 2000). In a related study, Klump and Preissler (2000) asserted that some inconsistencies and controversies related to the variants of the CES production function in growth models can be resolved by the "normalization" of the CES production function.

Our study is composed of seven sections. Sections 2 and 3 focus on first, to demonstrate that both the distribution and the efficiency parameter should depend on the elasticity of substitution; second, to prove that the distribution and the efficiency parameters are composed of the initial and the terminal conditions of the marginal product of factors of production, which are ignored in the ACMS definition of the CES production function; and third, to propose some crucial economic implications of the initial and the terminal conditions of the production function. Section 4 analyzes whether the method of "normalization" refines the parameters of the CES production function and makes any contribution to ACMS definition. Second, we investigate whether employing the initial and terminal conditions is capable of aligning the variants of the CES production functions. In Sect. 5, the analyses focus on the effect of elasticity of substitution on output per capita,[1] growth rate of capital–labor ratio, and the growth rate of output per capita, respectively. We

[1]Throughout the study, we use the terms output per capita, per-capita income, and income per capita interchangeably.

investigate whether there exists a "magic tool" to guarantee endless or perpetual growth rate of output.

In Sect. 6, we query the future path of the modern growth theory, its inconsistencies, and possible remedies under rare circumstances where the COVID-19 pandemic deteriorated the global supply chains and total demand in the economy. To do this, we exemplify both fiscal policy of US government and monetary policy of Federal Reserve amid COVID-19 pandemic, and we propose a simple deterministic time series model to interpret recent policy implications. Section 7 concludes.

2 Initial and Terminal Conditions of the CES Production Function

Proposition 1
Any production function which can be squeezed between two CES functions can be written in the form given by (1). Let $f(k)$ be per-capita production function, where the term $\frac{f(k_1)}{k_1.f'(k_1)^\sigma}$ is integration constant. This integration constant will be identified later, see Proposition 3.

$$f(k) = \frac{f(k_1)}{k_1.f'(k_1)^\sigma}.k.f'(k)^\sigma \tag{1}$$

For the proof, please see Eqs. (16), (17), and (18) in Appendix 1.

Proposition 2
The differential Eq. (1) has general solution for both $\sigma > 1$ and $\sigma < 1$, which are shown in (3) and (4), respectively.

Proof 2 Let $\vartheta = f(k)^{1-\frac{1}{\sigma}}$ and $\vartheta' = (1 - \frac{1}{\sigma})f'.f^{-\frac{1}{\sigma}}$.
Substituting these terms into (1) and integrating yields (2).

$$\vartheta(k) = \left(\frac{k_1.f'(k_1)^\sigma}{f(k_1)}\right)^{\frac{1}{\sigma}}.k^{1-\frac{1}{\sigma}} + C \tag{2}$$

where integration constant is $0 < C < \infty$. We note that if the constant C is equal to zero, $f'(k)$ must also be constant. On the other hand, if C is infinite, then $f(k)$ will be undefined. However, by definition of the production function, these cases are not possible. Therefore, the constant C satisfies the following limiting cases, (a) and (b):

(a) $\vartheta(0) = C$ if $\sigma > 1$ and (b) $\vartheta(\infty) = C$ if $\sigma < 1$.

Now we obtain the general solution for $f(k)$.

$$f(k) = \left(\left(\frac{k_1.f'(k_1)^{\sigma}}{f(k_1)} \right)^{\frac{1}{\sigma}} .k^{1-\frac{1}{\sigma}} + C \right)^{\frac{1}{1-\frac{1}{\sigma}}}$$

Inserting the possible values of C, we have (3) and (4), respectively. For the case $\sigma > 1$, the expression (3) determines the per-capita production function depending on the initial condition, namely $f(0)$.

$$f(k) = \left(\left(\frac{k_1.f'(k_1)^{\sigma}}{f(k_1)} \right)^{\frac{1}{\sigma}} .k^{1-\frac{1}{\sigma}} + f(0)^{1-\frac{1}{\sigma}} \right)^{\frac{1}{1-\frac{1}{\sigma}}} \tag{3}$$

For $\sigma < 1$, the expression (4) determines the per-capita production function depending on the terminal condition, namely $f(\infty)$.

$$f(k) = \left(\left(\frac{k_1.f'(k_1)^{\sigma}}{f(k_1)} \right)^{\frac{1}{\sigma}} .k^{1-\frac{1}{\sigma}} + f(\infty)^{1-\frac{1}{\sigma}} \right)^{\frac{1}{1-\frac{1}{\sigma}}} \tag{4}$$

First, we rearrange (3) and (4) in terms of production factors and second, we compute the term $\left(\frac{k_1.f'(k_1)^{\sigma}}{f(k_1)} \right)^{\frac{1}{\sigma}}$ which identifies different conditions for $\sigma > 1$ and $\sigma < 1$, respectively. Proposition 3 clarifies this issue.

Proposition 3
The distribution parameter and the efficiency parameter are composed of the initial and the terminal conditions of the marginal product of labor and of the marginal product of capital.

Whenever $\sigma > 1$, the production function is:

$$F(K, L) = \left((F_K(K,\ \ 0).K)^{\frac{\sigma-1}{\sigma}} + (F_L(0,\ \ L).L)^{\frac{\sigma-1}{\sigma}} \right)^{\frac{\sigma}{\sigma-1}} \tag{5}$$

For $\sigma < 1$, the production function becomes:

$$F(K, L) = \left((F_K(K,\ \ \infty).K)^{\frac{\sigma-1}{\sigma}} + (F_L(\infty,\ \ L).L)^{\frac{\sigma-1}{\sigma}} \right)^{\frac{\sigma}{\sigma-1}} \tag{6}$$

Proof 3 Computing the production function at limiting values of production factors, we have:

1. For $\sigma > 1$, the initial conditions of the CES function

$$\lim_{K\to 0} F(K, L) = F_L(0, L).L \quad \text{and} \quad \lim_{L\to 0} F(K, L) = F_K(K, 0).K.$$

The initial conditions with respect to input factors, $F_K(K,0)$ and $F_L(0,L)$, are also obtained in terms of per-capita (intensive) definition:

$f(0) = F_L(0,L)$ is defined for all $0 < L < \infty$ and is constant with respect to the input factors and does not vary with the elasticity of substitution.

$\left(\frac{k_1.f'(k_1)^\sigma}{f(k_1)}\right)^{\frac{1}{\sigma}} = F_K(K,\,0)$ is defined for all $0 < K < \infty$ and is constant with respect to the input factors and does not vary with the elasticity of substitution.

2. For $\sigma < 1$

$$\lim_{K\to\infty} F(K,\,L) = F_L(\infty,\,L).L \quad \text{and} \quad \lim_{L\to\infty} F(K,\,L) = F_K(K,\,\infty).K$$

The terminal conditions $F_K(K,\infty)$ and $F_L(\infty,L)$ can be written in terms of per-capita definition. These are:

$f(\infty) = F_L(\infty,L)$ is defined for all $0 < L < \infty$ and is constant with respect to the input factors and does not vary with the elasticity of substitution.

$\left(\frac{k_1.f'(k_1)^\sigma}{f(k_1)}\right)^{\frac{1}{\sigma}} = F_K(K,\infty)$ is defined for all $0 < K < \infty$ and is constant with respect to the input factors and does not vary with the elasticity of substitution.

The implications of the initial and terminal conditions are straightforward. Whenever $\sigma > 1$, the constant term $F_K(K,0)$ denotes the minimum marginal product of capital, whereas the constant term $F_L(0,L)$ is the minimum marginal product of labor. To observe the minimum product of capital, we have to consider the marginal product of capital without labor. Otherwise, the marginal product of capital is overvalued. That is, the sensitivity of output to capital without labor determines the minimum product of capital in the economy. Therefore, under competitive regime, $F_K(K,0)$ denotes the minimum rental price. Otherwise, the rental price is overvalued. Same argument is true for $F_L(0,L)$.

For $\sigma < 1$, $F_K(K,\infty)$ is the maximum marginal product of capital whereas $F_L(\infty, L)$ is the maximum marginal product of labor. To obtain the maximum product of capital, we must rely on the marginal product of capital under maximum possible labor. Otherwise, the productivity of marginal capital is undervalued. Hence, for competitive markets, $F_K(K,\infty)$ denotes the maximum rental price. Otherwise, the rental price becomes undervalued. Same argument is true for the maximum product of labor, $F_L(\infty,L)$.

We consider that each of the initial and the terminal conditions represents the structural properties of the production process and cannot be chosen arbitrarily.

To compare the economies, we have three possible cases which are based on the initial and terminal conditions and on the elasticity of substitution level as well. Let us tabulate them.

(i) The minimum (maximum) marginal product level may vary across the countries whereas the level of elasticity of substitution can be equal to each other, i.e., $F_{iK}(K,0) \neq F_{jK}(K,0)$ and/or $F_{iL}(0,L) \neq F_{jL}(0,L)$, and $\sigma_i = \sigma_j > 1$, where, i, $j = 1, \ldots, n$ and $i \neq j$ denote the country.

(ii) The elasticity of substitution differs across countries while the minimum (maximum) marginal products are the same.
(iii) The countries may have different values of elasticity of substitution and have different minimum (maximum) marginal products.

3 Aligning the Variants of the CES Parameters

Recall that the CES production function

$$Y = F(K, L) = (\beta.K^{-\rho} + \alpha.L^{-\rho})^{\frac{-1}{\rho}}$$

is written out more symmetrically (Arrow et al., 1961):

$$Y = F(K, L) = \gamma[\delta.K^{-\rho} + (1-\delta).L^{-\rho}]^{\frac{-1}{\rho}}$$

where $\alpha + \beta = \gamma^{-\rho}$; $\beta.\ \gamma^{\rho} = \delta$; $\frac{\beta}{\alpha} = \frac{\delta}{1-\delta}$; $\rho = \frac{1}{\sigma} - 1$ and σ is the elasticity of substitution.

Thus, the efficiency parameter equals to

$$\gamma = \left[\left(\frac{K.F_K(K,\ L)^{\sigma}}{F(K,\ L)}\right)^{\frac{1}{\sigma}} + \left(\frac{L.F_L(K,\ L)^{\sigma}}{F(K,\ L)}\right)^{\frac{1}{\sigma}}\right]^{\frac{\sigma}{\sigma-1}}$$

and the distribution parameter, δ should satisfy

$$\frac{\delta}{1-\delta} = \frac{F_K(K, L)}{F_L(K, L)}\left(\frac{K}{L}\right)^{\frac{1}{\sigma}}.$$

We have the following precise result: (5) and (6) demonstrate that the efficiency parameter depends only on the value of elasticity of substitution. Therefore, the efficiency parameter must be equal to (7):

$$\gamma = \begin{cases} \left(F_K(K,0)^{\frac{\sigma-1}{\sigma}} + F_L(0,L)^{\frac{\sigma-1}{\sigma}}\right)^{\frac{\sigma}{\sigma-1}} & \text{for} \quad \sigma > 1 \\ \left(F_K(K,\infty)^{\frac{\sigma-1}{\sigma}} + F_L(\infty,L)^{\frac{\sigma-1}{\sigma}}\right)^{\frac{\sigma}{\sigma-1}} & \text{for} \quad \sigma < 1 \end{cases} \tag{7}$$

In addition, (5) demonstrates that for $\sigma > 1$, $\beta = \delta.\ \gamma^{-\rho}$ must be equal to $F_K(K, 0)^{\frac{\sigma-1}{\sigma}}$, which depends on the elasticity of substitution. Similarly, from (5) it can be easily seen that $\alpha = (1-\delta).\ \gamma^{-\rho}$ must be equal to $F_L(0, L)^{\frac{\sigma-1}{\sigma}}$, which depends only on the elasticity of substitution as well. Above arguments lead to (8). Then, the distribution parameter δ must be equal to:

$$\delta = \begin{cases} F_K(K,\ 0)^{\frac{\sigma-1}{\sigma}} / \left(F_K(K,\ 0)^{\frac{\sigma-1}{\sigma}} + F_L(0,\ L)^{\frac{\sigma-1}{\sigma}}\right) & \text{for} \quad \sigma > 1 \\ F_K(K,\ \infty)^{\frac{\sigma-1}{\sigma}} / \left(F_K(K,\ \infty)^{\frac{\sigma-1}{\sigma}} + F_L(\infty,\ L)^{\frac{\sigma-1}{\sigma}}\right) & \text{for} \quad \sigma < 1 \end{cases} \tag{8}$$

Comparing (5) and (6) to (8), it is precise that whenever $\sigma > 1$, $\beta^{\frac{\sigma}{\sigma-1}} = F_K(K, 0)$ is the minimum marginal product of capital and $\alpha^{\frac{\sigma}{\sigma-1}} = F_L(0, L)$ is the minimum marginal product of labor.

On the other hand, for $\sigma < 1, \beta^{\frac{\sigma}{\sigma-1}} = F_K(K, \infty)$ is the maximum marginal product of capital, whereas $\alpha^{\frac{\sigma}{\sigma-1}} = F_L(\infty, L)$ is the maximum marginal product of labor.

Following (7), we easily see that the efficiency parameter identified by Arrow et al. (1961) is equal to a fixed point, namely $\gamma = F(1, 1)$. Moreover, homogeneity makes it equal to $\gamma = \frac{F(n,\ n)}{n}$. By the definition, we have

$$\delta.\gamma^{-\rho} = F_K(K, 0)^{\frac{\sigma-1}{\sigma}} = \left(\frac{F(K,\ L)}{K}\right)^{\frac{-1}{\sigma}} F_K(K, L)$$

Finally, the distribution parameter must be equal to (9).

$$\delta = \left(\frac{F_K(K,\ 0)}{F(1,\ 1)}\right)^{\frac{\sigma-1}{\sigma}} = \left(\frac{F(1,\ 0)}{F(1,\ 1)}\right)^{\frac{\sigma-1}{\sigma}} \tag{9}$$

Following (8) and (9), it is clear that ACMS implicitly set the point $F(1, 1)$ as the efficiency parameter and set the ratio $\frac{F(1,\ 0)}{F(1,\ 1)}$ as the distribution parameter. According to us, these implicit assumptions are groundless and inconsistent.

Now, we consider the behavior of the CES function as the substitution parameter, ρ takes the limiting values, 0 and ∞. Let us recall the argument and the proof developed by ACMS, which is one of the building blocks in the growth theory. That is: "The case $\rho = 0$ yields an elasticity of substitution of unity and should, therefore, lead back to the Cobb-Douglas function. This is not obvious from (13), since as $\rho \to 0$, the right-hand side is an indeterminate form of the type 1^{∞}. But in fact, the limit is the Cobb-Douglas function. This can be seen . . ."

Our findings (7), (8), and (9) demonstrate that both the efficiency parameter and the distribution parameter depend upon the elasticity of substitution and that above-given argument is false and should be corrected.[2] The CES production function does not fulfill the requirements of Theorem 3 of Mean theory in Hardy et al. (1934). In proof, taking logarithms of the production functions and then setting $\sigma \to 1$ in (5) and (6) are together sufficient to reach the desired result.

Moreover, in same page Arrow et al. (1961) claim that: "And as $\rho \to \infty$, the elasticity of substitution tends to zero and we approach the case of fixed proportions. We may prove this by making the appropriate limiting process on (13). And once

[2] Similarly, the approach of Pitchford (1960) is also inconsistent.

again the general theory of mean values assures us that as a mean value of order $-\infty$ we have. . . .”

Similarly, this argument is inconsistent too. Our result given by (6) is in sharp contrast with this finding of Arrow et al. (1961). Again, the CES production function does not fulfill the requirements of Theorem 4 of Mean theory introduced in Hardy et al. (1934).

In proof, we allow $\sigma \rightarrow 0$ in (6), and we obtain

$$F(K, L) = \min\left(F_K(K,\ \infty).K, F_L(\infty,\ L).L\right),$$

i.e., the minimum of the production shares having maximum marginal product.

More generally, Arrow et al. (1961) state that: “Apart from the efficiency parameter (which can be made equal to one by appropriate choice of output units), (13) is a class of function known in the mathematical literature as a “mean value of order -ρ”. . .”. However, this argument is misleading. The CES function is not a class of function defined as a “mean value of order -ρ”. On the other hand, to make the efficiency parameter equal to 1, we have to choose the initial and the terminal conditions such that $F(n, n) = n$, for all $n > 0$. However, it can be easily seen from (7) and (8) that efficiency and the distribution parameters depending on elasticity of substitution, σ, violate the fundamental hypothesis of both weighted means theorem and ordinary means theorem proposed in Hardy et al. (1934).

4 Normalization of the CES Production Function: Why Do We Need?

The “normalization” of the CES function at some arbitrarily chosen baseline values is initialized by de La Grandville (1989). In their theoretical study, Klump and de La Grandville (2000) apply the normalization method to compare the rate of growth of the economies which are distinguished by their elasticity of substitution.

In a related study, Klump and Preissler (2000) claim that there are certain inconsistencies and controversies arising from the variants of the CES production function in growth models. To align the use of the variants of the CES functions, the authors propose normalization of the CES parameters in terms of arbitrary chosen values for the capital–labor ratio, the per-capita production, and the marginal rate of substitution. Even though we give support to above-mentioned studies in the sense of investigating the implication and the interpretation of the CES parameters, our study differs from those by the methodology, the structure of the function, and the results. Our findings in Sect. 4 reveal the question whether “normalization” of the parameters of the CES function at some arbitrary chosen values is necessary.

Similar to Arrow et al. (1961), Klump and de La Grandville (2000) employ another partitioning of the CES coefficients and propose the following normalized CES per-capita production function[3]:

$$y = A(\sigma)\left(a(\sigma)k^{\frac{\sigma}{\sigma-1}} + (1-a(\sigma))\right)^{\frac{\sigma-1}{\sigma}}$$

where $A(\sigma)$ and $a(\sigma)$ depend on arbitrarily chosen values of three variables, namely capital–labor ratio, marginal rate of substitution value, and per-capita production.

Applying (5) and (6) to normalized CES function, we determine the normalization parameters in terms of initial and terminal conditions:

For $\sigma > 1$,

$$A(\sigma)^{\frac{\sigma}{\sigma-1}}.a(\sigma) = F_K(K,0)^{\frac{\sigma}{\sigma-1}}$$

For $\sigma < 1$,

$$A(\sigma)^{\frac{\sigma}{\sigma-1}}.a(\sigma) = F_K(K,\infty)^{\frac{\sigma}{\sigma-1}}$$

And for $\sigma > 1$, Proposition 3 leads to

$$F_K(K,0)^{\frac{\sigma}{\sigma-1}} = \left(\frac{F(K,\ L)}{K}\right)^{\frac{1}{\sigma-1}}.F_K(K,L).$$

which assure us that $A(\sigma)$ and $a(\sigma)$ denote the particular points:

$$A(\sigma) = F(1,1) \text{ and } a(\sigma) = \left(\frac{F_K(K,\ 0)}{F(1,\ 1)}\right)^{\frac{\sigma}{\sigma-1}} = \left(\frac{F(1,\ 0)}{F(1,\ 1)}\right)^{\frac{\sigma}{\sigma-1}} \tag{10}$$

One can easily compute the normalized parameters for $\sigma < 1$.

From (8) and (10), it is clear that Klump and de La Grandville (2000) formulation is same as that of Arrow et al. (1961). Moreover, our findings demonstrate that the inconsistencies and controversies reported by Klump and Preissler (2000) are eliminated by (5) and (6) (please see the expressions (19) and (20) in Appendix 1). Therefore, our results point out that we do not need normalizing the CES function parameters and that the initial and terminal conditions inherently identify the "structural" differences in economies.

Finally, unless the minimum (maximum) marginal product of input factors is shown to have more elementary components, all possible variants of the CES function should be written out in terms of the initial and terminal conditions.

[3] Klump and de La Grandville (2000) define the substitution parameter as $\frac{\sigma}{\sigma-1}$.

5 Endless Growth Regime: Is There Any "Magic" Policy Tool?

This part of study redetermines the effect of elasticity of substitution on output per capita, growth rate of capital–labor ratio, and growth rate of output per capita, respectively. We demonstrate that output per capita and growth rate of capital–labor ratio are decreasing functions of elasticity of substitution. The effect of elasticity of substitution on growth rate of output per capita depends on initial–terminal conditions of marginal products. We correct the misleading result that there is a threshold of elasticity of substitution for which perpetual growth is entailed.

Solow's example on the CES production function (Solow, 1956) demonstrates the condition under which perpetual growth would be possible. This finding leads to an extensive analysis on the relationship between the elasticity of substitution and the growth rate of income per capita. In addition, the investigation whether different growth rates among countries can be explained by the elasticity of substitution has taken considerable place in the literature of the growth theory.

This part of the study aims to extend our analytical results to make further contribution to the literature and we examine whether the minimum and maximum marginal product of input factors can be used as policy instrument to increase the growth rate of per-capita income for higher-than-unity elasticity of substitution or for lower-than-unity elasticity of substitution, respectively.

For our purposes, let us tabulate the major findings reported in the literature.

De La Grandville (2009, p. 94) states that for any capital and labor value and for any given value of the parameters of the CES production function, income and per-capita income are increasing functions of the elasticity of substitution.

De La Grandville (1989) finds out that there is a threshold of elasticity of substitution for which there is no steady-state equilibrium, implying perpetually increasing capital–labor ratio and per-capita income. Moreover, this threshold is increasing with growth rate of labor and is decreasing with saving rate.

Another crucial finding reported in de La Grandville (1989) is that the growth rate of per-capita income and the growth rate of capital per labor are increasing functions of the elasticity of substitution. For the case of steady state, de La Grandville (1989) shows that the steady-state per-capita income is an increasing function of the elasticity of substitution.

The findings in Klump and de La Grandville (2000) depict that if two countries have common initial conditions, the one with the higher elasticity of substitution will always experience, other things being equal, a higher per-capita income. Moreover, any equilibrium values of capital–labor and per-capita income are increasing functions of the elasticity of substitution. In a related study, Klump and Preissler (2000) point out that a higher elasticity of substitution leads to a higher steady state and increases the probability of permanent growth. Finally, de La Grandville and Solow (2006) claim that the elasticity of substitution can increase the growth rate of the economy and its effect may be greater than the contribution of the increase in the savings rate and/or technical progress.

Recall (5) and (6). Whenever $\sigma > 1$, the production function is

$$F(K,L) = \left((F_K(K,\ 0).K)^{\frac{\sigma-1}{\sigma}} + (F_L(0,\ L).L)^{\frac{\sigma-1}{\sigma}}\right)^{\frac{\sigma}{\sigma-1}}$$

For $\sigma < 1$, the production function is

$$F(K,L) = \left((F_K(K,\ \infty).K)^{\frac{\sigma-1}{\sigma}} + (F_L(\infty,\ L).L)^{\frac{\sigma-1}{\sigma}}\right)^{\frac{\sigma}{\sigma-1}}$$

Proposition 4

There exists no threshold of elasticity of substitution for which there is no steady-state equilibrium and for which ever-sustained growth entails. Therefore, there exists no threshold value for saving-investment ratio, s and growth rate of labor, n as well.

Proof 4 Please refer to (21) and (22) in the Appendix 2, which depict the CES function formulation given by de La Grandville (1989).

The parameter $\beta(\sigma)^{\frac{\sigma}{\sigma-1}}$ seemingly depends on σ. Following (23) and (24), it is straightforward to show that $\beta(\sigma)^{\frac{\sigma}{\sigma-1}}$ is a constant with respect to both capital–labor ratio and the elasticity of substitution: that is,

$$\frac{d\beta(\sigma)^{\frac{\sigma}{\sigma-1}}}{dk} = 0 \text{ and } \frac{d\beta(\sigma)^{\frac{\sigma}{\sigma-1}}}{d\sigma} = 0.$$

The same argument is also true for the other parameter denoted $\alpha(\sigma)^{\frac{\sigma}{\sigma-1}}$.

Our finding stands strictly in contrast to the result of de La Grandville (1989) and de La Grandville (2009, p.114).

De La Grandville (1989) claims that "there is a threshold of σ for which there is no steady-state equilibrium. This would imply perpetually increasing capital–labor ratio and income per capita."

De La Grandville (1989) claims that "the elasticity of substitution, as a measure of the efficiency of the productive system, has to be higher when the population growth rate increases or when the savings-investment rate decreases."

However, the argument and the computation behind these findings are completely wrong. De La Grandville (1989) erroneously assumes that $\beta(\sigma)^{\frac{\sigma}{\sigma-1}} = \frac{n}{s}$ and then determines the σ as a function of $\frac{n}{s}$ and $\beta(\sigma)$. The reader is referred to the expression (14) and to the expression (A9) in de La Grandville (1989).

5.1 *The Effect of Elasticity of Substitution on the Growth Rate of Output*

Proposition 5
An increase in elasticity of substitution decreases the growth rate of capital–labor ratio.

Proof 5 By definition of Solow (1956), the growth rate of capital–labor ratio is written:

$$\frac{\dot{k}}{k} = s\,\frac{f(k)}{k} - n.$$

Differentiating both sides with respect to σ leads to (11).

$$\frac{\partial}{\partial\sigma}\left(\frac{\dot{k}}{k}\right) = \frac{s.\beta.(1+m)^{\frac{\sigma}{\sigma-1}}}{(\sigma-1)^2}.\,ln\left(\frac{m^{\frac{m}{1+m}}}{1+m}\right) \tag{11}$$

Recall that $m = \left(\frac{\alpha}{\beta k}\right)^{\frac{\sigma-1}{\sigma}}$ equals $m = \frac{1-\pi}{\pi}$, namely the ratio of labor share to the capital share.

Expression (11) demonstrates that $\frac{\partial}{\partial\sigma}\left(\frac{\dot{k}}{k}\right) < 0$ for all k.

Proposition 6
Unless $\frac{dk}{dt} < 0$, increasing elasticity of substitution does not increase the output of production process.

For $\sigma > 1$, raising the elasticity of substitution may increase or decrease the growth rate of per-capita income depending on certain conditions, which are emphasized below. That is:

$$\frac{\partial\left(\dot{f}/f\right)}{\partial\sigma} \text{ is equal to } \begin{cases} >0 & if\ \dfrac{mlnm}{(1+m)\sigma}\left(\dfrac{\dot{k}}{k}+\sigma n\right) > ln\,(1+m)\left(\dfrac{\dot{k}}{k}+n\right) \\ \leq 0 & \text{otherwise} \end{cases}$$

Proof 6 The rate of growth of per-capita income is $\frac{\dot{f}}{f}$, and its derivate with respect to elasticity of substitution is defined in expression (12):
$\frac{\dot{f}}{f} = \left(\frac{df}{dk}\frac{k}{f}\right)\frac{\dot{k}}{k}$ and

$$\frac{\partial\left(\dot{f}/f\right)}{\partial\sigma} = \left(\frac{\partial}{\partial\sigma}\left(\frac{df}{dk}\frac{k}{f}\right)\right).\frac{\dot{k}}{k} + \left(\frac{\partial}{\partial\sigma}\left(\frac{\dot{k}}{k}\right)\right)\frac{df}{dk}\frac{k}{f} \tag{12}$$

$$\frac{df}{dk}\frac{k}{f}=\pi=\frac{1}{1+\left(\frac{\alpha}{\beta k}\right)^{\frac{\sigma-1}{\sigma}}} \quad \text{and} \quad \frac{\partial}{\partial\sigma}\left(\frac{df}{dk}\frac{k}{f}\right)=\frac{\frac{-1}{\sigma^2}\left(ln\,\frac{\alpha}{\beta k}\right)\left(\frac{\alpha}{\beta k}\right)^{\frac{\sigma-1}{\sigma}}}{\left(1+\left(\frac{\alpha}{\beta k}\right)^{\frac{\sigma-1}{\sigma}}\right)^2}$$

It is straightforward that the derivative of capital share to elasticity of substitution is obtained:

$$\frac{\partial}{\partial\sigma}\left(\frac{df}{dk}\frac{k}{f}\right) \text{ is } \begin{cases} <0 & \text{if } k<\frac{\alpha}{\beta} \\ =0 & \text{if } k=\frac{\alpha}{\beta} \\ >0 & \text{if } k>\frac{\alpha}{\beta} \end{cases}$$

We substitute $\frac{\partial}{\partial\sigma}\left(\frac{df}{dk}\frac{k}{f}\right)$ and (11) into (12), and then we obtain (13).

$$\frac{\partial\left(\dot{f}/f\right)}{\partial\sigma}=\frac{mlnm}{(1+m)^2(\sigma-1)^2}\left(\frac{sf}{\sigma k}+n-\frac{n}{\sigma}\right)-\frac{sf}{(\sigma-1)^2(1+m)k}\,ln\,(1+m) \quad (13)$$

By the definition of the capital–labor ratio growth rate, we must have

$$\frac{sf}{\sigma k}+n-\frac{n}{\sigma}>0.$$

Thus, if

$$m\leq 1 \quad \text{then} \quad \frac{\partial\left(\dot{f}/f\right)}{\partial\sigma}<0,$$

which is growth disturbing condition.

The case $m=\left(\frac{\alpha}{\beta k}\right)^{\frac{\sigma-1}{\sigma}}=\left(\frac{F(0,\ L)}{F(K,\ 0)}\right)^{\frac{\sigma-1}{\sigma}}\leq 1$
implies that the capital is at least as productive as labor, $F(0,L)\leq F(K,0)$.
To make progress, we rearrange (13) and obtain (14).

$$\frac{\partial\left(\dot{f}/f\right)}{\partial\sigma}=\frac{mlnm}{(1+m)^2(\sigma-1)^2\sigma}\left(\frac{\dot{k}}{k}+\sigma n\right)-\frac{1}{(\sigma-1)^2(1+m)}\,ln\,(1+m)\left(\frac{\dot{k}}{k}+n\right)$$

$$\frac{\partial\left(\dot{f}/f\right)}{\partial\sigma}=\frac{1}{(1+m)(\sigma-1)^2}\left(\frac{mlnm}{(1+m)\sigma}\left(\frac{\dot{k}}{k}+\sigma n\right)-ln\,(1+m)\left(\frac{\dot{k}}{k}+n\right)\right) \quad (14)$$

More precisely, we have:

$$\frac{\partial(\dot{f}/f)}{\partial\sigma} \text{ is } \begin{cases} >0 & \text{if } \dfrac{mlnm}{(1+m)\sigma}\left(\dfrac{\dot{k}}{k}+\sigma n\right) > ln\,(1+m)\left(\dfrac{\dot{k}}{k}+n\right) \\ \leq 0 & \text{otherwise} \end{cases}$$

Expression (14) demonstrates that, if

$$\frac{mlnm}{(1+m)\sigma}\left(\frac{\dot{k}}{k}+\sigma n\right) > ln\,(1+m)\left(\frac{\dot{k}}{k}+n\right) > 0$$

then $\frac{\partial(\dot{f}/f)}{\partial\sigma} > 0$,which is growth enhancing. To promote growth, $m > 1$ is a necessary condition, which implies that labor share should be greater. Otherwise, the production process is growth disturbing. Our findings given in (14) and in Proposition 6 stand in contrast to the findings of the literature.

Proposition 7

Let $v = \left(\frac{a}{bk}\right)^{\frac{\sigma-1}{\sigma}}$ and let $\sigma < 1$.

An increase in the elasticity of substitution may increase or may decrease the growth rate of output per capita. More precisely,

$$\frac{\partial(\dot{f}/f)}{\partial\sigma} \text{ is } \begin{cases} >0 & \text{if } \dfrac{vlnv}{(1+v)}\left(\dfrac{\dot{k}}{k}+\sigma n\right) > \sigma\left(\dfrac{\dot{k}}{k}+n\right) ln\,(1+v) \\ \leq 0 & \text{otherwise} \end{cases}$$

On the other hand, as σ gets closer to unity, $\frac{\partial(\dot{f}/f)}{\partial\sigma} < 0$ becomes more probable. Thus, under such a condition the economy should reduce σ to promote growth.

Proof 7 The proof applies same method used in Proof 6.

Finally, as σ gets closer to unity, $\frac{\partial(\dot{f}/f)}{\partial\sigma} < 0$ becomes more probable. Thus, under such a condition the economy should reduce σ to enhance the growth.

5.2 Comparison of the Economies with Different Elasticity of Substitutions

Proposition 8

Suppose that there are two economies: first one has an elasticity of substitution is lower than unity and that of the second economy is higher-than-unity. Suppose further that the maximum marginal product of labor in the first economy is equal to minimum marginal product of labor in the second economy, namely $a = \alpha$. Then, the economy which has the elasticity of substitution higher-than-unity enjoys faster capital growth than the other economy does.

Proof 8 Let $d \in R$ denote a finite number, $0 < d < \infty$.

For $\sigma > 1$, the derivative of capital per labor with respect to time satisfies:

$$\dot{k} > k(s\beta - n) + s\alpha \qquad F_L(K, d) > F_L(0, L)$$

For $\sigma < 1$, the derivative of capital per labor with respect to time satisfies:

$$\dot{k} < sa - nk \qquad F_L(K, d) > F_L(K, 0)$$

Since $k(s\beta - n) + s\alpha > sa - nk$, the proof is complete.

Proposition 9
Suppose that there are two economies. Suppose further that the elasticity of substitution of the first economy is $\sigma < 1$, and the other's is higher-than-unity $\sigma > 1$. Let the production functions be denoted g for $\sigma < 1$ and f for $\sigma > 1$, respectively.

Then, there exists a capital–labor ratio level $k = k^*$ such that at k^* level, $\frac{\mathrm{d}}{\mathrm{d}k} \times \left(\frac{g'}{f'}\right) = 0$. This stationary point means that increasing the capital–labor ratio initially makes the speed of growth in two types of economies converge, and then, the speed of the growth of the economies diverges from each other.

Proof 9 The proof is straightforward. To make use of the Rolle Theorem immediately gives the result.

5.3 *Policy Tools to Enhance the Growth Rate of Output Per Capita*

Proposition 10
For $\sigma > 1$, an increase in the ratio of minimum marginal product of labor to minimum marginal product of capital increases the growth rate of income per capita.

Proof 10 Make use of Proof 6, the derivative of $\left(\frac{\dot{f}}{f}\right)$ with respect to $\frac{\alpha}{\beta}$ must be positive.

Hence, raising $\frac{\alpha}{\beta}$ increases the growth rate of per-capita income.

Proposition 11
Apart from the case of $\sigma > 1$; for $\sigma < 1$, the effect of $\frac{a}{b}$ on the growth rate of per-capita income depends on the sign of $\left(\frac{\dot{k}}{k} + n\sigma\right)$.

Proposition 12
For both $\sigma > 1$ and $\sigma < 1$, increasing the limiting marginal product of input factors increases the steady-state growth rate of income per capita, respectively.

For $\sigma > 1$,

(i) $\frac{\partial\left(\dot{f}/f\right)}{\partial\alpha} = \frac{m^*.n}{\alpha(1+m^*)^2} > 0$; (ii) $\frac{\partial\left(\dot{f}/f\right)}{\partial\beta} = \frac{n}{\beta(1+m^*)^2} > 0$

For $\sigma < 1$,

(iii) $\frac{\partial\left(\dot{f}/f\right)}{\partial a} = \frac{v^*.n}{a(1+v^*)^2} > 0$; (iv) $\frac{\partial\left(\dot{f}/f\right)}{\partial b} = \frac{n}{b(1+v^*)^2} > 0$

Proof 12 For $\sigma > 1$, let us denote the steady-state capital share $m^* = \left(\frac{\alpha}{\beta k(\infty)}\right)^{\frac{\sigma-1}{\sigma}}$.

Similarly, for $\sigma < 1$, the steady-state capital share is denoted $v^* = \left(\frac{a}{bk(\infty)}\right)^{\frac{\sigma-1}{\sigma}}$.

6 Extraordinary Financial and Monetary Policy Applications amid Supply and Demand Shocks

The current crisis reveals some extreme properties of financial and economic systems, in the sense that extraordinary events can occur and cause persistent recursive shocks across the countries. Apart from the exogeneous shocks, these extreme events can occur inside the economic and financial system. The endogeneity is basically due to accelerating complexity of the financial system feeding real economic structure. This complexity has arisen from broadening economic networks which lead to an increasing number of financial innovations. In perspective of policy making, it is more reasonable than ever to expect high-speed transmission of endogenous shocks into economies through global financial channels. These complex and nonlinear process reveal that amplified in financial systems these shocks eventually hit the supply and demand sides of the economy and that create discontinuity in real economic activity. In the early stage of COVID-19 pandemic crisis, in April 2020 meeting (Minutes of the Federal Open Market Committee (FOMC), 28–29 April, 2020) the Federal Reserve observed that first, the shocks amplifying in financial system, weighed on economic activity and disrupted the supply chains: "…In the middle part of March, financial markets experienced record declines in the prices of risky assets, wide-spread illiquidity, and elevated volatility, as uncertainty regarding the effects of the coronavirus outbreak on the global economy jumped…Businesses that were able to remain open to some degree were also substantially affected by the pandemic, with many experiencing either substantial drops in new orders and sales or supply chain disruptions." Given these facts, we query the future path of the modern growth theory, its inconsistencies, and possible remedies under rare circumstances where the Covid-19 pandemic deteriorated the global supply chains and total demand in the economy. To do this, we exemplify both financial policy of US government and monetary policy of Federal Reserve. As a financial policy approach, the US government employs two instruments: first, cash injection to selected low-income families (Afro-American, East-Asian, Latin) and second announced a 50% increase in wage per hour at Federal contracts which will be issued in February 2022. Second, let us recall the Federal Reserve statement on

27 August 2021 "Booming demand for goods and the strength and speed of the reopening have led to shortages and bottlenecks, leaving the COVID-constrained supply side unable to keep up. The result has been elevated inflation in durable goods—a sector that has experienced an annual inflation rate well below zero over the past quarter century."

Many other advanced economies are experiencing similarly unusual conditions. On November 3, 2021, FED declares that supply and demand imbalances related to COVID-19 pandemic and reactivation of economy have continued to support elevated levels of inflation. The FOMC statement on December 15 confirms that shipping congestion and supply bottlenecks restrain overall trade in goods (see Minutes of the Federal Open Market Committee, December 14–15, 2021).

Now let us introduce a simple modeling for above arguments and propose a mathematical analysis of non-reachable steady-state domain of price levels.

In an economy, assume that there is a tradeable good at any continuous time t. Let $s(t)$ denote the supply at time t, $d(t)$ denote the demand at time t, and $p(t)$ denote price at time t. The parameters $a, b, c \in R$. The competitive price of the good occurs where supply is equal to demand.

$$s(t+1) = a.p(t) \tag{15a}$$

$$d(t+1) = -b.p(t+1) + c \tag{15b}$$

Market clearing condition implies the following differential equation.

$$-b.E[p(t+1)] + c = a.p(t) \tag{15c}$$

where $E[.]$ stands for expected value operator. Let the efficient market hypothesis be satisfied (Fama, 1970).

The steady-state price, if any, should satisfy above-given equation. Let p^* denote the steady-state (equilibrium) price. Thus, for any t, there exists a price level such that:

$p(t + 1) = p(t) = p^*$ and this brings about
$-b.\ p^* + c = a.\ p^*$, where $p^* = \frac{c}{a+b}$.

However, the query is not the value of steady-state price. The question is that: under which conditions there exists a unique, finite value of p^*?

For example, let $p(0) = 1$. If $a = 5$; $b = 2$; $c = 1$ then (15c) leads to the process $-2p(t + 1) + 1 = 5p(t)$ which generates $p(1) = -2$; $p(2) = \frac{11}{2}$; $p(3) = \frac{-53}{4}$, a divergent sequence. There is no steady-state price.

If $a = 0.2$; $b = 2$; $c = 1$ then (15c) leads to the process $-2p(t + 1) + 1 = 0, 2.\ p(t)$ which generates $p(1) = 0, 4$; $p(2) = -0.46$; $p(3) = 0.454$, a convergent sequence. The equilibrium price is $p^* = \frac{1}{2.2}$.

Thus, in order that we have a domain for stability in prices we have to assure that $|\frac{\partial s}{\partial p}| < |\frac{\partial d}{\partial p}|$. That is, the sensitivity of demand to price level should exceed the sensitivity of supply to the price level.

An appropriate policy would be supporting the prices which correspond to an increase in the sensitivity of demand to price.

In early stage of COVID-19 pandemic, the fiscal policy approach of the US Government aimed to trigger supply side of the economy. This policy approach can be complementary with the monetary policy. In the face of increasing concerns on slowing economic activity, US Treasury Secretary Steve Mnuchin told Congress that lawmakers should not fear for the increasing deficit of the national budget or the increasing size of Federal Reserve's balance sheet to delay additional Covid-19 relief. "Now is not the time to worry about shrinking the deficit or shrinking the Fed balance sheet...There was a time when the FED was shrinking the balance sheet and coming back to normal. The good news is that gave them a lot of room to increase the balance sheet, which they did" (CNBC reporting, September 14, 2020). In February 2022, the US government realized an increase in minimum federal wage rate by %50, which signals the increase in marginal product of labor and expectations on increase in growth rate. The executive order of that policy had already been released as "...Today, President Biden is issuing an executive order requiring federal contractors to pay a $15 minimum wage to hundreds of thousands of workers who are working on federal contracts." (Statement, April 27, 2021). These facts reveal that beginning from 2021Q4 the US Government predicts a considerable increase in economic activity and hence in real GDP.

However, according to our analysis this policy is not as efficient as it seems. According to expression (5), in a competitive economy increasing minimum marginal product of labor coincides with an increase in minimum marginal price of labor. Therefore, the expectations of policymakers on increasing growth rate lead to an increase in minimum wages. This policy measure would be better one given the substitution elasticity level higher-than-unity. However, the US economy historically has elasticity of substitution level lower than unity. A recent survey in Chirinko (2008) suggests that most evidence favors elasticities ranges of 0.4–0.6 for the USA. More recently, Knoblach et al. (2020) report that "Throughout the analysis, the hypothesis of a Cobb–Douglas production function is rejected. Based on our meta-regression sample, we estimate a long-run meta-elasticity for the aggregate economy in the range of 0.45–0.87." Therefore, given the result in expression (6), increasing maximum marginal product of capital would be a better policy choice in terms of fiscal approach.

On the other hand, monetary policy follows the path to augment price supports which implies increasing the coefficient b and hence the sensitivity of demand to price level. This policy approach is efficient and aims to establish steady-state domain for price stability.

7 Conclusion

We revise the aforementioned findings in the literature, correct the crucial errors, inconsistencies and misinterpretations on the implications of CES parameters, and substitution elasticity. We compared the economic growth rates of the two economies with differing elasticity of substitution which implies different technological progress and economic development levels. Moreover, our study corrects the misinterpretation that the elasticity of substitution is a "magic tool" for perpetual economic growth. Instead, increasing the minimum marginal product of labor and an increase in the ratio of minimum marginal product of labor to minimum marginal product of capital enhance the growth rate of per-capita income, each of which should be an appropriate policy tool. These policies can be independently set at the first place. Finally, we proposed a modeling of economic disequilibrium under extreme events causing demand and supply shocks. This model shows the conditions under which the equilibrium for the supply and demand functions cannot be converged. Our results suggest that amid COVID-19 pandemic, US fiscal policy and monetary policy do not optimally match and hence the fiscal policy should be calibrated. Otherwise, the economic growth path would be hampered sooner than expected. Therefore, we suggest policy implications to overcome these discontinuities. We believe that the extensive approach proposed in this study will be a source for different points of view. The future studies which will be based on existing literature on modern growth theory should consider our findings. We hope that our results shed light on future empirical studies focusing on the remedies to increase growth rate.

Appendix 1

The proofs stated in Appendix 1 are based on the results given in Ozkaya (2021).

The elasticity of substitution is defined in expression (16) (de La Grandville, 1997).

$$\sigma(k) = -\frac{f'(k)[f(k) - k.f'(k)]}{k.f''(k).f(k)} \tag{16}$$

such that $\sigma(k) \geq 0$ for $k \geq 0$. Reorganizing $\sigma(k)$, we get

$$\sigma(k) = \frac{1}{G'(k)} \cdot \frac{G(k)}{k},$$

where $G(k) = k - \frac{f(k)}{f'(k)} < 0$ and $G'(k) < 0$.

Suppose that $\sigma(k)$ is bounded and continuous on $k \in [0, k_1]$;

that is, $\sigma(0) - \varepsilon \le \sigma(k) \le \sigma(0) + \varepsilon$. Let $\sigma(0) - \varepsilon \le \sigma(k) \le \sigma(0) + \varepsilon \le \mu$ be satisfied and $\sigma(0) = \mu$ may or may not be equal[4] to 1. For notational ease,[5] let σ_- and σ^+ signify $\sigma_- = \sigma(0) - \varepsilon$ and $\sigma^+ = \sigma(0) + \varepsilon$, respectively.

In particular, let $\mu \in R$ and suppose that $\sigma(0) + \varepsilon \le \mu$.

Since $\sigma_- \le \sigma(k) \le \sigma^+ \le \mu$, which after plugging in elasticity of substitution (16) leads to $\sigma_- \le \frac{1}{\frac{dG(k)}{dk}} \cdot \frac{G(k)}{k} \le \mu$. Rearranging this as $\frac{1}{\sigma_-} \cdot \frac{dk}{k} \ge \frac{dG(k)}{G(k)} \ge \frac{1}{\mu} \frac{dk}{k}$ and integrating over the $k \in [0, k_1]$ yields

$$k - G(k_1)\left(\frac{k}{k_1}\right)^{\frac{1}{\sigma_-}} \le \frac{f(k)}{f'(k)} \le k - G(k_1)\left(\frac{k}{k_1}\right)^{\frac{1}{\mu}}.$$

Reorganizing this formulation and re-integrating, we get the per-capita production function demonstrated between lower and upper bounds

$$\frac{f(k_1)}{k_1}\left(\frac{\left(k^{1-\frac{1}{\sigma_-}} - \frac{G(k_1)}{k_1^{\frac{1}{\sigma_-}}}\right)^{\frac{1}{1-\frac{1}{\sigma_-}}}}{\left(1 - \frac{G(k_1)}{k_1}\right)^{\frac{1}{1-\frac{1}{\sigma_-}}}}\right) \le f(k) \le \frac{f(k_1)}{k_1}\left(\frac{\left(k^{1-\frac{1}{\mu}} - \frac{G(k_1)}{k_1^{\frac{1}{\mu}}}\right)^{\frac{1}{1-\frac{1}{\mu}}}}{\left(1 - \frac{G(k_1)}{k_1}\right)^{\frac{1}{1-\frac{1}{\mu}}}}\right).$$

Similarly, suppose that $\sigma(0) - \varepsilon \ge \mu$. The aforementioned calculation steps immediately follow that

$$\frac{f(k_1)}{k_1}\left(\frac{\left(k^{1-\frac{1}{\mu}} - \frac{G(k_1)}{k_1^{\frac{1}{\mu}}}\right)^{\frac{1}{1-\frac{1}{\mu}}}}{\left(1 - \frac{G(k_1)}{k_1}\right)^{\frac{1}{1-\frac{1}{\mu}}}}\right) \le f(k) \le \frac{f(k_1)}{k_1}\left(\frac{\left(k^{1-\frac{1}{\sigma^+}} - \frac{G(k_1)}{k_1^{\frac{1}{\sigma^+}}}\right)^{\frac{1}{1-\frac{1}{\sigma^+}}}}{\left(1 - \frac{G(k_1)}{k_1}\right)^{\frac{1}{1-\frac{1}{\sigma^+}}}}\right)$$

Squeezing $\sigma(0) + \varepsilon \le \mu$ and $\sigma(0) - \varepsilon \ge \mu$ and then, looking for the common condition satisfying $\sigma(k) = \mu$ for $k \in [0, k_1]$, yield the Eqs. (17) and (18). For conventional use, let us replace μ with σ.

$$\frac{k.f'(k)}{f(k)} = \frac{1}{1 - \frac{G(k_1)}{k_1^{\frac{1}{\sigma}}} k^{\frac{1}{\sigma}-1}} \tag{17}$$

[4]To analyze the case $\mu = 1$ is out of scope of the present study. For the case $\mu = 1$, please refer to Ozkaya (2021).

[5]The same applies for $\sigma(\infty)$, and we suppose that $\sigma(k)$ is bounded and continuous on $k \in [k_1, \infty)$; hence, $\sigma(\infty) - \varepsilon \le \sigma(k) \le \sigma(\infty) + \varepsilon$.

$$f(k) = \frac{f(k_1)}{k_1}.k.\left(\frac{\left(1 - \frac{G(k_1)}{k_1^{\frac{1}{\sigma}}}k^{\frac{1}{\sigma}} - 1\right)^{\frac{1}{1-\frac{1}{\sigma}}}}{\left(1 - \frac{G(k_1)}{k_1}\right)^{\frac{1}{1-\frac{1}{\sigma}}}}\right) \tag{18}$$

Inserting (17) into (18) and rearranging gives (1). That is,

$$f(k) = \frac{f(k_1)}{k_1}.k.\left(\frac{\left(\frac{f(k)}{k.f'(k)}\right)^{\frac{1}{1-\frac{1}{\sigma}}}}{\left(\frac{f(k_1)}{k_1.f'(k_1)}\right)^{\frac{1}{1-\frac{1}{\sigma}}}}\right) \text{ and } \frac{f(k)}{k.f'(k)} = \frac{f(k_1)}{k_1}.\frac{1}{f'(k)}.\left(\frac{\left(\frac{f(k)}{k.f'(k)}\right)^{\frac{1}{1-\frac{1}{\sigma}}}}{\left(\frac{f(k_1)}{k_1.f'(k_1)}\right)^{\frac{1}{1-\frac{1}{\sigma}}}}\right)$$

Thus, reinserting $\frac{f(k)}{k.f'(k)}$ into $f(k)$, we have

$$f(k) = \frac{f(k_1)}{k_1.f'(k_1)^{\sigma}}.k.f'(k)^{\sigma}$$

Normalization of the CES production function:
Klump and Preissler (2000) propose the normalized CES function:

$$F_t(K, L) = Y_0\left[\pi_0\left(\frac{K_t}{K_0}\right)^{\frac{\sigma-1}{\sigma}} + (1 - \pi_0)\left(\frac{L_t}{L_0}\right)^{\frac{\sigma-1}{\sigma}}\right]^{\frac{\sigma}{\sigma-1}},$$

where π_0, Y_0, K_0, L_0 are arbitrary initial values. π_0 denotes the capital share in total income at the point of normalization Y_0:

$$\pi_0 = \frac{r_0K_0}{Y_0}$$

whether $\pi_0 = \frac{r_0K_0}{r_0K_0+w_0L_0}$ is,
We should have

$$F_t(K, L) = F(K_0, L_0)\left[\frac{r_0K_0}{r_0K_0 + w_0L_0}\left(\frac{K_t}{K_0}\right)^{\frac{\sigma-1}{\sigma}} + \frac{w_0L_0}{r_0K_0 + w_0L_0}\left(\frac{L_t}{L_0}\right)^{\frac{\sigma-1}{\sigma}}\right]^{\frac{\sigma}{\sigma-1}}$$

$$F_t(K, L)$$

$$= \left[F(K_0,\ L_0)^{\frac{\sigma-1}{\sigma}}\frac{r_0K_0}{F(K_0,\ L_0)}\left(\frac{K_t}{K_0}\right)^{\frac{\sigma-1}{\sigma}} + F(K_0,\ L_0)^{\frac{\sigma-1}{\sigma}}\frac{w_0L_0}{F(K_0,\ L_0)}\left(\frac{L_t}{L_0}\right)^{\frac{\sigma-1}{\sigma}}\right]^{\frac{\sigma}{\sigma-1}}$$

where $F(K_0, L_0) = r_0K_0 + w_0L_0$.

Under perfect competition, π_0 this distribution parameter is equal to the capital income share but, under imperfect competition with non-zero aggregate mark-up, it equals the share of capital income over total factor income.

These are $\pi_0 = \frac{r_0 K_0}{r_0 K_0 + w_0 L_0}$ and $\pi_0 = \frac{r_0 K_0}{Y_0}$, respectively.

$$F_t(K, L) = \left[\left(\frac{K_0}{F(K_0,\ L_0)} \right)^{\frac{1}{\sigma}} r_0 (K_t)^{\frac{\sigma-1}{\sigma}} + \left(\frac{L_0}{F(K_0,\ L_0)} \right)^{\frac{1}{\sigma}} w_0 (L_t)^{\frac{\sigma-1}{\sigma}} \right]^{\frac{\sigma}{\sigma-1}}$$

$$\text{Then} \left(\frac{K_0}{F(K_0,\ L_0)} \right)^{\frac{1}{\sigma}} r_0 = F_K(K, 0)^{\frac{\sigma-1}{\sigma}} \tag{19}$$

where r_0 should be equal to $F_K(K, L)$ at a given normalization point. Since for any $K = K^*$, $0 < K < \infty$, we have $F_K(K, 0) = F_K(K^*, 0)$, which leads back to our definition.

$$\left(\frac{L_0}{F(K_0,\ L_0)} \right)^{\frac{1}{\sigma}} w_0 = F_L(0, L)^{\frac{\sigma-1}{\sigma}} \tag{20}$$

Similarly, w_0 does.

Equations (19) and (20) depict the normalized parameters for $\sigma > 1$, which correspond to initial and terminal conditions of the CES function obtained in (5).

Appendix 2

For our purposes, first of all, we have to focus on the formulation proposed in de La Grandville (1989), which introduces a variant of the CES production function. That is:

$$f(k) = A(\sigma) \left((1 - c(\sigma)) k^{\frac{\sigma-1}{\sigma}} + c(\sigma) \right)^{\frac{\sigma}{\sigma-1}} \tag{21}$$

De La Grandville (1989) defines the CES function parameters as:

$$A(\sigma)^{\frac{\sigma-1}{\sigma}} (1 - c(\sigma)) = \beta(\sigma) \quad \text{and} \quad A(\sigma)^{\frac{\sigma-1}{\sigma}} c(\sigma) = \alpha(\sigma) \tag{22}$$

Comparing the parameters in (22) with the CES production function in (5), for $\sigma > 1$, we obtain the relations given in (23):

$$\beta(\sigma) = F_K(K, 0)^{\frac{\sigma-1}{\sigma}} \quad \text{and} \quad \alpha(\sigma) = F_L(0, L)^{\frac{\sigma-1}{\sigma}} \tag{23}$$

On the other hand, assume the other case, $\sigma < 1$. Comparing the parameters of the production function (21) with the CES production function (6), gives the following identities depicted in expression (24):

$$\beta(\sigma) = F_K(K, \infty)^{\frac{\sigma-1}{\sigma}} \quad \text{and} \quad \alpha(\sigma) = F_L(\infty, L)^{\frac{\sigma-1}{\sigma}} \tag{24}$$

References

Arrow, K. J., Chenery, H. B., Minhas, B. S., & Solow, R. M. (1961). Capital-labor substitution and economic efficiency. *The Review of Economics and Statistics, 43*(3), 225–250.

Chirinko, R. S. (2008). σ: The long and short of it. *Journal of Macroeconomics, 30*(2), 671–686.

CNBC Reporting. (2020, September 14). https://www.cnbc.com/2020/09/14/steven-mnuchin-now-isnt-the-time-to-worry-about-the-deficit-fed-balance-sheet.html

De La Grandville, O. (1989). In quest of the Slutsky diamond. *American Economic Review, 79*(3), 468–481.

De La Grandville, O. (1997). Curvature and the elasticity of substitution: Straightening it out. *Journal of Economics, 66*(1), 23–34.

De La Grandville. (2009). *Economic growth: A unified approach*. Cambridge University Press.

De La Grandville, O., & Solow, R. M. (2006). A conjecture on general means. *Journal of Inequalities in Pure and Applied Mathematics, 7*(3).

Fama, E. (1970). Efficient capital markets: A review of theory and empirical work. *The Journal of Finance, 25*(2), 383–417.

Hardy, G. H., Littlewood, J. E., & Polya, G. (1934). *Inequalities*. Cambridge University Press.

https://www.whitehouse.gov/briefing-room/statements-releases/2021/04/27/fact-sheet-biden-harris-administration-issues-an-executive-order-to-raise-the-minimum-wage-to-15-for-federal-contractors/

Klump, R., & de La Grandville, O. (2000). Economic growth and elasticity of substitution: Two theorems and some suggestions. *American Economic Review, 90*, 282–291.

Klump, R., & Preissler, H. (2000). CES production functions and economic growth. *Scandinavian Journal of Economics, 102*(1), 41–56.

Knoblach, M., Roessler, M., & Zwerschke, P. (2020). The elasticity of substitution between capital and labour in the US economy: A meta-regression analysis. *Oxford Bulletin of Economics and Statistics., 82*, 62. https://doi.org/10.1111/obes.12312

Minutes of the Federal Open Market Committee. (2020, April 28–29). https://www.federalreserve.gov/monetarypolicy/files/fomcminutes20200429.pdf

Minutes of the Federal Open Market Committee. (2021, December 14–15). https://www.federalreserve.gov/newsevents/pressreleases/monetary20220105a.htm)

Ozkaya, A. (2021). Inada conditions asymptotically transform production function into the Cobb–Douglas. *Economics Letters, 201*, 109786. https://doi.org/10.1016/j.econlet.2021.109786

Pitchford, J. D. (1960). Growth and the elasticity of factor substitution. *Economic Record, 36*, 491–504.

Solow, R. M. (1956). A contribution to the theory of economic growth. *The Quarterly Journal of Economics, 70*(1), 65–94.

COVID-19: An Assessment in the Context of Its Economic Impacts and Market-State Relationship

Semanur Soyyiğit and Elife Akiş

Abstract The COVID-19 pandemic and severe issues of the twenty-first century such as food and climate crises have affected state-market interaction. Precautions against the spread of the virus such as social distancing, quarantine, and closures comprise direct intervention in social life and economic process such as production, consumption, and trade. This phenomenon makes us consider the future of the global economic order. How will capitalism, which received a blow from the global financial crisis of 2007–2008, be affected by the current pandemic crisis? Based on this research question, we first examine the pandemic's economic and social policy effects. Then, we compile different points of view about the future of capitalism. Some views advocate that capitalism will get over this issue by becoming more assertive, while others state that capitalism will never be like before and some structural changes will occur in terms of state intervention in the economic life.

Keywords Social protection policies · State intervention · Global economic order · COVID-19

1 Introduction

The COVID-19 pandemic has created a major challenge on a global scale for the world economy, by exacerbating the already-debated problems of the capitalist system such as climate change, global warming, and food and energy security. Accordingly, the United Nations (UN) described the pandemic crisis as "the most significant challenge in the organization's 75-year history" (UN, 2021). Although the COVID-19 pandemic appeared as a health crisis and had not been taken very

S. Soyyiğit (✉)
Department of Public Finance, Kirklareli University, Kırklareli, Turkey
e-mail: semanur.soyyigit@klu.edu.tr

E. Akiş
Department of Economics, Istanbul University, İstanbul, Turkey
e-mail: elifakis@istanbul.edu.tr

A. Ari (ed.), *Capitalism at a Crossroads*, Springer Studies in Alternative Economics,
https://doi.org/10.1007/978-3-031-23257-2_13

seriously initially, it requires us to be more serious about it day by day due to the risks it carries. As of this study, approximately 270 million coronavirus cases and 5.3 million related deaths have been announced on a global scale. Although various companies have developed vaccines against infection, vaccine production and vaccination have not reached a sufficient level globally, but the virus has reached a much higher rate of spread due to mutation.

When the coronavirus first emerged as a health crisis, neither China, where it originated from, nor the World Health Organization (WHO) had given much attention to it. Furthermore, the WHO declared the COVID-19 outbreak a pandemic on 11 March 2020, long after November 2019, when the first coronavirus cases emerged. In the face of the rapid spread of the coronavirus, healthcare services were insufficient to respond to the increasing number of cases, especially in some European countries such as Italy, France, the UK, as well as the USA and many other countries. To prevent the spread, several measures were implemented in countries. Although some countries announced that they will follow the path of herd immunity, the general trend was in the form of closure and quarantine. Mask, social distance, and hygiene have become the concepts we hear most in the last 2 years of our lives. Inevitably, these measures also had economic consequences. The pandemic has caused a severe increase in poverty on a national and global scale due to its supply- and demand-based effects on the economy. The UN Office for Disaster Risk Reduction (UNDRR) report states that the COVID-19 pandemic caused the first increase in extreme global poverty since 1998. The report also reveals that the pandemic pushed 71 to 100 million people into extreme poverty in 2020 (UNDRR, 2020). The importance of social protection policies has increased in this process, and there have been difficulties in integrating the poor into the social protection system since most of them are not registered in the system. Such developments brought along the debates on the necessity of reorganizing social protection policies.

Uncertainties due to the pandemic still prevail in the world. The first of these uncertainties is when the pandemic will be completely brought under control. The second uncertainty concerns the extent of the impact of the pandemic on the global economy such as economic contraction, inflation, unemployment, and public deficits. The third uncertainty is about how the global order will progress (Yong, 2020). Related to the last one, we come across questions about the future of capitalism within the scope of market and state relations. As the fragility of the current global economic system continues due to disruption of global value chains and high inflation rates, increasing poverty causes more state intervention to provide social protection for disadvantaged parts of the society. These problems also increase nationalism and populism in economic and political scene. Based on this, "what will be the future of capitalism?" and "how will the global economic order evolve?" are our research questions.

From that perspective, we first assess the economic effects of the COVID-19 in Sect. 2. Then, in Sect. 3, we focus on the social policy effect of the pandemic, by examining social protection policies and the increasing role of the state. In Sect. 4, we discuss the failure of the current economic system during the pandemic and debate if there is a paradigm shift in market-state relations. Section 5 concludes.

2 Economic Impacts of COVID-19

The COVID-19 pandemic, which emerged at the end of 2019 and caused a global alarm at the beginning of 2020, continues to have a devastating effect on the world economy. Researchers explain four reasons why the pandemic has had such an increasingly global impact (Yong, 2020). First, today's world is highly global and interdependent. The circulation of goods, capital, and people is more significant than at any other time. Second, they point out the slowness of governments and political leaders in understanding the significance of the crisis. While the length of the incubation period and the high rate of transmission of the virus make it difficult to notice, the opposition to masks; the approach of the Trump administration that underestimates the problem, initiating a trade war with China; and the negligent behavior of people in obeying the rules at the beginning are the issues observed in this process (Yigit, 2021).

Third, China and the USA, the world's two largest economies, are the pandemic's epicenter. While the pandemic spread in China affected the real economy at the global level through global value chains, its spread in the USA affected the real economy as it is the center of political, economic, technological, and cultural change in the world. Fourth, the pandemic has furthered the strategic race between countries by separating these two great powers and dragging the world into a new cold war.

Caracciolo et al. (2020) points out that the coronavirus has caused economic contraction due to five main reasons: (1) direct losses in labor supply due to death or infection, (2) additional losses in labor supply due to government shutdowns and social distancing measures, (3) decrease in households' consumption tendencies and firms' investment intention due to closures and increased uncertainty, (4) global interactions in the context of disruptions in global value chains and trade, and (5) a possible hysteresis effect that hinders the return to the pre-crisis economic situation.

From this context, it would not be wrong to say that the pandemic has caused economic contraction due to both supply and demand shocks. Accordingly, even if governments did not take any measures, there would be a supply effect resulting from a decrease in labor supply due to death or infection. The severity of this supply effect has however increased with governments' closure and social distancing measures, albeit with different severity. We can say that the supply effect has become more substantial due to the global supply chain and trade disruptions, especially via China, an essential supplier of intermediate goods in the global value chains and the source of the pandemic (Demiralp, 2020, p. 185). Moreover, the declining consumption propensity of the working people, who are deprived of income, and the decrease in consumption and investment propensities due to uncertainty deepened the economic contraction through the demand channel (Guerrieri et al., 2020). Das (2020) specifies that the current pandemic crisis is different from the one experienced in the 1929 crisis, because there was a problem on demand side, but not on supply side, during the Great Depression. So, Keynes' multiplier theory was practical, but the crisis experienced today is different because it simultaneously includes supply and demand shocks (Das, 2020). With the effect of the slowdown in production, practices such as layoffs and unpaid leave took place in many workplaces. Even when consumers are not deprived of income, quarantine practices and being unable to leave the house have changed the consumption habits of people. Note also that there is a global dimension of demand through imports. As the countries' income has decreased with the effect of the pandemic, foreign demand also started to decrease. Therefore, the decrease in countries' imports has caused a decrease in the export revenues of other trading partners (Demiralp, 2020, p. 186). To summarize, many macroeconomic indicators such as employment, national income and growth, import-export, inflation, income distribution, and poverty have deteriorated due to all these supply and demand effects.

2.1 *Impact on Economic Growth*

Before COVID-19, the global economy faced many issues that adversely affected international economic relations. These were problems such as the unrelenting effect of increased protectionism, trade conflicts and tensions between major trading partners, falling commodity and energy prices, and uncertainty about Brexit (Congressional Research Service, 2021). As the COVID-19 pandemic came on top of these problems, it suddenly lowered expectations for growth. While the IMF had predicted a global growth rate of 3.4% for 2020 in October 2019, it revised this rate to −4.4% in October 2020. The OECD revised its global growth forecast for 2020 from 2.9% in December 2019 to −4.2% in December 2020. On the other hand, the World Bank revised its global growth forecast of 2.5% in January 2020 to −5.2% in June 2020 (Congressional Research Service, 2021).

IMF (2021a) states that the most devastating impact of the pandemic was experienced in the second quarter of 2020. Accordingly, although there was a decrease in the components of GDP in the third quarter, we can see that this decrease was smaller compared to the second quarter. This improvement was observed in both developed and emerging market economies (excluding China). The IMF reported that this improvement in private consumption expenditures might result from a relaxation in demand, which was suppressed in the early stages of the pandemic, and adaptation to working from home (IMF, 2021a).

We can say that 2021 was a year in which the abovementioned devastating effects of the pandemic were partially recovered. Although there are inequalities globally, the spread of vaccination and the gradual normalization process have improved economic activities. In this context, we see optimistic figures in the economic growth forecasts of international organizations for 2021. The IMF announced that they predicted 5.9% growth in the global economy for 2021 in the WEO of October 2021. Their projections for 2022 were 4.9% (IMF, 2021b). On the other hand, the

OECD, which reports an unevenly distributed global improvement, predicted that there would be a 5.6% growth in 2021; however, the growth rate would decrease in the following years (OECD, 2021a).

The IMF's October 2021 WEO report looked at growth projections from a regional perspective. According to the report, there was a contraction of 4.5% and 2.1% in terms of GDP in developed and developing economies, respectively, in 2020. Among developed countries, the USA has the lowest rate of economic contraction (−3.4%), while Spain has the highest rate (−10.8%). The report shows that while the Chinese economy grew by 2.3%, the highest economic contraction was in Mexico (−8.3%) among emerging markets and developing countries. The forecast for 2021 was 5.2% growth in developed countries and 6.4% growth in emerging markets and emerging economies (IMF, 2021b).

2.2 *Impact on Unemployment*

Although the impact of the COVID-19 on employment differs from country to country, it is undeniable that it caused a sharp decline in employment in all countries. The OECD compared the decrease in working hours in OECD countries after the onset of the COVID-19 pandemic with the decline after the onset of the global financial crisis of 2007–2008: the devastating effect of the pandemic crisis was well above the effect of the global crisis (OECD, 2020).

In addition, we see that every sector and business line is differently affected by this crisis. The study by Del Rio-Chanona et al. (2020) is quite revealing. They have developed an index called Remote Labor Index (RLI). They calculated it for 740 sectors and NAICS—a two-digit sector category. This index takes a value between 0 and 1. If it is close to 0, it indicates that the opportunity to work remotely in the relevant line of business/industry decreases, while if it is close to 1, the opportunity to work remotely in the relevant business line/industry increases. The sectoral calculation shows that the information, finance and insurance, scientific, and technical services sectors have the highest value, and therefore they are most suitable for remote working, while agriculture, forestry, fisheries and hunting, accommodation, and catering sectors have the lowest value (Del Rio-Chanona et al., 2020).

2.3 *Impact on Inequality and Poverty*

Another economic and social issue caused by the COVID-19 pandemic is the increase in income inequality and poverty. According to a study, the richest five billionaires worldwide multiplied their total wealth by 59% in approximately 6 months, from 18 March to 10 September. In this period, unemployment, poverty, and indebtedness levels heightened at the global level (Paremoer, 2021). The number of people in extreme poverty is predicted to increase by 96 million in

2021 due to the global economic contraction of 5% in 2020 if no measures are taken to protect the most vulnerable. Also, the COVID-19 pandemic has impacted different sexes at different levels, and it has had a more serious effect on women. Accordingly, it is estimated that 435 million women and girls will live on less than $1.90 per day in 2021, including 47 million of whom will be pushed into poverty due to the pandemic (Azcona et al., 2020). The summary report of the UNDRR reveals that the COVID-19 pandemic caused the first increase in extreme global poverty since 1998; the pandemic pushed 71 to 100 million people into extreme poverty in 2020, which in turn canceled the progress made in reducing poverty since 2017. Also, low-skilled employees working for low wages in labor-intensive production areas in the Asia-Pacific region are in the highest-risk group following the pandemic (UNDRR, 2020).

The impact of the COVID-19 crisis on poverty should also be investigated in terms of rural poverty because the measures implemented to control the spread of the pandemic impose significant restrictions on movement. Del-Rio Chanona et al. (2020) shows that agricultural activities are one of the areas most affected by these measures, and this amplifies the pandemic's impact on rural poverty. Rural poverty affects farmers, stockbreeders, and people who make a living from fishing and forestry. Considering that the majority of poor at the global level need market access for seasonal agricultural work or the purchase of inputs, they have to reach public spaces to survive. In conclusion, the restrictions mean that this segment is deprived of its vital resources (FAO, 2020).

Furthermore, Paremoer (2021) also shows that the pandemic caused an 82% increase in the level of hunger. Moreover, the number of people experiencing food insecurity is expected to double, especially in countries affected by the economic crisis, climate change, conflict, etc.

2.4 Impact on Global Trade

The COVID-19 outbreak has also had a devastating effect on global trade. High unemployment and hindering mobility caused a decrease in the demand for tradable goods; hence, the supply lessened due to the interruption of production activities and the protectionist measures taken by countries (Beaulieu & Klemen, 2021).

The World Trade Organization (WTO) reported that in the second quarter of 2020—when the distorting effect of the pandemic on economic indicators reached the highest level—there was a decrease of 14.3% in trade volume compared to the first quarter of 2020. This decrease is more significant than the 10.2% decrease during the global financial crisis between the third quarter of 2008 and the first quarter of 2009 (Minondo, 2021). Looking at 2020 in general, there was a decrease of 6% in merchandise trade and 16.5% in trade of services, while global trade decreased by 9%. After the second quarter, in which the sharpest decline was experienced in global trade, the recovery that started in the third quarter became even stronger in the fourth quarter. This improvement in the second half of 2020 was primarily due to the rise in merchandise trade, while trade in services remained below average. In the last quarter of 2020, merchandise trade increased by 8% compared to the previous quarter, while trade in services remained below the average (UNCTAD, 2021). The UNCTAD report also includes both a regional and a sectoral evaluation of trade. Accordingly, this improvement in the last quarter of 2020 was realized thanks to developing countries. However, we cannot see any increase in developing country trade when East Asian countries are excluded. In other words, while South-South trade outperformed global trade, South-South trade decreased significantly in the fourth quarter of 2020 when East Asian economies were excluded (UNCTAD, 2021).

The sectoral assessment of UNCTAD reveals that the improvement in the second half of 2020 covers sectors other than the energy and transportation equipment sectors. The trade value of these two sectors is one-third lower than in the same period of 2019. However, while the recovery in the third quarter of 2020 was realized in sectors related to goods such as personal protective equipment and home/office equipment, where demand increased due to the pandemic, the improvement in the fourth quarter was broad-based (UNCTAD, 2021).

2.5 Impact on Inflation

The OECD Economic Outlook report states that inflationary pressures have occurred in all economies after the pandemic due to (1) disruptions in energy, food, and commodity markets, (2) high energy prices and fuel shortages limiting the manufacture of basic materials and intermediate goods, and (3) the bottleneck in production chains causing shortages of goods (OECD, 2021b). According to the report, the future course of inflation is expected to reach its highest value in late 2021 and early 2022 and then remain above the pre-pandemic level (OECD, 2021a).

According to the OECD (2021a), inflation rates increased in both developed and emerging market economies after the pandemic. The projection of OECD shows that there will be a decrease in inflation rates toward the end of 2022, but it will remain above the pre-pandemic level. According to the newly announced data, annual inflation in the USA, which has the highest inflation rate among developed economies, was 6.8% in November 2021, and this was the highest inflation rate since 1982 (Trading Economics, 2021).

The IMF's October 2021 WEO report forecasts inflation may return to its pre-pandemic level by mid-2022. However, it underlines that the estimations are made under severe uncertainties. It also states that inflation may remain higher for longer than expected in case of more persistent supply disruptions than the basis of simulations, the pressure of housing prices, and food prices that increase sharply in both developing and developed countries (IMF, 2021b).

3 Social Protection Policies in the Scope of COVID-19

The issue of state intervention in the economy was brought to the agenda again with the COVID-19 pandemic, because the lockdown policy and measures that countries had to implement to prevent the spread of the pandemic caused the deterioration of many economic indicators with the supply and demand channels mentioned above. Significantly, the decrease in employment and the increase in poverty have led states to implement more social protection policies. This section first addresses the importance and function of social protection policies and then social protection policies implemented within the scope of COVID-19.

3.1 The Function of Social Protection Policies

When we look at the concepts used together with social protection, we often see the concept of social security. However, the two concepts are quite different from each other. The concept of social security refers to the set of transfers arising from formal sector employment (Cichon et al., 2004, p. 19). Social security was founded as a fundamental human right in the Philadelphia Declaration of the International Labor Organization (ILO) in 1944, endorsed by the 1948 Declaration of Human Rights. Accordingly, social security is defined as ensuring the access of individuals and households to health services and guaranteeing income security, especially in cases of old age, illness, disability, work disability, birth, or loss of a family breadwinner (ILO, n.d.). Social security is associated with comprehensive and sophisticated social insurance and social assistance structures, especially in developed countries. Moreover, it is not considered appropriate for problems or debates in developing economies, where absolute poverty presents different challenges accompanying financial and institutional weaknesses (Norton et al., 2001). In this context, social protection is considered as a broader concept. On the other hand, it can be used in a narrower sense than social security, considering that it includes the measures attributed to the poorest, most vulnerable, or most marginalized segment of the society. They can be interchangeable concepts (ILO, 2011). However, we see that the concept of social protection is often used in a broader sense in the literature related to COVID-19.

Looking at the history of social protection, we see that social protection policies emerged for the first time in developing countries after the World War II. According to the ILO Convention No. 102 of 1952, social protection includes social security policies to protect workers from social risks (Merrien, 2013). Merrien (2013) points out that the concept of social protection was contrary to the mainstream development understanding until the early 1990s. The ILO, as the key organization in this area, continues its efforts to extend social protection coverage to workers but has not included the informal sector, because the extension of noncontributory social security to the unpaid population was thought to be an expensive way to strengthen the culture of poverty. However, the World Bank rejected social protection programs for workers because they were economically harmful and socially unjust. Safety nets, reserved only for the poorest segment of the socially vulnerable population, were considered minimally acceptable. The change in the dominant paradigm occurred due to disappointments with the results of the economic adjustment programs in late 1990s, the 1997 Asian crisis, and increased awareness about the negative consequences of global poverty. As a result, the World Bank started to promote social protection as international poverty reduction, so social protection became an essential tool for millennium development goals. The ILO has developed a global campaign (Social Protection Floor Initiative) to extend social security to developing countries. The United Nations Development Programme (UNDP) has underlined the role of social protection in development policy. Merrien (2013) notes that this consensus favoring social protection represents a fundamental shift of paradigm. With this change, social protection in developing countries is no longer a short-term tool against economic shocks. Instead, it is accepted as a global policy that includes cash transfer programs for the highly vulnerable segment of society, a new program that combines a social investment perspective with social transfer policies, and public and private social insurance programs for formal sector workers (Merrien, 2013). As a result of this structural transformation, especially in developing countries, within the scope of structural adaptation and globalization, social protection has turned into a policy framework based on poverty and vulnerability in the 1990s. In this context, social protection is defined as public actions taken in response to the levels of vulnerability, risk, and deprivation, all seen as socially unacceptable in a society (Barrientos, 2010).

Social protection is associated with institutions, norms, and programs that aim to protect workers and their households from unexpected events threatening their basic living standards. These are social insurance, social assistance, and labor market regulations. Social insurance covers programs that protect against life-cycle conditions such as birth and old age or work-related conditions such as unemployment and illness. Social assistance provides support to those in poverty. Under normal circumstances, social security is financed by contributions from the working and employer groups in the registered sector, while taxes finance social assistance. While there are institutions in developed countries within the scope of labor and employment regulations, the distribution of these institutions is unequal and uneven in developing countries (Barrientos, 2010).

While social protection prioritizes the continuity of income and the protection of living standards for everyone (but especially for the working population) in developed countries, it focuses on reducing poverty and providing support to the poorest segment of society in developing countries. Social protection has also focused on risk and vulnerability in developing countries. In addition, social protection has a more comprehensive role related to development beyond supporting the poor with income cuts in these countries (Barrientos, 2010). Three main functions of this role are (1) helping to maintain the essential consumption of those who are in poverty or at risk of falling into poverty, (2) enabling investment in people or productive assets that can provide permanent relief from intergenerational poverty, and

(3) empowering institutions that are in poverty to overcome their plight. There is also a global consensus that social protection provides essential support to achieving the Sustainable Development Goals, because social protection measures directly contribute to inclusive and robust growth through mechanisms such as human capacity building, social risk management, and broad macroeconomic impacts (OECD, 2019).

3.2 Social Protection Policy Practices with the COVID-19 Pandemic

The mentioned importance of social protection policies has increased with the coronavirus pandemic. Social protection expenditures extended from $653 billion during the global financial crisis to over $2.9 trillion during the COVID-19 crisis. This value corresponds to approximately 3% of the world GDP in 2021. In addition, this social protection expenditure level is approximately 4.5 times the expenditures made during the global crisis of 2007–2008 (Gentilini et al., 2021, pp. 14–15).

According to the study by Gentilini et al. (2021, p. 4), while 45 countries announced social protection measures in March 2020, this number reached 222 as of May 2021, and the number of measures planned or implemented by countries has increased from 103 in March 2020 to 3333 in May 2021.

When these increased measures are evaluated within the framework of the institutions, norms, and programs mentioned above in terms of social protection, the following practices are encountered (FAO, 2020):

- Social insurance measures: sick leave, health insurance provision, expanded pension schemes, expanded unemployment benefits for informal workers in some cases.
- Social assistance scheme: cash assistance, food and other in-kind assistance, childcare assistance, debt relief, etc.
- Labor market measures: wage subsidy, labor intermediation and training, emergency employment programs, changes in labor regulations.

Table 1 shows social protection expenditures made based on income groups and regions within the scope of these measures. Accordingly, we see that as the income level of the countries increases, the social protection expenditures per capita increase. We can reach a similar result according to the development levels of the regions. The study of Gentilini et al. (2021), covering 151 countries, shows that an average of $345 per capita social protection expenditure is made globally. However, the distribution of social protection expenditures is quite uneven across regions. Because while social protection expenditure was $4253 per capita in North America, this region is followed by Europe and Central Asia with $629 and East Asia and the Pacific with $369. Africa and East Asia have the lowest per capita social protection expenditures. Based on this, it would not be wrong to say that global inequality has

Table 1 Social protection expenditures (USD) by income groups and regions

Countries	Social assistance	Social insurance	Labor markets	Total spending ($)	Spending pc (average $/capita)
HIC ($n = 53$)	1,649,931,627,595	649,681,359,808	263,815,982,800	2,563,428,970,204	847
LIC ($n = 17$)	1,313,743,655		12,239,210	1,325,982,864	4
LMIC ($n = 35$)	8,533,105,616	886,751,359	1,471,655,886	10,891,512,860	30
UMIC ($n = 46$)	69,726,870,521	286,543,675,050	10,424,983,757	366,695,529,329	156
AFR ($n = 33$)	2,251,538,894	3,533,914,023	219,819,267	6,005,272,184	28
EAP ($n = 25$)	198,473,318,506	268,314,350,605	19,145,025,178	485,932,694,289	369
ECA ($n = 37$)	90,702,999,635	52,205,643,330	193,532,254,059	336,440,897,024	629
LAC ($n = 36$)	49,143,937,168	13,057,599,560	1,138,505,628	63,340,042,356	239
MENA ($n = 13$)	8,805,336,575	1,993,289,589	4,125,986,914	14,924,613,078	161
N. America ($n = 2$)	1,376,080,897,714	597,904,186,943	56,973,647,966	2,030,958,732,623	4253
SAR ($n = 5$)	4,047,318,896	102,802,166	589,622,642	4,739,743,704	17
Total ($n = 151$)	1,729,505,347,387	937,111,786,217	275,724,861,653	2,942,341,995,257	$345

Source: Gentilini et al. (2021, p. 16)

Note: LIC (low-income countries), LMIC (lower middle-income countries), UMIC (upper middle-income countries), HIC (high-income countries), AFR (Africa), EAP (East Asia and Pacific), ECA (Europe and Central Asia), LAC (Latin America and Caribbean), MENA (Middle East and North Africa), N. America (North America), SAR (South Asia) deepened with the pandemic. Because Table 1 reveals that low-income countries, which were more affected by the pandemic, also performed very poorly in responding to it.

On the other hand, it is obvious that these emergency social protection policies implemented against the COVID-19, which have a traditional approach, will not be sufficient. Hence, a new idea is necessary beyond governments' capabilities regarding social protection. Because closures have created a very strict inequality between those who have a stable income source and those who do not, this inequality continues to increase day by day (Lustig & Tommasi, 2020). In addition, since the informal sector has been affected much more severely by the pandemic, social assistance policies that take it into account have gained more importance. The ILO estimations reveal that six out of ten workers and four out of five businesses operate in the informal economy globally (ILO, 2021). Considering that those employed in the informal sector are more prone to poverty and risks but have less access to social protection mechanisms, the design and delivery of social assistance to this segment also emerge as an essential issue (UNDRR, 2020). Paremoer (2021) states that social protection measures such as tax cuts, cash transfers, unemployment benefits, and food and nutrition assistance do not reach people who need them the most, such as informal workers, immigrants, and the young population.

On the other hand, the need for assistance needs to be better evaluated and planned since the scale and duration of the pandemic cannot be predicted. People are endlessly encountering permanent restrictions due to the delays in the countries' economic recovery, the unequal distribution of the vaccination around the world despite the introduction of the vaccine, and the new waves in the pandemic because of the mutation of the virus. This leads countries to consider long-term investments that will maintain social protection and the effort to improve their economies (UNDRR, 2020). Hillson (2021) expresses that this new method should be a more inclusive and universal social protection centered on the new normal.

4 Post-Pandemic State-Market Relations

Because of the debates on the market's failure, the state's intervention in the economy and the level of this intervention come to the fore again in every deadlock of capitalism. Economic activities were partially or completely stopped in many economies to control the pandemic, and the negative supply shock caused by the cessation of production activities spread to other sectors through the supply chain. This effect also caused a contraction in income and demand. Since supply-demand mechanisms in the market could not solve this problem, it brought the state's role back to the agenda (Das, 2020).

Based on the view that the virus will cause a negative supply shock on a global scale, resulting in the closure of factories and affecting the global supply chain, Fornaro and Wolf (2020) sought answers within the framework of the New Keynesian model to some questions such as how deep and permanent this deterioration will be, how much aggregate demand will be affected, and what appropriate policies might be. Based on the worst-case scenario where the negative supply shock would be solid and permanent, the authors conclude that intense fiscal policy would be needed to get out of the global recession. As mentioned above, Das (2020) examined the pandemic and macroeconomic uncertainty in India and points out that the crisis caused by the pandemic is different from the one experienced during the Great Depression. He explains that there was a demand-based problem rather than supply in the Great Depression, and therefore the multiplier mechanism worked.

Nevertheless, the pandemic crisis, in which both supply and demand shocks are experienced simultaneously, is different. Das (2020) drew attention to the increasing importance of the state's role in solving this problem that the supply and demand mechanism cannot solve. Baqaee and Farhi (2020) voice that the shock caused by the pandemic is unusual and cannot be categorized as a supply or demand shock and will not affect all segments of the economy to the same extent. On the other hand, Mair (2020) evaluated the possible consequences of the pandemic from an economic perspective and mentioned four possible outcomes: barbarism, state capitalism, state socialism, and mutual aid. The author reveals that the current situation of countries facing coronavirus pandemic is state capitalism at the national level for now and adds that in case of a deep depression, deterioration in the supply chain, and the failure to increase the demand with standard Keynesian policies, the state's takeover of production may lead to state socialism. Before evaluating these future scenarios, it would be helpful to examine the failures of the laissez-faire model and the market during the pandemic process.

4.1 Failure of the Market During the Pandemic

Today, many countries can easily access the medical products needed for personal protection and medical diagnosis and treatment in the fight against the pandemic. However, during the pandemic, significant difficulties were experienced globally in accessing medical products related to COVID-19, which were collected into four categories (medicines, medical products, medical devices and technologies, and personal protective products) by the WTO (2020). Since all countries are trying to fight the virus globally, there has been a significant increase in the demand for medical products such as test kits, medicines, personal protective equipment, and ventilators. The struggle for access to these medicinal products has led to unilateral trade measures such as exporting countries stopping exports and importing countries lifting tariffs to facilitate imports. People witnessed extreme practices called "modern piracy" such as price wars, stopping the shipment of these vital products, and canceling contracts. In addition to these, the increasing demand for these medicinal products could not be met due to pandemic disruptions in production and supply, global logistics disruption, and ports closure (Vickers et al., 2020). While trade communities have intervened with incentives to lift export restrictions, this method has failed to solve the root cause of the problem, because the problem arose from the lack of capacity required to produce these goods in sufficient quantity. Baltzan (2020) examines this situation in the historical context and explains it as the result of the laissez-faire approach, developed in the eighteenth century. This approach claims that markets work better without government intervention. Later, as part of the New Deal, policymakers rejected this approach, realizing that state intervention was necessary to protect markets from the excesses of capitalism. However, the laissez-faire approach re-emerged with the rise of neoliberal policies in the 1980s, and governments started to prioritize the private sector decision process. The new trade rules liberalized movements of capital, leading to reduced regulation, pressure on wages and environmental protection, and ultimately a concentration of companies (Baltzan, 2020).

Baltzan (2020) says that although the coronavirus pandemic has natural origins, the shortage of medical equipment is due to human planning. The reason is the lack of capacity to meet the demand. This lack of capacity results from the economic regime that prioritizes economic efficiency based on low cost over strength/resistance based on flexibility in production. Maximizing efficiency means having a production capacity to meet demand at regular times. It is essential to minimize the labor cost. Since storage costs will reduce profitability, companies operate "just in time." For this reason, the system encounters insufficient capacity in the face of emergencies. The trading system became a part of our lives with multiple trade agreements after the 1990s. The rules of this system were designed based on the subordination of the state to private companies in matters of trade and investment. The system operates with the rules brought by the WTO, and it is shaped to benefit capital movements with low-cost and high-profit priority. In a sense, we can say that the WTO has institutionalized this system because capital can freely circulate globally within the framework of these rules. This global distribution of capital puts pressure on government regulations created to protect society. Investments made by multinational companies whose priority is profit maximization can be attracted by low cost of jurisdiction. The laissez-faire system, hence, causes the concentration of production in places that offer these conditions. This also leads to the destruction of labor and environmental problems as a negative externality (Baltzan, 2020).

Drezner (2001) talks about "race to the bottom theory" (RBT) regarding these circumstances. According to the theory, the mobility of trade and capital flows creates a convergence pressure on countries regarding policies. The magnitude of this capital flow weakens countries to engage in practices opposing market forces, because capital will look for locations where it will get the highest return. On the other hand, as high corporate taxes, strict labor laws, and harsh environmental protection measures would increase production costs and reduce profitability, capital will go to countries with the lowest regulatory standards. RBT's prediction is summarized as follows: (1) the more open a country is to global markets, the closer the tax and regulation policies in that country will converge to countries with international openness, (2) there is a negative correlation between the level of capital inflows to the country and regulatory standards, and (3) countries will be drawn toward other countries that implement laissez-faire policies the most (Drezner,

2001). Policies implemented in this context remove the obstacles to the global value chains (Nie, 2016). The global value chains emerged in the period when trade barriers were removed, the WTO was established, and policy prescriptions were presented within the framework of the Washington Consensus (Gereffi, 2015). In summary, we can say that the process that Baltzan mentioned emphasizes the formation of global value chains. At the point reached today, we face a structure where production is divided into small parts on a global scale, all sectors of all countries are interconnected, and input-output relations are complex. In a structure where interconnectivity between countries has increased, the pandemic process has undoubtedly caused vulnerabilities.

Baltzan (2020) summarizes the shortcomings encountered during the pandemic process with two crucial points: (1) concentration of production in a few countries and (2) insufficient capacity. The first problem showed itself with the emergence of the need for masks as mask production was concentrated in China. After people understood the importance of mask use in preventing the spread of the virus, there were problems in meeting the increasing demand for masks. Against this problem, countries have been able to find a solution in a short time since the mask has a relatively more straightforward technology. However, Baltzan conveys that the concentration of the production of such vital personal protective equipment in China is not based on comparative advantages but on the policies implemented by China, which has authoritarian political power, to attract capital. The Chinese government attracts capital by keeping labor costs and environmental standards low, currency manipulation, and various incentives. However, a deeper and more systemic problem was experienced in meeting the demand for ventilators. Since it is not easy to respond to the increasing demand for more advanced technology ventilators by increasing production, countries have experienced significant problems in accessing this medical device, which is vital for the treatment process.

Gruszczynski (2020) also underlines the possibility of significant changes occurring in the supply chain formation due to the pandemic. Stating that the early signs of such a process started with the pressures on American companies to move their production back to the country or at least out of China during the Trump era, Gruszczynski emphasizes that both the private sector and the governments may now be more interested in such changes. Shortening and diversifying the supply chain can eliminate the risk of supply constraints for private companies. It can eliminate the dependence on other countries and make them more resistant to future crises. These formations are closely related to how the global economic order will be following the pandemic. For this reason, we will emphasize various scenarios put forward for the future of the global economic order in the next part of the study.

4.2 The Post-pandemic Economic Order: The Beginning of a Paradigm Shift?

We have mentioned the future of the economic order as the last of the three significant uncertainties experienced after the pandemic. The "Great Reset" idea by the World Economic Forum (WEF) also supports the view that there will be a change in the global economic system with the coronavirus pandemic. Klaus Schwab, the founder and director of the WEF, indicates that the pandemic made the weaknesses of the current global economic system more evident and the crisis process presented the opportunity to make some institutional changes and policy choices to steer the economies toward a fairer and greener sustainable future in his book published at the beginning of the pandemic in 2020. Currently, we are at a crossroads. On one side of the road, there is a more inclusive, more egalitarian, and more respectful world. On the other side, there is a worse world than the one we left behind. At this point, the importance of the "reset" capacity is emphasized. The magnitude of a possible change is exemplified by mentioning the institutions formed with Bretton Woods after the World War II (Schwab & Mallaret, 2020).

It is possible to frequently encounter the expression of state capitalism in the literature regarding this change in the recent period. Bremmer (2010) explains the state capitalism process in four waves and points out that the fourth wave started with the 2008 crisis. However, note that state capitalist countries were also affected by the global crisis. For instance, Russia ran a budget deficit for the first time in 10 years, while China was less affected. India and Egypt also experienced less impact and a faster recovery. Therefore, the free market mechanism is expected to possibly undermine the view that private sector competition is necessary for long-term growth in this process (Bremmer, 2010). Bremmer highlights that understanding how state capitalism works in other countries, especially in Russia and China, and its strengths and weaknesses is essential in understanding how it will change our current life in the upcoming years. According to Bremmer's statements after the pandemic, this process can be a turning point in globalization (Bremmer, 2020a).

Considering the developments in the post-global crisis period, we see that even the USA, which is often stated to be the most liberal economy in the world, had a period of increased protectionist tendencies and got into a trade war with China in this period, which Bremmer refers to as the fourth wave of state capitalism. Sumner (2018) expresses that the Trump administration practiced a form of state capitalism. There have been talks about adopting the "Singapore model" in the UK in the post-Brexit period (Dixon & Alami, 2020). We have been living in a period in which interventionist policies have increased to fight against the coronavirus pandemic in the last year. We can see examples of that in the nationalization of private hospitals in Spain, the possibility of nationalization of various modes of transport in the UK, and France's statement that it is ready to nationalize large companies (Mair, 2020).

Can we say that a paradigm shift regarding the global economic order has taken place with the coronavirus pandemic? There are many scenarios mentioned in this regard. Mair (2020) talks about four possible outcomes of the coronavirus pandemic from an economic perspective. While making this assessment, he acts on two main factors: "exchange value" and "centralism." Exchange value is the value determined by the market according to the demand levels of goods and services, in other words, their usage value.

On the other hand, centralism is associated with whether the organizing process is carried out by a single commanding power or by many small units. There are four possible outcomes in this context: state capitalism, barbarism, state socialism, and mutual aid. The exchange value is also the primary guide of the economy in state capitalism, but we know that the market has failed to manage the crisis and the support of the state is needed. Barbarism, which is the worst-case scenario, is also based on the exchange value for the economy, and it refuses to provide support to those who have been pushed out of the market by illness or unemployment. In the scenario of state socialism, direct payments are made to everyone, regardless of how much value they create in the market. These payments are made to protect life, not to protect markets. State socialism is expected to occur due to the prolonged pandemic and the attempts at state capitalism. In case of a deep depression, deterioration in the supply chain, and if the demand cannot be increased with standard Keynesian policies, the state's takeover of production may lead to this result. Authoritarianism is the result to be avoided. The state does not have a defining role in the joint aid scenario. Instead, individuals and small groups organize support and engage with their communities. Mair (2020) expresses that the current situation of countries facing coronavirus pandemic is state capitalism at the national level.

Guinan et al. (2020) mentioned three possible scenarios for the future. The crisis is defined as an opportunity to establish a more productive, local, social, and democratic economic system. In "the good" scenario, the government and citizens work to build a more inclusive economy in cooperation and harmony with social solidarity and mutual aid. "The bad" scenario would be reestablishing global neoliberal capitalism by following the same process applied after the 2008 crisis. This scenario saves banks and companies, pays less attention to the remaining parts of the public, makes the public pay the bailout cost, forces the government to intervene less, and ultimately results in an increase in the economy's formerly existing injustices. "The ugly" scenario combines state authority with corporate capitalism, describing it as a "disaster." They state that such a result may threaten the democratic structure that is already under tension. Such a scenario could result in a new interventionist state capitalism where the government works to support big companies and the financial elite, with new laws created during the crisis that restrict fundamental freedoms.

Similarly, there are quite different views on the future of globalization after the pandemic. Some state that the end of globalization has come (Tsegaye, 2020; Toulan, 2020), others affirm that globalization will not be affected by the pandemic (Ishigaki, 2020; Antras, 2020), and another opinion is that further globalization will be needed after the pandemic (Thangavel et al., 2021).

Tsegaye (2020) states that globalization has taken a big hit, especially with the Trump administration. Since the USA is the biggest supporter of globalization and the country that benefits most from it, its withdrawal from international agreements cast doubt on globalization. Tsegaye thinks that post-pandemic globalization will be uncertain at best and will show a steady decline at worst. This decline will weaken both developed and developing countries, but the impact on developing countries will be more significant since the achievements of developing countries are directly dependent on the rapid development of globalization. Toulan (2020) also approaches the topic with a similar negative point of view: the pandemic has further increased the supply chain pressure, which has escalated since the beginning of the USA-China trade war. This happened to avoid being dependent on a single supply chain. As for the healthcare sector, governments also seem to be striving to secure the domestic supply of critical products. At this point, Toulan predicts that the centralized supply chain in low-cost countries may spread to high-cost countries with the help of the increasing use of robots and automation. In other words, the supply chain can evolve from centralistic to more imperialistic. Stating that the leadership styles of the dominant powers on a global scale will also be determinant in this course, Toulan draws attention to the possibilities of increasing populism, nationalism, and xenophobia. He also emphasizes that the world has come to a crossroads.

Ishigaki (2020) states that while it is necessary to seek ways to reduce the potential risk and harm of the pandemic by diversifying the supply chain and maintaining the flow of goods and services, this does not mean ending the existence of the global economy. One of the ways to ensure access to essential goods and services is to find local sources of supply, but this approach is not strong enough to replace all economic activities. Antras (2020) examines various globalization data and reveals that there has been a decrease in globalization, but this decrease is not surprising given the hyper-globalization period of the 1980s, 1990s, and early 2000s. According to Antras, it is difficult to say that technological development is likely to activate the era of deglobalization. Instead, policy factors have more influence on it. Even though new technologies increase inequality, which causes opposition to globalization, the main challenges for the future of globalization are institutional and political.

Stating that there is a need for more and new globalization, Thangavel et al. (2021) also remarked that COVID-19 and the political protectionism agenda would reduce the pace of globalization. However, the belief that globalization will disappear is exaggerated because the logic behind globalization still stands. According to the authors, the current failure of globalization cannot be solved either by protectionism or a return to the old form of globalization. The pandemic crisis has presented an opportunity to create new globalization that puts people's well-being and safety first. In this context, well-ordered globalization can also be a force for social good. While it provides cheaper goods and services and higher living standards for developed countries, it creates jobs for developing countries, reduces poverty, and improves women' economic and social power. According to the authors, the more mutually interdependent nations become, the less conflict they will have with each other. This is also what has been experienced with the greater prevalence of peace in the post-World War II era.

Among these views on the future of globalization, we are closer to Bremmer's view. In addition to the climate crisis, food crisis, and existing market-directing roles of states, the pandemic has triggered the tendency toward state capitalism. This matches the definition of state capitalism by Bremmer, which defines the domination of the state on markets primarily for political goals. Accordingly, capitalism will not emerge from this environment stronger.

5 Conclusion

The twenty-first century, which started with global economic crises, is about to complete its first quarter with the COVID-19 pandemic, which was considered as a health crisis in the first place but gradually evolved into an economic crisis. Regardless of the countries' development level, all countries were caught off guard because they did not take such a crisis seriously at first. After the first shock effect, many countries tried to take precautions with closure and quarantine. Of course, the emergence of the economic reflections of these practices started immediately. As the pandemic affected economies from both supply and demand aspects, the poverty rate has increased drastically worldwide. Since a significant part of poverty is from the informal sector, significant difficulties have been experienced in functioning the social protection system. Therefore, social protection policies have been better understood in this process.

There have been contractions in production, primarily due to disruptions in the supply chains during the pandemic. Accordingly, changing consumption tendency of segments whose income decreased due to layoffs and unpaid leave practices caused a decrease in investment tendency in general. So, the adverse effects deepened. These circumstances have caused negative consequences at national and global levels. Therefore, since the incomes of the countries decreased in this process, their foreign trade was adversely affected. The decrease in foreign demand and imports caused a decrease in the export revenues of the trading partner countries. As a result of all these supply and demand effects, many macroeconomic indicators such as employment, inflation, national income, growth, imports, exports, income distribution, and poverty have deteriorated. In particular, the increase in unemployment and poverty led the states to implement more social policies. However, we see a significant difference in the implementation of social protection policies between countries. While high-income countries can allocate more shares to social protection policies to protect their citizens from the adverse effects of the pandemic, this share is meager in middle and less developed countries. In this context, we can say that the pandemic has deepened the current global inequality even more.

As a result of vaccination and the efforts of countries to keep up with these new conditions, the uncertainties about the pandemic tend to decrease over time, but uncertainties continue about the direction of the global economic order. There are both optimistic and pessimistic views about the future of capitalism after the pandemic. We share the same approach with Bremmer that capitalism will transform into another structure in the post-pandemic world. Bremmer (2020b) states that this transformation had already started before the pandemic, and it has gained acceleration with the pandemic. According to Bremmer (2020b), three tendencies will be effective in this transformation. These tendencies are deglobalization, rising populism and nationalism, and an ascendant China. Deglobalization is wholly related to the disruptive effect of the pandemic on global value chains. Logistic difficulties due to the pandemic will lead countries to replace just-in-time supply chains with regional supply chains. The second tendency—rising populism and nationalism—is also related to deglobalization. Accordingly, the current rise in populist and nationalist political movements is expected to spread globally. The food crisis, which is triggered by the pandemic, and countries' restrictive policies are among the most typical cases.

References

Antras, P. (2020). *De-globalization? Global value chains in the post – Covid-19 age*. https://scholar.harvard.edu/files/antras/files/deglobalization_sintra_antras.pdf (02.05.2021).

Azcona, G., Bhatt, A., Encarnacion, J., Plazaola-Castano, J., Seck, P., Staab, S., & Turquet, L. (2020). *From insights to action: Gender equality in the wake of Covid-19*. UN Women.

Baltzan, B. (2020). *Covid-19 and the End of Laissez-Faire Globalization*. http://groundworkcollaborative.org/wp-content/uploads/2020/07/GWC2043_Globalization_2.pdf (accessed on: 15.02.2021).

Barrientos, A. (2010). Poverty reduction and policy regimes thematic paper – Social protection and poverty. *Social Policy and Development*, Paper no. 42.

Baqaee, D. R., & Farhi, E. (2020). *Supply and demand in disaggregated Keynesian economies with an application to the Covid-19 crisis*. NBER Working Paper, No. 27152.

Beaulieu, E., & Klemen, D. (2021). *Covid-19, the great trade collapse and Canadian trade policy, trade policy trends*. University of Calgary the School of Public Policy. https://www.policyschool.ca/wp-content/uploads/2021/02/Trade-Trends-Trade-Collapse.pdf (22.02.2021).

Bremmer, I. (2010). *Who wins the war between states and corporations?* Portfolio.

Bremmer, I. (2020a). *Why Covid-19 maybe a major blow to globalization*. https://time.com/5796707/coronavirus-global-economy/ (27.04.2021).

Bremmer, I. (2020b). How will the world be different after COVID-19? *Finance & Development*, June, 26–29.

Caracciolo, G., Cingano, F., Ercolani, V., Ferrero, G., Hassan, F., Papetti, A., & Tommasino, P. (2020). Covid-19 and economic analysis: A review of the debate. *Banca D'Italia Eurosistema Literature Review*, no: 3.

Cichon, M., Scholz, W., van de Meerendonk, A., Hagemejer, K., Bertranou, F., & Plamondon, P.. (2004). Financing social protection. *Quantitative Methods in Social Protection Series*. ILO-ISSA.

Congressional Research Service. (2021). Global economic effects of COVID-19. https://fas.org/sgp/crs/row/R46270.pdf (21.02.2021).

Das, P. (2020). *Covid-19 pandemic and macroeconomic uncertainty: Indian economic outlook*. https://mpra.ub.uni-muenchen.de/99757/1/MPRA_paper_99757.pdf (23.03.2021).

Del Rio-Chanona, R. M., P. Mealy, A. Pichler, F. Lafond & J. D. Farmer. (2020). *Supply and demand shocks in the COVID-19 pandemic: An industry and occupation perspective*. INET Oxford Working Paper, no: 2020-05.

Demiralp, S. (2020). Covid-19 Salgınının Ekonomik Etkileri. In D. Bayindir (Ed.), *Salgın: Tükeniş Çağında Dünyayı Yeniden Düşünmek*. Tellekt.

Dixon, A., & Alami, I. (2020). The specter of state capitalism. *Developing Economics*, March 26. https://developingeconomics.org/2020/03/26/the-specter-of-state-capitalism/ (12.02.2021).

Drezner, D. W. (2001). Globalization and policy convergence. *International Studies Review, 3*(1), 53–78.

FAO. (2020). *Social protection and COVID-19 response in rural areas*. http://www.fao.org/3/ca8561en/CA8561EN.pdf (20.02.2021).

Fornaro, L., & Wolf, M. (2020). *Covid-19 coronavirus and macroeconomic policy: Some analytical notes*. http://www.crei.cat/wp-content/uploads/2016/07/CMP.pdf. Accessed 29 May 2020.

Gentilini, U. et al. (2021). *Social protection and jobs responses to COVID-19: A real-time review of country measures*. World Bank. https://openknowledge.worldbank.org/handle/10986/33635; (16.12.2021).

Gereffi, G. (2015). Global value chains, development and emerging economies. *Research, Statistics and Industrial Policy Branch Working Paper*, UNIDO, no: 18/2015.

Gruszczynski, L. (2020). The COVID-19 pandemic and international trade: Temporary turbulence or paradigm shift? *European Journal of Risk Regulation, 11*, 337–342.

Guerrieri, V., Lorenzoni, G., Straub, L., & Werning, I. (2020). *Macroeconomic implications of COVID-19: Can negative supply shocks cause demand shortages?* NBER Working Paper, no: 26918.

Guinan, J., Leibowitz, J., McInroy, N., & Mckinley, S. (2020). *Owning the future – After Covid-19, A New Era of Community Wealth Building*. Centre for Local Economic Strategies.

Hillson, D. (2021). Covid-19, the social contract and the need for a new normal for social protection. *Pathways' Perspectives, 32*.

https://www.un.org/pga/75/2020/12/16/46th-plenary-meeting-reports-of-the-third-committee-opening/ (16.02.2021).

https://www.worldometers.info/coronavirus/. Accessed on 16.02.2021

ILO. (n.d.). *Facts on social security*. https://www.ilo.org/public/english/protection/socsec/pol/campagne/files/factsheet.pdf (21.03.2021).

ILO. (2011). Social security for social justice and a fair globalization, ILO conference 100th session, Report VI, Geneva.

ILO. (2021). *Informal economy (Employment promotion)* (ilo.org) (22.03.2021).

IMF. (2021a). *World Economic Outlook Update*. https://www.imf.org/en/Publications/WEO/Issues/2021/01/26/2021-world-economic-outlook-update (21.02.2021).

IMF. (2021b). *World economic outlook: Recovery during a pandemic – Health concerns, supply disruptions, and Price pressures*.

Ishigaki, T. (2020). *The future of globalization and multilateralism: Responding to and looking beyond the Covid-19 pandemic*. https://www.frstrategie.org/sites/default/files/documents/programmes/Programme-japon/Publications/2020-2021/N4-2020%20programme%20japon.pdf (02.05.2021).

Lustig, N., & Tommasi, M. (2020). Covid-19 and social protection of poor and vulnerable groups in Latin America: A conceptual framework. *UNDP LAC Policy Document Series, 8*.

Mair, S. (2020). What will the world be like after coronavirus? *Four Possible Futures*. https://theconversation.com/what-will-the-world-be-like-after-coronavirus-four-possible-futures-134085 (08.03.2021).

Merrien, F. X. (2013). Social protection as development policy: A new international agenda for action. International Development Policy, *Revue Internationale de Politique de Développement*. https://doi.org/10.4000/poldev.1525

Minondo, A. (2021). Impact of COVID-19 on the trade of goods and services in Spain. *Applied Economic Analysis, 29*, 58. https://doi.org/10.1108/AEA-11-2020-0156

Nie, M. (2016). *The transmission of trade policy shocks through global value chains: Evidence from China's processing trade regime* (Master Thesis).

Norton, A., Conway, T., & Foster, M. (2001). Social protection concepts and approaches: Implications for policy and practice in international development. *Centre for Aid and Public Expenditure Working Paper,* no: 143, London.
OECD (2019). *Lessons from the EU-SPS programme implementing social protection strategies.* http://www.oecd.org/dev/inclusivesocietiesanddevelopment/Lessons_learned_Implementing_social_protection_strategies.pdf (22.03.2021).
OECD (2020). http://www.oecd.org/employment-outlook/2020/ (20.02.2021).
OECD. (2021a). https://www.oecd-ilibrary.org/sites/66c5ac2c-en/1/3/1/index.html?itemId=/content/publication/66c5ac2c-en&_csp_=9b4ecb1aafc11518f34da944ee244a5b&itemIGO=oecd&itemContentType=book (16.12.2021).
OECD. (2021b). https://www.oecd.org/economic-outlook/ (16.12.2021).
Paremoer, L. (2021). Covid-19 pandemic and the social determinants of health. *BMJ, 372*(129), 1–5. https://doi.org/10.1136/BMJ.n129
Schwab, K., & Mallaret, T. (2020). *Covid-19: The great reset.* Forum Publishing.
Sumner, S. (2018). State capitalism, part 2. https://www.econlib.org/state-capitalism-part-2/ (08.03.2021).
Thangavel, P., Pathak, P., & Chandra, B. (2021). Covid-19: Globalization – Will the course change?. *Perspective,* Vision 1–4.
Toulan, O. (2020). Globalization after Covid-19: What is in store?. International Institute for Management Development. https://www.imd.org/contentassets/14944862a6914efc91e7af56a80c0e8c/tc041-20-print.pdf (02.05.2021).
Trading Economics. (2021). https://tradingeconomics.com/united-states/inflation-cpi (16.12.2021).
Tsegaye, K. K. (2020). Stay at home: Coronavirus (COVID-19), isolationism and the future of globalization. *African Journal of Political Science and International Relations, 14*(3), 84–90.
UN. (2021). https://www.un.org/pga/75/2020/12/16/46th-plenary-meeting-reports-of-the-third-committee-opening/ (16.02.2021).
UNCTAD. (2021). Global trade update. https://unctad.org/system/files/official-document/ditcinf2021d1_en.pdf (22.02.2021).
UNDRR. (2020). Disaster-responsive social protection: Lessons from COVID-19, UNDRR Asia-Pacific COVID-19 brief.
Vickers, B., Ali, S., & Zhuawu, C. (2020). Trade-in COVID-19-related medical goods: Issues and challenges for commonwealth countries. *The Commonwealth*, 159.
WTO. (2020). Trade-in Medical Goods in the Context of Tackling Covid-19, Information Note. https://www.wto.org/english/news_e/news20_e/rese_03apr20_e.pdf (22.04.2021).
Yigit, S. (2021). Trump vs China. In A. Günar (Ed.), *The trade wars of the USA, China, and the EU: The global economy in the age of populism*. Lexington Books.
Yong, W. (2020). The impact of the pandemic on China and its relations with the world. *Global Asia, 15*(3), 8–13.

Great Reset

Abdüsselam Sagin and Ünal Çaglar

Abstract This study discusses whether the great reset proposal can be implemented globally and be a remedy for the crisis of capitalism, dealing with the impacts of the COVID-19 pandemic and the fourth industrial revolution. The great reset proposal that was brought to the world's agenda by Klaus Schwab of the World Economic Forum (WEF) points out the need for creating a new social and economic order with a more resilient and more sustainable world economy. According to Schwab, since capitalism cannot sustain itself anymore as it is, a transition from shareholder capitalism to stakeholder capitalism is a must. This transition means the end of neoliberalism and the passing of a more interventionist economic order. The fourth industrial revolution, according to Schwab, makes the reset inevitable. However, what ensures that governments will make proper interventions and implement correct policies is not obvious. Schwab's proposal fails to determine the source of the systemic instability inherent in the domestic and international monetary system. Making the world more resilient and more sustainable requires international solidarity, which does not seem probable in the light of past experiences.

Keywords Great reset · Shareholder capitalism · Stakeholder capitalism · COVID-19 · Fourth industrial revolution

1 Introduction

The term great reset, which refers to the economic consequences of climate change, was used by Prince Charles and Chairman of the WEF Davos Summit Klaus Schwab to point out the need for a new social and economic order. The idea is that, as manifested by the COVID-19 pandemic crisis, capitalism can no longer sustain itself as it is. Hence, a great reset is needed to make capitalism sustainable. A "stakeholder

A. Sagin (✉) · Ü. Çaglar
Department of Economics, Kirklareli University, Kırklareli, Turkey
e-mail: abdusselam.sagin@klu.edu.tr; unal.caglar@klu.edu.tr

A. Ari (ed.), *Capitalism at a Crossroads*, Springer Studies in Alternative Economics,
https://doi.org/10.1007/978-3-031-23257-2_14

capitalism" must be created instead of the existing "shareholder capitalism." The aim is to rebuild the world economy as a more sustainable and more resilient one.

Schwab asserted his ideas on this topic in the book entitled *COVID-19: The Great Reset* which he wrote with Malleret. They think that the crisis caused by the pandemic is unprecedented in modern history in the sense that it will last for years, many aspects of life will change forever, and it will throw the world into a dangerous position economically, politically, and socially. Millions of companies, jobs, and many sectors are at risk of disappearing (Schwab & Malleret, 2020). What must be done is to create a fairer, sustainable, and resilient economic, social, and environmental system, harnessing rapid technological developments brought about by the fourth industrial revolution. This requires economically to depart from neoliberalism which has been hand in hand with financial globalization. That is, governments should have an interventionist approach rather than a liberalist one.

WEF's call for a great reset triggered some conspiracy theories. Skeptical ones believe that the great reset is a plan to provide the global elite with complete hegemony over humanity and the pandemic and resulting lockdowns are implementations aimed at persuading people. Many people are concerned that technology can undermine civil rights and liberties. Noninski (2021) asserted that there will be no great reset and the world will be as before after the pandemic. What the elite is doing is manipulation. According to Noninski, the main problem is the concentration of wealth among a small number of individuals, and until this imbalance is treated, the world will not be peaceful.

The WEF's idea of a great reset and its inevitableness is based on the impacts of the COVID-19 pandemic and fourth industrial revolution. As history shows, in their opinion, both have a transformative power on societies. Incredible transformations like the industrial revolution are triggered when a certain level of technological accumulation is reached, and the world is now at such a point. The point in question is the accumulation of digital technology such as artificial intelligence, nanotechnology, biotechnology, and quantum computing (Roth, 2021).

As the issue is quite new, there is not a comprehensive theoretical discussion. It seems like an undetailed program by the elite rather than being a theoretical issue. Therefore, the discussion has mainly to be the evaluation of what WEF offered. In Sect. 2, we will discuss the main problems of the world economy in the twenty-first century to determine the need for a reset. Section 3 is about the fourth industrial revolution (4IR) and the pandemic, the two transformative factors making a reset inevitable according to the WEF. In this section, we will evaluate the impacts of the 4IR and the COVID-19 pandemic to understand to what extent they make a transformation in the world economy inevitable. We will evaluate the proposal and submit our predictions on future developments in Conclusion.

2 World Economy in the Twenty-First Century

2.1 Features and Problems of the World Economy

The deficiency of the WEF view on great reset is that it does not show the roots or causes of the illnesses of the world system and gives no prescription. It is quite unclear how the illnesses will be cured. It would be rational to first ascertain the sources of the world's problems before putting forward a proposal. The reason may be that this will require criticizing the developments in the history of capitalism and even the system itself. Another deficiency is not to mention the unsustainable monetary and financial system, which is the main underlying factor that shaped today's economic system.

One of the main features of the global economic system is its addiction to growth. Every economy and business feels obliged to grow. We should ask if endless growth is possible and think about the results of this dependency on economic growth. Many questions will arise when we tackle this issue: For example, can the globe's resources allow us to grow forever? Can all the nations in the world industrialize and develop? Is there a limit to growth imposed by the environment? The belief that economic activities must accelerate or otherwise the economic system cannot be sustained is like a religious cult (Triodos Bank, 2020). Nobody knows what to do if economic growth gets slower than expected or stops.

The sources of the economic growth are increases in the number of factors of production and, more importantly, technological developments. Technological development and innovation increase labor productivity, which means producing the same amount of goods with less production factors or, put it differently, producing more with the same number of factors of production. Then, to protect the economy against unemployment, an increased amount of goods and services must be absorbed; in other words, demand must increase. Governments are also growth-addicted because their spending grows due to increases in population and aging. To afford this increased spending, tax income must increase. Since the base for tax income is economic activity, the economy must grow.

There is a relationship between the need for growth and debt, another addiction to the economic system. The economic system accumulates huge debt stocks inherent in the monetary system. Since debt is a claim on the future income, the ability of the economic agencies to pay it back is dependent on the increase in income. If income does not grow, the increasing debt-to-income ratio will rise the danger of insolvency. This addiction to growth, which destroys the environment and exploits the world's resources, has led to inequalities and violent conflicts, failing to bring prosperity to most human beings. Because growth rates are decreasing globally, the prosperity of the powerful minority is not sustainable. Crises have gained a global character, affecting wealthy nations, and a systemic collapse has appeared.

To understand the crisis-generating nature of the capitalist system, the relationship between money, credit, and banking needs to be analyzed. In the modern monetary system, banks are authorized to create credit out of nothing by lending deposits many times. Because credit functions as money, banks can create money that is not a physical entity but merely a number in a bank account. Considering that more than 90% of the money is supplied by banks in economies, it can be said that money emission was privatized in the modern economic system.

Under these circumstances, what can deter banks from creating too much credit money? Theoretically, if there is no constraint, banks can create an infinite amount of money. In the beginning, banks had to keep the same amount of reserve as credit. There was no money multiplier. When a fractional reserve system had been put in force, banks had the authority to create money with just account entries without needing a backing physical currency. They began to generate instabilities in economies by increasing and decreasing the quantity of credit and money. During the Great Depression, FED's nonactive behavior against a contraction in the money supply exacerbated the ongoing crisis. Learning from the Great Depression, the US government constrained financial activities, regulated banks' activities with the Glass-Steagall Act of 1933, and protected the US economy from excessive credit growths and busts, which caused instabilities in money supply and economic activity.

Following "the golden age of capitalism" from 1945 to 1971 came an age of slow growth. Ideas of removing constraints on financial activities were asserted, and in 1980, the US Congress eliminated restrictions on interest rates paid for bank deposits. Then, in 1996, the Glass-Steagall Act was abolished so that commercial banks could engage in investment activities in the finance sector. These developments freeing banks from the constraints on credit growth have undermined the tie between credit growth and GDP. Hence, the quantity of credit soared compared to GDP. In addition, credit turned toward financial activities which do not generate real income. As growth in credit and debt exceeded growth in real income, distinguishing or amortizing debt by increasing income became impossible, resulting in mounting debt.

In time, accelerating financial innovations (i.e., derivatives and securitization) led to an explosion in financial transactions and contributed to asset price appreciations. Moreover, expanding credit raised asset prices, leading to increased demand for credit, and so a vicious circle has started by credit expansion, asset price increase, and increasing interest rates. This unsustainable boom in financial markets made the economic system quite fragile, causing financial crises.

Today, the global monetary system can be described as a petrodollar system. Oil is sold in exchange for the US dollar, so every country must keep reserves in dollar. This creates extra demand for dollars. The US dollar functions as an internationally accepted means of payment, in other words, as the world money backed by nothing, and the increase in the world money supply is dependent on the deficit of the US balance of payments. This situation allows the USA to import goods and services without the obligation of selling goods and services produced in the USA and not having to keep foreign exchange reserves. Put it differently, the USA can finance its foreign deficits with its own money. This capability encouraged the USA to accumulate a vast debt stock. Though the international monetary and payment system puts the burden of balancing the trade imbalances on deficit nations, the USA, as an exception, has been able to sustain its debtor position.

Usually, the floating exchange rate system is expected to appreciate surplus countries' currencies. Accordingly, the Chinese renminbi and other surplus country currencies should have appreciated against the US dollar to eliminate their trade surpluses. However, China and other Asian surplus countries have preferred to intervene in the exchange market to prevent their currencies from appreciating and accumulating dollar reserves to continue to raise their exports and growth rates. This provided the Western countries, specifically the USA, with cheap goods imported from China and other emerging countries (Fidler & Nicoll, 2011). Lending these reserves in the US finance sector to get yield was a rational behavior for them. This financial flow from the surplus countries toward the USA due to global saving imbalances has fed the financialization in the world, starting from the USA.

The Asian crisis of 1997 also directed the export-oriented Asian economies to accumulate large dollar reserves to hedge against exchange rate volatility and thereby protect themselves from increasing fragility in the international financial system. Heading to the USA in search of profit, these reserves contributed to the overexpansion of the US financial sector, giving rise to excess speculation. Finance, instead of manufacturing, has become the primary source of wealth accumulation. Because there is no discipline on today's monetary system like gold imposed once, economies accumulated too many imbalances generating frequent dangerous boom and bust cycles (Table 1).

2.2 Policies of Capitalist Countries and Globalization

Today's economic system results from the developments since the industrial revolution in the eighteenth century. The industrial revolution provided the industrialized countries with consistent growth and material prosperity, but at the same time, the danger of demand insufficiency threatened the system. The solution was to find additional demand from abroad. In the early stages of capitalism, this was foreign trade, namely, exporting the excess production (Ivanova, 2013). The UK, the leading economy of the capitalist world, invested the trade surplus in deficit countries. This capital flow, together with the balancing effect of the international monetary system of the gold standard, contributed to keeping the system in balance.

After World War II, large companies which are known as multinationals—mainly the US origin—are in a struggle for the fields of profitable reinvestment for their growing profits and capital to avoid the potential crisis of demand deficiency and to benefit from low costs began to shift the production toward low-wage countries in Asia. That meant a new division of labor by the internationalization of production made possible by sharp decreases in transportation and communication costs. The restructured production created a system of high consumption in the West, chiefly in the USA, albeit the low rate of growth, and decreasing real wages and export-led growth of the newly industrialized countries. Production has shifted to Asia with low

Table 1 Total reserves (billion $)

	China	China	India	India	Japan	Japan	South Korea	South Korea	Russian Federation	Russian Federation
	Total reserves including gold	Total reserves minus gold	Total reserves including gold	Total reserves minus gold	Total reserves including gold	Total reserves minus gold	Total reserves including gold	Total reserves minus gold	Total reserves including gold	Total reserves minus gold
1996	111.73	107.04	24.89	20.17	225.59	216.65	34.16	34.04	16.26	11.28
1997	146.45	142.76	28.39	24.69	226.68	219.65	20.47	20.37	17.62	12.89
1998	152.84	149.19	30.65	27.34	222.44	215.47	52.10	51.97	12.04	7.80
1999	161.41	157.73	36.01	32.67	293.95	286.92	74.11	73.99	12.33	8.46
2000	171.76	168.28	41.06	37.90	361.64	354.90	96.25	96.13	27.66	24.26
2001	220.06	215.61	49.05	45.87	401.96	395.16	102.88	102.75	36.30	32.54
2002	297.74	291.13	71.61	67.67	469.62	461.19	121.50	121.35	48.33	44.05
2003	416.20	408.15	103.74	98.94	673.55	663.29	155.47	155.28	78.41	73.17
2004	622.95	614.50	131.63	126.59	844.67	833.89	199.20	199.00	126.26	120.81
2005	831.41	821.51	137.82	131.92	846.90	834.27	210.55	210.32	182.27	175.89
2006	1080.76	1068.49	178.05	170.74	895.32	879.68	239.15	238.88	303.77	295.57
2007	1546.36	1530.28	276.58	266.99	973.30	952.78	262.53	262.15	478.82	466.75
2008	1966.04	1949.26	257.42	247.42	1030.76	1009.36	201.54	201.14	426.28	411.75
2009	2452.90	2416.04	284.68	265.18	1051.65	1024.90	270.44	269.93	439.34	416.65
2010	2913.71	2866.08	300.48	275.28	1104.56	1069.99	292.14	291.49	479.22	443.59
2011	3254.67	3202.79	298.74	271.29	1295.84	1258.17	306.93	304.25	497.41	453.95
2012	3387.51	3331.12	300.43	270.59	1268.09	1227.15	327.72	323.21	537.82	486.58
2013	3880.37	3839.55	298.09	276.49	1266.85	1237.22	345.69	341.65	509.69	469.60
2014	3900.04	3859.17	325.08	303.45	1260.68	1231.01	362.83	358.78	386.22	339.37
2015	3405.25	3345.19	353.32	334.31	1233.10	1207.02	366.71	363.15	368.04	319.84
2016	3097.66	3029.78	361.69	341.15	1216.52	1188.33	370.15	366.31	377.05	317.54

2017	3235.68	3158.88	412.61	389.35	1264.14	1232.24	388.80	384.45	432.73	356.08
2018	3168.22	3091.88	399.17	374.43	1270.47	1238.94	403.08	398.78	468.65	381.58
2019	3222.89	3127.49	463.47	432.38	1322.44	1284.97	408.82	403.70	555.18	443.97
2020	3357.24	3238.78	590.23	549.09	1390.81	1344.28	443.46	437.11	596.77	457.02

Source: World Bank Data

consumption. These developments brought in saving imbalances and emerging economies addicted to exporting to the USA.

The developments mentioned above in production coupled with financial liberalization in advanced capitalist countries. Deregulation of the finance sector created highly liquid capital markets in the West, particularly in the USA. Dollar-denominated current account surpluses of China and other Asian countries flowed to the capital markets in the USA. These flows fueled the finance sector of the USA, leading to bubbles in sectors such as real estate, stock exchange, and derivatives. Additionally, they led to a growing interdependency between the USA and China and, on the other hand, turned China into a rival for the USA due to the shift of economic power toward it (Saull, 2012).

China also has some fragilities in this system. First, while China grows fast relative to the rest of the world, its growth depends on exports to a limited number of wealthy nations, particularly to the USA. That is, China needs a growing market in the West to sustain its high growth rate. As seen during the 2007–2009 crisis, any contraction in these markets is impeding the growth of China. However, China is quite growth-addicted because of the changes in its social and economic structures. Every year, Chinese citizens migrate to the big cities in bulk from rural areas in the hope of finding jobs there. Therefore, China has to sustain a high growth rate in order to create millions of new jobs every year. The last crisis that resulted from the COVID-19 pandemic showed that a negative development in production in China, supply chains, or consumption in developed nations threatens the world production-distribution system and brings out the possibility of the collapse of the world economy.

According to Charles Kindleberger, a liberal world economic order needs a hegemonic power or a multilateral institution to operate smoothly, curing imbalances and providing international cooperation (Funabashi, 2009). The imbalanced and interdependent world system implies that the USA as a world hegemon is in decline and no other power to substitute it is sighted on the horizon (Saull, 2012). A multilateral institution with that capability does not exist either. Unlike what happened after World War II, the whole system may collapse this time rather than a hegemon.

The USA–China relations occur at the center of the world economic system, and China has to preserve the pegged exchange rate policy to hold its competitive position. To be more precise, China has to control the renminbi's value and accumulate dollars. Any change in its exchange rate or foreign reserve policy will lead the system to a crash. Indeed, in addition to distortions in the production-distribution chain, China tries to get rid of substantial dollar reserves it accumulated to free itself from the fragile balance in the international monetary system. However, China's attention can undermine the dollar's value, which can trigger a global turmoil also involving China.

Additionally, because of the low level of wages, the demand in the USA is dependent on credit growth, and the financial flows from emerging countries make it possible to reduce interest rates. Any interruption in these flows can lead to turmoil in the US financial system. Resulting asset price deflation, credit constraint, bank failures, a sharp decrease in aggregate demand, and widespread bankruptcies can bring a total economic collapse which obviously will spread to the world, causing the collapse of the international system. Alternatively, burst of bubbles in the US financial system, leading to a sharp shrinkage in financial markets, can throw the US economy into a great depression and, at the same time, into hyperinflation because of the existence of too much dollars, used for financial transactions. As a result, the US dollar can become worthless, which will end with resulting chaos for the rest of the world. The dollar is steadily losing the confidence of the leading players in the world economy (Kotarski, 2009), creating a fragile environment that can quickly become chaotic with an unanticipated event.

2.3 Road to the Global Crisis

Outsourcing of production to low-wage countries, particularly China, as a solution to decreasing profit rates, substantial current account deficits in the USA coupled with sizeable current account surpluses of China and other Asian countries resulting in global saving imbalances, the worldwide large-scale domestic and foreign debt accumulation, the low level of interest rates in advanced capitalist economies fueling credit growth and leveraged speculative transactions, the explosion in financial derivatives, and financialization of the economies have laid flagstones of the road to the global crises at the end of the twentieth century and the beginning of the twenty-first century.

Emerging East Asian economies experienced a severe crisis in 1997. As the main reason for the crisis was excessive dollar-denominated debts that led to speculative bubbles in real estate, these countries transited to an export-oriented growth model instead of the one based on internal demand. They hedged themselves against instabilities in the international monetary system to avoid another foreign exchange crisis. Thereby, former dollar-debtor Asian countries became dollar creditors. They resorted to depreciated domestic currency policies and repressed consumption to accumulate foreign currency reserves using trade surpluses. This contributed to the saving imbalances in the world economy. Huge deficits of the USA offset excess savings in Asian countries. These dollar accumulations flowed to the US financial sector coupled with the FED's low interest rate policy as of 2001. After the dotcom crisis in 2000, trying to escape from deflation like Japan faced in the 1990s, the US monetary authorities followed an expansionary monetary policy, keeping interest rates around 1% and deregulating the banking sector. Negative real interest rates increased private indebtedness in the USA, at the same time encouraged the US banks for financial innovations and securitization.

This process was the main factor that created a great bubble in the US real estate sector. In addition to speculative investments in the financial sector, the consumption level of the American people increased, thanks to the borrowing opportunities with negative real interest rates, aggravating the debt accumulation of American households. Liquidity abundance due to capital inflows from the Asian surplus countries reduced long-term interest rates. Although the FED tried to restrict the credit growth by increasing short-term interest rates from 2005, abundant liquidity kept long-term interest rates on bonds below the short-term rates. Because of this inverted yield curve, the credit costs in the USA remained low, which prompted banks to give credit to even subprime people. Companies like Fannie Mae and Freddie Mac contributed to the banks' risk appetite.

Consequently, real estate prices kept rising until mid-2006 despite the restrictive monetary policy raising interest rates from 1% to 5.25%. The rise in interest rates resulted in defaulting risky debtors, and increases in real estate prices ended in the middle of 2006. Then, prices began to drop toward the end of that year. However, the bubble did not explode until rating agencies enunciated in August 2007 that some assets previously accepted as investable were toxic.

Saving glut in emerging Asian countries had flowed to the US financial sector in search of rent instead of being reinvested internally. Rent-seeking has become the leading economic motive, extending financial activities to the detriment of the real sector. Because this structure has not changed, the crisis-prone characteristic of the world economic system still prevails. In conclusion, the greatest threat to the capitalist world system is the fragile and unsustainable international monetary system designed in favor of the West, the USA in particular.

2.4 Postcrisis Policies

Central banks and governments' instant responses to the crisis were injecting liquidity into financial institutions, bailing out and/or nationalization of financial institutions, and urging them into mergers. As seen throughout history, economic crises are followed by recessions and even deflations. Therefore, central banks and governments announced rescue plans to prevent economic decline from leading to the collapse of the financial and economic system. Thus, governments of major capitalist countries resorted to stimulus packages following the financial rescue. However, these measures gave rise to a spike in government debts and money supplies, increasing the fragility of the world economy. Increasing budget deficits, debt stocks, and money supply cast doubt on the sustainability of the global financial system and the viability of growth-addicted capitalism. To what extent can growth be sustained by printing money and enlarging budget deficits? The measures taken by major economic powers contribute to the unbalanced global economic system. That means the problem faced by the world has turned into a vicious circle. Put it differently, it is a self-feeding process that the science of economics does not have any efficient formula to solve in the existing system. The problem is systemic rather than casual.

Conventional monetary policy is to lower interest rates and expand credits to prevent a decline in economic activities. However, during the global crisis, governments had to resort to unconventional monetary policies because interest rates had already fallen almost to zero but could not boost the economy. This unconventional policy is known as quantitative easing which is injecting money into the economy by purchasing financial assets of private companies. It meant unprecedented increases in money supplies of major economies and, at the same time, in the quantity of money in the world economy. After attempting to reverse the quantitative easing policy, the FED started asset purchases again in 2010 because of an economic slowdown. The massive dollar creation led to a decline in the value of the US dollar, starting capital inflows to the faster-growing emerging economies such as China and Brazil, bringing about appreciation of their currencies that undermines the competitiveness of their economies. They had to intervene in foreign exchange markets to prevent this danger, creating the threat of a currency war, trade retaliations, and protectionism (Fidler & Nicoll, 2011). Flaming up of the crisis again in the condition of the pandemic in 2020 compelled the FED, which was trying to decrease the money supply by selling assets to return to the quantitative easing and fiscal stimulus policies. Too much liquidity boosted financial markets, resuming the bubble-generating process.

The global crisis accelerated the shift of power from the West to the emerging countries, particularly China. However, the crisis and the pandemic also stroke Asian emerging countries, including China, which brought out a paradoxical outcome: the USA is preserving its position as the most secure place to invest savings (Marazzi, 2010). As the decline of the American hegemony is apparent, there is no appearance of a new hegemon to substitute it. The world is either unipolar or multipolar because the world cannot be governed unilaterally or multilaterally. Instead, all the major powers' fates are intertwined, but none of them can intervene in the catastrophic course of the world. This reality decreases the likelihood of international cooperation needed for an effective reset to save the capitalist system.

2.5 *Responses of Governments and Central Banks to the Pandemic*

Because of the fear of depression, governments and central banks have implemented expansionary economic policies during the global financial crisis of 2007–2009. Central banks have resorted to the unconventional monetary policy of unprecedented increase in money supply through liquidity injections, loan expansions, asset purchases, and lower interest rates. Governments have also intervened in the economy through a fiscal policy of expanding social safety nets, direct cash payments, public guarantees of private loans, and deferral of tax payments (Triodos Bank, 2020). The result of these massive interventions is soaring money supplies everywhere.

Increased government spending resulted from interventions in markets and decreasing tax incomes due to the decline in incomes stemming from widespread lockdowns deteriorated government budgets which led to substantial public debt accumulations and sharp increases in the quantity of money. Governments, particularly in advanced countries, have issued new government bonds, most of which are being purchased by central banks. The debt burden of companies and households also spiked. Resulting economic threats of repayment difficulties of emerging countries, zombie companies, and low effective demand will hamper economic recovery. It can also lead to an economic crisis and collapsing financial markets. Countries have resorted to printing money to support financial markets, which resulted in overexpansion in financial transactions and growing financial bubbles. As seen, the measures to which governments resorted made the capitalist world economy more crisis-prone, merely delaying the problems rather than solving them.

Another implementation that central banks have applied to support financial markets is buying equities. These efforts to conserve the status quo in the economic system contributed to risky unproductive investments, enlarging financial markets, repressing real wages, leading to deficiency in effective demand and tendency of deflation, and increasing the fragility of the economic system. Policies that placed financial transactions at the center of economic activities and made finance the primary source of profit resulted in increasing money supply, more rent-seeking behavior of economic agents, astronomical amounts of national debt, securitization-driven intricate and unmanageable ever-growing financial sector, low level of wages, and accelerating inequalities in income distribution.

Authorities in advanced countries tried to create moderate inflation to avoid deflation tendency in their economies. These efforts have been futile until recent times, but when significantly increased money supply coupled with the signs of recovery from the pandemic, inflation rates in developed countries climbed to high levels. Although the FED announced that it would complete tapering and begin to increase interest rates in 2022, it is not likely that interest rate increases will reach the level of inflation. In other words, we can expect that real interest rates remain negative because the large pile of debts cannot be sustained otherwise.

Negative real interest rates make saving accounts unattractive, which creates a tendency toward the withdrawal of money from the banks that can turn into a bank run. As known, because banks give long-term loans with short-term deposits, they cannot meet everybody's demand of withdrawing money at any given time. That is why there has been a tendency of restricting the use of cash in some countries. When people withdraw their money and hoard it, the gap between savings and investments enlarges, lowering total spending in the economy. It means a low level of economic growth. Because interest rates are already zero, there is no room for lowering interest rates to boost the economy in the framework of conventional monetary policy. Then, there are two possible measures to resort to, namely, quantitative easing and negative interest rates. Some economists like Krugman advocate negative interest rates to cure the imbalance between savings and investments (Middelkoop, 2016). According to them, to prevent bank runs due to negative interest rates, cash (physical) currency must be abolished globally so that currency must be mere digital numbers in bank accounts. Impacts of the pandemic and 4IR, the two so-called transformative developments, should be evaluated taking into consideration this framework in Sect. 3.

3 Impacts of Fourth Industrial Revolution and the COVID-19 Pandemic

3.1 *Impacts of the COVID-19 Pandemic*

One of the ideas on which Schwab builds his opinion of the need for a great reset is that the COVID-19 pandemic will trigger a radical transformation in the world that no return to the normal is possible. COVID-19, which started in late 2019 and turned into a pandemic in 2020, triggered significant changes in many aspects of life. Pandemic, impacting various microeconomic and macroeconomic indicators, has also led to disputes on the neoclassical economy and capitalism. The impacts of the pandemic can be summarized as follows.

3.1.1 Impact on Economic Growth

Since the pandemic started, the global economy has experienced substantial disruption in supply, production, and logistics (Yigit, 2021b). Additionally, shrinkage in the tourism sector due to countries closing their borders has led to significant decreases in the GDP of nations worldwide. For instance, G-20 economies slumped by 3.2% in the first quarter of 2020, while they grew by 0.3% in the last quarter of 2019. In the same quarter, G-7 economies and EU member countries slumped by 1.7% and 3.1%, respectively. Annual contraction in 2020 reached 6% in EU economies, 3% in G-20 economies, 5% in G-7 economies, and 3% in the USA (OECD, 2022a–d).

The condition threatening global economic growth has not been overcome yet. Consequently, the world economy shrunk by 3.4% in the same year. China, where the pandemic showed up, experienced only a 2.3% economic growth in that year (UN World Economic Situation and Prospects, 2022). Contractions at such a level were not witnessed even during and after the 2007–2009 crisis.

3.1.2 Impact on Financial Markets

During the pandemic, central banks have tried to prevent financial systems from falling into crisis, providing markets with low-cost borrowing facilities and liquidity. Credit expansion and loosening of regulations have promoted financial activities (IMF Global Financial Stability Report, 2021). Numerous countries, including Eurozone countries such as Germany, the USA, and the UK, had budget deficits unseen even during the 2007–2009 crisis. Additionally, substantial declines occurred in stock markets in 2020 (Eren et al., 2021). In essence, the impact of the COVID-19 pandemic on financial markets is expansionary in that governments had to increase the quantity of money extensively and give markets a great deal of liquidity in addition to lowering interest rates down to zero. As seen from Figs. 1,

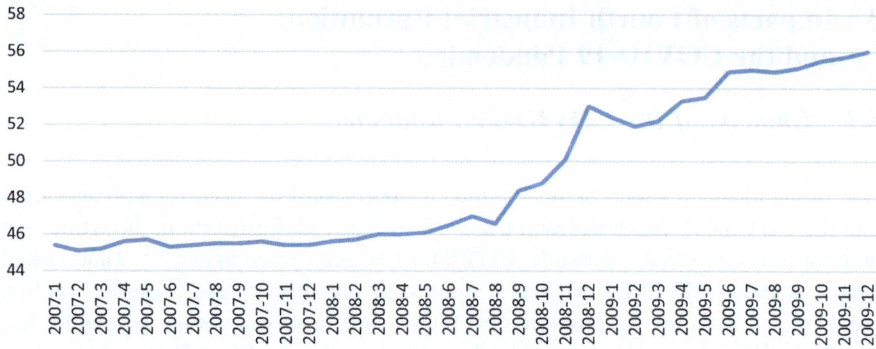

Fig. 1 FED money supply (monthly, 2015 = 100, 2007–2010). Source: https://data.oecd.org/

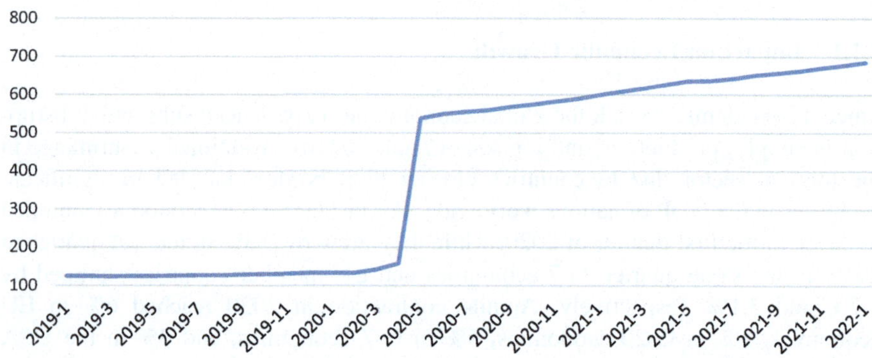

Fig. 2 FED money supply (monthly, 2015 = 100, 2019–2022). Source: https://data.oecd.org/

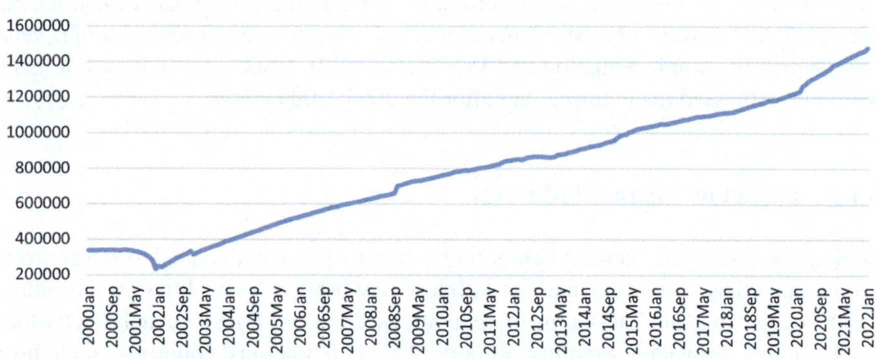

Fig. 3 ECB money supply (million €, 2000–2022). Source: ECB Statistical Data Warehouse

2, and 3, the money supply in the USA and the EU increased radically during the 2007–2009 and 2020 crises. Besides, as shown in Table 2, short-term interest rates that had increased before 2007 decreased substantially following the crisis. The same has happened after 2020.

Table 2 Short-term interest rates (yearly, 2003–2021)

Year	Canada	Germany	Japan	The UK	The USA
2003	2.96	2.33	0.09	3.74	1.15
2004	2.31	2.11	0.09	4.64	1.56
2005	2.81	2.18	0.09	4.76	3.51
2006	4.18	3.08	0.32	4.85	5.15
2007	4.63	4.28	0.75	6	5.27
2008	3.34	4.63	0.85	5.51	2.96
2009	0.69	1.23	0.58	1.21	0.56
2010	0.78	0.81	0.38	0.7	0.31
2011	1.17	1.39	0.33	0.87	0.3
2012	1.16	0.57	0.33	0.83	0.28
2013	1.16	0.22	0.24	0.51	0.17
2014	1.17	0.21	0.2	0.54	0.12
2015	0.82	−0.02	0.17	0.57	0.23
2016	0.82	−0.26	0.07	0.5	0.64
2017	1.06	−0.33	0.06	0.36	1.15
2018	1.79	−0.32	0.07	0.72	2.19
2019	1.89	−0.36	0.03	0.81	2.21
2020	0.64	−0.43	−0.04	0.29	0.53
2021	0.21	−0.55	−0.07	0.09	0.11

Source: https://data.oecd.org/

Consequently, markets began to get inflated, heading toward a financial bubble. Moreover, the increase in liquidity led to soaring inflation rates. This brought a dilemma: if monetary authorities, specifically FED, resort to tapering and increasing interest rates, a threat of asset price deflation can emerge. However, if they continue the quantitative easing policy, inflation will surge. The world seems locked between threats of deflation and inflation.

3.1.3 Impact on Prices

As COVID-19 spread worldwide in 2020, monthly consumer price indexes (CPI) began to decrease. Note however that during this period, changes in consumption habits of individuals—mandatory reductions in their spending on vacation, entertainment, cultural activities, etc., or they buy goods that they are not used to buy before because of the disturbances in production or supply—can cause deviations in CPI calculations (Blundell et al., 2020). In the same period, a sharp reduction in producer price indexes (PPI) at the beginning of 2020 was followed by perpetual increases in the before-mentioned countries (OECD Database). Countries reacted to the decrease in CPI by increasing the money supply to eliminate the deflationist tendency. However, recently, inflation rates started to increase as the last inflation rate announced by the FED in March 2022 is 7.9%.

3.1.4 Impact on Investment

The pandemic has had a significant impact on fixed capital investments. In the first quarter of 2020, when the pandemic reached a global extent, fixed capital investments decreased approximately by 7% in Germany and the USA and 18.4% in the UK. The average reduction in fixed capital investment in Eurozone economies was 19.7% for the same period (OECD, 2022a–d). In addition to the reduction in investment, emerging troubles in the security of supply exacerbated the adverse effects of the pandemic. In addition to the enclosure of countries, disruptions in working life, and contractions in production capacities, adverse effects of the pandemic on supply chains and logistics had substantial negative impacts on the security of the food supply (Shrestha et al., 2020). Specifically, the negative impact of the pandemic on China, which is the center of global production, caused heavy distortions in the production of many industrial goods.

3.1.5 Impact on International Trade

Due to the reduction in production, travel constraints, and shrink in demand throughout the world, international trade volume decreased in 2020 for the first time since the 2007–2009 crisis. Decreases in world international trade in 2009 and 2020 can be seen in Table 3. The rate of the decrease is expressed as 7.6%. After this decrease in the first half of 2020, economic activities rebounded. International trade also recovered (UN World Economic Situation and Prospects, 2021). However, while recovery in trade of goods is rapid, trade of services is lagging. China-the USA and the UK-EU decoupling remain elements of oppression on international trade (WTO, 2021). In addition, uncertainties about the future and the possibility that countries may increasingly rely on protective policies increase the likelihood of a downward trend in global trade (World Bank Global Economic Prospects, 2022). The future of the global GDP and trade volume is quite uncertain, which means that decisive steps should be taken to save the world economy.

3.1.6 Impact on the Labor Market

The labor market is one of the fields in which the effects of the pandemic are felt most. The pandemic led to high unemployment rates all over the world. Although countries began to ease lockdown measures and give financial aid to companies to boost employment, labor markets could not get over the effects of the pandemic. Production has reverted in quite a few countries, but a similar recovery has not seemed in employment figures. According to ILO 2021 report, in the third quarter of 2021, total working hours are fewer by 4.7% compared to before the pandemic. This indicates that approximately 137 million persons have lost their job (Soares et al., 2021). The emergence of new variants of COVID-19, a continuation of partial

Table 3 World International Trade data and GDP growth rate (2001–2020)

Year	Exports of goods and services (billion $)	World GDP growth (annual %)
2001	7669.29	2.00
2002	8004.53	2.34
2003	9401.51	3.16
2004	11461.03	4.48
2005	13011.46	4.05
2006	14970.47	4.50
2007	17447.99	4.44
2008	20015.23	2.00
2009	16017.85	−1.31
2010	19008.93	4.49
2011	22545.44	3.34
2012	22869.20	2.67
2013	23592.86	2.84
2014	23976.29	3.12
2015	21317.76	3.17
2016	20920.56	2.83
2017	23099.90	3.39
2018	25371.77	3.27
2019	24994.98	2.60
2020	22524.09	−3.29

Source: World Bank Data

lockdowns, and travel restrictions in some countries are primary factors that retard employment recovery, especially in the service sector (UN World Economic Situation and Prospects, 2022). Disadvantageous groups such as the young, women, and immigrant workers have been most affected by the pandemic, particularly in developing countries, during this period (Fabrizio et al., 2021). In terms of employment, the world economy has a problem that must be solved urgently, namely, in addition to slowing down, economic growth does not create enough jobs. This cannot be attributed merely to the pandemic, but rather it is inherent in capitalism.

3.1.7 Impact on Public Debts

We have witnessed an unprecedented rise in public debt during the pandemic era. Governments trying to avoid the threat of deflation have implemented expansionary fiscal policies resulting in huge budget deficits for which they have to resort to public borrowing since the beginning of the pandemic. This exacerbated a fundamental problem of the world economy: huge and increasing public debts. When the pandemic peaked in Europe, some European countries like Spain, Italy, and France were confronted with the problem of increasing public debt coupled with the health crisis (Briceno & Perote, 2020). In 2019, Spain's public debt reached 117% of its

GDP. This ratio was 154% for Italy and 123% for France, 136% for the USA, and 118% and 233% for the UK and Japan, respectively. In 2020, the debt-to-GDP ratio remained high for the countries mentioned above. For instance, the public debt of the USA reached 161% of its GDP while that of the UK and Italy increased to 148% and 183%, respectively (OECD, 2022a–d).

Figures in Tables 4 and 5 show that the crucial problem of debt in the world economy is aggravated by the pandemic and will worsen in the future. Accordingly, taking the necessary steps to save the system is getting more urgent. In their study on the sustainability of public debt of Eurozone countries, Briceño and Perote (2020) concluded that high public borrowing increases the precariousness of these countries and makes them more fragile in case of a decrease in terms of trade, an increase in global interest rates, or perpetuation of the pandemic. They stated that public debt at such a level was not sustainable for European countries and suggested macroeconomic policies such as debt restructuring and even debt cancellation.

3.1.8 Impact on Income Distribution

Another negative result of the pandemic is the increase in income inequality. It is predicted that the accelerating inflation in the medium and long term, increase in food prices, and interruptions in education will escalate the inequalities in income distribution (World Bank, 2022). In their study, in which they analyzed the effects of lockdowns and social distance implementations on income inequality and poverty in European countries, Palomino et al. (2020) concluded that the poverty rate in countries could range between 4.9% and 9.4%, depending on different lockdown scenarios. On the contrary, some studies found that developments and policies implemented during the period of the COVID-19 improved income distribution. For instance, Clark et al. (2021) concluded that Gini coefficients in France, Germany, Italy, Spain, and Sweden improved during COVID-19. O'Donoghue et al. (2020) found in their study on Ireland that although many households had economic difficulties, in general, the disposable income of households increased during the COVID-19 period. However, it should be noted that many governments provided households with financial support that cannot be sustained forever in this period.

3.1.9 Social Impacts

One of the significant effects of global pandemics is social unrest. Traumas and stress-related disorders drew attention as the most critical social problems (Rajkumar, 2020; Ni et al., 2020). Wong et al. (2021) observed highly depressive symptoms in most of the participants in the research they did in Hong Kong with 150 people. Research done by Winter-Ebmer et al. (2021) in the USA concluded that increasing unemployment and losses of life during the COVID-19 pandemic amplified people's emotional stress and economic insecurity. Saadi-Sedik and Xu (2020) analyzed the COVID-19 pandemic, considering the past pandemics. They concluded

Table 4 Budget deficit (% of GDP, 2007–2020)

	2007	2008	2009	2010	2011	2012	2013	2014	2015	2016	2017	2018	2019	2020
China	3.60	1.50	1.10	2.20	1.50	1.30	0.60	0.60	−0.60	−1.10	−1.40	−2.00	−2.30	−3.70
Germany	0.30	−0.10	−3.20	−4.40	−0.90	0.00	0.00	0.60	1.00	1.20	1.30	1.90	1.50	−4.30
Korea	4.00	2.10	−1.30	0.90	1.00	1.00	1.30	1.20	1.20	2.20	2.70	3.00	1.00	−2.30
The UK	−2.60	−5.10	−10.00	−9.20	−7.40	−8.10	−5.50	−5.50	−4.50	−3.30	−2.40	−2.20	−2.20	−12.90
The USA	−4.00	−7.30	−13.10	−12.40	−11.00	−9.20	−5.80	−5.20	−4.60	−5.40	−4.30	−6.10	−6.40	−15.30

Source: https://data.oecd.org/

Table 5 General government debt (% of GDP, 2005–2020)

Year	Canada	France	Germany	Italy	Japan	The UK	The USA
2005	93.9	82.1	71.6	117.2	172.3	52.1	88.6
2006	91.1	77.3	69.0	114.6	172.7	51.2	86.0
2007	87.0	75.9	66.3	110.2	174.3	52.9	86.3
2008	89.7	82.5	70.9	112.5	178.2	65.3	102.1
2009	102.7	97.6	77.7	125.5	199.4	78.4	115.5
2010	105.0	101.0	87.1	124.3	204.4	89.1	125.4
2011	107.7	103.8	86.1	117.2	218.0	102.7	130.6
2012	111.3	111.9	88.6	135.4	226.7	106.8	132.3
2013	107.3	112.5	84.1	143.2	229.7	102.6	135.9
2014	108.4	120.2	83.9	155.6	234.4	112.4	135.5
2015	114.7	120.8	79.8	156.9	233.3	111.7	137.0
2016	114.2	123.7	77.0	154.6	231.4	118.5	138.8
2017	108.6	122.9	72.4	152.0	230.3	119.1	135.5
2018	107.5	120.7	69.1	146.8	234.3	115.6	137.5
2019	106.9	123.1	67.5	154.1	234.5	118.5	136.0
2020	141.9	145.8	78.7	183.5	257.8	149.0	161.5

Source: OECD (2022), General government debt (indicator). DOI: 10.1787/a0528cc2-en (accessed on 17 March 2022)

that if governments do not take political measures about the COVID-19 pandemic, the income level will decrease, inequalities in income distribution will increase, and social unrest will be triggered.

3.1.10 Impact on International System

Despite problems and the possible solutions being global in today's world, a process of deglobalization was in effect before the pandemic. Nationalist populism has been on the rise, eroding international collaboration more and more. Specifically, the middle-class witnessing a decline in their real incomes supported the nationalist and anti-liberalist movements. The threats created by the pandemic have exacerbated this drift, resulting in the tendency of autism which limits governments' attention to events outside their border. As a result, people experiencing economic difficulties and risks began to see outsiders or migrants as economic burdens. Xenophobia emerged or grew more robust, especially in Western societies. However, the pandemic or other global economic, social, political, and environmental problems necessitate multilateral collaboration. Even if governments and leaders are aware that global efforts can overcome global problems, they have to prioritize their citizens because of the political pressure they face, which reduces the chance of a successful reset.

3.2 Impacts of Fourth Industrial Revolution

Schwab and Malleret (2020) point out three main characteristics of today's world: interdependence, velocity, and complexity. The world has become "hyperconnected" because of globalization and technological progress. Thus, all problems are interlinked and amplified, so no problem or risk can be handled individually, and no sector, area, or country can isolate itself. In addition, in today's world, every development occurs at an incredible pace, which the Internet and the Internet of Things are good examples. Besides technological developments, crises, geopolitical upheavals, and diseases spread fast among countries and regions. Moreover, today's world is so complex that the likelihood that things go wrong is very high and predicting what will happen in the future is impossible. We live in an uncertain world; hence, we have to be prepared for any surprise, even sudden turbulence.

One of the fundamental driving forces behind this globalized, complex, and uncertain world is some interrelated, widely used technologies such as artificial intelligence, including machine learning and deep learning, robotics, big data, the Internet of Things (i.e., devices with sensors like smartphones and other devices used in vehicles, workplaces, and public areas for monitoring), blockchain, and cloud computing (Ally & Wark, 2020). These interrelated technological developments brought our world to the brink of a technological revolution which is called by Schwab the fourth industrial revolution.

Schwab suggests that the first revolutionary change in our lifestyle was the transition from hunting and gathering to agriculture 10,000 years ago. Humanity managed this by domesticating animals. Compounding human effort with animals increased food production and made urbanization possible (Schwab, 2016). The agricultural revolution was followed by four industrial revolutions, starting from the second half of the eighteenth century. Based on the steam engine and railways, the first one lasted from 1760 to 1840. Coal was the new energy source, and this revolution carried the world from farming and feudality to manufacturing and industrial society (Xu et al., 2018). The second industrial revolution started in the 1900s with the invention of the internal combustion engine and used oil and electricity as primary energy sources, leading to rapid industrialization and creating mass production. The third industrial revolution started in the 1960s used electronics and information technology to automate production. We are starting the fourth industrial revolution, bringing about digitalization to almost every aspect of life.

What is different about the fourth industrial revolution is that the newly developed technologies are fast and intertwined. These technologies merging the physical, digital, and biological spheres change the world, affecting all socioeconomic dimensions of human life. According to Schwab, the future will be quite different from today, and there is no way for the world to stay as it is. Socioeconomic structures, states, cultures, and businesses will be different. Companies that miss the opportunity of digitalization cannot exist. Xu et al. (2018) assert that the resulting changes brought by technology are destiny; thus, people have no control over technology and its impacts. Hence, there is a consensus that technology will shape the future. The impacts of the 4IR can be listed as follows.

3.2.1 Impacts on Productivity, Costs of Production, and Growth

The pace of developing new products and their spreading worldwide is now much higher due to 4IR. Additionally, digitalization and resulting automation prevent decreases in economies of scale. Moreover, digital companies' marginal costs are close to zero. Many of them produce "information goods" with zero costs of storing, transporting, and duplicating (Schwab, 2016). Less initial capital is required to start an enterprise to bring a new product to reality, thanks to 3D printing (Xu et al., 2018). The cost of data storing is very close to zero. However, as Schwab (2016) pointed out, these developments did not increase productivity. This may bring a limit to growth in economies. Despite many optimistic expectations that 4IR will bring about a significant leap in production and incomes, increasing living standards, this outcome is in doubt because of the lack of persuasive observations.

3.2.2 Impacts on Market Structure

There is a consensus that 4IR will change the nature of work in almost all sectors because of the resulting automation. It is known that automation will substitute labor, but its extent is uncertain. New technologies create new jobs besides destroying many. Nevertheless, 4IR is estimated to destroy more than it creates. This can aggravate the unemployment problem, leading to social unrest. Besides, the share of labor in GDP will decrease, as has already been seen in the last years (Schwab, 2016). The effect of 4IR on jobs will not be neutral. Specifically, low-skilled and low-paid jobs will be affected most. This can increase income inequalities and cause disruptions in economies.

Furthermore, developing countries can lose comparative advantages in labor-intensive goods and sectors. As a result, the production that has shifted to countries and regions with cheap labor can return to high-income countries to be close to markets where high-income customers live in. This can increase polarization between regions and may create or aggravate political distresses.

It is asserted that the companies missing the digital revolution will not be able to survive. Accordingly, successful digitalized companies will dominate markets; thus, monopolization of markets will occur. In sum, knowledge and skill, rather than capital, will be the critical factors in markets. One of the dark sides of the resulting digitalization of the 4IR is that manufacturing systems will become more vulnerable to cyberattacks because they are connected to the Internet. It means substantial interruptions in production. Henceforth, security will become one of the most critical issues in economies.

4IR is expected to increase the gap between countries because today new technologies are not diffused evenly. These complex technologies will remain concentrated in a small number of economies. Data show that ten leading economies do 91% of the global patent application and 70% of the export related to these technologies (UNIDO, 2019). However, another division between developing countries and developed ones is that many low-capability and low-performance companies coexist with a few highly advanced ones. This will create a bottleneck in industries because this limited number of leading digitalized companies faces troubles in terms of backward links and supply chains.

3.2.3 Impacts on Employment

The main effect of 4IR on employment is expected that automation replace labor and thus many jobs will disappear. The future of job survey by WEF indicates that in the coming period up to 2025, 25% of a company's labor force will be affected negatively by the automation stemming from 4IR, and on average, 6% of them are predicted to lose their jobs (WEF, 2020). What is being discussed is the extent and pace and which sectors will be affected most. Frey and Osborne (2013) estimate that 47% of the labor force is at high risk.

The automation resulting from digitalization substituting less-educated, low-skilled, and low-paid labor more will give rise to downward pressure on the demand for this kind of labor, hence decreasing their wages. As a result, we should wait for an increase in inequalities and even a minority's domination of markets. In this setting, an increase in labor productivity will not result in wage increases. All the gains created by new technologies will be held by the minority dominating markets. As seen, 4IR will not make the world more equal by itself. On the contrary, it will increase inequalities and polarization in societies.

3.2.4 Impacts on Governments and Political Systems

Schwab asserts that innovations in web technologies can improve the performance of public administrations and can strengthen relations between the government and its citizens through promoting transparency and accountability. At the same time, new technologies can provide citizens with new ways to speak up, become organized against what they are opposed to, avoid government surveillance, and eventually cause a power shift from governments to citizens (Schwab, 2016). However, this argument is too optimistic; it is more likely that developments in surveillance technologies will bring much more powerful governments limiting civil rights. Schwab also mentions this probability. Consequently, 4IR can be expected to escalate power asymmetries in and among countries. Technological breakthrough does not ensure a bright economic, political, and social future.

4 Conclusion

As economic data show, the main characteristics of the world economy while it is approaching the COVID-19 pandemic were slow growth, low productivity, insufficient investment, the balance of payments and saving imbalances, financialization, and increasing speculative transactions. Labor productivity growth in advanced countries and emerging and developing economies were 1% and 4.1%, respectively, during the first decade of the twenty-first century (World Bank, 2021a). The COVID-19 pandemic worsened the situation by triggering a deep recession, increasing unemployment, decreasing productive investment radically, disrupting education, and distorting the global supply chain. The pandemic also exacerbated inequalities in and between countries. It must be stressed that the pandemic did not generate but merely aggravated these problems.

The global financial crisis of 2007–2009 brought down international trade and, consequently, the global growth rate. After the crisis, trade and production grew again but at a slower pace. The trade war between the USA and China significantly influenced it. The unexpected event of the pandemic reinforced the tendency of the slowdown in the world economy. One of the reasons for the decoupling between the USA and China was the rivalry on technology. The USA tried to restrict technology transfer to China through export control on technological products, and China retaliated (Yigit, 2021a). In addition to trade, technological investments have also been limited. Another technology decoupling was that the USA introduced a list of Chinese companies with which American companies are forbidden to conduct business (García-Herrero & Tan, 2020). Financial relations and cross-border capital flow declined but were not as severe as trade and foreign direct investment. Supply and logistic problems resulting from the pandemic and protective policies increased trade costs and limited recovery in global trade (World Bank, 2021b).

The response of the monetary authorities to the retrogressive economic situation is to manipulate the economic figures, trying to hide the reality. In addition, market control is gradually increasing; market powers are not determining interest rates, and asset prices do not reflect their value anymore. An unprecedented financial crisis that can lead anytime to the collapse of monetary systems globally is being impeded. The worldwide hyperinflation, the collapse of banking sectors and economies, and the following depression and economic shrinking globally should be expected. Therefore, the world economy's most urgent threat is a monetary and financial collapse, and the most urgent task is a monetary reset.

Avoiding an economic turmoil necessitates, first and foremost, a more democratic and peaceable economic and political world order. International organizations should be democratized and must be more participatory. The global economic system must be fairer. If there is no justice, then there will be no peace. The starting point should be the international monetary system. This requires global solidarity, especially among major economic powers, and coordination, particularly between the USA and China. As economic and political developments show, the likelihood of solidarity and cooperation is low, and that of the struggle between the West under the leadership of the USA and rivals of the West like Russia and China is high. This is not a struggle between different economic systems but rather an internal conflict of the capitalist system. Considering that Russia is one of the vital oil and natural gas suppliers and that the West and China are too interdependent economically, a global economic crisis is becoming more and more likely. The increase in the prices of oil and gas can accelerate inflation worldwide. Prices of other commodities and costs of transportation can also increase further. More deterioration in the supply chain and international trade can take place. An increase in food prices can make it challenging to afford foods and, at the same time, can cause a shortage. The possible economic slowdown of China will bring the global growth rate down, resulting in extensive unemployment worldwide.

It should be noted that a great reset is a must, but it must be participatory and inclusive in the sense that it must be planned through international cooperation rather than by an elite. Unequal relations must be eliminated. The international payment system must be modified in that the responsibility of balancing international accounts must be shared rather than being imposed solely on deficit economies. Hegemonic or multipolar world order is not likely to succeed in this task. A much more democratic world is needed. In other words, underlying power relations must be reformed to solve the significant economic problems and succeed in a great reset. If the economy becomes a zero-sum game, it ends sooner or later. It does not seem that the game can be reorganized fairly since it requires the world's great powers to give up some of the privileges brought by the power they have. History is full of evidence of power shifts rather than cooperation and collaborations. The way of the shift of power is through war. A great reset through war and economic turmoil seems more likely this time again.

References

Ally, M., & Wark, N. (2020). *Sustainable development and education in the fourth industrial revolution (4IR)*. Commonwealth of Learning.

Blundell, R., Griffith, R., Levell, P., & O'Connell, M. (2020). Could COVID-19 infect the consumer prices index? *Fiscal Studies, 41*(2), 357–361.

Briceño, H. R., & Perote, J. (2020). Determinants of the public debt in the Eurozone and its sustainability amid the Covid-19 pandemic. *Sustainability, 12*(16), 6456.

Clark, A., D'Ambrosio, C., & Lepinteur, A. (2021). *The fall in income inequality during COVID-19 in five European countries*. Ecineq working paper series, no: 565.

ECB Statistical Data Warehouse.

Eren, B. S., Göker, I. E. K., & Karaca, S. S. (2021). Covid-19 Pandemisinin Finansal Piyasalara Etkisi: Gelişmiş Ülkeler Üzerine Bir Analiz. *Hacettepe Üniversitesi İktisadi ve İdari Bilimler Fakültesi Dergisi, 39*(Covid 19 Özel Sayısı), 69–90.

Fabrizio, M. S., Gomes, D. B., & Tavares, M. M. M. (2021). *Covid-19 she-cession: The employment penalty of taking care of young children*. IMF working papers, no: 2021-058.

Fidler, S., & Nicoll, A. (2011). Out of balance: The fragile world economy. *Survival, 52*(6), 89–106.

Frey, C. B., & Osborne, M. A. (2013). *The future of employment: "How susceptible are jobs to computerization?"* https://www.oxfordmartin.ox.ac.uk/downloads/academic/The_Future_of_Employment.pdf

Funabashi, Y. (2009). Forget Bretton woods II: The role for U.S.–China–Japan Trilateralism. *The Washington Quarterly, 32*(2), 7–25.
García-Herrero, A., & Tan, J. (2020). Deglobalisation in the context of United States-China decoupling. *Bruegel Policy Contribution*, 21.
IMF. (2021). *Global financial stability report—COVID-19, crypto, and climate: Navigating challenging transitions.*
Ivanova, M. N. (2013). The Dollar as world money. *Science & Society, 77*(1), 44–71.
Kotarski, K. (2009). Structural imbalances and financial crises proliferation. *Politička Misao, 46*(3), 69–90.
Marazzi, C. (2010). The violence of financial capitalism. In A. Fumagalli & S. Mezzadra (Eds.), *Financial markets, social struggles, and new political scenarios*. Semiotext(e).
Middelkoop, W. (2016). *The big reset: War on gold and the financial endgame.* Amsterdam University Press B.V.
Ni, M. Y., Yang, L., Leung, C. M., Li, N., Yao, X. I., Wang, Y., & Liao, Q. (2020). Mental health, risk factors, and social media use during the COVID-19 epidemic and cordon sanitaire among the community and health professionals in Wuhan, China: Cross-sectional survey. *JMIR Mental Health, 7*(5), e19009.
Noninski, V. C. (2021). *No great reset*. Shakespeare.
O'Donoghue, C., Sologon, D. M., Kyzyma, I., & McHale, J. (2020). Modelling the distributional impact of the COVID-19 crisis. *Fiscal Studies, 41*(2), 321–336.
OECD. (2022a). *General government debt (indicator)*. Accessed March 17, 2022, from https://doi.org/10.1787/a0528cc2-en
OECD. (2022b). *General government deficit (indicator)*. Accessed March 15, 2022, from https://doi.org/10.1787/77079edb-en
OECD. (2022c). *Narrow money (M1) (indicator)*. Accessed March 18, 2022, from https://doi.org/10.1787/7a23d68b-en
OECD. (2022d). *Unemployment rate (indicator)*. Accessed March 10, 2022, from https://doi.org/10.1787/52570002-en
Palomino, J. C., Rodríguez, J. G., & Sebastian, R. (2020). Wage inequality and poverty effects of lockdown and social distancing in Europe. *European Economic Review, 129*, 103564.
Rajkumar, R. P. (2020). COVID-19 and mental health: A review of the existing literature. *Asian Journal of Psychiatry, 52*, 102066.
Roth, S. (2021). The great reset. Restrafication for lives, livelihoods, and the planet. *Technological Forecasting & Social Change*, 166.
Saadi-Sedik, T., & Xu, R. (2020). *A vicious cycle: How pandemics lead to economic despair and social unrest.* Available at SSRN 3744683.
Saull, R. (2012). Rethinking hegemony: Uneven development, historical blocs, and the world economic crisis. *International Studies Quarterly, 56*, 323–338.
Schwab, K. (2016). *The fourth industrial revolution*. Forum Publishing.
Schwab, K., & Malleret, T. (2020). *COVID-19: The great reset.* Forum Publishing.
Shrestha, N., Shad, M. Y., Ulvi, O., Khan, M. H., Karamehic-Muratovic, A., Nguyen, U. S. D., & Haque, U. (2020). The impact of COVID-19 on globalization. *One Health, 11*, 100180.
Soares, S., Bonnet, F., Berg, J., & Labouriau, R. (2021, March, 31). From potential to practice: Preliminary findings on the numbers of workers working from home during the COVID-19 pandemic. *ILO Brief.*
Triodos Bank. (2020). *Reset the economy*. Zeist.
UNIDO. (2019). *Bracing for the new industrial revolution*. Elements of a strategic response. Discussion paper.
Xu, M., David, J. M., & Kim, S. H. (2018). The fourth industrial revolution: Opportunities and challenges. *International Journal of Financial Research, 9*(2), 90.
WEF. (2020). *The future of jobs report 2020.*
Winter-Ebmer, R., Sunde, U., & Lackner, M. (2021). *Covid-19 and the forces behind social unrest.*

Wong, S. M., Hui, C. L., Wong, C. S., Suen, Y. N., Chan, S. K., Lee, E. H., & Chen, E. Y. (2021). Mental health risks after repeated exposure to multiple stressful events during ongoing social unrest and pandemic in Hong Kong: The role of rumination. *The Canadian Journal of Psychiatry, 66*(6), 577–585.

World Bank. (2021a, January). *Global economic prospects*.

World Bank. (2021b, June). *Global economic prospects*.

World Bank. (2022, June). *Global economic prospects*. Washington, DC.

WTO (World Trade Organization). (2021). *World trade statistical review*, 2021.

United Nations Department For Economic And Social Affairs. (2021). *World economic situation and prospects 2021*. UN.

United Nations Department For Economic And Social Affairs. (2022). *World economic situation and prospects 2022*. UN.

Yigit, S. (2021a). Trump vs China. In A. Günar (Ed.), *The Trade Wars of the USA, China, and the EU: The global economy in the age of populism* (pp. 67–84). Lexington Books.

Yigit, S. (2021b). The economic and political effects of COVID-19 on the Eurasian economic union. In B. Darici & C. L. Chiu (Eds.), *New normal and new rules in international trade, economics and marketing* (pp. 35–55). Peter Lang.

Degrowth Strategy to Sustain the Capitalist System

Süleyman Emre Özcan and Caner Demir

Abstract This study deals with the degrowth approach which was put forward to avoid the negative effects of economic growth. Especially since the industrial revolution, there has been a remarkable economic growth process in the world economy. Nations are trying to raise their growth rates to develop their domestic economies and to be ahead in competition with other nations. The planet on which we live and whose resources are limited is used recklessly for the sake of achieving economic growth. The process of capital accumulation, which is the main driver of economic growth, widens the income inequality between capital owners and workers. Can the degrowth movement, which was presented as an alternative to eliminate these negativities arising from economic growth, reveal a more sustainable economic model? Will the degrowth movement be enough to ensure the continuation of capitalism and to eliminate a possible collapse? In order to answer these questions, the study discusses comparatively current approaches and approaches to the degrowth movement.

Keywords Degrowth · Economic growth · Environmental economics · Economic inequality

1 Introduction

Since the industrial revolution, the global economy has experienced exponential growth due to high productivity increases. Although this exponential growth performance raised welfare in several countries, it is argued by many that such a growth-oriented strategy is not sustainable. The degrowth movement is one of the criticisms of the economic growth target of macroeconomic policies.

The modern macroeconomic theory with different approaches suggests that economic growth is one of the three main macroeconomic goals with price stability

S. E. Özcan · C. Demir (✉)
Department of Economics, Salihli FEAS, Manisa Celal Bayar University, Manisa, Turkey
e-mail: suleyman.ozcan@cbu.edu.tr; caner.demir@cbu.edu.tr

A. Ari (ed.), *Capitalism at a Crossroads*, Springer Studies in Alternative Economics,
https://doi.org/10.1007/978-3-031-23257-2_15

and full employment. None of the academics and policymakers are in doubt about the necessity of price stability and full employment. However, it is not that easy to suggest that there is a consensus on the necessity of economic growth. In the last decade, the degrowth movement has come up as an alternative to growth-oriented economic policies. The proponents of this movement suggest that higher levels of gross domestic product and household consumption are not convenient measures for welfare. The mainstream theory states that the welfare of the nation is the sum of the welfare of the households which theoretically depends on the level of consumption. Briefly, the more a country can consume, the more welfare it will have. However, the supporters of degrowth point out the need for some alternative measures of welfare. They assert that a higher need for consumption creates pressure for economic growth which finally leads to a decrease in resources. The degrowth movement is associated with the "limits to growth" hypothesis which emphasizes the limits of our world and asserts that it is not possible to sustain economic growth in its current way (see Meadows et al., 1972).

For years, both developed and developing countries try to raise their total output over time. Developing countries try to raise their output level to catch up with the developed countries, while developed countries raise the output to reach higher levels of welfare. However, how long will this increase continue? How will the Earth's limited resources sustain these objectives? These are crucial questions about the future of the growth-oriented policies. Both advocates and opponents of the mainstream economics should focus on these questions to find ways for a sustainable future of the planet. Hence, the study aims to discuss the opponent approaches, the critiques, and the propositions of the degrowth movement. To do that, we first present economic growth from a historical and theoretical perspective along with its negative externalities in Sect. 2. Then, in Sects. 3 and 4, we discuss the concept of degrowth as an alternative to current problems of capitalist system. Section 5 concludes.

2 Economic Growth as a Primary Economic Goal

2.1 A Brief History of Economic Growth and Basic Concepts

Although the history of economic growth can be traced back thousands of years, we may suggest that the considerable global economic growth started with the industrial revolution. Until then, the world's total real output was at a nearly constant level. According to Maddison (2010), in the sixteenth and seventeenth centuries, the per capita GDP growth rate in the world was around 0.04% per year. From the beginning of the eighteenth century to the last quarter of the nineteenth century, this rate increased to 0.20%. Since the last quarter of the nineteenth century, with the spread of the effects of the industrial revolution, the growth rate of world GDP per capita rose to 1.1%. By the second half of the twentieth century, improvements in many fields such as chemistry, energy, and automation systems caused this rate to dramatically rise to 2.26%.

The remarkable increases in economic growth rate have brought the question of what the basic dynamics of economic growth are. The sources of economic growth have been an important focus since the classical school. However, with the increasing effects of the industrial revolution, economic growth has become a much more popular area. The first growth models that emerged in the twentieth century mainly focused on the accumulation of capital stock. In the first half of the century, a Keynesian-based economic growth model emerged within the framework of the contributions made by Harrod (1939) and Domar (1946) to the literature. According to Harrod-Domar model, the multiplication of the marginal product of capital and the saving rate raises the growth rate of GDP, while the depreciation rate decreases it. By making some additional assumptions and considering the contributions of the Harrod-Domar model, the neoclassical school started to explain the sources of economic growth in the second half of the twentieth century. The fundamental neoclassical growth model, which was developed independently by Solow (1956) and Swan (1956), included the labor force as a factor of production. Besides, the Solow-Swan model differed from the Harrod-Domar model, since the ratio of capital to output was not fixed. In his 1957 work, Solow made it also possible to decompose labor productivity on basic components with the idea of growth accounting. This simple but functional method is still used today.

The second half of the century has been a period in which economic growth was studied from many different perspectives. In this period, beside the considerable use of mathematics, subjects such as intertemporal preferences, technology, and human capital began to be included in the models. In the 1960s, Cass and Koopmans developed the model based on intertemporal household consumption, which was introduced by Ramsey about 40 years earlier. Although it has a neoclassical content, this model differed from the Solow-Swan model because it was based on the fact that the saving rate was not constant over time. The endogenization of the saving rate brought the growth model very close to the flow of real life (see Ramsey, 1928; Cass, 1965; Koopmans, 1965). Even today, many modern growth models are built on the outcomes of this model.

In the Solow model, technological progress was considered as an exogenous factor. With the development of some early contributions to the literature in the 1960s (i.e., Arrow, 1962; Uzawa, 1965) and later in the 1980s, it became possible to define technological development within the model. This approach, which is called the endogenous growth theory, looks for the neglected sources of technological development and, accordingly, economic growth (see Romer, 1986, 1990; Lucas, 1988; Rebelo, 1991; Grossman & Helpman, 1991; Aghion & Howitt, 1992). All the studies dealing with the case from an endogenous perspective suggested that technological progress which was determined by some internal factors within the model is a substantial process that raises the productivity of inputs. Thus, investing in technology is important as is investing in capital. By engaging in research and development activities, firms and nations can enable innovative ideas to emerge.

Each of these innovative ideas has the potential to influence the total factor productivity.

The 1960s witnessed some pioneering studies not only in terms of the endogenization of technological development but also in terms of incorporation of the quality of labor into growth models. The idea that the quality of labor is important when making inferences based on the production function was put forward by economists such as Mincer (1958) and Becker (1962). In this context, human capital has been defined as a new form of capital. Later, some studies such as Mankiw et al. (1992) and Barro (2001) empirically examined the effects of differentiation in human capital on economic growth.

Almost all the growth models we have mentioned so far refer to the models that are expressed as the mainstream of the economic growth literature. It is seen that economic growth is an absolute goal in all these models, and to increase total production, the essential ways are sought. At this point, the following questions come to the front: Is it possible to satisfy such an endless desire for growth forever? Or, in other words, how possible is it to grow forever on the resource-limited planet we live on? Is it possible for all countries to grow together?

2.2 *Reducing Problems or Creating New Ones?*

Although economic growth is aimed to increase the welfare of humanity, the fact that growth becomes a dominant economic goal also causes some problems. As stated in the previous section, the main source of economic growth is capital accumulation. The capital accumulation is realized through the supply of household savings to the fund market and ultimately their transformation into investments. This cycle will not change as long as capitalism continues. In other words, capital owners—or firms—will always try to raise their total capital stock with increasing profit rates. Undoubtedly, maximizing saving rates to increase investments cannot become the primary objective. The ultimate purpose is to increase the consumption level of the society and accordingly the welfare. Therefore, Phelps (1961) emphasized the "saving rate that maximizes consumption" and expressed this situation as the "golden rule of capital accumulation." The fact that there is an optimal value between the shares of income allocated to savings and consumption also means that some problems will arise in case of deviation from this optimality. If we look critically, this situation actually presents us with another view of the conflict of interest between the capital owners and the households. It is only possible with high saving rates that capital owners demand abundant funds with the greed for profit. This means that the ratio of consumption to income will decrease. According to the golden rule perspective of Phelps (1961), if an optimal saving rate can be applied, this will yield higher output in the economy. Besides, since the total saving stock of the economy is nothing short of the multiplication of the saving rate and output, the economy will have higher savings and thus higher investment stocks. However, optimality is a possible but rarely seen situation in economics. So, ensuring the outcomes of this perspective is not that easy.

Consequently, the mainstream growth theory does not contain a contradiction or conflict of interest in itself. However, is economic growth the ultimate expectation of the capitalists? Does saving supply depend on an optimal saving rate? The answers will most likely be no. Briefly, the inferences of the mainstream growth models are consistent only if the conditions of the model are isolated from the real-world conditions.

Yet another problem with the capital accumulation statements of the mainstream theories is the linkage between savings and investments. The mainstream perspective suggests that savings and investments are equal by definition. In our era, it is easy to reach data for many countries. According to the data, savings and investments are almost never equal. There are many reasons for this inequality such as the outflow of domestic savings to foreign countries, the inflow of foreign savings into the domestic economy, and the existence of the shadow economy. Besides, incorporating the money market dynamics can also change the outcomes of the models. Any imbalance between money supply and demand will affect the share of the income allocated to savings. Depending on the increased amount of money, financing the investments may become easier, and the level of investment may increase. However, even in this case, potential investors may not make an investment decision due to insufficient demand in the market or some potential risks.

At this point, it is of great importance whether the profit greed of the capitalists is a desire that can be satisfied. Historical findings show that greed for profit and accordingly profit rates tend to increase, but this tendency leads to some economic problems (Piketty, 2013). Surely, in our era, the return on capital depends not only on physical capital investments but also on financial capital investments. In fact, the latter has a much greater impact on economic bubbles and turmoil. Piketty claims that if the rate of profit from capital is higher than the long-term growth rate, resource distribution and income inequality will deteriorate. He emphasized that to get rid of this possible bad situation, the income tax should have a progressive structure.

The relationship between the environment and the economic growth has been studied in many theoretical and empirical studies in the literature. Most of the studies are based on the environmental Kuznets curve (EKC) hypothesis. According to this hypothesis, the relationship between income per capita and environmental degradation draws an inverted U-shape curve. In other words, increases in per capita income will initially raise environmental degradation, but then this effect will be reversed (Stern, 1998). Dinda (2004) attributed this inconstant effect of the development process on the environment for multiple reasons. As societies develop, the share of production will pass from the agricultural sector, which produces cleanly, to the manufacturing sector, which harms the environment, and from there to the services sector, which produces cleaner. As another reason, Dinda stated that with increasing income level, the clean environment preferences of people will increase. However, if we criticize this inference, we may suggest that in developing countries the transition between manufacturing sectors to services sector is not smooth. Since firms in the developed economies outsource some polluting activities in developing world, increasing output may not reduce environmental deterioration even in the long run. Thus, the generalization of the EKC hypothesis is not possible (see also Liu et al., 2019).

Nevertheless, if we interpret the arguments of Dinda (2004) critically for developed countries, it is not that easy for this transition to take place so smoothly. Firstly, how long will it take for the polluting effect of the manufacturing sector to be replaced by the cleaner production of services sector? Secondly, is it possible for society to prefer a cleaner environment only with the increase in per capita income? Although it is difficult to give a clear answer to the first question, note that it will take a certain period to compensate for the environmental damage that will occur during the "long term" in question. The answer to the second question is no. Rather than per capita income, the income distribution, education level, functionality of institutions, and quality of governance determine the clean environment preference of the society.

As we mentioned above, as long as the desire for growth continues to become the primary goal, the deterioration in income distribution and environmental quality will continue to increase. The extent to which growth is sustainable in an economy where income is not distributed fairly is an important area of discussion. On the other hand, it is controversial how a society whose environmental resources are destroyed can continue production. Undoubtedly, these questions reveal the impossibility of endless growth. Even if economic growth will remain the primary goal, it is essential to get it in a sustainable form. Economics is a mix of preferences and concessions. The long-term damage caused by compromises must be taken into account.

Another issue for the economic growth goal is that it is not possible for all countries to grow together. The current global economic system contains inequalities between countries in many aspects. Trying to grow with debt burden, technological deficiencies, and limited educational opportunities makes the progress of developing countries difficult. Unfortunately, overcoming these obstacles is not only at the initiative of developing countries. The continuity of the system of developed countries causes developing countries to experience such problems.

2.3 Is Economic Growth Indispensable for the Mainstream Economic Ideology?

If economic growth is to be discussed as such a priority goal, it is necessary to examine whether economic growth is indispensable or not. In many ways, mainstream economics methodologically brings an abstracting perspective to the real-life notion of economics (see Colander et al., 2004). Heterodox schools argue that axioms and assumptions embedded in mainstream economics are defined to lay the groundwork for the defended economic ideology (see also Lee, 2008). While this abstracting and oversimplifying stance of mainstream economics makes it possible to theorize microeconomic relations, it also brings with it many problems on the macro side.

We cannot separate developments and paradigm shifts in economic theory from economic events. Although Keynesian economics gained significant support in the first half of the twentieth century, the weight of the neoclassical school began to be felt in macroeconomic policies as of the second half of the same century. At the same time, radical transformations took place in the global political economy. In this context, we can suggest that the last period in which today's mainstream economics took power coincided with the period when the global economic system also underwent a remarkable transformation. In this new order, in which capitalism has gained a global structure, uniform economic policies have been proposed in a general way to countries with different development paths and different social characteristics. Unsurprisingly, all these policies were aimed at satisfying the profit greed of the capitalist class and thus increasing investments. In short, economic growth is an indispensable goal for current mainstream global politics and economics.

However, at this point, the following question comes to mind concerning our discussions above: How can this indispensable economic growth goal be sustained on a planet of scarce resources? From this point of view, endless growth and the continuation of this system do not seem possible. Another mystery is whether the increase in economic growth and capital accumulation will cause a crisis due to the decrease in profit rates, as Marx (1894) stated. Or will the system be softened and continued with alternative solutions such as the degrowth movement? Of course, the degrowth movement alone cannot dispel the Marxist critiques on the end of capitalism. Because what is promised is a softened version of capitalism, for those who have a Marxist approach, this option will only delay the destruction of capitalism, nothing more. Among these two possibilities, it would be appropriate to touch on the details of the degrowth movement, which is relatively new and promises an alternative option.

3 An Alternative Movement: Degrowth

Ever since man began to use fire and tools, he has been shaping the world he lives on in line with his own needs and passions. In the era of hunting and gathering, man, who did not have the drive and power to consume the resources on the planet, quickly reached this power with science, discovery, and inventions. On the one hand, the needs brought about by the changing lifestyles and, on the other hand, the passions revealed by the changing motives increased consumption and production rapidly and almost declared war on the limited resources of the planet.

The struggle of man against nature and the planet, which will bring his own demise, has been going on for a very long time. But history is full of examples of how the unilateral exploitation of nature can destroy civilizations. The capitalist transformation, which started with Columbus sailing to the Atlantic Ocean, was one of the first steps of the destruction we are in today. The transfer of the wealth and labor power of the continents discovered by colonial activities to Europe led to the industrial revolution. While the industrial revolution changed the dimensions of production at an incredible speed, it also divided the planet into a center and a periphery (Foster, 2002, p. 15). A trading system was formed for the surpluses created after the agricultural and industrial revolutions. For the capitalist system to continue, consumption and production must constantly grow and reach new markets. That is why capitalism and growth are inseparable concepts. However, the view that the invisible hand of mainstream economics can solve everything with the price mechanism still does not seem to be able to realize the limits of our planet's resources.

The planet we live on has delicate balances. Greenhouse gases, which surround our planet like a blanket, keep the temperature of our planet at 15 °C, allowing living things to live. The greenhouse effect caused by fossil fuels, gases released into the atmosphere, the reduction of forests, the increase in industrialization, and consumption trends increase the temperature of the planet. However, for the health of the planet and the sustainability of life, the temperature rise must remain below 1.5 °C. The rate of greenhouse gases in the atmosphere increased rapidly after the industrial revolution, and this increase continues at a faster rate today. If greenhouse gases cannot be reduced, it is calculated that the global surface temperature will increase by 3–4 °C until 2100 (IPCC, 2018). Extreme weather conditions caused by temperature rise will destroy biodiversity. Floods, hurricanes, fires, and droughts caused by temperature changes will destroy many species and vegetation and turn much of the world into a desert. Agriculture will not be possible due to drought, and epidemics and deaths will increase due to lack of access to water and food. Rising sea levels will affect approximately 50 million people, resulting in mass migrations. In order not to encounter these disasters or to reduce the dimensions of the disaster as much as possible, humanity, who made the planet this way, needs to take immediate action (IPCC, 2018).

The main factor that reveals global warming and its indirect effects is carbon emissions. However, it does not seem possible to reduce carbon emissions without changing the capitalist mode of production, whose existence is indexed to growth. As a matter of fact, naturalist Boulding (1966) criticizes developmental economists: "someone who believes in infinite growth is "either a madman or an economist." Moreover, even the most well-known and simplest definition of economics says that resources are scarce.

Raworth (2017), who argues that there can be no endless economic growth, states that the approaching climate crisis is an opportunity to forget all the basics of economics and learn from the beginning. Raworth explains with the example of doughnut how to protect the planet on which we all depend and to establish a future that can meet the needs of all people on it. The interior of the doughnut represents the social base that everyone must reach, and the exterior represents the ecological ceiling that should not be crossed. The social basis consists of 12 items that include basic needs such as food, education, shelter, equality, and justice. The ecological ceiling represents issues affecting the future of the planet, such as climate change, acidification of the oceans, and loss of biodiversity. Four of these nine problems (biodiversity loss, climate change, nitrogen, phosphorus loading, and land conversion) have already crossed ecological boundaries.

Between the two sets of boundaries of the doughnut lies a sweet place, which is both an ecologically and socially safe and fair area. The first of Raworth's suggestions is to get rid of the GDP scale so that people can be in this sweet and beautiful part of the doughnut and save the planet. It is necessary to realize that human is a creature who does not act rationally and the economic system should be designed accordingly. A distributive system that eliminates inequalities should be established. Growth is not necessary, as mainstream economists put forward it. The important thing is not to grow, but to develop (Raworth, 2017; Steffen et al., 2015).

What Raworth is talking about is not new. In the 1950s, against the growth dependence of capitalism, the concept of zero growth (steady-state) economy which was based on Thomas Malthus, Adam Smith, David Ricardo, and John Stuart Mill was introduced. By considering the population and arable land limit, Malthus was one of the first economists to state that growth is far from sustainability. Mill, in his *Principles of Political Economy* of 1848, argues that the steady state of population and capital will not constitute an obstacle to the development of humanity. When the economic growth stabilizes, economic goals of the society will evolve from the quantitative side to the qualitative side, and the steady state will be reached. According to Mill, the best condition for human nature is one where no one is poor and no one wants to get rich (Ulucak, 2018, p. 128).

Mumford states in his 1938 work, *The Culture of Cities*, that "never before in recorded history such large masses of people lived in such a brutally degraded environment" (Foster, 2002, p. 67). It should be noted that 75 years have passed since this statement. Continuing with Mill's ideas, Mumford also stated that the stagnation economy is not just an ecological necessity; it should be combined with the basic concept of communism, which provides the households with a standard life and distributes the earnings to the entire society.

The 1970s is the period when Mill's views were deepened. Herman Daly (1974) made statements against growthmania, based on entropy, the second law of thermodynamics. The first law of thermodynamics states that matter and energy are fixed and cannot be created or destroyed. This change is from the usable to the non-usable, from the valid to the invalid, and from the regular to the irregular. The basis of the concept of entropy is based on the Roman Horace, who said that "time devalues the world." Entropy means that everything in the universe is inexorably heading toward chaos and extinction. Accordingly, all the mainstream economic theories which are based on the first law of thermodynamics, stating that the environment is inexhaustible, are wrong (Gündüz, 2006, p. 347–350).

The economist who adapted entropy to economic theory and is considered the founder of thermoeconomics is Nicholas Georgescu-Roegen with his 1971 work *The Entropy Law and The Economic Process*. Georgescu-Roegen, criticizing neoclassical economics based on Newtonian mechanics, argues that the energy used in economic processes is irretrievably destroyed. The increase in resource and energy use increases entropy and brings the inevitable ecological disaster closer.

The entropy that accelerated after the industrial revolution began to accumulate much faster in the 1960s when capitalism was in its golden age. Increasing concerns about the destruction caused by capitalism on the planet led to the establishment of the Club of Rome in 1968, which tried to make predictions about the future of the planet and humanity. The Club of Rome asked the US Massachusetts Institute of Technology to prepare a report on the future of the planet. The report "The Limits to Growth," which took 4 years to prepare and reveals the shocking facts, had a cold shower effect all over the world (Başçil, 2021).

The report shows that the planet's limits will be reached within a century if industrial production, resource consumption, environmental pollution, waste, population, and growth trends continue. Hall and Day (2009) indicate the main variables used in the modeling of the report. These are resources, births, deaths, services and industrial output per capita, food per capita, pollution, and population. As resources are being depleted rapidly, deaths are decreasing, and population and pollution are increasing. However, it is predicted that after 2010, industry and food production will decrease rapidly, and after 2030, the population will decrease very rapidly and fall to four billion people. It is predicted that the interactions of the relevant variables will collapse the ecological system (Meadows et al., 1972).

As long as the predicted trends continue and cannot be changed, sudden and uncontrollable decreases in population and production capacity will be encountered, and the limits of growth will be reached. However, it is possible to establish an ecological and economic balance by controlling growth. With this balance, it can be ensured that every individual in the world has equal opportunities to meet their basic needs and develop their human potential. The sooner and faster work is started for this, the higher the chances of humanity and the planet will be (Meadows et al., 1972).

Another important work that draws attention to the ecological disasters caused by capitalism and the growth problem in the 1970s is Ernst Friedrich Schumacher's *Small is Beautiful*. Schumacher (1973) criticizes neoclassical economics for not realizing or being unwilling to recognize the importance of ecological capital. The nonrenewable capital that the planet offers us is huge, but not unlimited. Therefore, it is necessary to abandon the understanding of growth and develop a new production-consumption order.

With "The Limits to Growth" report, Georgescu-Roegen's studies based on entropy, and Schumacher's book *Small is Beautiful*, the foundations of a new concept of shrinkage were laid to prevent the disaster that awaits the planet.

The cold shower effect created by "The Limits to Growth" report has diminished with the overcoming of the oil crisis and the rise of neoliberalism. The "Challenges of Degrowth" conference held in Montreal in 1982 was aimed at economic stagnation rather than degrowth (Turgut, 2014, p. 147). At the World Environment Summit held in Rio in 1992, "The Limits to Growth" report was updated and tried to emphasize the exceeded limits again. "The Limits to Growth 30 years Update" report, which was renewed in 2004, drew attention to the fact that there were 10 years left to the irreversible critical threshold. In the report, the only scenario where sustainability can be achieved is the scenario that coincides with the economic degrowth (Meadows et al., 2005). The report was last updated by climate strategist Jorgen Randers in 2012. The book *2052: A Global Forecast for the Next Forty Years* emphasizes that the world is much less sustainable now and talks about the impossibility of capitalism to solve these problems.

The first steps of the degrowth movement were taken in Lyon, France, in the early 2000s, 30 years after "The Limits of Growth" report. The degrowth special issue of *Silence* magazine also attracted attention. Afterward, a symposium was organized with the participation of well-known degrowthers (or degrowth advocates) by the Economic and Social Studies Institute for Sustainable Reduction. To keep the world's attention on the movement, François Schneider toured southern France by donkey. The first steps and ideas in France spread to Italy and Spain.

Founded in 2007, the Research and Degrowth organization sought to increase academic support by launching degrowth conferences. However, the First International Conference on Economic Degrowth for Ecological Sustainability and Social Equity held in Paris witnessed an important development for degrowth. At the conference, the word "degrowth" was used in English for the first time, and it was introduced into the academic literature. The importance of the use of the word in English is that the concept of degrowth is now open to international academic debate. At the conference, degrowth was defined as a voluntary transition to a just participatory and ecologically sustainable society (Degrowth Declaration of Paris Conference, 2008).

The first conference was followed by Barcelona in 2010, Venice in 2012, and Leipzig in 2014. At the conferences, the foundations of the degrowth movement were established, and public awareness began to rise. Publications on degrowth have increased, and the concept of degrowth has been placed in university curriculums. It is possible to talk about the positive effects of the COVID-19 epidemic, which we have experienced in the recent past and which has affected the whole world, on the degrowth movement. The closure of people in their homes has reduced the damage done to nature to a certain extent. It has also made it clear that the planet is trying to heal its wounds if given the opportunity. Studies show that when we choose to degrowth in a planned way, we can achieve a better life by working less and consuming less but with higher quality, less waste, and more recycling.

4 Degrowth (Décroissance, Decrescita, Decreixement, Decrecimiento)

The concept and idea of degrowth were first encountered in the works of André Gorz and Nicholas Georgescu-Roegen in the 1970s (Whitehead, 2013, p. 141). Georgescu-Roegen (1971) reminded that, like every human being, the planet Earth will eventually die and that this is an unchanging law of physics. But the real question is how fast and soon that will happen. Andre Gorz (1972) also asked whether it was possible to balance the planet in the current capitalist system. For this, he states that material production should not grow or even shrink (Kallis et al., 2014).

Kerschner (2010) defines degrowth as "...an equitable downscaling of production and consumption that increases human well-being and enhances ecological conditions at the local and global level, in the short and long term" (Kerschner, 2010, p. 544).

Degrowth is voluntarily trying to build a better society and a new post-development model within ecological limits. Although there is a definition of degrowth that is used by everyone, those who advocate degrowth state that there should not be a definite definition. The important thing is to focus on the goals of the movement, not the definition (Cosme et al., 2017, p. 323). Degrowth is a constantly changing and developing concept that cannot be placed in a single category, both intellectually and in terms of the actions of its followers (Koyuncu & Özer, 2017, p. 176).

Degrowth is a movement that opposes traditional growth economics because growth in developed countries is socially damaging, ecologically unsustainable, and uneconomical (Alexander, 2012). Degrowth, as a critique of the developmental hegemony, opposes Western uniform development proposals, green growth, or green development approaches (Demaria et al., 2013, p. 193). Degrowth is a political, economic, and social movement based on environmentalist, anti-consumerist, and anti-capitalist ideas, the symbol of which is the snail.

Degrowth is not synonymous of negative growth or stagnation, nor is a goal in itself. Although the degrowth includes reductions in resource-intensive production and consumption activities and a decrease in GDP, it is not a recession. Even if GDP decreases with degrowth, there will be positive qualitative, social, and environmental changes that we cannot use in the measurement of GDP (Schneider et al., 2010). As a matter of fact, Easterlin paradox states that there is not as strong a relationship between GDP and happiness as expected (Easterlin, 1974). For psychological welfare, relative income level is important, not absolute income. Although absolute income can increase happiness up to a certain level, financial gains do not make people happy after a point. What increases social welfare is not economic growth, but equality. Degrowth, which suggests voluntary simplicity and less consumption, also underlines this point.

Degrowth is not an argument against technology and knowledge. On the contrary, it expresses a more technological and information-intensive situation. With degrowth, we need to understand that technological innovation and productivity gains do not encourage more consumption and production.

Degrowth has emerged as a response to the triple crisis, environmental, social, and economic. Degrowthers come from different fields and movements of thought. Anthropologist Serge Latouche can be cited as the first source of degrowth. Latouche contributes to degrowth by criticizing the idea that Southern countries follow the growth development model of the rich North. The second source of degrowth is the desire to break the link between democracy, politics, technological system, education and information system, and short-term interests. The third source is ecological. Degrowth includes respect for nature and all living things in it. The fourth source is movements that embrace nonviolence, art, and voluntary simplicity. The final resource is the bioeconomy or ecological economy (Schneider et al., 2010).

The word degrowth is criticized by many economists because it is provocative. However, degrowth is a concept that covers many political, economic, and sociological problems. Degrowth is a step taken by academics who question the social, economic, and ecological crises of the dominant economic view. The degrowth movement seeks to deliberately downsize economies to create a life of greater social welfare by addressing climate change and working less.

Mainstream economics thinks that when limited resources are exhausted, science will solve this problem with alternative resources. But degrowthers agree that science and technology cannot solve this problem. Contrary to the growthist approaches of the mainstream economics, a policy call is made in which higher welfare, better ecological conditions, and a fair world can be created through a planned economic contraction.

Bilancini and D'Alessandro (2012) argue that it is possible to transit from suboptimal balanced growth to happy degrowth that increases welfare. Under reasonable parameters, downscaling of production, reduction of private consumption, and increase in leisure and welfare are necessary for an optimal balance. By increasing leisure time and strengthening social ties, positive dissemination of leisure time can be achieved. With the benefit obtained from this, the decrease in the benefit caused by less consumption is compensated, and even more benefits can be achieved.

As individuals adapt to the material improvements in their lives after a short time, the level of satisfaction they feel decreases over time. For the level of satisfaction to rise again, the individual must earn more income. However, when the income level rises, the same vicious circle will restart. This vicious circle shows that growth will never be enough. Income level and financial standards are at the forefront of the happiness of individuals. However, after a certain point where our basic needs are met, material gains do not increase our sense of satisfaction as much as expected. As a matter of fact, equality and simplicity are at the forefront in the degrowth movement, which states that social welfare can be increased with equality (Wilkinson & Pickett, 2009).

The degrowth movement emphasizes the need to adapt human well-being to the planet. Right here, it is important to mention five basic strategies generally accepted by degrowthers. The first strategy is to use alternative indicators instead of GDP to measure welfare. As long as development and welfare are measured by traditional GDP, it is not possible to give up growth. GDP is a variable that has no normative aspects, cannot distinguish between good and bad, and cannot show ecological-social costs. It also does not cover other important indicators such as equality in income distribution, women's labor, gender equality, education, and clean air, which are important for the degrowth movement. Therefore, degrowthers recommend using indicators that include ecological boundaries and equity. The United Nations' Human Development Index (HDI), which includes variables such as income, life expectancy, education, and inequality, is a recommended indicator. Another recommended indicator is the genuine progress indicator (GPI). GPI is a variable that includes all environmental and social factors that are not included in GDP.

The second key strategy is to identify sectors that are important for welfare. The growth of all sectors in the economy is not rational. As Georgescu-Roegen stated, an increase in resource and energy use rises entropy and brings our ecological disaster closer. Therefore, it is recommended to establish a democratic order in which it can be decided which sectors should be allowed to grow and which should be reduced. By making a voluntary reduction in production and consumption, the growth of sectors that harm the environment can be stopped or slowed down. On the contrary, the growth of sectors such as education, health, and renewable energy can be accelerated.

The third strategy is the redistribution of income and wealth. The mainstream economic theory proposes to increase global GDP to eradicate poverty. Supply-side economics approaches, especially after 1980, tried to increase the wealth of the rich to stimulate growth. Increases in the wealth of the riches would transform into more spending and productive investments, which would trickle down to the rest of society. This is called the trickle-down effect (Hickel, 2017). However, studies present that GDP growth does not benefit the poor. The benefits of growth are unevenly distributed. Degrowthers state that the resources on Earth will be enough for everyone to create a better life. They also underline the need for redistribution of income and wealth both within and between countries. To ensure redistribution, a progressive taxation system, in which high income and wealth are taxed more, is recommended. Unconditionally universal basic income application for every household individual in the country is another recommended method. To ensure equality and justice, those living in rich countries must learn to live with less property (Foster, 2011).

Reducing the environmental impacts of human activities is the fourth strategy. It is important to ensure the sustainability of the planet's limited resources and to minimize the damage done to the planet. It is necessary to protect biodiversity, reduce unnecessary consumption, and ensure a sustainable local food production.

The final strategy is to build a democratic and egalitarian society. The degrowth movement defends that all decision-making processes should be transparent and attended by all segments of society. People, and especially marginalized sections of society, should have a say in all decisions that affect their lives.

As a result, the degrowth movement seeks to provide a better life for all living things on the planet. It suggests enjoying life, increasing the well-being of all, voluntary simplicity, and slowing down. For this, the production and consumption frenzy of the Global North must be abandoned. The Global South needs to get rid of its former colonial connections and create a unique social and economic model. Both technical developments and social transformations are important to strengthen political participation and democracies, create localized economies, and solve ecological problems.

According to Latouche (2009), as long as the growth paradigm is adhered to, all productivity-enhancing activities we have done will increase consumption and production rather than decrease them. Making vehicles with lower emissions will lead people to drive more. Alternative energy sources will make people consume more energy. New and efficient technologies will lead to more consumption. The important thing here is to defeat the dictates of capitalism. Otherwise, what is done will not change the result. However, it should not be forgotten that productivity increases are also an important source for spending quality time by working less instead of producing more.

On the other hand, growth-oriented economic systems have intense psychological effects. Individuals who always want more and have to focus on the upper level are under intense stress. Long working hours, sleep disturbance, depression, and fatigue are the main indicators. Indeed, the use of antidepressants is increasing very rapidly. Degrowth seems to be a good solution to these problems with fewer working hours, slower, enjoyable, and quality living.

Andre Gorz states that as pollution on the planet increases, production will become more expensive and luxurious. In this case, it will be possible for only the rich and privileged to consume goods that have become more expensive. This will further increase inequality in society. Getting more scarcity of resources will make capitalism more brutal and increase the rent of resources even more (Gündogan, 2012).

Latouche underlines that if we do not reverse the situation, we will be condemned first to a controlled diet and then to a forced starvation. He finds activities such as advertising, tourism, transportation, automobile, agricultural industry (agribusiness), and biotechnology unnecessary. It is necessary to reduce or eliminate these unnecessary needs as much as possible by changing our lifestyle (Latouche, 2009, p. 79). Indeed, even the mainstream *Financial Times* portrays tourism as the world's number one environmental enemy (Latouche, 2009, p. 38). It is necessary to make serious changes in subjects such as people's consumption habits and transportation of goods. To reduce emissions during the transport of goods, it is important to produce and consume local products. However, these changes cannot occur spontaneously in a free market economy.

Decreases in growth rates in capitalist systems increase unemployment, disrupt equality of income distribution, and create problems in social, health, and education services. With degrowth, the problems that capitalist systems will face will be much more serious. Working less and consuming fewer goods and services will negatively affect people's standard of living. To compensate for it, it is recommended to increase public services. The fact that people do not have to spend money in areas such as health, housing, education, and transportation will lead to less work and will be able to compensate for the negative effects of degrowth. Cuba is a good example of this. Cuba is an indication that growth is not needed to make basic public services accessible to all. Although the Cuban economy is shrinking, it can provide quality health and education services to all citizens.

Latouche (2006) states that the main problem that prevents people from transitioning to a better society and compresses them into a narrow framework is capitalism. Ecologically compatible capitalism, while theoretically possible, is practically impossible. Latouche argues that radical change is necessary if we are to avoid a cruel and tragic catastrophe.

The targets put forward by the degrowth are the targets that cannot be realized in the current capitalist system. Nevertheless, degrowthers do not want to be imposed by an intellectual or political authority to implement the principles that they defend. Instead, it will be much more effective to achieve constitutional transformation with a bottom-up popular movement like Buen Vivir (Turgut, 2014, p. 154).

There are many criticisms and questions to be answered against the degrowth movement. The first criticism is that there is no clear explanation of what will be downsized. There are also criticisms about how the proposals for reducing production and consumption differ from the steady-state economy. Although the degrowth movement has drawn a general strategy with its ideas, projects, and policies, it is criticized that it does not have a clear scenario on how and by whom this will be done. It is also argued that degrowth is not politically feasible (Romano, 2012, p. 588).

How to create jobs without economic growth is another area of criticism. Degrowthers argue that in an economy where everyone works fewer hours, full employment is possible. They think that this problem will be solved by reducing working hours and sharing work. However, there is a critical balance between hourly divisions of labor between sectors in the economy, energy consumption, and production. Although it seems good to use fewer resources and energy, it does not seem possible to maintain the current order with fewer working hours. The low net energy production of alternative energy sources is already an important obstacle to reducing working hours (Şorman, 2012, p. 29–30).

To reach a fair, equal, free society with an increased quality of life that is desired to be achieved with degrowth, each society must take into account its dynamics and make good planning. However, cultural and social differences, uncertainties, insensitivity, lack of tolerance, and ignorance will create significant challenges that must be overcome.

Reducing energy consumption in some areas with degrowth will increase energy consumption in other areas. Increasing efficiency in energy and resource use will lead to more economic growth rather than less resource use. This situation is called the Jevons paradox. As more production will be made with more efficient machines and factories, resource usage will increase.

Another criticism suggests that degrowth may be an ideology rather than a practical way of life. Degrowth will not reduce carbon emissions to zero. A 10% reduction will only reduce carbon emissions by 10%. But degrowth of this rate will reveal a situation twice as bad as the Great Depression. The downsizing of the economy will affect the people who need energy and food the most.

How global inflation will develop after the universal basic income application and how people's production and consumption demands will be affected by this are also important problems. Degrowthers' suggestions for shortening working hours and applying basic income are not realistic within the capitalist system. In this respect, it is criticized by stating that the degrowth movement does not have a macro-integrative strategy and only looks at ecological problems. While examining the social consequences of the ecological crisis, degrowthists are also accused of not considering how the lower-income groups are affected (Koyuncu & Özer, 2017, p. 8).

5 Conclusion

Degrowth, drawing attention to climate change, speaks of a life with less consumption and production, less work, and high social welfare. It draws attention to the need to reduce the effects of human beings on the planet to a sustainable level. Degrowth argues that it is possible to redistribute income and wealth to a more just, sharing, participatory, and happy society.

A fairer, more sharing, and more enjoyable life can turn the world into a paradise for all people. The accessibility of the said world depends on human behavior. Be it mainstream economics or other views, they all talk about self-interested people. On our planet, where rational man is only in books, maximization behavior based on animal motives is ubiquitous. Humans want the most of everything in their limited lives and planet. While doing this, they do not care much about the situation of other people, just as they do not care about the resources and future of the planet. But what is overlooked here is that human existence depends on the health of the planet. The world existed before we were on it. It will continue to exist even when we are gone.

Studies show that our planet reboots itself. The planet warms, and the climate deteriorates and then enters an ice age. Then the same process happens again, just like the cyclical fluctuations of GDP, which mainstream economics attaches great importance to. The planet is renewing itself in this process that takes thousands of years. Fortunately, mankind has not yet witnessed this renewal process. However, if we continue to go full steam ahead in production and consumption, as degrowthers fear, we will be more likely to witness the beginning of the renewal process. With our current technology, is there any chance of us getting out of this process unscathed? Degrowthers, who have been criticized in many ways, try to answer this question before they reach the point of no return. What matters to those on the planet is not whether this answer is right or wrong; it will be the success of the degrowthers.

On the other hand, it should be stressed that the critiques made by the advocates of the degrowth movement point out important failures of capitalism. Although they strongly criticize the system, we may not suggest that the degrowth movement is an anti-capitalist movement. By offering some suggestions, they aim to fix the system. Since the history of the movement is relatively short, there are some debates on it. The socialists criticize the movement for not addressing the main points of exploitation of capitalism, while the advocates of free market criticize for ignoring the destructive consequences of the decrease in output. No doubt following the recommendations of the movement requires strong regulations made by national and international authorities, and it is not that easy. Yet another ambiguous point is the reactions of economic agents. It will be not that easy for households and companies to settle for less consumption and less profit rates, respectively. Thus, to establish a "new capitalism" based on the degrowth concept, microeconomic agents, national institutions, and international organizations should league together in a common acceptance.

References

Aghion, P., & Howitt, P. (1992). A model of growth through creative destruction. *Econometrica, 60*(2), 323–351.

Alexander, S. (2012). Planned economic contraction: The emerging case for degrowth. *Environmental Politics, 21*(3), 349–368.

Arrow, K. J. (1962). The economic implications of learning by doing. *The Review of Economic Studies, 29*(3), 155–173.

Barro, R. J. (2001). Human capital and growth. *American Economic Review, 91*(2), 12–17.

Başçil, H. (2021, Şubat 27). *Roma Kulübü Raporu: Küreselleşmenin Ekonomik ve Toplumsal İflası*. Gelenek ve Gelecek.

Becker, G. S. (1962). Investment in human capital: A theoretical analysis. *Journal of Political Economy, 70*(5, Part 2), 9–49.

Bilancini, E., & D'Alessandro, S. (2012). Long-run welfare under externalities in consumption, leisure, and production: A case for happy degrowth vs. unhappy growth. *Ecological Economics, 84*, 194–205.

Boulding, K. E. (1966). The economics of the coming spaceship earth. In H. Jarrett (Ed.), *Environmental quality in a growing economy* (pp. 3–15). Johns Hopkins Press.

Cass, D. (1965). Optimum growth in an aggregative model of capital accumulation. *The Review of Economic Studies, 32*(3), 233–240.

Colander, D., Holt, R., & Rosser, B., Jr. (2004). The changing face of mainstream economics. *Review of Political Economy, 16*(4), 485–499.

Cosme, I., Santos, R., & O'Neill, D. W. (2017). Assessing the degrowth discourse: A review and analysis of academic degrowth policy proposals. *Journal of Cleaner Production, 149*, 321–334.

Daly, E. H. (1974). Steady-state economics versus growthmania: A critique of the orthodox conceptions of growth, wants, scarcity and efficiency. *Policy Sciences, 5*, 149–167.

Degrowth Declaration of Paris Conference. (2008). Accessed February 22, 2022, from https://degrowth.org/wp-content/uploads/2011/05/Declaration-Degrowth-Paris-2008.pdf

Demaria, F., Schneider, F., Sekulova, F., & Martinez-Alier, J. (2013). What is degrowth? From an activist slogan to a social movement. *Environmental Values, 22*(2), 191–215.

Dinda, S. (2004). Environmental Kuznets curve hypothesis: A survey. *Ecological Economics, 49*(4), 431–455.

Domar, E. (1946). Capital expansion, rate of growth, and employment. *Econometrica, 14*(2), 137–147.

Easterlin, R. A. (1974). Does economic growth improve the human lot? Some empirical evidence. In P. A. David & M. W. Reder (Eds.), *Nations and households in economic growth* (pp. 89–125). Academic Press.

Foster, J. B. (2002). *Savunmasız Gezegen: Çevrenin Kısa Ekonomik Tarihi*. Epos Yayınları.

Foster, J. B. (2011). Capitalism and degrowth: An impossibility theorem. *Monthly Review, 62*(8), 26–33.

Georgescu-Roegen, N. (1971). *The entropy law and the economic process*. Harvard University Press.

Gorz, A. (M. Bosquet). (1972). 'Proceedings from a public debate'. Nouvel Observateur, Paris, 397. (19th June 1972, p. IV. Proceedings from a public debate organized in Paris by the Club du Nouvel Observateur).

Grossman, G. M., & Helpman, E. (1991). Quality ladders and product cycles. *Quarterly Journal of Economics, 106*(2), 557–586.
Gündogan, A. C. (2012). Ekonomik Küçülmenin Ahval ve Şeraiti: Başka Bir Küçülme Mümkün Mü? *Ekososyalist Dergi, 14*, 31–33.
Gündüz, M. (2006). Sosyal Yaşam ve Entropi Yasası: Dünyanın Sonuna mı Yaklaştık? *Atatürk Üniversitesi İktisadi ve İdari Bilimler Dergisi, 20*(1), 345–355.
Hall, C. A., & Day, J. W. (2009). Revisiting the limits to growth after peak oil. *American Scientist, 97*(3), 230–237.
Harrod, R. F. (1939). An essay in dynamic theory. *The Economic Journal, 49*, 14–33.
Hickel, J. (2017). *The divide: A brief guide to global inequality and its solutions*. Random House.
IPCC. (2018). Summary for policymakers. In V. Masson-Delmotte, P. Zhai, H.-O. Pörtner, D. Roberts, J. Skea, P. R. Shukla, A. Pirani, W. Moufouma-Okia, C. Péan, R. Pidcock, S. Connors, J. B. R. Matthews, Y. Chen, X. Zhou, M. I. Gomis, E. Lonnoy, T. Maycock, M. Tignor, & T. Waterfield (Eds.), *Global warming of 1.5°C*. World Meteorological Organization.
Kallis, G., Demaria, F., & D'Alisa, G. (2014). *Degrowth: A vocabulary for a new era*. Routledge.
Kerschner, C. (2010). Economic de-growth vs. steady-state economy. *Journal of Cleaner Production, 18*(6), 544–551.
Koopmans, T. C. (1965). On the concept of optimal economic growth. In J. Johansen (Ed.), *The econometric approach to development planning* (pp. 225–287). North Holland.
Koyuncu, M., & Özer, Ş. (2017). Büyümemek mümkün mü? 'Ekonomik küçülme fikri' üzerine tartışmalar. In H. Cömert, E. Özçelik, & E. Voyvoda (Eds.), *Kalkınma İktisadının Penceresinden Türkiye'ye Bakmak: Fikret Şenses'e Armağan* (pp. 175–196). İletişim Yayınları.
Latouche, S. (2006). *How do we learn to want less? The globe downshifted*. Le Monde Diplomatique.
Latouche, S. (2009). *Farewell to growth*. Polity.
Lee, F. S. (2008). Heterodox economics. *The Long Term View, 7*(1), 23.
Liu, J., Qu, J., & Zhao, K. (2019). Is China's development conforms to the environmental Kuznets curve hypothesis and the pollution haven hypothesis? *Journal of Cleaner Production, 234*, 787–796.
Lucas, R. E., Jr. (1988). On the mechanics of economic development. *Journal of Monetary Economics, 22*(1), 3–42.
Maddison, A. Historical Statistics of the World Economy: 1–2008 a.d. 2010. www.ggdc.net/MADDISON/oriindex.htm
Mankiw, N. G., Romer, D., & Weil, D. N. (1992). A contribution to the empirics of economic growth. *Quarterly Journal of Economics, 107*(2), 407–437.
Marx, K. (1894). Capital, vol. 3. In K. Marx & F. Engels (Eds.), *Collected works, 1975–2005* (Vol. 37). Progress.
Meadows, D. H., Meadows, D. L., Randers, J., & Behrens, W. W. (1972). *The limits to growth, a report for the Club of Rome's project on the predicament of mankind*. Universe Books.
Meadows, D. H., Randers, J., & Meadows, D. L. (2005). *The limits to growth: The 30-year update*. Earthscan.
Mincer, J. (1958). Investment in human capital and personal income distribution. *Journal of Political Economy, 66*(4), 281–302.
Phelps, E. (1961). The golden rule of accumulation: A fable for growthmen. *American Economic Review, 51*(4), 638–643.
Piketty, T. (2013). *Capital in the 21st century*. President and Fellows, Harvard College.
Ramsey, F. P. (1928). A mathematical theory of saving. *The Economic Journal, 38*(152), 543–559.
Raworth, K. (2017). *Doughnut economics: Seven ways to think like a 21st-century economist*. Chelsea Green Publishing.
Rebelo, S. (1991). Long-run policy analysis and long-run growth. *Journal of Political Economy, 99*(3), 500–521.
Romano, O. (2012). How to rebuild democracy, re-thinking degrowth. *Futures, 44*(6), 582–589.

Romer, P. M. (1986). Increasing returns and long-run growth. *Journal of Political Economy, 94*(5), 1002–1037.
Romer, P. M. (1990). Endogenous technological change. *Journal of Political Economy, 98*(5, Part 2), 71–102.
Schneider, F., Kallis, G., & Martinez-Alier, J. (2010). Crisis or opportunity? Economic degrowth for social equity and ecological sustainability. Introduction to this special issue. *Journal of Cleaner Production, 18*(6), 511–518.
Schumacher, E. F. (1973). *Small is beautiful.* Abacus Books.
Solow, R. M. (1956). A contribution to the theory of economic growth. *Quarterly Journal of Economics, 70*(1), 65–94.
Solow, R. M. (1957). Technical change and the aggregate production function. *Review of Economics and Statistics, 39*, 312–320.
Steffen, W., Richardson, K., Rockström, J., Cornell, S. E., Fetzer, I., Bennett, E. M., & Sörlin, S. (2015). Planetary boundaries: Guiding human development on a changing planet. *Science, 347*(6223), 1259855.
Stern, D. I. (1998). Progress on the environmental Kuznets curve? *Environment and Development Economics, 3*(2), 173–196.
Swan, T. W. (1956). Economic growth and capital accumulation. *Economic Record, 32*(2), 334–361.
Şorman, A. H. (2012). Planlı Ekonomik Küçülme Uygulanabilir ve Arzu Edilen Bir Çözüm Mü? *Ekososyalist Dergi, 14*, 27–30.
Turgut, G. (2014). Ekolojik Sürdürülebilirlik ve Küçülme. *Dokuz Eylül Üniversitesi İktisadi İdari Bilimler Fakültesi Dergisi, 29*(2), 137–165.
Ulucak, R. (2018). İktisatta çevreci dönüşüm: Ekolojik makro iktisat. *Erciyes Üniversitesi İktisadi ve İdari Bilimler Fakültesi Dergisi, 51*, 127–149.
Uzawa, H. (1965). Optimum technical change in an aggregative model of economic growth. *International Economic Review, 6*(1), 18–31.
Whitehead, M. (2013). Degrowth or regrowth? *Environmental Values, 22*(2), 141–145.
Wilkinson, R., & Pickett, K. (2009). *The spirit level: Why greater equality makes societies stronger.* Bloomsbury Publishing.

Can Green Deals Save Capitalism from Ecological Collapse?

Laurent Baechler

Abstract In response to the intensifying ecological crisis, a growing number of governments are adopting green deals designed to both revive their economies and put those economies on a sustainable development trajectory. The success of these plans will depend on their ability to put involved economies on a path to decoupling economic activities from their environmental impacts. The challenges are daunting in terms of financial capacity, institutional reforms, and international cooperation.

Keywords European Green Deal · NextGeneration EU · Ecological decoupling · International cooperation

1 Introduction

Karl Marx (1887) predicted in the middle of the nineteenth century that the capitalist system would collapse on itself because the accumulation of capital would be accompanied by a progressive exhaustion of the capacity to extract from the labor force the surplus value indispensable for the survival of the system. This did not happen, essentially because technological progress has so far allowed the growth rates of capital and labor income to be sufficient to raise living standards around the world, albeit at different rates. Since the publication of *Capital* in 1867, the average per capita income in the world has risen from about $900 (in 1990 dollars, in PPP calculation; Maddison, 2006) to over $18,000 (PPP estimate for the year 2019). And this process has taken place despite an increase in world population from about 1.3 billion to nearly 7.8 billion in 2020, thereby thwarting another famous prediction made in 1798, by Thomas R. Malthus, who believed that the rate of increase in world population would exceed that of agricultural production, leading to a steady state of the economies. The world economy came out of the Malthusian trap for the same reasons that the capitalist system did not collapse on itself, thanks to technological

L. Baechler (✉)
Centre International de Formation Européenne, Nice, France
e-mail: laurent.baechler@cife.eu

A. Ari (ed.), *Capitalism at a Crossroads*, Springer Studies in Alternative Economics,
https://doi.org/10.1007/978-3-031-23257-2_16

progress. Technological progress was not a sufficiently prominent element of the capitalist system in the first half of the nineteenth century to be considered the major engine of the system that it has become since. The predictions of Marx and Malthus have been overturned by economic history, which has been characterized for more than two centuries by a continuous increase in living standards, thanks in particular to a permanent injection of technological progress in the modern economy.

But the question of the durability of this phenomenon has recently arisen again in a renewed form, which the two authors could not have anticipated at the time they were writing. It is no longer a question of limits imposed on economic progress by world demographic trends or by the excess of capital accumulation. It is now a question of ecological limits imposed on human activities, for a reason that has become increasingly obvious over the last few decades: human societies are open systems whose evolution pushes them to expand; the terrestrial systems on which this expansion is based are closed systems, governed by unavoidable ecological laws.

This disjunction produced its most visible effects in the decades of the twentieth century, which saw a parallel acceleration in world population growth and living standards, implying in fact an explosion in the production of economic resources. The world's population increased by a factor of almost 2.5 between 1950 and 2000, while the world's average standard of living over the same period rose from $2100 to $5700 (in 1990 $ and PPP calculation; Maddison, 2006) at the same time, implying an enormous multiplication of the world's production of goods and services. These developments have led to what is known as the Great Acceleration (Steffen et al., 2011), a dramatic increase in ecological pressures of all kinds within a few decades after World War II. Ecological limits have been reached and exceeded for several of the major terrestrial ecological systems (Rockström et al., 2009): climate, biodiversity, phosphorus, and nitrogen cycles (essential for biomass formation). Others threaten to be reached soon if pressures continue to increase under current conditions: ocean acidification, land use, and freshwater withdrawals.

Contrary to the predictions of Marx and Malthus, those that announce for the near future a collapse of the Earth's systems in the absence of a rapid and vigorous reaction on the part of humanity have no chance of being thwarted by an element that has escaped the insight of recent observers. The diagnosis is clear: four centuries of capitalism, especially the last two associated with the industrial revolution, have brought the world economy and human societies to the brink of ecological collapse. But unlike the trajectories of the system that have invalidated predictions of collapse in the past, the one we are on now contains no mechanism that would allow it to deviate spontaneously from its logical endpoint. On the contrary, market economies are largely helpless to take into account the ecological impacts of human activities, insofar as all these impacts are externalities that escape the price and exchange systems on which the capitalist system is based. We have known since Arthur C. Pigou (1920) that only appropriate government intervention can correct these externalities. The vital question now facing human societies is whether governments have the means to thwart the looming ecological crises.

The remainder of the chapter is organized as follows: Sect. 2 presents the challenge of transforming existing economic systems, while Sect. 3 discusses the idea of new green deals with particular examples of the USA and the European Union (EU). Sections 4 and 5 emphasize the need for alignment of individual incentives with long-term objectives and for international cooperation, respectively. Section 6 concludes.

2 The Challenge of Transforming Economic Systems

It is a question of transforming the capitalist system to enable it to survive by overcoming these various crises. The purpose of this contribution is not to diagnose these crises in detail, but it is not possible to explore the solutions to a problem without exposing, even if only succinctly, the essential data. Let's take the climate crisis as an example, which is probably, along with biodiversity loss, the main threat to humanity. It is the result of almost two centuries of accumulation of greenhouse gases (GHG) in the atmosphere, mainly carbon, as a consequence of a radical transformation of energy systems that accompanied the rise of the capitalist system. Stabilizing global warming at a sustainable level[1] implies achieving climate neutrality, mainly carbon neutrality, by the mid of this century. It is important to keep in mind what this project implies to measure the magnitude of the challenge. The energy transition to carbon neutrality has little to do with previous energy transitions. The first one, which took place between the middle of the nineteenth century and the beginning of the twentieth century, progressively replaced biomass in the world's energy mix with coal, to the tune of 50% of the total, an amount that the latter has never exceeded (Smil, 2017). The second transition, spread over a comparable period of about five decades, saw coal dethroned by oil and gas between the 1920s and 1970s, with these two sources occupying a maximum of 65% of the global mix at their peak.

But the percentage perspective of the total energy mix is perfectly misleading, as it is accompanied by a considerable increase in energy demand over the same period, of the order of 1.7% per year on average during the nineteenth and twentieth centuries, comparable to the average increase in the world's standard of living. So, the two transitions described were not characterized by a replacement of old energy sources by new ones, but by a complementary accumulation of all these existing sources. The picture is actually worse than that, since not only have traditional energy sources not disappeared from the global energy mix, but their demand has continuously increased since the beginning of their exploitation.

The decarbonization of the world economy requires that this process be completely reversed so that renewable energies (mainly wind and solar) not only occupy an increasing share of the world's energy mix but almost completely replace

[1] Defined by the 2015 Paris Agreement to be between 1.5 and 2 °C of average global warming.

the other energy sources in this mix, whereas they currently represent 14% of annual primary energy consumption.[2] All of this should take place within three decades, to be in line with the objectives of the Paris Agreement on climate, compared to five to six decades for previous transitions. The challenge is enormous and involves a radical transformation of energy production and consumption systems. Comparable challenges are associated with the preservation of biodiversity.

3 The Idea of a Green New Deal

Such a transformation of economic systems requires governments to take charge. In the face of the ecological emergency, it is a question of rapidly mobilizing considerable resources to put these systems on a sustainable trajectory. The idea has recently emerged to draw inspiration from the American New Deal to implement this project. The New Deal, adopted by President F.D. Roosevelt's administration in 1933 to bring the US economy out of the Great Depression, aimed on the one hand to profoundly reform the economy to prevent such a crisis happening again and, on the other hand, to revive economic activity by injecting public funds into global spending. However, the Keynesian-inspired project[3] was criticized by the British economist in a famous open letter to the US president (Keynes, 1933), published by *The New York Times* on December 31, 1933, with the main argument that short-term economic stimulus policies should logically precede long-term reform measures for the US economy, contrary to what the US administration was doing at the time. Keynes' main idea was that rushing structural reforms before the benefits of the stimulus had been reaped would erode the impact of those reforms through a loss of confidence on the part of the actors involved, foremost among whom were investors.

Economic recovery and economic reform are also at the heart of recent plans to address the environmental crisis. The Green New Deal idea embraces environmentalism in general—and climate change more specifically—as a third pillar of a New Deal-type governmental intervention for the twenty-first century. The term, while in use since the 1990s, was popularized in a 2007 *The New York Times* op-ed by Thomas Friedman (2007) in which the author called not for a "Manhattan Project" for energy, but for a "broad range of programs and industrial projects to revitalize America." Friedman suggested that the presidential candidate who embraced this would have a "real leg up" in the 2008 election, emphasizing that "we will only green the world when we change the very nature of the electricity grid," which would be a "huge industrial project" (Friedman, 2007).

[2]Including hydro (2.5%), biomass (9.4%), and intermittent renewables (2.2%) (IEA, 2021). But the transition project must rely primarily on intermittent sources, as the potential for expansion of other two sources is limited.

[3]Even though the founding work of modern macroeconomics, *The General Theory of Employment, Interest and Money*, was not published until 3 years later.

The idea quickly caught on, and the first Green Deals appeared with the prospect of pulling the economies concerned out of the 2008–2009 financial crisis, which was the worst economic crisis since the Great Depression. Japan, China, South Korea, Europe, and the USA were the main actors of this impulse, which concentrated efforts in the field of energy transition: electricity production from renewable resources; building retrofits; efficiency technology upgrades; incentive schemes for low-carbon vehicles; energy network expansion; green transport infrastructure, including rail and mass transit; and clean energy research and technology investment. South Korea stood out by devoting 80% of its stimulus package to such measures, compared to 12% in the USA. The economic balance sheet of these first Green Deals seems more satisfactory than their ecological balance sheet, insofar as the stimulus effect was significant (up to 1.5% of GDP in the case of the EU), without any real reduction in energy consumption and carbon emissions (IEA, 2020).

The Green Deals conceived in the perspective of the COVID-19 crisis are far more ambitious, both ecologically and economically—ecologically since they all set major objectives, the main one being to achieve climate or carbon neutrality by the middle of the century, and[4] economically because they mobilize much greater resources than their predecessors did a decade ago. This is particularly true in Europe, where the stimulus policies adopted during the eurozone crisis of 2010–2012 were constrained by the fiscal and budgetary rules of the single currency.[5] The average fiscal stimulus in the eurozone was around 1% in 2010, but it was almost 10% in 2020. The explanations for this spectacular reversal of economic policy in the EU are multiple (Baechler, 2021): recognition of the ineffectiveness of fiscal austerity in reviving the economies of the southern part of the eurozone, recognition of the impact of austerity on the increase in income inequality and the rise of populist and Eurosceptic currents in Europe, new budgetary priorities given to investment in traditional infrastructure (transport, communications, water and energy distribution, etc.) and new infrastructure (digitalization), the evolution of governance in the eurozone toward greater mutualization of fiscal impulses, and a favorable macroeconomic context, with very low or even negative borrowing rates for some governments.

The challenge now is to mobilize sufficient resources to transform economies and put them on a sustainable development (SD) path. It is no longer a question of simply "repairing" an economic machine seized up by accumulated dysfunctions, as with the Rooseveltian New Deal, but of radically transforming this machine to avoid total collapse. In a way, it is the future of the capitalist system that is at stake with these programs. What exactly do they consist of? Several countries are now proposing to

[4]The difference between the two being that climate neutrality considers all other GHGs than carbon, mainly methane.

[5]Which limit the budget deficit of member countries to 3% of their GDP and the public debt to 60% of GDP.

launch such programs, but the most significant are those proposed by the USA and the EU.

3.1 The US Green New Deal

The US project, initially introduced to Congress by Senator Ed Markey and Congresswoman Alexandria Ocasio-Cortez (both Democrats) in February 2019 and mostly adopted by Senator Bernie Sanders in his run for president in 2020, deliberately echoes F.D. Roosevelt's plan as it seeks to convince Americans of the need for "rapid and far-reaching transitions in energy, land, urban and infrastructure, and industrial systems . . .unprecedented in terms of scale" (American Congress, 2019).

This unprecedented plan, with its most thorough costing detailed by the Sanders campaign, would have cost $16.3 trillion, or 5.7% of GDP annually over 10 years, a sum without comparison with any recently adopted stimulus programs. But, of course, Sanders did not win the presidency. Since then, although President Biden has tried to distance himself from the Green New Deal in search of a more bipartisan solution, he nevertheless proposed a $4 trillion infrastructure spending plan in his first address to a joint session of Congress on April 28, 2021. This speech followed a commitment on April 22, delivered at a summit of 40 world leaders on Earth Day, to reduce greenhouse gas emissions by 50% of 2005 levels by 2030. Biden's spending plan (in addition to the $1.9 trillion American Rescue Plan passed in January 2021 to alleviate the economic consequences of the COVID-19 pandemic) has seen comparisons drawn between Biden and Roosevelt. Since then, the spending plans, divided into a bipartisan $1 trillion infrastructure bill and the so-called Build Back Better Bill—a partisan bill held up by ongoing negotiations between the progressive caucus of the Democratic Party and right-leaning Democratic Senators Joe Manchin and Kyrsten Sinema—have been working their way through Congress.

As of writing, the $1 trillion bipartisan infrastructure bill is waiting to be passed by Congress. A condition of certain factions within the Democratic Party is that it will only be passed when agreement has been reached on the details of its sister bill, the so-called Build Back Better Bill. The politically difficult maneuver has taken most of Biden's first year in office, and much political capital, to reach a conclusion. While originally proposed as a $3.5 trillion spending bill, it has shrunk by 50% and now looks set to be worth $1.75 trillion. The social programs that have failed to make the final bill are not specifically focused on ecological issues, but many of the climate and clean energy policies have remained. The initial proposal earmarked $600 billion, while the current bill includes $555 billion for climate change. The main loss from the climate portion of the bill—after opposition from Senator Joe Manchin who represents the historic coal mining state of West Virginia—is a policy that would impose fines for utility companies that fail to switch to clean energy sources (The White House, 2021).

The ultimate bill that passes Congress will be smaller than Sanders' Green New Deal by a significant factor. Assuming the current bill of $1.75 trillion passes, it will amount to slightly more than 10% of the $16.5 trillion proposed by Sanders. Nevertheless, combined with the $1 trillion infrastructure bill, this amounts to around 13% of the US GDP. But there is still a great uncertainty about the conditions in which the plan will be adopted and even more so about the conditions in which it would be implemented. Europe has moved farther on both accounts, and the European Green Deal already appears as the model against which all other projects should be compared.

3.2 The European Green Deal

A reading of the text "The European Green Deal" (EGD) proposed by the European Commission (EC) on December 11, 2019, is edifying, more by its precision than by its scope. It does indeed contain the now usual "Green Deal" jargon, according to which it is about a "new growth strategy," which "aims to transform the EU into a just and prosperous society with a modern, resource-efficient and competitive economy, characterized by zero net GHG emissions by 2050 and in which economic growth will be decoupled from resource use." It also states that the strategy "also aims to protect, preserve and consolidate the EU's natural heritage, as well as to protect the health and well-being of citizens from environmental risks and impacts" and that "this transition must be fair and inclusive" (European Commission, 2019). Decarbonization of economies, climate neutrality, adaptation to climate change, transition to clean energy, fight against fuel poverty, circular economy, sustainable growth creating jobs, strategic security, digitalization in support of the protection of natural resources, decoupling between growth and environmental impacts, protection of biodiversity, etc. are there to describe European economies placed on a SD path.

If stuck to these generalities that have become almost commonplace, the EC text would be nothing more than an agreed-upon catalog of what it is desirable to do (or to dream about) to keep Europe (and the world) away from the prospects of a major ecological crisis. But it goes further, setting precise and ambitious quantified objectives in many areas. The one that has received the most attention is the increase of the GHG emission reduction target to 55% in 2030 compared to 1990 (a target finally adopted in June 2021), with a view to achieving climate neutrality by 2050, whereas at the time this strategy was proposed, the EU was on a 60% reduction trajectory by 2050, a considerable increase in its climate ambition.[6] But other objectives are just as ambitious: at least double the annual rate of retrofitting of the building stock from 0.4% to 1.2% in Member States; reduce GHG emissions from the transport sector by 90% by 2050; end fossil fuel subsidies; put into operation

[6]Not enough, however, to make it compatible with the 1.5 °C global warming target in the Paris Agreement, which is probably already out of reach. At a minimum, a 65% reduction in European emissions by 2030 would be needed to reach this goal (Storm, 2020).

nearly one million public charging and refueling stations for the 13 million zero- or low-emission vehicles expected on Europe's roads by 2025; invest 1.5% of the EU's annual GDP by 2030 to meet climate and energy targets; make the EU institutions themselves climate neutral by 2030, starting with the EC itself; etc.

The impression of ambition coupled with precision is even more pronounced when reading the National Recovery and Resilience Plans (NRRPs), the documents submitted by Member States for approval by the EU Council for the funds released under the NextGeneration EU (NGEU) plan, intended to help EU Member States to get out of the COVID crisis. The French plan (PNRR, 2021), approved on July 13, 2021, includes 815 pages of proposals with detailed milestones, targets, and timetables and detailed descriptions of costs and financing methods for the proposed measures, over the entire period of application of the strategy from 2021 to 2027, and in all areas concerned by the EGD.

The ambition is there, clearly stated, but we will have to wait for the results of this strategy to declare that it is indeed "Europe's man on the moon moment," as Ursula von der Leyen stated during her presentation of the EGD.

3.3 The Key Stake of Decoupling

The EGD is not in fact a recovery plan for the European economies in the classical sense of the term. A recovery plan aims to stimulate economic growth in times of crisis, to bring it back to a level as close as possible to the potential growth of the involved economy—this potential growth being the maximum level attainable in a situation of full employment of the available production resources. An economic crisis being characterized by a fall in effective growth below its potential level and by a sharp rise in unemployment, it is a question of filling the production gap by the so-called Keynesian measures to stimulate activity and bring down unemployment. This is not at all the case with the EGD, which, by the way, is not intended to reduce unemployment in Europe. Thanks to the employment protection measures put in place by EU member countries from the onset of the health crisis in 2020, unemployment has indeed not risen much in Europe, with a peak of 8.7% in the eurozone in September 2020, compared to 7.3% before the crisis, or 7.8 compared to 6.5% for the EU as a whole. Overall, the EU has returned to its pre-crisis GDP level by the third quarter of 2021, whereas it took 7 years to achieve the same recovery after the Great Recession of 2008–2009 (European Commission, 2022). The EGD has little to do with this; the credit goes to the unprecedented increases in public debt in all member countries. The real purpose of the EGD is to increase the EU's potential growth while decoupling it from its environmental impacts. This is the real ambition of the European plan: to create a new growth model based on decoupling.

The proponents of degrowth have been highly disappointed (Palahi et al., 2020; Ossewaarde & Ossewaarde-Lowtoo, 2020) and have not failed to express their frustration with a model that has no intention of challenging the foundations of the capitalist system established nearly four centuries ago. The SD according to the EGD is fed by technological progress, which is supposed to bring about an absolute decoupling between the continuation of economic development and the ecological footprint of activities,[7] whereas the proponents of degrowth consider that the decoupling can only be relative[8] and that SD can only be based on the moderation of needs and the means of satisfying them. A discussion of the notion of SD is beyond the scope of this contribution,[9] but it is a fact that, so far, no public institution in the world (let alone private) has chosen a SD strategy based on the notion of degrowth. One explanation may be that, by nature, moderation of needs can only be based on profound changes in individual preferences that cannot be imposed authoritatively, unless the foundations of political regimes are challenged. In fact, moderation is a choice made by a growing number of individuals (Büchs & Koch, 2019), although it is having a great difficulty in penetrating the field of public policy.

In any case, the EGD is betting on absolute decoupling, and a good part of the project's ambition lies in the idea that it can single-handedly put European economies on this SD trajectory, while the challenges to be met are considerable.

3.4 A Financial Challenge

The EGD is first and foremost a financial challenge. Achieving climate neutrality by mid-century, the central objective of the project, will require considerable investment. Is the EGD up to this challenge? The answer appears to be no, for two reasons: the sums involved in the plan proposed by the EC are insufficient to achieve the desired objectives, and the financial package proposed by the EC exaggerates these very sums.

On the first point, the EC estimates the investment gap to reach the objectives of the EGD by 2030 at 260 billion euros per year, a figure that several studies corroborate (Wolf et al., 2021). In other words, the additional investment effort to be made over the period 2020–2030 would be of the order of 2600 billion euros. But this estimate is in fact associated with the objective of reducing European GHG emissions by 40% by 2030 compared to 1990, an objective raised to 55% in the perspective of the EGD. The annual investment gap is therefore higher, estimated at 300–400 billion euros (Claeys et al., 2019) or 3000–4000 billion euros over the

[7] Absolute decoupling implies the possibility of increasing living standards while reducing the impacts of human activities in terms of resource extraction and environmental pollution.

[8] Relative decoupling implies an increase in living standards accompanied by a smaller increase in the associated extraction and pollution impacts.

[9] Let us just note here that there is a fundamental difference between extraction and pollution in terms of decoupling. Decoupling economic activity and environmental pollution is perfectly realistic, observable in many areas (Sanyé-Mengual et al., 2019), and at the very heart of the idea of decarbonizing economies. Decoupling economic activity from resource extraction is a completely different matter, and even the circular economy and the increasing dematerialization of activities are not certain to be able to solve it.

period in question.[10] The EC plan foresees "only" 1000 billion over the same period, a small part of the necessary sum.

This sum itself seems out of reach, as it does not really constitute additional efforts. The EC plan is presented as an additional investment effort of 1000 billion euros over the period 2020–2030. Half of this sum is supposed to come from the European budget, the part of which devoted to climate objectives is supposed to increase by 20–25%; but a budgetary sleight of hand, or more simply semantics, makes us consider this 25% as an additional contribution to the effort made, whereas it is really an additional effort of 5% compared to what was already planned. The remaining 500 billion euros of the additional investment effort would come from the following sources (not counting the Just Transition Fund, to which we will return later): private co-financing attracted by guarantees provided by the European Investment Bank (EIB), along the lines of the Juncker plan launched in 2015 (279 billion euros), public co-financing from national budgets (114 billion euros), and an increase in the EU's own resources through the auctioning of tradable emissions permits on the carbon market (25 billion euros). Here again, the sums seem overly optimistic: the Juncker plan is far from having proven itself in terms of additionality (Roggenbuck & Sol, 2019, more on this later); there is no reason to believe that member countries will mechanically increase investments compatible with the EGD without any change in the EU's fiscal rules (Claeys et al., 2019); the revenues from the sale of permits on the carbon market depend on their price, which cannot be anticipated with certainty since they are determined by the functioning of this market.

In total, the sums allocated by the EU to the EGD will be far from the estimated efforts needed to achieve its objectives. This remains true even if we add the contributions of the European recovery plan adopted on July 21, 2020, NGEU, with a view to helping EU member countries emerge from the COVID-19 crisis. This 750 billion euros plan, spread over the EU's 2021–2027 budgetary period, is the first European recovery plan based on a mutualized budgetary effort and financed by public debt issues by the EC, thus in a collective form and no longer on the basis of public debt issuance by Member States. Another major novelty of this plan is that part of the budgetary envelope (390 of the 750 billion euros) will be paid out in the form of grants, not loans, to the Member States. NGEU is a major step in the reform of the EU's economic governance; in terms of contribution to the EGD, it must dedicate at least 37% of the planned sums to ecological objectives, mainly climate. The additional resources are significant, but do not cover the total estimated cost of the EGD.

The missing sums will have to come from two alternative sources: complementary contributions from the Member States and, above all, private investment.

---

[10] By considering a linear relationship between the decarbonization of economies and necessary investment while it is known that the marginal cost of reducing GHG emissions is increasing, the more advanced decarbonization is, the more expensive it is to obtain an additional unit of decarbonization. This means that the required investment estimates are most likely optimistic.

3.5 Additional Contributions Are Essential

For the former, it is essential that the EU's budgetary/fiscal rules are to be adjusted in order to strengthen the capacity of Member States to invest in the ecological transition. The main avenues lie in the European Semester,[11] which, through country-specific recommendations, makes it possible to direct national public spending toward common objectives such as the energy transition, and above all in the relaxation of fiscal constraints in the eurozone (suspended for the moment, but which will return to the negotiating table once the COVID-19 crisis is over), which should be developed toward an exemption from the rule of structural budgetary balance in the medium term for national public investments compatible with the EGD. This latter adjustment would be perfectly justified by the fact that the investments in question are associated with a relatively high Keynesian multiplier[12] and that they generate benefits that are likely to cover all or part of the initial costs,[13] to the advantage of national budgets.

Regarding private investment, the co-financing mentioned above will play a decisive role and is expected to be an essential part of the project. In this respect, InvestEU will take over from the Juncker plan in 2021. The latter, adopted under the Juncker presidency of the EC (2014–2019), was intended to help boost the recovery of European economies hit by the eurozone crisis of 2010–2012, through a system of guarantees provided by the EIB to particularly risky projects. InvestEU should continue this scheme by focusing on projects compatible with the EGD. The effectiveness of the Juncker plan has been questioned by the European Court of Auditors itself, which found that it had attracted some investments (estimated at one third of the total) that would have been financed anyway without its existence (European Court of Auditors, 2019). This condition of additionality is essential to close the investment gap mentioned above and to avoid what is known in macroeconomics as a crowding out of private spending by public spending, in this case rather a crowding out of private investment by other investments supported by a public scheme. However, it is difficult to guarantee, and certain conditions must be met so that InvestEU does not fall into the same trap, mainly a strengthening of the additionality criteria and a systematic verification that the selected projects have no

[11] Introduced in the aftermath of the eurozone crisis to reinforce the budgetary and economic coordination within the EU, it makes it compulsory for EU Member States to present their national budget plans regularly to the EC in order to make sure they are in line with the commonly adopted rules.

[12] This multiplier calculates the magnitude of an increase in GDP generated by the injection of public spending into economic activity. It is estimated, for example, that investments in renewable energy are associated with a multiplier of around 1.1–1.5, compared to 0.5–0.6 for investments in fossil fuels (Batini et al., 2021).

[13] Among these benefits is, for example, the fact that switching to a fully renewable energy mix eliminates the need to import fossil fuels, a gain estimated at the EU level at 2000 billion euros over the period of the EGD (not even counting the benefits in terms of energy security, which cannot be calculated in monetary terms).

other financing options. Another major flaw must be avoided in the Juncker plan which, according to the data provided by the EIB itself before the health crisis broke out (EIB, 2018), was expected to have its maximum impact in 2020–2021, i.e., 6 years after its conception and almost 12 years after the start of the crisis that justified its creation, a time lag that is problematic, to say the least, for a recovery plan.

The EIB's role will be decisive in attracting private investment. To achieve this, it is planned to gradually transform itself into a climate bank, by ceasing to finance projects linked to fossil fuels and by increasing the share of its financing devoted to investments supporting the EGD from 28% to 50%, with the remainder going to projects compatible with the decarbonization objective.

From the point of view of the selection of investments eligible for co-financing, the EC's recent decision on the taxonomy for sustainable activities remains highly controversial. After lengthy negotiations, it finally proposes[14] to include some nuclear and gas infrastructure under certain conditions.[15] The issues related to either of these two energy sources in relation to the EGD are radically different. Adopting gas as a transitional energy source runs the risk of leaving part of the energy system locked into gas-related assets over the life cycle of the plants concerned, slowing the potential pace of transition to renewables in view of the 2050 carbon neutrality objective. On the other hand, without gas for this transition effort, there is a risk of having to face higher electricity access costs in the short term, which would also slow down the pace of the transition. In terms of electricity production, the larger the share of intermittent renewables (solar and wind) in the energy mix, the more baseload production capacity becomes an unavoidable constraint in the absence of large-scale storage or long-distance electricity transmission capacity. In this case, gas is the unavoidable candidate, along with nuclear power (Helm, 2022). It is a question of costs and decarbonization trajectory, and only a detailed assessment of these issues will allow to form an informed opinion (Gürsan & de Gooyert, 2021). The choice of nuclear power poses other, entirely different problems, linked to the safety of waste treatment, since it is given that its contribution to the decarbonization of the energy mix can only be positive, but at a cost that has recently become higher (Schneider & Froggatt, 2019) than that of intermittent renewables. The impact of this European taxonomy (which is likely to be adopted following the consultation of the European Council and Parliament) on the implementation of the EGD is impossible to anticipate. The future will determine the validity of this choice. It is certain, however, that it will have repercussions beyond the EU, as it appears to be a standard to which other comparable programs will probably refer (The Economist, 2022).

[14] The revision of the taxonomy received the EC approval on February 2, 2022.

[15] For nuclear facilities on condition that the conditions for the final disposal of their radioactive waste are guaranteed for 2050. For gas-fired power plants on condition that they commit to switching to renewable gas sources by 2035.

3.6 An Institutional Challenge for the EU

The EGD was proposed by the EC and supported by other EU institutions, but its success depends on the cooperation of the Member States, not least because competences are shared in all areas covered by the EGD. In the area of carbon emissions, for example, the EU can set collective guidelines for energy efficiency or vehicle emissions standards, but choices such as the energy mix or energy taxation are left to the Member States. The success of the EGD will largely depend on their commitment to its implementation, and, in this case, there are still significant differences from one state to another.

The Green Recovery Tracker (2021) provides a detailed analysis of this commitment in terms of how states are using the NGEU funds in line with the targets set by the EC, including the target of spending at least 37% of the funds on investments contributing to the EGD. By the end of 2021, the EC had approved 22 recovery plans submitted by Member States, of which EGD-compatible spending represented between 14% (Greece) and 42% (Finland) of the planned envelope. Of course, the release of the NGEU funds is conditional on meeting the 37% target set by the EC, but the implementation of the scheme is likely to be fraught with difficult negotiations, not to mention the specific difficulties concerning Poland and Hungary, as the EU Court of Justice recently validated the mechanism that makes the payment of EU funds conditional on the respect of the rule of law in these countries (COJ of the EU, 2022).

Clearly, the existence of the Just Transition Fund (see below), which provides for financial compensation for regions and sectors affected by the EGD, will not be enough to win Member States' support for the project. This is especially true since it falls far short of the estimated financial needs to compensate for the losses in the involved countries. The estimated losses in the coal sector in Eastern European countries alone (only a fraction of the total estimated impacts) amount to 130 billion euros, an amount that is already higher than the overall package (Storm, 2020).

4 Aligning Individual Incentives with Long-Term Objectives

It is clear that a massive transformation of economic systems, particularly energy systems, can only be based on a joint evolution of all production and resource use behaviors, in all strata of the economies. Private investment by companies and individuals (in housing) must therefore accompany the movement driven by public investment in infrastructure of all kinds. This concerns, if we take the example of energy systems, heating and insulation of buildings, individual and collective modes of transport, industrial and agricultural production processes, carbon capture and storage capacities (still embryonic), etc. At the very least, these changes require an alignment of individual incentives with long-term objectives, and, in this case, the essential parameter is carbon pricing[16] (not to mention methane, the other key GHG for climate neutrality), which must make it possible to internalize the environmental and social costs of climate change, in order to put all investment decisions involving carbon emissions on an equal footing, regardless of their intensity. This pricing can be based on taxing emissions or trading them on a dedicated market.

A carbon market, the Emissions Trading System (ETS), already covers nearly half of the EU's annual emissions, and the EGD plans to strengthen the mechanism in several ways: further lowering the overall emissions cap and raising its annual reduction rate, phasing out free emissions allowances for aviation, including shipping emissions in the ETS, and creating a new, separate emissions trading scheme for road transport fuel distribution and buildings (the two sectors in which there have been no recent emissions reductions). Taxing energy for environmental purposes is not part of the EU's remit, and it can only make recommendations in this case. The EGD proposes revising the Energy Taxation Directive to align energy product taxation with EU energy and climate policies, a cautious formulation, to say the least, that reflects the sensitivity of such measures, as illustrated by the Yellow Jackets uprising in France prior to the outbreak of the COVID-19 pandemic.

Any alignment of market incentives designed to accelerate the green transition involves losers, for two reasons essentially. The first is that this alignment increases the price of resources and activities responsible for the ecological crisis and that this increase is likely to have distributional effects to the detriment of individuals at the bottom of the income scale.[17] The second is that the transition leads to a loss of income and employment for those it penalizes. The EGD provides for compensation systems which are essential to ensure the participation of all the related actors. The Just Transition Mechanism provides for financial transfers to the regions and sectors most affected by the energy transition, such as the coal-mining regions in Poland (EC, 2020). It would be possible to go further by targeting the lowest individual incomes more directly, as is the practice in Switzerland and Canada, for example (Bureau et al., 2019), but this does not fall within the EU's competence.

5 The Need for International Cooperation

Beyond the EU, the success of the EGD will depend on its ability to draw in the wake of non-European actors. Achieving climate neutrality in the middle of the century at the European level will not solve the problem if the rest of the world does not follow the same trajectory, which is obvious in the case of a global public good such as the climate (the same observation applies to some extent to biodiversity as well). Europe

---

[16] The key parameter for the success of any decarbonization strategy for many economists, although there is still debate on this issue (Patt & Lilliestam, 2018).

[17] For example, the consumption of fossil fuels represents a larger share of the budget of the most modest households.

represents only about 9% of global GHG emissions, so its contribution to the stabilization of climate change is limited to this fraction. Of course, some of the benefits of reducing the impacts of the ecological crisis through the EGD will be strictly European, such as increasing the continent's energy security or market positioning on green technologies. But the main benefits, i.e., the purely environmental ones, are shared with the rest of the world, which implies that a European strategy, however ambitious and effective, cannot be the master of its own destiny in this area.

The project presented by the EC obviously considers this dimension of the European strategy and proposes ways to make the EU a pole of attraction in terms of ecological ambition, mainly four: the diplomatic path of environmental partnerships, aid for ecologically responsible development, bilateral trade negotiations that allow for the integration of ecological criteria, and production of exportable environmental standards (Hege, 2020). But there is no doubt that the main incentive must come from a constraint imposed on external actors, and, in this case, the main instrument is the carbon border adjustment mechanism, a tax on imported products calculated according to their carbon intensity, which is supposed to prevent carbon leakage to trading partners and protect European producers from unfair competition.[18] The scheme is under consideration, and the way it is designed and implemented will have a decisive impact on its economic and environmental effectiveness, as well as on its compatibility with multilateral trade rules imposed by the WTO (Mehling et al., 2019).

The EU's ability to leverage international cooperation is limited to the incentive instruments at its disposal. The EGD will have potentially profound geopolitical implications for EU relations with the rest of the world (Leonard et al., 2021), but its environmental impacts will remain dependent on the efforts that other countries are willing to make beyond the continent's borders. We have seen that the principle of the Green Deal is beginning to gain ground here and there. Many countries have now set a target of carbon neutrality by mid-century, but the gaps between promises and actions are still too wide to ensure that the Paris Agreement's climate target will be met (Climate Action Tracker, 2022). In this, the EGD may carry an additional responsibility, as its success may determine the willingness of other countries to follow Europe's lead.

[18] A joint effect, often forgotten, is that European consumers stop exporting part of their ecological footprint by importing goods associated with lower environmental standards than those in the EU, especially in the agricultural sector (Fuchs et al., 2020).

6 Conclusion

Will Green Deals save capitalism from ecological collapse? It would probably be giving them too much importance to answer in the affirmative to such a dramatic question. The ecological transition that must make human activities compatible with the limits imposed by the Earth's systems, if it is to happen, will be a planetary, multi-decadal process, involving all consumers and producers of resources derived from the transformation of natural resources. Such a process cannot be based exclusively on a plan devised by governments, however ambitious. Markets will have to contribute fully to this fundamental reorientation of individual and collective behaviors, and, beyond that, a fundamental change in these behaviors will be needed to bring about this change in the trajectory of the global economic system.

Green Deals can show the way and provide the initial impetus to launch the overall movement. Europe and perhaps soon the USA have begun a process whose outcome will have profound impacts on the way the ecological transition is conceived and implemented. The failure of this process would certainly be a catastrophe for the sustainability of modern economic systems. But its success would not necessarily be a guarantee that these systems could escape the looming ecological crises. The future will give its verdict on the validity of the experiment.

References

American Congress. (2019). *Resolution to recognize the duty of the federal government to create a Green New Deal, 116th congress, 1st session*. https://www.congress.gov/bill/116th-congress/house-resolution/109

Baechler, L. (2021). *D'un plan de relance à l'autre : ce qui a changé en dix ans*. CIFE policy paper, no: 119. https://www.cife.eu/Ressources/FCK/files/publications/policy%20paper/2021/CIFE_Baechler_crise_2021.pdf

Batini, N., di Serio, M., Fragetta, M., Melina, G., & Waldron, A. (2021). *Building back better: How big are green spending multipliers?* IMF working paper, no: 21/87. https://www.imf.org/en/Publications/WP/Issues/2021/03/19/Building-Back-Better-How-Big-Are-Green-Spending-Multipliers-50264

Büchs, M., & Koch, M. (2019). Challenges for the degrowth transition: The debate about wellbeing. *Futures, 105*, 155–165. https://doi.org/10.1016/j.futures.2018.09.002

Bureau, D., Henriet, F., & Schubert, K. (2019). *A proposal for the climate: Taxing carbon not people*. Notes du conseil d'analyse économique, no: 50. https://doi.org/10.3917/ncae.050.0001

Claeys, G., Tagliapietra, S., & Zachmann, G. (2019). *How to make the European Green Deal work*. Bruegel policy contribution, no: 14/2019. https://www.bruegel.org/wp-content/uploads/2019/11/PC-13_2019-151119.pdf

Climate Action Tracker. (2022). https://climateactiontracker.org/climate-target-update-tracker/

Court of Justice of the European Union. (2022). *Press release n° 28/22*. https://curia.europa.eu/jcms/upload/docs/application/pdf/2022-02/cp220028en.pdf

European Investment Bank. (2018). *Assessing the macroeconomic impact of the EIB Group*. https://www.eib.org/en/publications/assessing-the-macroeconomic-impact-of-the-eib-group

European Commission. (2019). *Communication from the Commission*. The European Green Deal. https://eur-lex.europa.eu/legal-content/EN/TXT/HTML/?uri=CELEX:52019DC0640&from=FR

European Commission. (2020). *The just transition mechanism: Making sure no one is left behind*. https://ec.europa.eu/info/strategy/priorities-2019-2024/european-green-deal/finance-and-green-deal/just-transition-mechanism_en

European Commission. (2022). *Winter 2022 economist forecast*. https://ec.europa.eu/commission/presscorner/detail/en/ip_22_926

European Court of Auditors. (2019, January 24). *European fund for strategic investments: Action needed to make EFSI a full success*. Special report 03. https://www.eca.europa.eu/fr/Pages/NewsItem.aspx?nid=11605

Friedman, T. L. (2007, April 15). The power of green. *The New York Times*. https://www.nytimes.com/2007/04/15/opinion/15iht-web-0415edgreen-full.5291830.html

Fuchs, R., Brown, C., & Rounsevell, M. (2020, October 26). Europe's Green Deal offshores environmental damages to other nations. *Nature*. https://www.nature.com/articles/d41586-020-02991-1

Green Recovery Tracker. (2021). *EU recovery: How green is recovery spending in different sectors?* https://assets.website-files.com/602e4a891047f739eaf5dfad/61c1c72f2784e84b32f53998_GRT_2021_FACTSHEET_20211221.pdf

Gürsan, C., & de Gooyert, V. (2021). The systemic impact of a transition fuel: Does natural gas help or hinder the energy transition? *Renewable and Sustainable Energy Reviews, 138*, 110552. https://doi.org/10.1016/j.rser.2020.110552

Hege, E. (2020, March 24). Can the Green Deal be the core of the EU's project for its external partnerships? *IDDRI Blog Post*. https://www.iddri.org/en/publications-and-events/blog-post/can-green-deal-be-core-eus-project-its-external-partnerships

Helm, D. (2022). *The first net zero energy crisis: Someone has to pay*. http://www.dieterhelm.co.uk/assets/secure/documents/The-first-net-zero-energy-crisis-someone-has-to-pay-7.01.22.pdf

International Energy Agency. (2020). *Green stimulus after the 2008 crisis*. IEA. https://www.iea.org/articles/green-stimulus-after-the-2008-crisis

International Energy Agency. (2021). *Key world energy statistics 2021*. https://www.iea.org/reports/key-world-energy-statistics-2021/supply

Keynes, J. M. (1933). *An open letter to President Roosevelt*. http://la.utexas.edu/users/hcleaver/368/368KeynesOpenLetFDRtable.pdf

Leonard, M., Pisani-Ferry, J., Shapiro, J., Tagliapietra, S., & Wolff, G. (2021). *The geopolitics of the European Green Deal*. Bruegel policy contribution, no: 04/2021. https://www.bruegel.org/wp-content/uploads/2021/02/PC-04-GrenDeal-2021-1.pdf

Maddison, A. (2006). *The world economy, Vol. 2: Historical statistics*. OECD. https://www.rug.nl/ggdc/historicaldevelopment/maddison/original-maddison

Malthus, T. R. (1798). *An essay on the principle of population*. McMaster University Archive for the History of Economic Thought.

Marx, K. (1887). *Capital: A critique of political economy. Volume 1, The process of production capital*. Progress Publishers.

Mehling, M., Van Asselt, H., Das, K., Droege, S., & Verkuijl, C. (2019). Designing border carbon adjustments for enhanced climate action. *American Journal of International Law, 113*(3), 433–481. https://doi.org/10.1017/ajil.2019.22

Ossewaarde, M., & Ossewaarde-Lowtoo, R. (2020). The EU's Green Deal: A third alternative to green growth and degrowth? *Sustainability, 12*(23), 9825. https://www.mdpi.com/2071-1050/12/23/9825/htm

Palahi, M., Hetemäki, L., & Potocnik, J. (2020). *Bioeconomy: The missing link to connect the dots in the EU Green Deal*. Blog. https://blog.efi.int/bioeconomy-the-missing-link-to-connect-the-dots-in-the-eu-green-deal/

Patt, A., & Lilliestam, J. (2018). The case against carbon prices. *Joule, 2*(2), 2494–2498. https://doi.org/10.1016/j.joule.2018.11.018

Plan National de Relance et de Résilience. (2021). https://www.economie.gouv.fr/files/files/directions_services/plan-de-relance/PNRR%20Francais.pdf
Pigou, A. C. (1920). *The economics of welfare*. Macmillan.
Rockström, J., Steffen, W., Noone, K., Persson, A., Chapin, F. S., Lambin, E., Lenton, T. M., Scheffer, M., Folke, C., Schellnhuber, H., Nykvist, B., De Wit, C. A., Hughes, T., van der Leeuw, S., Rodhe, H., Sörlin, S., Snyder, P. K., Costanza, R., Svedin, U., et al. (2009). Planetary boundaries: Exploring the safe operating space for humanity. *Ecology and Society, 14*(2) http://www.ecologyandsociety.org/vol14/iss2/art32/
Roggenbuck, A., & Sol, X. (2019). *The investment plan for Europe – A critical analysis of the pilot phase of the "Juncker Plan"*. Bankwatch Network. https://bankwatch.org/wp-content/uploads/2019/09/EFSI-final.pdf
Sanyé-Mengual, E., Secchi, M., Corrado, S., Beylot, A., & Sala, S. (2019). Assessing the decoupling of economic growth from environmental impacts in the European Union: A consumption-based approach. *Journal of Cleaner Production, 236*, 117535. https://doi.org/10.1016/j.jclepro.2019.07.010
Schneider, M., & Froggatt, A. (2019). *World nuclear industry status report*. https://www.researchgate.net/publication/336870789_The_World_Nuclear_Industry_Status_Report_2019
Smil, V. (2017). *Energy and civilization: A history*. The MIT Press.
Steffen, W., Grinevald, J., Crutzen, P., & McNeill, J. (2011). The Anthropocene: Conceptual and historical perspectives. *Philosophical Transactions of the Royal Society, 369*, 842–867. https://doi.org/10.1098/rsta.2010.0327
Storm, S. (2020). *The EU's Green Deal: Bismarck's "what is possible" versus Thunberg's "what is imperative"*. Institute for New Economic Thinking working paper, no: 17. https://www.ineteconomics.org/uploads/papers/WP_117-Storm-Green-Deal.pdf
The White House. (2021). *The build back better framework*. https://www.whitehouse.gov/build-back-better/
The Economist. (2022, January 8). The EU's green-investing taxonomy could go global. *The Economist*. https://www.economist.com/finance-and-economics/2022/01/08/the-eus-green-investing-taxonomy-could-go-global
Wolf, S., Teitge, J., & Mielke, J. (2021). The European Green Deal: More than climate neutrality. *Intereconomics, 56*, 99–107. https://doi.org/10.1007/s10272-021-0963-z

Green Technology and Smart Solutions for Capitalist Cities in the Twenty-First Century

Selin Calik

Abstract In the twentieth century, capitalist countries developed a model of urbanization that was based on industrialization, mass consumption, and the growth of large cities. The twenty-first century is characterized by environmental problems, especially climate change. In this context, sustainable development has emerged as a new paradigm for urban planning and design. A sustainable city is one that can meet the needs of its population in terms of social equity, economic prosperity, and environmental conservation. Green technology is the future of smart cities. Green technology will help us to solve many problems related to our environment. We need green technology to improve our cities and make them cleaner and better places to live. Green technology can also help us to create new jobs, reduce pollution, and increase productivity. The green revolution not only will improve our environment but also will help us to save money on electricity bills. In this paper, I examine how we can use green technology to make smart cities more efficient, productive, and better places to live. Smart cities use data and information technology to provide efficient services and solutions for their citizens. They are also sustainable, which means they have efficient resources and infrastructure that can be used with little or no harm to the environment. Smart cities can also be developed with green technology or technology that helps reduce pollution, waste, and energy consumption. The goal of green technology is to create sustainable environments where people live in harmony with nature.

Keywords Smart solutions · Smart cities · Green technology · Capitalism

1 Introduction

A smart city is a city that uses information and communication technology (ICT) to improve the efficiency of government services, increase urban productivity, manage sustainable development, and ultimately enhance citizens' life. These cities will also

S. Calik (✉)
London Institute of Directors, London, UK

A. Ari (ed.), *Capitalism at a Crossroads*, Springer Studies in Alternative Economics,
https://doi.org/10.1007/978-3-031-23257-2_17

have an integrated urban system, which includes 5G mobile networks, cloud computing, and data analytics. The term "smart city" was first used by the US Department of Commerce in its 2002 report titled "Building a Smarter Infrastructure for America's Economic Growth." In this report, it was mentioned that a smart city should be able to provide intelligent transportation systems and emergency response systems. Today, more people are talking about how to build a smarter infrastructure for America's economic growth.

Ahvenniemi et al. (2017) found that there was not a clear definition of what the term smart city means. They suggested that "smart city" should be used to describe an urban area that has invested in new technologies to improve the quality of life in the city. The authors also stated that there are many definitions of what a smart city is, and they suggest using multiple definitions so that we can better understand how our cities will change over time as technology advances and becomes more affordable to use in our daily lives. Smart cities can be found across the world from Singapore to New York City with many different approaches being taken by each. These cities are collecting data from sensors around town such as traffic signs or air quality monitors so they can better understand how their citizens are using transportation systems or if there are any environmental issues that need to be addressed like pollution in the air or water pollution caused by storm runoff. The twenty-first century is the era of technology. The development of technology is so fast that it changes the world. It has a great impact on our daily life. A smart city is a new concept that makes use of smart technology to improve the quality of life. It proposes an idea of sustainable urban development, using ICTs to enhance the efficiency and effectiveness of urban services through integration with other modes of transport, energy and water supply, environment monitoring, and management.

A city can be considered smart if it has the following characteristics:

- There is an effective use of technology which includes but is not limited to the Internet connection, digital payment systems, etc.
- The city has high-quality infrastructure, i.e., good roads, cleanliness, etc.
- It has efficient public transport systems such as trains, buses, etc.
- There are green spaces like parks, etc., where people can go out for recreation or just relax after work hours.

The idea of smart economies has been discussed since the 1990s. It was initially used in reference to advanced countries such as Japan and Germany, but it later became popular in developing countries such as China and India (Abdoullaev, 2011). In these countries, the term "smart economy" is often used interchangeably with "knowledge economy" or "creative economy." In recent years, governments have started to realize that ICT can be used as an effective tool for improving efficiency as well as for providing better services for citizens (Abdoullaev, 2011). However, most smart city initiatives still lack clear strategies and are often limited to isolated projects with little impact on the overall development of their regions.

This study shall be based mainly on the following research questions: What does it take to build a smart city? What makes it different from any other type of city? What challenges do planners face when designing these new communities?

The purpose of this study is to analyze the challenges and opportunities of green technology in capitalist cities. With the increasing demand for green solutions, there are a number of challenges that need to be overcome. The study uses an urban planning perspective to identify these challenges and opportunities. There are two main parts of this study: (1) analysis of challenges and (2) analysis of opportunities. In the first part, challenges are identified as social, economic, and political barriers to green technology implementation. These barriers are examined in terms of their causes, consequences, and implications for future policymaking. In the second part, opportunities are identified as market forces that may drive green technology adoption processes toward sustainability goals. These include demographic trends such as aging populations and emerging technologies such as solar energy.

2 Smart Economy

The smart economy is a digital economy that uses data to drive decisions, improve operations, and create value. It is the next step in digital transformation that unlocks new business opportunities, improves customer experience, drives innovation, and facilitates collaboration. The wealthy economy approach is an approach to urban development and planning, and it aims to provide policymakers with a more holistic understanding of cities as complex systems by combining insights from economics, sociology, and political science. This chapter explores how this approach can be used to develop green technologies for capitalist cities in the twenty-first century.

The wealthy economy approach has been developed within the framework of sustainability theory which argues that environmental degradation is caused by the interaction between economic growth, population growth, and technological development (Turner & Khondker, 2010). Under this theory, it is assumed that environmental problems are caused by capitalism because it has led to excessive consumption of natural resources and pollution which have resulted in climate change, biodiversity loss, etc. However, this theory does not explain how these problems could be resolved through sustainable development policies.

The Bennett Institute of Public Policy's "The Wealth Economy" project argues that the current economic model is not sustainable (Zenghelis et al., 2020). The authors argue that it is time for the UK to shift its focus toward a more sustainable model of growth. They suggest that this should be done by promoting green technologies and innovation in order to boost productivity. They also note that this will require a change in focus from consumption to investment and savings.

The wealthy economy approach is based on three principles:

- An economy should be designed for all people and future generations.
- It should be resilient against shocks from climate change and other sources.
- It should be fair so that everyone benefits from economic growth.

Lord Turnbull believes that the best way to achieve this shift is through an increase in productivity by using smart technologies such as artificial intelligence

(AI) and robotics. This would allow businesses and entrepreneurs to use their resources more efficiently while allowing them to cut down on costs associated with labor such as healthcare, pensions, or unemployment benefits. In addition, it would also reduce emissions from transport which accounts for almost half of all emissions since 1990 according to Lord Turnbull's report on the wealthy economy approach. The report also mentions that there has been a rise in automation, especially in manufacturing industries where robots have been replacing humans for years now due to their efficiency compared with human workers who are limited.

The literature review conducted by Basiri et al. (2017) shows that smart economies will be achieved through various approaches such as:

- Smart meters (for electricity generation), which can be used to control energy production and consumption efficiently, thus reducing energy costs and waste generation rates.
- Smart grids (for electricity distribution), which can be used to manage electricity distribution networks efficiently.
- Smart buildings (for water supply), which can monitor water use and detect leaks.
- Intelligent transportation systems (ITS), which can detect traffic flow patterns and autonomously redirect traffic flows during peak times.
- Smart parking systems.

To understand how a smart economy can benefit you, we must first understand what it means to be "smart." In the next section, we look at the concept of smart cities and how they can benefit from a smart economy.

3 Smart Cities and Smart Solutions

Smart solutions are the key to a sustainable future. The following literature provides a broad overview of the concept of smart cities, green technology, and sustainable development. Development (sustainable development) is an essential read for anyone interested in the future of cities, sustainability, and climate change mitigation. The urbanization represents one of the most pressing environmental challenges we face today and that cities must become sustainable if we are to maintain a habitable planet for future generations. It discussed on how urbanization can be made more sustainable through the application of new technologies such as smart grids and smart buildings; however, these technologies will not be sufficient without a radical transformation in how we live our lives as individuals within these urban environments.

In his paper, Abdoullaev (2011) argued that the world is moving toward a smart economy. He highlighted that the world population will increase substantially in the next few decades, leading to an increase in demand for goods and services. He argued further that there has been a shift in emphasis from material goods to information and knowledge-based products. He noted that this shift has been made possible due to changes in technology which have facilitated the development of new materials such as fiber optics and semiconductors.

Green technology is defined as a technology that reduces or eliminates negative environmental impact (Jackson & Victor, 2011). Green technology can be used in any field of science and sector such as agriculture, construction, manufacturing, and transportation among others. The main objective of using this type of technology is to leverage impacts negatively imposed on the environment by utilizing renewable resources rather than nonrenewable resources. It also aims at reducing waste by recycling materials or reusing them in another form (Jackson & Victor, 2011).

In the twenty-first century, cities are becoming more and more important in our lives. The global population is expected to reach ten billion by 2050, and the urbanization rate has increased rapidly in recent years, which means that more and more people have migrated to cities. The number of people living in cities has reached around 59% of the total population worldwide. It is estimated that this figure will reach 70% by 2050 (The Economist Intelligence Unit, 2017). The increase in population has led to an increase in energy consumption and carbon emissions from transportation. With a growing number of vehicles on the road and increasing traffic congestion, many cities have become increasingly polluted environments. In order to solve this problem and improve air quality, we need green technology for capitalist cities in the twenty-first century. Green technology refers to any technology that lowers the negative impacts on the environment by reducing the carbon footprint while providing solutions for our daily needs. Hence, it can ensure development that can sustain the inhabitants.

3.1 Smart Mobility and Transportation

Smart mobility, the next generation of transportation, is a journey that has already begun. It started with ride-hailing services like Uber and Lyft and has now moved to autonomous vehicles (AVs). As we move closer to a world where people do not need to drive or own cars anymore, it will be vital that cities are prepared to support this new way of life. Smart mobility will allow us to be more productive in our day-to-day lives by giving us more time to work and play while reducing congestion on our roads. We can also expect a reduction in CO2 emissions as the number of vehicles on the road decreases.

The mobility and transportation sector is one of the largest industries in the world, with a global market value of $7 trillion. The sector is also undergoing profound changes, driven by new technologies, shifting demographics, and changing lifestyles. Mobility and transportation are the keystones of economic growth. They provide access to goods, services, and jobs and create opportunities for trade and investment.

Smart mobility will help achieve sustainable development goals (SDGs) such as poverty eradication and gender equality. It will also contribute to climate change mitigation by reducing emissions and improving air quality through cleaner energy sources. Thanks to new technologies, we are now able to access transportation services at the touch of a button from anywhere in the world, at any time of day. We can also share rides with strangers and track our movements through GPS. These new technologies are disrupting the way people get around and redefining how we think about transportation. Smart mobility represents the next step in this evolution, as it uses data and analytics to provide a seamless experience for customers and drivers. But what exactly is smart mobility? And how does it differ from traditional mobility?

Smart mobility refers to a new class of products and services that help people get around more easily by improving their experience with public transit, taxi cabs, ride-sharing apps, and other forms of transportation. It considers data such as traffic patterns, weather conditions, and ridership numbers to optimize routing decisions and maximize efficiency for passengers and drivers alike. For example, if there is an accident on a major highway during rush hour traffic, smart mobility technology would reroute passengers away from that area so they can reach their destinations faster, or if there is less demand for rides during certain times of day, it would adjust its schedule accordingly.

3.2 Smart Energy

Smart energy refers to energy systems that can be controlled remotely, monitored, and managed by a computer or other device. The concept of smart energy is not new, but it has gained momentum in recent years due to its potential benefits to society.

It is estimated that worldwide sales of smart meters will reach $45 billion by 2024 (Al-Wakeel et al., 2016). It has been suggested that an efficient implementation of smart meters can lead to lower costs through reduced peak demand charges and reduced line losses during low-load periods. Smart meters also allow consumers to monitor their energy usage more accurately which leads them to use less energy per unit time than before they had access to these devices. Green technology can be applied to all areas of life, including energy consumption, and manufacturing processes. With the increasing population of cities and the growing demand for power, there is a need for sustainable energy that can be accessed by all people around the world. The use of green technology has proven to be cost-effective in saving money on utility bills, as well as reducing pollution levels in our environment. Smart technologies such as smart meters allow us to monitor our electricity usage and change our habits accordingly so we can avoid high bills at home or the workplace when possible.

Green technology is the generation of electricity from renewable sources such as solar, wind, hydro, and geothermal energies. The use of green technology is an effective way to reduce carbon emissions and help protect the environment. Green technology is being used more and more around the world to reduce air pollution and greenhouse gases produced by fossil fuels. We are looking at various aspects of green technology to include smart solutions for our future cities. Green economics is also sometimes called "clean capitalism."

Proponents argue that it will create more jobs than it eliminates by making the industry more efficient and eliminating waste. Opponents argue that it will require substantial changes in current forms of ownership or property rights that may be politically infeasible. Green technology has been used by many industries to reduce energy consumption and carbon emissions, but there are still many challenges to solve. The main challenge is how to make green technology affordable and accessible to all. If we want green technology to be more widespread, we need to find a way to make it more affordable for everyone.

According to a report from Bloomberg New Energy Finance (BNEF), "The cost of producing electricity from renewable sources such as solar, wind and hydroelectric power fell last year by 6 percent compared with 2016—down to $120 per megawatt-hour in 2021 terms—according to BNEF's latest New Energy Outlook (NEO). That is down from $126/MWh in 2017 and $220/MWh in 2020 terms." The report also shows that by 2040, solar will be cheaper than coal or gas in most places around the world including Europe and parts of Asia, while wind energy is already cheaper than coal in many places including China, India, and Brazil. Natural gas will remain competitive with rooftop solar until at least 2040 because it is cheaper than battery storage right now.

3.3 *Smart Grid and Intelligent Lighting*

The idea of a smart grid is not new, but it has been gaining momentum over recent years. A smart grid has been described as a system that enables a two-way communication between electricity generators, distributors, and consumers. Most of the time, the term refers to a network that can use digital technology to collect data from many points in the network and then use this information to help balance supply and demand in real time. A smart grid is a network of computerized devices that can connect to a power source. The smart grid network works with different devices such as sensors, meters, storage devices, microprocessors, etc. This technology is used to monitor and control the power distribution system. It helps in reducing energy losses by monitoring energy usage. A smart grid also helps in reducing greenhouse gas emissions by providing more efficient use of energy resources.

The smart grid relies on ICT to support advanced energy management, including a two-way communication between utilities and consumers, advanced metering infrastructure, automated demand response systems, and electric vehicle charging stations. It also includes features like remote disconnection of power supply in case of nonpayment or other contingencies.

Intelligent lighting is any lamp that uses light-emitting diodes (LEDs) as its light source. The term refers to both lamps which have been designed specifically to use LEDs as well as general-purpose lights where LEDs have been retrofitted into conventional sockets such as those used for incandescent bulbs or fluorescent tubes. Such fixtures are often referred to by the trademarked name "Lighting Science." Intelligent lighting systems reduce power consumption compared to traditional lighting systems like incandescent lights or fluorescent tubes. The cost of installation of intelligent lighting systems depends on the type of technology being used (e.g., LEDs or high-efficiency halogens).

Smart grids are an important component of the green economy because they enable more efficient use of renewable energy sources and help bring down carbon emissions. More efficient use of electricity also reduces energy losses during transmission, which means less fuel is required to produce power at a central facility. Smart grids have been deployed around the world with varying degrees of success. In Europe, there have been some notable successes such as in Germany which uses smart meters in over 70% of households.

3.4 Smart Infrastructure

Smart infrastructure is the most significant opportunity to achieve a smart city status (Dameri et al., 2019). For current cities, housing can be one large project as regards infrastructure. However, when it comes to smart infrastructure, the nature of these projects significantly differs. Smart infrastructure could entail the redevelopment of slums and encompass affordable housing. Smart infrastructure involves the development of such properties as retail, hospitality, residential properties, and offices. Improved urbanization would result in many people moving into the city, triggering more infrastructure development (Saba et al., 2020).

Further, the satellite towns around current cities are excellent opportunities for affordable housing development. The rolled out budgets are supposed to roll out the status of infrastructure to affordable housing projects in the city, and many players in the real estate sector are hiking on the bandwagon (Cardullo & Kitchin, 2019). Affordable housing propels forward the smart city initiatives.

3.5 Green Buildings

The construction industry is one of the pillars of critical interventions to achieve "smart, sustainable, inclusive" growth and economic transformation based on efficient resources and low carbon emissions. The wealthy economy approach is a model of capitalism that focuses on wealth creation and economic growth as the main indicators of its success. It is based on the idea that through investments in human capital, technology, and infrastructure, society can achieve economic growth and improve standards of living in the long run. Green buildings use the wealthy economic approach to promote sustainable development through smart solutions in smart cities. Green building policies are aimed at reducing environmental impact by using more energy-efficient materials and technologies, recycling wastewater, and minimizing waste generation. Green buildings also use renewable energy sources such as solar panels or wind turbines to generate electricity.

From many studies, the construction industry produces energy efficiency estimated, by 2022, about 30% of current consumption and could be exploited by effective interventions and costs (Suartika & Cuthbert, 2020). There is also a great deal of potential for building space that can be used to integrate renewable energy sources. In order to address climate change, many countries have started investing in green technology industries to reduce greenhouse gas emissions from fossil fuels and increase energy efficiency. For example, China has invested heavily in solar panel manufacturing plants which helped reduce its dependence on fossil fuels. Some European countries such as Germany have also invested heavily in wind power generation capacity which has helped reduce greenhouse gas emissions. In addition, in Europe, the population spends about 93% of its time inside buildings: inadequate building methods or poor construction can damage the health of residents and can make building management and maintenance itself more expensive, from cooling and heating to severe consequences, especially for older people and disadvantaged groups (Allam & Newman, 2018).

Concerning infrastructure, the aim is to promote the development of existing facilities, as well as government, especially in primary schools and public buildings through the efficient operation of heating systems and regular monitoring of their emissions (energy-saving measures), the promotion of the use of clean energy sources (the replacement of diesel with natural gas), renewable energy sources (solar thermal, solar photovoltaic, heat pumps) for air conditioning and domestic hot water production (clean energy measures), and measures to reduce dispersion using a construction envelope (power satisfaction measures).

Various cities have provided beneficial condom programs using the most effective solutions. Interventions to reduce air pollution and energy consumption also affect public lighting systems. Increasing in Europe are examples of the solar eclipse of existing historic buildings, from the photovoltaic cover of the historic Blackfriars Bridge to the 2014 natural regeneration on the first floor of the Eiffel Tower in Paris, which includes the integration of photovoltaic and wind technology (Kuecker & Hartley, 2020). The City of Paris relaunched in 2014 a major city development project sought by Mayor Anne Hidalgo, representing the most profound transformation of Ville Lumiere for 150 years (Appio et al., 2019). The "Reinventing Paris" project is about sustainable technology and green buildings: aquaponic farming, photocatalytic concrete, biofaçades, urban forests, urban farms, and green roofs are the 22 winning projects that will transform the French capital (Bohloul, 2020).

The city of Seoul has instead begun building a 12,000-square-foot urban park instead of a now demolished highway. Seoul Skygarden, designed by MVRDV, will be an encyclopedia of plants with more than 250 trees sorted according to Korean characters (Popov et al., 2019). The conversion, which will allow residents to take a shorter route to the train station, will let you walk 10 min instead of 30, walk through the trees and bushes, and look at the city 17 m high.

3.6 Smart Technology

ICT would play a critical role in developing current cities into smart cities (Kolotouchkina & Seisdedos, 2018). For instance, in the case of services to citizens, technology plays a significant role in offering easy access to the engagement and participation of citizens online. Smart technology could include delivering online and Wi-Fi services in all public places. ICT plays an integral role in improving the city's governance by building city operations and command centers. The current towns should line up their massive investment in this particular space. Because software development is significant in controlling water and power systems, superior body technologies specialized in infrastructure management services and digital analytics should be sought. An example of such is geo-design. The current cities can invest much in optic fiber cables for monitoring and controlling purposes.

3.7 Technological Innovation

Today, achieving these strategic goals is also possible, thanks to the availability of modern technologies that change user behavior, service performance, and the city's common feature: urban data, city applications, social media, smartphones and tablets, the Internet of Things, geolocation systems, broadband, ICT, innovative transport systems, advanced materials, and renewable energy. Over the next 8 years, Navigant Research's long-term forecasts track the steady market growth of smart cities that by 2024 will amount to 26.2 billion euros. This fixed amount means that 90% of urban projects will use technology to produce digital resources and improve urban efficiency. Areas of smart city land that will lead to growth include (Das, 2020):

- All the resources connected to urban data, made up of all the data produced by the city daily, are measured and translated into ideas, statistics, and facts.
- Intelligent systems to prevent damage to water resources.
- Smart travel, bike and car sharing, smart parking, mixed and electric cars.
- The latest public lighting, safety improvements, city pollution levels, and LED lights monitor traffic.

In particular, concerning urban data, according to Praharaj and Han (2019), the total amount of data collected by Google from the beginning of humanity to 2004 is equal to that currently produced in 2 days (Strielkowski et al., 2020). This act of massive knowledge growth often referred to as "Big Data" includes the need to filter and make these new information assets accessible (Keshavarzi et al., 2021).

Internet traffic from mobile devices will reach a capacity of 370 exabytes per year (Tan & Taeihagh, 2020). The amount of data is not easy to visualize since it equates to 7000 video clips on YouTube or sending or receiving 30 images per citizen of the world, day and year. Concerning urban data in Chicago, there is a highly named project called "Array of Things," which is being promoted by the Computation Institute of Chicago University to expand the Internet of Things to an urban scale (Yigitcanlar et al., 2020). The project involves building a network of 600 sensors located in strategic locations to balance all "critical parameters" and make it safer, healthier, and more efficient. In particular, the sensors will have the function of measuring and making available, in real time, data such as higher temperature, pedestrian and traffic, noise levels, pollution (ozone, CO, SO_2, NO_2), vibration, light level, rain, wind, air pressure, and temperature.

3.8 *Smart Governance*

A city is a place of great opportunity and potential, but it also poses many challenges. As the world's population continues to urbanize at an unprecedented rate, cities are faced with significant social, economic, and environmental issues that must be addressed in order to ensure sustainable development. Smart governance for smart cities is the new trend, and it has been gaining momentum in recent years.

Smart governance is a concept that focuses on improving cities through sustainable development and smart solutions. The idea behind this concept is to make cities more livable and efficient by using technology to maximize resources while minimizing waste. As the population grows and resources become scarcer, cities will need to find ways to provide adequate housing, services, and infrastructure for their residents. This can only be achieved by improving governance at all levels of government.

The concept of smart governance has been around for decades, but it has only recently gained traction as policymakers try to find ways to improve their service delivery systems. Smart governance refers to the ability of governments to effectively meet the needs of their constituents while balancing limited resources against competing interests. It involves using information technology (IT) tools like data analytics and management software systems (MSS) to improve efficiency within local governments (LGs).

3.9 *Smart Environment*

A smart environment is related to pure water supply, green area, and pollution-free. In the case of current cities, there is more pollution. Due to this, people are at risk of respiratory diseases. Further, water scarcity is a big problem for the environment and many parts of the world, because many vehicles in the cities release CO_2 emissions at a significant level. According to one survey, 630,000 die every year due to a bad environment (Cardullo & Kitchin, 2019). Also, in current cities, many factories in industrial areas release chemicals harmful to the town and the environment. One point is also noticeable that environment is not pure due to the lack of trees in many cities. So, to make a smart environment in current cities, the number of vehicles should be reduced, leading to less pollution by vehicles (Suartika & Cuthbert, 2020). Secondly, it should have sufficient resources of water for the city. Lastly, the government should take the initiative to plant more trees in space for a sustainable smart environment.

3.10 Smart Living, People, and Health

The substantial urban population has placed tremendous pressure on the present infrastructure, hence the necessity for big-scale capacity infrastructural growth to supply higher standards of living and accommodate the migrating population (Mozūriūnaitė & Sabaitytė, 2021). Current cities are presently experiencing significant issues with the urban population due to unexpected developments. However, the smart city idea is expected to facilitate renovation, affecting and replacing existing developments and designed environments. The idea is to promote the cocreation of the latest city layouts characterized by mixed land use and enhanced infrastructure. A smart city's diverse land-use side is ready to facilitate a mix of industrial land pockets, cultural, institutional, residential, and commercial. Changing current towns is set to take care of the problem of the urban area and improve the city's economic competitiveness. Creating efficient bus rapid transit systems (BRTS) and redeveloping the city's urban transport system can help to generate efficient, price-effective, and high-capacity transit solutions, which will fulfill the various infrastructural needs of the city.

4 Conclusion

It is clear that the ambition to develop current cities into smart cities is possible only with smart people since they must design, use, and interpret it to make it possible. Hence, social participation and innovation are essential. Also, smart organizations should take advantage of the available resources and existing opportunities. The possibilities of connection with the outside world are now more straightforward and immediate with new technologies. It has opened many areas to explore: health, people, environment, governance, economy, infrastructure, energy, and mobility. Thus, the responsible stakeholders in this project will be all the local authorities and citizens of different countries. As we can see, the application of green technology in smart cities is a must. It is the way to solve a great number of problems. Moreover, it creates the opportunity for futuristic solutions that would definitely change the way we perceive urban areas. After all, hope never gets lost. The future is ahead of us, and I believe that these cities are the first step toward making humanity's dream come true. The most positive aspect of green innovation is that technology has provided a way out of this global predicament. Technological innovation has led to the development of cost-effective, quick, and effective solutions to control anthropogenic-induced global warming. The world will benefit if municipalities and private and public sectors come forward and together find a smart solution in smart cities.

With increasing global concerns about the environment, especially in metropolitan areas, cities are taking measures to implement green technology. However, it is also important to consider that implementing green technology can help receive funding from other sources. Features such as "intelligent" windows that turn dark in the summer and clear in the winter (to control light and heat) are incorporated into the building of these smart cities—a play on terms that suggest innovation and planning on behalf of those designing these cities. A good example of this is the push to build eco-friendly apartment buildings that would be compatible with solar panels, wind turbines, etc.

References

Abdoullaev, A. (2011). A smart world: A development model for intelligent cities. In *The 11th IEEE international conference on computer and information technology*.

Ahvenniemi, H., Huovila, A., Pinto-Seppä, I., & Airaksinen, M. (2017). What are the differences between sustainable and smart cities? *Cities, 60*, 234–245.

Allam, Z., & Newman, P. (2018). Redefining the smart city: Culture, metabolism, and governance. *Smart Cities, 1*(1), 4–25.

Al-Wakeel, A., Jianzhong, W., & Jenkins, N. (2016). State estimation of medium voltage distribution networks using smart meter measurements. *Applied Energy, 184*, 207–218.

Appio, F. P., Lima, M., & Paroutis, S. (2019). Understanding smart cities: Innovation ecosystems, technological advancements, and societal challenges. *Technological Forecasting and Social Change, 142*, 1–14.

Basiri, M., Azim, A. Z., & Farrokhi, M. (2017). Smart city solution for sustainable urban development. *European Journal of Sustainable Development, 6*(1), 71–84.

Bloomberg. (2021). *New energy outlook*.

Bohloul, S. M. (2020). Smart cities: A survey on new developments, trends, and opportunities. *Journal of Industrial Integration and Management, 5*(03), 311–326.

Cardullo, P., & Kitchin, R. (2019). Smart urbanism and smart citizenship: The neoliberal logic of citizen-focused smart cities in Europe. *Environment and Planning C: Politics and Space, 37*(5), 813–830.

Dameri, R. P., Benevolo, C., Veglianti, E., & Li, Y. (2019). Understanding smart cities as a glocal strategy: A comparison between Italy and China. *Technological Forecasting and Social Change, 142*, 26–41.

Das, D. (2020). In pursuit of being smart? A critical analysis of India's smart cities endeavor. *Urban Geography, 41*(1), 55–78.

Jackson, T., & Victor, P. (2011). Productivity and work in the 'green economy' - some theoretical reflections and empirical tests. *Environmental Innovation and Societal Transitions, 1*, 101–108.

Keshavarzi, G., Yildirim, Y., & Arefi, M. (2021). Does scale matter? An overview of the "smart cities" literature. *Sustainable Cities and Society, 74*, 103151.

Kolotouchkina, O., & Seisdedos, G. (2018). Place branding strategies in the context of new smart cities: Songdo IBD, Masdar, and Skolkovo. *Place Branding and Public Diplomacy, 14*(2), 115–124.

Kuecker, G. D., & Hartley, K. (2020). How smart cities became the urban norm: Power and knowledge in New Songdo City. *Annals of the American Association of Geographers, 110*(2), 516–524.

Mozūriūnaitė, S., & Sabaitytė, J. (2021). To what extent we do understand smart cities and the characteristics influencing city smartness. *Journal of Architecture and Urbanism, 45*(1), 1–8.

Popov, E., Kortov, S., & Semyachkov, K. (2019). Intellectual capital of smart cities as objects for institutional modeling. In *European conference on intangibles and intellectual capital*. Academic Conferences International Limited.

Praharaj, S., & Han, H. (2019). Cutting through the clutter of smart city definitions: A reading into the smart city perceptions in India. *City, Culture and Society, 18*, 100289.

Saba, D., Sahli, Y., Berbaoui, B., & Maouedj, R. (2020). Towards smart cities: Challenges, components, and architectures. In A. E. Hassanien, R. Bhatnagar, N. E. M. Khalifa, & M. H. N. Taha (Eds.), *Toward social Internet of Things (IoT): Enabling technologies, architectures, and applications* (pp. 249–286). Springer.

Strielkowski, W., Veinbender, T., Tvaronavičienė, M., & Lace, N. (2020). Economic efficiency and energy security of smart cities. *Economic research-Ekonomska istraživanja, 33*(1), 788–803.

Suartika, G. A. M., & Cuthbert, A. (2020). The sustainable imperative—Smart cities, technology, and development. *Sustainability, 12*(21), 8892.

Tan, S. Y., & Taeihagh, A. (2020). Smart city governance in developing countries: A systematic literature review. *Sustainability, 12*(3), 899.

The Economist Intelligence Unit. (2017). *Safe cities index 2017*.

Turner, B. S., & Khondker, H. H. (2010). *Globalization east and west*. Sage.

US Department of Commerce. (2002). *Building a smarter infrastructure for America's economic growth*.

Yigitcanlar, T., Kankanamge, H. H., Butler, L., Vella, K., & Desouza, K. (2020). *Smart cities down under: Performance of Australian local government areas*. Queensland University of Technology.

Zenghelis, D., Agarwala, M., Coyle, D., Felici, M., Lu, S., & Wdowin, J. (2020). *Valuing wealth, building prosperity. Wealth economy project first year report to LetterOne*. Bennett Institute for Public Policy.

Solidarity Economy

Olivier Gajac

Abstract This chapter focuses on the solidarity economy as an economic model whose particularity is that it tends to articulate the aspirations of individuals to better social conditions of existence and the consideration of nature. This more democratic and egalitarian model of social protection, differing from liberal and socialist economic systems, tends to reduce the power of individuals to self-organize in a non-lucrative way and to democratically lead to a social change reconciling politics and economy. We consider terminological and linguistic aspects associated with the solidarity economy in Europe, in the West and South, from its associationist roots to the present day, to highlight the forces and characteristics that would bring it closer to and/or distinguish it from the social economy, the nonprofit sector, and the popular economy. Then, we apprehend the power of resistance of these noncapitalist organizations through the nineteenth and twentieth centuries in the face of capitalism and the political aims that the states in their own politico-cultural context will assign to them from a macroeconomic perspective. In spite of the will of the states to stifle the self-organization of individuals between the middle of the nineteenth and the last quarter of the twentieth century, solidarity initiatives seem today to be inescapable in the face of neoliberalism, and they demonstrate almost everywhere in the world that individuals are able to co-construct civic political models reconciling democracy and economy, which the states and local public authorities have difficulty in recognizing due to the fact that they are imprisoned in the hegemonic conception of the market economy.

Keywords Solidarity economy · Democracy · Noncapitalist organization · Self-organization · Market economy · Social change

---

O. Gajac (✉)
Centre Émile Durkheim de Bordeaux, Pessac, France
e-mail: olivier.gajac@scpobx.fr

A. Ari (ed.), *Capitalism at a Crossroads*, Springer Studies in Alternative Economics,
https://doi.org/10.1007/978-3-031-23257-2_18

1 Introduction

The idea of addressing the question of the solidarity economy is to demonstrate that these initiatives are constantly renewed throughout history in the face of a conception of the economy based on the market. As Karl Polanyi (1983, p. 65) pointed out, the market economy has not been the only form of economy in societies, and/or the market economy has not always been dominant. In fact, we would like to show that the solidarity economy has been a mode of resistance in history as well as in the present day to capitalism, which already in the nineteenth century amounted to "self-extraction," i.e., a system of "extraction of natural resources, which can turn against social and natural life, [and which is still today] at the origin of new forms of exploitation of people and the Earth" (Duverger, 2021, pp. 44–45).

Nevertheless, this form of resistance by civil society through what is known as the solidarity economy is not unique to Europe. It can be found on different continents and/or countries where states have gradually sought to mitigate the effects of this separation imposed by capitalism on living conditions and resources. "The welfare state, experiments in economic planning and the socialist economy were part of this same effort, depending on the specific characteristics of the different societies where these attempts took place. It was the socially and politically shaped diversity (. . .) that dominated these attempts to embed the economy in society" (Bugra, 2005, p. 45). These different societies may have taken the path of establishing a liberal democratic society where the social economy has been a regulator between politics and the economy. Conversely, they may have followed the constitution of socialist societies where the social economy (or cooperativism) is merged with the ideology of the state. Finally, they have been able to follow the path of political independence of the Southern countries coming out of the colonial yoke by making cooperativism an actor of economic development.

Among these political projects for the self-protection of societies in the face of capitalism, not all countermovements are "viable, morally acceptable or politically desirable forms" (ibid, p. 45) as were, among others, the totalitarian regimes in the twentieth century. In this way, "not all attempts to embed the economy in society (. . .) are humanly and politically acceptable" (ibid, p. 45). This brief historical review of societies politically limiting the effects of the market economy, whose terminological conceptualization of noncapitalist (or nonprofit) organizations has varied over time and cultural areas (social economy, cooperativism, solidarity economy, nonprofit sector, popular economy, alternative), tends to underline a common point. Noncapitalist organizations were deprived of their power of social transformation between the middle of the nineteenth century and the second half of the twentieth century, when their original model was based on a mode of self-organization. They were replaced by a political vision of the economy, either market, totalizing, or developmentalist, without it being possible for civil society to establish an alternative economy that is not limited to the accumulation of wealth and/or a state productivist model.

Within this framework, noncapitalist organizations were unable to establish a new form of democracy outside of representative democracy in liberal societies, and they were unable to institute freedoms of organizational action in socialist societies. Yet, these political attempts to embed the economy in social life came to an end in the 1980s, as "the economic order established in the aftermath of the World War II was challenged in favor of a return to a self-regulating market economy. The death of the Keynesian consensus and the questioning of 'Marshallian' social rights in the First World, the collapse of Soviet socialism in the Second, and the disintegration of the 'developmentalist state' under the pressure of macroeconomic stabilization and structural adjustment policies in the Third World, shaped the process of neoliberal globalization characterized by unregulated flows of goods, services and, above all, capital" (ibid, 45–46). In fact, the conception of the economy through the prism of the market has imposed itself on these different political regimes to become the natural and only perspective of societies today. This homogenization of thought, which makes the market economy the determining element in the structuring of social life, reveals a form of universal anomie. One reason is that wealth creation is measured by GDP, an indicator that does not take into account all social realities. GDP only considers private and public production activities without including and highlighting social inequalities, environmental impacts, and well-being (Gadrey & Jany-Catrice, 2016).

In fact, this conception of the market economy, considering its variables in national contexts, is the main factor of social inequalities, including gender and identity, and of environmental degradation. The capitalist and Soviet models of production have in common that, since the industrial revolution, they have set up mass production systems to the detriment of citizens' freedoms and their capacity to organize themselves democratically. While the market economy is a favorable medium for liberating social groups (Fraser, 2013, 47) from the administrative burden of dirigiste and socialist economies and allows them to access the labor market, the idealized vision of the market in favor of an equilibrium of social cohesion seems to be a pure illusion, because the market economy does not ensure full social integration; it creates marginality, precariousness, and extreme poverty. This phenomenon of exclusion is reinforced because it is based on political programs whose reforms have tended in recent decades to call into question labor law and social protection and even to weaken public policies in the Southern countries.

However, the old idea of social progress seems to have been consigned to the dustbin of history, unless one believes that social progress is solely a material quest for the accumulation of wealth. This haemorrhage of thought is de facto political because the different conceptions of social life that pluralism and political cleavages tend to defend no longer have a place and political parties have converted to the conception of the market economy and explicitly and/or implicitly defend the neoliberal economy despite a system of representative democracy or not: "Hence the persistent impression that electoral alternatives go hand in hand with the continuity of policies directed towards commodification" (Laville & Riot-Sarcey, 2020, p. 49), leaving financial capital free to circulate and assigning the most vulnerable the sole choice of being locked into a system of exploitation.

Worse, the plebiscite of the market economy leads to a frantic race of competition between countries, and in this way, in this hegemonic perspective, the rule of law no longer has as much value, as it did at the end of the World War II, to guard against the return of the tragedies of the twentieth century marked by dictatorships in Europe. In this sense, the return of a self-regulating market that subordinates human society to the logic of the market has, since the 1970s, helped to question the foundations of democracy (Bugra, 2005, p. 38). In fact, the market economy put on a pedestal as a miracle situation for progress can be worrying because it relies on states that are less and less democratic and on the construction of a majority political identity in favor of accepting the market economy. Today, the emergence of populisms as an alternative to the defense of national sovereignty tends to renew the historical thinking of extreme political forms that are not viable or even dangerous (Laville & Riot-Sarcey, 2020, pp. 10–11).

If this conception of the economy tends to become universal by reducing rights and freedoms or by excluding democratic principles, the consequences of the precariousness of living conditions are effectively accompanied by the degradation of the environment and the natural resources on which most of the world's population depends for their living. In fact, the multiple disorders and dangers facing societies originate in this conception of a separation between humans and nature, where the former impose themselves on the latter (Duverger, 2021, p. 23), making society an auxiliary of the market. "Instead of the economy being embedded in social relations, it is social relations that are embedded in the economic system" (Bugra, 2005, p. 41). Today, capitalism no longer seems to have any limits; it tends to integrate multiple forms of delinquency, and the financialization of the economy allows for new connections between bank managers and criminal networks (Laville & Riot-Sarcey, 2020, 46). Today, it is estimated that "the volume of money of dubious origin" is $200 billion, while "global criminal revenues amount to (...) 2100 billion dollars per year" (ibid, p. 46). This scale of crime is not the sole result of individual deviance but rather is part of a criminogenic institutional framework, established and known by the states.

The idea would be to establish a universal right to nature that its use be limited to ensure its renewal and that the modes of production or exploitation enrich rather than impoverish natural resources and that they be the support for economic models whose purpose is not only profit and the short term but also social cohesion inherited from a democratic mode of production where living together between man and nature is a reality. This perspective is not new; it is part of the practices and beliefs of ancient societies living in harmony with their environment. Their fate is well known; it resulted in their extermination in most cases for belonging to a past and/or for being perceived as an obstacle to progress such as a brake. Even today, the extermination of small indigenous societies or social groups in the face of the so-called democracies or multinationals, as in Brazil, continues without triggering an international outcry in the face of what can be called crimes against humanity, of which most countries and international organizations, opting for silence, become accomplices.

Consequently, talking about the solidarity economy means, paradoxically, first addressing a field of alternative initiatives that are poorly known (Laville & Riot-Sarcey, 2020, p. 9; Dreyfus, 2018, p. 132) even though they are attracting renewed interest (Demoustier & Richez-Battesti, 2010, p. 5). As such, there are 200,000 social and solidarity economy (SSE) establishments in France, representing 14% of salaried employment (MEF, 2022), whose employment growth rate can be higher than that of the competitive private economy in some years. On a European scale, these citizen economies represent approximately 10% of the economic landscape (Hascoët, 2005, p. 299). Despite their numerical weight, they are perceived as "marginal" (Demoustier & Richez-Battesti, 2010, p. 8) alongside the market economy and public power and even their "alternative projects, because they are subversive (…) are (…) denigrated or disdained [and set aside] from knowledge and debate" (Laville & Riot-Sarcey, 2020, p. 9). In this way, we shall endeavor, in Sects. 2 and 3, to provide linguistic and terminological precision regarding its history and to these conceptual variables constructed in various geographical contexts. In Sect. 4, we will try to trace its evolution as a noncapitalist organization in Europe, Latin America, Asia, and Africa to grasp its place and role in liberal democratic societies, socialist countries, and Southern countries. In Sect. 5, we examine the issue of solidarity economy from the end of the twentieth century to the present day in order to better understand how it is a force against capitalism in different geographical areas, including Turkey.

2 A Plurality of Concepts: Associationism, Social Economy, Nonprofit Sector, Popular Economy, and Solidarity Economy

The solidarity economy refers to a multitude of citizen initiatives driven by the ambition to bring values and principles into the economic field that are different from the market economy. These values and principles appear in different sectors of activity according to national contexts but evolve over the course of the nineteenth and twentieth centuries and in recent decades.

In the nineteenth century, it was more a question of an associationist movement seeking to establish other standards of work, more egalitarian, democratic, and solidarity between individuals in the face of capitalism. This associationist movement appeared in the first half of the nineteenth century in the form of self-organized collectives, associations, and cooperatives. However, since the French Revolution put an end to the intermediary bodies of the "Ancien Régime," the nascent democratic modernity was soon to oppose the freedom of association (Defourny & Develtere, 1999, p. 27), which could split sovereignty. The birth of this political modernity understood freedom in a restrictive way; it did not allow collective freedom between individuals, and on the contrary, it exposed them to the contingencies of the capitalist economy.

As a result, the associationist movement was doomed to die out, as civil society was not legitimate to intervene politically to regulate the capitalist economic order. It was not until the Third Republic, at the very moment when the French state achieved political democracy, that it institutionalized the democracy of civil society (Draperi, 2006, p. 40).

In fact, the legal recognition of cooperatives, associations, and mutual societies was part of the continuity of the revolutions and the social question of the mid-nineteenth century. From 1848 onward, the state intended to assume more and more the role of guarantor of solidarity to the detriment of a self-organized civil society. "Thus, the republican state resolved the dilemma of public power in a democratic context; it had to act on behalf of all and thus constrain, but within a legitimate framework provided by the 'general interest-public service' couple and without annihilating individual freedom and its corollary, the freedom of the market" (Duverger et al., 2020, pp. 22–23).

Thus, the three components (cooperative, association, and mutual) that are most often described as the social economy see their power of social transformation, present in associationism, marrying the market and the state. The collective freedom of association was accompanied by the promulgation of social rights until the establishment of an insurance-based social protection system in 1945. In this context, cooperatives, associations, and mutuals gradually specialized by focusing either on the interests of the members of their organization, such as cooperatives, or on the aims of the state's regulatory public policies or to supplement social insurance rights. In fact, the statutory recognition of the components of the social economy granting them a specificity regarding private enterprises and public authorities cannot avoid questioning their institutionalization.

However, the solidarity economy questions this institutionalization of the three components of the social economy for having generally adopted a service logic whose values and principles of equality, democracy, and mutual support (or the support of each other) have been increasingly subjected to management logics in connection with the new public management and the pressure of the neoliberal economy. In this sense, it can be pointed out that the reference to the solidarity economy that emerged in the last third of the twentieth century (Lévesque & Mendell, 2005) can be traced back to the reference to the social economy of the nineteenth century, more specifically to the associationist movement. In this way, one might think that "the various components of the social economy are being reinforced [today] by an associationism of solidarity that reflects a reaction against social injustices and ecological imbalances" (Hascoët, 2005, p. 299). This new solidarity associationism, whose project is a critique of the neoliberal economy through the constitution of democratic organizations of voluntary and free individuals, is part of a long process of emancipation from the state and market order, following the May 1968 movement, but also from the field of the social economy.

First, many new so-called cultural social movements were to mark the 1970s, making ecological, regionalist, identity-based, feminist, and economic demands (Gendron, 2001). As an alternative, we find the desire of city dwellers to return to the land by forming libertarian communities (Duverger et al., 2020, p. 1). Thus, this cultural dimension carried by the new social movements will gradually take on a socioeconomic dimension whose initiatives will be driven by the desire for autonomy and a different way of life by criticizing productivist societies and promoting "small is beautiful" (Schumacher, 1979). Very early on, we can see the beginnings of future socioeconomic experiments that will be found at the heart of the solidarity economy.

However, this historical process, which is specific to the European area, must first be qualified with regard to the Western world. In this respect, there is less talk of SSE in the Anglo-Saxon world and more particularly in American literature. SSE terminology is nonexistent in English-speaking countries (Demoustier & Richez-Battesti, 2010, p. 10). From this perspective, "Anglo-Saxon inspired works privilege the reference to civil society, while in French publications, the term SSE is more easily imposed" (ibid, p. 10). The equivalent of SSE in English is reflected in the commonly used term "third sector," which includes nonprofit organizations mutual and cooperative enterprises that have market activities and redistribute their surpluses to their members (Evers & Laville, 2004, p. 13).

In the USA, this notion of the third sector tends to refer more to nonprofit organizations (NPOs), "a sector that is different from both the state and the market, a sector that is able to fill the gaps in the market and the state, and thus cooperatives and mutual" (Salamon, 1990; Salamon & Anheier, 1998; Weisbrod, 1977 quoted by Lévesque & Mendell, 2005). NPOs defined as nonprofit and voluntary sector can include a wide range of predominantly nonmarket organizations but exclude "predominantly market organizations and collective enterprises" (Lévesque & Mendell, 2005) found within the third sector. In this case, the nonprofit sector is more restrictive than the social economy concept because it does not consider all these components and tends to move away from the values and principles that underpin the SSE.

Despite their voluntary and free nature, NPOs or the nonprofit sector do not always promote principles of equality and democracy. On the contrary, they may operate on a hierarchical and top-down basis vis-à-vis both their members and the target audiences of their activity. Moreover, they are subject to a strong interdependence of donors from the private sector, unlike in Europe where the state has ensured a redistribution of wealth as part of their public service mission. Thus, their obvious contribution to the general interest conceals their limited power to challenge the public authorities and the neoliberal economic order. In Anglo-Saxon societies, civil society must coexist harmoniously, without interference or in a minimal way, with politics and the economy. Consequently, the SSE differs from the nonprofit sector in that it claims a socioeconomic and sociopolitical dimension (Demoustier & Richez-Battesti, 2010, p. 8) with the aim of social transformation. The liberal conception of Anglo-Saxon civil society, the nonprofit sector, does not tend to promote another economy and is based mainly on market resources and philanthropic or charitable volunteering.

Nevertheless, over the last few decades in Anglo-Saxon countries, citizen solidarity initiatives have emerged that can be compared to solidarity economy initiatives in Europe, in the sense that if the new solidarity associationism gave a new impetus to the social economy at the end of the twentieth century, we can also mention that in the USA and the UK, the nonprofit sector is reinforced or criticized by initiatives with both sociopolitical and socioeconomic dimensions. In connection with social mobilizations critical of the neoliberal economy or with the dissemination of alternative economic models, initiatives for citizen self-organization have emerged. We can mention the "communities" or "intentional communities" (Lallement, 2021) rethinking the organization of work and social relations, but also the networks of multiparty actors investing the economic field such as agriculture to develop a strong alterity to the market economy such as community-supported agriculture (CSA).

In the same way, we need to better understand the language and terminology associated with noncapitalist organizations in the South. This phenomenon is therefore not unique to the West; we find it on most continents with variables linked to their context, but it tends to associate very early on both sociocultural and socioeconomic dimensions. In the South, the social economy is culturally influenced by the fact that it "is by definition the work of locally organized groups and communities [and is linked to the] specific cultures of these groups and communities" (Defourny & Develtere, 1999, p. 32). In these countries, many initiatives that are also called the popular economy arise from the field of the informal economy. In this component of the popular economy, there is no real separation between the economy and the social, as the production of these "specific forms of organization, with complex purposes that go beyond economic ones" (Fonteneau et al., 1999, p. 159), is geared toward the wider group and its market component is minimized to favor socialization and group culture (Laville, 2016, p. 54).

Indeed, it is perhaps daring to speak of the social economy in countries of the South where this term is little used, and to bring the popular economy closer to the social economy (Fonteneau et al., 1999, p. 160), or even to confuse the social economy with the informal economy and the domestic economy. This popular economy may stem in part from "the outsourcing strategies of capitalist enterprises" (Laville, 2016, p. 156) and is rather an adjustment variable to capitalism. From this perspective, neither it relies on collective and democratic impetus to address needs and expectations, nor it tends to become an actor instituting new alternative economic models. Conversely, the popular economy can be rooted in the domestic economy, and although it is marked by "hardship (. . .) the popular economy can also be a source of dignity when it allows people (. . .) to develop collective solutions to their problems of food, housing or health" (ibid, p. 58).

While the popular economy does not involve equality and equity (ibid, p. 156) in its developmental phase of the domestic sphere, the ties of belonging and reciprocal relations are of crucial importance to the emergence of solidarity practices (Defourny & Develtere, 1999, p. 32). These ties leading to solidarity practices are in traditional societies "very different from the relationships that prevail in formalized capitalist environments" (ibid, 32). The revival of the informal economy would be a form of rejection of capitalist standards to liberate traditional culture. In this perspective, some grassroots initiatives have been able to take on more egalitarian and broad extensions where peer reciprocity is at the heart of the relationships (Laville, 2016, p. 156).

The popular economy was, despite its emancipatory potential, more or less ignored during the colonial and postcolonial period to the detriment of one of the components of the social economy, the cooperatives. However, the emergence of cooperatives tends to participate in the economic development of the nation to assert their recent independence from the colonial yoke. More rooted in a logic of progress, cooperatives are often the initiative of the public authorities and/or NGOs (Fonteneau et al., 1999, p. 161). From this point of view, it appears that cooperatives in the South, as one of the most active components, have been able to deviate in their conception from the idea of the social economy that we have in Europe. While the social economy is defined by a purpose of service to members or the community rather than profit, management autonomy, democratic decision-making, and the primacy of people and labor over capital in the distribution of income (Defourny, 2017, p. 46–48; Defourny & Develtere, 1999, p. 38), they are not entirely based on a movement of citizen self-organization such as associationism and rarely rely on democratic functioning in the early stages.

This was not the case in the 1980s and 1990s, when local communities challenged the economic policies of their state and the pressure exerted by multinationals on natural resources. The emergence of socioeconomic alternatives combining the commitment of discriminated local populations and the fight against the commodification of natural resources was an attempt to counteract the reproduction of inequalities produced by the neoliberal economy. These solidarity economy initiatives, commonly referred to as the popular economy, emerge from social mobilizations to claim their rights and defend their natural resources and tend to become part of the institutional landscape at this time. While these economic alternatives aim to improve living conditions and incomes, this perspective is not limited to a commercial register; for many initiatives, it also implies a dimension of dignity. In the same way, the popular economy can be conceived for some of the populations facing poverty as a transitional process to integrate the market economy. The popular economy does not allow for a glimpse of contemporary social experiments known as alternative in the sense that they carry through their economic activity a political critique of the public authorities by promoting another economy that moves away from the market economy. Here, there are connections between the solidarity economy and the popular economy in that they attempt to convey the values and principles of equality, democracy, and fraternity.

If the solidarity economy and social economy were conceived in France and they all refer to the same pioneering associationism, it seems obvious to speak of SSE and to avoid opposing them (Defourny, 2017, 61). This hypothesis tends to be plausible in more ways than one. First, the components of what constituted the social economy are statutorily distinct from the public and private sectors. Moreover, they use the same legal statutes. Above all, they have been able to provide concrete and viable solutions where the public and private sectors have failed either individually or collectively. Nevertheless, it is not impossible that they lose the political project that led to their creation. What differentiates the solidarity economy from the social economy could be based on "a discursive indicator of internal typification" leading to the fact that "where the former intends to act 'against' in order to change the environment, the latter confines itself to an action 'in' the environment by aiming at a corrective effect of the environment" (Sorbets, 2004, p. 17).

In fact, "the social economy, by focusing on the organizational aspect, has not been able to counteract the institutional isomorphism generated by the division and complementarity between the market and the social state" (Laville, 2016, p. 329). It is indeed in reaction to their institutionalization that solidarity initiatives emerged at the end of the twentieth century. However, it is highly likely that what happened to the social economy will happen to the solidarity economy, i.e., that it will be subject to a process of institutionalization. Without anticipating the future, today, it seems that "the rapprochement of the two forms should not go too far, each being for the other, in a way, its external limit: a form close to but irreducibly different in nature" (Sorbets, 2004, p. 18).

The particularity of the solidarity economy comes from the fact that it promotes another conception of the economy that is not limited to the market economy. Although solidarity initiatives today are evolving in the context of the neoliberal economy, they tend to show that the economy is plural, that they do not rely solely on market resources, but combine nonmarket and nonmonetary resources. From this point of view, it "is characterized by a capacity to bring together a greater diversity of resources than other forms of organization (hence the term hybridization), due to collective aims defined on the basis of a democratic operation (hence an economy of solidarity)" (Lévesque & Mendell, 2005). According to this approach, the solidarity economy emerges under the reciprocal impetus of volunteers and a recognition of the various public and private stakeholders that ensure that the activities of goods and services will be jointly defined by producers and users, particularly in the case of proximity services (Laville, 1994, pp. 74–89). Consequently, the solidarity economy can be defined as "the set of economic activities subject to the will to act democratically, where social relationships of solidarity take precedence over individual interest or material profit" (Laville & Cattini, 2006, p. 303).

Thus, these organizations contribute to the creation of autonomous public spaces of proximity that make it possible to develop new ways of acting together and to strengthen social cohesion (Laville, 2004). However, these organizations cannot achieve these objectives without a strong investment in the functioning of a democracy that must be not only representative but also participatory and deliberative (Lévesque, 2003). In this sense, the solidarity economy is better understood in relation to the social economy through its dual socioeconomic and sociopolitical dimensions (Klein et al., 2017, p. 14; Laville, 2013, pp. 74–75; Demoustier & Richez-Battesti, 2010, pp. 8–10). This substantive conception of the economy inspired by the work of Karl Polanyi supports his thesis that the market economy has not always been historically dominant in societies. "Instead of considering the economy from a formal point of view, as neoclassical economists generally do (rational calculation in situations of scarce resources and unlimited needs), they take their inspiration from Karl Polanyi (1944) to define it from a substantive point of view, thus highlighting the three economic principles that are the market, which uses market resources, and the 'non-market', which is based on the concept of the market, the 'non-market' based on redistribution carried out mainly by the state, the 'non-market and non-monetary' based on reciprocity and giving which are exercised in civil society on a voluntary basis" (Mendell, 2002).

The current challenge for solidarity initiatives, including alternative or popular ones, "lies in the broadening of its project of autonomy in order to embed the economy not only in society, but also in nature" (Duverger, 2021, p. 45). It is this countermovement that Karl Polanyi refers to and from which the SSE must be inscribed to "conserve man and nature as well as the organization of production" (Polanyi, 1983, p. 182) while supplementing the inadequacies of representative democracy. The challenge is far from being won in the face of states that are autistic in the face of rising social inequalities and environmental degradation and intoxicated by the limitless national or supra-regional quest for the glory of material enrichment through monopolization and exploitation, especially since when they were an actor instituting other economic models, they were condemned in nineteenth-century France to die out; when they were more or less instituted by the state, they lost more or less their dimension of social transformation in twentieth-century Europe; and when they were used in the Southern countries, they were instituted in the name of the nation without being instituting.

3 A Look at the History

While we have seen that the SSE in Europe has its roots in an associationist movement of the first half of the nineteenth century, it is above all a movement that was formed in the capitalist era outside the interest and concerns of the state (Dreyfus, 2018, p. 133).

The new social class would not stop demanding the rights granted by the revolutions so that it could exercise them in everyday life (Laville & Riot-Sarcey, 2020, p. 72). In fact, the first decades of the nineteenth century were marked by popular revolts from England to Sicily but also in France with the Canut revolts in Lyon in 1831 and 1834, whose slogan was "live by working or die by fighting" (ibid, p. 73). Despite the prohibitions, "the workers experimented with emancipation through association" (ibid, pp. 73–74), and a plurality of spaces and meeting places served (*chambrées*, cabarets, street, clubs, and self-organization cooperatives initiated by Robert Owen) as a laboratory for the exchange of ideas and their dissemination for common action (ibid, p. 74). In this social effervescence, workers' and peasants' associationism resulted in "unprecedented experiments implemented" through associative practices, in which several currents of thought such as social Christianity, liberalism, Charles Gide's solidarism, and associationist socialism with Owen, Fourier, Simon, and Proudhon participated in their emergence (Defourny & Develtere, 1999, p. 28; Laville & Riot-Sarcey, 2020, p. 70).

This movement was not unique to Europe, but concerned other continents, such as Latin America, where the ideas of freedom were taken up by populations under the sway of empires. In Chile, Colombia, and Brazil, "those who have only their labor power" as property mobilize around democratic ideas to constitute "indigenous forms of mutual support" (Laville & Riot-Sarcey, 2020, p. 77). This type of society fights against injustice, as in the case of the quilombos, black Brazilians who seized land after emerging from their condition as slaves to establish republics. "This confederation of communities of 'fugitive Negroes' came into being in 1605 and grouped between 10,000 and 20,000 people. It stood up to the punitive expeditions of the colonists for over eighty years" (ibid, p. 78). Similarly, in North America, in the early nineteenth century, African Americans set up self-help groups.

While in France the February Revolution was bloodily suppressed in June 1848, "the Republic set itself up against these collective resistances by imprisoning its initiators in 1850" (ibid, p. 75). Conversely, the colonized people had to wait for the end of European supremacy, i.e., its weakening on the international scene, caused in part by the World War II, to lead European countries to being forced to grant them independence. In Europe, it was not until the end of the nineteenth century that the state became involved in the field of the social economy and the beginning of the nineteenth century that it really devoted itself to it (Dreyfus, 2018, p. 133). At the crossroads of the two centuries, laws will be enacted providing a legal framework for the forms of organization (cooperative, mutuality, and association) that will make up the modern social economy (Defourny, 2017, pp. 32–33; Defourny & Develtere, 1999, p. 28).

Indeed, in Europe, it appears that the components of the social economy were first an instituting actor before being instituted by the state. This movement from below has enabled the place of social economy organizations (or the third sector and the nonprofit sector) to be established in liberal democratic societies, the number of which has continued to increase throughout the twentieth century. Nevertheless, we can make a first remark about these liberal democratic societies. The legal recognition of cooperatives, associations, and mutuals from the second half of the nineteenth century onward will have the consequence of splitting up the values and principles that were combined within the associationist movement. For example, in the 1840s, cooperatives were "still linked to production, mutual support and protection, training and the defense of professional interests" (Duverger et al., 2020, p. 46).

In contrast to associationism, politics tends to lean on the increasingly dominant market while accepting the return of intermediary bodies, such as the components of the social economy, with the only difference that the latter will be institutionalized and broken up into specific objects that distance them from the spirit of the original associationist movement while reducing their capacity for self-organization and strengthening their dependence on politics (ibid, pp. 44–45). While associationism was confused with the values and principles of equality, liberty, and fraternity, the latter will constitute one of the specificities of the three components of the social economy. Thus, ". . . we witnessed an orderly division of the (. . .) components of associationism: economic functions, mutual support and solidarity functions and interest representation functions were entrusted to distinct institutional forms and carefully limited in their purposes" (ibid, p. 46). In this way, the workers' production associations of the first half of the nineteenth century lost their economic dimension with the 1901 law. The latter would be embodied in the cooperative movement.

In fact, during the Fordist period, these organizations were structured in a vertical and sectoral manner in close contact with the state, and they had access to public markets, public policies, and their funding (Demoustier & Richez-Battesti, 2010, p. 6). In this process, these three components of the social economy are specified in their status, and depending on the national context, their intervention will be further sectionalized. This institutionalization calls into question the specificity of their status, as these would only partially distinguish the organizations of the social economy from public authorities and private enterprises, without totally protecting them from a process of trivialization (Laville, 2016, pp. 296–322). The growing intervention of the state in Western Europe and North America led to the establishment of mediation processes from the end of the nineteenth century, which intensified until the 1970s; "The nascent social economy, far from being able to subvert and recompose the divided structure imposed by democratic modernity and industrial capitalism, was reduced to the role of mediating institutions intended rather to attenuate the tensions inherent in the overall social order" (Duverger et al., 2020, p. 44).

As such, one can trace the development of the cooperative movement in different national contexts and sectors. While the consumer cooperative movement started in England, in France, it was the producer cooperative movement that was predominant in its early years. At the end of the nineteenth and beginning of the twentieth century, the consumer or user cooperative movement dominated numerically. However, it cannot be denied that cooperatives in the industrialized countries have not changed from the initial self-management spirit of the nineteenth century. On the one hand, they would no longer differ too much from classical enterprises, and on the other hand, "their kinship with non-profit associative dynamics seems to have completely disappeared" (Defourny & Develtere, 1999, p. 42). Despite the great diversity of cooperatives, "including agricultural and housing cooperatives," "there is one constant in the institutionalization logics that have taken them into account: they are centered on their productive functions within the economic order, with the statutes having the ultimate aim of protecting their singular forms while facilitating their insertion into the market" (Duverger et al., 2020, p. 49).

The same applies to mutual societies, whose principle of mutual support or fraternity was at the heart of the first social experiments of the nineteenth-century associationist movement. They were characterized by self-management and egalitarian production activities, providing mutual support to members in a democratic manner. We can see here that they have both a socioeconomic and a sociopolitical dimension, as they combine the functions of protecting members from various risks and supporting social struggles until the Second Empire (ibid, p. 50). These social experiments had the virtue of preventing the risks of impoverishment of workers without social protection in the era of the industrial revolution. They thus instituted a democracy of solidarity in contrast to a philanthropic democracy based on a traditional conception of solidarity through religious, state tutelary, and secular philanthropic organizations to combat pauperism, whose operation was far from democratic.

In fact, the institutionalization of mutuals leads to the principle of mutual support being confused with the activity of production which "will also be embodied in specific institutional arrangements and kept at a distance from the other functions it assumed with the establishment of mutuality" (Dreyfus, 2001 quoted by Duverger et al., 2020, p. 50). In some industrialized countries, this system of mutuals will be linked to the system of insurance protection while giving them a place in the social security system (Defourny & Develtere, 1999, p. 35) in the form of complementary health insurance. This institutionalization of mutuals leads to the fact that they abandon "their nature as socio-political organizations, specializing through their insertion in state social protection," to become, before and especially after the World War II, quasi-insurance companies (Duverger et al., 2020, pp. 51–52).

Associations lose their economic dimension. In France, associations play a role in delegating services in the context of the redistribution of wealth in collaboration with the state to deal with the issue of exclusion. In England, associations or foundations maintain a philanthropic dimension in the field of exclusion without interfering in the political field. In fact, the approach of the statutes is insufficient to understand the SSE. While reading the legal statutes provides an initial overview to define the components of the social economy by distinguishing them from enterprises and public administration to address common challenges, the reality does not guarantee that practices comply with the statutory rules (Lévesque & Mendell, 2005). Similarly, the relevance of statutes relating to the components of the social economy in the South must be questioned on several counts.

First, they did not originate from below, but were instead instituted from above. Also, this diffusion of legal statuses in the geographical space of the South must be understood in the light of the political context of the North. The 1968s marked a critique of the order in which the youth uprising attacked colonialism and the liberal economy and fought against domination in all its forms (Laville & Riot-Sarcey, 2020, p. 96). In the process of independence in the countries of the South, some states adopted the statutes of the components of the social economy in their political project.

Here, they may have been a component of an ideological project as in socialist countries. "Several experiences have been inserted as the category of cooperatives in vast political projects where they have been institutionalized" (Defourny & Develtere, 1999, p. 31). "This is the case in countries where leaders have sought to reconcile national identity and experimentation with a third way of development between capitalism and centralized socialism," such as self-management in Yugoslavia and Ujamaa socialism in Tanzania (ibid, p. 31).

Second, they could be conceived as an actor of economic development and progress in the countries of the South coming out of the colonial yoke. Various postcolonial regimes have adopted cooperative dynamics in their national development plans, India, Peru, Chile, Jamaica, and Senegal, with an effort by governments to promote cooperatives. "In many countries of the South, cooperative development was a classic ingredient of the populist nationalist discourse of the 1960s and 1970s" (ibid, 31). Therefore, the use of the components of the social economy was mainly aimed at overcoming the global challenges of the newly independent countries. It was not initially intended to meet the expectations and needs of the people, let alone to promote their emancipation. Conversely, the nationalist cause has served in some geographical contexts as a means of using the social economy to promote local or regional development initiated and supervised by local communities.

These countermovements of the countries of the South in the face of the Western capitalist order, whose market economy is at the heart of the colonial model, do not eliminate the radical critique. Marxism and its variants oppose capitalism and its ideas of appropriation and exploitation which are at the origin of economic and social inequalities. Nevertheless, the solidarity economy does not espouse the revolutionary theses of socialist countries. The collectivization of the economy in the face of capitalist ideology is a political project imposed on civil society without the latter being free and willing to engage in a democratic deliberation process. In fact, the use of cooperative forms may follow an ideological will whose aim is to obtain the total adhesion of the population to the idea of collectivization.

Following the Cuban revolution, the state instituted the cooperative spirit in the agricultural sector with the aim of convincing small private owners to join the collectivist project. However, Cuba was first led to revise its ideological position regarding cooperatives, which were seen as contrary to collectivization. The use of cooperatives was even a political and economic necessity because the country was in deep crisis following the collapse of the USSR (Aureille, 2020). In this way, the cooperative form will become the dominant form in the agricultural sector to maintain the monopoly of its economic model over the state-owned enterprises. This project of collectivization of the economy has been partly maintained and has lasted by instilling a certain collective freedom of association of civil society through cooperatives, but without having put an end to private property. While Cuba has been able to structure its economy around state-owned enterprises, not all socialist countries have experienced the same developments.

In Vietnam, socialism put an end to the colonial system by imposing the collectivization of the means of production and by limiting the traditional communities perceived as a brake on collectivism. By creating the first cooperatives in the agricultural sector whose means of production were owned by the state, collectivism quickly reached its limits (Schaeffer, 1995). Even though the peasants' cooperatives had all the means of production at their disposal, they were more or less abandoned by the interested parties. In order to achieve the objectives of efficiency, the state maintained its collectivist model of cooperatives by granting greater management autonomy to the peasants of the cooperative commons and by taking measures of profit-sharing for the peasants (ibid). These policy orientations will not entirely curb the disinterest of peasants in cooperatives, who prefer to devote their time to family gardens from which they can earn an income.

The modernization and mechanization of agriculture, which proved to be costly for the state, failed to satisfy the expected production, which was at its lowest in the late 1970s. The collectivist project of the economy based on cooperative forms proved to be a failure and could not respond to the crisis and the needs of the population. In fact, from the 1980s onward, the state adopted the principles of the market economy while re-establishing the small private family farm. Private or semi-private family production units adopted either a "VAC" production model (vegetable garden/garden, fishponds, livestock) or an extensive production model (ibid). Nevertheless, the small family farm is facing increasing difficulties with the establishment of large estates and agribusiness groups. In this process of collectivization-decollectivization, the basic unit of the family farm is strongly challenged as an economic model of social integration and resource management by industrial units based on specialized production.

Whether we are talking about ex-colonized countries or socialist countries, it seems that the development of cooperatives is moving away from the idea that we can have of the potential of practices and solidarities in traditional societies (Yépez Del Castillo & Charlier, 1999, p. 161). This observation is in line with the idea that "the history of the cooperative movement in the South has often been marked by failure" (ibid, p. 163). Nevertheless, this failure is also primarily the result of the issues at stake between the communist and the capitalist bloc. The Latin America was confronted with the installation of military regimes and dictatorships. The price that many Latin American countries had to pay for the neoliberal doctrine is heavy in terms of freedoms and rights, but also in terms of human lives, with many citizens of civil society losing their lives to defend egalitarian, progressive, and socialist ideas. "This is the unacknowledged learning ground of neoliberalism: in order to avoid following the path of communist servitude and regain freedom through the market, Latin American military regimes have been considered as prototypes before the generalization of the policies tested in these countries" (Laville & Riot-Sarcey, 2020, p. 39).

Second, the failure is explained through North-South relations and structural adjustment programs (SAPs). Whether we consider Latin American or African countries, SAPs, whose objective is to reduce the debt of states, have harmful consequences on state interventionism and public policies, as they are forced to reduce public spending. The regulatory power of the state is limited to the detriment of privatization and the free movement of capital, "which allows Western companies to regain control of the economy of 'decolonized' countries" (Laville & Riot-Sarcey, 2020, p. 40).

Communism and liberalism have been violent regimes without being able to lead to a democratic emancipation of citizens. In their own way, they were violent toward the rights and freedoms of individuals by prohibiting individual and collective freedom of enterprise on the one hand and by promoting social inequalities as natural on the other. Faced with the hegemony of liberalism, the proponents of competition are faced with an immense challenge, i.e., to reconcile the market economy with environmental issues. The struggle of ideologies has been built around the unlimited exploitation of natural resources, often despite the lifestyles and economic models of people living in harmony with nature.

4 Solidarity Economy

Faced with this twenty-first-century challenge, "millions of people around the world are committed to saving the planet, developing democracy and challenging the iron laws of financial capitalism" (Laville & Riot-Sarcey, 2020, p. 8). Although capitalism has been able to bring most societies to heel, be it liberal democracies, antidemocracies, or the least developed countries, it continually faces citizen opposition as a countermovement seeking to curb its extension (Bugra, 2005, p. 44; Laville & Riot-Sarcey, 2020, p. 12).

In a way, citizens anticipate the glaring shortcomings of neoliberalism and/or its negative externalities. It is in this sense that we must understand the emergence of solidarity initiatives that will distinguish themselves from the components of the social economy to instill a new critique by proposing alternatives with a socioeconomic and a sociopolitical dimension. In this respect, since the 1990s, the solidarity economy has invested many sectors such as proximity services, management of urban services by inhabitants, knowledge exchange networks, self-production, sustainable agriculture, organic shops, collective kitchens, intercultural women's restaurants, solidarity tourism, solidarity finance, fair trade, creation of activities by unemployed people, and other forms of collective entrepreneurship (Laville & Cattini, 2006, p. 303).

Today, it still contributes to "the emergence of innovative solutions in new sectors: renewable energy, short circuits, circular economy, new forms of employment, housing, shared mobility, digital, etc." (Duverger et al., 2020, p. 32). Unlike the capitalist context of the nineteenth century and the societies of the twentieth century, environmental issues are now a major component of the solidarity economy. One could say that all these solidarity initiatives are driven by the idea of changing the "neoliberal world into a more humane, caring, compassionate and cohesive world, [making these elements a] source of inspiration for this ideology of change" (Kaya, 2017, p. 3). In this perspective, we would find a real counter-power (Lejeune, 2012, p. 142) that would be "at odds with the classical conception of economic transactions" (Rocha & Demers, 2007, p. 90).

In fact, this counter-power would no longer be limited to an internal critique, as illustrated by the components of the social economy that did not challenge the hegemony of the market economy. It would target and challenge both corporations and the state (Bélanger & Lévesque, 1991, p. 36), which leads Frère and Jacquemain (2013, pp. 242–244) to stress that "(...) anti-capitalism is not dead" as collective groups such as the *Faucheurs volontaires*, the *Casseurs de pubs*, or Greenpeace could demonstrate. Today, counter-powers can tend toward both internal and external criticism of the state. In this sense, solidarity initiatives can promote a critical externality to the market. This critical externality can be found, among others, in the free software movement, which responds to a deficit in the market offer of traditional companies (Demazière et al., 2006, p. 72).

These solidarity initiatives against the liberal economy tend to orient them toward other horizons and for the development of other things (Ion, 2017, p. 182). Faced with the negative externalities of the neoliberal economy, states can be seen as a brake for a more humane and nature-friendly world. In fact, many solidarity initiatives can develop, as in the nineteenth century, outside the concerns of the public authorities. Moreover, these citizens' commitments would respond to problems felt to be urgent, and they would be able to identify demands and needs and to conceive of themselves as users as well as promoters of services in the face of unsuitable market and public offers (Laville & Gardin, 2000, pp. 35–36). For some of them, it is a question of acting here and now, without waiting and seeking a blessing from the public authorities.

The idea that since the 1990s solidarity initiatives have displayed a more pronounced otherness toward the state and the market stems largely from the fact that the public authorities suffer from an inability to conceive of other economies outside the market economy. As such, one may get the impression that political representatives view with suspicion the initiatives of "a population accustomed to being spoken to by others" (Laville & Riot-Sarcey, 2020, p. 9), as "resistance can only be the immature reaction of an ill-informed population" (ibid, p. 9). This idea is in line with Karl Polanyi's thought that liberalism still denies the fact that "our society is still capable of using its ideas, hopes and conflicts to act on itself" (Touraine, 1999 quoted by Bugra, 2005, p. 49).

Nevertheless, it would be wrong to think that the public authorities have totally ignored the momentum of the solidarity economy movement. From the 1970s to the 1980s, "the social economy, which has also become 'solidarity', benefits from an increase in interest on the part of the public authorities, from an undeniable development of its activities and from a favorable ideological context" (Duverger et al., 2020, p. 68). Moreover, in some countries, the SSE field will be the subject of public recognition with the establishment of a Secretary of State for the SSE. This political will in favor of a public policy of solidarity economy is not limited to the European geography; it has been illustrated in some Latin American countries such as Brazil.

In France, this impetus from governments has resulted in a desire on the part of actors to structure themselves within the SSE field. "Previously fragmented and in institutional families that in reality ignored each other (. . .) their common characteristics and hence their inclusion in a group that would like to be homogeneous are much more clearly affirmed, and bodies that bring them together are appearing and multiplying" (ibid, p. 68). In fact, in France, there are national networks with regional or even departmental branches, but compared to other sectors, the SSE "suffers (. . .) from a weakness of networks and structures, which is detrimental to its development and influence" (Hascoët, 2005, pp. 299–300). In fact, the State Secretariat in France has not existed five times and for several years between 1984 and today.

In Brazil, a Secretary of State for Solidarity Economy was created within the Ministry of Labor and Employment in 2003 at the request of the actors concerned. This government policy provides political and material support to the various movements of solidarity economy actors such as the Brazilian Solidarity Economy

Forum, which includes agencies, municipal and state networks, associations promoting the management of microcredits, and networks of solidarity initiatives throughout the Brazilian territory (Singer, 2005, p. 292). In addition to this desire to structure the field of solidarity economy, the government has prioritized reintegration by developing numerous policies: support for family farming; material support for the use of water in semiarid areas for communities; and promotion of credit and social cooperatives in favor of mentally or physically handicapped people, but also of solidarity initiatives while including other secretariats, banks, and different ministries such as the Ministry of Social Development and Fight against Hunger, the Ministry of Agrarian Development, and the Ministry of Health.

These political conditions for the promotion and recognition of another economy that differs from the market economy and the state are often challenged by changes in political life. Consequently, the solidarity economy suffers from the instability of the social representations of the political class, as it can be the subject of a split between the opposition parties. A change of government can lead to freezing the measures taken by its predecessor or to maintaining and relegating the SSE field to one of the areas of the financially least supported public action by the state. Here again, we are faced with a form of denigration of the political class, because by refusing to bring to the attention of citizens or to debate the reality of the solidarity economy, it fuels certain prejudices.

In this respect, "the current vocabulary suggests that this sector eats up subsidies and that it is 'guilty' of financing it, when it seems normal to defiscalize a major merger of CAC-40 groups, to support the expansion or establishment of companies with tens or hundreds of millions of euros, even though substantial dividends will be distributed to shareholders at the same time" (Hascoët, 2005, p. 299). On closer examination, the market economy could not be sustained without states providing substantial financial resources or all forms of tax benefits. One only must look at the COVID-19 pandemic to understand that state intervention has been essential to the economic fabric and jobs. There is no doubt that other economic sectors are the ones that receive the most financial support, and to a much greater extent than noncapitalist organizations, which create more jobs than the market sector.

As a result, the solidarity economy today is marked by a great diversity of initiatives whose scale of intervention can vary from local to national or international. Depending on the geographical areas and political contexts, they do not experience the same development and consolidation process. Since it is impossible in the format of this text to relate in a transversal way all the dynamics specific to the solidarity economy regarding the different geographical cultural spaces between Europe, North and Latin America, Africa, and Asia, we will relate cases that have sought to establish, with varying degrees of success, a conciliation between politics and economy. These paths of conciliation, which today integrate environmental issues, may focus, with or without the collaboration of the public authorities and local governments, on territorial dynamics, sectors of activity, gender issues, the environment, and protest movements.

4.1 Living and Working Communities

Within the solidarity economy, it is not uncommon today to talk about the emergence of communities. These living community projects, which may or not be locally based, may emerge with varying degrees of otherness toward the state. Neglected by the public authorities and threatened socially and economically by the neoliberal economy, many communities have formed for various reasons and have sought to reconcile the economy and politics.

We could cite the emblematic example of Chiapas, whose model has since been adopted in Europe. The Chiapas movement has taken concrete form in a break with the Mexican state through the territorial affirmation of an economic production model that promotes social integration and respect for natural resources. Less divisive are the local communities in Canada that have initiated and generated, without entering open conflict with the state, "their own solutions to their economic problems in order to build long-term community capacity and promote the integration of economic, social and environmental objectives" (Ross & McRobie, 1989 cited by Lévesque & Mendell, 2005). Mondragon in Spain, on the other hand, is more the product of a stakeholder incubator in which the local government is a partner. The Mondragon project does not reject the market economy; on the contrary, it has been able to develop a territorial industry connected to the international market by promoting new, more democratic, and participatory wage relationships in its operation and decision-making process.

Nevertheless, communities of life can also emerge in a more spontaneous way without having a real local anchorage. The resistance movement of the "incorrigibles" of Notre-Dame-Des-Landes in France against the construction of a new airport was highly publicized. To defend an agricultural area and to avoid the increasing expansion of cities, many demonstrators came to the defense of the voiceless, i.e., the last farmers living modestly from their farms. The way of life and the natural space could be saved by the support of anticapitalist activists. Despite the use of the police and repression, as a tradition of state diplomacy against weak social groups, the resistance was not only limited to carrying a radical critique; it brought a positive response to the situation by making Notre Dame-Des-Landes a reference point for living together, but also a new place of experimentation of alternative life and production where practice and theory are regularly discussed (Laville & Riot-Sarcey, 2020, p. 30).

Unlike the libertarian communities established following the 1968 movement, these communities, which are being formed throughout Europe, the USA, and elsewhere and which some call "communities" or "intentional communities," have the particularity of putting work at the heart of their organization (Lallement, 2021). Nevertheless, their conception of work tends to structure group identity, but it differs from the dominant representation of work in capitalist societies in that it is extensive, including a range of tasks such as social, cultural, domestic, and activist activities (Lallement, 2021). In these organizations, there is also no logic of material appropriation of resources or means, nor of wage relations (Lallement, 2021). They rethink the social relations of work, but also of gender within the limits of maintaining the viability of their economic model. As such, they do not operate in isolation, but are open to the outside world, partly because of their commercial activity, and attempt to participate in movements of protest against neoliberalism (Lallement, 2021).

This process of emancipation of life from macroeconomic determinants with a view to establishing new, more egalitarian social relations of work and new modes of production that are more respectful of nature can be illustrated through various sectors (agriculture, industry, etc.). They tend to remove geographical areas and individuals from the law of the market economy while being vigilant of human living conditions and natural resources. Moreover, in Turkey, we find the constitution of living communities in the form of cooperatives. They have emerged from the consequences of the marginalization of certain geographical areas by the state. These initiatives, whose actors have a strong link with the territory, are now trying to improve their geographical environment by promoting the integrated development of cooperators who are more inclined toward agroecological agriculture. In another case, it stems from the desire of citizens from different backgrounds to establish themselves locally and to encourage a change in the mode of agroecological production in a region converted to agricultural productivism, which tends to impoverish farmers and make them dependent on state aid.

Indeed, "territories are at once a field of action, a resource and a product of transitions. However, if they are to be the site of social transformation, they must not be considered as islands preserved from the outside world, but rather as integrated into institutional arrangements that they have the capacity to modify" (Duverger et al., 2020, p. 14). Faced with these communities of life, the acceptance of public power is variable; the state can either have a repressive attitude, or work toward partnership, or simply control their regulatory and legal compliance.

4.2 Proximity Services

On a more sectoral level, the solidarity economy has revealed its effectiveness in the face of major changes in modern societies, confronted with a strong change in the labor market and greater professional mobility and demographic challenges linked to the aging of the population, but also the question of the vulnerability of certain social categories such as single mothers. These proximity services appear in various fields such as social action, health, gender, aging, early childhood, transport, rural and urban development, etc.

In fact, they assume that users are stakeholders in the service they will benefit from. In this case, mutual support or the support of each other "brings people together to resolve situations in which they are in difficulty. It is a question of pooling multiple resources for autonomous care. [Mutual support] does not separate the response from the people who carry it out" (Haeringer, 2002, p. 37). In Europe, there are many self-help initiatives linked to proximity services in countries such as

Sweden, Denmark, Germany, Austria, the UK, and France, but also in North America.

Nevertheless, they have questioned patriarchal gender relations in Europe in the domestic sphere. The proximity services such as childcare and care for the elderly are opportunities for women, especially those with low and middle incomes, to relieve themselves of some of their domestic tasks and to enter the labor market by gaining greater economic autonomy. These proximity services, which come from the women themselves, have been supported by the public authorities. Many of these initiatives have been recognized by the state and local authorities such as municipalities, which contribute to their funding. "Originally structured on a sectoral basis, this field is developing into a cross-sectoral logic that is largely based on partnership formulas" (Demoustier & Richez-Battesti, 2010, p. 11).

In the case of these proximity services, the economic model is based on a hybrid of resources, nonmonetary with volunteers, market with the financial contribution of users, and nonmarket with the redistribution of wealth by the state. In addition to being vectors of women's emancipation in the face of inequalities in domestic tasks between men and women, they provide new jobs. Nevertheless, these initiatives are not immune to a change in perspective by the political class. As an important and historical component, proximity services have been subject to strong constraints about the evolution of society's needs, but also regarding their competition with private operators, as in France in 2005 (Demoustier & Richez-Battesti, 2010, p. 11; Gajac, 2010, p. 320).

This attitude on the part of the public authorities is not new. In many cases, the innovations that noncapitalist organizations have been able to develop successfully in many sectors while devising a viable economic model are transferred to the market field, to large groups and/or private branches (Gajac, 2010, p. 319). Once these new economic sectors become economically viable, the public authorities tend to put them in competition with private operators. However, this appropriation by economic operators, with the explicit support of the public authorities, of social and civic engineering, which creates new viable economic models and new sources of employment, is not financially recognized.

Apart from the fact that noncapitalist organizations are not on an equal footing with the profit-making sector and that privileges persist between the regulated professions and the lambda professions subject to globalization, there is a paradox in this marketing of proximity services in that it tends to forget the initial objectives of these solidarity initiatives (i.e., the emancipation of citizens). In terms of gender, the competition of proximity services could weaken the emancipation of women from domestic tasks in favor of the rationality and profitability of proximity services. The state tends to defeat the emergence of self-organized and autonomous solidarity initiatives, as soon as it becomes a financial partner to create other public schemes on women's issues without women becoming the actors of their own emancipation.

In Turkey, solidarity initiatives have emerged in the field of education in view of the perceived inadequacy of public and private provision. Above all, they emerge from the will of families and their concerns to offer a better model of education where the child is at the center of the educational project by considering his or her development, well-being, and awareness of environmental and democratic issues (Gajac & Pelek, 2020, p. 20). The economic model is based on a hybrid of resources such as nonmonetary resources with the commitment of member and nonmember volunteers. In this phase of development, it is a reciprocity of peers in favor of a self-management model. In its consolidation phase, this model is reinforced by market resources, i.e., financial participation by families. Nevertheless, this economic model supports low-income families by granting scholarships and contributes to the social integration of families with more diverse social conditions.

Here, these initiatives carry both an internal criticism of the state and an external criticism of the market (ibid, p. 21). The paradox is that private institutions created by large business groups and/or political figures in the field of education (in the form of foundations) are finding recognition from the public authorities to compensate for their disengagement from education, whereas solidarity initiatives have not yet received any real and concrete sign of recognition from the state and local authorities.

4.3 *Maintaining Employment at All Costs?*

If the solidarity economy can formulate another economy through territorial and sectoral dynamics while taking into account the gender issue, it can tackle the macroeconomic consequences of neoliberalism, such as job losses and unemployment, by going beyond them to promote more democratic organizational forms.

In a way, one can speak of a cooperative revival with social and general interest objectives. In addition to the creation of new statutes such as social cooperatives in Italy in 1991, social purpose companies in Belgium in 1995, solidarity cooperatives in Quebec in 1997, and social solidarity cooperatives in Portugal in 1998, "these cooperatives favor social purposes and job creation, or even more broadly the general interest, in response to an economic context marked by mass unemployment and the withdrawal of the welfare state" (Richez-Battesti & Defourny, 2017).

In this case, we find the legendary example of the Lips movement of the 1970s, which sought to maintain employment. The latter "has given rise to vocations: cooperatives and associations are spreading throughout the different territories of European and American countries, in the North and the South" (Laville & Riot-Sarcey, 2020, p. 25). These initiatives, which most often opt for cooperative status, can implement different strategies. They may resort to fighting to recover their enterprises. This is the case in Argentina, where many enterprises, in a depressed economic context, have been taken over by employees and their number has continued to increase despite the reluctance of some governments (Quijoux & Ruggeri, 2019).

Here, the main motivations of the recovered enterprises are economic and less ideological, as the employees' primary focus is on work and job security, which is the basis for the adoption of a self-management mode. This process is not without difficulty due to the workers' limited resources and lack of knowledge about cooperatives. In Europe, these recovered enterprises affect industry and the tertiary sector, while in Argentina they can be small- and medium-sized enterprises, schools, hospitals, media outlets, and hotels (Quijoux & Ruggeri, 2019; Quijoux, 2019).

In Argentina, one government may institute public programs to support the recovered enterprises, while its successor may empty the program of content or keep it to a minimum. Nevertheless, the phenomenon of recovered enterprises may find support from local authorities in cases where the government is less ambitious or even reluctant to support the recovered enterprises. It appears that they are evolving in an uncertain political context, especially since they are subject to repression in their struggle process, but also in the continuation of their activity under a cooperative status to slow down their development.

However, the recovered enterprises and their economic viability in maintaining productivity can be affected by the neoliberal economic policies implemented by governments. The opening of the economy to imports in Argentina has resulted in the weakening of the economic fabric in general and SMEs in particular, but also in increased job losses and unemployment (Quijoux & Ruggeri, 2019). In this context, the recovered enterprises can also be impacted and lead to the closure of some of them.

Thus, it is difficult for governments to completely ban the recovered enterprises in the interests of the national economic elites when the country is hit by a 30-year structural economic crisis and when the only prospect for employees is unemployment. Cooperative self-management and recovered enterprises are the only alternative, and in this perspective, cooperatives and cooperators faced with production decreases, mainly linked to macroeconomic factors, are more inclined to lower wages and avoid layoffs (ibid).

In France, we find these initiatives of recovered enterprises, but also the more singular dynamics of the Scop movement. This is not limited to being a recovered enterprises movement; it tends to give itself legitimacy around the transmission of enterprises and enterprises creation (Quijoux, 2019). Nevertheless, the Scop remains little known to employees, and cooperatives in general have never been a favored option for trade unions until recent years when the idea of safeguarding jobs has become more acceptable. Moreover, it is not uncommon for these recovered enterprises to become part of the political agenda and to be publicized in the media, as some political parties, often reticent about this type of alternative, come to support the employees in order to safeguard jobs.

Nevertheless, these initiatives, like many others, are not perfect, as gaps can arise between the initial aspirations of employees for more democracy and the economic challenge the cooperative must face to be viable. Supported by the Scop movement, members may be bitterly surprised that the emphasis will be on adopting a classic division of labor scheme and that they are deprived of their decision-making power. These misunderstandings may lead the new management to take these disappointments into account and compensate for the democratic ideal with participatory tools inherited from their own trade union culture. Nevertheless, employees may also adopt a form of resistance to this lack of participatory democracy and be led to unionize the issue of work in the context of these covered enterprises accompanied by the Scop movement (ibid).

This kind of initiative is not absent in Turkey, although it is somewhat different from recovered enterprises. There is an example of a producer cooperative in the North that was revived after bankruptcy due to questionable management by the responsible bodies. The new managers and producer members took up the challenge of maintaining the cooperative and, as a corollary, of maintaining their own professional activity in their local living space. Here, one cannot deny the proximity between the left-wing political ideas carried by this cooperative and the surge of solidarity it will generate on a national scale. Their cooperative ideal could not be fully achieved in the early years in terms of self-management principles and values and participatory democracy, as they had to deal with the burden of debts and government suspicions.

This kind of initiative, where self-management is at the heart of the project with the idea of participatory democracy, does not seem to be to the taste of the government. The latter, via its administration, has been quick to carry out visits and regular administrative checks. Despite this negative perception and administrative obstacles, the challenge of clearing the debts is on the way to success. If there are disappointments in the face of the desire for self-management, the recovered enterprises not only have the virtue of demonstrating that employees are able to take charge of their own destiny and maintain their own jobs but can also place their project in the cycle of a more environmentally friendly production and in a dynamic of synergies with other actors.

4.4 Short Food Circuits

Short food circuits (SFCs) are a widespread phenomenon throughout the world. Whether we talk about AMAPs in France, Teikei in Japan, or community-supported agriculture in the USA, these solidarity initiatives challenge the model of conventional agro-industrial agriculture, whose social, economic, and environmental consequences resonate with citizens.

This postwar productivist model no longer tends to maintain good living conditions for farmers because globalization leads to a drop in prices as a result of competition (Prévost, 2014). In fact, the emergence of SFCs is rooted in the many consequences of this productivist model: the consequences of monoculture and environmental pollution in Japan, the reduction in the number of farmers in the USA (Lagane, 2011), and the maintenance of small-scale farming in France (Olivier & Coquart, 2010). One could add to this list the fact that the regulatory standards of the agro-industry have not prevented health crises, nor have they prevented the exposure of scandals and fraud (Prévost, 2014).

In this way, SFCs also raise the issue of food and public health policies. By re-personalizing the links between farmers and consumers, these initiatives focus on the quality of products while going against the law of the market-determining prices.

By criticizing market regulation, the notion of exchange is rethought to propose "an alternative conception of the regulation of agri-food exchanges for the benefit of another agriculture" (Prévost, 2014). As a result, numerous initiatives are emerging to bring consumers and producers closer together and allow better access to local products, but also to respond to multiple environmental concerns and to maintain small-scale agriculture.

Nevertheless, these initiatives tend to distance themselves from the criticisms leveled at the state over the past few decades in the face of the hemorrhaging of farmers and their casualization. These internal criticisms, followed by reforms, have only maintained a productivist system while benefiting from aid from their own state or from Europe in the case of European countries. Conversely, the SFCs have adopted the status of economic actors (Lanciano & Saleilles, 2011, p. 156), which tends to be similar to the concept of new economic social movements (Gendron, 2001). In this way, they have brought an external critique to the state and the market to seize economic issues themselves and establish economic models based on the principle of egalitarian and multilateral reciprocity. These alternative models call for the involvement of producers and consumers by eliminating intermediaries and promoting proximity links.

This movement has had the effect of drawing the attention of the authorities and all the official players (professional chambers, unions, networks, etc.) to the agricultural issue. Many of them were reluctant before changing their social representation of these initiatives. In France, it led the state to recognize and promote the SFCs. At the local level, municipalities have integrated farmers into the collective catering sector. In some cases, this can be explained by the municipality's desire to reduce the costs of cleaning up water related to agricultural pollution by supporting farmers in their conversion to organic farming and by opening collective catering as an economic opportunity (Prévost, 2014).

In this way, the SFCs make it possible to raise problems that are interconnected with conventional agricultural models, such as environmental and food issues, which public authorities can use to change the standards and content of public policies. In this sense, the issue of SFCs in France is increasingly the subject of a territory-wide policy. In a way, at their level, they extract agriculture from the logic of national productivism, or even from European policy, but also from the logic of financialization and speculators, in order to link it back to the territory, the citizens, and their living environment.

In fact, solidarity and citizen initiatives can create new production and consumption standards that are more respectful of the farming profession and the environment, apart from those imposed by the domination of the market, whose logic is solely profit without concern for the consequences on farmers' incomes and biodiversity. These forms of economic alternatives also have similarities with fair trade. Fair trade, whose principle is to remunerate producers in the South at a fair price, has gained momentum. Labels have been created through NGOs to make trade between the North and the South more ethical and to get away from the logic of exploitation by Western multinationals at the expense of small farmers in the South.

In Turkey, SFCs have developed over the last decade in the form of consumer communities, consumer cooperatives, and gardens (*bostan*). Similarly, they seek to reduce intermediaries, to value agricultural practices outside of conventional agriculture, and to differentiate themselves from the marketing of labeled products such as "organic certification" which fits the productivist model. It appears that the SFCs have been able to create new ecological standards outside the market sector (Gajac, 2022). If the focus is even on promoting local seeds, they ensure a better purchase price for producers, they help bring urban and rural people together, and they highlight farmers marginalized by conventional agriculture, but, most importantly, SFCs take into consideration social and gender issues related to vulnerable groups, such as women, seasonal workers, and refugees.

It can be said that they influence the government and public authorities in a certain way. The former was quick to carry out administrative controls, always confirming the idea that everything that comes from civil society is necessarily suspect. The latter are in a logic of imitation by letting people believe that they have carried out a participatory consultation process, only to decide unilaterally and initiate their own initiative (organic market, garden, internet sales), which is more top-down toward farmers and consumers and whose institutional durability remains fragile in the face of a probable change of municipal majority.

5 Conclusion

The solidarity economy initiatives that have appeared in the countries of the North and South since the 1990s tend to revive the associationist spirit of the nineteenth century. They invest in many sectors of activity to meet the expectations and needs of individuals while increasingly considering environmental issues. They distinguish themselves from the components of the social economy and the nonprofit sector by giving back to the associative, cooperative, and mutualist statutes the power to criticize the market economy and the public power. By democratically taking up diverse issues in the North and the South (threats to living conditions, exploitation of natural resources, abandonment of geographical areas, inequalities in wage relations, job losses, enterprises closures, unemployment, inadequacy and absence of public services, gender inequalities, productivism, pauperism, discrimination, health scandals, pollution), they are promoting other economic models to reconcile politics and the economy at different scales. In the face of liberal democracies and antidemocracies, states and local authorities, aware of the negative impact of neoliberalism, procrastinate between ideological blindness, rejection of civil society, and inability to promote another economy different from the market economy. However, many solidarity initiatives have already demonstrated that their economic model not only is viable and sustainable, more egalitarian, and democratic but also provides jobs and respects natural resources. The investment of the political class toward the solidarity economy is often uncertain, depending on the economic situation and political majorities, even if the solidarity economy has been supported on several occasions in the framework of public and local policies. Faced with public institutions, some solidarity initiatives have chosen a strong otherness to the state and to neoliberalism, and they seize, through self-management, the economic stakes in order to democratize societies conceived as commodities but also to recover a flavor of dignity. Nevertheless, they are rare those that have been able to establish in collaboration with the public power and local authorities, and on the long term, another economic model on the scale of a territory, but when it is the case, their cultural anchoring tends to demonstrate the democratic choice to find modes of organization of type "civic protection" reconciling democracy, economy and nature. Faced with the challenges of the twenty-first century, millions of people will continue to commit themselves and create solidarity initiatives, whether or not they break with public power and even if today neoliberalism via large groups and multinationals tend to give themselves an image of respectability, of social responsibility, and of benefactor of the protection of the environment and the fight against poverty, if it is a question of a moral solidarity to make the public opinion accept the continuation of the exploitation of the people and the Earth, but it is not a question of another economy seeking to reconcile democracy, economy, and nature.

References

Aureille, M. (2020). Des coopératives par défaut. Ambiguités autour de la place des paysans au sein du socialisme cubain. In A. Blin et al. (Eds.), *L'utopie au jour le jour. Une histoire des expériences coopératives (XIXe-XXe siècle)* (pp. 303–305). Editions Arbre Bleu.

Richez-Battesti, N., & Defourny, J. (2017). Les coopératives. In J. Defourny & M. Nyssens (Eds.), *Economie sociale et solidaire. Socioéconomie du 3ème secteur* (pp. 73–116). De Boeck Supérieur.

Bélanger, P., & Lévesque, B. (1991). La "théorie" de la régulation, du rapport salarial au rapport de consommation. Un point de vue sociologique. *Cahiers de recherche sociologique, 17*, 17–51.

Bugra, A. (2005). Karl Polanyi et la séparation institutionnelle entre politique et économie. *Raisons Politiques, 4*(20), 37–56.

Defourny, J. (2017). L'économie sociale. In J. Defourny & M. Nyssens (Eds.), *Economie sociale et solidaire. Socioéconomie du 3ème secteur* (pp. 29–72). De Boeck Supérieur.

Defourny, J., & Develtere, P. (1999). Origines et contours de l'économie sociale au Nord et au Sud. In J. Defourny et al. (Eds.), *L'économie sociale au Nord et au Sud* (pp. 25–56). Editions de Boeck.

Demazière, D., Horn, F., & Zune, M. (2006). Dynamique de développement des communautés du logiciel libre. Conditions d'émergence et régulations des tensions. *Terminal*, 71–84.

Demoustier, D., & Richez-Battesti, N. (2010). Introduction. Les organisations de l'économie sociale et solidaire: gouvernance, régulation et territoire. *Géographie, Economie, Société, 12*(1), 5–14.

Draperi, J. F. (2006). L'Etat et les associations. Du face-à-face au coude à coude. In M. C. Bureau et al. (Eds.), *Défaillances et inventions de l'action sociale* (pp. 37–57). L'Harmattan.

Dreyfus, M. (2018). Aux origines de l'économie sociale et solidaire à Grenoble au XIXe siècle, Simon Lambersens, campus ouvert, 2017. *RECMA, 2*(348), 132–134.

Dreyfus, M. (2001). *Histoire de l'économie sociale, de la grande guerre à nos jours*. PUR.

Duverger, T. (2021). *Utopies locale. Les solutions écologiques et solidaires de demain*. Les petits matins.

Duverger, T., Itçaina, X., & Lafore, R. (2020). *Les trois visages de l'économie sociale et solidaire. Institutionnalisation, trajectoires, territoires*. Le Bord de l'eau.

Evers, A., & Laville, J.-L. (Eds.). (2004). *The third sector in Europe*. Edward Elgar.

Fonteneau, B., Nyssens, M., & Fall, A. S. (1999). Le secteur informel: creuset de pratiques d'économie solidaire ? In J. Defourny et al. (Eds.), *L'économie sociale au Nord et au Sud* (pp. 25–56). Editions De Boeck.

Fraser, N. (2013). Marchandisation, protection sociale, émancipation: vers une conception néo-polanyienne de la crise capitaliste. L'actualité de Karl Polanyi. In I. Hillenkamp & J.-L. Laville (Eds.), *Socioéconomie et démocratie* (pp. 37–63). ERES.

Frère, B., & Jacquemain, M. (2013). Conclusion / Quoi de neuf sous le soleil de l'engagement ? In B. Frère & M. Jacquemain (Eds.), *Résister au quotidien ?* (pp. 241–256). Presses de Sciences Po.

Gadrey, J., & Jany-Catrice, F. (2016). *Les nouveaux indicateurs de richesse*. La Découverte.

Gajac, O. (2022). *La solidarité au cœur du mouvement des circuits courts alimentaires en Turquie: entre normes écologiques alternatives et visées socio-culturelles et socio-économiques*. Socioeco.org working paper. http://www.socioeco.org/bdf_auteur-5832_fr.html

Gajac, O. (2010). *Les associations face à la récurrence de l'exclusion*. PhD dissertation, Université Paris Dauphine, Paris.

Gajac, O., & Pelek, S. (2020). *L'économie solidaire en Turquie et son écosystème: un avenir encore incertain*. Working Paper CIRIEC, 2.

Gendron, C. (2001). Émergence de nouveaux mouvements sociaux économiques. *Revue POUR, 172*, 175–181.

Haeringer, J. (2002). Identifier les logiques institutionnelles. In F. Traversaz & J. Haeringer (Eds.), *Conduire le changement dans les associations d'action sociale et médico-sociale* (pp. 19–53). Dunod.

Hascoët, G. (2005). Le secrétariat d'état en France : un bilan provisoire. In G. Carvalho da França et al. (Eds.), *Action publique et économie solidaire* (pp. 297–302). ERES.

Ion, J. (2017). L'engagement des jeunes. *La Revue Lacanienne, 18*(1), 177–184.

Kaya, A. (2017). Right to public space: Social movements and active citizenship in Turkey. *Research and Policy on Turkey, 2*(1), 1–9.

Klein, J. L., Laville, J.-L., & Moulaert, F. (2017). *L'innovation sociale*. Eres.

Lagane, J. (2011). Du teikei à l'AMAP, un modèle acculturé. *Développement Durable et Territoires, 2*(2), 1–14. https://journals.openedition.org/developpementdurable/9013

Lallement, M. (2021). Les communautés intentionnelles: des utopies concrètes du travail. Entretien avec Michel Lallement, Réalisé par Simon Cottin-Marx, Auréline Cardoso. *Mouvements, 2*(106), 110–120.

Lanciano, E., & Saleilles, S. (2011). Le travail institutionnel du mouvement des Amap. *Revue Française de Gestion, 8*(217), 155–172.

Laville, J.-L. (2016). *L'économie sociale et solidaire. Pratiques, théories, débats*. Editions du Seuil.

Laville, J.-L. (2013). *L'économie solidaire. Une perspective internationale*. Fayard.

Laville, J.-L. (2004). Démocratie et économie: éléments pour une approche sociologique. *HERMÈS, 36*, 185–194.

Laville, J.-L. (1994). *L'économie solidaire. Une perspective internationale*. Desclée de Brouwer.

Laville, J.-L., & Cattini, A. D. (2006). *Dictionnaire de l'autre économie*. Gallimard.

Laville, J.-L., & Gardin, L. (2000). Économie solidaire: une approche européenne. *L'économie politique, 7*, 32–48.

Laville, J.-L., & Riot-Sarcey, M. (2020). *Le réveil utopique*. Les Éditions de l'Atelier.

Lejeune, C. (2012). L'organisation socio-politique des collectifs médiatisés. De quelques controverses internes à l'Open Directory Projet. In M. Jacquemain & P. Delwit (Eds.), *Engagements actuels, actualités des engagements* (pp. 141–153). Bruyant-Academia.

Lévesque, B., & Mendell, M. (2005). L'économie sociale: diversité des définitions et des constructions théoriques, *Revue Interventions Economiques, 32*. http://interventionseconomiques.revues.org/852

Lévesque, B. (2003). *Mondialisation, démocratie plurielle, économie sociale et solidaire* (pp. 103–121). Économie et Solidarités.
MEF. (2022). *L'économie sociale et solidaire*. https://www.economie.gouv.fr/leconomie-sociale-et-solidaire
Mendell, M. (2002). The social economy in Québec. Discourse and strategies. In E. Macdonald & A. Bakan (Eds.), *Critical political studies: Debates and dialogues for the left* (pp. 468–502). McGill-Queen's Press.
Olivier, V., & Coquart, D. (2010). Les AMAP: une alternative socio-économique pour des petits producteurs locaux ? *Économie Rurale, 4–5*, 20–36. https://journals.openedition.org/economierurale/2793
Polanyi, K. (1983). *La Grande Transformation. Aux origines politiques et économiques de notre temps*. Gallimard.
Prévost, B. (2014). Des circuits courts à la reterritorialisation de l'agriculture et de l'alimentation. *Revue Internationale de l'Economie Sociale, 331*, 30–44. https://doi.org/10.7202/1023483ar
Quijoux, M., & Ruggeri, A. (2019). Les entreprises récupérées face au gouvernement néolibéral argentin. *Mouvements, 1*(97), 140–148.
Quijoux, M. (2019). "Vous allez trouver une façon d'être dirigeant." formation coopérative et résistances ouvrières dans une usine reprise par ses salariés. *Politix, 126*, 193–215.
Rocha, L., & Demers, V. (2007). Nouveaux mouvements sociaux économiques et développement durable : les nouvelles mobilisations à l'ère de la mondialisation. *Natures Sciences Sociétés, 15*, 90–91.
Ross, D., & McRobie, G. (1989). *A feasibility study for a Centre for Community Economic Development at Simon Fraser University*. Community Economic Development Centre, Simon Fraser University. www2.sfu.ca/cedc
Salamon, L. M., & Anheier, H. K. (1998). Social origins of civil society: Explaining the nonprofit sector cross-nationally. *VOLUNTAS: International Journal of Voluntary and Nonprofit Organizations, 9*(3), 213–248.
Salamon, L. M. (1990). The nonprofit sector and government. The American experience in theory and practice. In H. K. Amheier & W. Seibel (Eds.), *The third sector. Comparative studies of nonprofit organization* (pp. 210–240). de Gruyter.
Schaeffer, D. (1995). L'élevage au Nord Vietnam : du collectivisme à la décollectivisation. *Cahiers d'outre-mer, 190*(48), 181–196.
Schumacher, E. F. (1979). *Small is beautiful: une société à la mesure de l'homme*. Le Seuil.
Singer, P. (2005). Le secrétariat d'état au Brésil : de la société civile au gouvernement fédéral. In G. Carvalho da França et al. (Eds.), *Action publique et économie solidaire* (pp. 285–295). ERES.
Sorbets, C. (2004). Institutionalisations. Façons de (se) dire ce que l'on fait dans le cadre de l'économie sociale et solidaire en Aquitaine. In X. Itçaina et al. (Eds.), *Un monde en quête de reconnaissance. Usages de l'économie sociale et solidaire en Aquitaine*. Presses Universitaires de Bordeaux.
Touraine, A. (1999). *Comment sortir du libéralisme ?* Fayard.
Weisbrod, B. A. (1977). *The voluntary non-profit sector*. Lexington Press.
Yépez Del Castillo, I., & Charlier, S. (1999). Origines et contours de l'économie sociale au Nord et au Sud. In J. Defourny et al. (Eds.), *L'économie sociale au Nord et au Sud* (pp. 25–56). Editions De Boeck.

Authors Index

A. Ari (ed.), *Capitalism at a Crossroads*, Springer Studies in Alternative Economics,
https://doi.org/10.1007/978-3-031-23257-2

Countries/Regions Index

A. Ari (ed.), *Capitalism at a Crossroads*, Springer Studies in Alternative Economics,
https://doi.org/10.1007/978-3-031-23257-2

Institutions/Organizations Index

A. Ari (ed.), *Capitalism at a Crossroads*, Springer Studies in Alternative Economics,
https://doi.org/10.1007/978-3-031-23257-2

Programs Index

A. Ari (ed.), *Capitalism at a Crossroads*, Springer Studies in Alternative Economics,
https://doi.org/10.1007/978-3-031-23257-2

Subject Index

A. Ari (ed.), *Capitalism at a Crossroads*, Springer Studies in Alternative Economics,
https://doi.org/10.1007/978-3-031-23257-2

The manufacturer's authorised representative in the EU is Springer Nature Customer Service Centre GmbH, Europaplatz 3, 69115 Heidelberg, Germany. If you have any concerns regarding our products, please contact ProductSafety@springernature.com

Printed and bound by CPI Group (UK) Ltd, Croydon, CR0 4YY
28/09/2026
02224062-0004